www.wadsworth.com

wadsworth.com is the World Wide Web site for Wadsworth and is your direct source to dozens of online resources.

At *wadsworth.com* you can find out about supplements, demonstration software, and student resources. You can also send email to many of our authors and preview new publications and exciting new technologies.

wadsworth.com
Changing the way the world learns®

The New Testament

HISTORY, LITERATURE, AND SOCIAL CONTEXT

FOURTH EDITION

DENNIS C. DULING

Canisius College

THOMSON

WADSWORTH

Australia · Canada · Mexico · Singapore · Spain
United Kingdom · United States

THOMSON

™

WADSWORTH

Publisher: Holly J. Allen
Religion Editor: Steve Wainwright
Assistant Editor: Lee McCracken
Editorial Assistant: Anna Lustig
Marketing Manager: Worth Hawes
Technology Project Manager: Susan DeVanna
Advertising Project Manager: Bryan Vann
Print / Media Buyer: Rebecca Cross
Permissions Editor: Bob Hauser

Production Service: G & S Typesetters, Inc.
Art Editor: Gretchen Otto
Photo Researcher: Sandra Lord
Copy Editor: Mike Nichols
Cover Designer: Andrew Ogus
Cover Image: Corbis
Compositor: G & S Typesetters, Inc.
Text and Cover Printer:
Transcontinental, Louiseville

For more information about our products,
contact us at:
**Thomson Learning
Academic Resource Center
1-800-423-0563**
For permission to use material from this text,
contact us by: **Phone:** 1-800-730-2214
Fax: 1-800-730-2215
Web: http://www.thomsonrights.com

Library of Congress Control Number: 2002115056

ISBN 0-155-07856-9

Wadsworth / Thomson Learning
10 Davis Drive
Belmont, CA 94002-3098
USA

Asia
Thomson Learning
5 Shenton Way #01-01
UIC Building
Singapore 068808

Australia / New Zealand
Nelson Thomson Learning
102 Dodds Street
Southbank, Victoria 3006
Australia

Canada
Nelson Thomson Learning
1120 Birchmount Road
Toronto, Ontario M1K 5G4
Canada

Europe / Middle East / Africa
Thomson Learning
High Holborn House
50/51 Bedford Row
London WC1R 4LR
United Kingdom

Latin America
Thomson Learning
Seneca, 53
Colonia Polanco
11560 Mexico D.F.
Mexico

Spain
Paraninfo Thomson Learning
Calle / Magallanes, 25
28015 Madrid, Spain

To Gretchen, Teddie, Eric, Stephen, and Flynn

Contents

CHAPTER FOUR   Paul: Apostle to the Gentiles   139

CHAPTER FIVE   The Letter and Paul's Early Letters   179

CHAPTER SIX   Galatians and Romans   219

Preface

The fourth edition of this textbook has many changes. My first priority has been to make the book more user friendly. Students at Canisius College helped by field-testing many portions of the text. I totally rewrote many parts of the book.

I also reorganized the book. Norman Perrin's original order in the first edition, which was mostly perpetuated in the second and third editions, was essentially Weberian in tracking the Jesus Movement from its "charismatic" beginnings to its institutional development. (I do not know whether Perrin was aware of this fact.) I more or less kept that overall structure. I also kept the placement of the Jesus chapter at the end of the book. For Perrin, this location was both theological and practical. It was theological because Perrin thought, like Rudolf Bultmann, that Jesus was the presupposition of the New Testament. It was practical because Perrin thought that students should take up the complexities of historical Jesus research only after gaining a better understanding of the history and literature of the period. An informal show of hands of scholars attending the Eastern Great Lakes Biblical Society revealed that they were evenly divided about whether this feature of the book should be changed.

Perrin developed the overall plan but I made numerous changes to this edition, even from my third-edition revision. My changes are mainly for pedagogical purposes. I reduced the first five chapters of the third edition to three and reorganized them. I combined Chapter Two, on the social-historical context of the New Testament, with Chapter Three, on the cultural and religious environment of the New Testament; they are now Chapter One. I updated and slightly expanded Chapter One, on modern interpretation of the New Testament; it is now Chapter Two. Finally, I combined Chapter Four, on the social history of early Christianity, with Chapter Five, on the earliest non-Pauline Christians; they are now Chapter Three.

Chapter Six, the general chapter on Paul, is now Chapter Four; I shortened this chapter, primarily by placing scholarly discussions about the letter genre at the beginning of the next chapter on Paul's letters. I divided the third edition's Chapter Seven, on the Pauline letters, into two chapters. In the new Chapter Five I discuss the letter genre and consider five letters (1 Thessalonians, 1 Corinthians, 2 Corinthians, Philippians, and Philemon). In the new Chapter Six I put Galatians and Romans together because of their similar content. The overall organization of the rest of the book is about the same as the third edition, although the epilogue, on ways of being religious, is omitted. And in addition to the appendix on archaeology, I included an appendix on the contents of Q and another on the canon of the New Testament.

A new feature of this edition is that many important terms (names and dates excluded) have been boldfaced in the text. The bold terms direct students to the glossary, which has been considerably expanded.

Another change is that the bibliographies at the end of each chapter have been replaced by an acknowledgment of scholars at the end of the book and a direction to refer to more complete bibliographies on a Wadsworth Web site. The lengthy bibliography that used to appear at the end of the textbook is updated and also on the Web site.

Though the order is similar to earlier editions, I changed the content significantly. This edition has even more social history and social-scientific interpretation than the previous edition. Chapter Two now includes brief introductions to hermeneutics in general, modernism, Liberationist Hermeneutics, Third World hermeneutics, and Socio-rhetorical Criticism. Chapter Five, on Paul's early letters, gives greater attention to 1 Corinthians, and Chapter Six emphasizes Romans. My intent was to allow students to focus on two of Paul's longer and most important letters, the first because of its social importance, the second because of its theological importance. I updated the discussions of Paul's letters and included some current rhetorical issues. Correspondingly, these chapters, except for a section of Chapter Five on 2 Corinthians, no longer defend letter-fragment theories. I also updated the chapters on the synoptic Gospels, especially with my own work on the Gospel of Matthew. The chapter on the Johannine literature now correlates the sectarian approach in the third edition with antilanguage and antisociety discussions. Chapter Twelve on Revelation has been buttressed with research on astrology. The most important change in Chapter Thirteen is the updated material on James. I also cut some text in the chapter on Jesus in order to add a survey of the three periods of quest for the historical Jesus. I took the new material partly from my book on that subject (*Jesus Christ through History*) and supplemented it with the so-called third quest issues.

I am obviously indebted to the many scholars cited at the end of the book. I am most grateful to the discussions of the Context Group and the social-scientific sections of the Society of Biblical Literature (SBL), the Catholic Biblical Association, and the Eastern Great Lakes Biblical Society (EGLBS). (I cochair SBL and EGLBS sections.) I am also much indebted to the Matthew sections of the SBL and the *Studiorum Novi Testamenti Societas,* sections in which I have given several scholarly papers and received helpful critical response. Those who have used earlier editions of this book will note that a few pages written by Perrin, the first author of this textbook, still remain.

I owe a special debt of gratitude to several members of the Context Group for offering critical remarks on various chapters. The members and their subjects of commentary are: Douglas E. Oakman, the social-historical context and the historical Jesus (Chapters One and Fourteen); John H. Elliott, methods and institutionalization (Two and Thirteen); Richard L. Rohrbaugh, the early non-Pauline groups and Mark (Three and Eight); John J. Pilch, Luke-Acts and Revelation (Ten and Twelve); K. C. Hanson, Paul and the deutero-Pauline letters (Four and Seven); and Bruce J. Malina, Matthew and John (Nine and Eleven). I would also like to thank a young friend and scholar, Dr. Matt Jackson-McCabe of Niagara University, for his comments on the Pauline letters (Chapters Five and Six), and to thank Carolyn Osiek for her kind assistance with a photo of the house of Vettii at Pompeii. Scholars in the field will recognize their influence at numerous points in the book. In some cases I inserted names of scholars in parentheses where I thought special recognition was due. None of these scholars is responsible for any errors in the book.

It is necessary to make a comment about language. For two reasons, many historians and social-scientific critics no longer use the terms *Jew, Judaism, Christian,* and *Christianity* when discussing the first and second centuries C.E. The first reason is ancient usage itself. Although *Christianos,* usually translated *Christian,* is found three times in the New Testament (Acts 11:26, 26:28; 1 Pet. 4:16), *Christianity* is not found. *Ioudaios,* usually translated *Jew,* is found many times. But this word can have different meanings in different contexts.

The second reason is that these terms carry many modern connotations about freestanding, independent religions that do not fit the ancient context. I emphasize that the problem is not simply that of using a different word for the same group; rather, the groups themselves are different from their modern counterparts. Language derives meaning from the social context. Although the problem of translating terms from another culture is not new, it is particularly complicated in this case because of modern Jewish-Christian relations. Moreover, there is no consensus on what should replace these terms. Increasingly, the most common alternative translation of *Ioudaios* is *Judean.* It has an advantage over *Jew* because place of origin is one of the marks of ethnicity. One problem with this translation is that in traditional English usage *Judean* is usually limited to the geographical region of Judea and not all *Judeans* (*Jews*) were from Judea. Therefore I have usually chosen the alternative *Israelite,* which has the advantage that *Israelitēs* is also common New Testament usage (e.g., Rom. 9:4, 2 Cor. 11:22). This is also true of *house of Israel* (Matt. 10:6, Acts 2:36), but the difficulty with the term *Israel* is that in the preexilic period it referred to the northern kingdom. It is found in this sense in Heb. 8:8 in a quotation from Jer. 31:31–34. The term has also been used by modern scholars, who call preexilic Israel "ancient Israel" and postexilic Israel "Judaism." (Some scholars question those terms today as well.) In place of *Christian* and *early Christianity* I use circumlocutions such as *members of the Jesus Movement* and *Christ believers.* For the rare term *Christianos* I use the neologism *Christ-ies* on the basis that pejorative epithets that originated in name calling have often become self-descriptions, as is the case, for example, with *Jesuits* and *Moonies.* The same situation applies to *Christianos.* I concede that my solution is not totally satisfactory, but I have decided that in these cases it is better to be odd than anachronistic.

Naturally, I have benefited greatly from the encouragement and expertise of my editors. In the early stages of this edition I worked with Susan Petty at Harcourt. More recently, Steve Wainwright at Wadsworth took charge and pushed the book forward. The professional staff at Wadsworth has been truly excellent and working with them has been a real pleasure. Gretchen Otto and the staff at G & S Typesetters worked diligently on the difficult tasks of editing and production. Sandra Lord worked on photos and maps.

I also want to thank the reviewers of this book: Edward C. Hobbs, Wellesley College; Robert D. Maldonado, California State University–Fresno; and Joseph B. Tyson, Southern Methodist University.

Finally, I dedicate this edition to members of my immediate family. I thank my spouse Gretchen for her constant encouragement. Our children are Teddie Anne (Duling) Granville and Stephen Lester Ngo Duling. Teddie's spouse is Eric Granville. Their son, our grandson, is Flynn Duling Granville.

Photo 1.1 Masada (Hebrew for "stronghold"), a majestic mesa 1900 feet by 600 feet, located about 50 miles southeast of Jerusalem near the shores of the Dead Sea. Originally built by the Maccabeans, it was further fortified and developed by Herod the Great (ruled 37–4 B.C.E.) who added a casemate wall around the top, a three-tiered palace-villa on the north end, enormous cisterns for water, a bath-house, and storerooms. Two ritual baths were also unearthed there. The dramatic story of the last stand of the Jewish rebels against Rome on Masada (73 C.E.) is recorded by the Jewish historian Josephus (*Wars* 7.8–9, paragraphs 252–406).

CHAPTER ONE

HISTORICAL, CULTURAL, AND SOCIAL CONTEXTS OF THE NEW TESTAMENT

People often think that Christian denominations and sects evolved historically from the one primitive church, that Christian diversity came from an original unity. It is true that the life and teachings of Jesus of Nazareth were distinctive; it is also true that Christianity has had its share of divisions throughout history. Nonetheless, scholars agree that diversity, not unity, was present from the very beginning.

At the same time, some scholars argue that there existed *another kind of unity* in the ancient world, namely, commonly accepted cultural values and behavior typical of "advanced agrarian" societies. They also say that these values were quite different from those held in the modern West. Such values included an allegiance to the group (family, relatives, village, region, ethnic identity) rather than the equality and rights of individuals; social status based more on **honor** and **shame** than on property and money; male dominance and patriarchy rather than gender equality; the divinely ordained rule of emperor and king rather than democracy; folk and popular medicine, including magic and miracle, rather than scientific medicine; and religion and economics rooted primarily in family and politics rather than independent religious denominations and a free market economy. Understanding of the various early movements and groups who believed in Jesus as the Messiah requires that we gain an understanding of both the general culture and some of the more important, specific historical contexts in which the various groups of what eventually became Christianity appeared.

This chapter will take up some of these historical, cultural, and social contexts. First, it will focus on the political and economic history of Palestine, then on intellectual life, religion, and cultural groups and ideas, and finally on some of the common cultural values that those who came to believe in Jesus as the Messiah shared and challenged.

PALESTINE IN THE PRE-ROMAN PERIOD

KEY EVENTS OUTLINE

B.C.E. (= Before the Common Era of Israelites and the Jesus Movement/Christianity [Christian B.C.])

1000	Independent Monarchy under Kings David and Solomon
921	Divided monarchy: Israel (north) and Judah (south)
721	Assyrians overcome Israel, deport and import foreign populations (origin of Samaritans)
587	Babylonians defeat Southern kingdom (Judah) and destroy Jerusalem and the temple
587–539	Babylonian Exile of leaders
539	Persians under Cyrus the Great defeat Babylonians
538	Edict of Toleration; some return
515	Second temple dedicated
437?	Nehemiah rebuilds Jerusalem's walls
428?	Ezra publicizes the "Law"
332	Greeks under Alexander the Great march through Palestine
301	Ptolemies (Greek-Egyptians) control Palestine
198	Seleucids (Greek-Syrians) control Palestine
167	Maccabean Revolt against Seleucids
142	Independent Maccabean (Hasmonean) kingdom
63	Romans assume control of Palestine; end of Israelite independence

Some recent scholars have called into question use of the terms *Jew, Judaism,* and *Jewish* to describe ancient groups. The Greek term *Ioudaios* from which these three terms derive is rare in the ancient world; moreover, the terms are loaded with modern meanings. As more accurate historical replacements, some scholars opt for *Judean* or *Israelite.* The problem with *Judean* is that although it avoids the anachronistic overtones of *Jew* or *Jewish,* it usually signifies in ordinary English coming from a geographical place called "Judea" (southern Palestine) and also has ethnic connotations. The problem with *Israelite* is that although it is a common New Testament term, it has been used most often by modern scholars for the period prior to the Babylonian Exile, which began in 587 B.C.E. Despite these difficulties, this textbook will use *Israelite* (often with the prefatory description *Greco-Roman* to indicate the later period) and *Judean.* A similar problem exists with *Christian.* Although the New Testament contains the word *Christian,* it never uses *Christianity.* This edition will use a variety of expressions, such as "(members of) the Jesus Movement," "those who believe in Jesus as the Messiah," "Christ believers," and the like, depending on the context. No solution to these problems is satisfactory.

Courtesy of U.S. Geological Survey, EROS Data Center

Figure 1.1 Palestinian Topography. This NASA photo shows the topographical features of present-day Palestine. The Jordan River flows from Mount Hermon southward into the "Sea of Galilee" (a freshwater lake), then further south into the Dead Sea, a salt lake below sea level. Galilee in the north is fertile; Judea in the south has much barren wilderness. The region east of the Jordan is the Transjordan. The region west slopes up to the Hill Country and then gradually slopes down to the Great (Mediterranean) Sea coast.

The Monarchic Period in Ancient Israel

"Palestine" is the name that fifth-century B.C.E. Greek historian Herodotus gave to what the Bible calls the "Land of Israel." This region lies at the southeastern end of the Mediterranean Sea and is only about 150 miles long and 60 miles wide. It is bounded on the north by the foothills of Mount Hermon, on the west by the Mediterranean Sea, and on the south by the Judean wilderness. On its eastern side, the Jordan River meanders southward from the mountains, first emptying into the Sea of Galilee (a large inland lake) and farther south into the Dead Sea, a great salt lake below sea level. Central and southern Palestine regions are dominated by a north-south range of hills that gradually slopes toward the Mediterranean Sea in the west and toward the Jordan River valley in the east. The northern and central regions have rich soil more suited to agriculture; the southern region becomes increasingly barren and rocky, and the southeastern region is a "wilderness" suited mainly for a few flocks or the life of a hermit, except for an occasional oasis along the Dead Sea. (See Figure 1.1.)

Palestine's climate is Mediterranean; it has a cool rainy season in winter, but it is hot and dry in summer. The rhythms of the seasons were the foundation of great agriculturally based religious festivals, and its regional contrasts in topography and weather created several different lifestyles. Although it has no great flood plain, it was predominantly agrarian, its chief commodities being figs and dates for export, along with olives and crops of wheat and barley. There was also a little mining, some fishing on the Sea of Galilee, small businesses in its cities, and a number of artisans. It was also important for the major overland trade routes that passed through it. Strategically positioned between the larger, more powerful agrarian empires, little Israel was coveted by them as a border and buffer region, and thus its history has been stormy.

In this strategically located land, there appeared groups who spoke **Hebrew** late in the second millennium B.C.E. About 1000 B.C.E., when the surrounding great powers were weak, David, a Hebrew bandit and mercenary from the town of **Bethlehem,** took over the city of **Jerusalem** in the south and made it the capital of an independent Israelite monarchy. His son Solomon, famed for wisdom, wealth, and wives, carried out King David's plan to build a great Jerusalem temple. However, about 921 B.C.E., the northern Israelite tribes revolted against Solomon's harsh labor policies and set up an independent monarchy. Its rival capital was the town of Samaria, where there was established a rival temple on Mount Gerizîm. Historians call this period "the Divided Monarchy," divided between the Northern Kingdom ("Israel") and the Southern Kingdom ("Judah," later "Judea").

Eventually, the great empires regained power. Assyria to the northeast crushed the Northern Kingdom in 721 B.C.E. In line with its policy it deported the people of Israel and imported other subject peoples in order to weaken opposition. The resulting mixed Palestinian population of the central region became **Samaria.** Then, in 587 B.C.E., Babylonia to the east conquered the Southern Kingdom, Judah. Jerusalem and its temple also were destroyed in 587, and the Israelite leaders were deported to Babylonia (the **Babylonian Exile**), marking the beginning of what is called the **Diaspora** (Greek for "dispersion"), or the "scattering" of Palestinian peoples from their homeland to foreign countries. (Traditionally scholars have called the Israelite people from this time forward *Jews* and their culture and religion *Judaism.* In this book they will be called mainly *Israelites* [see Preface and p. 2].)

The period after the Babylonian Exile is called the "post-Exilic period" or the "second temple period." Under Cyrus the Great, the Persians (still farther to the east) overcame the Babylonians in 539 B.C.E. Cyrus allowed the Israelites in Babylonia to return home. However, many exiles chose to remain. Those who returned hoped for the reestablishment of an independent monarchy. It did not happen. Yet, about 515 B.C.E. a modest "second temple" was dedicated. Despite Samaritan opposition the Israelites also rebuilt the walls of Jerusalem (ca. 437 B.C.E.). It was during this period that the **Aramaic** dialect, used internationally in the East, began to overtake Hebrew as the vernacular language of Palestinian Israelites.

Alexander the Great, Hellenization, and the Early Greek Period (332–167 B.C.E.)

In 336 B.C.E., young Alexander the Great (356–323 B.C.E.) of Macedonia (the Balkan region just north of modern Greece) launched a campaign eastward to capture the Persian empire. (See Figures 1.2a and 1.2b.) After several victories he subdued

Palestine in 332 B.C.E. Welcomed in Egypt as a conquering hero, he next moved eastward, defeated the Persians, and advanced into India in 326 B.C.E. By this time his battle-fatigued army resisted going any farther. He returned to settle in the city of Babylon but did not live long to enjoy his success. He died, apparently of a fever, in 323 B.C.E.

Alexander was a brilliant military strategist interested mainly in conquest and empire building. However, Aristotle was his tutor, and wherever Alexander went he spread the Greek language, culture, and civilization. Two of Alexander's activities can illustrate this "Greecizing" process, called "**Hellenization**" (*Hellas* is a Greek word for "Greece"). First, Alexander and his officers wed Persian women. Second, Alexander built a network of about thirty strategic cities as centers of trade, administration, and Greek culture. Alexandria, Egypt, named for Alexander, became one of the most important cities of the Greco-Roman world. Despite these pockets of Hellenistic culture, age-old traditional cultures persisted, especially in the heavily populated rural regions, where most people lived.

The death of Alexander in 323 B.C.E. led to a bitter power struggle among his Macedonian generals. By 301 B.C.E., four distinct Hellenistic kingdoms had emerged, two of which are very important for Israelite history: (1) the Seleucid kingdom ("Syria"), extending from western Asia Minor almost to India; and (2) the Ptolemaic kingdom, mainly in Egypt and the north African coast.

How did Palestine fare during the Hellenistic period? Under the Egyptian Ptolemies in the third century B.C.E., there seems to have been relative independence. When the aggressive Syrian Seleucids gained control of the region in 198 B.C.E., they were welcomed at first. However, the Romans defeated them in 190 and forced them to pay reparations, which they passed on to their subject peoples. In 175 B.C.E., the Seleucid king Antiochus IV Epiphanes ("[God] Manifest") sought to raise money from the Israelites and in the process to *force* Hellenistic culture on them. In Jerusalem the aristocracy, already somewhat Hellenized, carried out what scholars call a "Hellenistic reform." They abolished the ancestral laws and transformed Jerusalem into a Hellenistic city-state. However, when civil war broke out between rival priestly families, Antiochus appears to have interpreted the internal conflict as a revolt against him. He attacked the city, exterminated all males who resisted, and sold women and children into slavery. The city walls were torn down, and the old citadel of the temple was fortified as a Seleucid garrison (the Akra). Every town in Judea was commanded to sacrifice to the Greek gods. Syrian troops settled in Jerusalem, and they brought their gods with them. Antiochus forbade the Torah ("instruction" [often translated "Law"]) and religious practices dear to the people. Most offensive, the Seleucids erected an altar over the altar in the Jerusalem temple and offered sacrifices to the Greek high god, Zeus. This act became etched on the memory of the Israelites as **the abomination that makes desolate** ("the desolating sacrilege"; Dan. 11:31; 12:11; 1 Macc. 1:54; Mark 13:14).

The Israelite response to *forced* Hellenization was a war of social, religious, and national liberation. The initial phase was the **Maccabean Revolt (167–164 B.C.E.).** When Antiochus' emissary came to the Judean town of Modein northwest of Jerusalem in 167 B.C.E., he demanded that the people offer sacrifices to Greek gods. A priest named Mattathias refused. Seeing one of his fellow Israelites about to comply, the priest rushed forward and slew his countryman at the altar and then killed

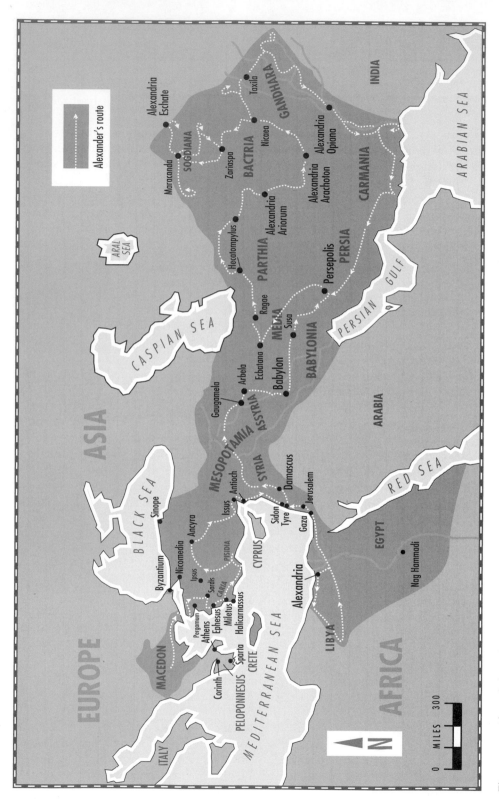

Figure 1.2a Alexander's empire.

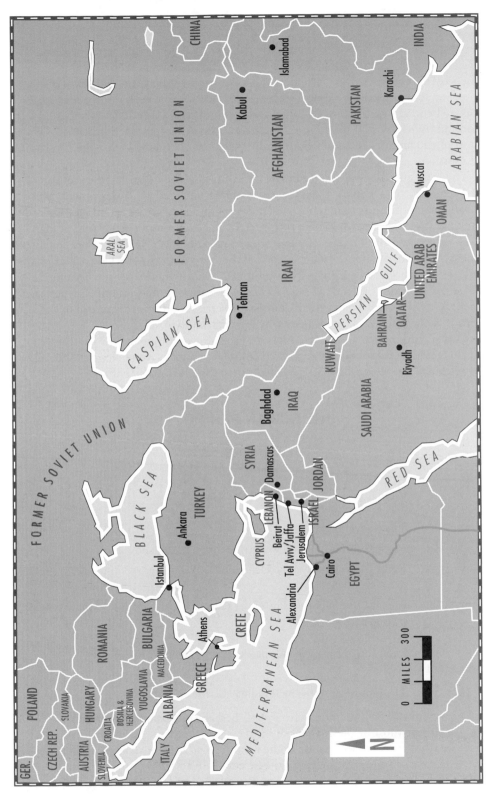

Figure 1.2b Modern area of Alexander's empire.

the king's emissary, "acting zealously for the law of God, as Phinehas had done" (1 Macc. 2:26). Then Mattathias and his sons fled to the hills. There they were joined by commoners from Jerusalem led by a group called the *Hasîdîm* ("Pious Ones," or scribal scholars of the Torah). At his death, Mattathias' son Judas Maccabeus (died 162 B.C.E.) assumed command and quickly became a national hero. He retook Jerusalem and in 164 restored and rededicated the temple. This event is the origin of the famous **Feast of Hanukkah** ("Dedication"), later called the "Festival of Lights."

The long guerrilla war that followed ended in Israelite victory and expulsion of the Seleucids from Jerusalem in 142 B.C.E. Thus emerged an independent Maccabean (or Hasmonean) kingdom, which lasted almost eighty years. Here we can note only three key developments: major territorial expansion, destruction of many Greek cities, and the forceful conversion and circumcision of many non-Israelite subjects. Despite the non-Davidic lineage of the Maccabeans—they were a priestly family—they began to see themselves as kings. Eventually the people became disenchanted with their rule. The independent Maccabean kingdom ended when the Israelites invited the Roman general Pompey to settle an internal dispute in 63 B.C.E. From this point forward, the Romans were in Palestine to stay.

This stormy period of history offers an excellent example of how the Israelites and their leaders responded to excessive "colonial" control. An analogous situation and response under the Romans occurred during the next two centuries.

THE ROMAN PERIOD

KEY EVENTS OUTLINE

B.C.E.

753	The Roman monarchy
509	The Roman republic
509–203	Rome controls Italy and western Mediterranean lands
203–27	Rome gains control of the Hellenistic empires in eastern Mediterranean
63	Roman control of Palestine under Pompey
27	Roman Empire

C.E. (= the Common Era of Israelites and the Jesus Movement/Christianity = Christian A.D.)

410	The capture of Rome by invading "barbarians"

During the old Roman monarchy, established about 753 B.C.E., Rome expanded its control over most of the Italian peninsula. (See Figure 1.3.) Under the republic after 509, Rome gained domination of the western Mediterranean lands and the eastern Hellenistic empires (the defeat of the Seleucids in 190 was noted earlier). Rome could not hold Alexander's conquered lands as far as India—the Parthian empire

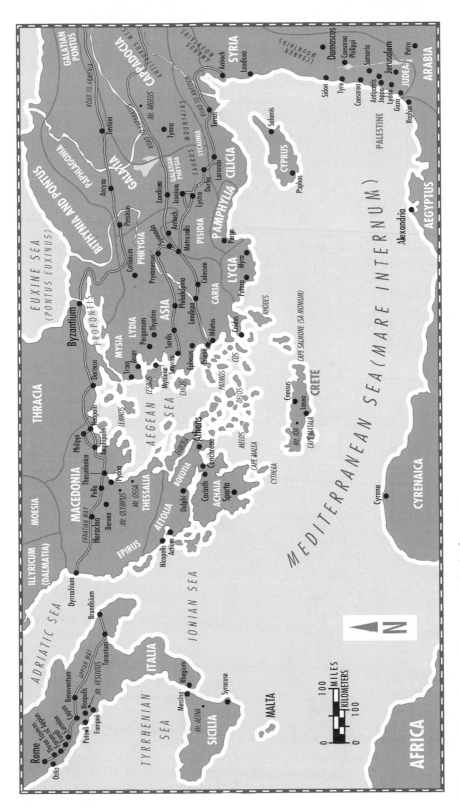

Figure 1.3 The southeastern Roman empire in the first century.

emerged there as a rival empire—but in the West, Rome's rule gradually included Spain, Gaul (modern France), southern Germany, and southern Britain. Palestine came under Roman control in 63 B.C.E. (by Pompey) and eventually became part of the Roman province of Syria.

The extension of Roman power during the first century B.C.E. put an immense strain on the republic. A stronger, more centralized rule became urgent, and the Romans looked for able rulers among their military leaders. The leaders, in turn, struggled with each other for absolute control. Pompey, successful in the East, was defeated by the western commander, Julius Caesar. After Caesar's assassination in 44 B.C.E., Octavian assumed power in the West and Antony in the East. Antony, however, began to lose the farthermost eastern territories to the Parthians. Moreover, although already married to Octavian's sister, he married Cleopatra VII of Egypt. Dishonored, Octavian convinced the Senate to declare war on Antony. In **31 B.C.E.**, Octavian routed Antony's forces on the sea at the Battle of **Actium.** The suicides of Antony and Cleopatra in Egypt in 30 B.C.E. left Octavian in full control of West and East. At Rome, he was made *imperator,* or supreme commander of the army. The Senate then conferred upon him the additional titles *augustus,* "the August," and *princeps,* "the first of the Senate." Thus in 27 B.C.E. the Roman Empire was born, and Octavian became Caesar Augustus, its first emperor.

ROMAN EMPERORS

27 B.C.E	**Octavian (Caesar Augustus)**
14 C.E.	**Tiberius**
37	**Gaius Caligula**
41	**Claudius**
54	**Nero**
68	Galba, Otho, Vitellius
69	**Vespasian**
79	**Titus**
81	**Domitian**
96	Nerva
98	Trajan
117	Hadrian
138	Antonius Pius
161	Marcus Aurelius (d. 180)

A brief look at the first-century Roman emperors will provide some indication of the vacillating political fortunes of the empire in which the Jesus Movement arose.

Caesar Augustus was a wise ruler. He secured the borders of the empire, built roads, and established a new era of peace and stability, the famous "peace of Rome" (Latin *pax Romana*). During his reign as emperor, Jesus of Nazareth was born. However, not all of Augustus' successors were as capable. Tiberius (14–37 C.E.) spent his last eleven years in a life of debauchery on the Mediterranean island of Capri. One of his infamous appointees was the governor of Judea and Samaria, Pontius Pilate (26–36 C.E.), during whose rule Jesus was crucified. Tiberius was followed by his grandnephew, the great-grandson of Augustus, Gaius Caligula (37– 41 C.E.). Caligula became consumed with power, demanded that he be addressed as a god, and proposed that his horse be made a consul (diplomat). He rewarded the animal with a marble stall and a purple blanket! He fomented a crisis among the Palestinian Israelites by demanding that a statue of himself be set up in the temple at Jerusalem. The crisis abated only when his private bodyguards assassinated him.

Caligula's uncle and successor, Claudius (41–54 C.E.), unexpectedly turned out to be a competent ruler. Under his rule came the early movements and writings of Paul the Apostle. The fourth wife of Claudius, Agrippina, poisoned him.

Nero (54– 68 C.E.), Agrippina's son by a previous marriage, succeeded Claudius. Nero's rule was marked by intrigue. He poisoned Claudius' son, executed his own wife, and arranged for the assassination of his mother. In 64 C.E., a fire devastated Rome, and Nero found his scapegoat in those who believed in Jesus as the Messiah. Finally, military commanders seized several provinces. Nero fled from Rome and eventually committed suicide in 68 C.E. According to church traditions, Peter and Paul were martyred during Nero's reign.

Widespread unrest led to a quick succession of emperors in 68– 69 C.E. (Galba, Otho, and Vitellius). Then Vespasian (69–79 C.E.), who had been dispatched to Palestine to crush the **Israelite Rebellion** (66–70 C.E.), was acclaimed emperor. Vespasian provided a decade of peace and prosperity for the empire. Vespasian's son and successor, Titus (79– 81 C.E.), who had concluded the war with the Israelites of Palestine, reigned for two years. Ancient Roman historians and Jesus Movement writers remembered his second son, Domitian (81–96 C.E.), as a tyrant. His reign provides the backdrop for the most anti-Roman book in the New Testament, Revelation. The following emperors were some of Rome's best: Nerva (96–98 C.E.), Trajan (98–117 C.E.), Hadrian (117–138 C.E.), Antonius Pius (138–161 C.E.), and the philosopher-emperor Marcus Aurelius (161–180 C.E.).

THE PALESTINIAN ISRAELITES UNDER THE ROMANS AND HERODIANS (63 B.C.E.–135 C.E.)

KEY EVENTS OUTLINE

B.C.E.

63	Romans under General Pompey control Palestine, ending Israelite independence
37	Herod the Great begins to rule
6/4	Jesus of Nazareth born
4	Herod Archelaus in Judea/Samaria
4	Herod Antipas in Galilee/Perea
4	Herod Philip in region northeast of Sea of Galilee

C.E.

6	**Prefects**/procurators (governors) replace Archelaus in Judea/Samaria
26	Pontius Pilate rules (to 36 C.E.)
37	Herod Agrippa I rules Philip's lands
39	Herod Agrippa I rules Galilee/Perea
41	Herod Agrippa I rules Samaria/Judea
44	Prefects/procurators again rule whole land
66	**Israelite Rebellion against Rome**
70	Destruction of Jerusalem and the temple
73	The **Masada** fortress taken by Romans
90	**Academy at Jamnia (Yavneh)**
132	**The Bar Cochba Revolt (to 135 C.E.)**
135	Jerusalem converted into a Hellenistic city; expulsion of Israelites

In the Roman Empire, there were mainly two types of provinces. Senatorial provinces were administered by the Roman Senate. Imperial provinces, considered politically volatile, were governed directly by a Roman military governor from the higher senatorial ranks. Called a "legate," he was directly responsible to the emperor. There were also *smaller* imperial provinces called "districts." They were also governed by a Roman governor a **prefect** (later called **procurator**), usually from the next highest, or "equestrian" rank. Like the legate, he was directly responsible to the emperor. The most famous of these today is Pontius Pilate. Finally, in some regions, the Romans permitted loyal native rulers to rule. These "client" rulers were of various ranks in descending order: "king," "ethnarch," and "tetrarch." An especially favored king was granted the title "friend of Caesar" by the emperor.

The Herodians

The **Herodians** were Herod the Great, his relatives, and his supporters and retainers. How did the Herodians come to power? In 63 B.C.E., the Roman general Pompey "settled" the dispute between the Maccabean priest-kings on the side of Hyrcanus II, whose crafty supporter, Antipater II of Idumea (just south of Judea), became governor of Idumea. After Antipater II gained Roman favor, his son Herod was granted rule of Galilee. Meanwhile the Parthians to the east appointed Antigonus II, Hyrcanus II's Maccabean rival, "client king" in Jerusalem (40 B.C.E.). Herod and his family members who were in Jerusalem at the time were forced to flee to Egypt. The ambitious Herod then went to Rome and secured the title "king" from the Romans. Returning to Palestine, he gathered an army. With Roman help he recaptured Jerusalem in 37 B.C.E. Thus an Idumean whose ancestors had been forcibly converted by the Maccabeans and who was later scorned as a "half-Israelite" by other Israelites became a Roman client king who ruled the whole of Palestine.

Flavius Josephus is the most important ancient source for the history of the Israelites during this period. He had fought in the rebellion against Rome but

AKG London/Peter Connolly

Figure 1.4 Modern reconstruction of Caesarea by the Sea, originally constructed along the Mediterranean coast by Herod the Great's builders. Since no natural harbor had existed there, it was an amazing engineering feat. It became the Roman "capital" of Palestine. (From Connolly, *Living in the Time of Jesus of Nazareth* [1983].) More recent excavations at Caesarea have shown that northwest of the theater on the land jutting into the sea was Herod's palace; north of it along the seacoast was a hippodrome; and all three—theater, palace, and hippodrome—were *inside* the wall. (K. L. Gleason, *Journal of Roman Archeology* 11 [1998] 23–52.)

nonetheless had endeared himself to the commander Vespasian, who then became emperor. So Josephus ended up in Rome as the official historian of the Israelite people, and his history, written in excellent Greek, is a fine example, though biased, of Hellenistic historical writing. Josephus wrote that Herod ("the Great," ruled 37–4 B.C.E.) was a competent ruler but also a tyrant who executed hundreds of his opponents, especially those of his family and entourage who were of royal Hasmonean descent and thus had some claim to his throne. For example, the brother of one of his wives, a Maccabean high priest, "accidentally" drowned at a pool party. Her grandfather, the old Maccabean ruler Hyrcanus II, was strangled. When Herod ordered his Hasmonean wife Mariamme executed should he not return from Rome, and the angered woman responded by refusing to have sex with him, he had her tried and executed for adultery. Then, however, he mourned her death and almost committed suicide. He also killed three of his sons. Because Herod attempted to abide by the Israelite Law, which prohibited eating pork, the pun arose, "It is better to be Herod's *hus* (Greek for "pig") than his *huios* (Greek for "son")!"

Herod was a Hellenizer and builder. He surrounded himself with Greek scholars and undertook many ambitious building projects. At Jericho he built a marvelous summer palace. The complete transformation of the Mediterranean coastal city, Strato's Tower, into the artificially constructed seaport of Caesarea was an amazing feat of ancient engineering, and it became the capital for the Roman governors. (See Figure 1.4.) At Jerusalem there was a hippodrome for races, an amphitheater, a theater, and a fortified palace. The modest second Jerusalem temple was rebuilt on a grand scale into a colonnaded Greco-oriental structure with courts, ritual baths, a central sanctuary, and a palatial Roman fortress, Antonia (named for

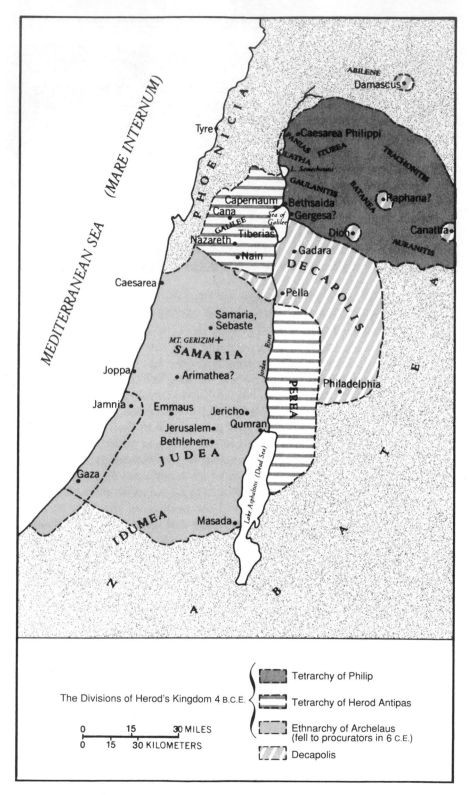

Figure 1.5 Herod's kingdom, as divided among his three sons.

Antony). Herod also built or rebuilt many outlying military fortresses, including the famous **Masada.** All of this building created a heavy tax burden on the people.

Herod had ten wives, and in his final years he was plagued by domestic problems. He passed away unloved and unmourned in 4 B.C.E. Indeed, at his death, there was a popular uprising. According to the Gospels of Matthew and Luke, Jesus of Nazareth was born near the end of his reign (ca. 6–4 B.C.E.). Herod's final will, slightly altered by Augustus, divided his kingdom among his three sons (see Figure 1.5.):

1. Philip (4 B.C.E.–33/34 C.E.) was named "tetrarch" (slightly lower in status than "ethnarch") of the largely non-Israelite regions northeast of the Sea of Galilee.

2. Herod Antipas (4 B.C.E.–39 C.E.) became "tetrarch" of Galilee and Perea beyond the Jordan River. He was finally exiled by the Roman emperor Gaius Caligula.

3. Archelaus became "ethnarch" (higher in status than "tetrarch" but lower than "king") of Samaria, Judea, and Idumea in the South. After ten years, because of opposition by his brother Antipas and the revolt of his subjects, Archelaus was dismissed and banished to Gaul in 6 C.E.

Archelaus' territory now fell to the prefects appointed by Rome. The fifth of these was Pontius Pilate (26–36 C.E.). According to the ancient Israelite philosopher Philo of Alexandria, Pilate was described by the Herodian King Agrippa I as ". . . by nature unbending and severe with the stubborn" and accused of ". . . the taking of bribes, wanton insolence, rapacity, outrages, countless and continuous murders, endless and most painful cruelty" (Philo *Embassy to Gaius* 38). This portrait contrasts with the more positive image in the New Testament gospels, but it is confirmed by Israelite historian Josephus. Although Palestine was again consolidated for three years under Agrippa I (41–44 C.E.), most of the region fell to the Roman prefects after Agrippa's death in 44.

It should be noted that these developments account for the complex political situation implied in the New Testament gospels. Herod the Great ruled as "king" at Jesus' birth. When Jesus was an adult, one of Herod's sons, the "tetrarch" Philip, who appears in the story of the beheading of John the Baptist (Mark 6:14–29), was ruling the region northeast of the Sea of Galilee. The second son, the "tetrarch" Herod Antipas, called in the gospel stories "king," but by Jesus "that fox" (Luke 13:32), was the ruler of Galilee, the location of Jesus' activity, and Perea. The third son, Archelaus, was "ethnarch" of Judea, Samaria, and Idumea soon after Jesus' birth. Because of unrest, he was replaced by **prefects.** The fifth prefect was Pontius Pilate, who appears in relation to the "trial" of Jesus at Jerusalem.

Social and Economic Conditions under the Romans and Herodians

It will be helpful for understanding the subsequent political history of Palestine to consider briefly what life was like under the Romans in general and in Roman-Herodian Palestine in particular.

In many respects, Herodian Palestine mirrored Mediterranean society as a whole. Some cultural anthropologists call it an advanced agrarian society, also known as a peasant society. There was some herding, mining, and fishing, but the focus of the economy was land and agriculture. The invention of the iron-tipped plow almost a millennium earlier allowed farmers to plow greater tracts of land. The agricultural surplus was then confiscated by a small ruling aristocracy, which under the Roman Empire was the emperor, the senatorial "classes," and regional kings and their families. These urban elite, perhaps 1–2 percent of the population, developed greater and greater power, privilege, prestige, wealth, and standing armies to defend their position. Like Alexander, they also built cities whose temples were filled with national treasuries.

Slightly lower than these ruling elite were the people who served them, or "retainers," that is, the priests, military personnel, and especially bureaucrats and technicians. Still lower were also a few large-scale merchants. Small merchants were still lower. Unlike in modern society, there was no "money economy" and no large, dominant "middle class." Still lower in rank—the vast majority, perhaps 75 percent or so—were the "peasants," mainly farmers, but also others of still lower status, such as fishermen. Those who were not able to hold on to their land (often younger sons who did not inherit) eked out their living as artisans or became impoverished and turned to beggary, thievery, and the like. These latter were expendable for the functioning of society, and in religious contexts many were considered impure.

A peasant or agrarian society was also a "limited-good" society. This means that the ranks lower than the governing elite understood that the "good things" in life—land, possessions, and wealth, but also power, privilege, prestige, status, honor, friendship, love—were limited in supply. Although some people were occasionally able to hold on to traditional family lands—the father in the Prodigal Son parable, for example (see Luke 15:11–32)—there was an increasing tendency for emperors, kings, military personnel, and urban aristocrats who taxed the peasants to hold large estates as absentee landlords when the peasants could not pay. The laborers on these estates became poor tenant farmers who paid the landlords rents. With the coming of the Romans, land was directly confiscated for imperial estates. Workdays were long and only rarely interrupted by holidays, feasts, or games. Most people were barely able to survive. The American dream of "getting ahead" or moving up the social ladder was rare, almost nonexistent.

This peasant, agrarian, limited-good society was also a slave society. Slavery in the ancient world was not usually like that in the pre–Civil War South (Bartchy). To be sure, mining and some agrarian slavery were terrible, and we hear of an occasional slave revolt in Italy. However, educated slaves could become teachers, librarians, administrators; household slaves were sometimes secretaries, tutors, or financial overseers. Slaves could accumulate assets, and some emperor's slaves had very powerful positions and owned land. Movements to abolish slavery were very infrequent. Loyal slaves were sometimes given their freedom, or if their assets were enough, they could occasionally purchase their freedom. Ex-slaves were "freedmen" or "freedwomen"; although technically free, they usually had obligations to their former masters. That the image of master and slave occurs very frequently in the New Testament is a reflection of its prevalence in the culture.

A region such as Palestine shared this general picture of social and economic stratification, although because it was a "colonial" region, the various governors and loyal client kings must be added to the ruling classes. Also, Israelites treated their

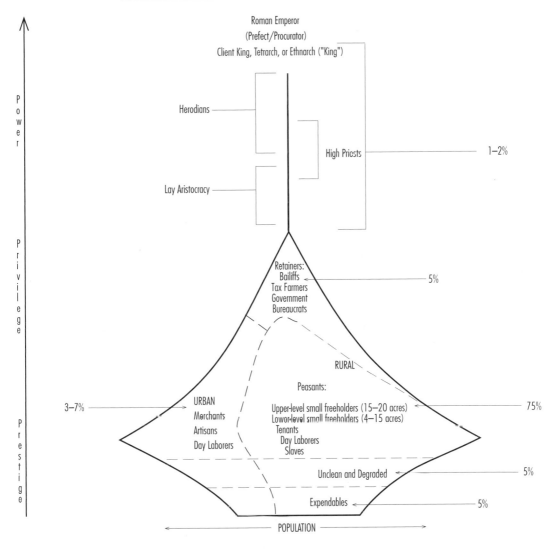

Figure 1.6   Adapted from D. Fiensy, *The Social History of Palestine in the Herodian Period,* p. 158, based on G. and J. Lenski, *Human Societies,* p. 203, and G. Alföldy, *Die römische Gesellshaft.*

slaves less harshly because they had once been slaves in Egypt. Rearranged, a model of social stratification in ancient Palestine would look something like Figure 1.6.

To get along in this vertically arranged, hierarchical social system, it was important to have "good connections." Thus there emerged a set of networks and informal contractual arrangements, little pyramids of power, within this giant pyramid of power, called **patron-client relations** (Elliott). Patrons, those of higher social status, provided protection, support, and favors for their clients. Clients offered something in return, such as loyalty, services, and military or political support. Ex-slaves usually became clients of former masters. There were also the necessary intermediaries, go-betweens, or "brokers." There were even patrons of whole cities, and, when the Roman emperor and Senate granted local rulers the status of "king," such rulers operated as "client kings." Such was Herod the Great.

At all levels of social stratification, **honor** and **shame** were core values (Malina). One could receive social status simply by being born into an honorable family or by being granted honor by an honorable person (**ascribed honor**). However, it was also possible to achieve honor by competing socially with equals, by winning a debate, for example (**acquired honor**). Loss of honor meant shame, and shame meant a decline in social status. It was very important to maintain the honor of one's family, clan, village, or gender—no matter what one's social level. Yet, it was also true that higher honor went with higher status. The fictional character Trimalchio was an ex-slave who acquired a vast fortune by investment in shipping—an investment strategy—and he ultimately purchased land. However, as an ex-slave, or "freedman," he was never able to achieve the honorable status he desired.

The most important social institution of antiquity was the family, which can be illustrated by houses and the arrangement of space (Balch and Osiek). The typical Mediterranean house did not look outward, with a porch and yard outside, but rather inward, with rooms facing in toward a central, open courtyard. In a mild-to-hot Mediterranean climate, this arrangement allowed for outdoor living inside. A common cross-cultural distinction in anthropology is the distinction between male space and female space. In Mediterranean antiquity, male space was predominantly public and political; female space was predominantly private and in the home. Yet, within the house there was also male space. In Greece and to the east, it was separate from women's space; in Rome, the boundaries were less rigid. It was also common for men of means to do business at home. Although the household was in many respects the domain of women, men tended to rule as the "head of the household" (*paterfamilias*) in three ways: As husbands they ruled over their wives; as fathers they ruled over their children (and instructed sons), although women shared in this rule; and as masters they ruled over slaves. This traditional pattern of household management is called the "**household code.**" Male dominance was even more pronounced in the traditional patriarchal societies of the eastern Roman provinces, which included Israelite society.

In general, the less fortunate urban folk lived in smaller, usually very crowded, apartments. The upper stories contained few amenities, such as plumbing or garbage disposal. People had to contend with lack of sanitation and its accompanying smells. The problem of feeding the increasing urban populations was never adequately solved; famine was a recurring phenomenon.

After 67 B.C.E., the high seas became mostly free of pirates. Cargo ships were the least expensive means of transport. Sea travel on the Mediterranean became common. There was also a network of Roman roads built mainly for military purposes. It was possible to use the roads for transport, but it was expensive, and tolls were charged. Travelers could stay at the many inns and wayside stations. For a traveler who found the inns too unruly and vulgar, entry to private homes became possible by engaging in correspondence between relatives, distant friends, or acquaintances and by carrying letters of reference. The host's **hospitality** for guests was an extremely important social virtue in antiquity.

As noted, Hellenization was primarily an urban phenomenon. Anyone who strolled through an ancient Greco-Roman city could observe Hellenistic design and architecture: walls around a city, walls within the city often coordinated with socially segregated districts, one or more central *agoras* (town squares used for marketplaces or government and administrative buildings), colonnaded streets and porticoes, stadiums, baths, temples, theaters, amphitheaters, hippodromes, gymnasiums, fountains, aqueducts, gates, and arches. Again, the Greek language and fashionable Greek dress were common. In the cities with stronger Roman influence, there was usually a *forum* with temples for the Roman gods, statues of the emperor and his family, statues of patrons, and buildings for the town council and legal and business transactions. One might also find Latin-inscribed monuments. Cities were also often dominated by temple and palace complexes related to indigenous religions.

Political power and economic power were heavily concentrated in the cities. In the countryside were poor peasants, mainly farmers under control of wealthy urban elites, often absentee landlords. Again, the great majority of people lived in rural areas, where traditional languages and age-old cultural patterns and religious ideas stubbornly persisted. Cities were networked to the countryside by trade, taxation, and the gathering of agricultural products for redistribution.

In older, established, local cultures, it was natural for people to perceive themselves as belonging to familiar groups such as family, clan, or village. Such groups dominated conventional morality and the individual's sense of **honor** and identity (for example, marriage according to kinship lines and taboos against incest). However, the shift to more Hellenistic urban settings, with their new, changing, international environments and political and economic repression of the poor, led to frequent social dislocation and conflict.

The chief responsibilities of the various Roman governors were the maintenance of civil order, the administration of justice, including the judicial right of capital punishment, and the collection of various taxes and tolls. This system was enforced by the military. Client kings had similar responsibilities, although their right to inflict capital punishment was often restricted.

The agents of the Romans and local client kings normally collected taxes on individuals and land. Tolls, however, were "farmed out" to the highest bidders. The income of toll collectors was whatever they collected in excess of the amount due to Rome. Greedy toll collectors abused this system and were commonly hated. In addition, client kings who had ambitious building projects—Herod the Great, for example—added their own taxes. Finally, there were religious taxes, such as the Israelite half-shekel "temple tax" for Israelite adult males, due once a year.

Roman Policy in Palestine

The Romans were sensitive enough to permit the stubborn Israelites special exemptions from performing military service, appearing in court on the Sabbath, having to portray the emperor's head on their coins (Israelite prohibition against images), and offering sacrifices *to* the emperor as a deity. This last duty was replaced by sacrifices "*for* Caesar and the Roman nation" in the Jerusalem temple twice daily.

In areas of heavy Israelite population, the Romans were not to represent the image of the emperor on their military standards.

However, these exemptions were not always implemented. At the death of Herod, demonstrators demanded that taxes be lowered, duties be removed, certain prisoners be freed, and a new high priest be instated. When a group protested Herod's execution of two teachers who had encouraged youths to remove the image of a golden eagle that Herod had placed on the temple gate, Archelaus' temple troops attacked and, according to Josephus (who liked to inflate figures), killed three thousand of them. Pilate brought military standards containing idolatrous images into Jerusalem at night. They were removed only when the people demonstrated their willingness to die for their religion. Pilate also confiscated temple funds to finance construction of an aqueduct, and when the people protested, he killed many of the unarmed protesters. For these and other abuses, Pilate was eventually removed by the legate of Syria.

In 40–41 C.E., the emperor Gaius Caligula (37–41 C.E.), who wished to be worshipped as a deity, took revenge for an incident of Israelite insubordination by commanding the legate of Syria to erect his statue in the Jerusalem temple. The wise legate delayed and held conferences with the Israelites, who vowed to go to war if he carried out the command. The incident was defused only when Gaius was assassinated. Herod Agrippa I's rule over the whole of Palestine for a brief period (41–44 C.E.) brought better times, although some members of the Jesus Movement remembered him for persecuting their leaders (cf. Acts 12:20–23).

After Herod Agrippa I's death in 44 C.E., the prefects/procurators assumed control over all of Palestine, and the situation worsened. Josephus claims that on one occasion twenty thousand Israelites were killed in a riot prompted by a Roman soldier's "mooning" some Passover pilgrims.

Resistance, Reform, and Terrorist Movements and Leaders in Palestine

Oppression, along with natural calamities such as drought and famine, contributed to much social unrest in the first century, especially among the urban poor and the rural peasants. Reform, resistance, and terrorist movements, known from other hot spots in the Mediterranean world, also arose in Palestine. The following are several types of such groups (Horsley).

Brigands (Social Bandits)

Members of one type of movement are often portrayed by Josephus as mere plunderers. Modern sociological study, however, suggests they might have been **social bandits,** that is, rural bandit-chiefs and their followers who rose from the ranks of the peasants, robbed the rich, sometimes gave to the poor, and sometimes found support among local villagers who hoped for a better future. In ancient Palestine, these bandits may have been influenced by millennial dreams and hopes. In any case, after 44, such bandit-led peasant groups, according to Josephus, increased. (Earlier, Jesus of Nazareth had been crucified between two such bandits.)

Popular Prophets

There were also self-styled, politically active, popular prophets. During Pontius Pilate's rule (26–36 C.E.), a Samaritan prophet led his followers to Mount Gerizîm to see sacred vessels supposedly buried by Moses. Josephus claims that they were armed and that many were killed, routed, or taken into captivity. A certain Theudas (cf. Acts 5:36) in the 40s C.E. led his followers to the Jordan River, telling them that at his command it would divide, presumably like the Red Sea at the command of Moses (Exod. 14:21–29). However, the prefect's troops attacked and killed many of them. Theudas was beheaded.

A third example was an Israelite named "the Egyptian" who in 56 C.E. told his followers that at his command the walls of Jerusalem would fall down, as in the story of Joshua (Josh. 6). They were attacked, many were killed, and "the Egyptian" fled.

These figures were probably influenced by apocalyptic thought and thus might be called "millennial prophets." Several such prophets appeared during the revolt against Rome in 66–70. John the Baptizer and Jesus were believed to have been prophets. Also, the author of Revelation considered himself a prophet.

Popular Kings or "Messiahs"

The term *messiah* comes from the Hebrew *m^eshîach,* "anointed (one)," translated in the Greek translation of the Bible, the **Septuagint,** as *Christos,* from which the English term *Christ* comes. In the Hebrew scriptures, priests, prophets, and especially kings were anointed as an act of inauguration into their "office." During the period under discussion, popular kings or messiahs were self-styled "strong men" with superior size or ability whose followers accepted them as royalty. Josephus says three such popular kings appeared at the unrest that followed the death of Herod the Great in 4 B.C.E.: Judas, son of the bandit-chief Hezekiah, who in "zealous pursuit of royal rank" (*Antiquities* 17.271–272) led a revolt against the Romans in Galilee; Simon of Perea, who donned the royal diadem, was proclaimed king by the masses, and, after plundering Herod's royal palace in Jericho, was finally caught and beheaded; and the shepherd Athronges, supported by his four brothers and their troops, who also donned the diadem, claimed to be "king," and went about ambushing Roman and Herodian troops.

During the wars with Rome from 66 to 70 B.C.E., two more popular kings surfaced: Menahem, who led a band of radical assassins called **Sicarii** (see following) and who entered Jerusalem as a king; and Simon bar Giora, whom the peasants obeyed "like a king" and who also joined the Sicarii in Jerusalem. At the end of the war, Simon appeared in royal robes and was taken to Rome, where he was executed.

"Fourth Philosophy"

The "Fourth Philosophy" seems to have been a group of nonviolent, activist intellectuals. As Herod lay dying in 4 B.C.E., two "teachers" incited their disciples to tear down the golden eagle on the temple gate; they and their followers were arrested and executed. In 6 C.E., a "teacher" named Judas the Galilean allied himself with the Pharisee Saddok and opposed the newly instituted taxes. Josephus wrote, "the nation was filled with unrest" (cf. *Antiquities* 18:3–9).

"Sicarii"

During the 50s C.E., an urban group called the **Sicarii** (Latin *sica,* "dagger"; *sicarius,* "dagger-man"; *sicarii,* "assassins") appeared in Jerusalem. They were clandestine, urban-based guerrilla terrorists named for their means of assassination, the dagger. They selected specific, symbolic targets for elimination among the aristocracy; they assassinated more generally and plundered the property of the elite; and they kidnapped hostages for ransom. Their religious philosophy was "No Lord but God." One of the group's leaders during the Israelite Rebellion against Rome, the popular king Menahem, was Judas the Galilean's (grand?)son as well as a "teacher" (Josephus *Wars* 2.445). Another leader who made the final defense of Masada, Eleazar, son of Ja'ir, was also related.

In summary, we have distinguished five movements: followers of social bandits, popular messiahs, prophets, the "Fourth Philosophy," and *Sicarii.* There appear to be certain family connections among some of their leaders. Whether these groups were a connected single movement or not, they shared what the Maccabees and *Hasîdîm* shared some two hundred years earlier: opposition to political, economic, and religious oppression by a foreign power in league with the native wealthy aristocracy. The social dimensions of some of these groups suggest that they were peasant revolts. Perhaps they were influenced by apocalyptic ideas as well. What was their relation, if any, to Jesus and the early Jesus Movement?

The War with Rome (66–70 C.E.)

Herod Agrippa I died in 44 C.E. His successor, Herod Agrippa II, was relatively powerless. The Roman prefects were again in control, now over all Palestine. Yet, incidents persisted. In the spring of 66 C.E., after a clash between Israelites and Greeks at Caesarea, the procurator Gessius Florus (64–66 C.E.) confiscated a large sum of money from the temple treasury "for governmental purposes." The outraged Israelite populace mocked him by taking up a collection in the streets. Florus responded by allowing his troops to plunder part of Jerusalem and to execute some prisoners. Attempts at mediation by the priests failed. When Roman troops did not react to friendly overtures by the crowds, the crowds slung insults at Florus. A bloody street battle broke out. The people gained the upper hand, took possession of the temple mount, and cut off the passageway between the temple and the Roman-held fortress of Antonia. Further attempts at mediation by Agrippa II, some leading Pharisees, and the priestly aristocracy failed. The fortress of **Masada,** taken earlier by the Romans, was retaken by *Sicarii* led by Menahem. At the direction of Eleazar, the rebellious son of the high priest, the sacrifices for the emperor were stopped. In modern terms, this act was a "declaration of war."

In Judea, bandit-led rebels routed the Roman army, and this initial success encouraged further resistance. The Israelites loosely organized the land for battle. The Roman emperor Nero (54–68 C.E.) dispatched his seasoned commander, Vespasian, who organized the legions at Antioch and sent his son, Titus, to Alexandria to bring up the Fifteenth Legion. The newly organized army marched on Galilee. Josephus, then a Galilean commander, attempted negotiations and offered only moderate resistance. More radical elements came to believe that Josephus was not fully committed to the cause. They may have been correct, because in 67 C.E. Josephus deserted to the Romans (thus eventually he became the official historian of the Israelites). Meanwhile, under the leadership of bandit-chief John of Gischala, more dedicated patriots were put in charge. A much-disputed ancient tradition in the Jesus Movement claims that just before hostilities broke out, believers in Jesus as the Christ fled to a town called Pella across the Jordan River.

Meanwhile, civil war broke out in Jerusalem. At first, aristocratic priestly royalists, wealthy families, and Roman soldiers were opposed by the populace and some lower-order priests led by the son of the high priest, Eleazar. However, when the "popular king" Menahem and his *Sicarii* killed Eleazar's father, the Eleazar group assassinated Menahem. The remaining *Sicarii*, now led by Eleazar ben Ja'ir, escaped to Masada, which other *Sicarii* had retaken from the Romans earlier. Despite the lack of unity, an assault on the city by the Romans was repelled.

Other factions arose in Jerusalem. The revolutionary **Zealots** (Greek *zealos,* "zeal" [for the Torah]) were able to overthrow the aristocrats, establish their own government, and choose their own high priest. However, they, too, broke into two competing factions. One was led by a priest, a certain Eleazar ben Simon; the other was led by the Galilean bandit-chief, John of Gischala, joined by some Idumeans. Then the Idumeans broke from John to form a third group who sought to overthrow John with the help of the popular king, Simon ben Giora.

Confusion reigned in Jerusalem. The experienced Roman commander Vespasian shrewdly decided to hold off and let the Israelites exhaust themselves. In 68 C.E., news of Nero's suicide arrived. Vespasian delayed longer. In quick succession, Galba, Otho, and the western commander, Vitellius, ruled the empire. In the eastern empire, Vespasian was acclaimed emperor and left for Rome to assume his new role, leaving his son Titus to conclude the war.

In the spring of 70 C.E., Titus began the siege of Jerusalem. The Israelite factions of the city now united under Simon ben Giora. While the Israelites fought valiantly, Titus' armies surrounded the city. Hunger and thirst began to take their toll. Gradually the walled sections of the city fell, one by one, and the fortress of Antonia was retaken. The temple was ravaged by fire. The Israelites refused to surrender. Women, children, and the elderly—all were butchered, and the city and most of its walls were destroyed. The major battle over, Titus set sail for Rome with seven hundred handsome prisoners for the victory parade through Rome, later commemorated by the Arch of Titus, still to be seen in the Roman Forum.

Although the victory belonged to the Romans, several fortresses remained to be subdued. The most difficult was **Masada,** commanded by Eleazar ben Ja'ir and the *Sicarii.* The task fell to Roman Commander Flavius Silva who, because of the steep cliffs, had an earthen bridge built across which a battering ram could be rolled into place. Josephus tells the story that when Eleazar saw that the Israelite cause was hopeless, he addressed the defenders of Masada, asking that they kill their families and then each other. The deed was done. Thus when the Romans finally breached the wall with the battering ram, there was no battle to be fought.

The destruction of Jerusalem and the temple was a tragic moment in Israelite history. What survived was an Israelite religion and culture reorganized by the **Pharisees** who were allowed by the Romans to meet not far from the Mediterranean coast at Jamnia (**the Academy at Jamnia**) about 90 C.E.

Still, hatred simmered. Between 115 and 117 C.E., Israelites in north Africa and on the island of Cyprus revolted. Then, between 132 and 135 C.E., Israelites again revolted in Judea. Rabbi Akiba acclaimed a certain bar Cochba ("Son of the Star," cf. the messianic star of Num. 24:17) to be "the king, the Messiah." The **Bar Cochba Revolt** probably arose in response to three events: the emperor Hadrian's empirewide ban on circumcision (not exclusively an Israelite practice), his attempt to establish Jerusalem as a Greco-Roman city (Aelia Capitolina), and his intention to build a temple to Jupiter Capitolinus on the site of the previous Jerusalem temple. This new revolt also failed. Bar Cochba's detractors renamed him "bar Koziba" ("Son of the Lie" = "Liar"). Hadrian's plans were then carried out. Although there is some archeological evidence that Greco-Roman Israelites and members of the Jesus Movement lived side by side in Galilee after the rebellion, Israelites living in Jerusalem were mostly driven out and, officially at least, not permitted to return upon punishment by death. From that time on, ancient Israelites survived primarily as "**Diaspora** Judaism," a people without a homeland until 1948, when the state of Israel was established.

In summary, the story of Palestine before and during the rise of the early Jesus Movement shows that it was the fate of the masses of ancient Israelites to live under the yoke of foreign oppressors and their agents. This situation brought about linguistic, cultural, and religious contact with powerful external, colonial forces. It also brought about social repression, economic deprivation worsened by heavy taxation, and periodic political turmoil. Although there is much evidence for assimilation to these influences, from time to time, religio-political resistance movements arose to combat them. These historical, economic, political, and religious elements converged in the late first century, precisely the period of the emergence of some of the earliest surviving Jesus Movement literature.

We must now look more closely at the cultural environment, especially Hellenistic intellectual life, Hellenistic religion, Israelite religion, and a few Palestinian groups.

HELLENISTIC INTELLECTUAL LIFE

Literacy and Education

In most Western cultures, illiterate adults—those who cannot read or write at some minimal level—are judged to be uneducated and often made to feel inferior. However, in *oral* cultures, one can be educated to *hear* appropriately (auraliteracy) and to *remember and recite* long passages orally or speak with eloquence (oraliteracy), both of which are highly valued. In an ancient Greco-Roman culture both, especially oraliteracy, were still respected in some quarters. Nonetheless, to *read* written alphabet letters (oculiteracy) was increasingly valued. Naturally, the ability to read and write enough to get along in a craft, trade, or business (craftsman's literacy) was also valuable. Of more status still was the ability to read and write *technical or professional literature* (scribaliteracy); indeed, scribes had power and prestige, in part because they could draw up legal and business contracts. Finally, only a very few politicians, poets, orators, playwrights, and scholars could read and write at highly sophisticated levels.

Education in schools across the Roman Empire was standardized and mostly of the Hellenistic type. At the primary level, students met wherever possible and studied reading, writing, and simple arithmetic, as well as physical education. At this level, girls and slaves sometimes attended. In addition to regular teachers, a *paidagōgos,* or male slave-guardian, would often accompany children safely to school and, if educated, drill them in their lessons. At the secondary level, normally for males only, the core curriculum was to read and recite from Greek classics such as Homer, the Greek playwrights, and in Latin schools the Latin orators. The focus was on copying, reading, translating, and interpreting. The "common" (*koinē*) Greek language was disparaged. Normally a *gymnasium,* where young men exercised in the nude, offered physical education. Finally, higher education was mainly for elite urban males, although a few women of means, especially among the Romans, were well educated. Advanced schools (Greek *ephēbeia;* Roman *collegia*) stressed philosophy, rhetoric, medicine, and law. One could also learn from wandering philosophers and public lectures. The goal of Hellenistic education was *paideia* ("culture"), or to become appropriately civilized.

Literacy among the Israelites was probably no greater than in the general population, that is, no more than 10 percent. Compulsory education for Israelite children was very unlikely. Some Israelite men attended Hellenistic schools. Others probably had an Israelite education based mainly on sacred texts. However, the two were often mixed. For example, ben Sira's writings about 180 B.C.E. exhibit the flowing together of Israelite wisdom and Hellenistic *paideia.* Five years later the "Hellenistic reform" of Jerusalem included Greek-style education, including a *gymnasium* and advanced schooling. There was also priestly education and a nonpriestly "synagogue of scribes" (1 Macc. 7:12). Eventually chains of interpretive tradition associated with great teachers arose, culminating in the learned schools of Palestine and Babylonia, which debated the finer points of the Torah (the **rabbinic literature**). Finally, there is some evidence of Israelite education for women in practical activities (nurses, weavers, midwives, and the like). In a few cases it appears that women of high status also received higher education.

Science and Literature

The flowering of the natural and mathematical sciences and philology took place during the last two centuries B.C.E. During the Roman period there were significant developments in international law and in literature: comedy, mime, and poetry, the revival of Greek tragedy, and the flourishing of historiography. Biographies of rulers and those endowed with great wisdom stressed their noble birth, education, teaching, conduct, and noble death. In biographies of popular heroes and heroines, these themes often merged with stories of miraculous healing. Fables, oracles, travel adventures, and erotic descriptions became typical of the Hellenistic romance.

Philosophical Schools and Popular Philosophies

One route to *paideia* was the philosophical school. Many schools were formed in Athens, the most famous being Plato's Academy, Aristotle's Lyceum, Epicurus' Garden, and Zeno's open-air Stoa (Greek *stoa,* a "colonnaded porch"). Despite many differences in these schools, there were also similarities. Alan Culpepper summarizes common elements of the philosophical schools like this:

> (1) they were groups of disciples which usually emphasized *philia* ["love"] and *koinōnia* ["fellowship"]; (2) they gathered around, and traced their origins to a founder whom they regarded as an exemplary wise, or good man; (3) they valued the teaching of their founder and the traditions about him; (4) members of the schools were disciples or students of the founder; (5) teaching, learning, studying, and writing were common activities; (6) most schools observed communal meals, often in memory of their founders; (7) they had rules or practices regarding admission, retention of membership, and advancement within the membership; (8) they often maintained some degree of distance or withdrawal from the rest of society; and (9) they developed organizational means of insuring their perpetuity.
>
> (*The Johannine School,* p. 259)

The Jesus Movement also seems to have developed informal "schools" that perpetuated the ideas of leaders.

What were some of the popular philosophies most related to the New Testament? We may note three.

Platonism

Plato (died 347 B.C.E.) argued that the changing, material world perceived through the senses is only a shadowy imitation of the true reality, which is the eternal world of abstract ideas known through reason, especially by the philosopher. In his famous allegory of the cave, Plato pictures humans who are chained and cannot move in an underground cave. They have been there since childhood. They can see only the shadows of moving objects on the cave wall before them, which have been cast by moving figures behind another wall outside the cave, with a blazing fire and finally the sun behind them. The chained humans hear voices they falsely think are coming from the shadowy figures. Then one of imprisoned figures gets loose, "ascends" from the cave, sees the true reality, the Light, which blinds him. "Descending" back into the cave, he is unable to convince the others of the amazing Truth that he has seen.

For Plato, the material, mortal body is a prison for the divine, immortal soul. The good and just person disciplines the body and its emotions and senses, allowing the reason in the soul to achieve the virtue of knowledge, to see what others cannot. Only philosophers can see the Truth at its fullest. Plato's view of humanity was elitist, as was his politics: The best ruler is the benevolent philosopher-king.

The Platonic view of the world is one example of philosophical **dualism,** the idea that there are two equal opposing powers in the universe (evil/good, light/darkness, but also mortal/immortal, material/immaterial, vice/virtue, and the like). Popular Platonism sometimes contributes to the view that this world is evil and that

Figure 1.7 Athens *agora,* Acropolis, and Stoa of Attalos. No letter of Paul to the Athenians survives, but Acts 17:17 claims that Paul spent time in the Athens *agora* or "market place," seen here at the foot of the famous Acropolis. Paul is also said to have delivered a speech on Areopagus Hill overlooking the *agora,* slightly below the entrance to the Acropolis (Acts 17:22–31). In the second century B.C.E. Attalos built the *stoa,* or roofed colonnade, to the left of the *agora* (now reconstructed). It provided shade from the sun and shelter from the rain; along the backside were entrances to shops. So this *stoa* was something like an ancient "shopping mall." In such a *stoa* Zeno (ca. 336–263 B.C.E.) was said to have taught; thus, his philosophy was called Stoicism.

our human origins and destinies lie in a higher world. Platonism probably influenced the Corinthians, the writer(s) of the Gospel of John, the Apostle Paul (1 Cor. 2–4; 2 Cor. 5), and especially the author of the Book of Hebrews. It also was an important influence on **Gnosticism** (see following).

Stoicism

Stoicism took its name from the Greek word *stoa,* meaning "a colonnaded porch or outdoor mall." (See Figure 1.7.) Its founder, Zeno (ca. 336–263 B.C.E.), taught under such a mall in Athens. In contrast to Platonic "dualism," Stoicism was "monistic": All reality is one. For the Stoic, the world was ordered by divine reason, the *Logos* (a Greek term meaning "word," "reason"), but a spark or "seed" of the *Logos* lived within human beings. If they obeyed it, they followed their true nature and were at home in the world. Stoics could also refer to the *Logos* as God, or Zeus, and they associated it with fire.

Stoics taught that happiness is attained by maintaining harmony with Nature, which was thought to lead to inner peace and contentment in a world full of troubles. Stoic virtues were self-sufficiency, tranquillity, suppression of emotion, freedom from external pressures and materialism, and the natural and innate rights of all people, *including slaves and women,* at least in theory. Stoics also stressed the importance of the will and detachment from property, wealth, suffering, and sickness. Stoics often formed associations that stressed these noble ethical themes.

Cynicism

Stoicism was related to **Cynicism.** Zeno, the founder of Stoicism, was a follower of Crates, and Crates, in turn, was a disciple of Diogenes. Diogenes accepted opponents' label "dog" (Greek *kyōn*), from which the word *cynicism* derives. The Cynics were not cynical in the modern sense; rather, they were counterculture street preachers who tried to convert people from normative human values such as the quest for fame, fortune, and pleasure to a life of austere virtue. This was the path to true freedom and happiness. Many Cynics wandered from town to town, restricted their diets, begged for food, wore short cloaks, carried only a wallet and staff, rejected social institutions such as marriage and the state, and sometimes attempted to shock people out of their complacency with witticisms and vulgar behavior. The Cynic way of life was revived as an ideal among first-century Stoics who wanted to appeal to the masses. The following sample of Cynic thought depicts the Cynics' nonnormative view that happiness lies in abandoning one's family and home to lead a wandering life of poverty:

> And how is it possible that a man who possesses nothing and who is naked, without house and hearth, untidy, without slaves and without a home town can live a happy life?
>
> Look at me. I am without house, without home, without property, without slaves! I sleep on the ground, I have no wife, no children, no palace from which to rule, but only the earth and sky and one rough coat. And what do I lack? Am I not without sorrow, am I not without fear, am I not free? . . . Who on seeing me will not consider that he is looking at his king and lord?
>
> (Xenophon *Memorabilia* 1.2.51)

There are a few parallels between the Cynic lifestyle and the lifestyle of some of the early apostles (Mark 6:8–10; Matt. 10:9–10). Also, the Cynic-Stoic literary device of arguing with an imaginary opponent (called the "diatribe") and the habit of listing virtues and vices are characteristic of Paul (Gal. 5:19–23).

HELLENISTIC RELIGIONS

In antiquity, religion, like economics, was not a separate institution, but rather always related to, or "embedded in," the family and political institutions (natural religion). There were, to be sure, "voluntary associations" in antiquity that one could join; moreover, some of them were specifically religious "cult associations," that is, associations that venerated some god or goddess. Such voluntary associations were hierarchically organized and had an ethos like that of the family; they thus became more pervasive when traditional family structures were in decline.

Traditional Gods and Goddesses

Political religions had traditional myths associated with city-states. Often the deities were thought to live in some sacred mountain to the north (Olympus), which also became heaven. Greco-Roman forms of such religions were polytheistic, although Zeus (Jupiter) arose to power to become the supreme, majestic deity (monarchial polytheism). He was a "sky god" who thundered, sent rain, and hurled thunderbolts. He and the other members of the Greek and Latin panthea were usually associated with the rhythms of the seasons. They were believed to descend occasionally to earth for some important redemptive mission on behalf of humankind; sometimes they were identified with historical figures. Essentially, however, they were *eternal* gods and goddesses, not exalted human beings.

Heroes and Heroines

However, there were accounts about special human beings thought to be so endowed with divine power that they were able to perform superhuman feats (see also the "Divine Man"). Often believed to be the offspring of divine-human unions, these beings were said to have wisdom, prophetic abilities, and other special powers, including the ability to work miracles, especially healing. Within the model of patron / client relations, they were considered to be the patrons or benefactors of all humanity. Among this group of special human beings were all manner of rulers, military conquerors, politicians, philosophers, physicians, healers, poets, and athletes.

Some of these supernormal humans were so special that they were thought to have been rewarded with the status of immortality at death. One of the most famous of these special "divine men" was the itinerant philosopher Apollonius of Tyana (Asia Minor), whose mother, it was said, was impregnated by the Egyptian god Proteus. Apollonius was said to have gathered followers, taught, helped the poor, healed the sick, raised the dead, cast out demons, and appeared to his followers after death to give a discourse on immortality. He lived through most of the first century C.E. Shortly after 217 C.E., the *Life of Apollonius of Tyana,* a type of ancient biography, was written by Philostratus. Scholars often compare his miracles to those found in stories about Jesus and the apostles.

Sympathy, Divination, Astrology, and Alchemy

In the Hellenistic period, the conviction arose that there are mysterious forces in heaven and on earth that unite everything (sympathy). On the one hand, some people believed that the universe is too mysterious for anyone to fully understand. For example, the early Greeks had accepted the view that each person has his or her own "Fortune," "Chance," or "Destiny," whether good or ill, deified as the goddess *Tychē* (Latin *Fortuna*). A somewhat more deterministic and less friendly deity was called "Fate" (Greek *Heimarmenē*). There arose specialists who sought to understand this mysterious order by **divination,** that is, either by intuitive skills akin to prophecy or by lots, involuntary acts of speech, animal entrails, oil floating on water, and the like. As the ancient Babylonians taught, one could investigate the effects on the earth of the impersonal, fixed order of the stars and planets, who were also deified as gods, goddesses, and demons (cf. Gal. 4:8–10; Col. 2:8). With the aid of Greek mathematics and astronomy, a person's "fortune" or "destiny" could be ascertained by the position of the stars at birth; by a knowledge of the stars, or **astrology** (from Greek *astēr,* "star"), one could learn about his or her fate. Astrology was extremely widespread in the Hellenistic world. The most obvious reference to astrology in the New Testament is the star of the "Magi" (Matt. 2:1–12, 16). Eventually there also emerged attempts to divine the process of transformation of base metals into precious metals and to hasten the process (alchemy).

Healing and Magic

Medical anthropologists say that to understand healing in antiquity it is necessary to have some grasp of the total "health care system," not just the individual healer. From this perspective "sickness" refers to two kinds of phenomena: disease and illness (Pilch). Sickness is the reality; disease and illness are concepts that explain the reality but from different perspectives: biomedical and socio-cultural. Disease and illness are not realities. "Disease" designates abnormal functioning of bodily organs or organ systems and requires diagnosis, prognosis, and therapy by biomedical experts. It is characteristic of most modern Western medical practice. "Illness," in contrast, is defined and experienced socially and involves cultural perceptions, values, expressions, and responses to what is experienced. It is typically found in most tribal and agrarian societies. Diseases are "cured" or not "cured"; illnesses are "healed" or not "healed." To heal disease is not simply to cure illness. It is to heal the whole self. To heal in this sense is to perform a symbolic action analogous to what takes place in Western psychotherapy. Finally, in antiquity there were professional, popular, and folk healers, although the boundary lines between them were fluid. Professional healers were recognized, authorized physicians, experts who treated diseases in customary ways and performed primitive surgeries. Popular healers were local family and village healers who attempted to maintain health; they were those within one's network of acquaintances. Finally, folk healers were well-known nonprofessional specialists, that is, shamans, magicians, and prophets who engaged in exorcising demons and healing the whole person.

Ancient healers mainly addressed illness and sought wellness. Famous health spas were associated with Asclepius, the Greek god of healing (for example, Epidauros, Pergamum, the island of Cos). Here the healing arts ranged from divine cures by the god Asclepius, who appeared in a dream in the holy sanctuary ("incubation"), to cures by attending physicians who used surgical tools. However, people also used family remedies such as herbal medicine. All manner of folk healers were believed to perform amazing cures. Such was Jesus of Nazareth.

A very common means of folk healing was the practice of magic. Borrowed from the Persian language, the Greek term *magos* originally referred to a Persian priest who attempted to combat the mysterious powers that determined one's fate and to provide protection against demonic powers often associated with stars (astrology). To know the correct formula and to recite it correctly were considered to be a scientific way of dealing with life's evil tragedies. The magical papyri of Egypt show that ancient magicians believed in the power of Hebrew language names, including the "god" whose name is "Jesus."

> **A tested charm of Pibechis for those possessed by daimons:** Take oil of unripe olives with the herb mastigia and the fruit pulp of the lotus, and boil them with colorless marjoram while saying, "IÔÊL ÔS SARTHIÔMI EMÔRI THEÔCHIP-SOITH SITHEMEÔCH SÔTHÊ IÔÊ MIMIPSÔTHIÔÔPH PHERSÔTHI AEÊIOYÔ IÔÊ EÔ CHARI PHTHA, come out from NN [*insert name*]" (add the usual). **The phylactery [amulet]:** On a tin lamella [a thin piece of tin] write "IAÊO ABRAÔTH IÔCH PHTHA MESENPSIN IAÔ PHEÔCH IAÊÔ CHARSOK," and hang it on the patient. It is terrifying to every daimon, a thing he fears. After placing [the patient] opposite [to you], conjure. **This is the conjuration:** "*I conjure you by the god of the Hebrews, Jesus,* IABA IAÊ ABRAÔTH AIA THÔTH ELE ELÔ AÊÔ EOY IIIBAECH ABARMAS IABARAOU ABELBEL LÔNA ABRA MAROIA BRAKIÔN, who appears in fire, who is in the midst of land, snow, and fog. . . ."
>
> (Paris Magical Papyrus IV.3008–25, in H. D. Betz, ed., *The Greek Magical Papyri in Translation,* p. 96)

Although magic was condemned by Israelites and Jesus Movement groups, paradoxically it was also practiced by both (Mark 8:22–26; Acts 8:9–24). Jesus' opponents accused him of deriving his power from the Prince of Demons (e.g., Mark 3:20–27), or, as later rabbis put it, he was a magician who led the people astray.

Mystery Religions

Many people during the Hellenistic period felt that the traditional Greek and Roman humanlike deities had become remote in their far distant heaven and too formal, too sedate, too impersonal. To fill the void, they turned to more exotic deities. Originally local, these deities had become internationalized, widespread, and very popular. These **mystery religions** were secret religious associations closed to outsiders. As with the voluntary associations, initiates joined and went through rites of cleansing and formal initiation. They took vows of silence not to reveal the most holy mysteries to outsiders. As a result, we do not know much about their most secret utterances, practices, and revelations.

However, the mystery religions also had a public side that displayed colorful pageantry. Usually there was a recital or reenactment of a myth to celebrate the death and resurrection of a hero or heroine, which had its parallel in the death and rebirth of vegetation during the cycle of the agricultural year. Often there was the theme of wandering in quest of some deity or attribute. Devotees also celebrated a sacred meal and were promised immortality, mystical communion with their god, membership in a close-knit community, and thus a true "home." The gods and goddesses of the mysteries, as well as other attributes and practices, tended to mix with those of the old Greco-Roman mythical deities (**syncretism**); thus, for example, the Greek high god Zeus was identified not only with the Roman high god Jupiter, but also with the Syrian high god Ba'al, god of thunder and lightning; similarly, the goddess of love and beauty, Greek goddess Aphrodite and Roman goddess Venus, was identified with the Syrian Ashtoreth, or Astarte, goddess of fertility.

While Mithraism was increasingly practiced by soldiers in the Roman army, other mystery religions attracted women devotees, for example, the Greek Eleusinian mysteries (Demeter and Persephone, archetypal mother and daughter), the Syrian Cybele or "Great Mother" mysteries, the (originally) Egyptian Isis mysteries, and the Greek Dionysiac mysteries. Such religions celebrated myths about the seasons and fertility, some explicitly sexual. By Israelite and Jesus Movement standards of taste, some were bizarre, for example, initiation by standing in a pit under a slain bull and drinking its lifeblood (the *taurobolium*) in the Cybele initiations.

Direct influence of the mystery religions on the Jesus Movement is difficult to show. However, it is agreed that they shared some similar practices, such as initiation rites and a common meal. No doubt many Greeks, Romans, and others would have perceived adherents of the Jesus Movement as members of some Israelite mystery cult. Certainly, later writers thought of the Jesus Movement as the truly sacred mystery.

The Emperor Cult (Emperor Worship)

The Emperor Cult, an excellent example of political religion, was an adaptation of Middle Eastern beliefs about the divinity of the Egyptian pharaoh or the "partial" deity of the oriental king. The Greeks and Romans cautiously tolerated such beliefs abroad as one means to political unity and stability, but they discouraged them at home. True, it was customary to pay worthy emperors divine homage after they died, but emperors who *claimed* divine prerogatives while still alive met stiff resistance, sometimes contributing to their "removal from office" by assassination! Nonetheless, titles of majesty were often bestowed on, or demanded by, the emperor. Examples were "Lord," "God," "Son of God," and "Savior," the same honorific titles that early members of the Jesus movements gave to Jesus. Moreover, in the provinces, some people believed that the emperor's birth, works, and enthronement brought about "good news" for the world. These same themes were associated with Jesus.

Gnosticism

Gnosticism, from the Greek word *gnōsis,* means "the belief in knowledge." However, it is not intellectual or scientific-technical knowledge, but rather a special, revealed, religious knowledge necessary for salvation. As the late second-century Gnostic Theodotus once summarized it, *gnōsis* is about our origins, identity, and destiny:

> Who we were, what we have become;
> Where we were, whither we were thrown;
> Whither we are hastening, from what we are redeemed;
> What birth is, and what rebirth.
>
> (Clement of Alexandria *Excerpts from Theodotus* 78.2)

Behind Theodotus' description are second-century Gnostic myths. In them this world "below" and matter are evil. They were not created by a good God, but rather by another, inferior deity. However, within each person is a true, good self, a divine spark of light from the world of light "above" ("who we were"; "where we were"). It is now trapped in an alien body with all of its sensual passions ("what we have become"; "whither we were thrown"; "birth"). The body-spirit dualism of Gnosticism, as noted, has some similarities to Platonism but is more radical. Expressed in Gnostic terms, the evil powers attempt to keep the true self in a state of "sleep" or "drunkenness" to hold the creation of the evil world together. The only possible means of liberation from this evil body and this evil world is *gnōsis,* secretly revealed knowledge about God; the world; and the origin, condition, and destiny of humankind. Those who have it ("rebirth") will be enabled to escape this evil world and the body's prison ("from what we are redeemed") to return to the world of light ("whither we are hastening").

In general, Gnostics believed that the salvation of *gnōsis* can be taught or transmitted through a secret ritual but ultimately that it comes from above as a "call." In mythical terms, a Gnostic Redeemer descends from the world of light, disguises himself in human form without becoming bodily, teaches *gnōsis,* and returns or ascends. However Gnostics gain their *gnōsis,* they learn that this world and this body are not their true homes, that they have been "thrown" into an alien world. Often they totally renounce the body and its passions (**asceticism**) or, knowing that the world is not their true place and cannot really affect them, allow themselves the utmost freedom (libertinism). Either way, they experience rebirth and become part of the privileged few. Clearly, Gnosticism was neither family religion nor political religion in the usual sense, but rather small-group, voluntary religion. There are certain similarities and differences between Gnosticism and the early Jesus Movement, such that some scholars believe in influences both ways.

ISRAELITE RELIGION

Three points should be kept in mind about Israelite religion. First, it was (and Judaism still is) primarily a religion of observance or practice, not belief or dogmas and creeds. Second, despite the Israelites' resistance to forced Hellenization during the Maccabean period, by the time of the New Testament, the Israelite religion had been influenced by Hellenistic religions. Indeed, the ancient Israelite religion *was* a Hellenistic religion. Third, one should think of many kinds of groups among the Israelites, not a single, unified religion. Nonetheless, for clarity the Israelite culture and religion will now be discussed separately, and the **Diaspora** will be reserved to the end of this chapter.

Clean and Unclean

From an anthropological perspective, classifications of "clean," "holy," "pure," or "sacred" are based on what is "in place" according to social norms. Contrariwise, classifications of "unclean," "defiled," "polluted," "impure," or "profane" are based on what is "out of place." The earth is "soil" in the garden; it is "dirt" and considered "unclean" in the house.

Traditional societies set aside people (priests, medicine men), places (temples, shrines), times (special days of the week or year), and things (sacrificial animals, important books) as especially holy, sacred, pure, or clean. They also set aside people (outsiders, lepers), places (other lands, places outside the community or city), and things (contaminated objects, certain foods) as especially unholy, profane, impure, or unclean. The two realms can be separated by physical boundaries: walls, gates, doors, and curtains. A tightly knit social group may also be symbolically mirrored ("replicated") by its attitudes about the human body, for example, as the social body avoids impure outsiders, so the physical body avoids impure food (pork, cf. Lev. 11) or impure fluids that come out of it (semen or menses). The cleanliness of the hands that control such functions is carefully regulated (ritual hand washing, toilet practices). Women in traditional Israelite culture are usually considered by men to be "unclean" more often than men (cf. Lev. 12, 15; cf. the woman with a hemorrhage, Mark 5:25–34).

Holy God, Holy People, Holy Land

A special belief among ancient Israelites was **monotheism:** "Hear, O Israel, Yahweh our God, Yahweh alone . . ." (Deut. 6:4). According to Gen. 15 and 17, the God Yahweh made a **covenant** or contract with Abraham that had two emphases: Yahweh's descendants would be many, and they would receive as their special inheritance the land of Canaan (Palestine). This covenant was ratified by a sign, namely, **circumcision** of every male child on the eighth day after birth. Thus the Israelites believed that they were Yahweh's elect, holy, and chosen people and that they should keep Yahweh's commands but also that they had a mission: to be "a light to the nations." Yahweh made other covenants, for example, with Moses or David. If the king or the people disobeyed the covenants, Yahweh would punish them. Thus, as Yahweh was holy, so the people of Yahweh had to be holy (Lev. 11:44–45; 1 Pet. 1:16); thus, also, God gave them a holy land. By New Testament times, God's name "Yahweh" had become too holy to utter. So one substituted *Adonai* ("lord"). All this meant that many strict, observant Israelites separated themselves from outsiders by all sorts of physical and social barriers, for example, by not eating with Gentiles.

Holy Temple and Holy Priesthood

In Israelite society, political religion and holiness went hand in hand. Within Yahweh's holy people and holy land, there were especially holy people, places, times, and things. Within the holy land was the holy city, Jerusalem, surrounded by walls; within the holy city was the holy temple, surrounded by walls; and within the temple were holy courts, surrounded by walls. (See Figure 1.8.) Non-Israelites were permitted only in the outermost "court of Gentiles." Indeed, Gentiles were warned by an inscription that if they proceeded beyond this point their penalty would be death. Moving inward, thus progressively more holy, was the Sacred Enclosure for Israelites, consisting of the Court of Women, then the Court of Israel (men), then the Court of Priests (especially holy men), and then the forecourt where the holy sacrifices (clean animals "without blemish") took place to atone for sin. In the very center was the Holy of Holies, where the presence of God was said to reside, and

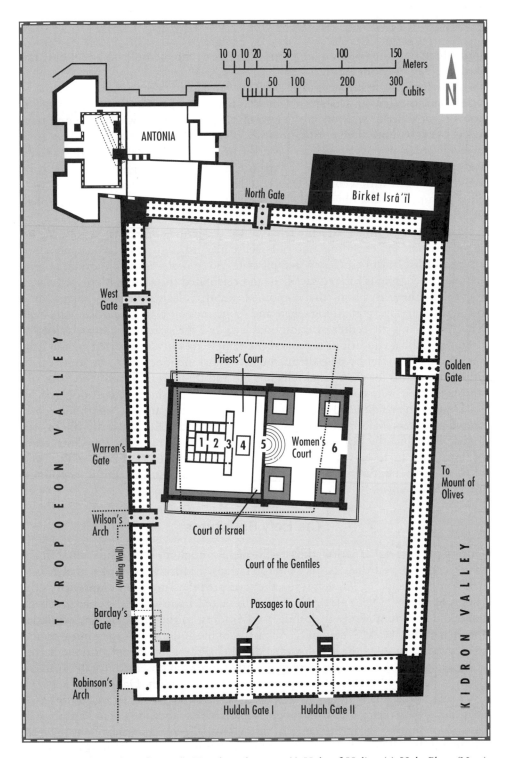

Figure 1.8 Floor plan of Herod's Temple and courts: (1) Holy of Holies, (2) Holy Place (Nave), (3) Porch, (4) Altar, (5) Nicanor Gate, (6) Beautiful Gate? (Based on Vincent-Steve [W. F. Stinespring, *IDB* R–Z, p. 556] and C. L. Meyers [*Harpers Bible Dictionary*, p. 1028, Maplewood, NJ: Hammond Incorporated]). For a photo of the remains of its western wall, see the beginning of Chapter Eight.

into which only the holiest of men, the high priest, entered only on a very holy fast day, the **Day of Atonement.**

Priests had to maintain purity. Priestly genealogies were necessary because a priest had to marry an Israelite virgin who had never been a divorcee, prostitute, convert, prisoner of war, or, in the case of the high priest, a widow. Among their many priestly duties were purification rites performed on those with diseases, especially disorders of the skin (Lev. 13; Mark 1:40–45) or physical impurities; preservation of holiness in the temple; and maintenance of their own purity, especially by avoiding contact with a corpse. They could not officiate in the temple if they were ritually impure, had a physical defect, were under the influence of alcohol, or had married an impure woman.

The center of official Israelite religion was the Jerusalem temple, a political, religious, social, and economic hub of Israelite life and culture. Indeed, some scholars have called Israelite society a "temple state," so central was the importance of the temple. There priests offered sacrifices and celebrated the seasonal festivals. There met the **Sanhedrin,** a body that combined executive, legislative, and judicial functions, thus serving as the ruling senate and "supreme court" of Greco-Roman Israel. The temple was the center of traditional laws and the system of courts, as well as more traditional education. It housed the temple treasury, supported by the half-shekel tax. The wealthy priestly aristocracy who functioned in the temple established the norms for traditional religious life and thought in Israel ("the great tradition"). These were emulated by the common people ("the little tradition").

Despite the religious ideology of holiness, the temple and its priesthood represented political religion. The priests were retainers and politically powerful; in "colonial" Palestine, the Romans actually appointed the high priests. The destruction of the temple in 70 C.E. meant not only the decline of the priesthood and the end of the central cultural institution of ancient Israel, but also the end of its political life as it was known.

The Holy Scriptures

During the post-Exilic period, the Israelite people sought to learn God's will through sacred writings and their correct interpretations. From the comment that Moses had written a book (cf. Deut. 29:20), they accepted the **Torah** or **Pentateuch** as the "book of Moses" (Neh. 13:1). According to sacred tradition, the Torah had been handed down from Moses to Joshua, to the elders, to the prophets, and finally to the men of the "Great Synagogue." All phases of life and thought were inspired and guided by it. To study the Torah was a "delight" (Ps. 1:2; cf. Ps. 19), and the heroes and heroines of the Israelites were frequently those who observed Torah norms of holiness despite adversity, war, or persecution (Tobit, Judith, Daniel).

There were actually different versions of the holy scriptures, as well as different attitudes toward them. The Torah of the Samaritans was the **Samaritan Pentateuch,** in which Mount Gerizîm in Samaria, not Mount Zion in Jerusalem, was the holy mountain. Israelites added to their Torah the Prophets and the Writings (Wisdom literature). Israelites living in the **Diaspora** added a few other books, and the whole made up the Greek **Septuagint.** Finally, some ancient Israelites believed that it was necessary to develop, elaborate, and apply Torah laws to specific everyday cases to protect the people from transgressing the central commandments themselves ("to build a fence around the Torah"). These legal interpretations became an "oral Torah" alongside the written Torah and became so authoritative that they were also attributed to Moses. In the New Testament, this oral tradition is called "the tradition of the elders" (Mark 7:3).

Feasts and Fasts

Feasts and fasts are holy times. Most Israelites followed a lunar-solar calendar. The length of the year was determined by the sun (from vernal equinox to vernal equinox), but the length of the months was determined by the phases of the moon (from new moon to new moon). Shorter thirty-day lunar months (= 360 days per year) required the intercalation of an extra month every few years. The six major feasts and one major fast of Israel follow the agricultural seasons and harvests. (See Table 1.1.)

Three feasts—Booths, Passover, and Weeks (in boldface)—were "pilgrim festivals," that is, (male) pilgrims were obligated to make a pilgrimage to Jerusalem to celebrate them.

Booths was celebrated at the time of grape harvest when booths were built in the vineyards for grape pickers (building such booths is still a Jewish custom); it eventually came to symbolize the story of wilderness wanderings. (The ninth day of Booths, called *Simhath Tōrāh* ["the Joy of the Law"], later became a separate feast [cf. 1 Esd. 9:50].) There may be hints of "Booths" in Mark 9:2–5.

Passover, a spring festival, referred in popular etymology to the time when the angel of death "passed over" the houses of the Israelites in Egypt if a house's lintel and doorposts were marked with the blood of the sacrificial lamb (Exod. 12:13). Originally it seems to have been a rite of sacrifice to maintain the fertility of the flock. Later it commemorated the exodus of the Israelites from Egyptian captivity to freedom. It became associated with the weeklong Feast of Unleavened Bread, originally marking the barley harvest.

In the first century, goats and lambs were ritually slaughtered at the temple on the afternoon before the Passover feast began ("the Day of Preparation" [Mark 14:12]), and the blood was sprinkled on the altar. While the sun was setting, the feast proper began with a common meal at a house or apartment within the city walls of Jerusalem. Later tradition says the pilgrim should find a room in the city; procure a male yearling sheep or goat for sacrifice; buy wine, unleavened bread dough, and spices; and celebrate with a minimum of ten males. In the gospels, this festival is the occasion for the Passion and death of Jesus.

The Festival of "**Weeks**" (New Testament **Pentecost**) was originally a celebration of the fertility of the land at the end of the grain harvest. It became associated with the giving of the Ten Commandments to Moses on Mount Sinai. In the New Testament, it is associated with the coming of the Spirit to the early church (Acts 2).

New Year (*Rōsh Hashānāh,* "Head [First (Day)] of the Year"), originally celebrating the ascent of the king to the throne, became a day of special sanctity marked

Table 1.1   Feasts and Fasts

Western Months	Mediterranean Season	Hebrew Calendar	Seasonal Festivals/ Fasts	Biblical Reference
September/ October	First (fall) rains	*Tishri* 1	1. New Year (*Rosh Hashānāh*)	Lev. 23:24
		Tishri 10	2. Day of Atonement (*Yōm Kippûr*), a fast	Lev. 16 and 23:26–32
		Tishri 15 (8 days)	3. **Booths** (*Succōth*) (See also *Simhath Tōrāh*, "the Joy of the Law")	Exod. 23:14–17; Lev. 23:34–36
November/ December	Main (winter) rains (olive harvest)	*Kislev* 25 (8 days)	4. Dedication (*Hanūkkāh*) (8 days)	1 Macc. 4:42–58; 2 Macc. 10:1–8 Also known as the "Festival of Lights."
(January)		*Tevet* *Shevat*		
February		*Adar* 14 (2 days)	5. Lots (*Purîm*)	Esther
March/ April	Spring rains (flax harvest) (barley harvest)	*Nisan* 15 (7 days) *Iyyar*	6. **Passover** (*Pesach*) and the Feast of Unleavened Bread (*Mazzōth*)	Exod. 12–13
May/June	Dry season (wheat harvest) (figs)			
July/August	Hot season (grape harvest begins)	*Sivan* 6 *Tammuz* *'Ab* *Elul*	7. **Weeks** (*Shāvuōth*) (in the New Testament, "Pentecost") 50 days after Passover	Lev. 23:15–16

by blowing the *shōphār,* or ram's horn. ***Hanūkkāh*** ("Dedication") was the "rededication" of the temple after its defilement by the Seleucid Greeks (see the Maccabean Revolt). *Purîm* ("Lots") celebrated the victory of Persian Israelites over Haman, who cast lots in his attempt to exterminate them; customarily the Book of Esther, which tells the story, was read on this day.

The only prescribed *fast* in the Hebrew scriptures—others developed—was *Yōm Kippūr,* the **Day of Atonement,** when purification from sins, or atonement, took place (Lev. 16). On this day of fasting, rest, and penance, the high priest sacrificed a bull for his sins and for the sins of the priests; then, and only on this day, he entered the Holy of Holies and sprinkled the bull's blood on the "mercy seat" of the Ark of the Covenant, that is, the symbolic throne where God dispensed mercy to his people. Two goats were presented by the people, one for God, one "for Azazel" (the goat? a place? a desert demon?). The high priest sacrificed the first goat to atone for the sins of the people. Then he placed his hands on the second goat, transferring to it the sins of the people. It was led into the desert to die, after which the high priest purified himself. In short, the sins of the community were driven off into the desert (the origin of the term *scapegoat*).

Sabbath

Israelite days began and ended at sunset, not midnight. Sabbath (Hebrew *shabbāt*) is the name given to the seventh day of the week, from sunset Friday to sunset Saturday. Popular priestly etymology explained that on the seventh day God *ceased* (Hebrew *shābat*, "he ceases") from his work of creation, blessed the day, declared it holy, and required that no one work on that day (Gen. 2:1–3; see also Hebrew *shāvuōt*, "period of seven days," from *sheva'*, "seven"). The requirement to observe the Sabbath became part of the Ten Commandments (Exod. 20:8). Similar ideas about refraining from work were associated with the holiness of the "sabbatical," or seventh, year when the land was not to be worked (Lev. 16:31, etc.), debts were to be released (Deut. 15:2), and taxes were not to be paid (Josephus *Antiquities* 14.202). The gospels report many controversies about Sabbath regulations.

(House-)Synagogue

The Greek word for synagogue, *synagōgē* ("gathering together"), is one of the two major translations of the Hebrew word in the scriptures for "assembly (of God)." Although the term is found frequently in the gospels and Josephus' writings, and although synagogue buildings outside of Palestine are well known (Philo of Alexandria; inscriptions), archeological evidence for synagogue buildings *in Palestine* prior to 70 c.e. is rare. The solution to this apparent discrepancy may be that the place to "gather together" in Palestine was a large room in a house (a "house-synagogue" or "meeting house"), an extension of domestic or family religion.

In contrast to the temple, no sacrifice was offered in the (house-)synagogue. Rather, services probably consisted of a recitation of the monotheistic *Shema'* ("Hear, O Israel, Yahweh our God, Yahweh alone . . ."), scripture readings, a sermon, blessings, and prayer. (House-)synagogues also became places for meditation and meetings. When separate buildings did come into existence, they became community centers for education, common meals, and in some cases places where Israelite travelers might stay.

Song and Prayer

Most of the psalms now found in the ancient Hebrew Bible were originally the "hymnbook" of the temple. In New Testament times these psalms and other chants had become the special province of a lower order of temple priests, the Levites. However, they were also no doubt sung in the house-synagogues. Prayers were also offered in house-synagogues or at any time and place. They were oriented toward Jerusalem—specifically the Holy of Holies—and it was customary to offer them three times a day: morning, midday, and evening. Standing or kneeling with hands raised to heaven was the usual praying position.

Wisdom

Wisdom had a venerable tradition in the religions of the ancient Near East. It was fostered by "wise men" who were part of the royal courts. Although the most characteristic form of Wisdom was the proverb, a wide variety of other forms existed, including the parable. Wisdom usually dealt with the practical knowledge about the world and human relations that would help the individual to prosper and lead a long and fruitful life. Examples are the Books of Proverbs, Job, Ecclesiastes, and some of the psalms. A number of Wisdom books after 200 B.C.E. also exist.

One example of everyday Wisdom comes from a male perspective: "A continual dripping on a rainy day and a contentious woman are alike" (Prov. 27:5). We should also note the Wisdom myth, that is, that Wisdom was the personified expression or extension of God. Here the term for divine wisdom is feminine gender in both Hebrew and Greek.

> Wisdom went forth to make her dwelling among the children of men,
> Wisdom found no place where she might dwell;
> Then a dwelling-place was assigned her in the heavens.
> Wisdom went forth to make her dwelling among the children of men, And found
>   no dwelling-place.
> Wisdom returned to her place,
> And took her seat among the angels.
>   (1 Enoch 42:1–2)

As in Greco-Roman religions at large, the descent/ascent motif is clearly present.

Practical Wisdom and the Wisdom myth were very important to many in the first Jesus movements. Jesus was a teacher of wisdom, and the Wisdom myth influenced their views of Jesus as a redeemer who came from heaven to earth and returned to heaven (Phil. 2:6–11; John 1:1–18).

Prophecy and Prophets

The word *prophet* comes from the Greek *prophētēs,* which in the Septuagint translates *nabî'* in the Hebrew Bible, literally "one who is called (by God)." Prophets could be a "seers"—persons who *see* in the Spirit—"diviners," or "soothsayers." They could also be unusually sensitive persons who have a special vocation, who "see" what others do not or do not care to (for example, political abuse, religious indifference, social injustice, or simply the outcome of a battle). They articulated revelations in concrete social situations; they spoke for the gods. In the Hebrew scriptures, prophetic messages often begin, "Thus says Yahweh . . ." It was believed that, as intermediaries between the divine and the human, prophets often had the power to work miracles. There was some emphasis on predicting upcoming events, but more often prophets interpreted current events.

Prophecy was most prevalent prior to the Babylonian Exile. There were official court and cultic prophets at religious shrines, whose oracles were consulted prior to war. There were also cult prophets (Isaiah) and prophets of priestly descent (Jeremiah and Ezekiel). There were also "shaman" prophets, that is, those who experienced altered states of consciousness (**ASCs**) such as spirit-possession or trances, hallucinations, and visions of the "out-of-body" sort. In such states, sometimes in-duced by musical rhythms, dancing, or self-flagellation, prophets were said to re-ceive revelations from Yahweh. Sometimes they uttered wisdom and performed miracles. Often they prophesied in bands or prophetic associations. A few wore un-usual garb, such as hairy sheepskins or leather loincloths. Two miracle-working shaman prophets from ancient pre-Exilic Israel were Elijah and Elisha.

"Free prophets," another type, were social and religious reformers who con-demned complacency and injustice and sought social, political, economic, and re-ligious change. They often came into conflict with aristocratic priests and kings. Claiming to know the will of the True King, Yahweh-God, they called upon people to return to God's just rule. Examples of "free prophets" are Amos, Hosea, Isaiah, Micah, Jeremiah, "deutero" [second]-Isaiah, and Ezekiel.

Prophecy continued in the post-Exilic period (after 538 B.C.E.) but was increas-ingly rare. Thus there arose a *hope* for a righteous prophet, either a new or return-ing Elijah or a "prophet like Moses," a new lawgiver. The prophet like Moses was expected among the Samaritans (the "Taheb") and is mentioned along with *two* hoped-for Messiahs in the **Dead Sea Scrolls.**

In the Jesus Movement, many sayings of the ancient prophets were consid-ered to predict the life and teachings of Jesus. Some members of the Jesus Move-ment identified John the Baptist with Elijah, and stories about both Elijah and Elisha are echoed in the miracle working of Jesus. Indeed, Jesus himself was con-sidered to be a prophet. There were also both male and female prophets in the early churches. Finally, the New Testament contains many examples of prophetic-type speech, as well as prophetic-type "call" scenes, prophetic visions, and prophetic-type symbolic actions.

Israelite Magic and Other Miracle Traditions

In the Greco-Roman world there were physicians, folk healers, and magicians. Palestine was no exception, although pious, educated Israelites believed that Yahweh was the ultimate source of healing. In the **Dead Sea Scrolls,** Abraham was said to have exorcised a demon from Pharaoh by praying, laying on of hands, and rebuk-ing the evil spirit. In other ancient texts, David was said to have done the same by playing his harp and Noah by using medicines and herbs. Moses was also believed to have been a great healer. Solomon's great wisdom was thought to include knowl-edge of magic and medicine, and the following account illustrates how these mag-ical beliefs were developed:

> He [the exorcist Eleazar] put to the nose of the possessed man a ring which had un-der its seal one of the roots prescribed by Solomon, and then, as the man smelled it, drew out the demon through his nostrils, and, when the man at once fell down, ad-jured the demon never to come back into him, speaking Solomon's name and recit-ing the incantations which he had composed.
> (Josephus *Antiquities* 8:2 [Loeb])

Josephus and the Talmud also mention a *Hāsîd* ("Pious One") named "Honi the Circle Drawer" who was remembered for bringing rain by prayer. Another *Hāsîd,* Hanina ben Dosa, was remembered for healing by prayer.

> When the son of Yohanan ben Zakkai became ill, Yohanan said, "Hanina, my son, pray for him that he may live." He put his head between his knees and prayed; and he lived.
>
> (Babylonian Talmud *Berakoth* 34b)

Again, the cure is said to have been effected by God, the real miracle worker, through prayer. Nonetheless, particular holy men were famous for the ability to heal. Jesus of Nazareth was one such man.

Apocalypticism (Millennialism)

The adjective *apocalyptic,* which comes from the Greek noun *apocalypsis,* meaning "revelation" (Rev. 1:1), can be used as a noun to encompass three overlapping phenomena: (1) apocalypses, or revelatory writings, thus literature; (2) apocalyptic eschatology, or revealed ideas about the end (Greek *eschaton,* "end") and the heavenly world; and (3) "apocalypticism," or groups or movements in which apocalyptic eschatology is the main religious ideology and in which apocalypses are sometimes written (P. Hanson).

An **apocalypse** refers to books or parts of books that record visual and auditory revelations. The revelations are typically said to come from an otherworldly medium such as a deity or an angel, sometimes in the form of dreams about the heavenly world. They are given to a human seer who "sees" in an ecstatic state ("in the Spirit"). In social-scientific terms, such a person is in an altered state of consciousness (ASC). Ancient apocalypses usually begin and end with a narrative but are dominated by revelatory visions in the central section. They usually conclude with the seer's return to a normal state and his reception of instructions about concealing or publishing the revelation. An apocalypse is normally said to be authored by some venerable worthy from the remote past—Abraham, Moses, David—who is represented as prophesying the future. Scholars call this false attribution **pseudonymity** (literally, "false name").

Most ideas found in apocalypses can be called **apocalyptic eschatology,** which may be defined as "revealed teaching about the end" (Greek *eschaton,* "end"). Thus apocalyptic visions stress *temporal matters* (world origins, past history, contemporary or future crises, resurrection of the dead, final judgment of sinners, salvation of the elect, the afterlife). They also include *spatial matters* (heavenly regions, heavenly beings [angelic or demonic], often revealed to one who takes a heavenly journey to one or several of seven heavens, where he is awestruck and receives assurance). The most important characteristic ideas are a sense of alienation and of despair about history that fosters a belief that the world is rushing to a foreordained tragic climax; a hope that God will act in the climactic moment to change things; and a conviction that it will be possible to recognize the signs of the end. All this is put in highly symbolic language.

Apocalypticism describes a movement that accepts (or whose leaders accept) apocalyptic eschatology as a dominant ideology. Apocalyptic eschatology helps to resolve the contradictory experience of despair about the terrible course of present human history and hope in the invincible power of God and his purpose for his chosen people. The vision is that the world will become much the same as it was in some earlier, more perfect time. Then God's elect people will be vindicated. This reversal of fortunes will be marked by historical and cosmic catastrophes. In the meantime, the movement that believes itself to be the people of God should prepare itself for the change and watch for the signs of its coming.

Anthropologists often call such groups "millenarian movements" or millennialist movements (**millennialism**). These terms come from the word *millennium* (Latin *mille,* "one thousand"), which is derived from the temporary, thousand-year reign of Christ and the martyrs before the Last Judgment (Rev. 20:4–8a ["a" refers to the first half of the verse]). Millennialism is a movement of people whose central ideology is that this oppressive world is in crisis and will soon end, usually by some catastrophic event, and that it will be replaced by a new, perfect, blissful, and trouble-free world, often imagined as a restoration of some primeval paradise; this hope is so intense that those who believe it sometimes prepare for the new world or even attempt to force its coming by political action.

Ancient apocalypses were written down by scribes who were "retainers" of the ruling classes but on occasion joined religious groups and movements. The extent of the scribes' influence among the nonliterate peasant classes of antiquity is not always clear, but apocalyptic ideas no doubt would have appealed to oppressed groups. Thus it is probable that apocalyptic movements were populated by peasants whose leaders appealed to millennial hopes and dreams.

Dan. 7–12 and the Book of Revelation are examples of literary apocalypses. An example outside the Bible is the *Assumption of Moses,* a work contemporary with the New Testament. In this book God will arise from his heavenly throne, will turn everything in the universe upside down, punish the evil Gentiles, and establish a purified kingdom without other gods. It is clearly the work of one who lives under sorrowful oppression and hopes for a better day. It also refers to "[God's] kingdom" (*Assumption of Moses* 10:1), the key theme of the teaching of Jesus.

Messianic Ideology

The Israelite literature points especially to two types of messiahs, political and apocalyptic. We have discussed the "popular messiahs" and bar Cochba as a messiah; some passages in the Dead Sea Scrolls expect "Two Messiahs," one of which was royal. These are essentially *political* messiahs. The best example of the political messianic *ideology* is found in the *Psalms of Solomon,* which was not really written by Solomon but rather by a member of a pious Israelite group about the time that Rome took control of Palestine under Pompey in 63 B.C.E. It expresses the hope that a descendant of David will come, overthrow enemies (especially Gentiles), and reestablish the Davidic kingdom as pure and holy, devoid of aliens and foreigners.

> See, Lord, and raise up for them their king,
>   the son of David, to rule over your servant Israel
>   in the time known to you, O God
> Undergird him with the strength to destroy the unrighteous rulers,

> to purge Jerusalem from Gentiles
> who trample her to destruction; . . .
> He will gather a holy people
> Whom he will lead in righteousness. . . .
>
> (*Psalms of Solomon* 17:21–22a, 26a)

The second major type of messianic ideology was the *millennial* type. It is best represented in the apocalypse of Dan. 7–12, specifically, the vision of a heavenly ideal ruler in the apocalypse of Daniel (ca. 165 B.C.E.). This vision speaks of "one like **a son of man.**"

> I saw in the night visions,
> and behold, with the clouds of heaven there came one like a son of man,
> and he came to the Ancient of Days [God] and was presented before him.
>
> And to him was given dominion and glory and kingdom,
> that all peoples, nations, and languages should serve him;
> his dominion is an everlasting dominion, which shall not pass away,
>
> and his kingdom one that shall not be destroyed.
>
> (Dan. 7:14–15)

"A son of man" in this text is an Aramaic idiom for "man" in the generic sense, that is, "human being" (see Ps. 8:4); thus "one like a human being" appears before God in the clouds of heaven. From this and other "son of man" texts, there appears to have been a common, widespread reference to a heavenly humanlike being to whom God would give great power to judge. The gospels go a step further: The "son of man" has become a *title* for Jesus, who has authority on earth, will suffer, die, be raised up, and return on the clouds as judge of sinners.

One other messiah type may be mentioned. In the **Dead Sea Scrolls** it is said that the demonic Belial is opposed by the heavenly high priest named Melchizedek (*11 Q Melchizedek*). A similar view occurs in the Letter to the Hebrews in the New Testament.

SOME GROUPS IN FIRST-CENTURY PALESTINE

Regional Groups: Galileans, Samaritans, and Idumeans

A person in antiquity was identified by his father and trade but especially by his place of origin, that is, city (Jesus of Nazareth) or region (Jesus the Galilean). People were stereotyped regionally by physical traits, skin color, personality types, language or dialect, beliefs and practices, and ethnicity. Philo, for example, said that Egyptians were jealous and envious. In the New Testament the author of Titus wrote, "Cretans [people from the Mediterranean island of Crete] are always liars, evil beasts, lazy drunkards" (Titus 1:12). Here we focus on Samaria, Galilee, and Idumea.

By the first century C.E., the Samaritans—Samaria lay between Galilee and Judea—were considered by purist Israelites to be the least pure of all peoples except the Gentiles. Samaritans accepted only the Pentateuch as scripture, and in their version of it (the **Samaritan Pentateuch**), Mount Gerizîm in Samaria, not Mount Zion in Judea, is the holy mountain. They also hoped for a "messianic" figure, the *Taheb,* who was a "prophet like Moses." Although relations between Israelites and Samaritans fluctuated, Israelites in the first century C.E. normally avoided Samaritans, and Jesus' listeners would have thought it very odd that he told a story about a good Samaritan.

Some Israelites from the region of Judea considered people from the region of Galilee, Jesus' region, to be not much better than the Samaritans (John 7:45–52; 8:48). At the very least they spoke with an accent, implying that Judean Aramaic was correct (Matt. 26:73). Josephus' views about Galileans are mixed, but he says that Judean leaders warned their people that it was not worth avenging the death of a Galilean pilgrim who had been murdered by Samaritans. Later rabbinic sources considered Galileans to be quarrelsome, ignorant of the Torah, and untrustworthy.

In Greco-Roman times, **Idumea** ("land of the Edomites") refers to the region just south of Judea. To this region refugees from ancient Edom, southeast of the Dead Sea, had migrated. Inhabitants of Idumea were forcefully converted to the Israelite religion under the Maccabeans. The Herodian kings came from this region, and, as already noted, Josephus says that they were considered to be only half-Israelites. In the civil wars in Jerusalem during the **Israelite Rebellion against Rome,** one of the major factions was a group of Idumeans.

"Religious" Groups

There were also "religious" groups—Josephus calls them "philosophies"—whose identity was associated primarily with special religious beliefs, norms, and practices related to the scope and interpretation of the Torah.

Sadducees

The **Sadducees** were a well-established religious group in Greco-Roman Israelite society. Because their own literature has not survived, our understanding of them must rely upon Josephus, the rabbinic literature, and the New Testament, which was not friendly to them.

The name "Sadducee" may have come from the Hebrew *tsaddîqîm* ("righteous ones"), but more likely it was derived from the high priest Zadok of David's and Solomon's time (tenth century B.C.E.). First mentioned during the rule of the Maccabeans in the second century B.C.E., this group was an important part of the Jerusalem aristocracy and dominated the powerful high court, the Sanhedrin. As political leaders, most Sadducees maintained cordial relations with the Romans. In the gospels, they are portrayed as opponents of Jesus from the Jerusalem temple establishment. When rebellion against Rome became imminent in the 60s, they attempted to mediate, but to no avail.

Despite some political accommodation to the Romans, the Sadducees seem to have remained conservative in religion. Among the Sadducees were priests who carried out sacrifices at the Jerusalem temple. Like the Samaritans, they accepted only the Pentateuch (but in its Israelite form) as scripture, and they seem to have interpreted it more literally. They therefore rejected the Pharisees' attempt to "build a fence around the Torah." A known objection was the Pharisaic interest in personal immortality, and there seem to have been many debates with the Pharisees about purity regulations, for example, Sabbath purity and the condition of women. There were also sharp differences with the Essenes. The Sadducees rejected fate and determinism and espoused a form of free will; thus God could not be held responsible for evil. In the New Testament, they are portrayed as not accepting belief in the resurrection of the dead, in contrast to the Pharisees and Jesus (Acts 23:6–10; Mark 12:18–27).

Pharisees

The **Pharisees** were a very different kind of group. Although we have sources—mainly Josephus, the New Testament, and the rabbinic literature that originally stems from them—they are difficult to describe. Their name was probably derived from the Hebrew *perûshîm* or the Aramaic *perishîn,* which means "the separated (ones)," although scholars debate what this separation means. Like the Sadducees, they are first mentioned in the second century B.C.E. In this early period they were a politically oriented reforming faction often in conflict with the Maccabeans and the Sadducees, but eventually they became a more established sect. Some continued political involvement during the reign of Herod (37–34 B.C.E.), and some were leaders of the revolt against Rome in 66 C.E. By the late first century C.E., when the synagogue was becoming a more important institution, they became synagogue leaders. They also may have become less political, although there are exceptions, and this generalization is debated. By this time, their renowned teachers were called **rabbis.** Unlike the Sadducees, most Pharisees were not priests, but rather laypersons, some of whom were scholars. They were divided into various schools, the most well known being those of Rabbi Hillel and Rabbi Shammai.

The early rabbinic literature agrees with the New Testament on certain crucial themes about pre-70 C.E. Pharisaic religious piety. Especially characteristic were the preservation and development of their oral interpretations of the Torah, an attempt to extend the laws of temple purity to everyday life. In these areas, the Pharisees "built a fence around the Torah" with respect to laws about Sabbath observance, festivals, oaths, tithes, lawful divorce, kosher food, and those with whom one eats. There nonetheless appears to have been a liberalization of attitudes toward the purity of women who were responsible for preparing food. In contrast to the Sadducees, the Pharisees accepted the larger body of scriptures and the oral Torah, as well as newer views such as angels, demons, and the resurrection of the dead.

After the war with Rome, the Pharisees were well situated to assert their authority and to reestablish Israel according to Pharisaic norms, values, and beliefs at an academy established at Yavneh (Jamnia) near the Mediterranean coast. At the **Yavneh Academy** certain books that were eventually accepted into the canon of the Israelite scriptures were debated and oral traditions were collected. Also, the Pharisees added the *Birkat Ha-Minîm* (Hebrew for "**Prayer against the Heretics**") to the Eighteen Benedictions (the twelfth benediction), so that it now has nineteen. Most scholars no longer think that the prayer was originally directed against the followers of Jesus alone, although they may have been included. A later edition mentions *Nōzrîm* ("Nazoreans," presumably implying Jesus of Nazareth). Here is one version of the Prayer against the Heretics:

12. For the apostates may there be no hope unless they return to your Torah. As for the [*Nōzrîm* and the] *Minîm,* may they perish immediately. Speedily may they be erased from the Book of the Life and may they not be registered among the righteous. Blessed are You, O Lord, who subdue the wicked.
(Translation after R. Kimelman)

In the New Testament, Jesus is pictured as frequently in debate with the Pharisees. Outside the gospels, evidence for Pharisees in Galilee is sparse; hence, some scholars think that they were primarily representatives, or "retainers," of the Jerusalem establishment.

The Dead Sea Assembly (Essenes)

Pliny the Elder and the Israelite writers Philo and Josephus described a group called the **Essenes.** Their name, "Essene" (Greek *Essēnoi, Essaioi,* "Pious Ones," probably from Aramaic *Hāsayyāh,* "Pious One," or perhaps *'asayyah,* "healer"), may reflect their origins among the *Hasîdîm,* which also means "Pious Ones," during the second century B.C.E. The Essenes were described as a strict group who withdrew from the rest of society and lived along the shores of the Dead Sea. Historical reconstruction suggests that the group surfaced during the period of the Maccabean high priest Jonathan (161–143/2 B.C.E.) but then disappeared during the wars with Rome, about 68 C.E. Most scholars, based on the discovery of the **Dead Sea Scrolls** in 1947 and the later excavation of nearby **Khirbet Qumran,** think that most of the scrolls came from the Essenes. This group lived mainly in nearby cliff caves, although some members seem to have lived in towns. Today a few scroll experts challenge the dominant Essene theory, and some archeologists make other suggestions about the Qumran ruins (a military outpost? a villa?). Yet, the Essene theory about the scrolls and the site prevails.

According to the scrolls, the founder of the group (groups?) was a certain Teacher of Righteousness, a Zadokite priest who opposed one of the Maccabean priests as "the wicked priest" sometime in the second half of the second century B.C.E. In fulfillment of Isa. 40:3 (". . . in the wilderness prepare the way of the Lord . . ."; cf. Mark 1:3), the Teacher took his followers to the Dead Sea and established a community there. Its leaders were disaffected priests, and its scribes interpreted the prophecies to refer to the community itself.

At Qumran the group worked, copied religious texts, wrote religious literature, worshipped according to their own calendar and customs, baptized, celebrated a common meal, and sought to live pure and undefiled lives. Their literature, community organization, and eschatological orientation have become extremely important for understanding the context of the Jesus Movement. The following passage illustrates their liturgical meal, which anticipates the great banquet that will take place when the *two* Messiahs, the Messiahs of Aaron and Israel, come.

[The Priest] shall enter [at] the head of all the Congregation of Israel, then all (13) [the chiefs of the sons] of Aaron, the priests called to the assembly, men of renown; and they shall sit (14) [before him], each according to his rank.

And afterwards, [the Mess]iah of Israel [shall enter]; and the chiefs (15) of [the tribes of Israel] shall sit before him, each according to his rank, . . . then all (16) the heads of the fa[milies of the Congre]gation, together with the wise me[n of the holy Congregation], shall sit before them, each according to (17) his rank.

And [when] they gather for the Community tab[le], [or to drink w]ine, and arrange the (18) Community table [and mix] the wine to drink, let no man [stretch out] his hand over the first-fruits of bread (19) and [wine] before the Priest; for [it is he who] shall bless the first-fruits of bread (20) and w[ine, and shall] first [stretch out] his hand over the bread. And after[wards], the Messiah of Israel shall [str]etch out his hands (21) over the bread. [And afterwards], all the Congregation of the Community shall [bl]ess, each according to his rank. And they shall proceed according to this rite (22) at every mea[l where] at least ten persons [are as]sembled.

(1QSa 11–22)

The New Testament never mentions Essenes or any Israelite group along the Dead Sea. However, it does say that John the Baptizer, a millennial prophet, came out of the Judean wilderness. It is thus possible that John had been associated with this group. In any case, its strict Torah interpretation and withdrawal to the desert were distinctive. Its eschatology, worship, messianic expectations, and interpretation of scripture offer many parallels to the New Testament.

By way of summary, we can show the three major groups in Table 1.2.

THE DIASPORA

Although the main focus of the preceding sketch of history, society, and religion has been Greco-Roman Palestine, many Israelites—indeed, the majority—had since the Babylonian Exile lived in foreign lands such as Babylonia and in cities such as Rome, Alexandria, Antioch, and Damascus. These were Israelites of the **Diaspora.** The largest of such communities was at Alexandria, Egypt, where it formed a legalized city ghetto (the *politeuma*).

The native tongue of most Diaspora Israelites was the commonly spoken *koinē* Greek. Thus there was a need in Diaspora synagogue worship for Greek translations of the Hebrew scriptures. The legend arose that seventy (or seventy-two) Greek-speaking priests from Jerusalem were invited to Alexandria, where they translated the Hebrew scriptures independently into Greek and miraculously arrived at precisely the same translations! The historical probability is that at least the Torah was translated by the third century B.C.E. and that, as the Prophets and the Writings began to be accepted as holy texts, they were also translated. These were supplemented by additions and a few other books and became the **Septuagint (LXX).** It had a very formative influence on language and thought of Greek-speaking adherents of the Jesus Movement.

Some other Israelite books in Greek were written at Alexandria, the most important of which were the works of a contemporary of Jesus named Philo of Alexandria (ca. 20 B.C.E.–45 C.E.). Platonic and Stoic ideas, as well as biblical Wisdom, influenced Philo. In his commentaries on the Septuagint, he sought to find and present to educated Greeks its deeper meaning based on **allegory.**

Greco-Roman Israelites in general were exempt from emperor worship and were permitted a number of special privileges based on their Sabbath observance

Table 1.2 Three Major Religious Groups

Category	Sadducees	Pharisees	Essenes
1. **New Testament**	Jesus' Jerusalem opponents	Jesus' main Galilean opponents	Not mentioned
2. **Place of activity**	Temple	House-synagogue, then synagogues	Khirbet Qumran
3. **Priest or lay**	Priests	Lay	Priests
4. **Relation to temple**	Control temple and Sanhedrin	Foster temple purity in everyday life	Do not sacrifice at Jerusalem temple; community is temple
5. **Focus of activity**	Sacrifice; purity	Teaching; purity	Communal life; interpretation; purity
6. **View of written sacred texts**	Torah only	Torah, prophets, and writings	Torah, prophets, writings, and Pseudepigrapha
7. **Interpretation of sacred writings**	Do not accept oral Torah; strict and literal	Develop oral Torah to apply Temple purity to everyday life: Sabbath and purity	Strict "sectarian" interpretations; some Pharisaic, some Sadducaic; Sabbath, purity, much else
8. **Group type**	Maintain society; strong purity boundaries	Reform within society; perhaps increasingly focused on piety; strong purity boundaries ("reformist")	Reform by leaving society's strong purity boundaries ("introversionist")
9. **Organization**	Priestly hierarchy; 24 "courses" (families) to serve at Temple	Possibly "brotherhoods"	Priestly hierarchy; Teacher of Righteousness, Three, Twelve
10. **Support**	Taxes; sacrifices	Work; trades	Communal farming
11. **Relation to Rome**	Cooperative	Mixed	Antagonistic
12. **Social status**	High; wealthy elite	Retainers of elites	Relatively low; "marginal"
13. **Beliefs**	Reject fate and determinism, immortality of soul, angels, and demons, resurrection of dead; less apocalyptic	Accept fate and determinism, immortality of soul, angels, and demons, resurrection of dead; some apocalyptic	Accept angels and demons, resurrection of the dead; highly apocalyptic
14. **Literature**	Do not survive	Reworked in Mishnah and Talmud	*Dead Sea Scrolls* (probably), 1947

and seasonal festivals. In the Diaspora, they sometimes formed political entities or synagogue organizations in their city quarters, were permitted to settle inter-Israelite legal disputes according to their own laws and traditions, to administer their own funds, and to send money to Jerusalem, especially the temple tax. Scholars debate whether Israelites also had *civic* rights as citizens of the Roman Empire, that is, participation in public life, election of magistrates, and the like. Josephus says they did; other sources say they did not, a condition that seems more likely. No doubt many Israelites of the Diaspora became less inclined to follow the Torah as strictly as Israelites in Palestine, especially because much of it dealt with issues about the temple.

Non-Israelite reactions to the Israelites were mixed. On the one hand, Israelite monotheism and practices such as the rite of circumcision and ritual purity kept them separate, and the formation of distinct ghettos along with their special privileges under the Romans brought them ill will. Various Gentile criticisms of circumcision, pork eating, and Israelite laziness (the Sabbath command!) have survived, as well as charges of hypocrisy by members of the Jesus Movement. Pro-Roman, anti-Israelite stories about the crucifixion of Jesus also testify to anti-Israelite ideologies (some modern writers call this "anti-Judaism"; "anti-Semitism" as a *racial* theory is modern). Yet, some Hellenistic writers admired the Israelites' high sense of morality and defended them (some modern scholars call this "philo-Judaism"). Indeed, as the stories of the Ammonite general Achior (Jth. 14:10) and king Izates of Adiabene (an independent kingdom far to the northeast) reveal, Israelites of the Greco-Roman period won "proselytes" (converts from another religion). Among them were especially women (who did not have to undergo the painful rite of circumcision) and what the Book of Acts calls "God-fearers," or men who were attracted to Israelite morality but were not circumcised.

Whereas some early Jesus Movement groups remained in Palestine, others quickly migrated to, or arose in, the urban centers of the larger Greco-Roman world where the Diaspora was already planted. Thus most early Jesus Movement literature, including the New Testament, was written in *koinē* Greek, and most of its scriptural citations were from the **Septuagint.**

This chapter has attempted to highlight some of the main features of Israelite history and society in the Greco-Roman period. It has included Hellenistic intellectual thought and religion, as well as Israelite religion and groups both in Palestine and the Diaspora. As a summary, one might attempt to answer the study questions.

Another task will be to narrow the focus to the early history and ideas of the Jesus Movement. Then it will be possible to take up in more detail particular Jesus Movement communities and their writings, specifically, the literature of the New Testament. First, however, it will be helpful to discuss modern scholarly approaches to the New Testament. That is the subject of the next chapter.

STUDY QUESTIONS

1. How does the strategic location of ancient Israel (Palestine) relate to its place in the history of the ancient Near East (Middle East)? In what sense is the history of Israel marked by oppression? What are some of its major regions, languages, and cities? What was the significance of the Babylonian Exile? Hellenization? Alexander the Great? The Maccabean Revolt? Hanukkah?

2. What were some common social values in ancient Mediterranean society? What were economic and social conditions in Palestine like under Romans? What was social stratification like in the ancient Mediterranean in general and in Palestine in particular? Who was Josephus, and why is he so important? How would you characterize Herod the Great, what were the major divisions of Herod's kingdom, and who ruled them? Why were there resistance, reform, and terrorist movements during this period? What were some key factors leading up to the rebellion against Rome? What was the significance of Jamnia?

3. What were some of the key ideas of Plato and the Stoics? What was the Cynics' alternative lifestyle? How would you distinguish a goddess/god from a heroine/hero? Why do you think that astrology and magic were so common in the Mediterranean world? Why were the mystery religions so popular? What was the political significance of the Emperor Cult? How did Gnostics look at the world, the self, and salvation?

4. Why do people distinguish the sacred from the profane, and what are some examples of this distinction in Greco-Roman Israelite religion?

5. How does the Jerusalem temple mirror beliefs about the holy? What are main Israelite feasts found in the New Testament, and what do they celebrate? What is the only fast prescribed by Torah (the "Law")? How would you describe the difference between the temple and the synagogue? How would you contrast wisdom and prophecy? What were ancient miracle workers like? What do the modern terms *apocalypticism* and *millennialism* signify, and what is their significance for the study of this period? What were some of the major groups in Greco-Roman Israel, and what did they believe? What were some major features of Israelite religion in the Diaspora, and who was Philo of Alexandria?

Photo 2.1   The scribe Eadwine, from the *Canterbury Psalter,* ca. 1150 C.E., Trinity College, Cambridge, England. Manuscripts were copied by hand (sometimes by groups of monks in monasteries) until the invention of the printing press in the 1450s. Despite great care, they were subject to error (and occasionally intentional changes to defend doctrine). From such handwritten copies that vary from each other, modern Textual Critics attempt to reconstruct what the New Testament writers originally wrote. See the modern Jewish scribe at the beginning of Chapter Nine.

CHAPTER TWO

INTERPRETING
THE NEW TESTAMENT

THREE BIBLES

One often sees a beautifully bound book inscribed with the words *Holy Bible*. Consider these two words. As observed in Chapter One, religious groups or their respected authorities tend to separate certain people, places, times, things, and actions apart as holy in distinction from their ordinary, everyday, or profane meaning or use. A book can be set aside as holy. The second term, **Bible,** comes from a Greek word for "book," *biblion*.

There is a third and related word: *canon*. **Canon** comes from the Greek word *kanōn*, meaning "reed." In the ancient world, a reed was often used as a measuring stick, like a ruler or yardstick. The term was then extended to mean a yardstick for true faith, thus orthodoxy ("thinking straight"). More generally, a sacred canon is a more or less fixed number of scriptures used as a guide or standard by which a group's religious faith and practice are measured. By the fourth century C.E., the term *canon* was being applied to the emergent Christian Bible. In short, the Holy Bible is literally the "sacred book," that is, a canonical selection of books that has been set aside by certain authoritative religious persons because they believe the collection is filled with the secret and mysterious truth of life (Gamble).

The Holy Bible is literally "the sacred book," but actually it is *several* collections of sacred books used by *several* historically related religions. Indeed, these religions do not have exactly the same canon. We shall consider three of these historically related religions—Judaism, Roman Catholic Christianity, and Protestant Christianity—and distinguish the canon for each of them.

The first of the three canons is the canon of Judaism. By the early second century C.E., religious leaders from "the land of Israel" had established a canon of thirty-nine books. Many Jews today call it simply "the **Bible.**" Some, however, call it the "**Jewish Bible,**" and some call it *Tanak.*

This term is an acronym based on its three ancient divisions: *Tōrāh, Nabî'îm,* and *Kitubîm.* The *Tōrāh* (Hebrew for "instruction") refers to the Pentateuch or first five books; the *Nabî'îm* is Hebrew for "Prophets"; and the *Kitubîm* is Hebrew for "Writings." This collection is also the Protestant Christian **Old Testament.** Most scholars call it the **Hebrew Bible** because virtually all of its original language is Hebrew. Whatever we call it, it is a collection of thirty-nine mostly Hebrew books that can be dated from about the tenth century to the second century B.C.E. Today it is the canon for Jews.

A second form of the Bible was not *officially* defined as a canon for many centuries; nonetheless, it functioned as sacred scripture. By the first century C.E., the **Aramaic** language had replaced Hebrew as the vernacular language for most native inhabitants of Palestine. Educated Palestinians used Aramaic paraphrases of the Hebrew Bible that have survived, called "**Targums.**" However, most Israelites were **Diaspora** Israelites living in Greco-Roman cities. Their native tongue was *koinē* ("common") Greek. They worshiped in **synagogues** and used the Greek **Septuagint,** which contained a few extra books and some books that were longer than those in the Hebrew Bible. Members of the Jesus Movement who spoke Greek as their native language also read or listened to the Septuagint as their Bible. In short, for a brief period, the longer Greek LXX became the Bible of both Greek-speaking Israelites and members of the Jesus Movement.

Early in the second century most Israelites began to follow a number of books in the thirty-nine-book Hebrew canon. Meanwhile, members of the Jesus Movement still used the LXX and began to add books of their own to it. The Greek Septuagint became the **Old Testament,** and this new collection of books became the **New Testament.** (The word *testament* here is a term for a **covenant.**) Eventually in the West both Greek testaments, Old and New, were translated into Latin, the language of Rome that gradually supplanted Greek as the language of the Roman Empire and the "Western" Christian church. One of these Latin translations, mostly that of Jerome, who worked on it from about 380 to 405 C.E. and who consulted the Hebrew Bible, the Greek LXX, and existing Latin translations (the Old Latin), gradually became the Christian Bible for Latin-speaking Christians. During the medieval period, the name given to Jerome's translation was the **Vulgate** ("common vernacular"). Thus the Greek Old Testament and Greek New Testament became the Christian Bible in the Greek-speaking East (and is generally the Bible of the Orthodox communities, with some exceptions). Their Latin translations became the Bible in the Latin-speaking West. The Christian Old Testament usually contained forty-nine books, and the Christian New Testament contained twenty-seven books (See Appendix Two for further discussion of the New Testament canon.) Finally, in the sixteenth century the Council of Trent, mainly in response to Protestant limitations of the canon (see the following), defined the *official canon* for the Roman Catholic church. Interestingly, it decided to exclude three books of the LXX/Vulgate. Today the Catholic Old Testament contains forty-six books, and some of them based on the LXX have additional portions and thus are longer.

We have defined the canonical Bible for what became Judaism and Catholic Christianity (the Syriac church in the Orthodox tradition never fully accepted some

New Testament books, especially Revelation; see Appendix Two). However, there is yet a third canon of the Bible. Sixteenth-century Protestant reformers thought that the additional Old Testament books (and sections of other books) in the LXX/Vulgate were the basis for certain doctrines and ideas they rejected. Thus the reformers returned to the thirty-nine books of the Hebrew Bible. During the 1520s they began to place the extra books and book parts of the Septuagint and Vulgate in an appendix called the **Apocrypha** (Greek for "hidden," *originally* meaning "sacred" but later to mean "hidden from the faithful or profane"). The Puritans disliked the Apocrypha so much that they soon omitted it from their Bibles altogether. In contrast, in 1615 the archbishop of Canterbury, head of the established (Protestant) Church of England, decreed that those who bound and sold Bibles *without* the Apocrypha would receive a year's imprisonment! In general, the Protestant Bible consists of the thirty-nine books of the "Old Testament" (= the books of the Hebrew Bible) plus the twenty-seven books of the Greek "New Testament." Its difference from the Catholic Bible is its shorter Old Testament. It needs to be added that there is another collection of Old Testament-type books that is not found in any of these three canons. This collection is called the Old Testament **Pseudepigrapha** (Greek for "false writings"). The books in this collection date from about 200 B.C.E. to 300 C.E. and are very important for understanding religious thinking prior to and during the rise of the Jesus Movement (see Appendix Three).

In summary, the canon for Jews is the thirty-nine books of the (mostly) Hebrew Bible. Roman Catholic Christians continued to accept a forty-nine-book Old Testament—the number of the Greek LXX and the Latin Vulgate—which was later reduced to forty-six books in the sixteenth century. They also accepted the twenty-seven-book New Testament. (The Eastern Orthodox canon in Greek is similar.) At that time, the Protestants returned to the thirty-nine-book Old Testament and placed the extra books and book additions of the LXX/Vulgate into the Old Testament Apocrypha—if they printed them at all. The general picture for Judaism, Roman Catholic Christianity, and Protestant Christianity is summarized in Table 2.1.

THE NEW TESTAMENT CANON

We may define the New Testament canon as a collection of twenty-seven books, originally written in ancient *koinē* Greek, written by and for members of the Jesus Movement, and set aside as sacred by certain church authorities during the first three centuries C.E. What books do they contain, what is the *form* of these books, and how did this canon develop?

In general, the twenty-seven books fall into *four literary forms* or "**genres.**" Table 2.2 shows the New Testament books in canonical order. Three facts are striking about this table. First, four different gospels or "biographies" are included, even though they cover essentially the same story. Second, the New Testament canon is dominated by the letter genre, even though the Old Testament contains no book of this genre. Third, the names of the books come from persons and places.

Canonical books were considered to be *apostolic,* a term that comes from the Greek *apostolos,* meaning "one sent out on a mission," originally a military term. In the Jesus Movement, **apostle** took on a more religious meaning. It had a narrower

Table 2.1 Three Canons

	Jewish Bible	Roman Catholic Bible*	Protestant Bible
	Hebrew Bible	**Old Testament**	**Old Testament**
Number of Books	39 books	46 books LXX; Vulgate	39 books; based on Jewish Bible
Original Language	Hebrew (and a little Aramaic)	Latin from Greek LXX plus Hebrew, Aramaic	Hebrew (and a little Aramaic)
(Modern) English Translation	Orthodox and Conservative boys learn Hebrew; there are also vernacular translations	Earlier translations from Vulgate (which consulted the Hebrew) have given way to translations directly from the original Hebrew	From the original Hebrew and Aramaic
Extra Material		From LXX and Vulgate; "deutero-canonical"	From LXX and Vulgate; Old Testament Apocrypha
	———	**New Testament**	**New Testament**
Number of Books		27 books	27 books
Original Language		Greek	Greek
(Modern) English Translation		Originally translated from Latin; now from original Greek	From original Greek

*The Greek Orthodox Bible also contains 3, 4 Maccabees (usually collected in the Old Testament Pseudepigrapha), and Psalm 151; the Russian Orthodox Bible also contains 2 Esdras, 3 Maccabees, and Psalm 151; the Coptic Church from Egypt omits 1, 2 Esdras, 3, 4, Maccabees, and Psalm 151, but contains the others, as well as three more New Testament books, the *Apostolic Constitutions* and *1* and *2 Clement* (Church Fathers). Other churches in the East accept most or all of the Apocrypha, and some accept or exclude other New Testament books, especially Revelation (see Evans, Bibliography).

sense, the twelve disciples (Matt. 10:1, 6–15; Luke 9:1–6), and a broader sense, Jesus' circle of the Twelve plus blood relatives and missionaries such as Paul. In Table 2.2, James and Jude were remembered as Jesus' blood brothers (Mark 6:3 [the perpetual virginity of Mary is not at issue]). Two fishermen, Peter son of Jonah, and John son of Zebedee, as well as Matthew, whom the Gospel of Matthew calls a "toll collector," are among Jesus' twelve disciples (Mark 3:16–19 par. ["par." abbreviates "parallels," or parallel passages in the first three gospels that contain the same or similar material]). The Book of Revelation claims to have been written by "John," whom later members of the Jesus Movement identified with John son of Zebedee, also one of Jesus' twelve disciples. Paul wrote to Philemon, a slave owner whom he had converted. Timothy, Titus, Mark, and Luke were Paul's companions (Gal. 2:1–10; Philem. 23–24), and Acts was attributed to Luke (Acts 1:1–2).

All but one of the remaining names of New Testament books—"Hebrews"—are derived from the *place* to which Paul purportedly wrote letters, that is, the cities of Rome, Corinth, Philippi, Thessalonica, Ephesus, and Colossae, and the region of Galatia. The Letter to the Hebrews was eventually attributed to Paul, as well. Although "apostolic" generally suggests apostolic *authors,* fixing the number of books was "apostolic" in at least two other senses. First, the books were used, especially for

Table 2.2   New Testament Books (Abbreviations in parentheses)

"Gospels" (4) ("biographies")	"History" (1)	Letters (21)	Apocalypse (1) ("revelation")
1. Matthew (Matt.)	5. Acts of the Apostles (Acts)	6. Romans (Rom.)	27. Revelation (Rev.)
2. Mark (Mark)		7. 1 Corinthians (1 Cor.)	
3. Luke (Luke)		8. 2 Corinthians (2 Cor.)	
4. John (John)		9. Galatians (Gal.)	
		10. Ephesians (Eph.)	
		11. Philippians (Phil.)	
		12. Colossians (Col.)	
		13. 1 Thessalonians (1 Thess.)	
		14. 2 Thessalonians (2 Thess.)	
		15. 1 Timothy (1 Tim.)	
		16. 2 Timothy (2 Tim.)	
		17. Titus	
		18. Philemon (Philem.)	
		19. Hebrews (Heb.)	
		20. James	
		21. 1 Peter (1 Pet.)	
		22. 2 Peter (2 Pet.)	
		23. 1 John	
		24. 2 John	
		25. 3 John	
		26. Jude	

public reading, in powerful urban churches purportedly established by apostles. That is an important historical and social fact: The canon was ultimately a choice of the leaders of prestigious, elite churches. Second, these books were important for apostolic beliefs and practices, that is, beliefs and practices held to be orthodox in those same churches. The development of the canon and the development of the orthodox Jesus Movement went hand in hand.

Narrowing down the twenty-seven-book New Testament canon took almost three hundred years (for details, see Appendix Two), and even then some books continued to be debated. Most historians think that ten of the fourteen letters eventually attributed to Paul were accepted as scripture in some circles already by the end of the first century C.E. Of the many gospels in use, the four canonical ones had achieved prominence by the second half of the second century. These two developments seem to have taken place partially in response to a second-century believer named **Marcion,** who accepted as authoritative only ten Pauline letters plus an edited version of Luke. (Marcion was subsequently judged by orthodox thinkers to be a "heretic.") In response, all four gospels continued to be used in major churches. One indication of this practice is that about 170 C.E. Tatian of Syria made a condensed version that wove precisely these four together into one gospel (the ***Diatessaron*** [Greek "through the four"]). It became "the gospel" in the Syrian church for about two centuries. Meanwhile, in 185 C.E. Irenaeus of Lyons (in modern France) defended the necessity of the fourfold gospel.

The **Muratorian Canon** (named for the man who discovered it), the first "official" canonical list of books at Rome, illustrates the developing canon, probably about 200 C.E.. In the list of twenty-seven books in Table 2.2, Hebrews, James, 1 and 2 Peter, and 3 John were missing from this canonical list, and on other lists these five were put into the category of "disputed" books. There was grave doubt about the Book of Hebrews in the West, and the Book of Revelation was so disputed in the East that it never received full canonical status in the churches of Syria!

Finally, in 367 C.E.—at least three centuries after the first Jesus Movement writings appeared—Athanasius, bishop of Alexandria, distributed his *Festal Letter* **(Easter Letter)** at Easter time. In it, he listed as "scriptures of the New Testament" the twenty-seven books that are almost universally accepted today.

The story of the growth of the canon is also the story of the emergence of influential urban churches and the books they accepted as sacred. Indeed, *a few* books in the canon imply guidelines about how to read *other* books in the canon! Some books hovered on the edge of canonicity; a few of them can be found in ancient manuscripts of the New Testament. Other books that almost became canonical were orthodox theological writings now collected as the **Church Fathers** or **Apostolic Fathers,** or simply the **Patristic Literature.**

Other books of the same general genre as the four New Testament genres were accepted in other churches. The orthodox churches judged them to be less valuable for reading or even heretical. Many of these books, some mentioned by the Church Fathers, did not survive; a few did, and some others have been rediscovered in modern times. These extracanonical books are now collected in the **New Testament Apocrypha.** Occasionally isolated sayings of Jesus are found quoted here and there in ancient manuscripts and elsewhere; these are called **Agrapha.**

Summarizing, the New Testament contains twenty-seven books of four genres: four biography-like "gospels," one "history," twenty-one letters, and one "apocalypse" (revelation). These twenty-seven were gradually accepted as the canonical New Testament by more powerful, prestigious churches over a period of almost three centuries. The canon was for all practical purposes closed by the time of St. Athanasius' *Festal Letter* in 367 C.E. Literature of the same type that did not become canonical but was passed down through the churches or rediscovered in modern times is collected in the New Testament Apocrypha. There also existed orthodox literature that almost became canonical; it can be found among the writings of the Apostolic Fathers (the Patristic Literature). We shall have occasion to study a few pieces of this extracanonical literature.

ACADEMIC STUDY OF THE NEW TESTAMENT

Dividing history into periods is a human endeavor that involves value judgments (for example, *Renaissance* means "rebirth," implying previous death). Yet, periodization is very practical. Some modern intellectuals think in terms of three broad periods called "Pre-Modernism," "Modernism," and "Post-Modernism." Pre-Modernism goes back many centuries. For practical reasons, in this section we can go back only to the period of the *Renaissance* (fourteenth to sixteenth centuries), the period of the invention of the printing press. Modernism begins in the eighteenth-century Enlightenment—some thinkers prefer the less ideological term *Industrial Revolution*—and continues until very recent times. (This general use of the term *Modernism* should not be confused with its very specific use for a heresy in the Roman Catholic Church.) Post-Modernism is usually considered to be relatively recent.

Period	General Time Frame
Pre-Modernism	Prior to 1776
Modernism	1776–1976
Post-Modernism	1976–

These three periods, although artificial, will provide a practical "big picture" for the following sketch of New Testament interpretation. The example passage throughout will be the most familiar of all New Testament passages, the prayer attributed to Jesus. Roman Catholic Christians call it the "Our Father"; Protestant Christians call it "the Lord's Prayer."

A familiar version of the Lord's Prayer in Matt. 6:9b–13 reads:

Our Father who art in heaven,
　　Hallowed be Thy name.
Thy Kingdom come.
　　Thy will be done,
　　On earth as it is in heaven.
Give us this day our daily bread;
And forgive us our debts,
　　As we forgive our debtors,
And lead us not into temptation,
　　But deliver us from evil.
For Thine is the Kingdom,
　　And the power,
　　And the glory forever. Amen.

This translation is very close to that of the influential **King James Version** (KJV), a translation of the Bible published at the time of King James I of England in 1611 C.E. Its wording is used in most English-speaking Protestant churches.

Roman Catholic Christians will immediately observe two major differences from what they pray, the Our Father. First, the last three lines, or concluding "doxology"—doxologies "praise" God (Greek *doxa*, "praise," "glory")—are not prayed immediately as part of the prayer but rather spoken in the liturgy of the Mass after a few intervening words by the priest. Second, they (and a few Protestant groups) pray "*trespasses*" and "*those who trespass against* us," not "debts" and "debtors." These two differences in the prayer illustrate the first two important critical problems for interpreting the New Testament in the following section.

METHODS OF ANALYSIS AND CRITICISM

Scholars use a number of methods of analysis and criticism in the study of the New Testament. The following methods are, despite divisions, numbered sequentially.

1. Textual Criticism

Protestants pray the final doxology of the Lord's Prayer immediately at the end of the prayer; Roman Catholics do not, but rather pray it slightly later in the Mass. This problem has a simple solution. The two versions are based on two different types of manuscripts. Let us look at this problem and its solution a little more carefully.

The study of ancient writing scripts and habits, called "**paleography**" (from the Greek for "ancient writing"), has demonstrated that the writing styles of the surviving manuscripts of the New Testament books are too late to come directly from the hand of their authors. In other words, they are all copies—and, indeed, for the most part, copies of copies. Like all ancient manuscripts, they were copied by hand down to the invention of the printing press in the mid-fifteenth century. Although hand copying of sacred texts was generally very careful, it was not perfect. Occasionally errors crept in to the manuscripts, and on occasion intentional changes were made for doctrinal reasons. Thus the surviving manuscripts contain many little variants, often called "readings," in words, phrases, and paragraphs. They pose this main problem: Which "readings" best represent what the author originally wrote? The analytical method used to solve this problem is called "**Textual Criticism.**" (The word *criticism* in this description and other "criticisms" that follow is not intended to be negative or destructive; rather, it calls attention to a "critical," that is, "scientific" method.)

Textual Criticism has two aims: to classify the surviving manuscripts and to evaluate them in order to reconstruct as best possible what the authors originally wrote.

A. Quantity: The Collection and Classification of Manuscripts

During the Modern period, a large quantity of hand-copied manuscripts was discovered, but the system for classifying them developed slowly and is not very logical. Some manuscripts are classified by the *material* on which they are written, papyrus ("paper" made from the ancient papyrus plant). Others are classified by the *kind of script* that they contain, namely, uncials, or block capital letters, and minuscules, or cursive script. Still others are classified by their *content,* such as lectionaries, that is, collections of biblical passages read on special church days.

Table 2.3 summarizes the known quantity and century of production of these most important classifications of New Testament handwritten manuscripts. This table shows that well over five thousand hand-copied Greek manuscripts of the New Testament (or parts thereof) were produced between the second century C.E. and the first printed editions in the sixteenth century (with a few thereafter). There are also two other important types of manuscripts. The first type is called "Patristic Citations," that is, quotations and allusions to scripture by the Apostolic Fathers. Because we know where and approximately when an apostolic father wrote, these quotations occasionally offer information about where and when certain types of

Table 2.3 Ancient Manuscripts of the New Testament

	Number of Manuscripts	Century Copied
		1 2 3 4 5 6 7 8 9 10 11 12 13 14 15 16 17 18 19
Papyri	96	▬▬▬▬▬ (2–8)
Uncials	300+	▬▬▬▬▬ (4–10)
Minuscules	2,800+	▬▬▬▬▬ (9–16)
Lectionaries	2,280+	
Uncial type		▬▬▬▬▬ (5–11)
Minuscule type		▬▬▬▬▬ (9–16)

manuscripts were in use. The second type is called "Versions," that is, translations of the original Greek into other languages. Examples already noted are the Latin Vulgate and the Syriac *Diatessaron*. Most all of the ancient New Testament manuscripts are located in the libraries and museums of Europe and the Middle East. A few are in North America.

B. Evaluating the Quality of Manuscripts and "Establishing the Text"

The 5,000-plus manuscripts contain more than 200,000 variant "readings"—more if one includes the lectionaries and versions. Given this vast *quantity*—today these variant readings are computerized—scholars have had to devise ways to evaluate their *quality* (the "best" readings) in order to "establish the text," that is, to reconstruct as closely as possible what the original authors of New Testament books originally wrote (the "autographs"). To solve this giant puzzle, they have developed several principles.

The most basic principle of Textual Criticism for establishing the text is this: When variant word(s), phrase(s), or sentence(s) occur, those that explain the origin of the other variant readings are most likely to be the earliest and best readings. This principle is related to both "external evidence" and "internal evidence." For Textual Critics, *external evidence* evaluates manuscripts according to their age, family relationships, length, and geographical distribution. *Internal evidence* evaluates the characteristic vocabulary, style, or ideas of the manuscripts, as well as changes typical of most ancient copyists. Good Textual Critics get to know certain ancient copyists and their writing habits quite well. Qualitative evaluation has produced a few very general "text types" and "genealogical trees" of the family relationships ("who copied whom") based on their resemblance. Two of the four major text types are especially important. The first type is represented by the *majority* of Greek manuscripts, most of which are cursive-script minuscules. During the Pre-Modern and early Modern periods, this text type was virtually sacred: It *was* the Greek New Testament. It was called the ***Textus Receptus*** ("Received Text"). This type was the basis for the first printed editions of the Greek New Testament in the sixteenth century and the first English translations.

With the discovery and publication of the earlier uncials and the papyri, mostly in the late nineteenth and early twentieth centuries, and with the development of scientific Textual Criticism, scholars realized that a second text type, the Alexandrian Text Type, centered in Alexandria, Egypt, was older and better. An excellent example is that in the *Textus Receptus* a copyist changed the Lukan form of the Lord's Prayer (Luke 11:2b–4) to conform to the more familiar liturgical form in Matthew (Matt. 6:9b–12). In the Alexandrian Text Type the differences stand out. Today, both the Protestant International United Bible Societies and the Roman Catholic Church accept a **Standard Text** based primarily on the Alexandrian Text Type.

We can now return to our first Lord's Prayer problem: Was the concluding doxology of the Lord's Prayer in Matt. 6:9b–12 original or added later?

With regard to *external evidence,* there are, unfortunately, *no surviving early papyrus manuscripts of Matt. 6.* The next-earliest and most reliable manuscripts are the block-capital letter uncials of the Alexandrian Text Type. They *do not contain the doxology.* Ordinarily one would need to go no further. However, there is an early Latin translation, "k" (about 400 C.E.), that may go back to a second-century Greek "parent," and it contains a *variation* of the doxology ("for thine is the power forever and ever"). Also, the *Didachē* (Greek for "Teaching [of the Twelve Apostles]"), usually dated to the early second century, contains a Matthean-like version of the prayer with a slightly different doxology ("for thine is the power and the glory forever"). Nonetheless, because the earliest surviving manuscripts do not contain the doxology, external evidence suggests that it was added from an early liturgy in the Jesus Movement. This probability is suggested also because copyists tended to *add* clarifications to their manuscripts to improve them, not the reverse.

With respect to *internal evidence,* the question is this: Would a later copyist have added or omitted the doxology? Adding it is much more likely. There is a very similar doxology in the Hebrew Bible (1 Chron. 29:11–13, especially 11). In either private devotion or public worship, it would have been natural to add such a conclusion in the liturgy.

In short, external evidence and internal evidence combine to conclude that very early—perhaps as early as the early second century C.E. (*Didachē*)—a doxology was recited after the prayer, perhaps then written beside the prayer in the margins of manuscripts of Matthew, and eventually tacked on to the prayer itself.

Summarizing, Textual Criticism attempts to classify the surviving manuscripts and to evaluate them in order to best reconstruct what the authors originally wrote. It shows that the Protestant liturgical form of the Lord's Prayer containing the final doxology, derived from the King James Version, rests on later, less reliable minuscule manuscripts (the *Textus Receptus*). It therefore shows that the Catholic liturgical form omitting the doxology, derived from the Latin Vulgate, follows the earliest, the best-surviving Greek manuscripts (*in this case;* very often the Vulgate rests on the later *Textus Receptus*). It is likely that the doxology was added, perhaps as early as the second century C.E. Thus recent editions of the New Testament usually put the doxology of the Lord's Prayer in a footnote at the bottom of the page (often prefaced with the comment, "Other ancient authorities read . . ."). Finally, it should also be noted that Textual Critics of Matthew have pointed us toward a very high historical probability, namely, that *Jesus did not teach his disciples a prayer that included the doxology.*

2. English Translation

The second difference between the Catholic and Protestant forms of the Lord's Prayer is "debts" and "debtors" in the Protestant prayer and "trespasses" and "those who trespass against" in the Catholic prayer. This difference can be explained easily. They are alternative translations of the Greek terms *opheilēmata/tois opheiletais.* We should, however, clarify two matters: There is a long history behind these different translations, and there is still the question about which is the *better* translation.

There was a long history behind these translation alternatives. The early Latin Vulgate translated the two Greek words with the Latin *debita/debitoribus.* Toward the end of the fourteenth century C.E., a "Middle English" translation of devotional and liturgical text selections translated the two key words like this:

> And foryeue us oure *dettys,*
> as we foryeue oure *dettourys.*

The Middle English translation *dettys* and *dettourys* looks like the Latin. Yet, about the same time an English translation associated with John Wycliffe (ca. 1330–1384 C.E.) read:

> And forgeve vs oure *treaspases,*
> even as we forgeve *them whych treaspas* vs.

In these very early translations we see the roots of the modern *debts* and *trespasses.*

The rest, as they say, is history. "Trespasses" was perpetuated by the sixteenth-century Protestant translators Tyndale (1526) and Coverdale (1535), picked up in the Church of England's official prayer books (1537, 1549, 1552), primers, ABC books, and by the Roman Catholic Church in England and then North America. "Debts" found its way into the Coverdale Bible (1535, *"dettes"/"detters"*), the official "Thomas Matthew" Bible (1537), the Great Bible (1539–1568), and most important, the highly influential Protestant-sponsored King James Version (1611).

This simple sketch clarifies the history of English language translation. But which translation is *better?* This question is not easy to answer.

Let us first observe the language. The Greek terms in Matthew, *opheilēmata* and *tois opheiletais,* come from the verb *opheilō,* literally, "I owe (a debt to someone)." *If* the author of the Gospel of Matthew was being literal, the meaning implies something about people who owe money (or an equivalent exchange), and it might have implied poverty and low social status, as is also suggested by "daily bread" in the previous line. The "trespasses" translation suggests a different meaning. Although "to trespass" in early English referred to property (contemporary "No trespassing"), thus implying something about higher status, it could *also* have a more general sense, "to offend against," "to wrong," "to violate a person," and thus "to sin." This sense of "trespass" is not common today, except perhaps when Christians think "sins" when they pray "trespasses"!

There are other translation wrinkles. A second version of the prayer, as just noted, occurs in the Gospel of Luke (see Luke 11:2b–4), and that version contains a Greek term usually translated "sins," not "debts" or "trespasses" (Luke 11:4: *tas hamartias*). Furthermore, behind the Greek of *both* the Matthean and Lukan prayer terms might be an *Aramaic* term (*ḥōbā'* [cf. Mark 11:25]) that can mean *either* "debts" or "sins"! What did the author of the Gospel of Matthew mean? Or what did the author of Matthew think that *Jesus* meant? This is not yet the question, "What did *Jesus himself* mean?" What, then, did the translators think that Matthew thought that Jesus meant? It may be that "trespasses," which was already in the translation tradition (Wycliffe and his successors) was selected by some sixteenth-century translators because they were elite scholars who naturally chose a term related to ownership of property. More likely, it was plucked from the translation tradition because they thought that Matthew meant (that Jesus meant) something like "sins," a *secondary* meaning of *opheilēmata* in English, which was also found in the *Lukan* form of the prayer.

In summary, "debts," not "trespasses," *is a better translation of Matthew*. It comes closer to the literal rendering of the Greek than does the modern, *ordinary*-language meaning of "trespasses." It opens up historical possibilities of meaning for the author, his sources, his traditions, and perhaps Jesus himself!

HERMENEUTICS

A relatively accurate Greek text of the New Testament and a reasonably good translation of it *are* only the beginning of interpretation. There exists a whole body of modern theory about *how to interpret texts,* ancient and modern. It is called **hermeneutics**—some prefer the singular *hermeneutic* for the *general* range of theory—from the Greek word *hermēneuō,* "I interpret." Hermeneutical questions include: Should I interpret an ancient text to mean what its Greek-writing author *intended* it to mean when he or she put "pen" to papyrus? Does it mean what the Greek-speaking *first readers* (or listeners) would have understood it to mean? Would that not require understanding Greek and the whole cultural and social context of the "world" in which the text was written? In the case of Jesus and his first disciples, isn't Greek already a translation that implies an interpretation? In other words, is the main task of interpreting a text from the past to *bring out* the meaning of what it meant in the past (**exegesis**) before pondering what it means in the present? Yet, can one avoid *bringing into* the text merely what one wants to see there (**eisegesis**), for example, personal religious beliefs? However, to see the other side, does a text after all really mean what readers *think* (or believe) it means, regardless of what the original author intended? *Which* readers? Believers and atheists, rich and poor, men and women, First World and Third World people, conquerors and oppressed—do all these ask the same questions and hear the same answers from sacred texts? Do Jewish and Christian interpreters have pride of place in the act of interpreting texts that "belong" to the synagogue or church? Do scholars who study sacred texts in an "academic" field have the best insights? What kinds of scholars are best equipped to interpret? Historians? Literary critics? Theologians? Do authors sometimes say *more* than they intend, and is it therefore legitimate to see *more* in a text than its original author intended? Is there an imaginary world "inside" the text, as there is in modern fiction, that is the more appropriate concern of interpretation? Is it better to take the text *as it is* and try to interpret that inner world? Should one take into account all the different interpretations down through the centuries? *Where is meaning,* anyhow? Is it simply different for different people?

These questions open up many interesting possibilities for interpreting texts. The following treatment of academic study of the New Testament is roughly chronological and takes up several of the main hermeneutical approaches. It will then be necessary to briefly state at the end of the chapter the interpretive approach of this textbook.

HISTORICAL CRITICISM

One type of hermeneutics—indeed, the most common type—is interested in historical questions about "what really happened." These are questions about who, when, where, and why a text was written, as well as analysis of written sources, oral traditions, original authors' intentions, and the actuality of the events portrayed. The attempt to find answers to these sorts of questions has been called "Higher Criticism," a designation that is meant to be a contrast with Textual Criticism, which has been called "Lower Criticism." Historical questions arose especially during the eighteenth century and have dominated academic interpretation of the New Testament during the Modern period. Six common "critical" methods, to which it is possible to add "biblical" archeology, attempt to answer these sorts of historical questions. Building on the numbering thus far, they can be listed as follows:

3. (Old) Literary Criticism
4. Source Criticism
5. General Historical Criticism
6. Form Criticism
7. Redaction Criticism
8. Social-Scientific Criticism and Social-Historical Criticism
9. Archeology

We shall now take up these seven approaches, again using the Our Father or Lord's Prayer as a model text.

3. (Old) Literary Criticism

One aspect of **Literary Criticism** is analysis of vocabulary, grammar, syntax, and style, and it is quite ancient. Already in the third century, Alexandrian scholars argued that the Book of Revelation, attributed to "John" (Rev. 1:9), was not written by Jesus' disciple, John son of Zebedee, believed to be the author of the Fourth Gospel and three letters. Similarly, the ancient Alexandrians realized that the Book of Hebrews was not written in Paul's style. Origen of Alexandria (185–253 C.E.) said: "But who wrote the letter [of Hebrews], God really knows" (Eusebius *Ecclesiastical History* 6.25.11–14). In the nineteenth century some scholars argued that only four of the fourteen letters attributed to Paul were authentic. In short, literary analyses raise the question of what moderns would call "forgery," although in the ancient world *pseudonymity* (false author) is often a better term. Much more will be said about this topic.

Literary Criticism remains a very important tool of interpretation, and its results are critical for historical interpretation. It will be used to analyze the language of the Lord's Prayer that follows.

4. Source Criticism

Also part of Old Literary Criticism is **Source Criticism.**

There may be echoes of the Lord's Prayer in the Gospel of John (John 17), and a third version occurs in the noncanonical *Didachē.* The main versions, however, are in Matthew and Luke. Compare the two versions in the New Revised Standard Version (1989, slightly modified to fit the Greek). They are based on the more accurate **Standard Text** of Greek established by Textual Criticism. If we place the two versions side by side, they look like this:

Matthew 6:9b-13	Luke 11:2-4
Our **Father** in heaven,	— **Father,** — ———
hallowed be your name.	**hallowed be your name.**
Your kingdom come,	**Your kingdom come.**
Your will be done,	—— —— — ——
On earth as it is in heaven.	— —— — — ——
Give **us** this day **our daily bread;**	*Give* **us** each day **our daily bread;**
And forgive us our debts,	**And forgive us our** sins,
As we **also** *have forgiven*	As we **also** *have forgiven*
Our debtors.	everyone who is indebted to us;
And do not bring us to the test,	**And do not bring us to the test.**
But rescue us from the Evil One.	— —— — —— —— ——

The varying typefaces in the parallels represent words and phrases in Greek that are **exactly alike** (**boldface**), *somewhat alike* (*italics*), and different (plain typeface). Four obvious possibilities to explain these differences emerge:

1. The Lukan writer used the *written* Gospel of Matthew as a source, shortening the prayer.

2. The Matthean author used the *written* Gospel of Luke as a source, lengthening the prayer.

3. Both Matthean and Lukan authors used the *same written* source (or a version of the same source), but each changed it in a different way.

4. Both authors independently modified an *oral/liturgical* tradition.

Which possibility is most likely? Although the oral/liturgical hypothesis (no. 4) should be kept in mind, exact linguistic parallels demand that *written* source or sources, that is, direct literary relationship (nos. 1–3) be considered. This question requires addressing first the bigger question of sources in the gospels in general.

The first three gospels have the same general outline and share much of the same or similar content. They can be compared and contrasted in vertical side-by-side parallels called a "synopsis" (Greek *syn:* "together"; *optic,* from "to see") and are therefore labeled the "**synoptic gospels.**" The attempt to explain the similarities and differences of the synoptic gospels in both order and content is called "**the Synoptic Problem.**"

The ancient solution to this problem, already defended by Augustine of Hippo (354–430 C.E.), was that the gospels were composed by the persons whose names are in the superscriptions in the order as they are now found in the canon, each author having built on his supposed predecessor(s). The First Gospel was written by Matthew, Jesus' disciple; then Mark, a follower of the Apostle Paul, shortened Matthew; Luke, also a follower of Paul, used both Mark and Matthew as sources but rearranged them; and John, another of Jesus' disciples, knew and used all three, but wrote a "spiritual gospel." This became the "official" view of the church, and it was scarcely questioned until the Modern period. From this perspective, solution 1 is right: Luke shortened Matthew's more original version of the Lord's Prayer.

However, there are difficulties with this theory. First, the Gospel of John is so different from the other three that *direct* literary dependence is not likely. Second, it is incredible to think that the Lukan writer copied from the Gospel of Matthew but omitted the Sermon on the Mount and totally changed the birth, infancy, and resurrection of Jesus. Solution 1—thus also its reverse, solution 2—is therefore highly unlikely.

What then, of solution 3, that the authors Matthew and Luke used the same source independently? To answer this question, it is necessary to study parallel passages. Two samples are offered here, the story of Jesus' baptism, which is in *all three* gospels ("the triple tradition"), and the account of the Lord's Prayer, found only in *two gospels* ("the double tradition").

Matthew 3:13–17	Mark 1:9–11	Luke 3:21–22
Then *Jesus came from Galilee* to John at the Jordan, to be baptized by him. (*14*) <u>John would have prevented him, saying, "I need to be baptized by you, and do you come to me?"</u> (*15*) <u>But Jesus answered him, "Let it be so</u>	In those days *Jesus came from* Nazareth of *Galilee*	Now when all the people were baptized

now; for it is proper
for us in this way to
fulfill all righteousness."
Then he consented.

(16) **And when Jesus had been baptized,** just as *he came up from the water,* suddenly the heavens were opened to him and *he saw* **the Spirit** of God **descending like a dove** and alighting on him; (17) **and a voice from heaven** said" <u>This</u> is **my Son, the Beloved, with** whom **I am well pleased."**	**and was baptized** by John in the Jordan. (10) And just as *he was coming out of the water, he saw* the heavens torn apart and **the Spirit** descending *upon him* **like a dove** on him; (11) **and a voice** *came* **from heaven** "*You* **are my Son, the Beloved; with** *you* **I am well pleased."**	and when **Jesus** also **had been baptized** and was praying, the heaven was opened (22) and **the** Holy **Spirit** descended *upon him* in bodily form **like a dove. And a voice** *came* **from heaven,** "*You* **are my Son, the Beloved; with** *you* **I am well pleased."**

If you study these triple-tradition parallels carefully, you will see that there are at least three types of relationships. First, some words and phrases are found in all three gospels (**bold**). Second, some words and phrases are found in only one gospel (ordinary font, some underlined). Third, some words and phrases are found in two gospels over against the third (*italics*). Fourth—this is the main observation—in this "triple tradition" *Matthew and Luke do not agree with each other against Mark.* This pattern—that Matthew and Luke differ from Mark at different places—suggests that *the Gospel of Mark is the common thread or source of the gospels of Matthew and Luke* (note one minor exception: the heaven[s] *open*).

This pattern with respect to *content,* or sayings, also exists in the *order* of major events throughout the synoptic gospels: *Matthew and Luke do not agree to disagree with Mark at the same place.* Again, *Mark seems to provide the common thread.*

A third related argument is that it is easier to explain how and why the Matthean and Lukan writers changed the Gospel of Mark than why the Markan and Lukan writers changed Matthew or the Markan and Matthean writers changed Luke. This argument becomes much clearer in relation to another critical method (**Redaction Criticism**).

A fourth argument stresses the length of the gospels in comparison with the length of the various passages within them. Note the following statistics:

	Matthew	Mark	Luke
Verses	1,068	661	1,149
Words	18,293	11,025	19,376

It is clear that the Gospel of Mark is the *shortest* gospel. Yet, in the triple tradition, individual Markan passages are often the *longest*. If the Markan author had known important passages in Matthew or Luke such as the birth, infancy, resurrection, and Sermon on the Mount, would he have omitted them and expanded other shared passages and at the same time shorted his gospel? It is much more likely that the authors of Matthew and Luke shortened Markan passages and lengthened their gospels to make room for their other source material—birth, infancy, resurrection, teachings, and the like.

A fifth related argument is that the Gospel of Luke *consistently* lacks the Matthean "additions" to the triple tradition. How could this be if he was using the Book of Matthew as a source?

Note two other common arguments. One is that the Matthean and Lukan authors revised the Markan author's cruder and "inferior" grammar; another is that they explained Aramaic terms, colloquialisms, and redundancies in the Gospel of Mark. By themselves these arguments are less impressive. However, they look more impressive when added to the previous, weightier arguments.

Taken together, these arguments have led to the theory that the Gospel of Mark was the earliest of the synoptic gospels. This theory is called **the Markan Priority.**

However, if the author of Luke did not know and revise the Book of Matthew (or the reverse), and the Gospel of Mark was first, we face a new problem. Study the following example (Luke NRSV; Matthew revised to follow the **Standard Text**).

Matt. 3:7-10	Luke 3:7-9
3:7 But when he saw many Pharisees and Sadducees coming for baptism, he said to them, **"You brood of vipers! Who warned you to flee from the wrath to come? (8) Bear** fruit **worthy of repentance. (9) Do not** presume **to say to yourselves, 'We have Abraham as our father'; for I tell you, God is able from these stones to raise up children to Abraham. (10) Even now the ax is laid to the root of the trees; every tree therefore that does not bear good fruit is cut down and thrown into the fire."**	3:7 He said therefore to the multitudes that came out to be baptized by him, **"You brood of vipers! Who warned you to flee from the wrath to come? (8) Bear** fruits **worthy of repentance, and do not** begin to **say to yourselves, 'We have Abraham as our father'; for I tell you, God is able from these stones to raise up children to Abraham. (9) Even now the ax is laid to the root of the trees; every tree therefore that does not bear good fruit is cut down and thrown into the fire."**

The question is this: If the authors of Matthew and Luke did *not* know each other's gospels, as the Markan Priority suggests, how can the Lukan and Matthean authors be *exactly, word for word, the same* (in Greek, as well) in passages where there is no Mark (the double tradition)? A common oral tradition is not sufficient to account for such verbal exactness. The usual solution is that these verses come from *a written source that has not survived.* In the late nineteenth century, scholars began to call this hypothetical source "**Q**" (German *Quelle,* "source," is the usual explanation, although there are others). Although the precise extent of Q passages is debated, it must have included at least the sixty-eight Matthean-Lukan passages not in Mark, or about 235 verses. Scholars usually argue that because the Lukan writer follows the Markan order more carefully than the Matthean writer, the Lukan writer also followed the sequence of Q passages more carefully. They infer that the Lukan Gospel also represents the *order* of Q better. Thus they designate Q passages by the *Lukan* chapter and verse preceded by the letter "Q" (that is, Q 3:7–9 is Luke 3:7–9 [= Matt. 3:7–10]). This custom of designating Q passages with the Lukan chapter and verse does not mean that the Lukan writer always preserved the best *wording* of Q. (An example can be found in the Lord's Prayer.)

The Markan Priority and the Q hypothesis are the most common explanations of passages in the triple tradition and the double tradition. What about the passages found in only *one gospel,* the "single tradition"? Because most of the Gospel of Mark has parallels in the gospels of Matthew and Luke (about 94 percent of Mark), the single tradition refers *mainly* to passages found only in either Matthew or Luke, that is, "**Special M**" (for Matthew) and "**Special L**" (for Luke). Usually it is thought that each was a written source. However, it is sometimes difficult to tell, precisely because they have no parallels; in some cases such passages might have derived from oral tradition, and in other cases they appear to have been composed by the author (e.g., Matt. 3:14–15 in preceding parallels [underlined]).

It is time to present one of the standard diagrams for illustrating the preceding "solution" to the Synoptic Problem. This solution, shown in Figure 2.1, is usually called the "**Two-Source Theory,**" "two" referring to the two main sources, Mark and Q. Those who have considered Special M and Special L to have been from written source documents have sometimes called it the "*Four*-Source Theory." However, given the possibility that some of Special M and Special L may have been oral or composed by the writer, we shall use the more common designation "Two-Source Theory." The Two-Source Theory, built on the acceptance of the Markan Priority and the existence of Q, is the simplest and most widely held solution to the Synoptic Problem.

Note again that without maintaining the independence of Matthew and Luke there is no real basis for the Q hypothesis in the Two-Source Theory. The traditional *Matthean* priority needs no Q hypothesis because the Lukan writer copied what the gospels of Matthew and Luke share word for word from the Gospel of Matthew. If he did not know the Gospel of Matthew, Q becomes very probable.

We shall say more about Q in Chapter Three. At this point, note that the final edition of Q seems to have been mainly a collection of Jesus' sayings. Because of the exact linguistic parallels between the gospels of Matthew and Luke, the version that their authors used was *written,* and written in *Greek,* although the original version was probably composed in Aramaic. It should also be noted again that the **Gospel of Thomas** discovered at Nag Hammadi, Egypt, in 1945 is an analogous "sayings gospel." It lends credibility to the hypothesis that the Q source once existed.

Nonetheless, some scholars do not accept the Two-Source Theory and its corollary, the Markan Priority. One major reason is that in a few instances of the triple tradition, the gospels of Matthew and Luke *do* agree against Mark. An example in

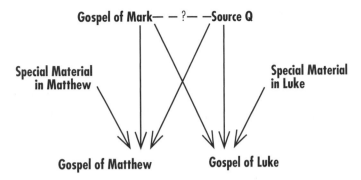

Figure 2.1 Gospels.

the baptism story quoted earlier is that Matthew and Luke agree that heaven or the heavens were "opened," whereas Mark says that they were "torn apart." There are about a half-dozen impressive examples. How can such agreements against Mark exist, these scholars ask, if the Lukan author did not know the Gospel of Matthew (or vice versa)? Could these be only coincidence? These "minor agreements," as they are called, have led some scholars to an alternative solution, a variant of the traditional solution (no. 1). In this solution the Gospel of Matthew came first, the writer of the Gospel of Luke used it, and the writer of the Gospel of *Mark* knew both, but wiggled between them and shortened them (a renewal of the nineteenth-century "Griesbach [or Two-Document] hypothesis"). Thus Q is unnecessary. Defenders of the dominant Two-Source Theory usually respond that in these few instances Mark and Q have the same material, that is, there are "Mark–Q overlaps." The preceding Two-Source Theory diagram illustrates this phenomenon with a dotted line and question mark between Mark and Q.

Finally, it needs to be said that other scholars have put forth much more complicated theories, some of which include multiple editions of gospels.

This textbook accepts the Two-Source Theory but recognizes that the challenges to it have important points to make and that the multiple gospel theories have merit. Thus it should be recognized that the form of the theory represented by the preceding diagram is a simplified model of what may have been a more complex set of interrelationships. At the same, it should be stressed that there is scientific merit in finding the simplest working hypothesis, even though it may not answer all the questions adequately at every point.

After this detour into Source Criticism in general, let us return to the Lord's Prayer. This time, we shall *number* the prayer "petitions" in the Matthean form.

Matt. 6:9b–13	Luke 11:2–4
Father	Father,
of ours in heaven	— — — —
[Greek word order],	
1. hallowed be your name.	hallowed be your name.
2. Your kingdom come,	Your kingdom come.
3. Your will be done,	— — — —

On earth as it is in heaven.   — —— — — —— — ——

4. Give **us** this day **our daily bread;**   *Give* **us** each day **our daily bread;**

5. **And forgive us our** debts,   **And forgive us our** sins,

    As we **also** *have forgiven*   As we **also** *have forgiven*

        Our debtors.   everyone who is indebted to us;

6. **And do not bring us to the test,**   **And do not bring us to the test.**

7.   But rescue us from the Evil One.   —— —— — — —— — —— —

In this layout, there are three parts to the Matthean prayer: (1) an initial address to God; (2) a second section containing three petitions to God with second-person singular pronouns (nos. 1–3); and (3) a third section containing four petitions to God, more directly about human beings, with first- or third-person plural pronouns (nos. 4–7). The **boldface** terms are exact shared words in both gospels, and the *italics* represent the same word in Greek but in a different grammatical form.

It is obvious that the Lukan form of the prayer is shorter and that not all the words agree as closely as our preceding example, the baptism story. You will naturally ask: Are there enough words in common (**boldface** and *italics*) to show that the prayer—or at least these words—was in Q? Although opinion is not unanimous, many scholars believe that it was in Q, a position reinforced by the fact that the word here translated "daily" (Greek *epiousion*) in the NRSV is very distinctive *and* found only in this prayer in Matthew and Luke (and the *Didachē*).

Let us accept as a working hypothesis the likelihood that a version of the prayer came from Q. Immediately a second question arises: Did the Lukan author omit "Our . . . in heaven" and the third and seventh petitions from Q, or did Matthew add them to Q? The latter is more likely. Why? First, the division into three sections suggests that the extra words fall at the *end* of each section (in Greek "our . . . in heaven" comes *after* "Father"). Second, the language in Matthew—"Our . . . in heaven," "earth . . . heaven," "the Evil One"—is *very* typical of the Matthean author. The best hypothesis is that the shorter Lukan gospel represents Q better and that Matthew added the extra words and phrases to his copy of Q (**Redaction Criticism**). Yet, scholars also argue that Matthew, not Luke, *sometimes* preserved the best wording from Q, for example, "each day" and "sins" are very Lukan and probably represent Lukan changes of Q. On this basis, a hypothetical reconstruction of the Q form of the Lord's Prayer closer to that found in Luke, but using a little Matthean wording (*italics*), reads in English:

Father,
Hallowed be your name.
Your kingdom come.
Give us *this day* our daily bread.
And forgive us our *debts,*
As we also have forgiven *our debtors.*
And do not bring us to the test.

Summarizing, the probable reason why the Lord's Prayer is found in the First Gospel is not because a disciple-eyewitness of Jesus' life named Matthew heard what Jesus had said and recorded it, and later Luke, a follower of Paul, shortened his

Matthean source. Rather, an unknown author of the First Gospel derived it from the Q source and expanded it, although he preserved a couple of the words found in Q (still represented by the Lukan version). *A historical result is that the earlier,* reconstructed Q form is *much* closer to the Gospel of Luke.

However, is it possible that the author of the Book of Matthew knew (also?) an *oral* form that influenced his version of the prayer—for example, a form used in worship in his day—or alternatively, that behind the shorter Q written form were two or three decades of *oral* history (no. 4)? Although theories of written sources and oral traditions occasionally compete, it need not always be the case. Thus it will be important to consider oral traditions and the method used to study them: **Form Criticism.**

It is clear from the preceding discussion that (the Old) Literary Criticism and Source Criticism lead to all sorts of historical questions and answers. If two books have a totally different vocabulary and style, it is much less likely that the same person wrote them both, and that is also a *historical* conclusion. Similarly, if the writer of Source B used Source A, Source A preceded Source B. That is also a historical conclusion. Thus Old Literary Criticism and Source Criticism can also be seen as part of **General Historical Criticism.**

5. General Historical Criticism

Who wrote the gospels of Matthew and Luke? When? Where? Why? These are some of the "what actually happened?" sorts of historical questions that have arisen during the Modern period. They obviously cross over into the area of **Literary Criticism** as well. To illustrate such problems we can concentrate on the Gospel of Matthew because it contains the familiar version of the Lord's Prayer.

Let us begin with what scholars call the "superscription" in the ancient manuscripts. The superscription of a book within an ancient manuscript is analogous to the title of a chapter in a modern book. The superscription of the Gospel of Matthew reads simply "According to Matthew." Presumably this is a reference to Matthew the tax collector, who according to the "First Gospel" (and this gospel only!) was one of Jesus' twelve disciples (Matt. 9:9, 10:3). If this reference were historically correct, one might logically deduce that the gospel is an eye-witness account written in Galilee by a Galilean tax collector who spoke Aramaic and remembered certain events about the life and teaching of his teacher/master. That was the accepted conclusion in the second century c.e. However, historical method requires that we deal with several other facts.

First, in contrast to modern books, not one of the four canonical gospels identifies its author apart from the superscription just mentioned. Second, the superscriptions to the other canonical gospels have the same exact formula as the Gospel of Matthew, that is, "According to X." This suggests that superscriptions were later written into manuscripts that contained several gospels to distinguish one gospel from the other (according to then-current opinion). Third, we have no full manuscripts that contain superscriptions before the third century. Fourth, we have no descriptive information about authors, places, and the like from Church Fathers prior to 150 c.e. However, about 150 c.e., Papias, a bishop in Asia Minor (modern Turkey), offered his opinion about "Mark" and "Matthew": "Matthew collected the 'sayings' (*logia*) in the Hebrew language, and each interpreted them as best he could" (Eusebius *Church History* 3.39.16). This **Papias tradition** became the accepted opinion in the late second century C.E., the period when the superscriptions were added. Papias says nothing about when or where the First Gospel was written, but later Apostolic Fathers placed it in Palestine.

In short, what we have is Papias' opinion, which probably represents general opinion about 150 C.E., and superscriptions that were probably added about the same period or later.

The modern historian asks this question: Does Papias' information tally with *internal evidence?* The answer is this: not very much. First, our Gospel of Matthew is not, as Papias says, a collection of "sayings" of Jesus; rather, it has a long *narrative framework* (twenty-eight chapters) that contains *within it* sayings and shorter narratives. Second, language experts are convinced that our Greek Book of Matthew was not originally written in either Hebrew or Aramaic. Third, most analysis shows that the First Gospel used *Greek* sources—at least Greek Mark and Greek Q—which is more natural for a Greek writer. None of this seems to tally with Papias' comments about "Matthew." There are also complications about the implied date. References within the gospel (24:15–16, 22:7) suggest that the author knew about the destruction of Jerusalem by the Romans in 70 C.E. Most scholars also accept the Two-Source Theory and say that the Matthean author used the Gospel of Mark, usually dated about 70 C.E. In this post-70 period there was heightened conflict between Israelite members of the Jesus Movement and the **Pharisees.** And the conflict between Jesus and the Pharisees is especially sharp in this gospel. All this suggests a date about 85–90 C.E. Although this late date does not rule out the possibility that one of Jesus' disciples wrote it, he would have been a very elderly person, especially so in the ancient world.

Finally, was the First Gospel written in Palestine, as later church tradition thought? Today some scholars argue strongly for Palestine, especially because this location fits a particular Israelite interpretation of the gospel. However, most modern historians have thought that it was written in or near Antioch, Syria, north of Palestine. All together, these arguments suggest that Papias' information about "Matthew" is inaccurate and that slightly later inferences by certain Apostolic Fathers about time and place are at least debatable. Most modern critical opinion says that the gospel was written in Greek by an unknown Greek-speaking Israelite who believed in Jesus as the Messiah about 85–90 C.E., *perhaps* in Antioch, Syria.

This conclusion, especially with respect to authorship, may seem unduly skeptical. However, it is important to remember that **pseudonymity** (Greek for "false name") was not considered immoral or illegal among the ancients. Books could be associated with an author's opinion, or *believed* to have been written by an author, or to have been "titled" with the conscious intention to give the book authority, or all these reasons, and more, simultaneously.

In short, modern historical analysis suggests that the Lord's Prayer was not written down because Jesus' disciple and follower, a toll collector named Matthew, heard it directly from Jesus and then wrote it in his memoirs. Rather, some unknown author decades after Jesus' death either took the prayer from some written source or learned it from some familiar oral or liturgical tradition. Indeed, we must ask whether he totally rewrote it.

6. Form Criticism

You will easily recognize patterned forms of oral discourse in our own culture (e.g., the three-part joke). You will also be able to recognize the typical contexts in which they are spoken and say something about how they function (e.g., ethnocentric humor). You might also know something about their history (e.g., that people often adapt jokes to fit their own ethnic heritage). People often understand something about how oral tradition works if they have played the game of "Telephone," otherwise known as "Rumor."

Oral forms and traditions are common in all cultures, including the ancient Mediterranean culture. Indeed, one ancient member of the Jesus Movement valued oral tradition more highly than the written word (Papias in Eusebius *Church History* 3.5). In the nineteenth and early twentieth centuries—the middle of the Modern period—German scholars began to theorize about oral traditions behind ancient written documents, especially the Bible. Indeed, ancient oral communication is still a major area of research, although it is now informed by communications theory and anthropology. This study of oral traditions in the academic study of the Bible is traditionally called **Form Criticism.**

Classical Form Criticism scholars were mainly interested in three matters:

1. *The forms.* These are the smaller, isolated, individual units (called "pericopes" [*puh-ri´-koh-peez*])—short sayings, parables, miracle stories, proverbs, hymns, prayers, and the like—that lend themselves to retelling. They are taken out of their present literary contexts and compared with the same or similar forms in the ancient culture. Jesus' parables, for example, can be isolated and compared to ancient rabbinic parables.

2. *Socio-religious settings.* German *Sitze im Leben* ("settings in life") and the singular *Sitz im Leben* are commonly used in English to refer to the socio-religious contexts in which sayings and stories were told. The early German Form Critics analyzed early church settings such as worshipping, teaching, entertaining, and convincing outsiders ("propaganda"). Today there is more attention to broader social contexts (see following **Social History** and **Social-Scientific Criticism**).

3. *The history of the tradition.* As the settings and the way the units functioned in them changed, the sayings and stories themselves were modified in their new social and religious contexts. Traditional Form Critics usually argued that simpler, purer, or shorter oral forms developed into more complex, mixed, or longer forms, like a growing onion. By removing the outer layers it is possible to discover the inner core, that is, the earliest form. The reverse is also true; it is possible to imagine how the core grew into its present shape. Form Criticism can thereby become an aid to recovering the history of the earliest Jesus Movement (German *Formgeschichte* is literally "*form* history"). A drawback is that growth was not always from simple to complex, and thus contemporary analysis often considers other options.

For *some* Form Critical scholars, the following aim should be added:

4. *Rediscovering Jesus' teaching and typical aspects of Jesus' life.* The historical Jesus is usually sought in the reconstructed, earliest stages of the oral tradition.

Returning to the Lord's Prayer, all of its forms in Luke, Matthew, and the *Didachē* contain "couplets," or "parallel members" typical of ancient oral prayer and poetry. This time, we shall arrange the Q form of the prayer in metrical structure (Jeremias and Fitzmyer). We then offer a translation into Aramaic (the native tongue of Jesus and his first followers). This translation (right column of list) will be written in English characters (transliterated) so it can be pronounced in English. We also renumber its lines.

1. Father,	1.	*'Abbā',*
2. Hallowed be your name.	2.	*yit-qaddāsh sh^emāk*
Your kingdom come.		*tetē malkutāk*
3. Give us this day	3.	*lachmān d^elimchār*
Our daily bread.		*hab lān yoma dēn*
And forgive us our debts/sins		*ush^eboq lān chobēnan*
As we also have forgiven our debtors		*k^edish^ebāqnan l^echayyabēnan*
4. And do not bring us to the test.	4.	*w^ela' tā`elînnan lēnisyōn.*

Say aloud the right column of the list. You will hear that the prayer *sounds poetic.* The *form* of this shorter Q prayer can be outlined formally like this:

1. An "invocation" (addressing God, asking for God's presence)

2. Two short "petitions" (requests)

3. Two long (positive) petitions

4. A short, closing (negative) petition

The invocation and short petitions (nos. 1 and 2) are more general and center on God; the two long and the short negative petitions (nos. 3 and 4) are more concrete and center on humans. Form Critics carry this formal analysis further and raise historical questions: Was this simply a "model prayer" that could be expanded? Was it really a prayer *in this form,* or have various individual, separate emphases been brought together? Did the whole prayer go back to Jesus? Did he say different parts of it at different times? Did only some of its parts go back to Jesus? Which? Much more might be analyzed about the oral form of the prayer, but enough has been said to illustrate its potential in oral settings.

Finally, what were some of the possible socio-historical settings, that is, what were the *Sitze im Leben* for the prayer? We must first note what ancient *writers* in the Jesus Movement say about certain settings

There is a very Matthean-sounding version of the Lord's Prayer in the *Didachē,* usually dated to the early second century C.E. The *Didachē* is not specific about a socio-religious setting; yet, it is a teaching document, and its version of the Our Father occurs in a section about worship (*Did.* 7 baptism; 8 fasting and Lord's Prayer; 9–10 Eucharistic meal). This suggests that the prayer was used at this time *to instruct initiates to the Jesus Movement on how to pray.* In Matthew, the *larger* context for the prayer, the Sermon on the Mount (Matt. 5–7; see 5:1), is also teaching, public teaching, but the *narrower* context *within* the sermon has the command to pray "in secret," *not like the hypocrites* (Matt. 6:5–8), who for the author are the Pharisees. The command not to babble on and on *like the Gentiles* when they pray also suggests teaching; yet, the addition of a doxology in the manuscripts of

Matthew and the *Didachē* suggests a setting of *corporate* prayer. So in addition to teaching there are statements about private prayer and hints at public worship in Matthew. In Luke, the context is Jesus praying *alone*. However, when the disciples request *teaching* on prayer like John teaches his disciples, Jesus illustrates with the (shorter) Lord's Prayer, although the analogy with John could suggest something more public (J. M. Robinson). The narrower gospel contexts have a common denominator: *teaching about prayer, mainly in private* (Matthew: "in secret," not like the hypocrites; *Didachē:* "not like the hypocrites"; Luke: Jesus praying *alone*). Yet, again, there are hints about public, communal contexts (overhearing; like John; an added doxology; the form itself), which are suggested also by the larger context of Matthew and the *Didachē*. Finally, in speculating about the function of the prayer in Q, one is left primarily with an internal analysis of the prayer itself.

The initial address contains the term "Father." The letters of the Apostle Paul in the 50s show no clear knowledge of the prayer itself. However, the Aramaic cry *'Abbā' was used in the worship* of Paul's churches (Gal. 4:6; Rom. 8:15). This foreign language utterance could have recalled Jesus' address to God. Was the expression "'Abbā', Father!" a liturgical cry (cf. present-day "Hosanna!" and "Amen") or an indirect reference to a longer prayer? If the latter, Paul's reference would support a *public worship context*. We may add that other expressions in the Lord's Prayer are very similar to public prayers in the synagogue.

In short, written sources indicate that from the last decades of the first century on, the Lord's Prayer was taught, memorized as a model and example prayer in religious instruction, and prayed in corporate (not yet necessarily "public") worship. Was this the setting earlier in the century?

The question leads to the historical Jesus. Did Jesus pray an Aramaic version of the Q prayer or parts thereof? This is a difficult question to answer. At this point we can say that *some* interpreters have argued that the preceding reconstructed prayer in Aramaic was at least close to what Jesus prayed and taught others to pray. If so, Jesus would have addressed God as *'Abbā'*, seen God's name as holy, preached about the Kingdom of the Heavens (of God), petitioned God for "daily bread," and stressed God's forgiveness of debts/sins. It is plausible that the original *Sitz im Leben* of Jesus was Jesus' everyday meals with his disciples and disreputable people (Matt. 8:11, 11:16–19). Other interpreters have argued that Jesus prayed only some of the individual phrases of the prayer and that later they were assembled as a more formalized prayer. But *which phrases?* Whether the interpreter accepts the whole or only some of the parts as going back to Jesus, historical Jesus scholars would claim that we are closer to the Jesus of history (at least the "echo of his voice"). This is one goal of some Form Critics.

7. Redaction Criticism

The method of **Redaction Criticism** studies how ancient biblical writers expanded, shortened, reformulated, regrouped, and repositioned their written sources and oral traditions and often composed new materials in and around them, the object being to clarify their changes and their motives for them and thus illumine the writers' intentions and points of view, sometimes called the writers' "theology" (Perrin). How would a Redaction Critic understand the Our Father?

If you examine the Lord's Prayer in its *Lukan context,* you will see the following sequence of passages:

11:1–2a	Setting: Jesus at prayer privately in a certain place; the disciples' request to be taught prayer, as John the Baptizer taught his disciples
11:2b–4	**The Lord's Prayer**
11:5–8	Parable of the friend making a demand that is answered at midnight
11:9–10	**Exhortations and promises about "ask," "seek," and "knock"**
11:11–13	**Rhetorical questions about asking and answering in human situations and "how much more" the Heavenly Father will give the Holy Spirit to those who ask him**

The boldface passages are from Q; the Lukan author makes five major emphases. First, he keeps statements about "asking" and "answering," statements that the Matthean author chooses to place elsewhere (see Matt. 7:7–11). Thus he is interpreting these statements in relation to people's asking and God's answering *prayer.* Second, he inserts into Q a parable, probably from **Special L,** about God's response to a person who is persistent (11:5–8). Luke's lesson: *Be persistent in prayer!* Third, he prefaces the whole section with an account of Jesus himself praying "in a certain place" (11:1). This introduction is not casual. The Lukan author inserts Jesus at prayer at other key turning points in the story: baptism (3:21); escape from crowds (5:16); call of disciples (6:12); Jesus' self-identity at Caesarea Philippi (9:18); transfiguration (9:28); the Garden of Gethsemane (22:41, 45); and on the cross (23:34). Fourth, he has the disciples request that Jesus teach them to pray as John the Baptizer taught his disciples (Luke 11:1–2b). John's subordinate relationship to Jesus is very important in the gospel (1, 3:15–18, 16:16; see Acts 19:1–7). Fifth, the Lukan writer also says that if a member of the Jesus Movement asks God for the Holy Spirit, it will be granted (Luke 11:12). The gift of the *Holy* Spirit is also a persistent Lukan theme.

Finally, the Lukan author has placed this set of passages in the context of Jesus' journey from Galilee to Jerusalem (Luke 9:51–18:14). During the journey, Jesus' teachings and actions show that his message of salvation is *available to all.*

Summarizing, for the Lukan writer the Lord's Prayer was instruction from the Jesus who prayed at decisive moments in his life, in this case on the way to Jerusalem. It was a model prayer for any Jesus Movement member who had been baptized, who had received the Holy Spirit (granted in prayer), who was part of the ongoing church in time, and who prayed, whether Israelite or Gentile, man or woman, rich or poor. If the believer prayed persistently, God would answer.

The Gospel of Matthew used the Lord's Prayer quite differently. Jesus was not on the way to Jerusalem but rather still in Galilee. He was not on a journey but rather sitting on a mountain before large crowds teaching (the Sermon on the Mount, Matt. 5–7). The key Matthean theme is that Jesus is a more authoritative teacher than contemporary Pharisaic "hypocritical" teachers (7:28–29; cf. 23:8). The more immediate context is this:

6:1	Beware of showing off your piety before others.
6:2–4	Do not show off your almsgiving like the hypocrites; give in secret.
6:5–6	Do not show off when you pray, like the hypocrites; pray in secret.

6:7–8   Do not pray like the Gentiles who heap up empty phrases.

6:9–13   Lord's Prayer

6:14–15   Forgive others their transgressions.

6:16–18   Do not show off when you fast like the hypocrites; fast in secret.

In the Matthean context, the Lord's Prayer from Q (boldface, Matt. 6:9–13) and the forgiveness of sins from Mark (italics, Matt. 6:14–15; Mark 11:25) have been *inserted into* a section found only in Matthew that teaches about three common acts of piety in Israelite religion: almsgiving, prayer, and fasting. (The Q section about "asking," "searching," and "knocking" from Q [Luke 11:9–13] has been deferred until later in the sermon [Matt. 7:7–11].) The major Matthean point is that when Jesus' followers practice these three acts of piety they should not show off like the hypocritical religious leaders (6:1, 2, 5, 16; cf. 23:1–36). Rather, they should practice these acts *in secret,* and their heavenly Father will reward them *in secret* (6:1, 4, 6, 18). Moreover, one should not "heap up empty phrases as the Gentiles do." One should, then, "pray like this . . ." Then comes the Lord's Prayer, followed by the correlation between human and divine forgiveness (Matt. 6:14–15; Mark 11:25).

In short, the Matthean context for the Lord's Prayer is the Sermon on the Mount in Galilee. The prayer instructs and serves as a model and an example of a superior way that contrasts with that of long-winded Gentiles, but much more, with that of hypocritical religious leaders, the Pharisees. "For I tell you, unless your righteousness exceeds that of the scribes and Pharisees, you will never enter the kingdom of heaven" (Matt. 5:20).

Redaction Criticism can also help the interpreter to discover the earlier, perhaps original, wording of the prayer. On the one hand, the interpreter can see that the Matthean author made wording changes to the Q Lord's Prayer suggested earlier.

1. "*Our . . . in heaven*" is typical Matthean editorial practice, that is, he surrounds references to "Father" with "heavenly" or "my/your . . . in the heavens" (e.g., 5:45; 6:1).

2. "*Your will be done*" corresponds to the Matthean emphasis on doing the "will of the ("my") Father" (e.g., 7:21; 26:42) or "your will" (6:10; 18:14).

3. "*On earth as it is in heaven*" is especially typical of the heaven/earth contrast in Matthew (Matthew thirteen times; Mark two times; Luke five times).

4. In the NRSV's "do not bring us to the test," which can also be translated, "*But rescue us from the Evil One,*" the "Evil One" is a special Matthean term for the devil (Matt. 13:19, 13:38).

On the other hand, the Lukan author sometimes changed the Q wording, and in these instances the original wording is probably better preserved in Matthew. Thus it is probable that:

1. The Lukan author changed the more immediate "this day" in Q (= Matt. 6:11) to "each day" (Luke 11:3), which conforms to the Lukan emphasis that time is marching on and that the Spirit guides the ongoing church (see Chapter Ten).

2. The *Greek tenses* of "give" ("keep on giving") and "forgive" ("keep on forgiving") in Luke also imply a continuation of time; Q probably contained the more immediate Matthean verb forms.

3. The Lukan author changed "debts" in Greek Q to "sins" because it conforms to the Lukan emphasis on the forgiveness of sins/sinners; moreover, "debtors"/"everyone indebted" is in the Q context (Matt. 6:12 = Luke 11:4).

Summarizing, Redaction Critics try to uncover the special emphases of an individual writer by seeing where the writer places sources and traditions and by observing how these sources and traditions have been modified, reworked, reordered, expanded, and developed by new composition. The trained eye can usually see the author's special perspective in the details of vocabulary, style, emphases, insertions, omissions, creation of new material, and the like. Redaction Criticism is a literary analysis, but it adds valuable historical information about the author's intentions in relation to the time, place, and circumstances of writing. When there are no earlier sources to compare, or when the scholar is interested in the book as a whole, some scholars prefer the expression "**Composition Criticism.**" Looking at a whole book from this perspective also contributes to understanding its genre, or larger literary form in relation to comparable literary forms of the period. This is sometimes called "**Genre Criticism.**" Finally, by *removing* the author's special emphases, the interpreter can more easily see sources and traditions that the author used and can often move backward through time. Thus Redaction Criticism works hand in hand with Source Criticism and Form Criticism and can even aid in the quest for the historical Jesus.

8. Social-Historical Criticism and Social-Scientific Criticism

General Historical Criticism of the Bible has sought to write "scientific" history in relation to "world history." This sort of history was mainly the history of ancient empires and great individuals. In the late nineteenth and early twentieth centuries, many historians became more and more interested in the history of *all of society,* including the "little people." In the New Testament they are farmers and fishermen, women and children, slaves and ex-slaves, poor and oppressed. Stimulated by the writings of Karl Marx and development of the social sciences, some historians became interested in the importance of climate, geography, ecology, political "colonialism," economic oppression, family life, and culture in general. In other words, history writing was being challenged to develop perspectives generated by the emergent *social sciences.* (Note a parallel: Several decades ago, high school students took courses in "history"; now they take courses in "*social* studies.") For New Testament study, this meant that the church-related socio-*religious* settings of Form Criticism needed to be broadened.

Social questions were asked by some New Testament scholars in the early part of the twentieth century, but such research declined, in part because of theological reasons. About 1960 a renewed interest in social questions began to take place. Answering them has never been easy because the ancient sources do not give direct information about, or explain, social structures and social relations. Moreover, there is no way of generating new data comparable to the modern opinion poll or of joining an ancient group and observing its behavior ("participant observation"). Rather, it is necessary to "read between the lines," to try to compare and contrast the New

Testament information with what is otherwise known about social arrangements in the larger society or in comparable societies. Two related methods have arisen to deal with these questions: Social-Historical Criticism and Social-Scientific Criticism.

Social-Historical Criticism

The practitioners of Social-Historical Criticism—it is usually called simply **Social History**—are primarily interested in describing social change over time. They recognize the paucity of information about social organization and social relations in the ancient texts. Therefore, they emphasize the usual sources of historical reconstruction but ask social questions about them. They speak of "social description," "social location," and "social context" (Theissen; Meeks).

How does such study help to interpret the Lord's Prayer? A Social History approach tries to determine the *successive social* contexts in which the prayer was used and transmitted. Form and Redaction Critics had already observed how the prayer was being used by the late first century. Moving back through time, analysis of Q suggests that it was preserved by early Galilean believers in Jesus who were from the lower social and economic strata and who opposed the rich and powerful. In the villages of Galilee, where Jesus' ministry took place, the Lord's Prayer might have been seen as revolutionary "wisdom" and "prophetic" teaching, perhaps passed on by educated scribes. From here one moves further back to Jesus' own social context. Some elements of the prayer speak about the need for daily bread, forgiveness from debt, and deliverance from the Evil One. The net result is that one can reverse the process and track the prayer not only through worship contexts, as the Form Critics did, but also through communities about which the scholar has gained some deeper social understanding.

Social-Scientific Criticism

Social-Scientific Criticism is in many respects like Social-Historical Criticism. However, in Social-Scientific Criticism scholars are more interested in two matters: (1) examining social structures and social relations described in the Bible with the aid of *general theories* developed in the fields of sociology, social anthropology, and cultural anthropology and (2) using interpretive cross-cultural *models* of social arrangements and patterns of behavior developed in the social sciences to understand and explain biblical patterns of social relations, organization, and conduct (Elliott; Malina; Osiek). This approach holds that we all formulate models or "mental maps" to understand and interpret our worlds and that it is important to make them as conscious as possible. This is especially important in interpreting the Bible because ancient Mediterranean mental maps are quite different from modern Western ones (northern Europe and North America), and modern Western interpreters constantly run the risk of confusing the latter with the former. For example, we can examine male dominance and hereditary family arrangements in either the Far East or in closer Mediterranean societies to generate clues about understanding and explaining male dominance and the reaction against it in various parts of the New Testament. *Models* for understanding the social relations and perceptions of the rich and the poor can be developed from the economies of preindustrial agrarian or peasant societies. The study of social conflict, its causes and consequences, or the study of the way cultural symbols work can help us to understand New Testament society and culture.

The Lord's Prayer also can be illumined by Social-Scientific interpretation. "Worship" in antiquity is related not only to the church but also to family, kinship, male-female roles, and village life, as well as the politics of empire and the economics of agriculture. "'Abbā' Father" fits cultural patterns about family relations dominated by males over females and parents over children in ways quite different from those of modern culture; for example, the woman and son honor and obey the male head of the house. "Hallowed be your name" is associated with the holiness of the Divine Name. "Your kingdom come" derives its imagery from ancient Middle Eastern agrarian monarchies. "Give us this day our daily bread" suggests meal customs, different types of meals, where meals are eaten, when meals are eaten, honored status and the position of reclining around the table, "extended family" structures, hosts, guests, invitations, hospitality; who cooks and who serves, pure/impure foods, the order of foods served, and so on.

Social-scientific critics hold that all language is social. Examining language will therefore yield clues about social relations. Here are some specific examples in the prayer. Describing God as "father" requires understanding the dynamics of ancient family relationships, especially royal ones, and what is honorable and shameful to the family (**honor** and **shame**). "Daily" in "daily bread" suggests having enough bread to survive, as poor folk would need. "Forgive us our debts" is bound up with economic debt in agricultural societies, that is, the confiscation of land by the Romans, control and redistribution of agricultural products, the system of lenders and debtors, social status, urban and rural forms of poverty, the political burdens of taxes and tolls, hereditary wealth and inheritance by sons, repression of peasants and peasant revolts, "social welfare" in relation to family and village life, almsgiving and begging, and so on. "Lead us not to the test" could imply persecution.

In short, Social-Scientific Criticism based on theories, models, and cross-cultural parallels helps to analyze and explain social phenomena in the Lord's Prayer.

9. Archeology

There are two senses of the term *archeology*. In the narrow sense, *archeology* refers to the "science" of recovering and evaluating the material remains of everyday life from past periods of history, for example, buildings, statues, objects of worship, tombs, magical paraphernalia, tools, pottery, and the like. The narrow sense also includes literary remains written on material objects, that is, inscriptions on stones, coins, and burial stones and writing on pottery and amulets. In the broad sense, *archeology* refers to material remains and newly discovered manuscripts, some of which are not found at an actual archeological site.

There is perpetual debate about whether archeology should be considered together with historical reconstruction, mainly because its conclusions sometimes conflict with the ancient literary sources for historical reconstruction. Archeologists also debate the extent to which archeology is a "hard science" of facts or an "soft (interpretive) science." Such issues obviously have great importance when related to the reconstruction of biblical history and culture and, from a theological perspective, the nature of "truth" in the Bible. Whatever one decides, it is certain that material remains have political, social, religious, economic, and thus general cultural relevance for interpreting texts from any period of history. With respect to the Lord's Prayer, archeology makes it easier to understand the language of "father," "kingdom," "daily bread," and "debts." For example, it sheds light on opulence of the kingdoms and religious practices of the day, as well as daily life in Palestinian and Hellenistic villages and cities.

Discovery of new texts by archeologists or others can radically alter historical perspectives. The two most important manuscript discoveries for the early Jesus Movement are the **Dead Sea Scrolls** and the **Nag Hammadi Library** (see Appendix Three). The Dead Sea Scrolls, discovered by Bedouin tribesmen at Khirbet Qumran near the Dead Sea in 1947 (see Figure 1.5), have totally transformed historical views of pre-70 C.E. Palestinian Israel. The scrolls offer first-hand information about an Israelite group, most probably the Essenes. This group (these groups?) baptized, celebrated a sacred meal with bread and wine, held beliefs about messiahs, and preserved divine revelations in a context of social, economic, and political oppression. There are distinct parallels here with the groups who preserved the Lord's Prayer. More specifically, the scrolls also contain prayers and songs that sanctify God's name and offer information about sin and temptation. The absence of the address of God as 'Abbā', combined with a similar form in the scrolls (Aramaic *Genesis Apocryphon* 2:19, 24; 3:3), reinforces the much-debated view that Jesus' address to God in Aramaic was at least unusual in this period.

The **Nag Hammadi Texts** ("Library") came to light in 1945. It consists of thirteen books that contain Israelite and Greco-Roman booklets, including some from the Jesus Movement. One of these booklets is the ***Gospel of Thomas,*** a collection of sayings attributed to Jesus. It is very important for understanding unconventional wisdom in the Jesus Movement, and for some scholars it is crucial for understanding the teaching of Jesus. In relation to the Lord's Prayer, for example, this gospel contains many supposed sayings of Jesus about "the kingdom of the Father." The *Gospel of Thomas* is more unconventional about the traditional Israelite practices of fasting, praying, and almsgiving than is Matt. 6. *Thomas* says, "If you fast, you will give rise to sin for yourselves; and *if you pray, you will be condemned;* and if you give alms, you will do harm to your spirits" (Saying 14).

In summary, archeology, whether in its narrow or broad sense, sheds light on the culture of a particular period and can often help to interpret quite specific terms, ideas, and practices in a socio-historical context. Thus it belongs with Historical Criticism.

The seven methods just discussed have been developed during the Modern period to solve interpretive problems that are in part literary, but *primarily historical:* reconstructing the text from manuscript copies; translating it; determining the original author's vocabulary, style, time, place, occasion, social setting, sources, oral traditions, special interests, and readers. The hermeneutical bias is this: Unless the interpreter first attempts to "bring out" what the authors of these texts originally *meant* in the past (**exegesis**), she or he cannot really understand what they *mean* in the present. Without such patient work, the interpreter will simply "read into" the text contemporary or personal prejudices (**eisegesis**). Furthermore, to understand what the texts meant in the past, it is necessary to understand the way people thought and behaved, thus to understand something about "the real world" *behind* the text, which is also "the real world" *outside* the text, the whole historical, social, and cultural context. The text becomes something like a window through which to view an ancient author's thoughts and context at the time and place of writing.

ALTERNATIVES TO HISTORICAL CRITICISM

During the 1960s and 1970s, some New Testament interpreters began to take up interpretive methods, the majority of which do *not,* strictly speaking, have the preceding historical, social-historical, and social-scientific orientation. Most of them are related to what might be termed "Formalism," that is, the analysis of "formal" features of narratives, an analysis common for several decades among "secular" literary critics. The theory for these methods came mainly from Russia and France. To understand it, one must do an about-face. Analyses included the *form* of folk tales, the *structure* of languages, and the *structure* of tribal rituals. Unlike **Form Criticism,** which is interested in the historical evolution and successive socio-religious contexts of the forms of stories, the emphasis here is on the formal *structures* of narratives themselves. It is stressed that meaning is *not what some author intended* to say in the past (the "intentional fallacy"), but rather is located in literary conventions, that is, genres, or in what lies in, *beneath, or "in front of"* the text. These all sounds very abstract, but the student should attempt to grasp the main point of each as a reaction to the various forms of Historical Criticism.

10. Structuralist Criticism; Deconstructionism

Analysis will show that there are some typical kinds of actors and actions in stories. One way to think of these patterns is to suggest that there are also underlying ways that people think. Some analysts have suggested that human minds think in oppositions, analogous to positive and negative electrical charges or computers and that there is an attempt in language and narrative to resolve these oppositions. This sort of abstract, formal analysis is called Structuralist Analysis (Patte). Although such interpretations have been used primarily with narratives, one might suggest that the Lord's Prayer also contains structural oppositions. Examples are heaven versus earth or "Thy" (reference to God) versus "us" (reference to humans). Structuralists would say that these oppositions, or tensions, are being mediated by prayer. In reaction, Post-Structuralist interpreters (Deconstructionists) challenged not only these "formalist" thinkers, but also the validity of virtually *all* previous attempts at systematic interpretation of meaning in Western civilization! Such systematic interpretations include grand theories of historical reconstruction implied by the methods described earlier.

11. Psychoanalytic Criticism

Other interpreters base their insights on the psychoanalytic theories of Sigmund Freud and Karl Jung (Kille). Might one, for example, relate the "Our Father" to Freud's view of God as a loving, judging "father figure" created by dependent personality types unable to grow and mature out of childhood superstitions?

12. New Literary Criticism

More widespread is the **New Literary Criticism.** Old Literary Criticism had analyzed vocabulary, grammar, syntax, and style of whole documents and genres. However, this analysis was in the service of Historical Criticism. The New Literary Criticism reacted against Modernist Historical Criticism.

Some well-known "secular" literary critics of modern literature in Britain and North America had already argued that *historical objectivity is impossible* and that traditional Historical Criticism is at best inadequate, at worst totally misguided. Think about what happens when you go to a good movie. You enter an *imaginary world* guided by a *creative author* (script writer and film director) who takes a *particular perspective.* A text, they argued, has *its own internal structure,* and that takes on *a life of its own.* A text is *not* like a window through which one catches a glimpse of the past, but rather like a maze of mirrors, each one reflecting the other, though which one catches a glimpse of oneself. This form of New Literary Criticism turned away from authors, original intentions, sources, and history mainly to the text itself, or in some cases the audience of the text. There are several types.

A. The "New Criticism"

The first type of recent Biblical Literary Criticism is *not author centered,* like Historical Criticism and its subtypes, *but rather is text centered.* It attempts to understand the imaginative world inside the text. Drawing on the "New Critics" of modern fiction, a text is considered to be a creative work of art. Once produced, it is autonomous, that is, it takes on "a life of its own." It is not adequate to probe a biblical text for the author's original intention ("the intentional fallacy") or the author's first readers or hearers (labeled "the affective fallacy"). An analysis is not about the text's author, date of composition, place of writing, social context, and so forth. Rather, analysis should focus on the perspective or contribution of the interpreter. Indeed, numerous legitimate interpretations are possible. One should concentrate on the text's own *imaginary* "world," a world that understands life in subtle, indirect, metaphorical, sometimes ironic ways. With respect to the New Testament, analysis can include the forms of Form Criticism and Genre Criticism, but the emphasis would be on *how* the text communicates, not its historical context.

B. Narrative Criticism

Narrative Criticism follows the theory of certain recent "secular" literary theorists as well. It also stresses the text rather than the author and the way that the text creates meaning. It seeks to recapture the *story* features of a text. A story has a beginning, middle, and end. Analysis stresses *how* the story is told (conflict and resolution), *how* scenes are used, *how* the plot unfolds, and *what* the characters are like. It analyzes the "point of view" *implied in the text:* Thus it distinguishes between the flesh-and-blood author who actually writes and the "implied author" whom the reader experiences when (s)he reads. The "implied author" whom one learns about by reading may or may not hold a "point of view" that is the same as that of the real author. Rather, the text is designed to appeal to *intended* readers. Some hold that the author also creates an image of her or his intended reader. When the real author is long dead, the point of view and impressions of the implied authors and readers live on with the text. This distinction helps one to avoid the intentional fallacy (stressing the *real* author's intentions) as well as the affective fallacy (stressing the readers' intentions).

Some Narrative Critics also analyze and distinguish the "narrator," the fictional teller of the story, such as the "voiceover" in film, and the "narratee," the fictional hearer of the narrator's voice. For example, Holden Caulfield narrates the story in *Catcher in the Rye,* but his point of view is not like that of J. D. Salinger at the time he wrote. A "reliable narrator" in the story continuously represents the beliefs, values, and norms of the "implied author," which are not necessarily those of the real author.

Like Redaction Criticism and Genre Criticism, Narrative Criticism is concerned with the genre as a whole, not just the parts. However, the critic's main interest is on the impact or effect of the total story as an imaginative work of art, not an author's careful remolding of sources and traditions to create a "theology." Narrative genres in the New Testament are the gospels and Acts. However, some Narrative critics go on to suggest that even nonnarrative genres, such as letters, have a "story" underlying them. For example, behind Paul's letters (the letter genre is not a story) stands the *story* of Paul's relationship with his churches. To this extent, some Narrative Criticism scholars remain interested in historical matters.

C. Reader-Response Criticism

Whereas Historical Criticism focuses on the author (or speaker), and New Criticism and Narrative Criticism focus on the text (or speech), Reader-Response Criticism focuses more on the reader (hearer or audience). Whereas Historical Criticism stresses authors and the world "behind" the text, and New Criticism stresses the world "within" the text, Reader-Response Criticism stresses readers or the world "in front of" the text. Readers read texts differently depending on their backgrounds, experiences, interests, competencies, gender, race, ethnicity, and the like. Some Reader-Response critics say that a text lies dormant and means nothing until *a reader creates meaning as (s)he reads.* Others speak of an *interaction* between text and reader. Moreover, there are multiple levels, stories within stories, with multiple audiences. The narrator of the Book of Mark tells a *story* to narratees about Jesus, who teaches by telling *another story,* a parable, in which there are still more speakers and respondents. This second story, which has its own characters and plot, serves as a teaching to hearers within the larger story but also to implied readers of the whole story. In any case, *actual* readers, past or present, may not conform to what the text implies about its *intended* readers. Modern readers, for example, are not like ancient readers, let alone ancient hearers of Jesus' parables within the story. Such multilevel analyses often leave us one or two steps away from what were the first, "actual" authors/speakers and readers/hearers external to the text.

It should be added that some recent Narrative critics, also following secular theorists, argue that there is *some correspondence* between real authors and implied authors on the one hand and real readers and implied readers on the other. Similarly, there is in a general way *some correspondence* between the first actual readers/hearers and the implied readers/hearers because they shared the same general cultural context. Moreover, authors, if they wish to communicate, intend to be "considerate" authors; and readers, if they wish to understand, intend to be "considerate" readers. These points are important for dealing with biblical authors, texts, and readers from the past because it is difficult for people from different cultures to be "considerate." Thus for some critics Historical and Social-Scientific Criticism can be coordinated with the more recent Literary Criticism to help readers become "considerate" and thus reestablish the contract originally intended. Such modifications also open the door for correlation with more traditional historical, social-historical, and social-scientific methods.

How do these recent literary approaches affect the interpretation and meaning of the Lord's Prayer?

The Lord's Prayer is not a narrative text as such, but it is set within a narrative text, the *whole Matthean story* about Jesus. That story reveals an "implied author" (who in this case corresponds to the real author) and "implied readers" (who in this case correspond to real first readers). The "narrator" is an unnamed, unidentified, unnoticed figure behind the scenes. All seeing and all knowing, this narrator/story-teller is able to transport readers (or hearers to whom the story is read) from scene to scene. The narrator gains the readers' trust and confidence. If successful, the narrator convinces the readers of the "right" point of view—note the "ethical" implications—which coincides with the point of view of the implied author, which in turn is a claim to represent *God's* point of view (Matt. 16:23). This is confirmed by "proof texts" from scripture; these demonstrate God's plan.

The major *characters* in the Matthean story are the heroic protagonist, Jesus, his immediate followers, and the opposing religious leaders who create the conflict to be resolved. Jesus is portrayed as the Messianic King descended from King David, the special Son of God (not God), and an authoritative preacher, teacher, and healer. The immediate followers, the disciples, are of "little faith" and come into minor conflicts with Jesus, but ultimately they will carry on his mission. The opponents on the supernatural level are the Evil One and his demons; on the natural level they are Israelite leaders who by the end of the story are joined by the crowds. The *plot* turns on the greater and greater conflict between good and evil. Jesus wins the supernatural conflict by not yielding to the test of the Evil One (see "lead us not to the test") and by overcoming the evils of disease and demon possession in healings and exorcisms; moreover, he has authority over nature itself. He appears to be defeated by his human adversaries, but, ironically, his resurrection shows that he is ultimately victorious. Readers do not get the "point of view" of the Israelite leaders; that story would look quite different!

In the Gospel of Matthew, the unfolding of the narrative plot is interrupted by five speeches that portray Jesus the protagonist as the authoritative teacher in contrast to the Israelite leaders. In his first sermon (Matt. 5–7), the narrator takes the reader to a mountain in Galilee (Matt. 5:1) where Jesus interprets the "Law and the prophets" (5:17–20) to disciples and crowds. Jesus' teaching about prayer as private prayer includes the Lord's Prayer (6:9–13); in context it is the correct way to pray in contrast to the showy piety of the Pharisees. Thus it contributes to generating opposition by religious leaders and contributes to the plot on Jesus' life (Matt. 12, 14). It is thus part of the plot's conflict. It also is a prayer for the original "implied readers," who are similar to actual ancient readers. However, it may speak to other, unintended readers as well. Insofar as the text has a life of its own, the teaching does not have one simple interpretation; it may bring forth a number of different responses not only from readers, but also from those who pray its final form in worship.

Summarizing, Literary Criticism poses an alternative to General Historical Criticism and its subfields. New Criticism shifts attention away from what is behind the text, looking through the text to reconstruct history, social context, and the like, to the *text itself,* which has its own intrinsic qualities. It claims that historical questions cannot be answered objectively and do violence to the artistic quality of literary texts. Their meanings are always greater than their author intended. For the more radical New Criticism scholars, even modern historical writing is a form of fiction, not "objective" history. Narrative Criticism also concentrates on the text but is concerned to explore how the text works. It explores plot and characters but also "point of view," "implied author," "implied reader," "narrator," "narratee," and the like on the analogy of modern fiction. Within this perspective Reader-Response Criticism shifts the accent to the *reader,* how readers read texts, implied readers, and in some cases the extent to which these readers correlate with the first actual readers because of their shared cultural context. Insofar as implied authors correspond to real authors and implied readers correspond to real first readers, this last interest opens the door for some point of contact with historical and social-scientific interests.

LIBERATIONIST HERMENEUTICS

Liberationist Hermeneutics refers to interpretations of the New Testament that challenge any form of oppression, thus that liberate. Those who have experienced domination or oppression have developed this kind of hermeneutics. They often share some of the perspectives of other critics. However, they see Jesus and the early Jesus movements as catalysts for liberating subjected peoples from political, economic, racial, ethnic, and gender injustices. Typical "oppressors" are people who consciously or unconsciously accept the superiority of their own culture, people of a certain race who think consciously or unconsciously that their race is superior to other races, and genders who think consciously or unconsciously that they are superior to other genders. Typical Liberationists challenge Western imperialism and colonialism, attitudes of white superiority, and expressions of male dominance. Some interpreters write on homosexuality and the Bible, but as yet no major Gay and Lesbian Liberation Hermeneutic has surfaced, although it exists in certain forms of culture criticism. One might add that there are also scholars who attempt to sensitize modern Christians about "anti-Judaism" in the New Testament.

Two prominent perspectives are what might be called Third World Hermeneutics and Feminist Hermeneutics.

13. Third World Hermeneutics

Scholars in especially two areas of the Third World—Latin America and sub-Saharan Africa—have developed their own interpretive perspectives on the New Testament. In Latin America, "Liberation Theology" originated especially among Roman Catholic priests who served poor, usually peasant, Native American congregations who experienced harsh political and economic oppression from political leaders, Spanish-descended landowners, and North American business interests. These priests formed "base communities," that is, religiously oriented social reform groups who sought to better conditions and achieve land reform. Influenced by their reading of the New Testament and Karl Marx's revolutionary politics and economics, they argued that legitimate Christian theology should begin with *praxis,* that is, "practice" or concrete action, not abstract thought, as has been the tendency in Euro-American theology and historical research. There should be, as Liberation Theology put it, a "preferential option for the poor." It is not accidental that the basis for this position is a particular interpretation of the historical Jesus and his followers as "liberators" of the poor and suffering. Abstract, intellectualistic thinking about the Christ, they say, has the danger of failing to see him in his concrete historical and social context. As Jesus worked among suffering, poor village peasants to liberate them, so to truly understand his message and life one must do the same. Here, New Testament interpretation is in the service of a theology that stresses social and economic reform at a grass-roots level. It is as much a practical, strategic liberation hermeneutic as it is an academic method.

14. Feminist/Womanist Hermeneutics and Criticism

The quest for liberation in general and Liberation Theology in particular has spawned a number of liberation thinkers and movements. The most dominant and visible in Euro-America is Feminist Hermeneutics, which on a broader scale has been called "Womanist Hermeneutics." This approach reflects the emergence of women's liberation and the increase of women professionals, including women biblical scholars, especially since the 1960s, as well as concern for the oppression of women with respect to male dominance wherever it occurs. "Gender" issues had been mostly neglected by mainly male interpreters interpreting mainly male-centered texts written mainly (if not exclusively) by males down through the centuries. The latter gap is being closed. Some feminist interpreters have taken Archeological, Historical, and Social-Historical Critical approaches. For example, they have refined historical research about women's roles in the male-dominated family, women's space in houses, women leaders in Greco-Roman religions, women leaders in Israelite synagogues, women leaders in the early churches, and the like. Others have taken Redaction Critical and Literary Critical approaches and concentrated on the characterization of women in the gospels or the possibility that some texts were composed by women. Reader-Response Criticism has opened up the possibility of understanding texts from the perspectives of modern women readers. Some more radical critics have argued that the mentality of the Historical critics—the quest for external, objective, hard truth—is itself a form of male dominance and power. The most radical feminist positions have contended that males interpreting males writing about males who believed in a male God revealed in an "incarnate" male contributes to the oppression of women. Strategically it is important for women to write about women to and for women. Some have charged that the Bible is a main contributor of the oppression of women.

It is possible to take many options about the Lord's Prayer in Feminist Hermeneutics. One might state at one extreme that the name "Lord's Prayer" or "Our Father" as used throughout this chapter simply perpetuates the oppression of women. Thus I write about a male writing about males who write about a male whose prayer to a male father is called by a male name, the Our Father or the Lord's Prayer. Women, read no farther! Perhaps more common would be feminist interpretations of the Gospel of Matthew showing either that this ancient male scribe (13:52) is predominantly male or perhaps transcends his maleness with inclusive themes and therefore has some liberationist strains that go beyond his maleness. More particularly, what is the historical, social-historical, and social-scientific significance of the address of God as a patriarch, that is, as a "Father" who reigns as a "king"? However one looks at these interpretations, there can be no doubt: Feminist/Womanist Hermeneutics has significantly changed the landscape of recent New Testament interpretation.

15. Post-Modernism

For some observers, intellectual currents such as Deconstructionism, Literary Criticism, and Liberationist Hermeneutics, especially Feminist/Womanist Hermeneutics, are signs of the end of the usual Modern attempts to find "Truth." Thus Deconstructionism challenges the construction of grand schemes of meaning, Literary Criticism removes the sharp distinctions between fact and fiction, Liberationist Hermeneutics observes that history is a point of view dominated by male selection and interpretation. From these perspectives, historical methods are the *outmoded* remnant of Modernism. Historical texts do not tell us "what really happened" as much as they are *narratives,* with their own biases and points of view, about what happened and, indeed, about what is still happening. They do not really "refer" to anything "out there"; rather, they represent particular viewpoints. Consciousness of multiculturalism reinforces the point: Each group has its own competing version of the Truth, and none is truer than the other. Indeed, there is no one Truth, but only truths. There is no "real" objective history, but only narratives about history. Thus for some, "history" is really fantasies of the past, and docudrama is as good. All this represents our new cultural "condition," in which the Modern consensus about the past, who we are, where we came from, our norms and values is dissolving before our eyes. Indeed, there is no single "we," but only you and I.

OTHER PERSPECTIVES

16. Socio-Rhetorical Criticism

The term *rhetoric* has both specific and general meanings. Historically, rhetoric was the ability to communicate effectively in specific contexts (persuade, praise, defend, and the like), an ability that in Greco-Roman antiquity was taught to the educated elite. Modern Socio-Rhetorical critics at this level attempt to read ancient texts with an eye to identifying the various rhetorical techniques used by ancient writers and thus to understand better their rhetorical strategies, cultural ideologies, and social relations. However, more generally, Socio-Rhetorical Criticism is a hermeneutical method that attempts to combine historical, literary, social-scientific, and theological methods. Using "text" in a broad sense, it takes account of the modern interpreter's presuppositions, that is, social situation and ideology. Then it analyzes "the text's" literary techniques and argumentation (traditional rhetoric and literary criticism), relation to other "texts" (quotations, allusions, but also social and cultural knowledge in the text), social and cultural contexts of "the text" (social-scientific analysis), and political ideology (Robbins).

17. Theological Criticism

There is one very important traditional criticism called "New Testament Theology," a subcategory of Biblical Theology. Theology attempts to think rationally, creatively, constructively, and consistently about faith and ethics for the modern world, within the context of a religious community. The New Testament does not offer a consistently unified view of God, Christ, human beings, the church, the spirit, salvation, the end, and so on. Yet, there have been attempts to discover what is common in the various perspectives of the various authors and groups in the New Testament literature. This is the attempt to find unity within all the diversity of the canon. It is a formidable task. The books of the New Testament represent a variety of perspectives in a multicultural Mediterranean world, and most of us live in a multicultural world as well. Yet, if there is to be modern Christian theological reflection, some attempt to gain such a perspective on the New Testament, some believe, is worth the effort.

SUMMARY AND POINT OF VIEW IN THIS TEXT

In this chapter we have covered some of the main approaches to interpreting New Testament texts, usually known as hermeneutics. There are others. Worth mentioning is the New Historicism, which also treats ancient texts as narratives but retains something of a free-ranging historical and cultural context, with a focus on marginal people similar to what is found in Social History, Social-Scientific Criticism, and Liberationist Hermeneutics. However, enough has been said to demonstrate that in this multiculture we now have multimethods. We have noted that a couple of these methods emerged in the Pre-Modern period, that most appeared in the Modern period, and that several others have emerged in what some scholars like to describe as the Post-Modern period. The following list gives a very brief description of the problem and the method used to solve it. The list is then repeated with a bar graph to show periods of origin and dominance.

1. Manuscripts to reconstruct the New Testament — Textual Criticism

2. Foreign language documents — English translation

3. Vocabulary, grammar, syntax, style — (Old) Literary Criticism

4. Written sources used by New Testament authors — Source Criticism

5. Authors, dates, places, recipients, intentions — General Historical Criticism

6. Oral traditions, their histories, and settings	Form Criticism
7. Ideology/theology of authors	Redaction/Composition Criticism
8. Structures, conflicts, symbols of groups	Social-Historical, Social-Scientific Criticism
9. Material remains and newly discovered texts	Archeology
10. Human thought expressed in narrative	Structuralist Criticism
11. Discovering psychoanalytic insights	Psychoanalytic Criticism
12. Plot, characters, implied authors and readers	New Literary Criticism
13. Reorientation to colonialist oppression	Third World Hermeneutics
14. Reorientation to women's issues	Feminist/Womanist Hermeneutics/Criticism
15. Objective interpretation deferred	Post-Modernism
16. Synthetic literary and social-scientific hermeneutics	Socio-Rhetorical Criticism
17. Reflecting about God, Jesus, church	Theological Criticism

If placed in a chronological table, the critical methods and other orientations look as shown in Table 2.4.

As you might infer from the areas of concentration in the preceding sketch, the emphasis in this textbook will be methods from the Modern period, although some attention will be given to more recent developments. This strategy in no way intends to deny the importance of Literary Criticism, Structuralism, Feminist/ Womanist Hermeneutics, Socio-Rhetorical Criticism, and various methods related to Post-Modernist thought. It is a choice based on predominantly historical hermeneutics. Several reasons may be offered.

First, the Modern period covers the longest span of time in attempting to address a variety of critically interpretive questions related to the New Testament; not surprisingly, methods related to historical hermeneutics have gained something of a normative status. One hopes that this is not an abuse of power. Second, historical (and at points social-historical) contextual questions have dominated the Modernist period of academic New Testament study. Third, some forms of Literary Criticism such as the New Criticism have relatively little interest in history writing as practiced by professional historians, and to adopt them as an overall perspective would require a totally different book. Fourth, it is not impossible to adopt this perspective but remain open to Post-Modernist perspectives and critiques. Fifth, the author of this approach has moved increasingly toward Social-Historical and Social-Scientific Criticism. Sixth—a very practical reason—historical, social-historical, and social-scientific methods are most consistent with previous editions of this textbook.

Although this chapter has focused primarily on the New Testament documents, some other literature in the early Jesus Movement has been mentioned. In accord with the approaches sketched out earlier, Chapter Three will examine the earliest Jesus Movement, its traditions, and its literature.

Table 2.4 Criticism Methods

	Pre-Modern	Modern				Post-Modern		
	1500 1700	1775 1800	1890	1910	1950	1970	2000	
English Translation	▬▬▬▬▬▬▬▬▬▬▬▬▬▬▬▬▬▬▬▬▬▬▬▬▬▬▬							
Old Literary Criticism	▬▬▬▬▬▬▬▬▬▬▬▬▬▬▬▬▬▬▬▬▬▬▬▬▬▬▬							
Textual Criticism	▬▬▬▬▬▬▬▬▬▬▬▬▬▬▬▬▬▬▬▬▬▬▬							
General Historical Criticism	▬▬▬▬▬▬▬▬▬▬▬▬▬▬▬▬▬▬							
Theological Criticism	▬▬▬▬▬▬▬▬▬▬▬▬▬▬▬▬▬▬							
Source Criticism	▬▬▬▬▬▬▬▬▬▬▬▬▬▬							
Archeology	▬▬▬▬▬▬▬▬							
Form Criticism	▬▬▬▬▬▬							
Redaction/Composition Criticism	▬▬▬							
Social-Historical; Social-Scientific Criticism	▬▬▬							
New Literary Criticism	▬▬▬							
Structuralist Criticism	▬▬▬							
Feminist Hermeneutics	▬▬							
Psychoanalytic Criticism	▬▬							
Third World Hermeneutics	▬▬							
Post-Modernism	▬▬							
Socio-Rhetorical Criticism	▬							

STUDY QUESTIONS

1. Why do some people pray "debts," whereas others pray "trespasses"? Why do some Protestants pray a concluding doxology, whereas Catholics do not? In which two gospels is the Lord's Prayer found? Is it found elsewhere in ancient literature?

2. What are the "synoptic gospels"? Why is there a "Synoptic Problem"? What is the usual solution to this problem? What is Q? What are some of the key historical problems about the Gospel of Matthew? How do modern historians solve them? How was oral tradition passed on in the Jesus Movement, and what happened to it?

3. What is the meaning of the major terms in the Lord's Prayer? Do you think that Jesus prayed about debts, trespasses, or sins? What are some social dimensions of the prayer? Why do you think that the authors of the Matthean and Lukan Gospels put the prayer where it is in their stories?

4. How does studying the gospel writers' tendencies help understand what the original prayer might have looked like? How do Social-Historical and Social-Scientific Criticism help to understand the prayer? How can archeology be of help? Why have some interpreters turned to newer approaches to literary criticism, and what do these approaches have to offer about the interpretation of the prayer? Can you describe any other approaches?

Photo 3.1   The Egnatian Way (*Via Egnatia*) was the major Roman road across Macedonia, linking the Adriatic and Aegean seas. Paul probably traveled this road between Philippi and Thessalonica. (See map of the Roman empire, p. 9, and the map of important cities and regions of Paul, p. 164).

CHAPTER THREE

THE EARLIEST NON-PAULINE GROUPS AND THEIR BELIEFS AND PRACTICES

HISTORICAL SEQUENCE

The first object of this chapter will be to gain some impression of the historical sequence of the traditions, sources, and books of the New Testament as a whole. To do this, the historical and social context sketched in Chapter One and some of the methods explained and illustrated in Chapter Two will be important. Using this chronology we can then turn our attention to the earliest groups in the Jesus Movement apart from the Apostle Paul, whose writings will be studied in the following two chapters.

WRITINGS OF THE JESUS MOVEMENT

In the last chapter we gave a table of the twenty-seven books of the New Testament canon distributed into four general literary types or genres (Table 2.2). The student should review that table before proceeding further. The table raises several questions. The first is this: What is the origin of the *names* given to these twenty-seven books? Over a period of about three centuries, the majority of believers in the Jesus Movement came to believe that Jesus' relatives and eyewitnesses to his life on the one hand and the Apostle Paul on the other wrote these books. James and Jude were thought to be Jesus' blood brothers (Mark 6:3; Gal. 1:19). Simon called Peter, John son of Zebedee, and Matthew the Toll Collector are listed among Jesus' twelve Galilean disciples (Mark 3:16–19). John of Patmos claims to be the author of Revelation, and he was eventually identified with Jesus' disciple, John son of Zebedee.

Paul recruited Philemon, Timothy, Titus, Mark, and Luke "the Physician" to the Jesus Movement, and they became Paul's close companions (Gal. 2:1–10; Philem. 23–24). To Luke was attributed a gospel and the Acts of the Apostles (Acts 1:1–2). Later Church Fathers said that Paul also wrote a book to the Hebrews. The remaining names come from the *place* to which Paul or someone writing in his name ("a Paulinist") wrote. All these locations but one, the region of Galatia in Asia Minor, are cities: Rome in Italy; Corinth, Philippi, and Thessalonica in Greece; and Ephesus and Colossae in Asia Minor.

In which chronological sequence were these books written? Would this chronology reveal something important about the history of the Jesus Movement? Scholars do not always agree on the answers to these questions. To gain some perspective, consider first the one book that purports to offer a history of the early church, the Acts of the Apostles.

The Acts of the Apostles

The Acts of the Apostles contains stories about the early Jerusalem church and the shift of the Jesus Movement from Jerusalem to Rome. The main heroes and heroines in the first part of the book are Jesus' disciples (Peter, John son of Zebedee, Philip), and Jesus' brother James. Mary, the mother of Mark, is also mentioned. The heroes and heroines in the last part of Acts are Paul, his companions, associates, and converts. The genre of the Acts of the Apostles is usually called "history." But is Acts *really* historical writing as modern Western people think of historical writing? Consider the contrast between Paul's letters and Acts on several points in Table 3.1. It is clear from this table that in these three cases the Acts of the Apostles and Paul's Letter to the Galatians disagree in certain details. Another example of difference about subjects is found in Acts and 1 Thessalonians in Table 3.2. A third example compares Acts and Romans on a very important "theological" idea in Table 3.3.

Acts and Paul's letters do not always disagree, and that is very important. However, these cases raise certain questions. Did Paul have a poor memory? Did he intentionally distort his version of the truth in order to make a point? Or was Acts sometimes inaccurate? Although one can never rule out the former two questions completely, most historical critics prefer the third solution. There are several reasons.

First, Acts was written a number of decades later than the events it records, whereas Paul's letters were closer in time to those events. Second, most modern historians think that the author of Acts was not Luke "the Physician," the companion of Paul, as later tradition says, but rather an anonymous person relying on hearsay. Third, and most important, although most historians think Acts belongs to the "history" genre, they mean *history* in the *ancient* sense of the term, not modern history. Among ancient Greek, Roman, and Israelite historians, history was usually not written to record "the way it actually happened," although there is occasional testimony that it was. Instead, it was normally written to illustrate the greatness of the state and the virtues of its heroes and heroines. Moreover, ancient historians felt free to create speeches on the basis of what they thought an orator might have said or what seemed appropriate for the occasion. A study of the speeches in Acts shows

Table 3.1   Selected Events in Acts and Galatians Compared and Contrasted

Topic	(Paul's Letter to the) Gal. 1:18–24	Acts of the Apostles 9:19b–30; 11:25–26
1. **Length of Paul's stay in Damascus, Syria**	*Three years*	An indefinite number of *days*
2. **Source of directions for Paul's movements**	*God* orders or sends Paul "by revelation"	*Jerusalem authorities* order and send Paul
3. **Those who know Paul at Jerusalem**	Paul *virtually unknown;* visits only Jesus' disciple Peter and meets Jesus' brother James	Paul a hero who *publicly disputes* with "Hellenists" (Israelites who speak Greek and follow Greek ways)

Table 3.2   Acts and 1 Thessalonians

Topic	1 Thess. 1:9, 14	Acts 17:1–9
Who persecuted members of Jesus Movement at Thessalonica?	Their own countrymen, that is, Gentiles	Israelites from the local synagogue

Table 3.3   Acts and Romans

Idea	Rom. 1–3	Paul's Speech in Acts 17
Is ignorance of the knowledge of God an excuse for sin?	There is no ignorance of the knowledge of God, either on the part of Israelites or Gentiles; thus not to do God's will is sin	There is Israelite and Gentile ignorance of the knowledge of God; however, God overlooks it

that although different heroes spoke them at different times and places, they have a number of common themes. Also, ancient authors often used whatever sources were available—often oral—in very creative ways.

Literary Criticism of the language, style, and content of Acts shows that it was written by the same person who wrote the Gospel of Luke. Because this author extensively rewrote and rearranged his gospel sources (the **Two-Source Theory**), it is likely that he did the same with Acts. Finally, history writing in the Hebrew Bible, which was the Bible of the Jesus Movement, had a religious purpose. It claimed that Yahweh, the God of Israel, was in control of history and guided his people. It is the same in Acts: God is guiding the course of the Jesus Movement through his "Holy Spirit."

In short, the Acts of the Apostles is the genre "history," but a special kind of history, a ancient history based on limited sources and written with religious themes and ancient historical conventions. Based on limited sources, it is what the ancient author imagined to have happened and interpreted according to certain canons of ancient historical writing, including heroes' speeches. It was also religious writing. In the case of Acts, the attempt was to show how God was guiding the early church through his "Holy Spirit." This position about Acts—that it is not as straightforward and "objective" as we moderns would like—is normative in modern critical study (for more on historical writing in Acts, see Chapter Ten).

The principle used for reconstructing history from Acts in this textbook is that priority will be given to Paul's letters where Paul disagrees with Acts because Paul was actually present at the events recorded. The same principle will hold with respect to Paul's ideas, especially when it is clear that the speeches attributed to Paul in Acts follow the general pattern for all the speeches in Acts.

This perspective on the only book in the New Testament called "history" may sound unduly negative. However, Acts covers much more ground about Paul (as well as other events) than Paul himself explicitly mentions; in many cases it is the *only* source. Read cautiously and critically, therefore, it can be very helpful in historical reconstruction.

More important for the earliest period of the Jesus Movement are other methods that recover some of what was going on in the earliest phases of the Jesus Movement. Historians, like Textual Critics, usually refer to two kinds of evidence: internal evidence and external evidence. **Internal evidence** is evidence within a particular book itself. For example, a New Testament book sometimes gives hints about its author, sources, traditions, social context, place, time, and recipients. **External evidence** is evidence outside the book, that is, what can be known about comparable persons, places, events, and the like from archeology, inscriptions, and other literary documents. Acts can then be used as a supplement.

All these tools help to put the early traditions, sources, and books of the Jesus Movement in chronological sequence. That will offer at least some plausible sequence in which to read the New Testament books. A good beginning point is to attempt to date those books that say something about Jesus.

The Four Canonical Gospels and the *Gospel of Thomas*

In the Gospel of Mark there is a millennial speech ascribed to Jesus (Mark 13). This speech is about forthcoming natural disasters such as earthquakes and drought and the end of the present social order. It contains a very vague reference to the "desolating sacrilege" (Mark 13:14). The Lukan author in his parallel passage omits these precise words and substitutes an interpretation, "Jerusalem surrounded by armies" (Luke 21:20); the Lukan Jesus also prophesies that Jerusalem will be destroyed in another passage (Luke 19:43–44). The Gospel of John does not refer to the desolating sacrilege, but it mentions the fear of Jesus' Israelite opponents that ". . . the Romans will come and destroy both our holy place and our nation" (11:48). However, the author of the Gospel of Matthew includes the reference to the desolating sacrilege in his expanded version of the Markan speech (Matt. 24–25). Moreover, he has Jesus *imply* a reference to the destruction of Jerusalem in an allegory. It tells of an angry king who will destroy a city as punishment for the people's not accepting God's invitation to a banquet for his Son (Matt. 22:7).

The "desolating sacrilege" reference and its interpretations, as well as references to the destruction of Jerusalem, offer the most important possibility for dating the gospels in relation to Palestinian history in the Roman period. About 235 years earlier, the "desolating sacrilege" referred to the defilement of the temple by the Seleucid Greeks (167 B.C.E.), an event that helped trigger the Maccabean Revolt (e.g., Dan. 9:27 [**Abomination That Makes Desolate**]; 1 Macc. 1:54). In the first century C.E., the expression seems to have become a code word for a comparable defilement. In the gospel stories it was put into the mouth of Jesus as a prophecy. Historical critics conclude that the author of the earliest gospel, the Gospel of Mark, must have known about the event and was therefore writing *during or just after* the event. In other words, it was written *during or just after 70 C.E.* The interpretation in Luke about Jerusalem being surrounded by armies and the comment in John suggest that they were also written after 70 C.E. All this is reinforced by the **Two-Source Theory.** In short, *all four gospels can be dated in relation to the fall of Jerusalem in 70 C.E.;* more precisely, the Gospel of Mark was written during or just after 70 C.E. and the others in the decades afterward.

The *latest* possible date for the Gospel of Matthew is the early second century about 110 C.E. This date is suggested by **external evidence,** that is, a bishop named Ignatius of Antioch appears to have quoted a phrase *composed* by the author of Matthew (Matt. 3:15). This conclusion can be supported by other internal/external arguments. For example, Jesus' much heightened conflict with the Pharisees in Matthew (see Matt. 23) is a conflict between *Israelites and members of the Jewish Movement* in the late first century (**Historical Criticism; Redaction Criticism**). A plausible outside date for Matthew would be 110 C.E., probably about a generation earlier. Thus Matthew is dated about 85–90 C.E. A similar control for the *latest* possible date for the Gospel of Luke (and Acts) does not yet exist. However, drawing on the **Two-Source Theory,** most scholars suggest about 85–90 C.E. as well. The *latest* possible date for the Gospel of John is fixed differently. It is based on the earliest known papyrus fragment of that gospel (P^{52}), which paleographers date about 125 C.E. As in the case of Matthew, Jesus' conflict with Jesus' opponents in the Gospel of John (especially John 9) may point to the conflict between Pharisees and members of the Jesus Movement in the late first century. The usual view is that John was written slightly later than Matthew and Luke, about 90–100.

In short, the four gospels were written in the last third of the first century. The sequence was the Gospel of Mark (ca. 70 C.E.), then the Gospels of Matthew and Luke (ca. 85–90 C.E.), and finally the Gospel of John (ca. 90–100 C.E.).

We have concentrated on dating the four canonical gospels. A very important fifth gospel needs to be mentioned, however. It is the ***Gospel of Thomas*** discovered at **Nag Hammadi,** Egypt, in 1945. This gospel contains 114 sayings attributed to Jesus. Like the other gospels, it has to be critically evaluated. Its opening line attributes it to a certain Judas Didymos Thomas, no doubt a reference to Judas, the brother of Jesus (Mark 6:3), considered to be Jesus' "twin" (Greek *didymos* and Aramaic *thomas:* "twin"). However, modern scholars hold that the *Gospel of Thomas* is **pseudonymous** ("false name," that is, falsely attributed authorship). The Nag Hammadi version was written in Egyptian **Coptic,** probably in the late fourth century C.E. However, this version was a translation of a Greek version written before

200 C.E. because fragments of such a Greek version have survived. Thus the Greek *Gospel of Thomas* was known in the second century. Some scholars argue that the most original version was composed about 120 C.E.; however, some push it back to about 70–100 C.E., and still others date it as early as 50–70 C.E. There is obviously an important controversy here. The last date would make it earlier than all four canonical gospels and put it at the time usually suggested for **Q,** to which it is analogous in form. One possible dating for the four canonical gospels and the *Gospel of Thomas,* then, is the following:

Gospel of Thomas, ca. 50–70 C.E. (70–100? 120?)

Gospel of Mark, ca. 70 C.E.

Gospel of Matthew, ca. 85–90 C.E.

Gospel of Luke, ca. 85–90 C.E.

Gospel of John, ca. 90–100 C.E.

The dating of the writings themselves is not the only point of importance; it is also important to try to date the sources in them, and some sources in later books may be earlier than some early books (and their sources).

The Letters

There are also twenty-one letters and letter-like books that must be dated, as well as Acts and Revelation. The letters can be divided into three groups of seven: (1) seven undisputed letters attributed to Paul, (2) seven disputed letters attributed to Paul, and (3) seven letters attributed to Jesus' apostles and probably two siblings:

Undisputed Pauline Letters	Disputed Pauline Letters	Other Letters
1 Thessalonians	2 Thessalonians	James
1 Corinthians	Colossians	1 Peter
2 Corinthians	Ephesians	1 John
Philippians	Hebrews	2 John
Philemon	1 Timothy	3 John
Galatians	2 Timothy	Jude
Romans	Titus	2 Peter

The order of books in this list is not the New Testament order. Rather, each column has a chronological sequence of its own, and the three columns themselves, from left to right, are roughly chronological. What is the basis for these sequences?

Study for a moment the first column. It is usually held that 1 Thessalonians was written to Thessalonica (in Macedonia [northern Greece]) from Corinth (Achaia [southern Greece]). Can it be dated? Here **Literary Criticism, Historical Criticism,** and **archeology** are of great help. Acts 18:1–3 says that when Paul came to Corinth, he found two Israelite members of the Jesus Movement, Aquila and his wife Priscilla. They had just arrived there from Italy because the emperor Claudius had commanded all Israelites to leave Rome. Another ancient source suggests that Claudius issued this **Edict of Claudius** about 49/50 C.E. Thus Paul would have arrived at Corinth about 49/50 C.E. Further, Acts 18:11–12 says that the Israelites dragged Paul before the Roman proconsul (governor) Gallio. Now a **Gallio Inscription** has been found at Delphi, Greece. Scholars' analysis of it shows that Gallio was proconsul about *July 1, 51 C.E. to July 1, 52 C.E.* Other inscriptional evidence seems to agree. Acts says that Paul had been in Corinth *eighteen months* when he appeared before Gallio. If the Book of Acts is right, Paul would have arrived at Corinth eighteen months earlier, again about 49/50 C.E. In short, archeology—the Gallio Inscription—agrees with Acts and thus helps to establish the time of Paul's arrival at Corinth.

Two very important historical results follow. First, if 1 Thessalonians was Paul's first surviving letter, as scholars usually say, it can be approximately dated. Indeed, this information helps to establish a chronology of his whole life, because now it is possible to look at Paul's autobiographical statements in Galatians and relate them to his arrival in Corinth. Second, if he was martyred about 60 (the latest would be 64 C.E.), we can place Paul's surviving letters roughly in the decade 50–60 C.E. (**Historical Criticism**).

Consider the second column. A reading of 2 Thessalonians shows that it is very similar to 1 Thessalonians. However, it is different *enough* that historical critics have questioned Pauline authorship (**Literary Criticism, Historical Criticism**). That will be the procedure here. Five other letters (omitting Hebrews) are different in vocabulary, style, ideas, and implied social relationships from those in the first column. The third letter, Ephesians, copies phrases from Colossians (B); it therefore must follow Colossians (**Literary Criticism**). Moreover, the earliest manuscripts of Ephesians do not have the words "who are at Ephesus and faithful" in the first verse (**Textual Criticism**). Scholars conclude that Ephesians was not written by Paul; some also conclude that it was not written to a specific location and might have circulated as a "cover letter" for a collection of Paul's letters (the seven in column 1 plus the first three in column 2 = ten, the number of Paul's letters known about 150 C.E.). Writing in someone else's name was not unusual in the ancient world. It is usually described by the term **pseudonymity,** literally, "false name." Thus, on the basis of vocabulary, style, ideas, social relationships, and the use of Colossians by Ephesians, we conclude that the first three letters in column 2 were written by persons who knew the thought of Paul well but who lived in a somewhat later period, probably after 70 C.E. We call these three second-generation Pauline letters "**deutero ('secondary')-Pauline.**" More will be said about these issues in the chapter that takes up the deutero-Pauline letters (Chapter Seven).

Passing over the Book of Hebrews for the time being—it is a special case—there is a second set of three letters in the second column, 1 and 2 Timothy and Titus. Traditionally, they are called the "**Pastoral Letters**" because they purport to be Paul's advice to two of his missionary companions, Timothy and Titus, about pastoral oversight of their churches. However, vocabulary, style, and ideas show that they were probably composed early in the second century C.E. by a third-generation follower of Paul. Some scholars also call them "deutero-Pauline," although they are really "trito (third-stage)-Pauline."

The result is that there are three generations of Pauline letters in columns 1 and 2. Because the latest six letters—most of those in column 2—appear to have been written in Paul's name, the theory has arisen that there was group who accepted and followed his ideas and wrote in his name, that is, a "**Pauline School.**" This theory gains some further support from a few insertions ("**interpolations**") into the Pauline manuscripts (**Source Criticism**).

The last letter in column 2 is called the Letter to the Hebrews. However, it is *radically* different from the other thirteen letters attributed to Paul. It is not even a letter in the strictest sense. Its vocabulary, style, and ideas are nothing like what we find in the other thirteen attributed to Paul (**Literary Criticism**). As noted in Chapter Two, even the ancients doubted that Paul wrote Hebrews, and it was almost rejected for the canon. Modern scholars do not include it in the Pauline School. Its date is uncertain, but most favor about 80–90 C.E.; if so, it was written before the Pastoral Letters (hence its place in the list).

In summary, if Paul arrived in Corinth about 49/50 C.E. and stayed eighteen months (the **Gallio Inscription;** Acts 18:1–3, 11–12), he wrote 1 Thessalonians there about 50/51 C.E. If he was martyred at Rome, as tradition says, and that took place about 60, or perhaps as late as 64 C.E., the seven undisputed letters in column 1 were probably written in the 50s. Thus **Literary Criticism** and **Historical Criticism** converge to make conclusions about the Pauline letters. The thirteen letters of the Pauline School plus Hebrews can now be rearranged according to their probable dates.

Pauline (50–60)	Early Pauline School (70–90)	Totally Non-Pauline (80–90?)	Later Pauline School (100–125)
1 Thessalonians	2 Thessalonians	Hebrews	1 Timothy
1 Corinthians	Colossians		2 Timothy
2 Corinthians	Ephesians		Titus
Philippians			
Philemon			
Galatians			
Romans			

The letters in columns 2 and 3 were written during the period of the canonical gospels. Thus *the undisputed Pauline letters in column 1 are the earliest written books in the New Testament.* One of the synoptic sources, **Q**, was probably written during the period of the undisputed Pauline letters, and if one accepts the early dating of the *Gospel of Thomas,* it was also from that period.

We have discussed fourteen letters that the Jesus Movement attributed to Paul. Seven other letters and letter-like books remain, those in column 3 of the previous list designated "Other" (nos. 20–26 in the twenty-seven-book list). Traditionally they have been called the "**Catholic Epistles**" because they are not written to a single person or a group meeting in a house-church, but rather are very general (*catholic* means "universal"). Specific arguments about vocabulary, style, and content show that they are also pseudonymous. This whole group of letters represents the interests and concerns of communities in the Jesus Movement that are on the way to becoming more established groups in the Greco-Roman world. All are judged to have been written between 90 and 125 C.E. or slightly later.

Revelation

A reasonable date for the Book of Revelation, or the Apocalypse, is about 95 C.E. This dating arises because its references to persecution and martyrdom fit fears of a local persecution related to Christ believers who refused to worship Domitian in western Asia Minor about that time. As already noted, its author, John of Patmos, was later identified with John son of Zebedee, Jesus' disciple. He was also believed to have written the Fourth Gospel and the three Johannine letters. However, the language, style, ideas, and context of Revelation are so different from the Gospel of John and 1, 2, and 3 John that it does not belong in this "Johannine School." Thus if Jesus' disciple wrote the rest of the Johannine books, he did not write this one. However, it is not likely that Jesus' disciple wrote the other Johannine books, either! At the same time, neither is it likely that John of Patmos was Jesus' disciple (who was an illiterate fisherman). Thus Jesus' disciple did not write Revelation.

The New Testament Apocrypha

The twenty-seven books of the New Testament canon, along with the *Gospel of Thomas,* have been given relative dates. Although in practice the *Gospel of Thomas* is often considered along with the rest of the Nag Hammadi Texts, in theory it belongs with the **New Testament Apocrypha.** This refers to books of the New Testament type in general, but they are not in the New Testament canon. Actually, more than fifty gospels from the ancient Jesus Movement are known. Some are known only by name. Others are fragmentary. There are some subcategories, for example, gospels about Jesus' infancy and childhood and gospels by relatives of Jesus. There are also gospels by apostles, by women, and by those judged to be heretics. A few scholars believe that the *Gospel of Peter,* which is an account of Jesus' death, empty tomb, and resurrection, is valuable as an early source for the **Passion Story** (see following). The *Secret Gospel of Mark* was probably a longer version of Mark; it is mentioned in a certain letter of Clement to Theodore, discovered in 1957 (apparently). It reinforces the theory that other versions of Mark existed (note: there are four endings in the manuscripts of Mark). Egerton Papyrus 2 also contains a few variant passages of the gospel stories. Among the other gospels, some are very Israelite, and some are Gnostic in orientation. However one judges their worth in relation to Jesus, these gospels are certainly valuable for understanding beliefs in the Jesus Movement of the second and third centuries C.E.

With regard to the other three genres of the New Testament, there are also apocryphal letters. Examples are "Paul's" letter to the Laodiceans (probably based on mention of such a letter in Col. 4:16) and the exchange between Paul and Roman philosopher Seneca. Apocryphal "acts" existed, such as the fascinating romance legend, the *Acts of Paul and Thecla,* a second-century C.E. book that heightens the interpretation of Paul as an ascetic and defends the place of asceticism as an option for women. Finally, there are apocryphal apocalypses. (Those who wish to pursue the controversial and fascinating **New Testament Apocrypha** should consult the bibliographies on-line.)

The Earliest "Church Fathers"

The "Church Fathers" are writings of eminent men in the Jesus Movement and thought to be very valuable by modern orthodox Christians. The earliest such writings that should be considered with the New Testament are the letters of *1 Clement* (90–95 C.E.) and *2 Clement* (90–110 C.E.), the *Didachē* (ca. 90–110 C.E.), the letters of Bishop Ignatius of Antioch (ca. 110 C.E.), perhaps the letter of Polycarp *To the Philippians* (ca. 110–115), and the *Letter of Barnabas* (100–125 C.E.). These books overlap the dates of the latest New Testament writings. (Those who wish to pursue the Church Fathers should consult the bibliographies on-line.)

SOME WRITTEN SOURCES OF THE JESUS MOVEMENT

So far, the main emphasis in this chapter has been on canonical books from about 50 C.E. to 125 C.E. If one wants to learn about the early period, it is possible not only to interpret the earliest books of this period, but also to hypothesize about underlying written sources of both these and later books in the Jesus Movement. Literary critics and especially Source Critics are specialists in this sort of research. Some of the most important examples will now be considered. At this point they will be summarized; further discussion of some of the earliest materials will come later in this chapter.

Mark, Colossians, and Jude

Recall that the gospels of Matthew and Luke used the Gospel of Mark as a source (**Two-Source Theory**) and that the writer of Ephesians appears to have used Colossians. A third example of this type is that the author of 2 Peter used Jude (Jude 4–16; 1 Pet. 2:1–22). Again, sources are obviously earlier than the books in which they are found, and thus **Source Criticism** leads to a historical result.

The Q Source

Some written sources can be isolated by critical analysis. Scholars account for the verbal exactness between the gospels of Matthew and Luke in passages where they are not dependent on Mark with a source called "**Q**" (see Chapter Two). Recall that Q is primarily a collection of Jesus' sayings. Although it must have been written prior to Matthew and Luke, there is unfortunately no saying in the reconstructed Q that determines its date. In general, scholars think that because Q has no reference to the destruction of Jerusalem in 70 C.E., it was probably written prior to that time, or about 50–70 C.E.

Parable Collections

Most literary analyses of Mark 4 suggest that the author's vocabulary and style are best represented by the Introduction (verses 1–2), the Conclusion (verses 34–35, 36), and an Interlude giving an explanation of the purpose of the parables (verses 10–12). If one attributes these three sections to the final writer (**Redaction Criticism**) and removes them, what remains are six short, pithy sayings called "**aphorisms**" (4:9, 21, 22, 23, 24, 25) and three **parables** and an **allegory.** The latter two are of special interest because they have the *same theme: seed or sowing.*

4:2b–8	The Parable of the Sower (one who sows seed)
4:13–20	Explanation of the Parable of the Sower (an allegory)
4:26–29	The Parable of the Seed Growing Secretly
4:30–32	The Parable of the Mustard Seed

The usual conclusion of Form and Redaction critics is that at least the three Seed parables were gathered together during the early period of oral tradition to form a little cluster or collection in order to illustrate Jesus as a teacher. The fourth item, the allegory, which has themes and words uncharacteristic of either Jesus' parables or the Markan writer, was no doubt added to explain the parable of the Sower before the Markan author wrote. If so, there emerged a little thematic "Sower/Seed" collection—Seed parables and an allegory explaining the Sower—put into writing prior to their inclusion in the gospel by the author of Mark.

Miracle Story Collections

In contrast to what modern Christians often think, ancients would not have thought that Jesus was distinctive simply because of his miracles. There were many miracle workers in antiquity, and many miracle stories were told about them. Form and Redaction critics think that many miracle stories about Jesus were taken from written miracle story collections. The trained eye can spot them in the gospels, especially in Mark and John. Those who made these collections may well have been certain members of the Jesus Movement who thought of Jesus as a great miracle worker and wanted to impress not only outsiders, but also believers in the movement. Indeed, it is possible that those who saw Jesus this way were in competition with those who believed in other miracle workers.

Controversy Story Collections

Controversy stories are question/answer debates that Jesus has with his opponents. **Social-Scientific** critics call these debates "**challenge and riposte (response)**" and observe that the victorious respondent achieves **honor** by his public victory. A possible example of a collection of such stories is in Mark 12. Jesus is in the Jerusalem temple precincts (Mark 12:1–37). In this setting, different opponents—Pharisees and Herodians, Sadducees, scribes—pose three challenging questions to Jesus. Jesus responds by winning these challenges and then poses his own challenging question to the opponents, which they finally cannot answer. When placed in this context, the controversy collection progressively heightens the opponents' opposition to Jesus.

Testimony Books?

Examples of lists of scriptural passages from the Israelite Bible (Old Testament) to support arguments of those who believed in Jesus against nonbelieving Israelites are known from the second century C.E. Perhaps some of these proof text collections, or "testimony books," existed very early. This possibility is suggested because scribes in the Jesus Movement use and reuse—sometimes reinterpret—some important passages in various parts of the New Testament.

Ethical Lists, Household Codes

Writers in the Jesus Movement also cited commonly known lists of virtues and vices (e.g., Gal. 5:19–23). Such lists were common among the Stoic philosophers. Duties of household members meant to regulate households (e.g., Eph. 3:18–4:1) were also well-known means of moral instruction in Greco-Roman culture. There are several examples of such "**household codes**" in the New Testament (e.g., Eph. 3:18–4:1).

"Special M" and "Special L"

Finally, you will recall that the **Two-Source Theory** posits that the authors of the gospels of Matthew and Luke had access to, and used, the Gospel of Mark and Q. Additionally they used their own special sources, although parts of these "strata" were probably oral.

ORAL TRADITIONS BEHIND WRITTEN SOURCES AND DOCUMENTS

If the preceding suggestion about a parable collection in Mark is plausible, one can see at least three pregospel stages behind Mark 4:

1. Individual aphorisms and Sower/Seed parables
2. The collection together of three Seed parables illustrating Jesus as a parable teacher and (added at the same time?) the addition of the allegory to explain the Sower

3. The placement of the aphorisms and the Seed/Sower collection into the Markan Gospel, with the writer creating two settings: a public seaside and private teaching setting

Granting the possibility of these three "layers" or "strata," the first stage represents an oral period in which isolated sayings and parables circulated before being gathered together in thematic clusters. Another possible example of this phenomenon is the prewritten prayer lines that were brought together as the **Lord's Prayer,** as suggested in Chapter Two. A third example is that *some* sayings that are clustered together in the canonical gospels are found scattered separately through the *Gospel of Thomas*. This suggests that there was a stage in which they circulated separately.

The "Jesus Tradition"

The same sort of analysis applies to other forms of the "Jesus tradition." This expression refers to gospel oral traditions spoken by or told about Jesus. To gain an impression of the Jesus tradition, the following is a catalogue of the types of oral traditions with respect to Jesus divided into two major categories: (I) words or sayings *of* Jesus and (II) actions or narratives *about* Jesus.

I. Sayings of Jesus
- A. **Aphorisms:** separate, individualistic, wisdom-like sayings that often go against conventional wisdom; they can generate anecdotal contexts similar to the following category
- B. **Anecdotes** ("*Chreiai*," "Pronouncement Stories"): sayings spoken by Jesus in a brief narrative or dialogue context. Whether the context is integral or not, these can be subdivided as follows:
  1. Controversy dialogues
  2. Teaching dialogues
  3. Biographical accounts
- C. Prophetic and apocalyptic sayings
- D. Sayings about Torah laws and behavior among Jesus' followers
- E. **Similes** ("X is *like* Y")
- F. **Metaphors** ("X *is* Y")
- G. **Parables** (stories about nature or everyday life that tease the imagination and challenge the listener/reader to make some response)
- H. Example stories ("Go and do likewise")

II. Narratives about Jesus
- A. Miracle stories
  1. Exorcisms (a demon is mentioned)
  2. Healings (no demon is mentioned; healing by word or touch [see the discussion of healings in Chapter One])
  3. Miraculous feedings (feeding many people with little food)
  4. Resuscitations from the dead (the person will eventually die [again])
  5. Nature miracles (e.g., calming the sea)
- B. "Biographical" legends and action-oriented anecdotes
- C. The Passion Story

Liturgy: Sermons, Hymns, Confessions, Creeds, Prayers, Benedictions

Form Criticism is also very useful for isolating liturgical traditions. For example, writers occasionally quoted all or parts of sermons, hymns, songs, confessions, creeds, baptismal liturgies, liturgical meal liturgies, prayers, benedictions, and other elements from worship in the Jesus Movement. The Lord's Prayer is a special example.

Scriptural Proofs

As noted earlier, members of the Jesus Movement may have used "testimony books." Some of these proof texts would surely have been circulating in the oral tradition.

After such forms have been analyzed, isolated, and described, Form Critics try to compare variations within the same classification in order to determine which is earlier and later; then they theorize about their sequence and the history of developing oral traditions. It is often possible to observe shifting interpretations of scriptural proofs in the same manner.

As we have seen, the third task of Form Criticism, analyzing the concrete historical and social "settings" in the various groups of the Jesus Movement (*Sitze im Leben,* "settings in life"), was often neglected in the earlier period of **Form Criticism.** Recently, there have been attempts to update Form Criticism in this regard. Contemporary Literary critics have suggested that more attention should be paid to the *function* of a particular form within a given community. These scholars have been led to evaluate the significance of "orality" based in part on anthropological and social-scientific research into oral traditions and their transmission in other cultures. In ancient Mediterranean cultures, people were often trained how to listen (auraliteracy) and trained to speak well, as in the case of rhetoric or oral recitation (oraliteracy). Some scholars believer that the shift from oral to written communication had a major social impact (one may compare the social effect of the development of the computer). Finally, you will recall that whereas the earlier Form critics were interested primarily in "church settings"—again, worship, teaching, and the like—Social-Scientific scholars try to learn more about *everyday* social factors, that is, social relations, social conflict, family life, social stratification, and the like. Although modifications like these are taking place, Form Criticism in *the broad sense* remains a useful tool for attempting to understand the history of oral traditions and their functions in the Jesus movements.

SOCIAL-HISTORICAL FACTORS THAT HELP TO DATE SOURCE MATERIALS OF THE JESUS MOVEMENT

We have concentrated heavily on dating of early documents and their sources and traditions, mainly by internal and external evidence. Now we turn to social factors that influenced the change of these traditions over time.

From Oral to Written

It is estimated that in the ancient world about 90 percent of the people were illiterate. As far as anyone knows, Jesus wrote nothing. Indeed, a case has been made that Jesus, like the peasant farmers and fishermen of his day, could not read and was therefore illiterate (despite Luke 4:16); at best his writing skills were probably limited (craftsman's literacy). This judgment says nothing about his intelligence. Oral communication and dramatic action were both highly valued in Israelite culture (oraliteracy), and they were Jesus' forte. Moreover, oral communication did not suddenly cease when writing became important in certain quarters of the Jesus Movement. Yet, the power of reading and writing at higher levels (scriba-literacy) should not be underestimated. Mediterranean societies, to use a double negative, were not "nonliterate societies." *Texts,* especially *holy texts* and their *interpretation,* were increasingly important, and those elite specialists who possessed the ability to preserve and interpret them gained power within their communities (textual communities). In the Jesus Movement, even if popular writing preserved some of the dynamics of oral discourse, there was some shift from an oral environment to communication by the written word. Eventually there was a corresponding shift to groups interested in preserving the Jesus tradition in writing and in collecting documents for posterity—presumably with realization that history would continue.

From Palestine to the Larger Greco-Roman World

The Jesus Movement gradually moved beyond the networks of Galilee and Jerusalem to the larger Greco-Roman world. This implies a shift in cultural environment: from the Palestinian Israelite homeland, with its dominant Israelite holiness—holy people, holy city, holy temple, holy persons, and holy texts—to an environment of much greater cultural and religious diversity. That is related to the following two shifts.

From Majority Israelite to Majority Gentile

Jesus and the first disciples were Israelites who in diverse ways derived their beliefs from the Torah, although their interpretations of it often differed from those of other Palestinian parties and factions. There is evidence for continuing groups of Jesus believers among Israelites in Galilee, Jerusalem, and other eastern localities. Yet, over time—the length of time is now debated—the new movement eventually succeeded among non-Israelite Gentiles who were attracted to moral, rather than ritual, teachings and practices.

From Aramaic (and Some Hebrew) to Greek

The Greek language was used in Hellenistic cities and for trade and commerce. It was also used in Palestine. However, the traditional language was Hebrew, the language of the holy texts, and, as archeology shows, it was still in use. The commonly spoken language of Palestinian Israelites had long since become Aramaic. As the Jesus Movement moved into the larger Hellenistic world, Greek predominated. Among Greek-speaking Israelites and Greek-speaking members of the Jesus Movement who could read, the holy texts were learned and studied in the Greek **Septuagint.** The shift from the Semitic languages, Hebrew and Aramaic, to Greek was a cultural shift already present in the Hellenistic cities of Palestine and among Greek-speaking Israelites everywhere. Jesus spoke Aramaic; the New Testament was written in Greek.

From Rural to Urban Environments

The Jesus Movement seems to have had its initial successes among the villages and towns of Galilee; archeological evidence suggests that some groups of Jesus Movement members remained there. Its greatest success, however, was in the urban centers: Jerusalem, Caesarea, Damascus, Antioch, Ephesus, Philippi, Thessalonica, Corinth, and Rome. Thus an Israelite movement of the Galilean countryside soon became primarily a Hellenistic urban religion with the attendant problems of, and accommodations to, especially Greco-Roman urban life.

From Reforming Faction to Emergent Institution

The Jesus Movement was initially an Israelite faction led by spontaneous, prophetic, Spirit-filled leaders. It spawned a variety of factions whose members experienced themselves standing against society. Eventually more-ordered groups emerged. We can see in this process a response to opposition by outsiders, increasing self-definition, and growing organization, institutional authority, fixed offices of leadership, and internal struggles. Much of this process can be seen in the literature of the New Testament itself.

The Development of Beliefs about Jesus

The sayings and actions of Jesus that survived were interpreted for new contexts and in the process often transformed; it was also believed that after Jesus died, he continued to speak through Spirit-filled prophets. Who, then, was this Jesus? A prophet? A "messiah"? A miracle-working hero? Even a god? Christologies—reflections about Jesus as the Messiah ("Christ")—are found throughout the New Testament literature. They become quite explicit in the hymns, creeds, and confessions and are also implied in titles of honor reserved for people of power and high status in the culture, as well as those believed to be descended from the gods. Such titles include "Messiah," "Lord," "Son of God," "Son of Man," and "Son of David."

After Jesus was executed, many members of the Jesus Movement believed that he was vindicated by God; death could not contain him. Certainly, he was still alive! As opposition to these believers increased, so did the intensity of their belief. For many it included the view that the social order as it was understood would end and that a different and more perfect social order would be created. Thus Israelite millennialism was transformed into Jesus Movement millennialism. Millennial thinking seems to have dominated most of the early Jesus movements. Many expected that Jesus would return as "Son of Man" or "Lord" to judge the evil and redeem the good. Several New Testament writers used the Greek term *parousia,* a technical term for the official "visit" of a high official or deity, for the expected return of Jesus. However, months and years passed by, and the *parousia* did not take place. The hope for his return was revitalized with the fall of Jerusalem (Mark 13: the desolating sacrilege) and again when the believers in Christ in Asia Minor felt threatened by persecution (the Book of Revelation). Still Jesus did not return. Much literature in the Jesus Movement had to come to terms with the "delay of the *parousia.*"

Broadly speaking, the hope of members of the Jesus Movement took three forms. First, it was intensified, as if doubts could be overcome by shouting louder (2 Peter). Second, the hope was maintained but softened by pushing it into the more distant future and combining it with the attempt to make sense of the extended interim period or present (the Lukan writings). Third, the claim was made that the *parousia* had *already* taken place. The reasons are that the cross and resurrection of Jesus were considered to be part of the millennial period and that the new life was already being experienced by believers in the present (the Gospel of John; some believers in the Pauline mission group at Corinth).

The Jesus Movement began as a series of responses to the life and teachings of Jesus. One response was to preserve his sayings and parables, to make collections of them, to apply them, to find interpretations of them, and to apply them to life. A related response was to tell stories about him. Still another was to continue his lifestyle. In the process, there were preserved traditions, interpretations, and new creations of Jesus material in a variety of Jesus movements. In short, a variety of beliefs went through a variety of transformations in a variety of groups.

A CHRONOLOGICAL SUMMARY OF TRADITIONS, SOURCES, AND DOCUMENTS IN RELATION TO EXTERNAL EVIDENCE

We are now in a position to summarize what we have observed about traditions, sources, literature, and groups in the Jesus Movement, arranging them chronologically as much as we can in relation to external events.

6/4 B.C.E.–30 (?) C.E.:   Jesus of Nazareth was born under Caesar Augustus (reigned 27 B.C.E.–14 C.E.) and Herod the Great (reigned 37–4 B.C.E.) and died under Caesar Tiberius (14 C.E.–37 C.E.), Pontius Pilate (reigned 26–36 C.E.), and Herod Antipas of Galilee (4 B.C.E.–39 C.E.). Jesus apparently did not write anything. He wandered from town to town; spoke aphorisms (challenging proverbial-type sayings), parables, and prophetic sayings; associated and ate with peasants, expendables, and outcasts; exorcised and healed; and was crucified for sedition against the state (see Chapter Fourteen).

30–150 C.E.:   Oral traditions. Circulation of **aphorisms,** other wisdom-type sayings, **parables,** simple stories punctuated by a pronouncement (**anecdotes**), miracle stories, some Passion materials, baptismal and meal traditions, scriptural testimonies, and liturgies, creeds, confessions, hymns. These are found in **Q,** the *Gospel of Thomas,* Mark, **Special M,**

Special L, pre-Pauline materials, James, Acts, and the Gospel of John. There are a few isolated sayings in manuscripts and early Church Fathers (**agrapha**).

30–70 c.e.:   Parables collections; miracle collections; controversy collections; *testimonia* (scriptural proof collections); Passion stories.

50–60 c.e.:   (**Gallio Inscription**): Paul writes 1 Thessalonians; 1 Corinthians and (the collection of letters that is now) 2 Corinthians; Philippians; Philemon; Galatians; and Romans probably in that order, although we cannot be sure of the place in the order of the individual elements in 2 Corinthians and Philippians. Paul's undisputed letters are the earliest New Testament writings to survive intact.

50–70 c.e.:   The **Q** source; perhaps the *Gospel of Thomas.* Except for Paul, **Q,** and *Thomas,* all traditions and books in the Jesus Movement come after the fall of Jerusalem to the Romans and the destruction of its temple in 70 c.e. **Special M** and **Special L.**

70–90 c.e.:   Pupils and followers of Paul write the earliest **deutero-Pauline** letters: 2 Thessalonians, Colossians, and Ephesians.

Unknown members of the Jesus Movement write what we now know as the gospels of Matthew, Mark, and Luke, the Acts of the Apostles, the Letter to the Hebrews, and perhaps the letter of James. Some scholars would add a few extracanonical gospels or their sources here.

90–100 c.e.:   The Gospel of John and the letters of John are produced most probably not by one individual but rather by persons who are members of a tightly knit group. Their names are unknown, but scholars often refer to them as "the Johannine School."

A church leader named John writes the Book of Revelation while in exile on the island of Patmos; it is usually dated more precisely in relation to fears of persecution in Asia Minor.

1 Peter, which reflects persecution, is probably from this period.

100–125 c.e.:   Leaders in various churches write the pseudonymous literature of the merging institutional church: the Pastorals, Jude, and 2 Peter.

To this period we may assign early extracanonical literature, the "**Apostolic Fathers.**" These include the *Didachē, 1 Clement, 2 Clement,* the letters of Ignatius of Antioch, the *Epistle of Barnabas,* and perhaps the letter of Polycarp *To the Philippians.*

You will observe that this outline covers the first century and the first third of the second century, roughly divided into *four stages of about equal length,* although there are some overlaps:

Stage 1: The period of the life of Jesus (4 b.c.e.–30 c.e.)

Stage 2: The period of early oral traditions, two written "gospels" (Q and *Thomas*), and the letters of Paul (30 c.e.–70 c.e.)

Stage 3: The period of the written gospels and several other books of the New Testament (70 c.e.–100 c.e.), although oral tradition continues

Stage 4: The period of the rest of the New Testament, although oral tradition continues (100–125 c.e.)

This general outline offers a way of proceeding through the rest of this textbook. Its bias is historical, social-historical, and social-scientific.

The life and teachings of Jesus (Stage 1) will be considered last (Chapter Fourteen). In the rest of this chapter, the second third of the century (Stage 2) will be examined, except for Paul. This is the period of early oral traditions, Q, and *Thomas*. In what follows, these traditions and sources will be considered more carefully. To set the stage, some groups and gatherings in which these materials may have circulated will be noted.

SOME EARLY GROUPS AND GATHERINGS
OF THE JESUS MOVEMENT

The Galilean Groups

If we critically sift the sources, it appears that the earliest groups of believers came from, or lived in, the towns and villages of Galilee and the city of Jerusalem.

The gospel sources claim that Jesus himself did not remain in Nazareth but rather settled in Capernaum, a village on the northwestern shore of the Sea of Galilee. At the same time, he seems always to have been on the move from village to village in the Galilean countryside and around the sea. His followers, the early "apostles," also moved about from village to village. Their lifestyle is suggested by a tradition of instructions that Jesus gave to them—take no money, no bread, no bag, no change of tunics (Matt. 10:9–10 = Luke 10:4; Mark 6:8–9; the accounts vary about whether they should take a walking staff and sandals). This tradition has several similarities to the lifestyle of wandering **Cynic** philosophers (who, however, stressed the bag, a sign of their self-sufficiency). Another important saying says that Jesus' recruits might have "nowhere to lay their heads" (Q 9:57–60). Some scholars have concluded from such traditions that Jesus and his immediate disciples *voluntarily* left their homes, families, possessions, work, and security and went from village to village proclaiming the good news of the Kingdom of God, prophesying, and working miracles. Other texts seem to confirm this when they report that although there was a certain distrust of outsiders and "false prophets," wandering prophets should be shown hospitality and social support. Was all this itinerancy *voluntary?* The texts as they now read make it appear so—Jesus *commands* his disciples to live this way. However, recent critics increasingly think that social, economic, and political pressures may have *forced* Jesus and his disciples into this lifestyle, and thus originally their mission may have been to bring not only words of hope and healing, but also social reform for the peasantry. If so, the mission speech of voluntary poverty represents a slight but important revision of Jesus' program.

The writings of Paul, Acts, and the *Didachē* indicate that some early missionaries in the Jesus Movement spread the message about Jesus by moving from town to town and staying with folks in their homes. Families were important in the spread of the religion. However, villagers distrusted outsiders, and criteria emerged for distinguishing true apostles and prophets from the wandering frauds and swindlers. One tradition says that a true prophet does not stay more than one or two days, does not accept more food than will carry him to the next place, does not ask for money for himself (especially while prophesying in the Spirit, an altered state of consciousness). Also, he does not eat from a table he has "marked out" while in the Spirit (a table for the Lord's Supper?). Authentic prophets and teachers who want to settle down have the right to be supported, but a traveling artisan who settles down should work for his living (*Didachē* 10:7–13:7). These tensions between itinerants and householders may also be a development from a later time.

All of this shows members of the Jesus Movement negotiating problems about outsiders, recruitment, spiritual gifts, itinerant versus local leadership, and a growing tendency toward organization.

The Jerusalem Group

Paul's letters and Acts agree that some members of the Jesus Movement remained in Jerusalem, some awaiting the return of Jesus. Here they met in homes for meals and social occasions. Acts puts forward the picture that their poverty was not voluntary. Paul's letters speak of "the poor" at Jerusalem, indicating some level of poverty. Acts says that they shared their goods in common, a sort of ancient "voluntary communalism" (Acts 2:43–47), probably similar to that found at Qumran. Acts also says that initially Peter the Galilean fisherman assumed a leadership role in Jerusalem and reorganized "the Twelve" (1 Cor. 15:5; Acts 1:15–26).

Paul says that he went back to Jerusalem and met Peter and James the brother of Jesus (Gal. 1:19; cf. Mark 6:3). At a conference at Jerusalem some years later he mentions only Peter, James, and John (Gal. 2:1–10; cf. Acts 15:13). This raises the question: Did at least some of the disciples continue the mission to the Palestinians, as well as to **Diaspora** Israelites? Acts says that Philip went to Samaria (Acts 8) and the coast, later residing in a coastal city, Caesarea by the Sea (Acts 21:8). Peter went to the Palestinian town Lydda and the coastal cities Joppa and Caesarea; he also went to Antioch of Syria (Gal. 2:11) farther north. A late first-century source says that he was martyred at Rome (*1 Clement* 5:2–7). "People from James (Jesus' brother)" apparently remained in Jerusalem (Acts 21:18) and also visited Antioch (Gal. 2:11–12). Peter or his one of his followers may also have gone to Corinth (1 Cor. 1:12; 9:4). Certain portions of Paul's letters point to rival Israelite apostle-missionaries, with positions about Jesus very different from those of Paul (Gal. 2; 2 Cor. 10–13). Acts indicates that when the Hellenists were run out of Jerusalem (8:1) they went to Cyprus, Phoenicia, and Antioch (11:19). They are also credited with establishing the Jesus Movement at Antioch (11:19–26) and perhaps at places like Damascus as well (cf. 9:10–25).

Such memories of the Jesus Movement may have been preserved and interpreted by the people who lived and worked in all of these places; nonetheless, they indicate a movement gradually spread by apostle-missionaries.

Communal Gatherings

The ancients, like all peoples, gathered for social and religious occasions at people's houses. We gain impressions of such occasions in the Jesus Movement, some of which come from Israelite practices.

Meals

Gathering for meals was a widespread social practice in Hellenistic society in general and among Israelites in particular. Festive meals were held in all sorts of "voluntary associations" in the Greco-Roman world (trade guilds, artistic guilds, religious cults, burial societies, and the like). Such occasions normally had rather clear patterns of social etiquette such as procuring the banquet hall, sending out advance invitations, reclining at meal by social rank, and engaging in conversation. There were also meal customs in Israel, for example, the **Passover** meal, the gatherings of religious groups such as the Pharisees, and the "messianic banquet" of the Essenes. Israelite meals normally began and ended with a blessing. During the Essene meal, for example, "the priest" was said to utter "a blessing over the first portion of the bread and wine, and [stretch out] his hand over the bread first of all" (1QS 6:4–5).

A more specific social context for creative interpretation of teachings and stories, then, would have been meals in homes where believers gathered ("**house-churches**"). Acts idealizes this custom when it says, "Day by day, as they spent much time together in the temple, they broke bread at home [or from house to house] and ate their food with glad and generous hearts, praising God and having the goodwill of all the people" (2:46).

Elsewhere in the New Testament, meal traditions have survived and reflect religious and social relations. The various sources mention Jesus' meals with "tax collectors and sinners" (Mark 2:13–17; Q 7:24–35). The result was a charge by opponents that Jesus was "a glutton and a drunkard, a friend of tax collectors and sinners" (Q 7:34). This saying implies meal practices that included people who were judged by persons of strict religious observance and high status to be unclean and of lower status. Other sayings about meals in the Jesus tradition reinforce this perspective. "Blessed are you that hunger now, for you shall be satisfied" (Q 6:21a; *GTh* 69:2) implies poverty. "And I tell you, many will come from east and west and sit at table with Abraham, Isaac, and Jacob in the kingdom of heaven" (**Q** 13:29, according to Matt. 8:11) possibly points to an expectation for a "messianic banquet." Jesus' parable of the Dinner Party concludes by sending invitations to "street people" (Q 14:16b–23; *GTh* 64). It is certainly not accidental that members of the Jesus Movement preserved meal traditions that broke with the usual social ranking of the larger society!

A number of sayings and controversy dialogues also combat rigorous laws about pure and impure foods, as well as who could eat with whom (Mark 7; *GTh* 14:3). For example, Paul talks about "certain people from James" (Jesus' brother) who pressured Peter into adhering to stricter Israelite meal practices at Antioch (Gal. 2:11–14). Similarly, religious and social distinctions about Jesus' last meal created problems for Paul in the house-churches at Corinth (1 Cor. 11:17–34; 8; 10).

In short, gatherings of believers for meals that included people of various social strata would have been ideally suited for "table talk" of just the sort in which "inclusive" Jesus traditions were transmitted, interpreted, and enlarged and in which a variety of beliefs about Jesus himself flourished.

Worship in the Early Jesus Movement

Information about gatherings for worship in the very early churches is sparse and scattered. Letter writers quoted fragments of hymns, confessions, creeds, benedictions, and other elements from early liturgies. Paul says, "when you come together, each one has a hymn, a lesson, a revelation, a tongue, or an interpretation" (1 Cor. 14:26). A "hymn" in this passage is literally "a psalm"; it could mean an antiphonal chant, as existed in the Israelite synagogues, or some other kind of song (Col. 3:16; Eph. 5:19). "A lesson" (*didachē*) is a teaching, and it is likely that some teachings included "words of the Lord," as well as beliefs about Jesus' death and resurrection. "A revelation" (*apocalypsis*) probably refers to the spiritual gift of apocalyptic prophecy (1 Cor. 14). "A tongue" is what Paul calls a "spiritual gift," in this case an unintelligible guttural utterance by a person in an altered state of consciousness, or *glossolalia,* "speaking in tongues." Finally, "interpretation" refers to the gift of interpreting *glossolalia.* Paul emphasized that the apostle's main function was preaching.

Other spiritual gifts that might be associated with worship are utterances of wisdom, utterances of knowledge, faith, healing, other miracle working, and discernment of spirits (1 Cor. 12:8–11). In other contexts, Paul speaks of prayer (1 Cor. 14:13, 15). There are also various liturgical terms connected to early worship, for example, *'Abbā', 'Amēn,* and *Hosanna,* and the cry for the return of Jesus, *Maranatha,* "Our Lord, come!"

It is clear from all this that Israelite worship provided the main raw material for worship in the Jesus Movement. Hellenistic influences were also present, for example, banquet customs and spiritual phenomena.

The Lord's Supper

Form Critics can often isolate formal, liturgical traditions with some or all of the following indicators:

1. Interruptions of an author's general line of argument to make a point
2. Commonly used terms for transmitting traditions (for example, "received" and "handed on," technical terms for handing on tradition in an Israelite text, *Sayings of the Fathers* 1:1)
3. Introductory words, such as "that" or "who"
4. Poetic or hymnlike style
5. Basic ideas about Jesus *not* typical of the author
6. Terms and phrases *not* typical of the author

On the basis of such indicators, it is possible to spot what is probably the earliest tradition about Jesus' *words* at his last meal with the disciples:

> For I *received* from the Lord what I also *handed on* to you, *that* the Lord Jesus on the night when he was betrayed took a loaf of bread, and when he had given thanks, he broke it, and said, "This is my body that is for you. Do this in remembrance of me."

In the same way he took the cup also, *after supper,* saying, "This cup is the new covenant in my blood. Do this, as often as you drink it, in remembrance of me."
(1 Cor. 11:23–25)

Scholars judge that Jesus did not say all the words recorded here in precisely this form. The point here, however, is that Jesus' words were still being connected with a "supper" or everyday meal. Indeed, no special Passover meal or custom is clearly indicated. Further, some meal accounts elsewhere refer to "breaking of bread," which sounds like a common meal (Acts 20:7, 11; 2:42, 46; cf. Luke 24:30). In short, most Form Critics think that the Lord's Supper grew out of common everyday meals that would have included taking bread, giving thanks, eating a supper, and passing the cup (*Didachē* 9–10; 14:1–3; Acts 2:46). Paul's recommendation that the wealthy Corinthians first eat at home if they are hungry (1 Cor. 11:33–34) also suggests that the Corinthian meal was a common everyday meal. Indeed, Paul's recommendation probably contributed to separating a solemn and holy ritual practice (what became the "sacrament") from its original context, the everyday meal.

In the Gospel of John, Jesus' last meal was *not* a Passover meal. This seems to support the view that the Last Supper was not originally a Passover meal. In the synoptic gospels, however, Jesus' last meal was interpreted as a Passover meal (Mark 14:22–25 par.). This interpretation is also reflected by certain believers of Israelite origin in Asia Minor, the Quartodecimanians, who continued to celebrate Jesus' last meal on the very same night as the Israelite Passover, the date of which varied according to the lunar calendar.

Baptisms

Followers of Jesus would have passed on their traditions about what he said and did at other special occasions as well. Baptisms were a likely occasion. As far as we are aware, members of the Jesus Movement did not practice frequent ceremonial washings and ritual purifications like the Israelites. Rather, baptism was a *one-time* initiation rite derived from the practice of John the Baptist (Mark 1:2–11). Preliminary instruction probably preceded it, and whole families and extended families were often baptized together. Baptism was also a rite of inclusion, which is reflected in a baptismal formula that says that "in Christ Jesus" there should be no distinction between Israelite and Greek, male and female, slave and free (Gal. 3:28). At the same time, there was undoubtedly an emphasis on a new kind of life, a separation from worldly values, norms, and practices. This was symbolized by the act of removing one's old clothing and putting on new clothing at the time of baptism, symbolizing dying and rising with Christ to a new life (Rom. 6). These baptismal rituals reinforced the critique of social and ethnic exclusion in some groups of Christ believers.

Other Early Gatherings in the Jesus Movement

There must have been many other occasions for gatherings of followers of Jesus. Israelite believers would have come together for the naming of children and circumcisions. We know a little about wedding customs from the parable of the

Ten Bridesmaids (Matt. 25:1–13), the wedding at Cana (John 2), and the fact that "mixed marriages" between believers and nonbelievers were a controversial issue (1 Cor. 7). Anointing the sick with oil (James 5:14), death, contact with corpses (Luke 10:31–32), preparation of bodies and embalming (Mark 16:1), burial (Mark 15:42–47), cemeteries, tombs, burial inscriptions, mourning, memorial meals, re-burial practices, beliefs about the afterlife, and the like were immensely important in antiquity. Indeed, there were voluntary associations in Greco-Roman society that included the practice of burial of members. We have almost no information about early funeral practices and rituals in the Jesus Movement apart from the Passion Story of Jesus (Mark 15:42–16:2) and Paul's mysterious statement about "baptism for the dead" (1 Cor. 15:29). Certainly, there was concern about the departed dead in connection with hopes for an imminent return of Jesus (1 Thess. 4:13–5:11). We may speculate that members of the Jesus Movement gathered for such occasions, followed local customs, had meals, and discussed matters related to sayings of Jesus about marriage, life, and death.

Summarizing, we have attempted to be more specific about some of the groups in which the sayings, stories, practices, and beliefs of the early followers of Jesus were transmitted. We have singled out missions and meals, key ritual contexts such as the Lord's Supper and baptism, and other social and religious settings such as weddings and funerals. We now turn to some of the main teachings passed on in these groups.

WISDOM, PROPHECY, AND APOCALYPTIC IN THE JESUS MOVEMENT

In Chapter One we noted two orientations to Israelite wisdom: the Wisdom myth and practical wisdom sayings. In this section, the focus will be on the latter type, wisdom sayings, although they will be of a special kind. We also indicated that prophecy was revitalized in the Jesus Movement. Finally, we noted that apocalypses were produced in Israel and in the Jesus Movement from about 250 B.C.E. to 250 C.E. and that apocalyptic groups and apocalyptic movements were common contexts for millennial reflection and action. We shall now explore these three areas using the hypothetical Q document and the *Gospel of Thomas* as our basis for discussion.

The Q Source

The **Two-Source Theory** requires that the non-Markan passages in Matthew and Luke that have the same or very similar wording come from a lost source, or **Q.** Q scholars contend that the 235-plus verses in Q come from the first generation of believers and that Q was preserved in Galilee (or perhaps nearby southern Syria) in a "Q community." It was anonymously put into writing at least by the second generation of the Jesus Movement, 50–70 C.E. (A complete list of Q passages and the forms of the Q sayings is found in **Appendix One.**)

Again, there were basically two kinds of Jesus material circulating as oral traditions: *sayings* of Jesus and *narratives* about Jesus. Q has only two major narratives:

the temptation of Jesus story (Q 4:1–13) and a miracle story (Q 7:1–10). Although some anecdotes take on a narrative quality, the rest of the passages are in the form of *sayings,* almost all spoken by Jesus (a few sayings are spoken by John the Baptizer). Thus, Q apparently contained no **Passion Story,** so important for the four *narrative* gospels.

This Q collection of sayings has no clear chronological references, although its story of the temptation of Jesus (Q 4:7–8) hints at the desire of Gaius Caligula (37–41 C.E.) to be worshipped as a god (Theissen). There is also no neat order to the collection, although there is some evidence of clustering around themes (Kloppenborg). Analogies to such sayings collections have been sought in Old Testament collections of prophetic sayings and wisdom sayings, in Israelite wisdom collections, and in early sayings collections such as the *Didachē* and the *Gospel of Thomas.* All this suggests that there were members of the Jesus Movement interested in collecting Jesus' sayings as *the words of a sage or wise man.* Thus the *form* of Q, which some scholars call a "sayings gospel," is important for attempting to understand its significance and function.

Some recent scholars of Q emphasize that it contains two types of sayings material—wisdom and apocalyptic—and that these two types tend to fall into alternating clusters. In other words, wisdom about how to live alternates with apocalyptic judgment, especially against "this generation." While this division is debated, these same scholars try to theorize about which is earlier. Look first at the "wisdom speeches." These speeches contain practical wisdom sayings, beatitudes ("Blessed are . . ."), exhortations ("Do thus and so . . ."), and some oracles (visionary utterances). With regard to *content,* the wisdom material has a strong stress on poverty, for example, "Blessed are you who are poor" (Q 6:20b). It appears that some Q missionaries not only were poor but also took on poverty voluntarily to identify with the poor (Q 10:4; 12:13–14). It is God who provides for life's necessities (Q 11:3, 9–13; 12:22b–31).

Another ethical ideal in Q is "turning the other cheek" (Q 6:29), or what we would call nonviolence. Thus discipleship requires radical commitment (Q 13:24). It is based on forgiveness and mercy, as God forgives and extends mercy (Q 6:27–29, 32–38). Radical commitment may include rejecting family (Q 9:57–60; 14:26) and being prepared for poverty and homelessness—even martyrdom (9:57–58; 16:13). Some sayings stress that Jesus is the Son of Man *already in the present.* An example is this saying about homelessness: "Foxes have holes, and birds of the sky have nests; but the Son of Man has nowhere to lay his head" (Q 9:58).

In Q parables, we discover that a tree is known by its fruit (Q 6:43–44) and that it is important to build one's house on a rock (Q 6:46–49). Again, these teachings reflect "following," "coming to," or "listening to" Jesus (Q 6:40; 9:57–62; 14:26–27). There is little sympathy for Gentiles in this stratum (6:33, 12:30), despite some looseness about food laws (10:8).

Apocalyptic, the second main type of material in Q, consists of "apocalyptic speeches." Typical *forms* in Q are prophetic judgment sayings and apocalyptic words (Q 3:7b–9, 16–17; 17:34–35) and sayings that warn or threaten those who fail to respond to the message of the Kingdom of God. With regard to *content,* what dominates is judgment of "this generation" that is, judgment of those who fail to respond to John the Baptist, Jesus, and the Q missionaries (7:31–35; 11:16, 29–32; 12:57–59). Thus "this generation" is blind, stubborn, a "brood of vipers" (3:7); it follows Satan; it is an "evil generation" (7:31–34; 11:29). The Kingdom of God is dawning (Q 6:20b; 9:62; 10:9; 11:2; for further discussion, see Chapter Fourteen), and it will be accompanied by violence. Judgment will be soon (3:9, 17; 11:51b; 12:51–53, 54–56), and the *parousia* of the Son of Man will be universal, visible, sudden, and without warning (12:39–40; 17:23–24, 26–30, 34–35, 37b). There will be forgiveness for the insiders (e.g., 17:3b–4) and (in this stratum) openness to the Gentiles (7:1–10), all the more proof of judgment on Israel. A number of scholars argue that ecstatic prophets in the Jesus Movement spoke many of the apocalyptic sayings attributed to Jesus, for example, Son of Man sayings.

Some recent Q experts have concluded from the two major orientations in Q that the two different strata represent *redactional layers.* One position is that the earliest layer was apocalyptic prophecy. This view has often been connected to a widespread interpretation that the historical Jesus was an "eschatological prophet." Others hold that the wisdom layer was earlier. They argue that this wisdom is not *traditional* wisdom, which tends to support cultural values, but rather "subversive wisdom," which tends to challenge them. Some conclude that this early wisdom layer helps to prove that the historical Jesus was primarily a sage. Clearly analysis of Q by Redaction Critics has had an effect on scholars' views of Jesus (again, see Chapter Fourteen). Whatever view one takes on the stratification and sequence of strata, Q as it now exists is dominated by *apocalyptic,* especially the return of Jesus from heaven as Son of Man with power to execute the final judgment (Q 12:8–9). In characteristic fashion, eschatological hopes in a time of alienation drew on prophetic and apocalyptic ideas and images from the other apocalyptic and prophetic literature. It seems likely that the developing Q community was led, at least in part, by Spirit-filled, eschatological prophets who spoke for the now departed, but soon to return, Jesus.

Representative samples will illustrate some of these themes. A wisdom oracle that condemned Jerusalem stresses the persecution of prophets:

> Jerusalem, Jerusalem, the city that kills the prophets and stones those who are sent to it! How often have I desired to gather your children together as a hen gathers her brood under her wings, and you were not willing! See, your house is left to you. And I tell you, you will not see me until the time comes when you say, "Blessed is the one who comes in the name of the Lord."
>
> (Q 13:34–35)

A woe that preserved wisdom-like teaching, but comes from the apocalyptic stratum, condemned the Israelite "fathers" and "this generation" in an environment of persecution:

> Woe to you! For you build the tombs of the prophets whom your ancestors killed. So you are witnesses and approve of the deeds of your ancestors; for they killed them, and you build their tombs. Therefore also the Wisdom of God said, "I will send them prophets and apostles, some of whom they will kill and persecute," so that this generation may be charged with the blood of all the prophets shed since the foundation of the world, from the blood of Abel to the blood of Zechariah, who perished

between the altar and the sanctuary. Yes, I tell you, it shall be charged against this generation.

(Q 11:47–51)

Similar condemnations were especially directed at the Pharisees, who were leaders of "this generation":

But woe to you Pharisees! For you tithe mint and rue and herbs of all kinds, and neglect justice and the love of God; it is these you ought to have practiced, without neglecting the others.

(Q 11:42)

The beatitudes (Q 6:20–23) hint at the social class of some members of the Q community when they affirm that human values will be reversed. The poor, the hungry, those who weep—all will be vindicated in the forthcoming Kingdom, and those who will yet be hated on account of the Son of Man will be happy. "In that day" there will be great reward, especially for those who love their enemies (Q 6:35). Attachment to riches is also problematic because one cannot serve God and money (Q 16:13). In short, the loving and well-grounded disciple, although perhaps poor and hungry, although persecuted, although hated because of the Son of Man, will receive a reward in the coming Kingdom.

Discipleship, then, is no easy task. Unlike the animals and birds, the Son of Man had no permanent home (Q 9:57); followers cannot stop even to bury the dead (Q 9:60). Disciples may be sent out like lambs in the midst of wolves, living off those who will take them in, healing the sick (Q 10:2–20) as Jesus healed (Q 7:22) and exorcising the demons (Q 11:20) as Jesus did. In line with the prophetic precedent (1 Kings 19:19–21), the true disciple of the Kingdom should not even go back and say goodbye to his family (Q 9:62); in fact, following Jesus is bound to lead to family divisions (12:51–53). The most extreme form of this tradition is:

Whoever comes to me and does not hate father and mother, wife and children, brothers and sisters, yes, and even life itself, cannot be my disciple.

(Q 14:26)

In short, Q is primarily a collection of sayings and discourses, almost exclusively attributed to Jesus. It is not a narrative "gospel" because it lacks notations of time and place and a Passion Story. Its focus is not on the suffering, death, and resurrection of Jesus, but rather on his ethical teaching and on his imminent return as apocalyptic Son of Man who will bring salvation to his true followers, the elect. Judgment on this evil generation and its leaders, who most certainly include the Pharisees, is included. Jesus is apparently God's wisdom in the sense that he inspires prophets who speak in his behalf and who, like himself, give wise teachings to sustain the community until he returns. Hence, Q has a special interest in prophets and prophetic forms as well as wisdom and wisdom forms. Such teachings, which are often exhortations of a practical sort, sustain the apocalyptic community, perhaps composed of the poor and disinherited. The disciples of Jesus are persecuted now, but they expect their reward in the future. They may, like the earthly Son of Man, have no real home. But they are sustained by a morality strongly rooted in love, even love of enemies; moreover, they have a mission to Gentiles and, like Jesus, are expected to heal.

If one attempts to describe the social context of Galilean Israelites in the Jesus Movement, Q provides much information. Generally, the community seems to be composed of poor peasants. We may imagine that the prophets of the Q community, although they had a home base in Capernaum, went from village to village. Perhaps under economic and political pressure, they did not maintain the usual family ties and did not seek wealth and security. Yet, there were also local leaders and many sympathetic disciples in the villages. In this case, one might think of related, networked communities. In them, the model for the one who is alienated is the alienated Son of Man, while the hope of the one who is alienated is the hope for the Son of Man who will come as judge and savior.

PARABLES AND PARABLE COLLECTIONS

Mark 4 contains a parable collection with an allegory. C. H. Dodd has offered a classic definition of **parable** that will serve as a starting point for discussion:

> At its simplest the parable is a metaphor or simile drawn from nature or common life, arresting the hearer by its vividness or strangeness, and leaving the mind in sufficient doubt about its precise application to tease it into active thought.
> (*The Parables of the Kingdom*, p. 5)

The definition refers to two figures of speech: metaphor and simile. A **metaphor** is a comparison of two kinds of reality that literally are quite different but figuratively make a point. New metaphors shock the imagination and "tease the mind into active thought" ("he's a racecar with no motor!"). Literary theorists say that metaphors create a kind of participation in that to which they refer; they "draw you in." A **simile** is a figure of speech that contains the comparison word *like* or *as* ("You have a memory *like* an elephant").

Parables expand these figures of speech into very short stories. They are secular, not religious narratives like myths. Yet, they can have religious figures in them ("a priest passed by . . ."). They mainly speak about everyday persons, places, and things ("nature": seeds, bushes, trees; "common life": farmers, fishermen, merchants, women baking bread). Nevertheless, they are *imaginary*—we would say "fictional"—not real persons. They *point beyond themselves to a reality that is very difficult to describe.*

Another dimension of parables is that they are subtle and often paradoxical. They *engage* the hearer (or reader). They are like a good play or film whose story provokes discussion or disagreement. They share this quality with their shorter companions, the **aphorisms.** Scholars usually contrast **parables** and **allegories.** Parables tend to have one central focus; allegories intentionally exploit many points of comparison, *each* of which refers to some hidden meaning, a meaning outside the narrative. To understand allegories, the hearer or reader must know what each of the persons, places, or things in the story symbolizes; one must have the keys that will unlock their mysterious meanings. Such symbolic interpretations tend to get passed on from allegory to allegory. It is possible to compose allegories from scratch (*Pilgrim's Progress*), but it is also possible to interpret nonallegorical narratives— myths, for example—as allegories. By this means one can give them "deeper" symbolic meanings. For example, characters in ancient Greek myths could be interpreted as symbolizing virtues or vices, such as love, justice, hate, and the like. Philo of Alexandria interpreted complex biblical epics allegorically. Similarly, Jesus' followers often interpreted his subtle, mind-teasing parables allegorically in order to use them as teaching about moral truths.

Modern scholars generally agree that Jesus' most original utterances can be found in his parables, which were spoken in Aramaic, mainly to challenge opponents. However, in oral and written transmission their meanings changed. They were translated into Greek and were affected by other, especially Greco-Roman, environments. Adding scripture and folk-story themes embellished them. They were given generalizing conclusions with universal, not specific, meanings. Most of all, they were understood as allegories with moral applications, mainly answers for concrete problems such as ethical matters and the fact that Jesus the Messiah had not returned to finish what he had started ("the delay of the *parousia*"). Changes also came when they were grouped in collections with particular themes and author-created settings in the gospels.

This discussion is fairly abstract. It can be illustrated from the gospels with the Sower/Seed cluster in Mark 4. Here is the outline of the key verses and their parallels in the *Gospel of Thomas*.

4:2b–8	The Parable of the Sower	*GTh* 9
4:14–20	**Allegory explaining the Sower**	————
4:26–29	The Parable of the Seed Growing Secretly	*GTh* 21:4
4:30–32	The Parable of the Mustard Seed	*GTh* 20

This list shows that *Thomas* preserves the three parables *separately*—they are *not* in a cluster—and there is *no allegorical interpretation*. It adds strong weight to the hypothesis that the parables in Mark 4 once circulated separately, that one was later interpreted allegorically, that they were collected into a cluster still later, and then finally incorporated into Mark.

A second point to observe is that the Sower parable occurs in *four different versions*: Matthew, Mark, Luke, and *Thomas*. Let us compare *two* of them, Mark and *Thomas*:

Mark 4:3–8

"Listen! A sower went out to sow. And as he sowed, some seed fell on the path, and the birds came and ate it up. Other seed fell on rocky ground, where it did not have much soil, and it sprang up quickly, since it had no depth of soil. And when the sun rose, it

GTh 9

"Behold, the sower went out, took a handful (of seeds), and scattered them. Some fell on the road; the birds came and gathered them up. Others fell on the rock, did not take root in the soil, and did not produce ears.

was scorched; and since it had no root, it withered away. Other seed fell among thorns, and the thorns grew up and choked it, and it yielded no grain. Other seed fell into good soil and brought forth grain, growing up and increasing and yielding thirty and sixty and a hundredfold."

And others fell on the thorns; they choked the seed(s), and worms ate them. And others fell on the good earth and it produced good fruit; it bore sixty per measure and a hundred and twenty per measure."

We can see that the Markan version is repetitious ("not much soil . . . no depth of soil . . . was scorched . . . no root"). The shorter and more compact version in *Thomas* is probably earlier and adds "the worms ate them." Matthew mostly follows Mark. However, the Lukan Gospel also has a shorter version, more like that of *Thomas.* By comparing the four versions, the scholar hypothesizes that the Luke/ *Thomas* version is probably closer to what Jesus said and that the author of the Mark/Matthew version offers some *embellishing touches.* Why? A hint of the solution emerges by interpreting first the parable and then the allegory.

The original parable stressed a rather general point: the mystery that although many rejected Jesus' teaching (the Kingdom of God), some unexpectedly accepted it. Jesus may have told his parable to illustrate his own failures and successes as parable teller. If so, the original parable illustrated the challenge of telling parables by a parable teller! The allegorical interpretation that follows in the gospels of Mark, Matthew, and Luke (4:14–20 par.), but that is absent in *Thomas,* spells this out in much greater detail, with secret, deeper meanings:

Sower	= speaker of the word
Seed	= word, with potential to "take root" and "bear fruit"
Path	= hearers who are susceptible of evil
Birds	= Satan (evil) who takes away the word sown in them
Rocky ground	= hearers who do not have "root in themselves" and fall away when tribulation or persecution comes
Thorns	= hearers who are consumed with secular matters, wealth, and materialism, which choke the word so it cannot bear fruit
Good soil	= hearers who accept the word and bear fruit

The technical language on the left is nothing like Jesus' language elsewhere (or the language of the Markan writer) but rather is much like that of some other writers in the early churches. Scholars have concluded that Jesus spoke the parable, but the allegory was a later interpretation designed to offer moral teaching in the early church. The "word" is preaching, but Satan is at work; when persecution comes, some fall away, others are caught up in materialism that chokes the word, but others accept it and "bear fruit." In short, the allegory details the various kinds of soils, which are the various kinds of people who heard the gospel in the churches. We can see clearly the *moral embellishments* or repetitions in Markan parable: They *em-*

phasize that hearers/readers (members of the Jesus Movement) are too concerned with tribulation and persecution or wealth and materialism to truly "hear" and respond to Jesus' message. Yet, although most people rejected it, some mysteriously accepted it!

It would be possible to offer a similar analysis of the other two parables in the cluster; however, enough has been said to indicate that the parable is undergoing interpretation, first in the little elaborations of Mark/Matthew and then in the allegory. Let us proceed, then, to make some generalizations. Reference to the three Seed parables *separately* in the *Gospel of Thomas* adds weight to the hypothesis that the parables originally circulated independently and were only subsequently clustered together on the basis of the theme Sower/Seed. Perhaps the allegorical interpretation was also added at that time. In any case, the whole section points to the activity of interpreting and gathering together parables around a common theme.

First, the Sower, which originally pointed to Jesus' failures and successes in a general way, has received elaboration in the repetitions of the soil on rocky ground, which emphasis anticipates the tribulation and persecution allegorical interpretation.

Second, some of the parables have been combined with aphorisms, received additions from scripture, and accrued apocalyptic interpretations.

Third, the allegorical interpretation is much more precise in relation to the various responses. It has an ideology of the "word" and Satan and includes attitudes toward the world, materialism, and the like.

Fourth, the allegory stresses conflict and persecution in the congregations of the Jesus Movement, which has affected Mark's version of the parable itself.

The allegorical interpretation continued to have an effect on the section in Matthew and Luke: The emphasis on the four types of soils (hearers) is stronger and has blunted the contrast between the bad and good seeds in Mark. The second parable in the cluster, the Seed Growing Secretly, seems to have recommended patience, has become an apocalyptic lesson. Similarly, the third parable, the Mustard Seed, stresses that the tiny seed becomes a great shrub and has received apocalyptic embellishments from scripture (Ezek. 17:23; Dan. 4:10). Probably the cluster as a whole was intended to instruct believers about the failures and successes of the mission, as well as patience until the return of Jesus.

ANECDOTES

A number of Jesus' witty, figurative, or argumentative sayings seem to have generated brief narratives that provided them with a living context; others seem to have been connected with a brief story context from the beginning. Sometimes the climax to such stories was an action of Jesus, such as a controversial healing, or a saying plus an action. These "pronouncement stories" or "**anecdotes**" had several functions. They could offer a teaching in response to a question by friend, neutral listener, or foe; illustrate a conflict about the Torah or early church teaching or practice; or simply give a "biographical" snapshot of some event in Jesus' life. Although some of the individual sayings in the anecdotes may actually have gone back to Jesus, the narrative stories in which they are placed are usually scenes that are *typical* of what happened in Jesus' life, whether they happened *precisely* that way or not. In general, the anecdotal settings were formed in the communities. Consider the following anecdote collection.

Mark	Passage	Form
2:1–12	**The Healing of the Paralytic**	**Miracle/conflict anecdote**
2:13–14	Call of Levi	Biographical anecdote
2:15–17	**Tax Collectors and Sinners**	**Conflict anecdote**
2:18–20	**Question of Fasting**	**Teaching/conflict anecdote**
2:21–22	Old and New	Aphorisms
2:23–28	**Disciples Pluck Grain on Sabbath**	**Conflict anecdote**
3:1–6	**Sabbath Healing**	**Conflict anecdote**

The first story is a miracle story into which is inserted a conflict anecdote. The anecdote stresses the point about the ability of the Son of Man (in this context, Jesus) to forgive sins like God forgives sins (2:5b–10). The second story is Jesus' call of Levi sitting at the tollgate. It stresses Jesus' authority ("Follow me!"). It sets the stage for the third conflict anecdote, a controversy about Jesus' eating with tax collectors and sinners, which emphasizes the saying, "Those who are well have no need of a physician, but those who are sick. I have come to call not the righteous but sinners" (2:17). In the fourth, a question about fasting by John's disciples and the Pharisees evokes Jesus' reply that the wedding guests will fast when the bridegroom is taken away. The saying reflects a context when Jesus, the bridegroom, is no longer alive. Aphorisms about the old not being able to contain the new (patch; wineskins) follow. Then come two conflict anecdotes. The first tells about the disciples' plucking grain on the Sabbath, which went against the Sabbath Law; it concludes with the punch line, "The Son of Man is Lord also of the Sabbath" (2:28). In the last conflict anecdote, Jesus heals a man with the withered hand on the Sabbath, provoking a controversy in which Jesus asks whether it is lawful to heal on the Sabbath.

This section by its connecting links forms a unity. The section turns on conflict and has a climax in 3:6: "The Pharisees went out and immediately conspired with the Herodians against him, how to destroy him." Clearly, the hand of the Markan author is present. Yet, at least part of the collection may have predated Mark. One possibility is represented by the boldface stories in the list. That these anecdotes go back to early Palestinian groups is suggested by the *issues* of the conflict: Israelite Sabbath, fasting, and meal practices. A solution to these conflicts is attempted by appealing to the sayings or practice precedent of Jesus.

A second anecdote collection comes from Mark 12.

Mark	Passage	Form
12:13–17	Taxes to Caesar	Conflict anecdote
12:18–27	The Resurrection	Conflict anecdote

| 12:28–34 | The Greatest Commandment | Teaching anecdote |
| 12:35–37 | The Son of David Question | Conflict anecdote |

The present location of these four stories is the Jerusalem temple precincts. In the first story, Pharisees and Herodians attempt to trap Jesus by asking whether taxes should be paid to Rome. After examining a coin with Caesar's image on it, Jesus says, "Give to the emperor the things that are the emperor's, and to God the things that are God's." The second anecdote, a question about the resurrection, is another trap, this one set by the Sadducees who do not believe in the resurrection. Again Jesus eludes the opponents. Third, the question of the scribe about the First Commandment is more neutral in Mark, but Matthew and Luke have made it into a conflict anecdote by omitting the praise of the scribe (Matt. 22:34–40; Luke 10:25–28). Finally, Jesus himself poses a question about how the scribes can say that the Messiah is the Son of David, thereby implying that the title, or at least the usual meaning of the title, is insufficient.

These anecdotes also form a unit in the synoptic gospels, but it is possible that they were already clustered in the pre-Markan tradition. It was typical for four types of question to be raised to the rabbinic teacher, and these questions correspond to those rabbinic types.

We have hardly mentioned "biographical" anecdotes. Examples would be stories about Jesus' birth, family, youth, baptism, and rejection at Nazareth, conflict with Herod, and the cleansing of the temple.

EARLY MIRACLE STORIES AND MIRACLE COLLECTIONS

Miracles were considered to be unusual, but not unique, in the ancient world. In the Hebrew Bible, miracle stories were recorded about Moses and the prophets Elijah and Elisha. In Israelite texts of the New Testament period, Moses, Solomon, and others took on the aura of magicians and miracle workers. Fascinating miracle stories were told about the famous Galilean holy men, Honi the Circle Drawer and Hanina ben Dosa. In the larger Hellenistic world, where Israelites were characterized by Gentiles as magicians, miracle stories about the so-called heroes and heroines—physicians, philosophers, political leaders, generals, athletes, and the like— were told to demonstrate their powers. Jesus of Nazareth was also remembered as a miracle worker. Stories of his exorcisms, healings, miraculous feedings, resuscitations from the dead, and control over nature were told not only to entertain, but also to demonstrate his divine power.

Members of the Jesus Movement interested in propagating the movement no doubt collected miracle stories. Scholars have isolated two major pregospel collections: one behind the Gospel of Mark, the other behind the Gospel of John. In Mark 4:35–8:26 there are ten miracles. Perhaps the Markan author rearranged two of them—the Woman with a Hemorrhage (5:24–34) and the Blind Man of Bethsaida (8:22–26). By placing them back in their original sequence, one arrives at two

Table 3.4   The "Signs Source"

Unit	Passage
The Opening	
John's Testimony	1:6–7, 19–23, 26b–27, [33d], 29–34
First Disciples Find the Messiah	1:35, 37, (38a), 38b, 39–42, 43b–47, 49
The Signs of Jesus: Galilee	
1. Water to Wine (Cana)	2:1–3a, 5b–11a, (11b[himself]), 11c
2. The Official's Son Restored to Life	2:12a; :46b, (47), 49b, 50ac, 51–52, (53), 54
3. The Catch of Fish	21:(1), 2–4, 6–7, 8b, 11, 14
4. Feeding the Multitude and Walking on the Lake	6:1, (3), 5, 7–11, (12–13a), 13b–14, 15c, 17–20, 21b, (22, 25)
The Signs of Jesus: Jerusalem	
5. Lazarus Resuscitated from Death	11:1, 2c–3, 7, 11, 15c, 17, 32–34, 38–39a, 41, 43b–45
6. A Blind Man Sees	9:1, 6–7, (8)
7. A Crippled Man Walks	5:2–3, 5–9

miracle collections that have a parallel sequence and are virtually parallel in content (Achtemeier):

	Mark 4:35–6:44	Mark 6:45–8:26
1. Nature (Sea) Miracle	4:35–41 Stilling of the Storm	6:45–51 Jesus Walks on the Sea
2. Healing (or Exorcism)	5:1–20 Gerasene Demoniac	*8:22–26 Blind Man of Bethsaida*
3. Healing	*5:25–34 Woman with a Hemorrhage*	7:24b–30 Syrophoenician Woman
4. Healing (Resuscitation?)	5:21–23, 35–43 Jairus' Daughter	7:32–37 Deaf Mute
5. Feeding Miracle	6:34–44, 53 Feeding of 5,000	8:1–10 Feeding of 4,000

Although this particular order-plus-content has not turned up in any other known miracle collection, it is worth noting that Moses was said to have performed a sea miracle and a feeding (Exod. 13–17)—the types that begin and end both these "cycles." In any case, the collection displays Jesus' divine power. Because the climactic feeding stories are clear reminiscences of the breaking of bread (cf. Mark 6:41, 8:6 with Mark 14:22, 1 Cor. 11:24), Jesus' meals may have been the context in which the stories were told.

A similar type of group may have collected the miracles ("signs") behind the Gospel of John, the so-called Signs Source. It includes an opening unit about John the Baptist and the first disciples. Then come seven signs ("seven" is a number of completeness). The source can be rearranged to fit a chronological-geographical order from Galilee to Jerusalem (Fortna). (See Table 3.4.)

These two possible miracle sources behind the gospels of Mark and John, who share a few stories (Mark 6:33–52; John 6:1–21; 11:1–57), suggest that there were members of the Jesus Movement who collected stories about Jesus as a powerful miracle-working holy man in the way that some Israelites looked at Solomon, Moses, Honi, or Hanina ben Dosa. Believers of Hellenistic background would have transferred to these stories motifs about Hellenistic heroes or heroines. In other words, miracle stories evolved and increasingly *demonstrated Jesus' authority and power.* This was very important because the Jesus Movement was relatively without authority and power. But not everyone agreed about this importance. A group of missionaries who challenged the Apostle Paul's authority at Corinth (2 Cor. 3:7–8; 10–13) appears to have stressed Jesus' power in contrast to Paul's emphasis on humility ("weakness"). Moreover, most members of the Jesus Movement came to the conclusion that miracle collections, like sayings collections, were by themselves not sufficient to say who Jesus was. Thus they incorporated them into larger narratives that included Jesus' suffering, death, and resurrection.

A MILLENNIAL SPEECH:
THE "LITTLE APOCALYPSE" OF MARK 13

Millennial speeches detailing the events that will occur at the end are a feature of apocalyptic or millennial literature. The particular *form* of the millennial dreams and hopes held by the writer provided the overall pattern, but the actual *content* came from two sources: the sacred scriptures and the experience of the writer and his group. The scriptures themselves were used in two ways: direct quotation and allusion. Sometimes the writer wished to reinterpret an existing text; sometimes the writer made a connection *between* texts by association of ideas, words, or even the sounds of words (in the ancient world, a person normally read aloud, even when reading to oneself; see Acts 8:30). So a millennial speech was in the first place a mosaic of scriptural quotations and allusions.

However, millennial thinking did not arise in a vacuum; usually it emerged in millennial movements that experienced or at least feared social and economic oppression. Thus millennial speeches also contain references to the experiences of the writer and his group.

The apocalyptic discourses of the Jesus Movement vary from this general pattern by including ethical sections in which the writer exhorts his readers. An example is Mark 13 and its parallels (Matt. 24; Luke 21), which make up an apocalyptic speech attributed to Jesus. This "Little Apocalypse" has often been thought to be a revision of an earlier, perhaps Israelite, apocalyptic discourse. We now offer a sketch of Mark 13 following the analysis of Lars Hartman in *Prophecy Interpreted.*

13:1–5a: An *introduction* composed by the evangelist Mark to give the discourse its present setting on the Mount of Olives just outside Jerusalem. It includes Jesus' prophecy of the destruction of the temple.

13:5b–8: *The first section of the discourse proper.* This section combined with verses 21–23 warns about false prophets and false messiahs coming in Jesus' name. It gives signs of the beginning of the end. It quotes or alludes to many scriptural references, especially in the apocalyptic Book of Daniel.

13:9–13:   *The first exhortation section.*   It couches references to the actual and antici-pated sufferings of members of the Jesus Movement in language deliberately reminiscent of the sufferings of Jesus during his **Passion** but also alluding to various scriptural passages.

13:14–20:   *The second section of the discourse.*   It quotes and reinterprets Dan. 11:31 and 12:11, the **"Abomination That Makes Desolate"** (in Daniel this is the altar to Zeus set up in the Jerusalem temple by the Seleucids; in 2 Thess. 2:1–12 it might have referred to the emperor Caligula's attempt to set up his statue in the temple). Many modern commenta-tors suggest that Mark could have had in mind the events surrounding the defeat of Israel and the destruction of Jerusalem and the temple in 70 C.E., thus giving a clue as to the date of Mark. The command to "flee to the mountains" is a quote from Gen. 19:16, as is the command for the man in the field not to turn back in verse 16. In verse 19 the description of the tribulation quotes Dan. 12:1.

13:21–23:   *The second exhortation section.*   The reference to the false prophets uses language taken from Deut. 13:1–5, but the whole addresses itself to concrete problems faced by the churches in a period of intense apocalyptic expectation. It is often connected with 13:5b–7.

13:24–27:   *The third section of the discourse.* Here the quotations are frequent. Verse 24 quotes Joel 2:10 (the sun being darkened) and Isa. 13:10 (the moon not giving its light). Verse 25 has the stars falling and the powers of heaven being shaken (from Isa. 34:4). The Son of Man reference in verse 26 is from Dan. 7:13, and verse 27 is a mosaic of Deut. 30:3–4 and Zech. 2:10 (in the LXX version). There are allusions to Isa. 11:10–12, 27:13 and Dan. 7:14 at various places.

Verse 27 ends the apocalyptic discourse proper. The remaining verses 28–37 form a loose-knit, final section of ethical exhortation that does not contain a single scriptural quotation but does show a good deal of traditional material. It was almost certainly added to the original discourse by Mark himself.

What the precise form and original date of this discourse might have been is difficult to say, although scholars have often suspected that it was written in re-sponse to the crisis brought about by Gaius Caligula's attempt to set up his statue in the temple in 40 C.E. (e.g., Theissen). It is the nature of apocalyptic writers to interpret and reinterpret texts, even their own, so that any discourse text we have represents the version of it that came from the hand of the particular evange-list concerned.

A PRE-PASSION PASSION STORY?

In the long Passion Story about Jesus' last days in Jerusalem, the four canonical gospels have many common features. Overlaps between the synoptic gospels and John, a quite different gospel usually thought to be independent of the others, raise this question: Did a longer "**Passion Story** source" circulate in the early church prior to the writing of gospels?

Three answers have been given to this question. The first theory is that there was indeed a connected Passion Story in the *oral tradition* of the early church. Today this view is undergirded with the mention of names, places, and dates in the story, perhaps suggesting a tense time connected with the rule of Agrippa I

(37–44 C.E.), who had Jesus' disciple James put to death (Theissen; cf. Acts 12:2; Mark 10:35–45).

The second theory is not so concerned to isolate a pre-Markan Passion Story, but to show that there is a *literary* relationship between the Gospel of Mark and the Gospel of John. It is based on three observations. First, there are a few *exact* verbal parallels between the gospels of Mark and John in the Passion Story.

Mark	John	Words or Phrases
14:3	12:30	ointment of pure nard
14:5	12:5	300 denarii [*denarius* = a coin, about a day's wage]
14:54, 67	18:18, 25	Peter warming [*thermainomenos*] himself
14:54	18:15	Peter goes "into" the courtyard
15:14	19:15	the cry "crucify him" in the Greek imperative case
15:17	19:2, 5	the purple cloak
15:42	19:15	mention of the Day of Preparation

Second, the order of the Gospel of John is most distinctive where the Johannine author wants to develop his own point of view (18:4–9, 14; 18:28–19:16). Third, a special Markan literary technique is the placing of one account inside another ("sandwiching"; "**intercalation**"; see, for example, 3:20–35). The author of John appears to be following this Markan technique in the "trial" scene:

Mark	John	Intercalation
14:54	18:15–18	Peter's denial
14:55–65	18:19–24	"Trial"
14:66–72	18:25–27	Peter's denial

These three points have suggested that the author of *the Gospel of John had at some time read the Gospel of Mark* but preferred his own presentation. No pre-Markan Passion Story is necessary. Some scholars have tried to make a similar argument with the Passion Story in the gospels of *Luke* and John.

The third theory is that the synoptic gospels and the Gospel of John are indebted to a *written* Passion source rather than oral tradition. In one version of the theory, a Passion source was joined to the "Signs Source" (the miracle source) to make a narrative "Signs Gospel" (R. Fortna). The writer of the Gospel of John then used this source. A second version of the theory is that passages from a written "Cross Gospel" can be traced behind all four canonical gospels and the apocryphal *Gospel of Peter* discovered in 1886–1887, with fragments found in 1972 (J. D. Crossan).

JESUS' PASSION: SUFFERING, DEATH, AND RESURRECTION IN THE LIGHT OF SACRED TEXTS

Using the Form Critical principles for isolating sources, scholars have found what appears to be the earliest New Testament source about Jesus' death and resurrection. It is tucked away in Paul's letter 1 Corinthians:

> For I *handed on* to you as of first importance what in turn had *received,*
> that Christ died for our sins
>   in accordance with the scriptures, and
> that he was buried, and
> that he was raised on the third day
>   in accordance with the scriptures, and
> that he appeared to Cephas, then to the twelve.
>   (15:3–5)

Paul continues:

> Then he appeared to more than five hundred brothers and sisters [Greek: "broth-
> ers"] at one time, most of whom are still alive, though some have died. Then he ap-
> peared to James, then to all the apostles. Last of all, as to one untimely born, he ap-
> peared also to me. For I am the least of the apostles, unfit to be called an apostle,
> because I persecuted the church of God.
>   (15:6–9)

Scholars see in the four initial "*that* clauses" a traditional confession or creed quoted
by Paul. This judgment is supported not only by its formal qualities ("that . . ." and
the balanced lines) and Paul's tendency to quote such traditions, but also by the
terms "handed on" and "received," technical terms for handing on tradition in Israelite contexts, noted earlier in connection with the Last Supper (1 Cor. 11:23). It
is supported further by a number of terms and phrases not characteristic of Paul (the
plural "sins"; "according to the scriptures"; the Greek tense of "was raised"; "on the
third day" and its form in Greek; and "the Twelve"). Some scholars also argue that
these phrases contain "Semitisms," that is, Greek words that translate Hebrew or
Aramaic idioms. If so, the tradition might have gone back to very early Palestinian
Aramaic-speaking members of the Jesus Movement, perhaps even the Jerusalem
group where Cephas (Peter), the Twelve, James, and "all the apostles" who would
have remembered these events had authority. In any case, the creed was current in
the generation before Paul wrote 1 Corinthians (ca. 54 C.E.). We shall now consider
its emphasis on Jesus' death, resurrection, and earliest appearances.

Two of the four "*that* clauses," the death and resurrection clauses, have an extra
phrase, "according to the scriptures." Jesus' painful suffering and death by crucifixion, a punishment reserved primarily for political criminals, would have been
considered by most all people as a shameful event. Nonbelieving Israelites must
have responded by quoting scripture: "Cursed is everyone who hangs on a tree [=
a cross]" (Gal. 3:13). Thus members of the Jesus Movement had to develop interpretations of the crucifixion embarrassment "according to the scriptures."

One way to do that was to retell the stories about Jesus' Passion by using details
from the fourth "messianic" song about Yahweh's Suffering Servant (Isa. 52:13–
53:12). The song says, "He was despised and 'rejected' (from *exoudenō*) by men"
(Isa. 53:3). Mark 9:12 says that it is written of the Son of Man that he will suffer
many things and be "treated with contempt" (from *exoudenō*). The song also says
"His soul was 'delivered up' (from *paradidomi*) to death" (Isa. 53:12). On three
occasions the Gospel of Mark uses the verb "delivered up" (from *paradidomi*) as a

description of what happens when the Son of Man is betrayed (9:31; 10:33; 14:21). Although Markan redaction is present in all these passages, they also hint that reflection about the suffering and death of the Suffering Servant was one way to explain Jesus' dishonorable suffering and death.

Another way to explain the Passion by scripture was the use of the Psalms, regarded by Israelites of the first century as prophecies by David. Psalm 118 was important for Israelite worship (the so-called Hallel). Ps. 118:22 says that the "rejected" stone becomes the chief cornerstone. In the gospels this verse is quoted at the end of the allegory about the slaying of the vineyard owner's "beloved son," an indirect, but nonetheless clear, reference to Jesus, who is called "beloved son" by God in the baptism and transfiguration stories (Mark 1:11 par.; Mark 9:7 par.). Thus God's "beloved son" was the "rejected stone" who nonetheless became chief cornerstone.

The details of the betrayal, the agony in the Garden of Gethsemane, and most especially the crucifixion also show a great deal of reflection on the Psalms. The following list will illustrate some of the more prominent allusions (there are others), especially to what are often called the "Suffering Psalms," Pss. 22 and 69.

Mark	Psalm Reference (NRSV)
14:18: "one of you will betray me, one who is eating with me."	41:9: "Even my bosom friend in whom I trusted, who ate of my bread, has lifted the heel against me."
14:34: "I am deeply grieved, even to death."	42:6, 11; 43:5: "Why are you cast down, O my soul?"
15:23: And they offered him wine mixed with myrrh . . .	69:21: "They gave me poison for food, and for my thirst they gave me vinegar to drink."
15:24: they divided his clothes among them, casting lots to decide what each should take.	22:18: "they divide my clothes among themselves, and for my clothing they cast lots."
15:29: Those who passed by derided him, shaking their heads. . .	22:7; 109:25: "All who see me mock at me; they make mouths at me, they shake their heads"
15:34: "My God, my God, why have you forsaken me?"	22:1a: "My God, my God, why have you forsaken me?"
15:36: And someone ran, filled a sponge with sour wine, put it on a stick, and gave it to him to drink . . .	69:21: "They gave me poison for food, and for my thirst they gave me vinegar to drink."

The Jesus Movement was not alone in using sacred texts as prophecies to show that it was fulfilling them. Scribes at Qumran quoted passages of scripture and interrupted them by brief interpretations to show that the prophecies referred specifically to them. For example, they believed that the true messianic "Son of David"/ "Son of God" or "seed of David" of 2 Sam. 7:14 is also the messianic *Shoot* of David" (Jer. 23:5) or *Branch* of David which is fallen" (Amos 9:11) and that he was their royal Messiah, the Messiah of Israel. With a slightly different method, members of the Jesus Movement also used 2 Sam. 7:14, combined with others, as a prophecy about Jesus as the royal Messiah who will be raised from the dead. Rom. 1:3–4 contains one of those early pre-Pauline creeds about the "gospel concerning his [God's] son" Jesus:

> who was descended from David
> > according to the flesh
> and was declared to be Son of God with power
> > according to the spirit of holiness by resurrection from the dead.

This creed suggests the enthronement of the Davidic king as Son of God that is found in many places in the Hebrew scriptures. However, the Davidic king is Jesus, and the enthronement is in heaven (see also Luke 1:32; Acts 2; 13:16b–41). The crucified one is believed to be vindicated.

The third element in the pre-Pauline creed stresses appearances to Peter and "the Twelve," to which Paul adds five hundred brethren at one time (most of whom are still alive), James, "all the apostles," and finally himself. The term "appeared" here comes from the verb "to see." Paul does not describe these experiences, although he elsewhere claims to have seen "the Son" (Gal. 1:12, 15–16), and in Paul's "Damascus road conversion," described in Acts three times (Acts 9:1–19a; 22:6–16; 26:12–18), Paul is said to "see" a light from heaven and hear Jesus' voice. Similarly, in the gospels no description of Jesus' resurrection survives; rather, we have empty tomb stories, promise-of-appearance accounts, and appearance narratives, sometimes combined. On the one hand, these stories emphasize "spiritual" rather than physical elements, for example, seeing a spirit, forbidding touch, lack of recognition, and sudden appearances, usually behind closed doors. On the other hand, Jesus' resurrection is clearly described as "physical," especially in Luke and John. Thus appearance traditions played a much stronger role in belief about Jesus' resurrection than did the empty tomb. In some of the earliest traditions the honor of having "seen" Jesus first fell to Peter (1 Cor. 15:5; Luke 24:34), although in other traditions it fell to Mary Magdalene (John 29:14).

NEW TESTAMENT CHRISTOLOGICAL HYMNS

In the worship of the Jesus Movement hymns were sung or chanted. Christological hymns are isolated by Form Critics on the basis of critical principles noted earlier in connection with Jesus' last meal. They portray Jesus as a divine Christ-being who comes to earth and returns. They are called "**Christological hymns**" because in the early second century C.E., a Roman governor wrote that followers of Jesus were known to "recite a *hymn* antiphonally to Christ, as to a god" (for the full text, see the correspondence between Pliny, governor of Bithynia in northern Asia Minor, and the emperor Trajan, Chapter Twelve).

Philippians 2:6–11

Who, though he was in the form of God,
    did not regard equality with God
    as something to be exploited,
But emptied himself,
    taking the form of a slave,
    being born in human likeness.
And being found in human form,
    he humbled himself
    and became obedient to the point of death—even death on a cross.
Therefore God also highly exalted him
    and gave him the name
    that is above every name,
So that at the name of Jesus
    every knee should bend,
    in heaven and on earth and under the earth,
And every tongue should confess
    that Jesus Christ is Lord,
    to the glory of God the Father.

Colossians 1:15–20

He [Who] is the image of the invisible God, the first born of all creation;
for in him all things in heaven and on earth were created . . .
All things have been created through him and for him
He himself is before all things,
and in him all things hold together
He is the head of the body (the church).
Who is the beginning, the firstborn from the dead . . .
For in him all the fullness of God was pleased to dwell,
and through him God was pleased to reconcile to himself all things.

Hebrews 1:3

He (Who) is the reflection of God's glory
and the exact imprint of God's very being,
and he sustains all things by his powerful word.
When he had made purification for sins,
He sat down at the right hand of the Majesty on high,
Having become . . . superior to the angels . . .

These hymns portray the pattern of a redeemer who descends to the earth from a higher sphere, achieves his redemptive purpose on earth, and ascends again to the higher, heavenly sphere. It reflects the Wisdom myth (see Chapter One), and it occurs where the Jesus Movement has come in contact with Gentiles. The Q materials, early Johannine strata, and the Book of Acts show that Greeks were admitted to the Jesus Movement at a relatively early date.

SUMMARY

In this chapter we have attempted to look at the some of the earliest communities in the Jesus Movement apart from the Pauline communities, along with their beliefs and practices. Because our only history, the Book of Acts, is from a later time and presents a highly interpreted version of the story, we resorted to early oral traditions and sources critically reconstructed by modern scholars. Believers from these strata were primarily from the peasant social strata. They continued to meet in houses on special occasions, such as common meals and religious celebrations. At such times, the Jesus traditions were transmitted, supplemented, and interpreted.

Some of those traditions were sayings of Jesus or of prophets speaking in his name. These teachings gave guidance to the groups who preserved them. Typical were wisdom sayings, parables, and prophetic sayings, all of which became increasingly apocalyptic as the Jesus movements encountered opposition. Other traditions were narratives, such as miracle stories that demonstrated Jesus' power and anecdotes about his life and controversies. There were also traditions about his suffering, death, and resurrection as fulfillment of prophecy and stories about his last days in Jerusalem. Finally, we can see the emergence of Christological hymns that give him the highest possible evaluation as one descended from God.

Not all early members of the Jesus Movement accepted all of these traditions, however. Some of them were accepted by being incorporated in the canonical gospels. Others were rejected. One major figure had a totally different emphasis. That was the Apostle Paul, and to his life and thought we now turn.

STUDY QUESTIONS

1. How many books are in the New Testament, and what are the four main genres? Which genre dominates, and why is that significant? How do modern scholars evaluate Acts for history?

2. What is the difference between external evidence and internal evidence? How do scholars date the literature of the New Testament in order to establish some sort of chronology? Of what importance are the Delphi Inscription, the *Gospel of Thomas,* the Pauline School, the New Testament Apocrypha, and the Church Fathers for reconstructing this history?

3. What are some of the earliest written sources and oral traditions? What are some of the key social factors in the history of the early Jesus Movement? What are the major stages for the chronology of New Testament documents? What kinds of early practices in the Jesus movements fostered group activity?

4. What is the Q source, how is it isolated, and what are some of its major ideas? What kind of early group(s) in the Jesus Movement seem to have preserved Q? Can you

define and compose a simile, a metaphor, a parable, an allegory, an anecdote, and a miracle story? What is the Johannine "Signs Source"? What is probably the earliest death/resurrection account in the New Testament? Do you think that there once existed a Passion Story before it was incorporated into the gospels, and what was the role of the Psalms in telling the Passion Story?

5. What is the "Little Apocalypse," and what appears to be the context of the people to whom it gives hope and encouragement? What are Christological hymns, and what image of Jesus do they seem to stress?

Photo 4.1 The Apostle Paul as portrayed in a mosaic medallion in the Chapel of St. Andrew in the Archbishop's Palace, Ravenna, Italy. An imaginative description of Paul in the apocryphal *Acts of Paul (and Thecla)* (second century C.E.) reads: ". . . a man small of stature, with a bald head and crooked legs, in a good state of body, with eyebrows meeting and nose somewhat hooked, full of friendliness; for now he appeared like a man, and now he had the face of an angel" (W. Schneemelcher in E. Hennecke and W. Schneemelcher, *New Testament Aprocrypha,* trans. R. McL. Wilson, vol. 2, p. 354).

CHAPTER FOUR

PAUL: APOSTLE TO THE GENTILES

Paul is a major player in the Jesus Movement. In terms of the amount of material, Paul's letters—combined with those attributed to him—make up more than one-fourth of the New Testament. In addition, over one-half of the lengthy Acts of the Apostles (twenty-eight chapters) is given over to the life, journeys, and speeches of Paul.

In terms of ideas, Paul's letters offer one of the great foundations of later Christian theology. He inspired many of the church's most influential thinkers and reformers. Some of the most famous examples are St. Augustine of Hippo, St. Thomas Aquinas, Martin Luther, John Calvin, John Wesley, and more modern thinkers such as Swiss theologian Karl Barth. At the same time, some of his ideas are, as one New Testament writer says, "hard to understand" (2 Pet. 3:16), and they have often been, like Paul himself, the occasion of sharp controversy and division. In recent times, Paul has been accused of distorting Jesus' simple message, of laying the groundwork for Christian anti-Semitism, and of perpetuating chauvinistic attitudes about race, politics, sex, and gender! Yet, as one modern Jewish scholar put it, Paul was a genius. Thus an honest study of Paul and his letters can be not only exasperating, but also a challenge well worth the effort.

This chapter lays some groundwork for the study of Paul's letters. It evaluates the sources for his personality, life, and thought, especially his undisputed letters and the Acts of the Apostles. From this relative chronology for his career, a sketch of his life emerges, with special attention given to his personality, background, "conversion" to the Jesus Movement, deep conviction that he is an apostle ("call"), and mission. Finally, it will be important to take up Paul's authority in relation to the church at Jerusalem and in the churches he established, taking into account his opponents and his general social world.

SOURCES AND CHRONOLOGY FOR THE LIFE OF PAUL

Four kinds of ancient sources claim to offer information about Paul. Three of them are in the New Testament, namely, letters written by Paul himself (undisputed letters), letters attributed to Paul but considered by scholars to have been written later by Paul's followers, and the Acts of the Apostles. The fourth kind of source consists of works attributed to, or written about, Paul that are *not* in the New Testament. These books are collected in the **New Testament Apocrypha** (see Chapter Three).

A basic interpretive problem is that the four kinds of sources offer at least a half-dozen different portraits of Paul! In this chapter, as before, apocryphal works and their portraits of Paul will be considered only in passing. Although they are very important for historical and social information about mainly second-century interpretations of Paul, they are of little value for understanding the historical Paul in the first century. Therefore, we shall use first-century sources, which, of course, need to be evaluated. The goal is to get behind these various portraits to the historical Paul in order to understand his life, teaching, and social setting.

Evaluating the Sources

As discussed in the last two chapters, the canon adopted by the churches in the fourth century C.E. contains fourteen letters attributed to Paul. Thirteen of them explicitly bear his name (the one that does not is the Letter to the Hebrews, which came close to being omitted from the canon). However, modern scholars do not think that Paul wrote (or dictated to his *amanuensis,* or secretary) all fourteen letters attributed to him because some of them differ on the basis of language, style, and content. These fourteen letters can be ranked on an ascending scale of probability, from those that contemporary scholars do not dispute to those that they do dispute (early Pauline School) to those that they think did not come from Paul (later Pauline School) to the one that they almost universally reject. Our conclusions about those letters were:

UNDISPUTED PAULINE (50s)	PAULINE SCHOOL (70–100)	PAULINE SCHOOL (100–125)	NON-PAULINE (70–100?)
1 Thessalonians	2 Thessalonians	1 Timothy	Hebrews
1 Corinthians	Colossians	2 Timothy	
2 Corinthians	Ephesians	Titus	
Philippians			
Philemon			
Galatians			
Romans			

More detailed arguments about whether Paul wrote these books will be offered in later chapters. Here a summary will suffice. Beginning with the last column, the Letter to the Hebrews is almost universally *rejected* as Paul's letter for three main reasons. First, its style and vocabulary are totally different from those of *all* other letters. Second, Paul wrote letters, and its form is not a typical letter form. Third, and most important, its dominant theme, the heavenly high priesthood of Christ, sounds nothing like the ideas of Paul in the remaining Pauline letters. As observed in the last chapter, even the ancients doubted that Paul wrote it, and it had an uphill battle being accepted in the canon. It can be safely excluded as coming from Paul himself and will be discussed independently later.

The letters in the next column from the right, 1 Timothy, 2 Timothy, and Titus, might be considered to be a second stage of "deutero-Pauline" letters, but a traditional name persists, the "**Pastoral Letters,**" sometimes shortened to simply "**the Pastorals.**" They purport to be Paul's pastoral advice to his coworkers, Timothy in Ephesus (1 Tim. 1:3) and Titus on the island of Crete (Titus 1:5). There are, again, three main reasons for rejecting them as Paul's letters. First, these letters, especially the supposed letter to Titus on Crete, cannot be coordinated with what is generally accepted as the movements of Paul—unless one accepts the speculative theory that he was released from prison in Rome to carry out a later mission in Crete. Second, there are very significant differences of language and style from Paul's undisputed letters in column 1. Finally, these three letters contain evidence for a well-developed church organization (strict standards for bishops, elders, deacons, widows) not found in the other letters but typical of church organization emerging in certain churches about a half-century later. (The evidence for such organization is found in Church Fathers from the very late and early second century.) Most contemporary scholars therefore conclude that the Pastorals date from a later period long after Paul's death, probably the early second century, when such organization is known to have emerged.

Finally, the letters in column two, 2 Thessalonians, Colossians, and Ephesians, are debated and should be treated with more caution with respect to authorship. Least likely to have come from Paul is the third, Ephesians. It contains also many differences from the undisputed letters in language, style, and content. It lacks Paul's usual personal touch. It copies parts of Colossians. Finally, the reference to Ephesus in 1:1 is not present in our earliest manuscripts, suggesting that it might have circulated at first as a general summary of certain features of Paul's thought. Perhaps the congregational reader inserted a specific location, and then a later scribe gave it a destination, Ephesus.

Some scholars accept Colossians as Paul's letter. Yet, there are still a large number of distinctive terms and some new ideas in comparison with the undisputed letters. Thus many do not accept it, and that conclusion will be accepted in this textbook.

Finally, most debated with respect to Pauline authorship is 2 Thessalonians. This letter is clearly very close to Paul's thought in 1 Thessalonians, which is usually accepted as Paul's. Nonetheless, some scholars think that its content implies that it was written soon after (a very few speculate before!) 1 Thessalonians and seems to imitate it, yet it has a different point of view that suggests a delay of the *parousia*. Despite its similarity to 1 Thessalonians and Paul's thinking, then, it will also be considered as non-Pauline, that is, as deutero-Pauline. Thus these three deutero-Pauline letters will be dated about 70–100 C.E.

Summarizing, on the basis of three main factors—language, style, and content—most scholars hold that Hebrews cannot have come from Paul and that at least five, and perhaps even six (the position taken here) of the letters attributed to him come from Paul's later followers. These six can on the basis of historical reasons be divided into two periods of a "Pauline School." Scholars call them "deutero (secondary)-Pauline letters."

Thus only seven of the fourteen letters—those in column 1, the "undisputed letters"—should be used as direct historical sources for the life and thought of Paul. Six of these letters were written to congregations in Turkey or Asia Minor (Galatia), northern Greece or Macedonia (Thessalonica, Philippi), southern Greece or Achaia (Corinth), and Italy (Rome). The seventh, Philemon, was addressed to a single person but was also intended to be read to an assembled congregation (Philem. 3: "you" is plural).

Letter Fragments and Interpolations

We have reduced the number of undisputed Pauline letters from fourteen to seven, those in column 1. However, these seven letters may actually be more than seven because at least one of them (2 Corinthians) is usually thought to contain several **letter fragments** written by Paul. Some scholars hold the same view for two others (Philippians, Romans). Scholarly conclusions accepted about letter fragments and the sequence of their writing affect judgments about the course of Paul's life, thought, and social relations at Rome. Hypotheses about letter fragments were once very common, but today scholars are more cautious about them, especially because more is understood about ancient letter writing. In this edition, letter fragments will be considered only for 2 Corinthians. The issue may now be illustrated.

It is a striking feature of Paul's letters that there are occasional sharp interruptions in the flow of his thought. Some of them can be explained by his own spontaneous, dramatic tendency to deviate from, and return to, the main course of his argument. Some can be demonstrated to be insertions by a later follower of Paul (or perhaps a still later manuscript copyist). An insertion like this is called an **"interpolation."** Some, however, appear to be passages from other letters, fragments that were somehow accidentally misplaced. In such instances, one can follow the natural flow of Paul's thought by removing these sections and picking it up a few verses, passages, or even chapters, later.

The most convincing examples of letter fragments can be found in 2 Corinthians. Consider how the natural flow of thought in 2 Cor. 6:13 is interrupted but resumes again in 2 Cor. 7:2, as certain key terms help to show:

2 Cor. 6:11–13:   Our mouth is open to you, Corinthians; our *heart* is wide. You are not restricted by us, but you are restricted in your affections. In return—I speak as to children—widen your *hearts* also.

2 Cor. 7:2–4:   Open your *hearts* to us; we have wronged no one, we have corrupted no one, we have taken advantage of no one. I do not say this to condemn you, for I said before that you are in our *hearts,* to die together and to live together. I have great confidence in you; I have great pride in you; I am filled with comfort. With all our affliction, I am overjoyed.

Perhaps the deviation and resumption of flow of thought by themselves would not be convincing. However, the intervening passage, 2 Cor. 6:14–7:1, contains words and ideas that are strikingly characteristic of the **Dead Sea Scrolls** but not at all characteristic of Paul. These are:

1. "Belial" (Greek: *Beliar*) is a name for the Prince of Demons
2. Light-darkness dualism
3. The particular way that the term "righteousness" is used
4. The necessity of separation from unbelievers

Scholars usually conclude that 2 Cor. 6:14–7:1 is a letter fragment, in this case *one that did not come from Paul.* Just how it found its way into the letter is uncertain. Perhaps part of another letter (an opponent's letter?) was copied in the manuscript margin—marginal glosses were common—and later inserted into the main text of Paul's letter when the whole collection of Paul's letters was first assembled near the end of the first century. Again, if these few verses are omitted, the thought flows quite naturally.

In another example in 2 Corinthians, Paul is recounting his itinerary:

2 Cor. 2:12–13: When I came to Troas to preach the Gospel of Christ, a door was opened for me in the Lord; but my mind could not rest because I did not find my brother Titus there. So I took leave of them and went on to *Macedonia.*

2 Cor. 7:5–6: For even when we came into *Macedonia,* our bodies had no rest but we were afflicted at every turn—fighting without and fear within. But God, who comforts the downcast, comforted us by the coming of Titus. . . .

This time a rather long section of several chapters intervenes, 2 Cor. 2:14–7:4 (which *includes* the non-Pauline, Qumran-type fragment just discussed!). Initially a reader might imagine that Paul has simply engaged in a lengthy digression and is returning to his itinerary. However, the interrupted itinerary is not the only problem. The *tone* of this long section is quite different from what precedes and follows it. In this long section, relations between Paul and the Corinthians are clearly *deteriorating.* In the surrounding section, relations between Paul and the Corinthians are *being patched up.* A reasonable hypothesis is that the two sections represent two different periods of Paul's relations with the Corinthians. The content of the two sections reinforces the view that there is an interruption of the natural progression of Paul's itinerary.

There are other examples in 2 Corinthians. One is that Paul's sudden, angry self-defense against opponents who hold a different view of Jesus in 2 Cor. 10–13 is often thought to be at least part of a "tearful letter" that Paul mentions in 2 Cor. 2:3–4 and 7:8. Another is that 1 Cor. 8 makes a break by taking up a new theme, the **collection** of money for the poor among the "saints" (believers) at Jerusalem. Then, oddly, 2 Cor. 9 discusses this collection as though it had never been mentioned in the previous chapter! (Because of content, we can be fairly certain of the logical sequence of four references to the collection; these are 1 Cor. 16:1–4, 2 Cor. 8, 2 Cor. 9, and Rom. 15:25–29; indeed, they conform generally to a reconstructed order of his letters.) Thus 2 Cor. 8 and 9 appear to be different, independent letters about the collection.

Summarizing, leaving aside the un-Pauline fragment in 2 Cor. 6:14–7:1, the five remaining fragments can now be arranged in a logical and chronological sequence:

1. 2:14–7:4 (minus 6:14–7:1)   deteriorating relations
2. 10–13, a "tearful letter"   sharply hostile relations
3. 1:1–2:13 and 7:5–17   reconciling relations
4. 8   the collection
5. 9   the collection

Note again that solving this problem is not just solving an interesting literary puzzle. A logical and corresponding chronological sequence will influence the interpreter's opinion about Paul's changing relations with the Corinthians. There are three other factors to consider. First, the preceding logical-chronological sequence needs to be elaborated in relation to what can be reconstructed about the movements of Paul and his coworkers, and for that the Acts of the Apostles is a helpful supplement (see Chapter Three). Second, in 1 Corinthians, Paul mentions a "previous" letter to the Corinthians (1 Cor. 5:9) and another from them to him (1 Cor. 7:1), but these have disappeared. Third, 1 Cor. 14:33b–36, Paul's presumed advice about women keeping silence in the churches, is most likely a later addition (again, an "interpolation") by a follower of Paul. The reasons are that this passage breaks the context, contrasts with Paul's own views about women even in this letter, and looks like the very different view of a later, deutero-Pauline author of one of the Pastorals (1 Tim. 2:11–15).

Taking all these factors into account, the following tentative literary sequence and picture of Paul's relations with the Corinthians emerge (again, omitting the non-Pauline fragment, 2 Cor. 6:14–7:1).

A Reconstruction of Paul's Relations with the Corinthians

1. Paul leaves Corinth and resides in Ephesus (1 Cor. 16:8); eventually he writes what he calls his "previous letter" (1 Cor. 5:9).   **Letter 1 by Paul (lost)**

2. There comes back an oral report from "Chloe's people" about factions at Corinth (1 Cor. 1:11).

3. With the oral report there also arrives a letter asking Paul to address certain problems at Corinth (1 Cor. 7:1); perhaps it was brought by Fortunatus, Stephanus, and Achaicus (1 Cor. 16:17).   **Letter 2, from the Corinthians (lost)**

4. Paul responds with another letter. Timothy's visit is announced (1 Cor. 4:17;   **Letter 3 (our 1 Cor. minus 1 Cor. 14:33b–36**

16:10; cf. Acts 19:22). Paul also gives instructions about the collection (1 Cor. 16:1–4).

[an interpolation])

5. Paul sends Titus to hurry up the collection (2 Cor. 8:5–6, 10; 9:2; 12:18).

6. Paul learns (from Timothy or Titus?) that Israelite members of the Jesus Movement have come to Corinth, have challenged Paul's authority, and have said that he lacks charisma (3:1; 11:4–5, 13, 22; 12:11).

7. Paul writes a letter in which the congregation is still loyal, but relations are deteriorating.

Letter 4 (2 Cor. 2:14–6:13; 7:2–4 [minus 6:14–7:1])

8. Paul now makes a "painful visit" (2 Cor. 2:1; 12:14, 21; 13:1), which includes an attack against him by a member of the congregation (2:5; 7:12).

9. Paul returns to Ephesus and writes the "tearful letter" defending himself against the competing Israelite missionaries in the Jesus Movement (2 Cor. 2:3–4; 7:8). This may have been delivered by Titus (2 Cor. 2:12–13; 7:5–7).

Letter 5 (2 Cor. 10:1–13:10)?

10. Paul is now imprisoned in Ephesus (2 Cor. 1:8–11), and it is probably from there that he writes a letter to Philippi and a letter to Philemon at Colossae.

(letters not written to Corinth)

11. Paul is released from prison, heads north to Troas, then to Macedonia to meet Titus, who reports that the situation at Corinth has much improved (2:12–13; 7:5–16).

12. Paul writes a letter of reconciliation that clarifies why he has not yet visited the Corinthians on his way to Macedonia and what to do about the person who has so offended Paul (2 Cor. 1:15–2:4; 2:5–11).

Letter 6 (2 Cor. 1:1–2:13; 7:5–16)

13. Paul now writes a letter about the collection; he sends the letter with Titus from Macedonia.

Letter 7 (2 Cor. 8)

14. Leaving Macedonia, Paul writes a second letter (Greece) about the collection to all the believers of Achaia.

Letter 8 (2 Cor. 9)

15. Paul visits Corinth, apparently for the third time (cf. Acts 20:2–3).

The preceding reconstruction of letters and letter fragments in relation to the Corinthians is very widely accepted and helps to sort out Paul's vacillating relations with the Corinthians. This sequence will be followed in Chapter Five.

Do similar theories exist in relation to the other letters? Yes. However, more recent literary analysis will prevail, namely, that these letters, despite their problems, are unified.

The final step is to place the undisputed letters and letter fragments of 2 Corinthians into a logical and chronological sequence, noting where possible the location from which they were written in relation to what is known of Paul's movements. In such a sequence, 1 Thessalonians was Paul's earliest letter because of its apocalyptic orientation, and it was probably written from Corinth. It is generally agreed that Romans (minus the doxology in 15:25–27) was Paul's latest letter, primarily because Rome was last in Paul's itinerary and Romans is the most developed and least apocalyptic. It was probably written from Corinth. We have just seen that Paul wrote the Corinthian correspondence from Ephesus. Paul's imprisonment there was probably the occasion for his letters to the Philippians and to a person named Philemon (2 Cor. 1:8–11; Phil. 1:12–26). Finally, the time, place from which, and place to which Galatians was written are also much debated; here the view that Galatians was written relatively late because of its similarity to Romans will be accepted. It will be placed before Paul's last letter (Rom. 15:24–29). Putting all this together, the following tentative sequence of Paul's letters emerges:

Letter	Origin
1. 1 Thessalonians	Corinth? (2:2; 3:1, 6)
2. "Previous letter" to Corinth (1 Cor. 5:9)	Ephesus?
3. 1 Cor. (minus 14:33b–36)	Ephesus (16:8)
4. 2 Cor. 2:14–6:13; 7:2–4 (deterioration)	Ephesus?
5. 2 Cor. 10–13 ("tearful letter")	Ephesus?
6. Philippians	Ephesus
7. Philemon	Ephesus
8. 2 Cor. 1:1–2:13; 7:5–16 (reconciliation)	Macedonia (7:5)
9. 2 Cor. 8	Macedonia (8:1)
10. 2 Cor. 9 (to Cenchreae?)	Macedonia (9:2, 4)
11. Galatians (to north Galatia? cf. 4:13)	Macedonia?
12. Romans	Corinth? (15:25–26)

This sequence of letters and letter fragments combined with what Paul says about his movements becomes a plausible basis for developing a relative chronology of Paul's career and a corresponding sketch of his life. To these literary products it is possible to add an occasional reference from ancient writers and inscriptions (**external evidence**); thereby the chronology of Paul's life can be anchored in ancient history. You will recall that there are some apocryphal sources about Paul. Several of these and some Church Fathers will be noted in passing but primarily for the sake of interest. There are also some church traditions about Paul's family and martyr-dom that add speculative possibilities for Paul's life and death.

A Possible Chronology of Paul's Career

Again, the most important piece of evidence for dating Paul's movements is the **Gallio Inscription** as it related to the Acts of the Apostles. Recall the major point that correlating Acts 18:11, the Gallio Inscription, and the "**Edict of Claudius**" shows that Paul would have arrived in Corinth in 49 or 50 C.E. (see Chapters Two and Three). Although chronologists do not always agree, they usually develop their chronology of Paul's life by working backward and forward from this pivotal date, and that will be the procedure here.

In Galatians, Paul says that after his "conversion" he was in Damascus *three years* (or, by Israelite reckoning, at least two). He also says that he had been in Syria and Cilicia *fourteen years* (or, by Israelite reckoning, at least thirteen). This is a to-tal of seventeen (or at least fifteen)—if the three is not included in the fourteen (Gal. 1:17–18; 2:1)! Then he went to the Jerusalem Conference, then to Antioch, and eventually to Macedonia and Achaia, where Corinth is the capital city. Work-ing back fourteen to seventeen years from his arrival at Corinth in 49/50 C.E., his "conversion" and call would have taken place between 32 and 36 C.E., probably closer to the former.

This dating generally fits Paul's comments about Damascus. In Galatians, Paul says that after his "conversion," he was in Damascus (Gal. 1:17–18). In 2 Cor. 11:32, he mentions additionally that he escaped from the governor of Damascus while King Aretas (IV of Nabatea) ruled the Arabs. Aretas' dates are thought to be from 9 to 40 C.E. (Josephus *Antiquities* 1.12.4; 16.9.4; 18.5.1–2). Thus prior to 40 C.E., Paul had been in the region of Damascus three years.

In short, if Paul arrived in Corinth in 49/50 C.E., composed his surviving letters thereafter, and was recruited to the Jesus Movement about seventeen years earlier than his arrival at Corinth, a chronology of his life would look like this:

Event	Approximate Date
Paul's date of birth	not known (0?)
Crucifixion of Jesus	not known exactly (ca. 30)
"Conversion" and call (Gal. 1:12–16)	ca. 32/33 (perhaps as late as 36)
Visit to Arabia; return to Damascus (Gal. 1:17)	ca. 32/33
First visit to Jerusalem after three years (Gal. 1:18)	ca. 36
Jerusalem Conference (Gal. 1:17–18; 2:1)	ca. 49, fourteen years after "conversion"
Paul's first arrival in Corinth (Acts 19:1, 10, 22)	49/50 (winter) until summer of 51
Activity in Galatia, Asia, Macedonia, and Achaia	50–56

Paul in Ephesus (including imprisonment)	ca. 52–55
Last stay in Macedonia and Achaia	probably winter of 55/56
Journey to Jerusalem with collection and arrest there	spring of 56
Prisoner in Caesarea	ca. 56–58
Taken prisoner to Rome	ca. 58/59
Two years' imprisonment in Rome	ca. 59–61 (cf. Acts 28–30)
Martyrdom under Nero (54–68 C.E.)	61–64?

This chronology is necessarily tentative. Its dates are based partly on vague comments in the Book of Acts and an otherwise unattested early tradition in a Church Father that Paul was martyred in Rome (*1 Clement* 5:7, 6:1). This would have been during the reign of Nero, who blamed members of the Jesus Movement for the great fire of Rome in 64 C.E. Finally, the chronology assumes that Paul was not released to carry on a mission in Spain, an event that would be necessary if Paul wrote the **Pastoral Epistles.**

PAUL'S INDIVIDUAL AND SOCIAL CONTEXT

Having attempted to line up a sequence of sources and establish a chronology for Paul's life, it will now be important to fill in the gaps and present a sketch of Paul's individual and social context. Again, the undisputed letters will be the primary sources, but occasional details can be furnished where the accounts in Acts will permit.

Paul as a "Collectivist" Personality

Paul was an ancient Mediterranean person. Some of the prevailing cultural patterns and core values of ancient Mediterranean culture were presented in Chapter One. Examples are **honor** and **shame;** a high level of vertical social stratification; a large agrarian peasantry with power concentrated in a tiny, powerful urban elite (emperors, kings, governors, temple priests) and "retainers" who served the elite (military, urban wealthy, scribes); a "redistributive" economy; primary orientation to family; male dominance; arranged marriages; political and family-oriented religion; and patron-client relations. Here the first focus will be on the notion of ancient "collectivist" or group-centered personalities.

Most modern Euro-Americans are "individualists," not "collectivists." They naturally identify and value themselves primarily in terms of their personal individual identities and goals and are so rewarded. With reasonable intelligence and hard work, one can "be a success," which usually means to have power or material wealth. Modern individualists tend to be psychologically introspective. They can be found reflecting about their identities and have "identity crises," and most speak freely about their inner motivations or what they think and feel. Studies show that ancient Mediterranean persons were more "collectivistic," group centered, or what social-scientific analysts call "dyadic." Although there were a few individualists about—

recall the deviant philosophers, healers, and prophets—most persons were more prone than moderns to identify themselves and stereotype others by their groups. Those they deemed most important tend to fall into three categories: group of origin, place of origin, and male/female relationships, that is, *generation, geography, and gender* (Malina and Neyrey). *Generation* refers to kinship, that is, ancestors, clan, tribe, family, father, and children. *Geography* refers to place of origin, that is, village, town, city, region, and country. Gender judgments are self-evident: The male gender was considered to be superior (at least by literate males). People could also be identified in terms of religious or political affiliation or "work." Also, although appearances were sometimes deceiving, especially in the case of liars and cheats, and distrust of outsiders was common, it was thought that one *ought* to be able to identify a person in terms of his or her group affiliations and external appearances.

We can illustrate this Mediterranean collectivist orientation from the New Testament in two ways: names and physical features. Consider the following names:

1. Jesus *of Nazareth* and Mary *of Magdala* (geography: village)
2. Saul *of Tarsus* (city)
3. James and John, *sons of Zebedee* (gender and generation)
4. Simon *the Tanner* (work)
5. Zadok *the Pharisee* (religious group [with political overtones])
6. Simon *the Zealot* (political group [with religious overtones])

A second way to identify people was by physical features. One figure in the New Testament is called "Simon the Leper" (Mark 14:3 = Matt. 26:6), a designation that stresses the appearance of his skin: He was impure (Lev. 13, 14). Some ancient writers believed that it was possible to determine the race, disposition, and character of a person by studying ". . . a person's movements, postures, colors, facial expressions, hair, type of skin, voice, flesh-tone, parts of the body and overall physique" (*Physiognomics* 806a, pp. 22–33). This is called "**physiognomics.**" For example, it was thought that the male is strong and has great endurance; thus he is suited to public space out of doors; females, who are weaker, belong indoors (anthropologists call such categories "male space" and "female space"). Small-minded men are small-limbed with small eyes and a small face, "like a Corinthian or Leucadian" (Pseudo-Aristotle, *Physiognomics* 808a, pp. 30–33). *Animal* types include lion-like rulers, who are strong and savage; serpent-like people, who have a small, thin, round head and move their heads quickly and easily and who are considered to be murderers and devoted to evil-doing. Finally, there are *anatomical* types. Brave persons were supposed to have stiff hair and be erect, strong, with a flat belly and broad shoulders. Generals were said to be short and bow-legged (firmly planted on the ground, on two feet), and a warrior was thought to have bushy eyebrows that meet, a hooked nose, and slightly bowed legs. One could learn about another's character and moral type especially by looking into the eyes.

Such group categorizations are **stereotypes.** Many are ethnocentric, or centered on one group's limited perceptions and generalizations about other groups. Anecdotes from ancient literature illustrate such ethnocentrisms. "Can anything good come out of Nazareth?" (John 1:46). "Cretans [people from the Mediterranean island of Crete] are always liars, evil beasts, and lazy drunkards" (Titus 1:12).

We make two observations about collectivist personalities, ethnocentric stereotypes, and Pauline literature. First, Paul occasionally placed barriers between his believing congregations and outsiders; that is, he established "group boundaries." He did so on the basis of sacred and profane, clean and unclean, especially in the domain of moral behavior. 1 Corinthians is especially concerned with Paul's attempt to preserve the unity and purity of the congregation at Corinth against corruption from outside influences (for example, 1 Cor. 5). However, Paul also sought to break down some traditional stereotypes that separated people, especially in the areas of national identity, slavery, and gender. He wrote, "There is no longer Israelite or Greek, there is no longer slave or free, there is no longer male and female; for all of you are one in Christ Jesus" (Gal. 3:28). Such a statement could lead to all kinds of problems for a house where members of the Jesus Movement met, or **house-churches.** In such houses, some Israelites might refuse to eat with Gentiles, slaves served meals to their masters, and men's quarters were separate from women's quarters. Paul's "in Christ Jesus" statement is in conflict with such cultural norms and establishes a new kind of group centeredness, the inclusive family.

Second, the second-century, ascetic-minded apocryphal *Acts of Paul and Thecla* contains a famous imaginative description of Paul as short, bald, bow-legged, with a good state of body, meeting eyebrows, a nose somewhat hooked, and full of friendliness (*Thecla* 3). This is an idealized description, and it comes from a later time; it apparently has no historical value for Paul himself. Yet, it shows how a later writer wanted Paul to be remembered: brave, courageous, commanding, just, and full of confidence.

A Few Biographical Inferences

Paul's most important autobiographical statement is found in his letter to the Philippians. In defending himself, he says, "circumcised on the eighth day, a member of the people of Israel, of the tribe of Benjamin, a Hebrew born of Hebrews; as to the law, a Pharisee; . . .) as to zeal, a persecutor of the church; as to righteousness under the law, blameless" (Phil. 3:5–6). This statement says a great deal about what had been Paul's ethnic, religious, and group identity. He had been a proud Israelite of the strict, law-abiding Pharisee party, and he had the evidence on his body to prove it. Yet, as a proselyte to the Jesus Movement, Paul rejected his heritage; as he says in the next verse, "whatever gains I had, these I have come to regard as loss because of Christ."

The statement is very important. However, it says nothing very *specific* about Paul's family of origin. That must be inferred. A Christian tradition says that Paul's parents migrated to Tarsus from Gischala, a small town in Galilee (Jerome *On Illustrious Men* v; *Epistle to the Philippians* 23), which would imply that they were Galileans. However, the tradition is very late (fourth century C.E.), and its source is unknown. The Acts of the Apostles says that Paul had a sister and that her son, thus Paul's nephew, was living in Jerusalem (Acts 23:16). It is not impossible that Paul himself had been married, but we have no evidence for that, and he was certainly single when he wrote, "To the unmarried and the widows I say that it is well for them to remain unmarried as I am" (1 Cor. 7:8). If he was born a Roman citizen, as Acts claims (Acts 22:28—see following), *perhaps* his father had earned citizenship, *perhaps*—again—by serving honorably as a mercenary in the army (although there was no conscription of Israelites because they often would not do battle on the Sabbath). Or perhaps Paul's father was a colonist who had been granted citizenship because he was an inhabitant of the free city of Tarsus.

All this is, of course, pure speculation.

The physical description of Paul in the *Acts of Paul and Thecla*—short, bald, bow-legged, meeting eyebrows, a nose somewhat hooked—is probably a late, idealized portrait based on **physiognomics.** There is also a traditional image of Paul in early Christian art (see photograph on p. 138), but most scholars think that it is late and stereotypical and that no one really knows how Paul looked. Yet, Paul must have been physically strong. He walked many miles, endured many physical trials, and was often in prison (2 Cor. 11:22–12:1; the "prison letters").

Paul also had some sort of personal problem: "And to keep me from being too elated by the abundance of revelations, a *thorn was given me in the flesh,* a messenger of Satan, to harass me to keep me from being too elated. Three times I besought the Lord about this, that it should leave me; but he said to me, 'My grace is sufficient for you, for my power is made perfect in weakness'" (2 Cor. 12:7–9). There has been much speculation about what Paul calls his "thorn in the flesh." Was it psychological? Was it spiritual? Or was it physical? Theories range from malaria to the possibility that Paul was gay. There is no solid evidence.

Paul as a Hellenist

With the general picture of Paul as an ancient collectivist personality and a few biographical inferences in mind, four more specific features of Paul's background can be mentioned: Paul as a Hellenist, a Roman citizen, an Israelite, and a member of the Jesus Movement.

Paul was a *Hellenist,* that is, one who spoke, wrote, and thought in Greek. According to Acts, he was "a man of **Tarsus** named Saul" (Acts 9:11). Acts calls him *Saulos* (Hebrew transliterated in Greek letters) up to the time of his missionary work on Cyprus, after which he is called in Greek *Paulos* (Acts 13:8–9). In his letters he always refers to himself as *Paulos,* the Greek form. Apart from its being the usual Greek form, Paul may have preferred it because the term *saulos* in Greek could describe the waddling gate of a tortoise, the prancing of a horse, or even the sexually suggestive walk of a courtesan or devotee of the Dionysiac rites. This, too, is speculative!

Acts says that Paul was *born* in **Tarsus** (Acts 22:3) and that he was *a citizen* of that city (Acts 21:39). Tarsus was the capital of Cilicia (southeastern Asia Minor or southeastern Turkey). It was a flourishing commercial city and contained many of the religions prevalent throughout the Greco-Roman world. It also had a well-known Stoic philosophical school. Indeed, as an educational center Tarsus rivaled Athens and Rome.

In this connection, it is possible to say something about Paul's early *education*. Paul's letters demonstrate at least a secondary-level Greek education and, according to some scholars, a higher level of education. He wrote and dictated Greek well. He displayed knowledge of Greek rhetoric and its devices, and in some of his ethical discussions he cited lists of virtues and vices of the type known in Cynic-Stoic philosophical schools (Gal. 5:19–23; see Chapter Three). Anyone who knew the mystery religions (see Chapter One) would not have been surprised to hear of dying and rising with Christ (Rom. 6:5). Others would have found the tradition that Jesus Christ was in the form of God, took the form of a servant, and was highly exalted by God (Phil. 2:6–11) a congenial way of thinking not unlike the notion of descending-ascending redeemers widely known (see Chapters One and Three). These factors are another reason why the apostle preferred the Greek form of his name, "Paul," not the Hebrew form, "Saul." However, more about his education needs to be said later in relation to his background as an Israelite.

Paul as a Roman Citizen

The Book of Acts claims that Paul was a citizen not only of Tarsus, but also of Rome (e.g., 21:39; 22:22–29), although some scholars reject the claim because Paul never mentions it in his letters. Originally only those who lived in Rome received Roman citizenship. However, eventually it was extended to select individuals and whole groups of non-Romans. Children of citizens received citizenship at birth and could prove it by means of a small double-folded document that could be carried on one's person and produced upon demand (like a passport), although it was valuable enough that one would most likely keep it in a safe place. If Paul was a Roman citizen, this honorable status would have offered him certain advantages. Included were easy access to Roman roads and Roman colonial cities (e.g., Philippi or Corinth). Most important, he could not be beaten without a fair trial and right of appeal for such before the emperor. According to Acts, he eventually made use of this privilege (Acts 25:11–12), although some scholars think that a person of Paul's status would not have been granted such an appeal.

Paul as an Israelite

Saul of Tarsus in Asia Minor had a Hellenistic background, spoke and wrote Greek, and possessed Roman citizenship. However, he was also an Israelite—indeed, the preceding statement from Philippians indicates that in his own self-description that was what had mattered. Just what sort of Israelite he was has been one of the most debated questions of modern New Testament scholarship. No less debated is whether he *remained* an Israelite after he affiliated with the Jesus Movement.

Paul's most complete autobiographical statement has already been quoted. It stresses his ethnic, religious, and party affiliations as a pure Israelite. Here it is again, with his Mediterranean collectivist group identity references put in parentheses:

> circumcised on the eighth day (sign of a religious/national group; male), of the people
> of Israel (religious/national group), of the tribe of Benjamin (tribal subgroup), a
> Hebrew born of Hebrews (national/ethnic group, perhaps with language implica-

tions); as to the law a Pharisee (religious party affiliation); as to zeal a persecutor of the church (devotion to his religious subgroup), as to righteousness under the law blameless (purity within his religious group)

(Cf. 2 Cor. 11:22; Rom. 9:3–5; 11:1)

To Paul, honor had meant being a man who belonged to the Israelite people and was a zealous member of the Pharisaic party.

Paul was from Tarsus, a city known for education, and as noted previously he was reasonably well educated. Did he also have a special *Israelite* education, even an advanced *rabbinic* education? Such questions are not easy to answer. The author of Luke-Acts says that Paul was brought up in the city of Jerusalem "at the feet of Gamaliel" (Acts 22:3). **Gamaliel** is known in both rabbinic and New Testament sources as a highly respected Jerusalem rabbi of the party of the Pharisees (Acts 5:34–40; Babylonian Talmud *Sota* 9.15). According to our principle of source evaluation, these comments must be measured against what Paul himself says in his letters. He certainly claims to have been a member of Pharisee party (Phil. 3:5). A complication is that the main sources for understanding rabbinic education, including the rabbis' distinctive interpretation of scripture, are mostly later than the time of Paul. Some scholars think that Paul did not have a formal rabbinic education. One argument is that Paul's interpretation of the Torah is not literal enough to be like that of the later rabbis. Another is that the Gamaliel comment betrays the tendency of the author of Luke-Acts to anchor the early phase of the Jesus Movement in the Jerusalem "mother" church and thus to show a relatively smooth transition from Jerusalem into the larger Greco-Roman world. Thus the Gamaliel tradition is part of the Lukan literary imagination. Others, however, say that Paul's biblical interpretation was *in the main* rabbinic. For example, he used some common rabbinic methods of interpretation, although he used them somewhat differently and had an uncharacteristic view of legal questions in the Torah. Further, rabbinic education was itself influenced by Greek education. Finally, a Diaspora Israelite who had received a Hellenistic education and later became a Pharisee and then a member of the Jesus Movement could have interpreted the Greek Old Testament (**Septuagint**) in ways rather different from later Hebrew and Aramaic rabbinic interpretations. This could have happened especially when he was developing interpretations for Hellenistic *members of the Jesus Movement*. It should be remembered also that certain aspects of Paul's thought can be illuminated by what are known to have been originally Palestinian rabbinic ideas, although they are no longer prominent in the rabbinic sources. Most important in this regard is the apocalyptic orientation in much of Paul's writing.

In summary, it can be neither absolutely affirmed nor denied that Paul was educated at the "feet of Gamaliel" in Jerusalem. Yet, it is possible, even likely, that he received *some* sort of Israelite education along with (after?) his Hellenistic education.

Paul's "Conversion" and Call

Some recent scholars from the Jewish tradition have seen Paul as a Greco-Roman Israelite but so deviant that he was no longer in continuity with "Judaism"—however one conceives it. Other scholars have seen Paul as an Israelite who, despite his

deviant beliefs about Jesus, was still mainly an Israelite. To what extent did an Israelite have to give up his ethnic and religious heritage when he or she affiliated with
the Jesus Movement? There were several possibilities—because there were different
kinds of Israelites and different kinds of Jesus movements. In Paul's case the critical
point is that he came to believe that Jesus was not only the hoped-for Messiah, but
more: God had revealed his Son to him, Paul, and had summoned him to announce
the good news about Jesus Christ to the Gentiles (Gal. 1:15–16). In other words,
Paul was a Greek-speaking **Diaspora** Israelite who also became a Jesus Messiah believer. This could have led to some radical views, particularly his abandonment of
the requirement of circumcision. How did this happen?

As far as scholars can determine, there was never a systematic persecution of
members of the Jesus Movement by Israelites in the Greco-Roman period. Yet,
there were occasional *local* persecutions. According to Acts, Paul first came into
contact with the Jesus Movement as a bystander at the martyrdom of Stephen in
Jerusalem (Acts 7:58), and subsequently Paul persecuted the infant community of
Christ believers in **Damascus** (Acts 9:1–2). Paul never referred to the Stephen incident in his letters, but he did emphasize that he had persecuted members of the
Jesus Movement on three separate occasions. In his statement about his religious,
ethnic, and party affiliations (noted earlier), he wrote, "as to zeal a *persecutor* of the
church" (Phil. 3:6). In commenting that the resurrected Jesus had appeared to him,
he remarked, "For I am the least of the apostles, unfit to be called an apostle, because I *persecuted* the church of God" (1 Cor. 15:9). A third reference is made to the
congregation at Galatia in Asia Minor: "For you have heard of my former life in
Judaism, how I *persecuted* the church of God violently and tried to destroy it; and I
advanced in Judaism beyond many of my own age among my people, so extremely
zealous was I for the traditions of my fathers" (Gal. 1:13–14). These three statements show that Paul considered his zeal in persecuting followers of Jesus to be a
mark of his sincere convictions as an Israelite and as a Pharisee.

Modern Jews have little interest in making proselytes of non-Jews. Jewish identity has more to do with kinship than conversion of others. In the Greco-Roman
period, group identity did not lend itself easily to individual conversion. Yet, certain,
especially ethical, teachings of the Israelite religion were attractive to non-Israelites
who commonly affiliated with more than one religion. The ancient historian Josephus (*Antiquities* 14.110; *Wars* 7.45) and the writer of Luke-Acts (10:7; 17:4, 12) refer to "God-fearers," that is, *partial* proselytes who were very attracted to the Israelite religion but resisted total conversion because they were reluctant to accept
strict holiness, especially dietary laws, and, for males, circumcision. Paul claims that
at one time *he* had "preached circumcision" (Gal. 5:11). This suggests that he had
been an active *Israelite* missionary in the Hellenistic world. If so, he might well have
come into contact and conflict with competing missionaries in the Jesus Movement
who were active outside Palestine (Acts 8:1b–3). These missionaries would have attracted the "God-fearers" precisely because they did not require strict adherence to
ceremonial laws and circumcision. Perhaps it was Paul's conflict with such missionaries that led him to persecute them—and perhaps this led to his eventual rejection
of circumcision when he became a missionary for the Jesus Movement. In any case,
he persistently linked persecution of the members of the Jesus Movement with his

"conversion" and call (Gal. 1:11–17; 1 Cor. 15:9; Phil. 3:6–7). From a modern perspective, this raises the question of whether Paul had a guilty conscience. Indeed, Paul's "conversion" naturally raises a number of fundamental issues: his attitude toward other forms of Israelite religion, his conception of Torah law and covenant (circumcision), and his view of Jesus. It also raises questions about modern forms of Christianity that lay emphasis on conversion. We therefore need to be a little more specific.

The ancient sources offer no evidence that Paul had never known Jesus of Nazareth personally, which ironically was a prerequisite for becoming an "apostle" for the author of Luke-Acts (Acts 1:20–26). Yet, Paul considered himself to be an apostle, and he expressed this claim by saying that his apostleship was not of human origin but rather came directly from God. As the Letter to the Galatians puts it, "Paul an apostle—not from men nor through man, but through Jesus Christ and God the Father" (Gal. 1:1). Paul connected this revelation of the resurrected Christ to the "good news" or gospel as he saw it. Using typical Greek rhetoric, he reminded the Galatians, "For I would have you know, brethren, that the gospel which was preached by me is not man's gospel. For I did not receive it from man, nor was I taught it, but it came through *a revelation* (*apocalypsis*) of Jesus Christ" (Gal. 1:11–17). After telling of his former persecution of Christ followers, Paul continued,

> But when he who had set me apart before I was born, and had called me through his grace, was pleased to reveal his Son to me (literally "in me"), in order that I might preach him among the Gentiles, I did not confer with flesh and blood, nor did I go up to Jerusalem to those who were apostles before me, but I went away into Arabia (Nabatea), and again I returned to Damascus.

The stress in this passage is not on "conversion," that is, on an Israelite's becoming a proselyte to a special form of Israelite religion, the Jesus Movement. Rather, Paul believed he had received a *direct, divine call to be an apostle who proclaimed "the Son" to the Gentiles.*

A striking pattern for this description of direct recruitment by God is found in the biblical stories about the call of Isaiah and Jeremiah. They were said to have been set apart while they were still in their mother's womb (Isa. 49:1; Jer. 1:5). Paul uses the same kind of language. Like them, he claims that he had no real choice about his vocation; it was his destiny, the plan of God. This conclusion does not deny that Paul had some intense religious experience. He elsewhere speaks vaguely about his having been transported to the third heaven, to Paradise (2 Cor. 12:2). In Galatians, he says that God revealed his Son "in him" in order that he might preach him among the Gentiles (Gal. 1:16). So this experience is in the first place a "vision" of the Son. In 1 Cor. 9:1, Paul says, "Am I not free? Am I not an *apostle?* Have I not *seen* Jesus, our Lord?" In 1 Cor. 15:8, he writes, "Last of all, as to one untimely born, he *appeared* also to me" and again mentions his apostleship and persecution of the church (15:9). Elsewhere he mentions his "visions and revelations of the Lord" in which one might *hear* things; indeed, he claims that he had been transported to the third heaven, to Paradise (2 Cor. 12:1–5). Clearly, Paul had an experience of the sort found in most cultures of the world.

In these texts, again, Paul's focus combined his experience of the revelation of Jesus with his call to be an apostle to the Gentiles. Moreover, he related these two facts to his previous persecution of the church and spoke of a change from his "former life." This led him to have difficulties accepting observance of certain details of the Torah law as sufficient for maintaining a relationship with God (see Rom. 7). The most prominent was the requirement of circumcision, which he rejected as a prerequisite for Gentiles who wanted to join the Jesus Movement. Yet, his pride in his Israelite heritage suggests that Paul was *not* plagued with a guilty conscience for persecuting members of the church. Indeed, he seems to have been quite proud of it as evidence of his identity as an Israelite.

This last observation raises the question of whether the term "conversion" is appropriate. The key autobiographical text and its context (Phil. 3:4–9) reinforce this hesitation. Paul's Israelite background was, he said, reason for "confidence in the flesh" (verse 4). After giving his heritage "as a member of the people of Israel, of the tribe of Benjamin, a Hebrew born of Hebrews" (verses 5–6), he concluded, "But whatever *gains* I had, these I have come to regard as loss because of Christ. More than that I regard everything as loss because of the surpassing value of knowing Christ Jesus my Lord" (verses 7–8). It was this conviction that led him to state the major theme of much of his writing: "the righteousness of God based on *faith*" (verse 9).

The author of the Acts of the Apostles lays great weight on what has traditionally been called "Paul's conversion" or "Damascus road experience" because he relates the story three times (9:1–19a; 22:1–15; 26:4–20). In fact, his stress on the intensity of the experience has probably contributed to its interpretation as an emotional "conversion" experience in modern conversion-oriented Christian traditions. There are three constant elements in all three of the Acts accounts—*persecution, a vision of Jesus, and the voice of Jesus.* Here is one of those accounts:

9:3: Now as he journeyed he approached Damascus, and suddenly a *light from heaven flashed about him.*

9:4: And he fell to the ground and *heard a voice* saying to him,
"Saul, Saul, why do you *persecute* me?"
"Who are you, Lord?"
"I am Jesus, whom you are *persecuting.*"

In this kind of material, Form Critics usually think that the central dialogue is the oldest part, the nucleus around which the other details cluster as the tradition is transmitted. It is worth considering whether the detail of the vision of blinding light (9:3; 22:6; 26:13) was originally connected to the central dialogue in this triple account. Yet, enshrined in the Acts "conversion" stories are elements that are not inconsistent with what Paul himself says: persecution, visual revelation of Jesus Christ, verbal communication—clearly an altered state of consciousness.

However one evaluates the accounts of Paul's so-called conversion, it is clear that he stresses an *apocalypsis* of Christ and that his letters reflect the vitality and power of one who, because of this experience, is driven to accomplish what he believes is God's will for his life.

In summary, it is possible to say that Paul associated his persecution of the church with two interrelated experiences: a direct revelation of Jesus Christ as God's Son and a call to become apostle to the Gentiles, which he related to biblical prophetic calls. In Paul's own statements, there is no emphasis on a guilty conscience followed by repentance. Rather, these sources indicate that Paul had thought of himself as a good and loyal Israelite. He had been confident, to use his terms, "in the flesh." Thus the accent in these accounts falls on the experience of his "call" to become apostle to the Gentiles. The revelation itself undoubtedly had visionary and auditory elements—which seems to be further supported in Acts. Acts, however, elaborates the stories with legend and theological interpretation related to Paul's connections with Jerusalem.

Paul's Social Status

Paul's social status has also been the subject of much debate. The main reason is that two types of information seem to be in conflict. On the one hand, his ideas, his language and style, his rhetorical techniques, his knowledge of the **Septuagint,** his apparent acquaintance with popular Stoic philosophy, and, if Acts is correct, his Roman citizenship point to a person of relatively *high* social status. However, his trade, which clearly involved working with his hands (1 Cor. 4:12; 1 Thess. 2:9), suggests a relatively *low* social status. The issue of Paul's social status needs to be considered more carefully.

Ideas, language, style, rhetoric, and the like point to the question of Paul's education, discussed earlier. It was common for boys of the lower social strata to learn their *"Alpha-Beta-Gammas"* ("ABCs") from a "teacher of letters." Boys of the upper strata usually went on to secondary school, where they learned, among other things, letter writing and introductory rhetoric from a secondary school teacher called a *grammaticus.* Whereas letter writing apparently did not follow precise rules, rhetoric—the principles used to convince people in *oral* discourse—did follow such rules, at least in principle, and rhetoric tended to carry over into letter writing (Stowers). The teacher's method was to get students to analyze and imitate the great classics of history, literature, and oratory. They could then advance to more sophisticated rhetorical training under the tutelage of a specialized teacher. Paul's letters display knowledge of letter writing at a rather high degree of skill.

But just as Mark identifies Jesus as an artisan, the author of Luke-Acts identifies Paul as an artisan. The term for his trade is usually translated as "tentmaker" (Acts 18:3), although the underlying Greek term can mean "leatherworker," that is, an artisan who made things out of leather, of which tents were only one item. You will recall that in the ancient Mediterranean, artisans had a *low* social status. People from the upper social strata thought that working with one's hands was degrading. "Stigmatized as slavish, uneducated, and often useless, artisans, to judge from scattered references, were frequently reviled or abused, often victimized, seldom if ever invited to dinner, never accorded status, and even excluded from one Stoic utopia. Paul's own statements accord well this general description" (R. Hock, *Tentmaking,* p. 36).

The question, again, is this: Can these two contrasting views of Paul's social status be reconciled?

One option is to suggest that Paul accepted the rabbinic ideal and practice of combining Torah study with a trade. That would have allowed him to be independent. This solution implies that Paul did not accept the usual Hellenistic view that working with one's hands was degrading. Another option is that by working at a trade Paul symbolically "enslaved"—better, "entraded"—(1 Cor. 9:19) and "demeaned" himself and offered the gospel "free of charge" (2 Cor. 11:7), which allowed him to relate to, and thus to recruit for the Jesus Movement, people of any status. This option suggests that Paul did, in fact, hold the usual Hellenistic aristocratic view—working with one's hands was shameful—but opted for it as a mission strategy anyhow.

A third option combines these two. Paul's self-description focuses on his Israelite identity (Phil. 3:5). Thus he could have had some notion of an Israelite rabbinic-like view of his trade, that is, positive. Another model, however, was the wandering philosopher, especially the Cynic, who sometimes supported himself by work, as well (see Chapters One and Three). However, Paul could have taken the demeaning "entradement" as defense rhetoric against those who criticized him for being unable to support himself by gifts from others. This would seem to allow for some positive value for a working artisan like Paul.

Paul's Strategy as an Apostle to the Gentiles

What was Paul's missionary strategy? First, the impression from both Paul's letters and the Acts of the Apostles is that Antioch in the Roman province of Syria (not too far from Tarsus in Cilicia) became his first headquarters and that Ephesus in the Roman province of Asia (western Turkey) became his second. Paul also established house-church communities in other major urban centers of Asia Minor (Galatia) and Macedonia-Greece (Philippi, Thessalonica, and Corinth).

How did he recruit people into this new movement? Here Acts and Paul's letters are not always easy to coordinate. Acts illustrates two possibilities for Paul's strategy, and only the second seems to conform to the letters.

> (4) Every sabbath he [Paul] would argue in *the synagogue* and would try to convince Israelites and Greeks. (5) When Silas and Timothy arrived from Macedonia, Paul was occupied with proclaiming the word, testifying to the Israelites that the Messiah was Jesus. (6) When *they opposed and reviled him* [Strategy A], in protest he shook the dust from his clothes and said to them, "Your blood be on your own heads! I am innocent. *From now on I will go to the Gentiles"* [Strategy B].
> (Acts 18:4–6)

Passages such as this one suggest that Paul argued his case first in the Diaspora synagogues and that when the Israelites there did not accept him, he turned to the Greeks. The pattern is first to the Israelites, then to the Gentiles.

However, the previous verses in this passage suggest a possibility that might be better coordinated with his defense of his working with his hands in the letters, namely, that he networked first with those of the same trade, perhaps in the leather-working trade guild.

> (1) After this Paul left Athens and went to Corinth. (2) There he found an Israelite named Aquila, a native of Pontus, who had recently come from Italy with his wife Priscilla, because Claudius had ordered all Israelites to leave Rome. Paul went to see them, (3) and, because he was of the same trade, he stayed with them, and they worked together—by trade they were tentmakers.

On the basis of passages like this one, some scholars have suggested that Paul's strategy might have been to enter a city and set up a leatherworking shop on the first floor of a local *insula* (Latin: "island"). This was a sort of ancient apartment building let out to poorer folk, and it usually had such shops on the street level. Although there is literary evidence for *insulae* in this period, archeological evidence suggests that they were only beginning to be built. Thus it is just as possible that Paul relied on the hospitality of those who lived in houses, as the Acts passage suggests. Some of them may have become **house-churches** where members of the Jesus Movement met for social life and worship.

Whatever his strategy, Paul continued to work at his trade. Yet, his strong desire to support himself, to remain self-sufficient, opened him up to the charges by competing missionaries that he was not a *legitimate* apostle, not "charismatic" enough to win the hospitality and gain the financial support of others (perhaps according to the pattern of the itinerant Jesus).

PAUL'S EARLY ACTIVITY AS AN APOSTLE

Paul's First Activity in Arabia and His Return to Jerusalem

After his "conversion," which may have taken place as early as 32 or 33 (although perhaps as late as 36), Paul says that he spent three years in Arabia (Nabatea), the Gentile district east of the Jordan River, and Damascus (Gal. 1:17–18). Considering his zealous character, it is possible that he was already working as a missionary for the Jesus Movement. If he was, his missionary activity may have been unsuccessful, although it apparently aroused enough hostility that he had to flee Damascus (2 Cor. 11:32–33; Acts 9:23–25).

Paul also says that he left Damascus and paid a brief visit to Peter, the primary leader of the movement, in Jerusalem (Gal. 1:18). Because he always referred to Peter by his Aramaic name (Cephas), perhaps they talked to one another in Aramaic. It is a pity that Paul does not say anything about their conversation. In view of his vehemence about his gospel not coming from human agency (Gal. 1:12), it is unlikely that the visit was to take part in a crash course in missionary work. Yet, C. H. Dodd once wryly asked whether they were just talking about the weather. Perhaps Paul learned of some Jesus traditions he later quoted in his letters. Examples are knowledge of Jesus' lifestyle (1 Cor. 9:14), Jesus' teaching on marriage and divorce (1 Cor. 7:10), what was said at the Last Supper (1 Cor. 11:23–25), Jesus' death and resurrection "according to the scriptures," and Jesus' appearances to his followers (1 Cor. 15:3b–9). However, if Paul learned more about Jesus from Peter, why did he not emphasize it in his letters?

Paul says that after his visit to Jerusalem he went to his own native district of Cilicia (the province where Tarsus lay) to carry on missionary activity (Gal. 1:21–23). Again, we can only speculate about the extent of his missionary activity there.

Paul's First Activity at Antioch

Sometime during the next fourteen years, Barnabas, a leader of the congregation in Antioch, may have brought Paul to Antioch to help in the missionary activity in Syria (so Acts 11:26). Antioch on the Orontes River was the capital of the Roman province of Syria. It was located on the best land route between Asia Minor and Syria and hence between East and West. It was the most important city in the Roman Empire after Rome and Alexandria. Here the cultural crosscurrents of the Hellenistic world came sharply into contact. Here Greek civilization and philosophy interacted with oriental culture and religion more directly and on more equal terms than almost anywhere else. Here the establishment of a community of believers was an extremely important event for the growth and development of the Jesus Movement. Acts says that "in Antioch the disciples were for the first time called 'Christ-ies'" (Acts 11:26), probably a derogatory name at first.

Paul's arrival at Antioch marked the beginning of the most important phase of his life and work as an apostle. At Antioch he had the active support of a strategically located congregation. This major city thus became his first headquarters, or base of operations. From here began the spread of the Jesus Movement that is the major theme of the Acts of the Apostles.

Acts distinguishes *three* distinct missionary journeys launched from Antioch. It claims that Paul's first missionary journey with his companions was to the island of Cyprus and the southern part of Galatia in Asia Minor (13:2–14:26). Acts puts this first journey after a visit by Barnabas and Paul to Jerusalem, the so-called famine visit (Acts 11:27–30; 12:25) and before the Jerusalem Conference (Acts 15; see following). Indeed, the conference is said to have been a direct result of Paul's success of this first journey. However, Paul himself never mentions either the famine visit or an initial, separate journey to Cyprus and Galatia. Many scholars conclude, therefore, that the Jerusalem Conference became necessary because of Paul's success in and around Antioch. If so, Paul's travels to Cyprus and Asia Minor came *after* the Jerusalem Conference, which authorized Paul and Barnabas to go into the Gentile world (the Jerusalem Compromise; see following). Thus it may have been more closely connected with the other journeys, thus not a separate journey (**Historical Criticism**). Also, from Paul's account, we cannot be sure when "certain men from James" came to Antioch. Speculation is that some time may have elapsed; thus it may have been after some initial missionary activity. A possible sequence based mainly on the letters looks like the right-hand column of Table 4.1.

Table 4.1   Reconstructed Sequence Based on Paul's Letters

Acts	Paul's Letters	Reconstructed Sequence
Persecution of members of the Jesus Movement (9:4; 22:4, 7; 26:11, 14)	Persecution of members of the Jesus Movement (Gal. 1:13)	**Persecution of members of the Jesus Movement**
"Conversion" on road to Damascus (9:1–19a; 22:1–15; 26:4–20)	"Conversion" and call (Gal. 1:12, 15–16)	**"Conversion" and call**
Damascus (9:8–25)	Damascus (Gal. 1:17; 2 Cor 11:33)	**Damascus (missionary work?)**
	Arabia (Gal. 1:17)	**Arabia**
Famine visit to Jerusalem (Acts 11:27–30; 12:25)	————	————
	Jerusalem visit to Cephas (Gal. 1:18)	**Jerusalem visit to Cephas (Gal. 1:18)**
	To Syria and Cilicia (Gal. 1:21)	**Paul's successful missionary work in Antioch of Syria**
		Israelite members of the Jesus Movement want Paul's converts to be circumcised (Gal. 2:3)
First missionary journey (13:2–14:26)	————	————
Jerusalem Conference and the "Apostolic Decree" (Acts 15:4–29)	Jerusalem Conference (Gal. 2:1–10) (No "Apostolic Decree")	**Jerusalem Conference** **No "Apostolic Decree"**
Paul, Barnabas, and others to Antioch with "Apostolic Decree"	Peter to Antioch (Gal. 2:11–14)	**Peter to Antioch**
	"men from James" to Antioch (Gal. 2:12)	**"men from James" to Antioch**
	Missionary journeys (Antioch base)	**Missionary journeys (Antioch base)**
Second missionary journey (15:36–18:22)		**Missionary journeys**
Third missionary journey (18:23–21:16)	Missionary journeys	**Missionary journeys (Ephesus base)**

The Jerusalem Conference and the Jerusalem Compromise

It was suggested earlier that Paul's missionary success in Antioch was the impulse for the **Jerusalem Conference** (Gal. 2:1–10; cf. Acts 15). This conference was a major event in the early phase of the Jesus Movement. The conference is usually dated about 48 C.E.; Paul says that he went to the conference with Barnabas and that he took Titus with him. One probable reason was Paul's missionary success in Syria and Cilicia, especially at Antioch. Yet, Acts is undoubtedly on target in saying that the conference was occasioned by Israelite members of the Jesus Movement who came to Antioch demanding that other members be circumcised, because Paul states that Titus, a Greek, was not compelled to be circumcised (Gal. 2:3). The central is-sue was adherence to Torah commands and the covenant and how they were related to the influx of Gentiles into the movement. To what extent, if at all, did a Gentile have to become a "law-abiding" or Torah-observant Israelite to become a member of the Jesus Movement (Gal. 2:3, 7; Acts 15:1, 5–6)?

At the Jerusalem Conference, there appear to have been three parties to the controversy:

1. A group of conservative Israelite members of the Jesus Movement who considered that the Torah was still in effect and that circumcision was necessary (in Gal. 2:4, Paul calls them "false brethren" to whom he did not yield)

2. The Jerusalem leaders, James (Jesus' brother, not Jesus' disciple), Peter, and John (both Jesus' disciples)

3. Paul and his companions, Barnabas and Titus

What lay in the balance was the mission to the Gentiles, the heart of the apostle Paul's program in Syria and Cilicia and, presumably, the Antioch congregation. If we take Paul's statements seriously—he said that the Jerusalem leaders, or "pil-lars," James, Peter, and John gave him and Barnabas "the right hand of fellowship" (Gal. 2:9)—the first, or conservative, group lost the debates, and a compromise was reached between the second and third groups. The **Jerusalem Compromise** was that Peter was entrusted with the mission to "the circumcised," or Israelites, and that Paul was entrusted with the mission to the Gentiles (Gal. 2:7), or uncircum-cised. It was the first major decision of the Jerusalem Conference. There is reason to question whether it held.

The second major decision of the Jerusalem Conference was "only they (the pillars) would have us remember the poor, which thing I was very eager to do" (Gal. 2:10). As a result, Paul developed a strategy to gather a **collection** of money from members of the Gentile mission congregations for "the poor" at Jerusalem. As noted earlier, this collection is mentioned four times in Paul's letters (1 Cor. 16: 1–4; 2 Cor. 8; 9; Rom. 15:25–29). The recipients included actual (not just spiritual) poor persons in the Jerusalem congregation (Rom. 15:27). We can understand how the collection was eventually gathered from 1 Cor. 16:1–4:

> Now concerning the collection for the saints (members of the Jesus Movement): you should follow the directions I gave to the congregations of Galatia. On the first day of every week, each of you is to put aside and save whatever extra you earn, so that collections need not be taken when I come. And when I arrive, I will send any whom you approve with letters to take your gift to Jerusalem. If it seems advisable that I should go also, they will accompany me.

Paul elsewhere encouraged giving and complimented the generosity of those who contributed (2 Cor. 8, 9). The importance of this collection to Paul is illustrated by his willingness later to take it to Jerusalem, even though his life might be in danger. Rom. 15:25–28a states:

> At present, however, I am going to Jerusalem in a ministry to the saints; for Mace-donia and Achaia have been pleased to share their resources with the poor among

the saints at Jerusalem. They were pleased to do this, and indeed they owe it to them; for if the Gentiles have come to share in their spiritual blessings, they ought also to be of service to them in material things. So, when I have completed this, and have delivered to them what has been collected, I will set out.

Thus Paul eventually kept his promise made at the Jerusalem Conference. He took the collection to Jerusalem despite his anticipation of harm from unbelieving Israelites and his fear that the collection might not be accepted (Rom. 15:30–31). We shall note the collection again in relation to his opponents.

The Antioch Incident

Did the Jerusalem Compromise—the first agreement—hold? How did the various parties accept it? The **Antioch Incident** suggests that the various parties severely tested the compromise and that perhaps it did not hold. Here it is necessary to be a little imaginative.

Paul wrote that "certain men from James," whom Paul calls "the circumcision party," later came to Antioch and that after their arrival Peter felt compelled to withdraw and not eat with the Gentiles (Gal. 2:11–14). Although Paul calls the opponents "the circumcision party," the main issue this time was Israelite purity in relation to food. If "the circumcision party" represented James honorably, as envoys normally did, perhaps James had in the interim moved toward a position closer to the conservative party that lost as a result of the Jerusalem Compromise. In other words—the first point—James may have altered his position.

Second, Paul implies that Peter's behavior was inconsistent and two-faced. He *had* been eating with Gentiles; now, under pressure—the influence of "certain men from James"—he withdrew from table fellowship, a purity stance that Paul as apostle to the Gentiles had abandoned.

Finally, Paul himself may have been inconsistent. The compromise, as Paul reports it, was, "we go to the Gentiles, and they to the circumcised" (Gal. 2:9). Yet, he later wrote: "To the Israelites I became as an Israelite, in order to win Israelites. To those under the law I became as one under the law (though I myself am not under the law) so that I might win those under the law" (1 Cor. 9:20). Of course, the statement says nothing about when Paul acted as an Israelite. In any case, it needs to be emphasized again that this later became one of the most fundamental issues of all Christian history: the relationship of Christians and Jews. The beginnings of this problem were at the heart of the message of Paul. If the Jerusalem Conference compromise did *not* hold, and if Paul's status as apostle at that time was *not* absolutely clear, the conservatives might have had a legitimate case against him. Did the conservatives sway the more moderate pillars to take a harder line, so that they in effect sided with the conservatives?

In conclusion, whereas initially Paul seems to have won against the conservatives with the Jerusalem Compromise, it may well be that he eventually lost to them at Antioch, perhaps in the wake of the Antioch Incident. In any case, it is telling that Paul eventually shifted the center of his missionary activity from Antioch in Syria to Ephesus in western Asia Minor. (See Figure 4.1.)

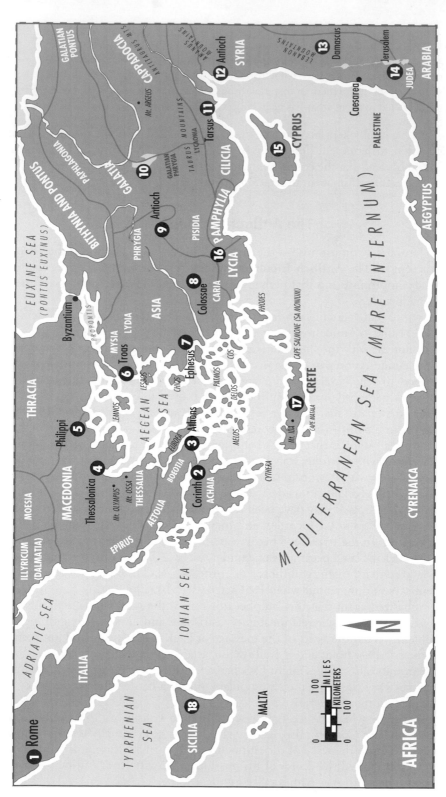

Figure 4.1 Major cities and regions of Paul's missionary activity and travels.

PAUL'S MISSIONARY JOURNEYS

The Mission to Galatia

At Antioch, Paul began the most active phase of his missionary work, deliberately going out into the Gentile world. Again, Acts portrays him as carrying out three separate, neatly defined, missionary journeys: one to Cyprus and southern Galatia (central Asia Minor or Turkey; 13:3–14:26); one through northern Galatia to Macedonia and Achaia (Greece), concluding at Ephesus in Asia Minor (15:40–18:22); and a third in generally the same region (18:23–21:17). Although three neat journeys suggest an ordering by the author of Acts, the general picture of the regions to which Paul went seems correct. At some point Paul would have worked on the island of Cyprus and in southern Galatia, readily accessible from his base in Antioch. Then he must have moved west following the overland route through northern Galatia. The author of Acts writes a mission speech for Paul at this point in another Antioch in central Asia Minor, that is, Antioch of Pisidia (Acts 13:13–52). Finally, at some point Paul made the momentous decision to go farther northwest into Macedonia and Achaia (Greece). Other options would have been southwest to the coastal region of **Asia,** whose congregations are the concern of the Book of Revelation, or northeast to the area of Bithynia and the Black Sea, where other missionaries went (1 Peter; Pliny-Trajan correspondence [see Chapter Twelve]). Acts 16:6–10 presents this decision as a result of a direct revelation to Paul.

The Mission in Macedonia (Northern Greece)

Paul's itinerary, going to cities in Macedonia (northern Greece) and Achaia (southern Greece), seems reasonably accurate because Paul's letters and Acts agree on the essentials:

Itinerary in Greece	Paul's Letters	Acts
Philippi	1 Thess. 2:2	Acts 16:11–40
Thessalonica	1 Thessalonians	Acts 17:1–9
Athens	1 Thess. 3:1	Acts 17:16–34
Corinth	1 Thess. 1:1; 3:6	Acts 18:1–17

Letters to three locations (Philippi, Thessalonica, Corinth) survive.

Paul says that he and his companions had "suffered and been shamefully treated at Philippi" (1 Thess. 2:2). This comment receives support from Acts 16:19–24, where the text says that they were whipped by command of city officials and thrown into prison (the account is expanded with miracle stories). Nonetheless, Paul had a special affection for the Philippians, and he later thanked them for their financial support, even though it did not coincide with his strategy of self-support by his trade (Phil. 4:15–16; cf. 2 Cor. 11:8–9).

After leaving Philippi, Paul probably followed the main highway westward across Macedonia (the Via Egnatia) to Thessalonica (modern Saloniki), a seaport and the capital city of ancient Macedonia (northern Greece). In 1 Thessalonians,

Paul encouraged the Thessalonians, among whom he had worked so hard (2:9), for their steadfast faith in the face of persecution by their countrymen (2:14). This comment implies that they had been recruited to his version of the Jesus Movement as Gentiles (1:9; contrast Acts 17:1–9). The letter has a strong dose of apocalyptic eschatology, which fits the situation of persecution.

The Mission in Achaia (Southern Greece)

According to Acts, Paul was forced to leave Thessalonica (Acts 17:5–9, 13–15). Whether forced or not, he moved on to Athens. In 1 Thessalonians, he mentions that Timothy was dispatched from Athens to Thessalonica (3:1–2). The author of the Acts of the Apostles presents one of the most magnificent mission sermons in the mouth of Paul (Acts 17), but no Pauline letter to the Athenians survives.

From Athens, Paul went westward to Corinth (Acts 18:1, 18), where Timothy probably rejoined him from Thessalonica (1 Thess. 3:6). Corinth was a thriving cosmopolitan seaport and capital of Achaia. As we noted in connection with the **Gallio Inscription,** Paul arrived there in 49 or 50 C.E.—the fulcrum for Pauline chronology—and stayed about eighteen months. There he established (at the house of Stephanas? 1 Cor. 1:16; 16:15) a lively **house-church** of mainly Gentiles. It was nurtured by Apollos (1 Cor. 1:12; 3:5–6), whom Acts claims had been a Diaspora Israelite from Alexandria and an eloquent man well versed in the scriptures (18:24–28). Having received Timothy's report about the Thessalonians, Paul probably wrote 1 Thessalonians, the first of his surviving letters, at this time. We have already illustrated Paul's back-and-forth correspondence with the Corinthians when he was at Ephesus later. It indicates many problems related to the Gentile background of the Corinthians. We have also noted his conflict with other apostles of the movement who challenged his authority. We shall say much more about these subjects in the following chapter.

From Corinth in Greece, Paul crossed the Aegean Sea eastward to Ephesus, a major port city in the province of Asia, the western coast of Asia Minor. The Acts itinerary then takes him from Ephesus back to Palestine and then up to Antioch.

The Mission in Asia (Western Turkey)

According to Acts, Paul retraced his steps through Asia Minor back to Ephesus (Acts 18:18–23; 19:1), thus launching a third missionary journey (down to 21:17). Although this account is full of legendary material, it is certainly accurate in placing Paul at Ephesus for a long period of time, perhaps two and a half years (19:8, 10). Hence, as we have suggested, he in effect shifted his headquarters from Antioch to Ephesus. 1 Corinthians was written at Ephesus (1 Cor. 16:8), as well as parts of 2 Corinthians (**letter fragments**). If Paul was imprisoned there, as most scholars think (2 Cor. 1:8–11), he probably wrote the "prison letters" Philippians and Philemon there. (In the preceding chronological sequence, Philippians and Philemon are located in the midst of Corinthian letters written at Ephesus.) He appears to have made a quick trip to Corinth, the "painful visit" noted earlier, and back (2 Cor. 2:1;

12:14, 21; 13:1). Eventually he made a journey through Macedonia, where he continued his correspondence with the Corinthians (2 Cor. 1:8–10, 15–16; 2:12–13; 7:5; 9:2). He may also have written Galatians about this time, although some scholars put it earlier.

Paul's Last Journey to Corinth

Finally, Paul made a third and final trip to Corinth (2 Cor. 13:1). Earlier we stressed his interest in the **collection** of the Corinthians for "the poor" among the believers at Jerusalem (1 Cor. 16:1–4; 2 Cor. 8, 9; Rom. 15:25–28). When he arrived at Corinth from Macedonia, Paul probably wrote his most lengthy and mature letter, Romans. In it he clearly indicated his intent to fulfill his promise to "remember the poor" by taking the collection back to Jerusalem, despite the dangers involved from opponents in Judea (Rom. 15:31).

Paul's Last Journey to Jerusalem

It seems likely that Paul's anxiety about the "unbelievers in Judea" (Rom. 15:31) was correct. The author of Luke-Acts tells the story that in Jerusalem Israelites from Asia claimed to the crowd in the temple that Paul had been speaking everywhere against the Law and the temple and had defiled it by bringing a Greek there. The crowd tried to beat Paul to death. However, he was rescued by the Romans and taken to the barracks. Eventually there was even a plot on his life. According to Acts, Paul appealed his case to Caesar, such appeal being, as we have noted, the right of every Roman citizen (Acts 21:1–28:16).

Paul's Journey to Rome

As yet, Paul had never been to Rome, despite his lengthy letter to the Romans. Now he went to Rome as a prisoner. The journey probably took place about 58/59 C.E. According to the conclusion of Acts, Paul spent two years in Rome under house arrest but preached "quite openly and unhindered." Although this comment reflects the perspective of the author of Luke-Acts, it is not implausible that Paul was an active missionary even while a prisoner.

New Testament knowledge of Paul ends at this point because Acts ends at this point. No undisputed letters are preserved from any later period. Some scholars hold that Philippians and Philemon were written during the Roman imprisonment, although most situate them in connection with the imprisonment in Ephesus. Church tradition says that Paul was released from his captivity, visited Spain, and returned to Rome a second time as a prisoner. Those who have tried to defend Paul's authorship of the Pastorals have placed a mission to Crete in this period. However, the later tradition of Paul's mission to Spain appears to be an attempt to make history out of Paul's plans in Rom. 15:24–29. Thus it is likely that Paul's first imprisonment in Rome ended with his death, probably as a martyr under the reign of Nero, as another church tradition says (*1 Clement* 5–6).

THE AUTHORITY OF PAUL AS APOSTLE

It is clear from both Paul's letters and Acts that he encountered delicate problems in his claim to be an apostle to the Gentiles. He had never known Jesus. He had been a persecutor of the church. Although he was no doubt dependent on various traditions of the Jerusalem and Damascus churches, and although "pillars" in the Jerusalem church confirmed his mission to the Gentiles, Paul claimed that his call originated in divine revelation, that it was independent of human agency. Moreover, the Gentile churches that Paul established had a special relationship with him; indeed, he attempted to gather a collection from them to take back to Jerusalem. It should come as no surprise, then, that there were those who constantly challenged his authority as an apostle—perhaps even his motives.

The issues surrounding Paul's authority and opposition to his authority have generated a great deal of discussion. Where do Paul and "his" churches fit within a spectrum of possibilities from a small sect in Greco-Roman Israel to a rational-legal institution accommodating itself to Hellenistic society? When religious assimilation begins to occur, some members of a group will want to hang on to the traditional ways, whether they are conservative or radical, whereas others will think it necessary to adjust.

In considering such important questions, three issues need to be highlighted: (1) Paul's relationship to the Jerusalem church, (2) his authority in the Gentile churches, and (3) opposition to him.

Paul and the Church at Jerusalem

Paul's precise relationship to the church in Jerusalem has been hotly debated. It is affected, perhaps even determined, by the relative weight scholars put on Galatians and Acts, as well as by the interpretation of Paul's emotional statements in Galatians and the way one interprets the Jerusalem church's willingness to accept the collection.

In his letters, Paul claimed that he went to Jerusalem to meet with the pillars "by revelation" (Gal. 2:2). Thus he said he was not sent. Indeed, he apparently considered himself to be the dominant figure at the conference. In the Acts version, however, Barnabas and Paul were *sent* as delegates from the Antioch church, and it was James and especially Peter who dominated the conference. Although Paul wrote Galatians some years after the conference, and although he wrote in the heat of controversy, Acts was written even later and written by one who was presumably not present at these events. Moreover, its author betrays an overall tendency to reduce conflict and see a smooth development in the early churches. According to our interpretive principle, then, Galatians must be the primary source. From its perspective, Paul did not "report in" to his "superiors," but rather maintained a degree of independence.

Yet, Paul knew some sayings of Jesus as well as confessional Christ creeds. How did he arrive at this information? It is possible that he learned at least some of it from the Jerusalem group. If so, Paul could not have been *totally* independent of Jerusalem. This conclusion is also suggested by his willingness to risk his life to take the collection back to Jerusalem. How should this collection be interpreted?

Some scholars suggest that the collection was equivalent to a tax, an analogy being the annual temple tax required of all adult Israelite males (see Chapter One). If this is correct, Paul would have been a representative of the Jerusalem "mother church" and presumably submissive to it. However, the limitation of the collection to Paul's "Gentile" churches, its one-time (not annual) occasion, and its destination for "the poor" in a literal sense make the Israelite temple tax an inadequate analogy. Yet, the collection was more than *only* an act of charity; it was for Paul also an act of gratitude, an indication of the independence of the Gentile churches, and—despite Paul's defense of his apostleship in Galatians—a sign of the unity of the church. In short, it appears that if Paul did not submit to the Jerusalem church, neither did he wish to offend it.

Paul's Authority in the Gentile Churches

Paul warned the Corinthians that they should not set their allegiance to him over against their allegiance to Christ. For Paul, Christ is the church's one and only foundation (e.g., 1 Cor. 1:10–17; 3:5–14). Nonetheless, it is hard to deny that he was an authority figure in "his" churches. He counseled those in his communities to imitate him (1 Thess. 1:6; Phil. 3:17; 1 Cor. 4:16). His letters are full of commands about what believers should be and do as well as pastoral comments that comfort. He had many coworkers, some of whom were clearly subordinate to him. In one instance, he ranked persons on the basis of spiritual gifts (1 Cor. 12:28); in so doing, he ranked his one self-designation, "apostle," at the very top (1 Cor. 12:28; cf. Eph. 4:11) and those who were causing problems, "speakers in various kinds of tongues," at the very bottom. In another instance, he mentioned in passing local roles, sometimes translated as "bishops" and "deacons" (Phil. 1:1 [RSV, NRSV]). If Paul's letters represent his demeanor—his opponents said they did not—Paul must have been an imposing figure. Certainly he could be very testy and occasionally nasty. Thus he generated opposition. Was Paul rebelling against the authority of the Jerusalem church while at the same time establishing his own authority in far-away lands? At first glance it might seem so; but the issues are more complicated. They need to be examined more carefully.

Paul's exhortation to imitate him should be seen in the context of his view that the gospel is a gospel of lowliness exemplified by "the Cross of Christ." Thus the true apostle "imitates Christ." "Be imitators of me, *as I am of Christ*" (1 Cor. 11:1; cf. Phil. 3:17). For Paul, this theme was a theological paradox with social and political implications: *God's power lies in weakness* (1 Cor. 1:10–4:21). He often cited this form of authority—indeed, boasted about his trials and tribulations—but he did so against opponents who boasted to honor themselves, as was common and acceptable. Yes, Paul would boast (2 Cor. 10:8; 11:16–28), but he would quickly say, "If I must boast, I will boast of the things that show *my weakness*" (2 Cor. 11:30). Moreover, this authority expressed itself in *love*. Behind his commands was the one who loved his churches and wanted to see them grow. "Knowledge (*gnōsis*) puffs up, but love (*agapē*) builds up" (1 Cor. 8:1).

There are many examples of authority expressed in weakness and molded by love in Paul's letters. Paul was bold enough to believe that as an apostle "in Christ" he could *command* the slave owner Philemon to release his slave Onesimus, but he preferred to appeal to him "for love's sake" (Philem. 8), giving him the freedom to make his own decision (Philem. 14). Although he saw some of his coworkers as subordinate, the relationship was an intimate and personal family-type one, characterized by such terms as "faithful," "trusted," "beloved." His ranking of spiritual gifts from "apostles" to "speaking in tongues" noted earlier needs to be seen in the broader context of 1 Cor. 12. There his stress was on the *unity* of a congregation being torn apart by social and religious conflict, and his fear was that people would think that "speaking in tongues" was a superior gift. Finally, the terms in Phil. 1:1 that have been translated "bishops" and "deacons" were simply mentioned and not explained by Paul. Many scholars think that they were not clearly defined offices with qualifications. That came later, perhaps in the deutero-Pauline Pastoral Letters. Some scholars and translators thus translate the terms as "overseers" and "ministers" (NAB) or "overseers" and "helpers" (NRSV margin). Paul as apostle also thought of himself as a "minister" (2 Cor. 11:23, *diakonoi* = "ministers" [NRSV]). In short, although the works point to *some* local function, their precise meaning in this early period remains uncertain.

In short, Paul did have authority in his churches, but it was the authority that certain social-scientific scholars call "charismatic leadership" (Max Weber). This sort of authority emerges not by virtue of some well-defined office passed on from generation to generation, but rather by virtue of the personal attraction that some leaders have for their followers. Whatever we call it, many believers in Paul's communities must have responded to him as a powerful religious figure. He was literate and a genius, a special human being in touch with the Divine. Paul used this recognition to challenge the *status quo* in the name of what as a divinely appointed apostle he believed to be the gospel of Jesus Christ and freedom from Torah commandments. Others, of course, could challenge him or claim to have a greater "charisma" and oppose him.

Paul's Opponents

In Paul's churches, there were those who denied his authority, did not follow him or heed his advice, imputed bad motives to him, or even considered him to be an imposter. Scholars usually call such persons Paul's "opponents." It is usually difficult to identify them with precision. In the first place, what they say about Paul has to be reconstructed from what he says about them, which is always a precarious historical procedure. Second, what he says about them is usually based on hearsay from his coworkers who traveled back and forth between him and the **house-churches,** or from letters, not first-hand information. Third, Paul's comments are often phrased in the style of ancient Greek rhetoric, not literal description. When was the rhetoric representative of reality? Finally, there is the pervasive tendency of Acts to smooth over Paul's conflicts with opponents, especially those in the Jerusalem church.

These critical problems have contributed to several different theories about the identity or identities of Paul's opponents within the Jesus Movement. Consider the missionaries who challenged his authority. Some modern interpreters argue that they are the same everywhere. Others maintain that they differ from place to place. Still other interpreters think that there are different types of opponents at the same place at different periods. One scholar argues that often Paul is not sufficiently informed to know precisely *who* they are, and so modern historians cannot know either! Nonetheless, the attempt to identify Paul's opponents within the Jesus Movement persists. One important reason is that it has potential to shed light on the possible diversity within the Jesus Movement and, most important in this context, Paul's own point of view when he counters them. Because Philemon is a personal letter to an individual, it does not reflect Paul's opponents (at Colossae? Cf. Col. 4:9); therefore, possibilities at the other major locations will be stressed. (Paul's opponents will be discussed also in later chapters; here it is enough to get a taste of frequent opposition to him, a major feature of his life.)

Jerusalem and Antioch

The James group at Jerusalem, who had originally agreed to the **Jerusalem Compromise,** apparently came to terms with the conservatives about purity matters. How would these Jerusalem conservatives have responded to Paul's continuing rejection of circumcision as a mark of God's covenant people or to Paul's eating with Gentiles? Would they have received Paul's collection for the poor from the Gentile churches? One recent study concludes:

> from the time of the [Jerusalem] conference, at the latest, the Jerusalem church assumed a preponderantly anti-Pauline attitude. Their rejection of the collection, which only a few years before had been a bond of unity between the two churches, was a clear public indication of the hostility to Paul of the Jerusalem church, from which James cannot be excluded.
>
> (Lüdemann, *Opposition to Paul,* pp. 62–63)

Although some scholars might see this as an extreme reading about opposition to Paul at Jerusalem, no one would doubt that Paul experienced some degree of opposition there. Neither would they doubt that this opposition spilled over into the Antioch church or that Paul placed hope in the collection as a way of helping to build unity.

Thessalonica

In 1 Thess. 2:1–12, Paul is defending the manner in which he had presented the gospel to the Thessalonians. He says that he and his companions were *without* error, uncleanness, guile, *without* seeking to please men, to use words of flattery, to cover their greed, *without* attempting to gain glory from men. Were there opponents who, in Paul's view, did just that? Paul is not specific, and his style in this passage is rhetorical. Some scholars even think that it was inserted later. In short, it is difficult to isolate a group of opponents from within the Jesus Movement at Thessalonica.

Philippi

In Phil. 3:2–3, Paul writes, "Beware of the dogs, beware of the evil workers, beware of those who mutilate the flesh [*katatomē*]. For it is we who are the circumcision [*peritomē*], who worship in the Spirit of God and boast in Christ Jesus and have no confidence in the flesh." These two sentences contain a pun on the terms *incision* (*katatomē*) and *circumcision* (*peritomē*). To pun on Paul's pun, this is one of Paul's occasional "cutting remarks." Paul is warning the Philippians against those who stress circumcision. Their identity is not clear. Probably they were Christ believers of Israelite background. However, their apparent tendency to think of following Torah regulations, especially circumcision, *as a means of attaining spiritual perfection, opens the possibility that* they were Gentile opponents like those whom Paul encountered in the congregation at Corinth (1 Cor. 9, 15). Perhaps they were Gentiles influenced by more conservative Israelite missionaries of the Jesus Movement. As in 1 Corinthians, Paul counters their arrogance with the weakness and lowliness of the crucified Christ (Phil. 3:18–21).

Corinth

In the Corinthian community, there were several kinds of opponents. What is more, the problem of opponents shifts when we move from 1 Corinthians to 2 Corinthians.

Paul was aware that Jesus and his disciples—including Peter—had elected to accept hospitality and financial support for their work (1 Cor. 9:14; see Q [Luke] 10:7b). He had encountered Jesus' disciple Peter at Antioch. Now he learned of a divisive faction at Corinth who alleged that they "belong to Peter" (1 Cor. 1:12). Paul also claimed the apostolic *right* to be supported by the Corinthians; nonetheless, he renounced this right in favor of working at his trade (1 Cor. 9:3–6). Thus some person or group must have been challenging his apostolic style. Paul's defense gives a reason for his self-support: He should not boast but rather exemplify "weakness," and the gospel should be free of charge. A similar opposition to Paul may be implied in 1 Cor. 15. There he defends his apostleship by claiming to have seen the resurrected Lord, just as have Jesus' disciples Peter and the Twelve, the Five Hundred, and Jesus' brother James—all from Jerusalem!

Another sort of opposition in 1 Corinthians came from those who were involved in what Paul deemed to be spiritual excesses (1 Cor. 1–4). Certain factions were proud of their special relationships with those associated with their baptism: Paul, Apollos, and Peter (1:10–17). Perhaps these same persons or groups boasted of their special human wisdom (1:26–30; 3:18–23) and their unique spiritual gifts (2:12; cf. 12, 14). Apparently claims were also being made that they had achieved spiritual perfection because some of the Corinthians believed that they were living the life of resurrection *already* (15) and that the community was already a redeemed heavenly body (11–12). Others interpreted their freedom to mean they were "strong," not "weak" (8–10). Some bragged about their special knowledge (*gnōsis,* cf. 8:1–3); their behavior may have derived from a very early form of Gnostic thinking ("proto-Gnosticism") that emerged within the congregation (4:18–21). Paul responded that God operates through weakness, as is indicated by the cross of Jesus and the low status of most of the Corinthians.

In 2 Corinthians Paul talks about other kinds of opponents. Some man had done injustice to Paul (2 Cor. 1:23; 2:4–5). After receiving Paul's "tearful letter" (partly 2 Cor. 10–13), the Corinthians punished the offender, whereupon Paul counseled love (2:6–8). There also seems to have been some criticism of Paul's gathering the collection for the poor. Probably some thought that he would mismanage (steal?) the funds (2 Cor. 7:2; 8:16–24).

More prominent in 2 Corinthians and also most discussed among scholars are the outside agitators in the Jesus Movement whom Paul labels sarcastically "super-apostles" (2 Cor. 11:4–5; 12:11). They were envoys of Israelite background (11:22), were complimentary to each other (10:12, 18), and bore "letters of recommendation" (3:1–3). Reportedly they performed miracles. They attacked Paul by saying "his letters are weighty and strong, but his bodily presence is weak, and his speech contemptible" (10:10; cf. 11:6). They also attacked Paul for supporting himself by his trade, but at the same time they claimed that he took advantage of them with the collection (11:7–9; 12:6, 13). For them, Paul was not a true "charismatic" and lacked the proper authority to be an apostle.

Paul's defense employed the rhetoric of accusation and "boasting." He accused the super-apostles of being "deceitful workers, disguising themselves as apostles of Christ" (11:13). He objected that they preached "another Jesus"—probably Jesus as a hero—and had "a different spirit" (11:4). He could also boast—like a fool, he says—but he boasted about his trials as an apostle: God demonstrates his divine power through weakness exemplified in the cross (13:4; cf. 1 Cor. 9). Paul, too, claimed to have had "visions and revelations of the Lord" (12:1) and to have performed "signs, wonders, and mighty works" (12:12) when he was among them.

Paul seems to have made some headway with the Corinthians because the letter fragments indicate reconciliation (2 Cor. 1:1–2:13; 7:5–16), and Paul finally made his visit to gather in the collection (2 Cor. 8, 9).

Galatia

After Paul had established a congregation at Galatia and moved on, there appeared a group who unsettled the church. According to Paul, they preached a "different gospel" (Gal. 1:6). They were probably members of the Jesus Movement who, like Paul, were of Israelite background. However, they pressured the Galatians to accept circumcision, attacking Paul for dispensing with it to "please people" (1:10). With much anger Paul charged that they had "bewitched" the Galatians (3:1) and in a two-edged comment that they wanted "to make a good showing *in the flesh*" (cf. 6:12). His sharpest cutting remark was, "I wish those who unsettle you would castrate themselves" (5:12).

Who were these Israelite opponents? Some scholars have suggested that they were purists from Jerusalem, perhaps strict Pharisees who dogged him wherever he went (2:3–4, 11–12). But would Jerusalem conservatives have held polytheistic, syncretistic views such as worshipping the "elemental spirits" (probably demonic angels or stars, or both) and observing days, months, seasons, and years (an astrological calendar [see Gal. 4:3, 9, 10])? A complicating factor is that these opponents seem to have charged that Paul is too dependent on Jerusalem leaders (chapters 1–2)!

These problems have led to other alternatives. One view is that there were two sets of opponents: the conservative group and the **syncretistic** group. Others have proposed that the opponents were recently circumcised *Gentile* members of the Jesus Movement who combined their old views with the necessity of circumcision. Still others argue for a group of *Israelite Gnostics* in the Jesus Movement!

Probably the most common view today is that the opponents at Galatia were *syncretistic Israelite missionaries in the Jesus Movement, that is,* missionaries who accepted a form of Israelite religion native to Asia Minor (were they similar to the Corinthian opponents in 2 Cor. 10–13?). If so, they did not follow the precise position of the Jerusalem conservatives but were *at one with them in what for Paul was the essential issue: the Torah and circumcision.*

Ephesus

In his letters to the Corinthians, Paul writes, "I fought with beasts at Ephesus" (1 Cor. 15:32) and speaks of facing death in Asia (2 Cor. 1:8–10). Most scholars think that Paul was imprisoned in Ephesus and that Philippians and Philemon were written during that imprisonment. The precise circumstances are not known.

Rome

The problem of identifying possible opponents at Rome is very complex, and, again, a variety of solutions can be defended. Although Paul may have known that he had real opponents at Rome, the language in Rom. 14:1–15:13 and 16:17–20 is mainly like the language about opponents in his other churches (Gal. 2:12; 4:10; 1 Cor. 8; 10; Phil. 3:19). Therefore, it is likely that Paul, who has not been to Rome, is engaging in rhetoric.

In concluding this section, an important historical question needs to be asked. Was continual opposition to Paul simply the natural response to a person who claimed authority for himself and by such claims elicited negative responses from others? Perhaps. But it should be recalled that in the ancient world there was often distrust of wandering philosophers and religious vagabonds. Moreover, it can hardly be doubted that Paul was a religious genius, a man of "charisma," who felt called and who carried out his call, despite amazing hardships. Indeed, for that reason he may have provoked envy and hostility.

PAUL'S URBAN CHURCHES

The gospels and their sources indicate that the main setting for Jesus' life was in the fields, towns, and fishing villages of rural Galilee and that he avoided the cities, except for Jerusalem. In contrast, Paul's letters reflect settings in key cities of the Roman Empire. Jesus' native language was Aramaic. Paul's native language was Greek, the primary spoken language in Greco-Roman cities. Paul was reared and at least partially educated in the city of Tarsus, and he appealed to Greek-speaking Gentiles in the cities. In short, the Pauline mission was basically an urban phenomenon (Meeks).

Urban members of the Jesus Movement normally worshipped together, had communal meals together, talked together, heard letters from apostles, and carried on their social life in **house-churches** (1 Cor. 16:19; Philem. 2; Rom. 16). In some cities there might be more than a single house-church. Residents were often members of an extended family that included relatives, household slaves, hired hands, and occasionally professional or trade partners and tenants. Urban households were often places of business, with an office as the most conspicuous room. Finally, the physical environment of Mediterranean houses was relatively open and partly open to view to outsiders. There was no porch in front or deck in back, but rather an open courtyard, or courtyards, in the center, and the rooms surrounded the court-

Courtesy of Carolyn Osiek

Figure 4.2 House of Vettii, Pompeii, Italy, the main garden or colonnaded "Peristyle." The Jesus Movement gathered in houses that scholars call "house-churches." In Greek and Roman houses the roof was open to the sky, like the house of Vettii, and people could be "outside" while being inside the house. The Pauline branch of the Jesus Movement was supported by patrons such as Stephanas (1 Cor. 1:15; 16:15) and Phoebe (Rom. 16:1–2) who probably owned larger houses. Were any of them as grand as the House of Vettii?

yard. In a Mediterranean climate, therefore, people could spend much more time out of doors but remain within the house. (See Figure 4.2.)

Whole households as distinct from individuals were often baptized into the Jesus Movement (1 Cor. 1:16). This undoubtedly created some conflict at home because a typical household was hierarchically organized from the head of the household (*pater familias*) down, as described in the **household codes,** whereas Paul's goal "in Christ Jesus" was the removal of customary social rankings (Gal. 3:28). The house-churches were local; there was as yet no centrally organized, hierarchical "universal church." Nonetheless, Paul was often in contact by letter and reminded the house-churches that they were networked with other house-churches in their own region (2 Cor. 1:1) and, indeed, with the whole "church of God" (1 Cor. 1:2). One way by which Paul himself symbolized this unity was the collection. The **Pauline School** in the late first century then developed the idea of a cosmic or universal church (Colossians, Ephesians).

We have discussed the problem of Paul's social status and noted the problem of the "educated artisan." What kinds of people did Paul attract to the Jesus Movement? This question has been studied especially in relation to Corinth. In the recent past, some scholars argued that earliest proselytes to the Jesus Movement were from the lower social strata. This judgment still pertains to the rural Palestinian Jesus Movement as portrayed in the gospels.

However, much recent social-historical and social-scientific work shows that this judgment is too general for Paul's urban Hellenistic churches (Judge; Theissen; Meeks). To be sure, the Pauline wing of the movement attracted many people from the lower social strata. Included were artisans, freed persons, slaves, and the poor, groups who were alienated from social and political power. However, Paul implied that at Corinth there were at least *a few* of "noble birth" and perhaps also *a few* "wise" and "powerful" in the worldly sense (1 Cor. 1:26). A study of particular individuals in Paul's churches, some of whom had political positions or offered special services or could afford to travel, bears this out.

Although social and religious conflicts arose inside the Pauline communities, members strove to maintain a united front so that the movement might be perceived favorably by "outsiders" or nonbelievers. This approach had precedent in **Diaspora synagogues.** The distinction between insiders and outsiders—social boundaries—is also implied by rituals of entrance (baptism, Rom. 6) and perpetuation (the Lord's Supper, 1 Cor. 10:16–17; 11:23–25). Paul thought of ethical behavior in terms of "imitation": His "children" were to imitate him as he imitated Christ (1 Cor. 11:1). A radical nonconformist in the community was excluded (1 Cor. 5:2, 11). Believers in Jesus as the Christ were "chosen," "beloved," and "saints" (literally, "holy ones"). Thus for all his difficulties with more conservative views of purity, Paul was developing his own sense of purity. However, it would be incorrect to leave the impression that the Pauline communities were withdrawn and exclusive. If social boundaries were being drawn, they were also fluid. For Paul, the new era had as its ideal the abolishment of the distinctions between Israelite and Gentile, slave and free, male and female (Gal. 3:28). This was a new "fictive" family with new norms and values (Bartchy). Moreover, in practice Jesus Movement peoples were not to break off all ties with outsiders (1 Cor. 5:9–13). They could be entertained at the homes of nonbelievers and even eat "meat offered to (pagan) idols," *if* the practice did not offend the conscience of a weaker believer (1 Cor. 8; 10:23–30). Were these communities "sectarian"? Yes—and no. W. Meeks writes:

> In the letters, we see Paul and his followers wrestling with a fundamental ambiguity in their conception of the social character of the church. On the one hand, it is formed as an eschatological sect, with a strong sense of group boundaries, reinforced by images of a dualistic tendency and by foundation stories of a crucified Messiah raised from the dead as the root symbol of the way God's action in the world is to be perceived and followed. On the other hand, it is an open sect, concerned not to offend those outside but to attract them to its message and if possible to its membership. It has other forms of self-description. It also has basic symbols that point toward universality and comprehensiveness: it is the people of the one God, including both Israelite and Gentile. Indeed, Christ is the "last Adam," the "new *anthropos* ['man']," the image of God and therefore the restoration of humanity to its created unity.
>
> ("Since Then You Would Need to Go Out of the World," p. 41)

SUMMARY

In this chapter the canonical sources for Paul's personality, life, and thought have been examined. The seven undisputed canonical letters are primary sources—they come from Paul himself—and the Acts of the Apostles is secondary. Five letter fragments in 2 Corinthians can be isolated and placed in sequence and then used (with some help from Acts) to develop a chronological progression for one phase of Paul's career. Then, after developing a sequence of all the letters and using archeological evidence as a fulcrum along with Acts, it becomes possible to fill in many of the gaps to expand the Corinthians sequence and arrive at a relative chronology for Paul's career. With this chronology as a skeletal outline, a sketch of what is known about Paul's life can be made. Much can be said about his personality, background, "conversion" to the Jesus Movement, conviction that he is an apostle ("call"), and activity as a missionary. Another important feature is Paul's authority in relation to the Jerusalem church and to the congregations he himself established, taking into account his opponents. Finally, it needs to be emphasized that Paul's main social context was the Greco-Roman city. With this background, it is hoped that a foundation has been laid for studying Paul's letters in sequence, the subject of the next two chapters.

STUDY QUESTIONS

1. What are the undisputed Pauline letters? How do scholars attempt to reconstruct the sequence of Paul's life from his letters? What are letter fragments, and how are they discovered?

2. What are the Gallio Inscription and the Edict of Claudius? Why is Phil. 3:5 so important? What and where was Paul's hometown? What was Paul's ethnic and religious background, and why was it well suited for his role as "apostle to the Gentiles"? What was his trade and its significance for his social status and mission? Why do scholars put quotation marks around the word *conversion* in relation to Paul? What city was Paul's first home base for his mission?

3. What were the Jerusalem Conference and its results? Where were the key cities of Paul's mission? Why did Paul generate so much conflict? Who were his opponents? What was Paul's mission strategy?

4. What were house-churches? What do you think about Paul's authority in the churches he started?

Photo 5.1 Old Corinth, the *bēma*, and the Akrocorinth. Acts 18:12–17 says that at Corinth, the capital city of Achaia (southern Greece), Paul was dragged before Gallio, the proconsul or governor, who sat in judgment on a raised platform called a *bēma*. Since a church was built over the ruins of this raised platform, perhaps it was that very *bēma*. In the background is the Akrocorinth, a hill on which in the classical period was found the temple of Aphrodite, said to have housed 1,000 temple prostitutes (probably an exaggeration).

CHAPTER FIVE

THE LETTER AND PAUL'S EARLY LETTERS

In the last chapter, the stage was set for understanding Paul's letters by looking at the way the Pauline letters can be analyzed and then by studying Paul's background, life, social context, missionary strategy, and opponents. In this and the next chapter the task will be to study Paul's individual letters.

Although not all ancient manuscripts had exactly the same sequence of Paul's letters, the sequence that became *the canonical order* in the New Testament manuscripts is as follows (undisputed letters in **bold**; others in brackets):

Romans → **1 Corinthians** → **2 Corinthians** → **Galatians** → [Ephesians] → **Philippians** → [Colossians] → **1 Thessalonians** → [2 Thessalonians] → [*1 Timothy*] → [*2 Timothy*] → [*Titus*] → **Philemon**→ [Hebrews]

This canonical sequence was based on three factors: (1) the formation of letter collections, (2) the length of the letters (from the largest to the smallest) within the collections, and (3) Hebrews as a much-disputed book (see Chapters Two, Seven). Collections of letters were common in the ancient Mediterranean, especially letters attributed to philosophers and politicians. Such letter collections helped to create an honorable impression about some venerable person within a community of admirers.

The first Pauline collection may have consisted of the seven undisputed letters. The collection appears to have grown to ten letters sometime in the early second century C.E. Thus the first three deutero-canonical books—2 Thessalonians, Colossians, and Ephesians, not written until 70–100 C.E.—were added. Marcion's canon about 150 C.E. contained ten Pauline letters, and that was probably his canon. The three Pastorals (in *italics*)—1 Timothy, 2 Timothy, Titus—were probably written in the early second century c.e. and were also collected together. They were personal letters, and Philemon, also a personal letter, was eventually put with them in a collection. Two types of collections emerged: letters written to churches (the first nine) and letters written to persons (the next four). Then the two collections were converged to make a collection of thirteen. Eventually, as the Book of Hebrews (underlined) gained acceptance, it was tacked on to the thirteen-letter collection.

This chapter will take up *five of the seven undisputed* Pauline letters, which have the following probable chronological order:

1 Thessalonians → 1 Corinthians → 2 Corinthians → Philippians → Philemon

Discussion will deviate from this suggested chronological order in one instance: the letter to Philemon. This little letter will be considered first because it offers the simplest and best example for examining the genre and rhetoric of Paul's letters in relation to letters in general in Greco-Roman antiquity. Most attention in the chapter will be given to 1 Corinthians because of its length and importance for social relations in the Jesus Movement. The next chapter will take up the remaining two undisputed Pauline letters—Galatians and Romans—because they share some of the same themes and because Paul probably wrote them last. The chapter after that will consider the early deutero-Pauline letters because they come next chronologically. It will also consider Hebrews.

A good place to begin is with a discussion of genre and rhetoric and with Paul's use of early traditions and scripture.

THE PAULINE LETTER: ITS GENRE AND RHETORIC

When Paul had been away from one of his newly founded congregations for a while, he continued to maintain communication through oral reports and letters. For example, Paul says in 1 Cor. 1:11 that Chloe's people brought him (oral) reports about factions and certain moral questions, to which Paul responded (1 Cor. 1–6). In 1 Cor. 7:1, he turns to matters about which the Corinthians had written to him in a letter (now lost). Paul's coworkers or other travelers in the Jesus Movement carried these oral reports and letters. With the possible exception of his letter to the Romans, the content of a letter was related directly to problems in the particular congregation (except the personal letter to Philemon). Sometimes members of the congregations communicated good news to him about their life and activities. Sometimes—more frequently!—they communicated problems and sought his advice. As you know, Paul often had to defend himself against opponents, both insiders and outsiders, sometimes made known to him through such communications.

In short, Paul's letters were expressions of good news, joy, gratitude, opinion, advice, clarification, recommendation, anger, self-defense, his own situation and plans, and his teaching about God, Christ's death and resurrection, salvation, scripture, the nature of the church, and morality.

How was the letter written? Recall first that not many people could read or write. Paul could, but he also followed common practice, that is, he dictated letters to a person who had special skills in writing, a professional "secretary" (Hebrew: *sōphēr,* "scribe"; Greek *grammateus,* "scribe," "secretary"; Latin: ***amanuensis,*** "of the hand"). One secretary of Paul's is mentioned by name in Rom. 16:22: "I, Tertius, writer of this letter, greet you in the Lord." Sometimes Paul would add at the end of a letter his personal touch and stamp of authority by adding a greeting (1 Cor. 16:21), a promise (Philem. 19), or a summary (Gal. 6:11) in his own hand.

Paul wrote to his communities in a specific geographical area or city. Community members would gather, usually for worship and social life, at some wealthy patron's house, that is, a **house-church.** In 1 Thess. 5:27, he explicitly requested that the recipients of his letter read it to the gathered house-church (Paulinists later imitated this tradition; cf. 2 Thess. 3:14–15). Even his most personal letter, Philemon, was meant to be read openly to those in the house-church (Philem. 2).

Content considerations and Paul's "signing off" at the end of his letters raise the question of the letter **genre.** It is fortunate that in this case there exist for comparison not only more formal types of letters in classical literature, but also a large number of everyday "nonliterary" papyrus letters discovered in modern times. These include personal letters to friends and relatives, business letters, and various kinds of governmental, military, diplomatic, and legal correspondence. These letters include a number of personal, friendly, cordial letters that show what relationships between authors and those to whom they wrote were like. Paul's letters have some of the same elements (especially 2 Cor. 1:1–2:13; Phil. 4:1–20). Most important, these ancient letters follow a rather set pattern, or form. Paul modifies this standard form by giving it special meaning for believers, and that will be examined.

To illustrate this letter genre, it will be instructive to consider a typical personal letter from the papyri, Apion's letter to his father Epimachus, and compare it to Paul's shortest, most personal letter, the letter to Philemon. At this point *form,* not content, is more important. Content will be considered later.

Apion's Letter to His Father Epimachus

Apion to Epimachus his father and lord, many greetings. Before all things I pray that you are in health, and that you prosper and fare well continually together with my sister and her daughter and my brother. I thank the Lord Serapis that when I was in peril on the sea he saved me immediately. When I came to Miseni, I received as *viaticum* ["journey money"] from the Caesar three pieces of gold. And it is well with me but I urge you, my lord father, to write me a little letter: first, about your welfare; second, about my brother and sister; third, so that I may do obeisance to your hand, because you have taught me well and I have hopes therefore of advancing quickly, if the gods are willing. Greet Capito much and my brother and sister and Serenilla and my friends. By Euctemon I am sending you a little picture of myself. Furthermore, my name is [now] Antonis Maximus. Be well, I pray. Centuris Athenonica [my military unit]. The following send their greetings: Serenus the son of Agathus Daemon, and . . . the son of . . . and Turbo the son of Gallonius and . . . the son of . . . (Farewell!)

[On the back:]

To Philadelphis for Epimachus
from Apion his son
Give this to the first cohort of the Apamenians to [?]
Julianus An . . . the Liblarios,
from Apion so that he may convey it to
Epimachus his father.

The Letter to Philemon as a Comparison

Briefly, when Paul was in prison, probably in Ephesus, he met a slave, Onesimus, whom he probably convinced to join the Jesus Movement. Despite his affection for Onesimus, Paul decided to send the slave back to his master Philemon. However, Philemon belonged to the Jesus Movement; indeed, he may have been a patron of a Colossian house-church. This state of affairs posed a delicate problem for Paul: How should a slave owner in the Jesus Movement treat a slave who had also become a Christ believer and who was—presumably illegally—absent from his master's household? Paul carefully composed a short, delicately worded letter to indicate his wishes in the matter. A comparison of Paul's letter to Philemon to a letter of Epimachus will illustrate the extent to which Paul uses the conventional letter form. (See Table 5.1.)

It is clear that Paul's letter to Philemon conforms to the customary ancient Greek letter genre, although he makes some changes. First, consider the beginning of the letter. Paul alters the typical Greek opening *Chairein* ("greetings") to the similar Greek term *Charis* ("Grace"), which refers to God's free gift of salvation in Jesus Christ. Thus he shifts from the normal greeting to a specialized religious greeting. Second, Paul adds to this Greek greeting the typical Israelite greeting, *Shalōm* ("Peace"). Such changes are typical of Paul. Thus Paul's letters usually begin with a short formula such as "*grace* to you and *peace* from God the father and our Lord Jesus Christ." Third, Paul sometimes includes liturgical traditions in his salutations.

The central section of Paul's letters normally falls into two subsections: the body and the moral exhortation. The body usually covers the major themes of the letter. Paul's most sophisticated ideas usually occur here. The moral exhortation often begins with a formula of request ("I implore you . . .") or disclosure ("I would not have you ignorant . . ."). However, Paul sometimes begins with a formula that simply marks off specific topics of discussion ("Now concerning . . ."). These "hortatory" or moral encouragement and advice sections are unlike typical Greco-Roman letters in two ways. First, the Greco-Roman letters usually make rhetorical moral appeals on the basis of individual character and virtue; in contrast, Paul usually appeals to group solidarity and divine power. Second, Paul's hortatory sections usually close by adding some statement about his travel plans or itinerary. He omits this feature only in Galatians because he has no intention to return (Gal. 4:12–15). Some letters have very little moral teaching in the central section. In such cases, Paul's

Table 5.1 Two Letters Compared

	Papyrus Letter	Letter to Philemon
A. Introduction		
I. Salutation		
1. Sender	Apion	Paul; Timothy;
2. Recipient	Epimachus	Philemon; Apphia; Archippus; his household
3. Greeting	"Greetings" Prays for their well-being	"Grace" to you and "peace" from God our Father and the Lord Jesus Christ
II. Thanksgiving and prayer	Gives thanks to God for a safe journey	I thank God always when I remember you in my prayers
B. Central Section		
III. Body	Statement about wages; hopes for advancement	Paul asks Philemon to "accept" the slave Onesimus
IV. Moral exhortation or other commands	Urges father to write to him about the family	Receive him as you would me . . . Charge that to my account . . . Refresh my heart in Christ . . . Prepare a guestroom for me . . .
C. Conclusion		
V. Greetings to . . .	Capito; my Brother; my sister; Serenilla	Absent but present in other letters; implicit in "you" (= recipients)
Greetings from . . .	my friends Serenus; -?-; Turbo; -?-	Epaphras; Mark; Aristarchus; Demas; Luke; my fellow workers
VI. Closing or benediction	Absent due to text mutilation; usually, "Farewell"	The grace of the Lord Jesus Christ be with your spirit

usual pattern is to put longer moral exhortations near the end of the letter, before the conclusion. These moral sections are like little homilies or "sermonettes." One might say that in letters of this sort there is a natural progression: What God has done for believers ("theology") brings forth what believers ought to do in response ("ethics"). In other letters, however, shorter clusters of moral maxims and exhortations about virtues and vices (common in Hellenistic moral philosophy; see Chapter Three) may crop up almost anywhere. Indeed, much of 1 Corinthians is moral advice or ethical exhortation.

You can see that Paul modifies the typical letter genre to fit special needs and circumstances. The letters are therefore "occasional letters," designed to fit the specific occasion. 1 Thessalonians has much more thanksgiving and consolation because the Thessalonians held on to their faith in times of persecution. In Galatians, Paul is very angry because, as we have seen, his opponents were seducing church members at Galatia into practicing the rite of circumcision. Thus two uncharacteristic changes occur: His initial salutation becomes a defense of his apostolic authority, and he omits the customary complementary "thanksgiving" altogether! In Romans, Paul's salutation contains a long summary of his gospel and definition of his apostolic mission (1:1–7) because he has not yet been to Rome and is introducing himself.

Finally, Paul also modifies the customary conclusion. Whereas the Greek letter usually had a simple "farewell" as a closing, Paul's letters contain several closing elements that express his distinctive thought. The "peace wish," like the term "peace" in the greeting, reflects the Hebrew *Shalōm,* that is, well-wishing for one's health, although Paul sometimes uses it as an occasion for recalling a major theme in the letter (1 Thess. 4:9). There are usually greetings to recipients and from senders. Often there is another reference to "grace." As Paul opens with "grace" and "peace," so he often closes with "peace" and "grace." Hellenistic letters often contain a prayer request, and Paul sometimes adds this (1 Thess. 5:25; Rom. 15:30). Greeting one another with a kiss sometimes has been thought to have been a liturgical sign, that is, after the reading of the letter, members of the Jesus Movement would celebrate the liturgy. It is more likely to have been a sign of affection within the new family. Exhortations or apostolic commands sometimes follow. Finally comes the benediction with its word of grace occasionally related to a threat (1 Cor. 16:23; cf. 1 Thess. 5:27; Gal. 6:17). A variant is an apocalyptic cry, "Our Lord, come!" (1 Cor. 16:22; cf. Rev. 22:20), probably taken from the liturgy in which the Last Supper was celebrated, that is, the "eucharistic liturgy" (Greek *eucharisteō:* "I give thanks").

In short, Paul transformed many of the formal features of the ancient Greek letter; he tailored them to fit the insider language of the Jesus Movement. It became something of an insider's genre, both in form and content.

In considering the form of the letter, Paul's most personal letter has been compared to a soldier's personal letter to his family. This comparison is not arbitrary. Study of Paul's language in Philemon shows that its language is much like the language of the familial letters of the period. It is "fictive kin" language. Even the more personal letter to Philemon, however, has its public side. Paul intended it to be read publicly in Philemon's house (Philem. 2). Although like a familial-type letter, Philemon is *also* a typical letter of mediation. In such letters, a third party writes to another person, usually a friend, on behalf of somebody else to mediate some conflict.

Before leaving the topic of Paul's language, note again his ability to use rhetoric. Students from the upper strata of society learned introductory rhetoric and letter writing at the secondary level of education. More advanced rhetorical skills were learned from a rhetorician-tutor. Typically students imitated famous speeches. These models were the basis for a set of precise rhetorical rules. Although no comparable rules for letter writing have survived, it appears that letter writers adapted rhetorical rules. In other words, guidelines for letter writing overlapped guidelines for speech giving. Recent study of Paul's letters has examined these rhetorical rules. Briefly, there were three types of rhetorical persuasion:

1. The rhetoric of the *courtroom,* which accuses or defends people on trial on the basis of what is deemed just or unjust ("judicial rhetoric")

2. The rhetoric of *public, political debate,* which argues for an expedient course of future action ("deliberative rhetoric")

Table 5.2 Use of the Rhetorical Appeals in Philemon

Exordium (4–7)	Proof (8–16)	Peroration (17–22)
My **prayers** (4)		Your prayers (22)
Your **love** (5)		
Your **love** (7)	Because of **love** (9)	
All the **good** (6)	The **good** (14)	
The **fellowship** of your faith (6)		If therefore you have me as a **fellow** (friend)
The **hearts** of the saints have been refreshed through you (7)	Onesimus . . . my very **heart** . . . beloved brother (11, 12, 16)	Yes, brother, I want some benefit from you in the Lord. Refresh my **heart** . . . (20)

3. The rhetoric of *victory celebrations, funerals, weddings,* and the like, which *praises or blames persons or actions* ("epideictic rhetoric")

Most scholars of rhetoric think that Philemon contains mainly the second type, or deliberative rhetoric, because it stresses arguments for expedient action. Paul offers advice to his believing "brother" and attempts to convince him of a course of action, just the way that a friend might counsel a friend or, better, a close family member might offer advice to another family member. He appeals to Philemon's honor and what is of advantage to him, as well as his good character and love. He does all this with emotional appeals to what is reasonable.

In short, the letter to Philemon is similar to a speech of deliberative rhetoric. (See Table 5.2.) Its three parts—introduction, body, and conclusion—have parallels to the three parts of the "deliberative speech":

- The *exordium,* a complementary introduction *meant to gain the favor of the speaker/reader* by using praise related to the subject (the body)
- The *proof,* or main body, that is, the *advancement of arguments* that make use of direct appeal, emotion, and reason
- The *peroration,* or *summary restatement,* to win over the hearer/reader, amplify the argument, and put the hearer/reader in an emotional frame of mind *to take action*

The form and rhetoric of the letter to Philemon have several characteristics. It is typified by "deliberative rhetoric" related to advice in a very personal, familial style. It even includes a little humor. There are other subtypes of letters in the Pauline corpus and still other types mentioned by Paul. For example, Paul mentions his opponents' letters of recommendation (cf. 2 Cor. 3:1–3), to which we might compare Paul's own (letter of?) recommendation of Phoebe (Rom. 16:1–2). As already observed, some letters stress thanksgiving (1 Thess. 1:2–3:10; cf. Phil. 1:3–3:1a; 4:10–20) or responses to others' specific questions (1 Cor. 7–15) or defense (Gal. 1–2) or thanksgiving, consolation, and moral exhortation (1 Thessalonians) or general beliefs in a kind of "letter-essay" (Rom. 1–15). All are well-known letter subtypes in the Greco-Roman world.

For comparison, Table 5.3 is an outline of the structure of Paul's other six letters.

Table 5.3 Outline of Letter Structure

		1 Thess.	1 Cor.	2 Cor.	Gal.	Phil.	Rom.
Introduction	I. Salutation						
	A. Sender	1:1a	1:1	1:1a	1:1–2a	1:1	1:1–6
	B. Recipient	1:1b	1:2	1:1b	1:2b	1:1	1:7a
	C. Greeting	1:1c	1:3	1:2	1:3–5	1:2	1:7b
	II. Thanksgiving	1:2–10 2:13 3:9–10	1:4–9	1:3–7	None!	1:3–11 4:10–20	1:8–17
Central Section	III. Body	2:1–3:8 (possibly 3:11–13)	1:10–4:21	1:8–9:15 (letter fragments) 10:1–13:10 (letter fragment)	1:6–4:31	1:12–2:11 2:19–3:1a 3:1b–4:1	1:18–11:36
	IV. Ethical Exhortation and Instructions	4:1–5:22	5:1–16:12 16:13–18 (closing moral exhortation)	13:11a (summary)	5:1–6:10 6:11–15 (summary)	2:12–2:18 4:2–6	12:1–15:13 15:14–32 (travel plans and closing moral exhortation)
Conclusion	V. Closing						
	A. Peace Wish	5:23–24	—	13:11b	6:16	4:7–9	15:33
	B. Greetings	—	16:19–20a	13:13	—	4:21–22	16:3–15(?), 21–23
	C. Kiss	5:26	16:20b	13:12	—	—	16:16(?)
	D. Apostolic Command	5:27	16:22	—	6:17	—	—
	E. Benediction	5:28	16:23–24	13:14	6:18	4:23	16:20(?)
	(F. Doxology)	—	—	—	—	—	(16:25–27)

(Reprinted with slight revisions from *The Letters of Paul: Conversations in Context* by Calvin J. Roetzel, 2nd ed. (slightly modified), John Knox Press. Used by permission.)

PRE-PAULINE TRADITIONS IN PAUL'S LETTERS

Paul stressed that his message came through a revelation of Christ and that there-fore he was not *taught* it by some human (Gal. 1:12). Yet, he also says that he remained at Damascus and Arabia (among members of the Jesus Movement?) for three years. Then he visited Peter and James at Jerusalem for a little over two weeks, associated with believers in the regions of Syria and Cilicia, and went again to Jerusalem for the Jerusalem Conference (Gal. 1:13–2:10). At locations such as these, he must have become acquainted with at least aspects of worship in the Christ-believing communities, for example, confessions and hymns about Jesus as "the Christ," liturgical phrases, and some traditional "words of the Lord." It is also clear from his letters that he was deeply immersed in the Scriptures and argued his case from them in ways he might have learned from his training as a Pharisee and as a leader in the Jesus Movement. As we have seen, he also had some level of education in Greek rhetorical devices, literary conventions, and parenetic traditions similar to those found among the Stoics and Cynics. Again, Paul had at least a secondary education—and perhaps more.

Recall that there are ways of recognizing and isolating sources and traditions in ancient texts. With respect to Paul, they often interrupt his line of argument (more than usual!), are sometimes introduced by terms for transmitting oral traditions well known from Israelite texts, and have a certain poetic or hymnlike style. They usually contain basic confessional statements about Jesus as "the Christ" (not always Paul's). Finally, they contain a number of terms and phrases not typical of Paul. Here we cite a few typical examples.

- *A death and resurrection-appearance tradition* is recognizable by technical terms for transmitting oral traditions ("handed on . . . received"), by a formal pattern, and a number of atypical terms and phrases (1 Cor. 15:3b–5; see Chapter Three)
- *A **Christological** confession:* ". . . if you confess with your lips that Jesus is Lord and believe in your heart that God raised him from the dead, you will be saved" (Rom. 10:9)
- *A Christological creed* that does not accord precisely with Paul's views of Jesus as the preexistent Son of God (Rom. 1:3–4; see Chapter Three)
- *A Christological hymn* in Phil. 2:6–11 (see Chapter Three)
- *A Lord's Supper tradition* with the technical terms for transmitting tradition (see Chapter Three)
- *A baptismal liturgy:*

  > (For as many of you as were *baptized* into Christ have put on Christ.)
  > There is neither Israelite nor Greek,
  > There is neither slave nor free,
  > There is neither male nor female;
  > For you are all one in Christ Jesus.
  > > (Gal. 3:27–28; cf. 1 Cor. 12:13; Col. 3:11)

- *A prayer doxology* (Greek *doxa:* "praise"): "Thanks be to God through Jesus Christ our Lord." (Rom. 7:25)

- A *"word of the Lord"* (that is, a tradition about what Jesus said): "To the married I give this command—not I but the Lord—that the wife should not separate from her husband . . . and that the husband should not divorce his wife." (1 Cor. 7:10–11)
- A *catalogue of vices and virtues* (such catalogues were commonly used by Hellenistic moral philosophers): (Now the works of the *flesh* are plain:) immorality, impurity, licentiousness, idolatry, sorcery, enmity, strife, jealousy, anger, selfishness, dissension, party spirit, envy, drunkenness, carousing, and the like . . . (But the fruit of the *Spirit* is) love, joy, peace, patience, kindness, goodness, faithfulness, gentleness, self-control . . . (Gal. 5:19–23; cf. 1 Cor. 6:9–11)
- A *proverb:* "Bad company ruins good morals." (1 Cor. 15:33)

PAUL AND THE SCRIPTURES

Paul the Pharisee was immersed in the scriptures of ancient Israel, and he frequently used them as a source to buttress his arguments. Most of his allusions and quotations came from the Greek version, or **Septuagint,** but many of his arguments relied on methods that, however strange to modern ears, were familiar to Israelite scholars of his day. Here are two examples:

- An Israelite *"midrash"* used to give the scriptures meanings for the Jesus Movement (see the Exodus and Wilderness Wandering [Exod. 13:21–22; 14:22; 16:4–35; 17:6; Num. 20:2–12; Ps. 105:39; Num. 21:16–18; Tosefta *Sukkah* 3:11])

   > I do not want you to be unaware, brothers and sisters, that our ancestors were all under a cloud, and all passed through the sea, and all were baptized into Moses in the cloud and in the sea, and all ate the same spiritual food [e.g., manna], and all drank the same spiritual drink. For they drank from the spiritual rock that followed them, *and the rock was Christ.* Nevertheless, God was not pleased with most of them, and they were struck down in the wilderness. Now these things occurred as examples for us, so that we might not desire evil as they did. . . .
   >
   >   (1 Cor. 10:1–6)

- A *word association* between two different meanings of the Greek word *diathēkē,* "will" and "covenant," combined with an interpretation of a grammatically singular noun that has a plural or collective meaning, namely, the Greek word *sperma,* meaning "offspring" or "descendants." Such an interpretation needs to be studied carefully:

   > Brothers and sisters, I give an example from daily life: once a person's *will* (*diathēkē*) has been ratified, no one adds to it or annuls it. Now the promises were made to Abraham and to his *offspring* (*sperma*); it does not say, "And to offsprings (*spermata*)," as of many; but it says, "And to your offspring (*sperma*)" (Gen. 12:7, etc.), that is, to one person, *who is Christ.* My point is this: the law (of Moses), which came four hundred thirty years later (than the covenant with Abraham), does not annul a *covenant* (*diathēkē,* here meaning "covenant") previously ratified (like a *diathēkē,* meaning "will") by God, so as

to nullify the promise. For if the (willed) inheritance comes from the law (of Moses), it no longer comes from the promise (to Abraham); but God granted it to Abraham through the promise. Why then the law? It was added because of transgressions, *until the offspring ["seed"] would come to whom the promise had been made* . . .

(Gal. 3:15–19a)

In interpretations of Paul's letters in the following chapter, such traditional elements will often be noted.

As an aid for study in what follows we offer interpretive outlines. *They are not meant as a substitute for reading Paul himself; rather, they should be used to help focus on the major points of what Paul says.*

FIRST THESSALONIANS: CONSOLATION AND INTERPRETATION OF THE MILLENNIUM IN THE FACE OF PERSECUTION

Background

According to the itinerary reconstructed in Chapter Four, Paul entered Macedonia (northern Greece) and established his first European congregation at a city called Philippi. He then traveled from Philippi on a major Roman highway, the Via Egnatia or "Egnatian Way," westward across Macedonia to Thessalonica. Thessalonica, named for the sister of Alexander the Great, was the capital of Macedonia. It was also the province's chief seaport and most populated city. In line with his strategy of going to major cities, then, Paul established a congregation at Thessalonica.

Paul says in 1 Thessalonians that while he was at Thessalonica he and his companions worked hard to support themselves by their trade but that they were treated shabbily (1 Thess. 2:2). By whom? Answering this question requires taking a position on the divergence between Acts and Paul's letters (**Historical Criticism**), a problem discussed in Chapter Three. Acts 17:1–9 suggests that Paul's major opponents were local *Israelites* who resented Paul's activity in their synagogue and who were jealous of the conversion to the Jesus Movement of some of its Israelite members and Gentile "God-fearers," including some "leading women." These *Israelites* incited the rabble to riot. Also a certain man named Jason, whose house had been the center of Paul's and Silas' activity, along with some of "the brethren" were brought before the city authorities and charged with treason for claiming that Jesus was "another king." However, if 1 Thess. 2:13–16 is not an "interpolation" from a later Paulinist—Paul is not usually so harsh in condemning his fellow Israelites—Paul's letter sees it differently: Both the converts and the opponents were *Gentiles* (1 Thess. 2:14). There may also be a slight discrepancy between Acts and 1 Thessalonians in time: Acts 17:2 says the small band of missionaries stayed only three weeks, whereas 1 Thessalonians suggests that they were there for some time.

According to Acts, the Thessalonians immediately sent Paul and his companions by night to the coastal town of Beroea farther south (Acts 17:10). When they were pursued, Paul himself was urged on to Athens, presumably joined by his companions later. In 1 Thessalonians, Paul says that they wanted to return to Thessalonica but that "Satan blocked our way" (2:18); so he sent Timothy from Athens (3:1). When Paul's preaching at Athens did not find much response, he went on to Corinth, arriving there about 49 C.E. (the **Gallio Inscription**). According to Acts, he stayed about eighteen months (18:12–17). Thus, in lieu of his desired return to Thessalonica, Paul wrote what is now called "1 Thessalonians," probably from Corinth about 51 C.E.

With respect to *form,* the first sections of 1 Thessalonians are dominated by Paul's thanksgiving because the Thessalonians persevered under persecution (1:2–10 plus 2:13 plus 3:9–10), apparently by their own countrymen (2:13–16). Indeed, the extension of elements of thanksgiving into the body is formally distinctive.

With respect to *content,* the primary teaching of 1 Thessalonians is **apocalyptic eschatology** (1:10; 4:13–5:11). Paul presents the faith as essentially **millennial:** Jesus is God's Son; God has raised him from the dead; the risen Jesus will shortly return to the earth as judge and redeemer (the ***parousia***); and he will deliver the believers forever from this world of persecution and suffering. Thus members of the Jesus Movement must prepare themselves for this great event. Interestingly, the synoptic gospel source **Q** has a similar understanding of faith and life in the Jesus Movement. It also has the same concern to give form and content to the expectation of the *parousia.* However, although 1 Thessalonians is in many respects close to Q and to most millennial thought in the movement, it is also distinctively Pauline. In 5:9–10 we find a first statement of themes that were to become characteristic of Paul's thought: the concept of Jesus offering to human beings salvation from the wrath of God and that of Jesus dying "for us, so that . . . we may live with him." Paul also includes a strong ethical exhortation about the holiness of marriage and sexual relations in contrast to what he considers to be Gentile "pagan" behavior. As in Philippians, there is much fictive kin language because, again, Paul thinks of the congregation as a new family.

Outline

1:1	Salutation
1:2–3:13	Thanksgiving and body (mixed)
4:1–5:22	Moral exhortation and instructions
4:1–12	Moral exhortation
4:13–5:11	Instruction about the coming of the *parousia*
5:12–22	Final moral exhortation
5:23–28	Conclusion

1:1: *Characteristic Pauline salutation*

1:2–3:13: *Thanksgiving and body* (thanksgiving: 1:2–10, 13; 3:9–10; body: 2:1–12, 14–20; 3:1–13). Paul normally uses this to set the tone of the whole letter and to express his understanding of the situation he is addressing.

1:2–10   is a more customary thanksgiving. Verse 1:3 contains Paul's famous combination of faith, love, and hope (e.g., 1 Cor. 13:13). Verse 1:10 is a formula-like representation of millennial or apocalyptic faith. The coming "wrath of God" is known in Israelite expectation (e.g., Isa. 13:9; *Sibylline Oracles* 3.555–62 [ca. 140 B.C.E.]; cf. 1 Thess. 2:15).

2:1–16:   *Recollection and interpretation* of Paul's work in Thessalonica.

2:1–12   may imply Gentile opponents who thought of Jesus as a hero (see Chapter One) but could also be rhetorical, that is, not applying to any "real" situation. It contains two of Paul's intimate analogies for his relationship with the Thessalonians, that he was "gentle . . . like a nurse" (2:7; cf. Gal. 4:19) and encouraging "like a father with his children" (2:11). Verses 2:5–6 may reflect the well-known philosophical view that a true friend is not a flatterer (Cicero, *On Friendship* 25; Philodemus, *Concerning Frank Speech*). Evidence for trade associations has been found at Thessalonica. Verse 2:9 mentions Paul's pride in supporting himself as an artisan (see discussion, Chapter Four).

2:13–16,   which looks like a second thanksgiving, is possibly a later addition, thus a letter fragment not from Paul. If it is from Paul, he is adopting anti-Israelite polemic known in other Israelite groups who wage verbal warfare against other Israelites (1 QM 4.2 [Dead Sea Scrolls]), in anti-Israelite groups, in other Jesus Movement groups (Matt. 23:31; Luke 11:49), and in Roman anti-Israelite thinking (Tacitus *Histories* 5.5).

2:17–3:13:   *An expression of Paul's affection and concern* for the Thessalonians and Timothy's encouraging report about them.

4:1–12:   *Moral exhortation.*   An exhortation to holiness and love. "Control your own body" is literally "control your own vessel." "Vessel" has also been interpreted as either "wife" or "the male genitalia." Self-control was a virtue, and in contrast to modern ideas, men were thought to be more capable of control than women. Vengeance belongs to God alone (see Rom. 12:19 [Deut. 32:35]).

4:13–5:11:   *Instruction with regard to the coming of the **parousia**.*   This section is the real concern of the letter. Inscriptions show that most Thessalonians did not believe in life after death. Paul has apparently taught the Thessalonians that Christ's *parousia* and resurrection would come very soon. Meanwhile, they have become concerned about their departed loved ones in the interim. In traditional apocalyptic language—the cry of command, the archangel's call, and the sound of God's trumpet (Isa. 27:13; Joel 2:1; Zech. 9:14)—he reiterates the millennial hope that the resurrected Jesus will return "like a thief in the night" (5:2; see Matt. 24:43). Then the resurrected Thessalonians would join the Messiah and the living Thessalonians in the journey to heaven. However, Paul uses the title "Lord" rather than the "Son of Man" of Daniel for Jesus as apocalyptic judge and redeemer. He goes into physical details not found in the words of the Q prophets or in the apocalyptic discourses of the synoptic gospels. He still expects this *parousia* to come in his own lifetime (4:17), and he uses this belief to comfort the Thessalonians who are concerned about what will happen to their departed dead. As noted, 5:9–10 is important as a first statement of the themes that came to be characteristic of Pauline thinking.

5:12–22:   *Final moral exhortation.*   A hint at some early form of church organization in 5:12 is followed by a stress on work—again, there were associations of artisans at Thessalonica—and a *cautious* encouragement about charismatic gifts (cf. 1 Cor. 12, 14).

5:23–28:   *Conclusion.*   The peace wish, request for prayer, kiss, command for letter to be read, and benediction.

THE CORINTHIAN CORRESPONDENCE

The city of Corinth in the Roman province of Achaia (southern Greece) is strate-gically situated on a narrow isthmus that joins the Greek mainland with what is called the Peloponnesus, a very large peninsula. Destroyed by Rome in 146 B.C.E., Corinth was rebuilt by Julius Caesar in 44 B.C.E. and became a Roman colony. It rapidly grew, and Caesar Augustus made it the capital of Achaia in 27 B.C.E.

The strategic location of Corinth made it a natural location for a major seaport. It had a northwestern harbor area on the Gulf of Corinth called Lechaeum and a southeastern harbor area on the Saronic Gulf (nearer Athens) called Cenchreae. It became a center for shipbuilding, commerce, industry, and government. The city was also one of the four major sites for the Isthmian athletic games held every two years. This bustling city was cosmopolitan, populated with Roman officials, mer-chants, businesspersons, soldiers, sailors, and from time to time, athletes. Corinth also gained a notorious reputation in ancient literature as a "city of sin," so that the verb *korinthiazesthai,* "to live like a Corinthian," took on the connotation "to have sex with," and the expression *korinthia korē,* "a Corinthian girl," became synony-mous with a prostitute. Strabo, the famous geographer, quotes the proverb, "Not every man's concern is a trip to Corinth."

The city also had a religious life typical of a Hellenistic city (see Chapter One). The Isthmian games and ruins of a temple to the emperor indicate the presence of the imperial cult or "emperor worship." Remnants of both traditional Israelite and Greek religion, as well as the popular Hellenistic mystery religions, still survive. The temple of Aphrodite Pandemos, a goddess of love, stood above the city on a mas-sive rock. Strabo speaks of this famous temple and says it had a thousand temple prostitutes, although the comment surely comes from his imagination. Sanctuaries of Demeter (of the Eleusinian mysteries in the hills northwest of Athens), Asklepios (the god of healing), and Poseidon (the god of the sea, in connection with the games) have been preserved in what is today called "Old Corinth." Columns of the Temple of Apollo, the sun god, still stand. There were also sanctuaries to the Egyp-tian goddess Isis and god Serapis and the Asian mother of the gods, Cybele. There has been discovered on the Lechaeum Road leading into Corinth a damaged marble slab that preserves a partial inscription in Greek letters, which might be rendered in English as ". . . **GOGEBR** . . . ," that is, originally "[SYNA]**GOG[UE OF THE H]EBR**[EWS]." Although its writing style shows that it comes from a time several centuries later than Paul (probably fourth–fifth century C.E.), such buildings were continually built on traditional sites; thus there might have been a synagogue there in the first century. There are many remains of dining rooms where religious ban-quets were held; these are very important in relation to Paul's comments about Corinthian excesses at the Lord's Supper (see following).

In the center of the marketplace at Corinth was the famous *bēma,* or "tribunal," a high raised platform where speeches and judicial decisions were made (see p. 178). No doubt Paul was brought before the governor Gallio here (cf. Acts 18:12–17). We should also note the famous "Erastus Inscription" cut into the pavement of a square of the theater floor at Corinth. This Erastus was an *aedile,* or city "business manager." Perhaps—this is speculative—he was the very same Erastus converted by Paul because that Erastus is called an *oikonomos* (Rom. 16:23) or city "steward," that is, he could have been at an earlier stage of his career a Corinthian bureaucrat.

As the **Gallio Inscription** helps to show (see Chapter Four), the apostle Paul reached Corinth from Athens about 49 or 50 C.E., and he may have stayed there about eighteen months (so Acts 18:1, 11). There he established a community of believers with at least one major house-church, although there may have been satellite house-churches (for example, at Corinth's port area, Cenchreae, about five miles southeast [see Rom. 16:1]). As we have seen, the apostle returned to Corinth twice (2 Cor. 13:1) and wrote at least seven letters to the Corinthians (see **letter fragments** in Chapter Four). They reveal the Corinthians' tendencies to quarrel with each other, to break into factions, to lapse into their old ways before joining the Jesus Movement (especially ecstatic trances), and to become influenced by other Hellenistic Israelite missionaries who challenged Paul's right to call himself an apostle, thus his authority.

Because we have already studied these problems, we shall proceed to our interpretive outline of 1 Corinthians.

First Corinthians

1 Corinthians is unique among Paul's letters in indicating precisely the place from which he wrote the latter, namely, Ephesus, a city on the western coast of Asia Minor, across the Aegean Sea from Corinth (cf. 1 Cor. 16:8). The letter was probably written about 53 or 54 C.E. Although now called "1 Corinthians," it was not his first letter to Corinth (see following, 1 Cor. 5:9).

The body of the letter falls naturally into two parts. The first part (1:10–6:20) deals with matters reported *orally* to Paul by "Chloe's people" (slaves or relatives of a Corinthian woman named Chloe?). The second part (7:1–15:58), which begins with "Now concerning the matters about which you *wrote* . . . ," takes up questions that the Corinthians raised in a letter sent to Paul from the Corinthians. Both sets of problems seem to be associated with the Corinthians' claim to superior knowledge (*gnōsis*), often manifested in ecstatic spiritual experiences. Paul's response to these Corinthian "enthusiasts" or "pneumatics" (Greek *pneuma:* "spirit")—were they proto-Gnostics?—stresses the necessity of love and unity in the face of differences. Thus the Corinthian correspondence offers very interesting source material for the study of social relations in the early Jesus Movement.

1 Cor. 9, a defense of Paul's apostleship, and 1 Cor. 10:1–22, a section on the dangers of idolatry, seem to interrupt Paul's argument about meat offered to idols (chapter 8; 10:23–11:1). A few scholars have posed the possibility of a fragment from another letter in these sections. As I shall indicate with more detail in relation to Philippians and Romans, there has been a tendency in recent scholarship to be more cautious about partition, or letter fragment, theories, primarily because of arguments related to ancient rhetoric. Because theories of **letter fragments** have received relatively less assent in 1 Corinthians than in 2 Corinthians, we shall follow this trend and consider 1 Corinthians as a unity.

Outline

1:1–3: *Pauline salutation from Paul and a certain Sosthenes.*   It is impossible to be certain whether this is the Sosthenes, a "ruler of the synagogue," who is mentioned in Acts 18:17.

1:4–9: *Thanksgiving,* characteristically setting the tone of the letter and noting some of its major themes: the apocalyptic hope, the spiritual gifts of the Corinthians, and their "call" to affiliate with the Jesus Movement.

1:10-6:20: PART I: THE PROBLEMS REPORTED TO PAUL BY "CHLOE'S PEOPLE" (1:11) IN EPHESUS

This section of the letter has four main parts:

1. The factions in Corinth (1:10–4:21) and "theology of the cross"
2. Purity issues, that is, incest and sexual sins in general (5:1–13)
3. Litigation before pagan law courts (6:1–11)
4. Sexual immorality, or the claim of some with spiritual gifts that "all things are lawful for me" (6:12–20)

1:10–4:21: *The factions in Corinth.*   A faction is a small, unstable group that is recruited by some leader to achieve some limited purpose; it is in conflict with other factions and often with some other authority. In the Corinthian church, factionalism centered on religious fervor, sometimes called "enthusiasm" by scholars. Certain Corinthians had developed a view of baptism in which the baptized persons identified themselves with some prominent church leader (Paul, Cephas [Peter], Apollos, "Christ"). Because we have no knowledge that Jesus or Peter had ever been to Corinth, perhaps some local leaders had in some way identified with them. Recall that initiation was a prominent, dramatic feature of joining a mystery religion. Evidently these Corinthians regarded baptism as a kind of mystery rite by which they came to share the power they attributed to the person whom they associated with their baptism. Once baptized they felt themselves to be truly "spiritual" in a way other people were not and thus to possess a special "wisdom" or "knowledge" (**gnōsis**) in a way other people did not. The quarrels between the factions were, therefore, quarrels among a spiritual and wise elite, all of whom claimed their distinctiveness from the rest of the world.

Paul's argument against the factions and their basis includes his claim that he, himself, did not come to baptize—he had baptized no one except Crispus, Gaius, and the household of Stephanas (16:15, 17; Rom. 16:23; Acts 18:8)—but to preach the gospel. His most important reason, however, is that the Corinthians do not fully understand the significance of the gospel of Christ's death by crucifixion, or Paul's "theology of the cross" (1:18–25). You will recall that crucifixion, or being publicly displayed naked on a cross in a prominent place for all to see, was an extremely painful, humiliating, and dishonorable punishment, a deterrent designed especially for criminals and deserters from the military. Clearly, Jesus' crucifixion was something of an embarrassment. To center one's message of hope and salvation for the world on one so executed seemed the height of folly. However, Paul deftly gave it a theological spin in the form of a paradox. The wisdom of the world is folly to God, and what the world would count as folly—"Christ crucified, a stumbling block [*skandalon*] to Israelites and foolishness to Gentiles"—is the power and wisdom of God. The focus is on Christ's *humility and weakness,* to which Paul will return again and again.

For Paul the proof of this paradoxical truth lay in the social realm, as he argued in the following section (1:26–31; cf. 6:11). *Most* of the Corinthians were from the lower strata of society. As he puts it, "not many of you were wise by human standards, not many were powerful, not many of noble birth." Paradoxically, Paul says, God chose them, precisely to shame the wise. (Later critics of the Jesus Movement such as Celsus were led to say that it attracted only the foolish, dishonorable, and stupid, his examples being slaves, women, and children.) "Not many" suggests that a few of the Corinthians, however, were from the upper strata of society. Examples are the leaders of the congregations in whose houses members of the movement met. Some of the problems that surface later in the letter betray tensions between the elite minority and the nonelite majority. Indeed, it is clear that *some* of Paul's advice was directed to the elites (cf. 8:10–13; 10:23–30; 11:23–34). Here, however, Paul uses as his example the nonelite majority: God works through the lowly, just as he worked through the lowly Crucified One.

In chapters 2–4, Paul develops this theme of true wisdom for the initiated in more detail. It is divine, not human, wisdom. God's wisdom is also human foolishness because he effects salvation through the crucifixion of Christ. The Corinthians do not fully understand this secret wisdom; had they understood it, they would not have been so proud and arrogant, so taken up with themselves. They are still influenced by "the flesh," their lower natures (which sin attacks), and thus they are not well-developed spiritually. They are immature children, still in need of baby's milk, not solid food. That is the reason why they split into factions. The church has only one foundation: Jesus Christ. Paul and Apollos—Cephas is not mentioned again (!)—are only servants (or slaves) of Christ. In passing, Paul's view that they are—or ought to be—spiritual leads him to say that they are God's temple where, Israelites believed, God's spirit dwells. So the congregation is God's true temple, as also the Essenes believed (1QS 8:5–9).

The theme of the "weakness" of God symbolized by the cross as the basis for unity in the movement will be a constant theme in the letter as Paul attempts to "build up" the congregation. When Paul's "enthusiastic" missionary opponents claim that he is a weak person, Paul puts his own spin on the criticism: He imitates Christ's weakness.

5:1–13:   *Incest and sexual sins in general.*   As noted earlier, Corinth was notorious in antiquity for "sexual immorality" (Greek *porneia*). For Paul, the Corinthian congregation was too tolerant of one of its members, a man who has had sexual intercourse with his step-mother. They should have mourned (as in a funeral rite?) but did not. The man has committed what for anyone of Israelite background is legal incest (see Lev. 18:6–18), and for Paul this act was worse than even pagan immorality. Paul again tried to establish norms for group purity. He recommended that the community should assemble and carry out a ritual act that appears to be a magical exclusion rite, a curse to ban the sexual offender. He argued that just as leaven must be excluded from the house during Passover, so the impure person must be excluded from the group. The reference in 5:3–5 is a formula referring to God's final judgment.

Recall that 5:9 mentions Paul's "previous letter" to the Corinthians, lost to us. Paul's revived purity norms are for insiders, not outsiders, "since you would then need to go out of the world" (5:10). He is especially concerned about morality *within* the Corinthian house-churches.

6:1–11:   *Litigation before pagan courts.*   There are various recommendations for solving disputes internally among Israelites. They are usually based on not allowing grudges to simmer in one's heart, Lev. 19:17 ("You shall not hate in your heart your brother, but you shall surely reprove [confront and make amends with] your neighbor, lest you bear a grudge [LXX: "sin"] against him"). See, for example, ben Sira 19:13–17; *T. Gad.* 6:1–6. Matt. 18:15–17 seems to incorporate such an internal process. Some Hellenistic philosophers also claim that going to court is dishonorable. For the Cynic Epictetus, one must avoid courts and preferably suffer insults rather than dishonor oneself publicly; only Zeus is the final judge. In this passage, Paul recommends that members of the Jesus Movement should also settle their disputes out of court and within their own group. His reasons, however, are communal and eschatological: Believers will participate in Christ's final judgment of the world, including judgment of its magistrates. Note that Paul presumes that there is no local leader to judge at Corinth, such as a bishop/overseer or elder/presbyter (contrast 1 Timothy).

1 Cor. 6:9 is one of three important passages from the Pauline letters and later Pastorals (see also Rom. 1:26–27; 1 Tim. 1:10) that are much debated in the modern discussion about homosexuality and the Bible. There were varying views about same-sex relations in antiquity. In the earlier Greek period, some philosophers valued male-male relationships, especially older male–younger male (often teacher-pupil) relationships, over male-female relationships. However, although opinions differed, more philosophers by Paul's day were condemning male–male relationships as "unnatural" and especially objectionable was the sexual abuse of prostitutes and young male slaves. In this verse, Paul does not dwell on the subject but condemns certain kinds of sexual relations in a typical Stoic-like "catalogue of vices" (verses 9–11; see Chapter Three). The two terms he uses are rare and thus difficult to translate. *Malakoi*

means "soft ones," "gentle ones," perhaps "effeminate ones"; and *arsenokoitēs* (ar-se-no-koí-tace) comes from two words, *arsen,* "male," and *koitē,* "bed" (English "coitus") and seems to refer to "a male who has sexual intercourse." Because the word *arsenokoitai* is so rare, it may be Paul's translation of the Torah expression for the prohibition against same-sex relations in foreign worship in Lev. 18:22, *mishkav zakur,* "lying with a male" (referring to the active, rather than the passive, partner).

The terms could refer respectively to the passive and active partners in a homosexual relationship, but it is more likely that they refer to adolescent boys who sold themselves for sexual favors and to their older, more dominant male sexual partners. (The modern term *sodomites,* sometimes used—incorrectly—to translate *arsenokoitēs,* comes from the biblical story about men from the city of Sodom who demanded to have sex with [i.e., to gang rape] figures who appeared to be Lot's male guests. In an unusual display of hospitality for his honored guests, Lot instead offered the men his daughters, but they refused and pressed against Lot's door. The guests, however, happened to be "messengers from God" [i.e., angels]. They struck the men blind, and the men then found it difficult to find Lot's door [Gen. 19:1–11; cf. Judg. 19:22–30]). Levitical laws of purity that distinguish Israelite behavior from that of surrounding peoples, the Canaanites ("we" versus "they"), said that Israelite men should not have sex with other Israelite men (Lev. 18:22; 20:13). (See further, Rom. 1:26–27, 1 Tim. 1:10, and the general discussion of "homosexuality" at the end of Chapter Six.)

6:12–20:   *Sexual morality: The claim of the enthusiast opponents that "all things are lawful."*   A popular view in antiquity was that sex is simply satisfying natural urges; sexual indulgence was common. Similarly, some Corinthians, claiming to be truly "spiritual" people (proto-Gnostics?), were indifferent to matters of the body and argued for total sexual freedom (libertinism), even freedom to visit Corinth's notorious brothels. These Corinthian opponents of Paul cited slogans to legitimate their behavior: "All things are lawful." Against this Paul argues that the physical body must maintain its purity if the social body is to maintain its purity. Some philosophers—Musonius Rufus, for example—also argued that sex belongs in marriage.

7:1–15:58: PART II: THE QUESTIONS RAISED BY THE CORINTHIANS IN THEIR LETTER TO PAUL

The Corinthians have written a letter to Paul asking for guidance on a number of practical problems (7:1). Paul frequently introduces a new subject with the words *peri de,* "now concerning," as he does here (7:1; cf. 7:25; 8:1; 12:1; also 16:1, 12). Thus he shifts from discussing the problems communicated orally by Chloe's people to those mentioned in the letter. He responds as a pastor to his people, and the result is a fascinating account of an attempt in the Jesus Movement to face much-debated social, religious, and moral problems—and perhaps also an illustration of the adage, "The more things change, the more they remain the same." Six important topics are treated:

1. Marriage, sex, and celibacy (7:1–40)

2. Meat sacrificed to other gods ("idols") (8:1–11:1)

3. Dress and status of women in worship (11:2–16; [cf. 11:33b–36, probably an interpolation])

4. The proper practice of the Lord's Supper in worship (11:17–34)

5. Spiritual gifts and the gift of love (12:1–14:40)

6. The future resurrection of the dead (15:1–58)

7:1–40: *Marriage, sex, and celibacy.* Paul has to respond to Corinthian questions about marital and sexual relationships. The opposite moral position of the libertinism just discussed has also surfaced among the Corinthians, namely, a religious **asceticism.** Although this term can be defined differently in different religious and social contexts, in general *asceticism* is the denial of bodily pleasure or comfort in order to pursue the spiritual and/or moral life. Some Corinthians are opting for sexual asceticism; that is, they are refusing to have sexual relations with their wives and husbands. Thus there were extremes in moral behavior at Corinth: Some avowed libertinism and visited prostitutes (6:12–20), and some practiced asceticism and avoided sexual relations altogether. These extremes also occurred in later forms of **Gnosticism,** that is, they were alternatives based on the presumed "knowledge" (*gnōsis*) that one's true self is not at home in this evil body and this evil world. Perhaps the sexual extremes at Corinth offer a glimpse of an early form of Gnosticism ("proto-Gnosticism") within the Jesus Movement (see Paul's lengthy discussion of wisdom and *gnōsis* in 1:10–4:21). Another possibility is that Paul's discussion represents a century-old debate between the Cynic philosophers, who renounced marriage as the backbone of the institutions of the city-state (Greek *polis*) and the Stoic philosophers, who upheld marriage as a way of preserving those institutions (so Deming).

To understand Paul, it is important to observe the perspective from which his advice is given: ***apocalyptic eschatology,*** *or the imminent end.* In verses 26–31 he argues that the Corinthians should maintain the *status quo* because "the appointed time has grown very short" (verse 29), and the mission will be better served by concentrating on it. He applies this principle through the chapter to Israelite and Greek (verses 17–20), to slave and free (verses 21–24), and to the married and unmarried states (verses 8, 25–27, 32–35, 37). Ultimately, then, slavery is of no account because—here Paul sounds like the Stoic and Cynic philosophers—internally slaves are truly free, and the free (their masters) are truly slaves, although for Paul joining the Jesus Movement means becoming a slave of Christ. However, if there are those who are "burning" to get married, let them do so; it is no sin (verses 9, 28, 36).

A second point to note when reading this passage is that Paul, although retaining many of the patriarchal biases of his culture, nonetheless develops a certain equality insofar as he balances genders. Here are some examples:

Verse	Male	Female
2	Each man . . . his own wife	Each woman her own husband
3	The husband should give to his wife her conjugal rights	Likewise the wife (should give to her husband his conjugal rights)
4–5	The husband has authority over his wife's body—do not deprive one another	The wife has authority over her husband's body—do not deprive one another
10	The wife should not separate from her husband	The husband should not divorce his wife

12–13	A husband should not divorce his unbelieving wife	A woman should not divorce her unbelieving husband
16	Wife . . . you might save your husband	Husband . . . you might save your wife
32	The unmarried man is anxious about the affairs of the Lord, how to please the Lord	The unmarried woman is anxious about the affairs of the Lord, how to please the Lord
33–34	The married man is anxious about the affairs of the world, how to please his wife	The married woman is anxious about the affairs of the world, how to please her husband

Thus Paul's patriarchy is qualified in the congregations by his ideal of gender inclusion on the one hand (cf. Gal. 3:28) and his practice of having women leaders on the other (Rom. 16:1–2; Phil. 4:2–3).

Returning to the first section of the chapter with these orientations, Paul clearly prefers that the unmarried Corinthians maintain the *status quo,* that is, remain single, *as he himself is* (7:1, 7, 8; the background for his present nonmarried state is unclear: Has he ever been married?). He considers this single state not to be obligatory, however, but rather a gift. He also acknowledges that for some this single state could easily lead to sexual immorality (promiscuity? visits to the brothels?) before the end arrives. So he concludes this section, "it is better to marry than to be aflame with passion" (7:9). Later he will argue that marriage leads to divided loyalties (verses 33–34), a teaching similar to the Cynic view that marital obligations are a distraction from devotion to God.

Nonetheless, Paul is no ascetic. He strongly recommends that partners fulfill their mutual sexual obligations (3–5). They should separate only for a time of prayer, a custom found also among the Israelites (*Testament of Naphtali* 8:7–9).

With respect to divorce, Paul draws on a tradition from Jesus or "word of the Lord"— most likely oral because the gospels have not been written yet!—which forbids the woman to separate from her husband and the man to divorce his wife (cf. Mark 10:1–12). This rigorous Jesus tradition agrees with the strict Israelite interpretation in the Dead Sea Scroll Sect (*The Damascus Document* 4:19–5:3). It is based on Gen. 1:27 ("male and female he created them"; Gen. 2:24: "they become one flesh"). However, it contrasts with the rabbinic traditions (descended from the Pharisees?) that permitted divorce based on Deut. 24:1–4 (the husband gives the wife a certificate of divorce because there is "something objectionable about her"), although the rabbis did not agree on what was objectionable (cf. Mark 10: 1–12 discussion). The conservative school of Shammai interpreted this to mean that adultery was the only basis for divorce, but the liberal school of Hillel said it meant for "any cause." Jesus spoke mainly to Israelites. In the Jesus Movement of the larger Greco-Roman world, however, the problem and its solution are different. With regard to *mixed marriages* between those in the movement and those outside it, Paul advises that insiders should *not* divorce their spouses. The believing partner "consecrates" the unbelieving partner and makes their children "holy." Nonetheless, Paul suggests that the *unbelieving* partner may "separate"—meaning divorce. This is clearly a modification of the "saying of the Lord," adjusting it for members of the Jesus Movement living in a non-Israelite, Gentile world. Curiously, Paul says nothing about procreation as the purpose of sex in marriage, a view found in both the Torah command to produce children (Gen. 1:28) and Hellenistic views of marriage (Musonius Rufus, *What Is the Chief End of Marriage?*). Perhaps Paul thinks that the coming end makes having children unnecessary. Paul finally turns to the question about how a man should behave toward his "virgin" (verses 36–38). The term "virgin" in this passage has been much debated. Traditionally it was thought to mean "daughter," that is, the refusal of fathers to allow their daughters to marry. However, in verses 25–35, Paul is clearly referring to those who are *betrothed;* thus the same meaning is probable for one's "virgin" in verses 36–38.

8:1–11:1:   *Freedom and love: The problem of eating meat sacrificed to other gods.*   Many problems faced the new member of a tiny group living in a Greco-Roman city. For example, if you dined at a "pagan" friend's house, you might—presuming that the host was from the upper social strata—have been served meat from the marketplace. However, meat from the marketplace would have been previously sacrificed to "pagan" gods in the temples, a common practice in Greek and Roman cities. Usually the meal would have implied worshipping at the god's table, or at least an acknowledgment of the god. Such meat would have been forbidden to purist Israelites and, as the **Apostolic Decree** in Acts shows, within some circles of the Jesus Movement (cf. Acts 15:28)! Or you might have been invited to dinner at one of the many pagan sanctuary dining rooms, where you would have been offered a succulent menu of roast pork, recently sacrificed. Clearly, no pious Israelite could eat this meat. Could one who now affiliated with the Jesus Movement eat it? These were crucial questions that the Corinthians asked Paul. Paul had to respond to them.

The passage is complicated. As noted earlier, chapter 9, a defense of Paul's apostleship, seems to break his train of thought, and 10:1–22 about idolatry also seems to be a digression. These sections have given rise to the theory that they might be fragments from other letters. Again, we are considering 1 Corinthians as a unity.

In both 8:1–13 and 10:23–11:1, Paul seems to agree initially with the (proto-Gnostic?) Corinthian enthusiasts when he says (1) "we know that all of us possess knowledge (*gnōsis*)" (8:1), (2) that idols do not really exist (8:1, 4–6), and (3) that therefore it is permissible to eat food offered to "idols," as the new freedom in Christ allows (8:8; 10:26–27, 29b–30). This is the view of those who possess the new wisdom; here Paul leans to the libertine side (Paul is not speaking of sexual morality!). However, (4) he is concerned that "the weak" might be troubled in conscience if they see a brother banqueting "at table in an idol's temple" (8:10). They might also be troubled if someone (a nonbeliever?) informs a believer at a nonbeliever's house or temple banquet that the meat has been (purchased in the marketplace and) offered in sacrifice to the gods (10:28). In these cases, the believer should be most concerned about the conscience of the "weak." Who are "the weak"? Philosophers and satirists of the day considered them to be the uneducated and uncultured, those who are guided by emotion, not reason, thus often those who are superstitious. Usually they are those of the lower strata. For Paul, here is a dilemma. He concedes that there is a superior *gnōsis,* but those who have it, "the strong," presumably the wealthier, more educated "few" at Corinth (1:26)—who no doubt are patrons—should curb their freedom because of the conscience of "the weaker" brothers and sisters in the community.

Note the *course* of Paul's argument here. His orientation is stated at the beginning: "Knowledge (*gnōsis*) puffs up, but love (*agápē* [ah-gáh-pay]) builds up." "We know that all of us possess knowledge" is a slogan of the "enthusiasts," and Paul himself has granted a *certain kind* of knowledge, represented by the folly of the cross (1:18–25). Nonetheless, for the sake of unity, *agápē* is superior to *gnōsis,* and freedom operates out of love for one's brother or sister.

Paul may not have been totally consistent in his statements about the extent of freedom in these passages, but his main point seems clear enough: He encourages freedom but opposes it when it leads to superior knowledge without love. Thus the attitude of spiritual superiority is the major danger of "enthusiasm"; it tramples on the free conscience of the brother or sister, creates a basic moral dilemma, and threatens unity in the group (see the conclusion to this chapter).

Paul is also engaged in an issue related to social status. Apart from occasional festivals, usually hosted by a wealthy patron, peasants and urban poor in antiquity normally did not—could not afford to—eat meat; it was the "caviar" of the ancient world. Paul was grappling with a problem that pertained to elite and nonelite believers. His solution impinged on not only those with religious scruples, but also those of higher and lower status in the Corinthian community. We shall see that he has to deal with this social issue again in troubles related to Last Supper observance (1 Cor. 11:17–34).

In the midst of the "meat offered to idols" discussion, Paul defends his apostleship (9:1–27) on the grounds that, first, he has had a vision of the Lord and, second, his missionary activity has been successful. He also repudiates the argument that he is not really an apostle because he earns his own living as an artisan rather than living off the results of his missionary labors, as did other wandering apostles (including the Palestinian Jesus Movement!) and Hellenistic philosophers (see the discussion of Paul's social status in Chapter Four). We have already seen Paul defending his self-support as an artisan in 1 Thessalonians (2:9).

Isthmian games were held at Corinth every two years. This section contains Paul's most complete reference to athletic competition. He compares the life of a believer to winning a footrace, the athlete's exercise in self-control (self-control was also an important philosophical virtue), the prize (not a perishable, but an imperishable wreath), not running aimlessly, and—shifting metaphors—shadow boxing. He stresses that his own discipline must be a model for others (9:24–26). Paul refers to athletic competition only rarely, but there are other comparisons of the new life with "struggle" (Phil. 4:3) and "running" (Phil. 2:16; 3:13–14; Gal. 2:2; 5:7).

In 10:1–22, another digression begins with the *midrash* about Christ as the spiritual Rock noted earlier. The section continues with exhortations against sexual immorality and idolatry.

11:2–34:   *The regulation of worship in the community.*   The apostle now turns to a series of problems connected with worship: the dress and status of women (11:2–16); abuses of the Lord's Supper (11:17–34); and *glossolalia,* or "speaking in tongues" (12–14).

The first problem has to do with women who dishonor their husbands by their appearance when they pray and prophesy in public worship. However, the precise issue is extremely difficult to isolate, and problems abound.

There is the question of whether Paul is talking about a woman's head covering or her hair ("veil" in the modern Middle Eastern sense is not meant). In line with his use of "head" in general, a widespread interpretation is that women, in contrast to men, should have their *heads* covered when they pray and prophesy in public worship (1 Cor. 11:2–16). In favor of this interpretation is the fact that head coverings in worship were in discussion elsewhere. The Greeks did not cover their heads in worship, but the Romans did. The question of whether *men* should cover their heads in worship was seriously discussed by moral philosophers; one suggested that the covering of the head symbolized the concealing of the soul by the body (Plutarch *Moralia,* "The Roman Questions" 10). (The modern custom of Jewish men wearing a "skull cap" [the *ya(r)mulka*] in worship seems not to have existed this early.) In any case, the passage concentrates on *women who pray and prophesy in worship,* not men (see comments on 1 Cor. 14:33b–36 following).

Alternatively, some interpreters think that the issue is not head *coverings* for women, but rather the appearance of the *hair itself* when women pray and prophesy. Verse 5 refers literally to a woman's hair flowing down (like some priestesses? or prostitutes who "let their hair down"?). Verse 13 refers to hair "loose" or unbound. Verse 14 says that for men to have short hair is "natural," and there were philosophical discussions elsewhere about what hair length was "natural" (Musonius Rufus, *On Cutting the Hair;* Epictetus, *Discourses*). Does Paul, then, think that women ought to have their hair bound up on their head, which was customary for women appearing in public?

Whether the issue is the head covering or the hair itself, it is clear that the woman who prays or prophesies this way in public worship dishonors her "head." How shall we understand this? It is clear that Paul uses the word "head" in both literal and metaphorical senses in this passage. The literal is the physical head of the body. The metaphorical may refer to someone who is above or over someone else in rank. However, it is more likely that it refers to "source" or "first" in order or sequence, as it does in the "first" of the year, which in Hebrew is "New Year" (*Rōsh Hashānāh*). Correspondingly, in verse 8, Paul has in mind the *sequence* of the creation story, which suggests to him that God is the "head" of Christ, Christ the "head" of man, and man the "head" of woman. Does he then think also of social hierarchy? In any case, the woman dishonors her "head," the man. Included in the dishonor is probably the possibility that her appearance is dishonorable, perhaps "suggestive" to men.

Another interpretive problem is Paul's statement that dishonoring her "head" is the same as having her head shaved (verse 5b). However, what does this mean? Does he refer to certain pagan priestesses? To women caught in some immoral act? Further, what does it mean that a woman ought to have a "symbol of authority" on her "(literal) head" *because of the angels* (verse 10)? Was the widespread view that worship took place in the presence of angels accepted by Paul (Col. 1:18)? Did members of the Jesus Movement think that they joined the angels when they worshipped (cf. **Dead Sea Scrolls** 4Q 403 1.30–46)? Did the head covering ward off lusting angels who wanted to descend and mate with human women (see Gen. 6:1–8) and who among Israelites of this period were thought to be demons?

It is noticeable how ill at ease Paul becomes in discussing this issue. It is certain that he wants to distinguish between men and women in worship. However, his argument limps along, and in the end he falls back on an argument found in the philosophers, namely, what is "natural" (verses 14–15), as well as a "church rule" (verse 16)—definitely not his usual kind of solution! We shall return to this passage at the end of Chapter Six.

A second section about worship deals with the observance of the Lord's Supper (11:17–34). As our discussion in Chapter Three indicated, meals were an occasion for all kinds of social practices and distinctions, including advance invitations, seating arrangements, order of food and drink, and the like. Here Paul's terms "received" and "handed on" (11:23) point to an oral tradition about Jesus' last meal (the same terms occur in 15:3). The words "after supper" (verse 25) indicate that Jesus' last words were sacred words still being spoken in the context of an ordinary communal meal. However, this meal was in danger of becoming just another Hellenistic banquet with the usual kinds of social status distinctions between people of upper and lower status, as well as heavy drinking. Presumably it was the rich who provided the food and were eating and getting drunk; moreover, they were humiliating those who had nothing. Paul's response was to recall the tradition about the words of Jesus at the Last Supper (verses 23–25) and to indicate that the sacred meal in connection with Jesus' death was to be a solemn occasion. If they were hungry, they should eat at home. Ordinary meals and sacrament were thereby separated, perhaps for the first time.

12:1–14:40:   *The problem of speaking in tongues and the true nature of spiritual gifts.* A major feature of Corinthian religious enthusiasm was the proliferation of religious phenomena connected with religious ecstasy: making utterances of wisdom and knowledge, having faith, healing, working miracles, prophesying, "distinguishing between spirits," speaking in tongues, and interpreting tongues (12:8–10). This in itself would not be extraordinary because other religions in the Hellenistic world exhibited at least some of the same phenomena. Indeed, these are spiritual gifts. What is interesting is Paul's cautionary perspective about speaking in tongues.

There are two interruptions in the flow of chapters 12–14. As in the previous section, the middle chapter (chapter 13) is an interruption. In this case, it is a self-contained "poetic" section similar to Hellenistic and Israelite wisdom poetry of the period, only loosely connected with chapters 12 and 14 (12:31; 14:1). The material contains Pauline ideas and probably, as in the previous case (1 Cor. 9), comes from Paul himself.

A second passage on denying women the right to speak at house-church meetings (14:33b–36) also interrupts the context; however, in this case the evidence for a later interpolation is quite strong and will be considered again later. It will be better to take up chapters 12 and 14 first.

In chapter 12, Paul's remarks show that he has encouraged various spiritual phenomena at Corinth, although he denies that a member of the Jesus Movement can say "Jesus be cursed!"— perhaps an ecstatic cry of the enthusiasts, perhaps in contrast to the cry "Jesus as Lord" (1 Cor. 12:3). Paul also draws on the general Hellenistic and Roman political notion of the body politic and its members (e.g., Livy's *History of Rome* 2.32.9–12), although he stresses the importance of the lesser members in order to support the unity of the church. In short, the physical body replicates and symbolizes the corporate body.

In chapter 14, it is clear that at least some of the Corinthians consider "speaking in tongues" (Greek *glossolalia*) to be the highest spiritual gift. What form of speaking is this? Contemporary Protestant Pentecostals and Catholic Charismatic believers claim to "speak in tongues," that is, they fall into a trance and utter guttural sounds during worship; often they believe that they, like those in the early church, are filled with the Spirit and are spontaneously speaking another, real language. Scientific observers and linguistic analysts reject this interpretation of what was happening at Corinth. To be sure, Acts 2:4–11, on which this modern interpretation rests, stresses that at Pentecost the apostles spoke other languages (2:4) and that foreigners *heard* their *own* languages being spoken (2:8). However, this is the Lukan perspective and does not fit Paul's description. Thus it is necessary to distinguish spontaneously speaking foreign languages (*xenoglossia*, as in the Acts story) and so-called speaking in tongues (*glossolalia*, as in 1 Corinthians). The latter is a jumble of ecstatic, unintelligible, usually guttural, utterances emitted by persons who are spiritually agitated while they are in an altered state of consciousness. There are well-known examples of ancient ecstatic speech among prophets and devotees of the mystery religions, and apocalyptic writers also talk about "angelic speech." These seem to be the closest parallels.

In chapter 12, Paul has prepared for his judgment on glossolalia by giving his own ranking of charismatic gifts: the interpretation of glossolalia is next to last, and glossolalia is the
very last (12:27–30). In chapter 14, he reinforces this view. On the one hand, glossolalia is
indeed a "spiritual gift," and he claims that he speaks in tongues more than anyone at
Corinth (14:18). Yet, he thinks that it must be strictly regulated. In worship only two or
three persons should speak in tongues; each person should do it in turn; and an interpreter
should interpret such utterances (14:27–28), which, again, is also a "spiritual gift" (12:10;
cf. Philo's *Life of Moses* 2.35.191). Unless there is order, speaking in tongues does not contribute to the "upbuilding" or "edification" of the whole group, in contrast to prophecy,
which people can understand and which Paul much prefers. Paul stresses, then, the higher
gifts: being an apostle (like himself!), prophecy, and teaching (12:28), and he ranks speaking in tongues last.

Sandwiched between chapters 12 and 14 is a "hymn" of three stanzas (chapter 13). Its
theme is that the highest spiritual gift of all is "love." The term is not *eros,* or "sexual love";
it is not *philia,* or "brotherly love"; it is *agápē,* the "higher love," which is best described by
reading the hymn. Not only speaking in tongues, but also prophecy and many other gifts
and virtues—having knowledge of God, working miracles, giving one's possessions to the
poor, and suffering martyrdom—are absolutely nothing without *agápē* love (13:1–3). In
beautiful and powerful language—the short section contains fifteen verbs!—Paul then describes the nature of *agápē* love and its power (13:4–7). He concludes with the eschatological theme that whereas the other gifts will pass away, love is indestructible (13:8–13).

14:33b–36   *is most probably an interpolation by a Paulinist.*   It says that a woman
ought not to speak in worship; rather, she ought to ask her husband at home. This advice illustrates a generality proposed by modern anthropologists—also found in many
other texts from Greco-Roman society—that men's space is public space and women's
space is private space. Plutarch, for example, says that public debate is for men; women
should consult their husbands at home (Plutarch *Moralia,* "Advice to Bride and Groom"
31–32). There are several reasons why this passage is considered to be an interpolation
inserted by a later Paulinist. It interrupts the context, but unlike other interruptions in
1 Corinthians (9; 10:1–22; 1 Cor. 13), it does not easily agree with Paul's previous statements that women prophesy (therefore, uncharacteristically speak) in worship (1 Cor.
11:2–16). It also appeals to the Law in a rather un-Pauline way. Finally, and most important, it sounds almost exactly like a passage about the public silence of women found
in 1 Tim. 2:11–15, which is held to come from the Pauline School in the early second
century about three generations later. In other words, this passage about women reveals
an assimilation to commonly accepted cultural values about women that were not typical of Paul. Most likely a later Paulinist inserted it. See the discussion of 1 Timothy in
Chapter Thirteen.

15:1–58:   *The future resurrection of the dead.*   Many people in antiquity did not believe in life after death. Tomb inscriptions in Latin often read "*NFFNSNC,*" an abbreviation for *non fui, fui; non sum, non curo,* or "I was not, I was; I am not, I care not." A Greek
variant said, "I did not exist, I was born; I existed, I do not exist; so much for that." In contrast, others believed that by their initiation into the mysteries, by their special *gnōsis,* or perhaps some other means they were *already* participating in the new life! The enthusiasts at
Corinth appear to have held this latter view, that is, they seem to have believed that by their
baptism they had *already* come to participate in the resurrection life. Against this view, Paul

had to argue for the apocalyptic view, that the *general* resurrection of the dead was yet to take place (cf. 1 Thess. 4:13–5:11). Second, a related problem that Paul faced was the widespread view that the physical body does not survive death, that is, some spiritual essence survives. Plato had stressed that the material body is the "prison of the (immortal) soul"; thus Socrates had been content to drink hemlock so that, he thought, his soul could finally escape the confines of his physical body and return to its true home. Similarly, Gnostics believed that the true self had been thrust out of the world of light into an evil body that is trapped in a world of darkness; at death it would escape and return to the world of light. In contrast to these negative views of the body, Paul had to argue in typical Israelite fashion for the resurrection of *the body*. Further, Paul gave the resurrection a new interpretation by assuming that only members of the Jesus Movement would be raised (cf. 1 Thess. 4:13–5:11).

1 Cor. 15:3b–5 has already been discussed in some detail. It is an early, oral tradition ("handed on . . . received"), perhaps liturgical, about the death and resurrection of Jesus (see Chapter Three). Paul understood his call to be an apostle in relation to a revelation to him of Jesus as the resurrected Son of God; indeed, he used the appearance of the resurrected Son of God to him as a defense of his apostleship (cf. Gal. 1:12, 15–16; see Chapter Four).

Chapter 15 also contains one of Paul's two statements about Adam and Christ (cf. Rom. 5:12–21). A little background for this idea is in order. If Adam was created in God's image, how could he have sinned? The philosopher Philo of Alexandria, an Israelite of the **Diaspora,** argued that there were *two* Adams. The first was the ideal Adam in Gen. 1; he was perfect, created in God's image, without sin. The second was the material Adam in Gen. 2 (the forbidden fruit story); this Adam sinned and was punished. There is no evidence that Paul or the Corinthians had any direct knowledge of Philo's theory of two Adams. If Paul did, he reversed the Adams in a sense. He claimed that it was the "old (*first*) Adam" who sinned— he did not mention two Adams in Genesis itself—but it was the "new (second or last) Adam," or *Christ,* who reversed Adam's sin (15:20–28), at least for believers.

In chapter 15, Paul also mentions the mysterious practice of baptism on behalf of the dead (15:29). The chapter becomes increasingly dynamic as it concludes with Paul's view of Christ's dramatic victory over death: "Where, O death, is your victory? Where, O death, is your sting?" (verse 55).

16:1–18: *Some further matters.*   Paul concludes his letter by discussing the arrangements he was making concerning the collection for the poor in Jerusalem and his own future itinerary (see following, 2 Cor. 8, 9). Verses 16:13–18 are a typical concluding moral exhortation.

16:19–24:   *His closing*   includes greetings from Asia by his own hand, the kiss, a curse, the *Maranatha* ("Our Lord, come!"), which is an Aramaic prayer going back to the earliest days of the Palestinian Jesus Movement (cf. Rev. 22:20), and a final benediction. Note that Aquila and Prisca (the Priscilla of Acts 18) are currently in Ephesus (verses 8, 19; cf. Acts 18:1–3; Rom. 16:3–5), the place from which the letter was written. Finally, it appears that Timothy is on his way to visit the Corinthians (16:10).

Second Corinthians

In Chapter Four, it was stated that 2 Corinthians contains several **letter fragments** written by Paul to the church at Corinth. These fragments may have been put together when the apostle's letters were collected as a group toward the end of the first century. Most scholars think that they were written shortly after the writing of

1 Corinthians, thus about 55 C.E. They can be isolated and reordered chronologically to shed light on Paul's vacillating relationships with the Corinthians. The first two parts were probably written in Ephesus. Once again, we offer our reordered sequence and corresponding chronology, with the letters numbered:

1. Some time shortly after Paul has written his "previous letter" (1 Cor. 5:9) and 1 Corinthians, he writes a (third?) letter to the Corinthians (2 Cor. 2:14–6:13 and 7:2–4 [minus 6:14–7:1]); various statements imply that relations between him and the Corinthians are deteriorating because those he sarcastically calls "super-apostles" have come in from the outside and challenged his authority.

   Paul makes a "painful visit" from Ephesus to Corinth (2 Cor. 2:1; 12:14; 12:21; 13:1), at which time he is attacked by a member of the church (2:5; 7:12).

2. Upon his return to Ephesus, Paul writes to the Corinthians a fourth letter, the "tearful letter" (2 Cor. 10–13, [2:3–4; 7:8]); in it he vigorously defends himself against the "super-apostles."

   (Paul's "prison letters," Philippians and Philemon, are probably written in Ephesus; if so, they may have been written next. We shall, however, consider them after 2 Corinthians.)

   Paul is released from prison and heads for Macedonia (cf. 1 Cor. 16:5; 2 Cor. 7:5).

3. Paul writes a letter of reconciliation to the Corinthians, probably in Macedonia (2 Cor. 1:1–2:13 plus 7:5–16; note, again, 7:5).

4. Paul writes a letter about the collection, perhaps in Macedonia (2 Cor. 8; cf. 8:1).

5. Paul writes a second letter about the collection, perhaps also in Macedonia (2 Cor. 9; cf. 9:2). Was it written to a satellite house-church in the area of Corinth, such as the port city Cenchreae (cf. Rom. 16:1)?

   In short, 2 Corinthians contains parts of five Pauline letters plus a non-Pauline fragment, 6:14–7:1. To read the first three fragments in the preceding historical sequence is to become caught up in Paul's dramatic conflict with both Corinthian insiders and missionary outsiders, that is, the so-called super-apostles who came in and challenged Paul's authority. We shall offer our interpretive notes in the preceding hypothetical sequence.

   2:14–6:13; 7:2–4: *Paul's first letter of defense against his new opponents, the "super-apostles."* This is part of a letter in which Paul's relationship with the Corinthians is deteriorating. Paul writes to defend himself and his authority against opponents who have come to Corinth bearing letters of recommendation from other communities in the Jesus Movement in which they have previously worked (3:1) and who seem to have rapidly assumed positions of authority in the Corinthian community. Paul later labels them "super-apostles" (11:5; 12:11) and calls them "peddlers of God's word" (2:17). He offers in his own behalf a moving account of the humility and reconciliation of the true ambassador for Christ, for which the sufferings of Jesus are the model. Apocalyptic ideas of present/future and final judgment are combined with Hellenistic ideas of the inner and outer person.

   A few details of the text will illustrate some of Paul's rhetorical technique. 2 Cor. 2:14 contains imagery suggestive of Roman victory parades in which vanquished prisoners of war were forced to march. In 71 C.E., for example, the Romans forced seven hundred captured

Israelite warriors carrying confiscated Jerusalem temple vessels to march through the streets of Rome to mark the victory of the Romans over the Israelites (Josephus *Wars* 7.5.3–6). This triumphal procession culminated in the execution of the "popular messiah" Simon ben Giora, one of the Israelite leaders of the revolt (see Chapter One). A representation of the forced march can be seen today on an inside façade of the famous victory Arch of Titus in the Roman Forum, erected in 81 C.E. The messenger who brings either the aroma of life or death in the following verse (2:15) is also mentioned elsewhere (*Testament of Abraham* 16:7–8; 17:16–18).

In 2 Cor. 2:17–3:18, Paul defends himself as the true, sincere apostle of the unwritten law on one's heart and the new covenant (Jer. 31:31). The unwritten law on one's heart has Hellenistic philosophical parallels, and elsewhere Paul himself stresses circumcision (= the law) of the heart (1 Cor. 7:19; Gal. 6:16; Rom. 2:25–29). Paul also responds to his opponents, who are recommending themselves with letters (3:1), with the view that the Corinthians are a spiritual letter written on the apostles' human hearts.

In 3:7–18, he uses the common rabbinic argument called "from the lesser to the greater"—see "how much more . . ." (verse 8)—in his interpretation of Exod. 34:29–35, where Moses' face shone brightly when he descended from receiving the Ten Commandments on Mount Sinai. Israelite expositions of this theme also stressed the brightness of Moses' face (e.g., Philo of Alexandria, *On the Life of Moses* 2.70; cf. Mark 9:2–10). The bright light theme continues with the "glory" of God and the "glory" of the gospel (4:1–6).

2 Cor. 4:8–10 is a "catalogue of sufferings" that Paul sometimes uses when he stresses that one can boast, but only of one's weakness or sufferings. The most extensive example is 2 Cor. 11:16–33 (see following).

In 2 Cor. 5:1–9, Paul's "longing to be clothed with our heavenly dwelling" could have referred to the general resurrection of the dead, but the contrasts between the temporary and permanent are well known from Greek philosophy, including views about the immortality of the soul (cf. Phil. 1:23). His letter of reconciliation is climaxed by one of the apostle's most powerful statements about the ministry of reconciliation (5:11–6:10): "if anyone is in Christ he is a new creation!" (5:17).

10:1–13:14: *The "tearful letter": Paul attacks the "super-apostles" head on* (cf. 2:3–4; 7:8). Apparently Paul's letter of defense against these new opponents failed in its desired effect. First, he paid a quick visit across the Aegean Sea to Corinth. However, he found the church in open rebellion against him. One opponent was even able to dishonor him publicly (cf. 2 Cor. 2:5; 7:12). We do not know who this person was, although it has been proposed that he was the man whom Paul had earlier condemned for having sexual relations with his stepmother (1 Cor. 5:1–8).

Paul returned to Ephesus and wrote another, even stronger, letter to Corinth "out of much affliction and anguish of heart and with many tears" (2:4). This is traditionally known as the "tearful letter," and 2 Cor. 10–13 is probably part of it (this section does not mention the person who had humiliated him).

In these four chapters an interesting picture of Paul's opponents emerges from his parody of, and attack against, them. These "super-apostles" represent an Israelite form of the Jesus Movement. They boast of their achievements in the name of Christ and of their Israelite heritage. They claim to have been given visions and revelations as a special sign of their status. They offer "signs and wonders and mighty works" as proof that Christ speaks through them. Indeed, Paul thinks that they proclaim "another Jesus" (11:4).

Moreover, they charge that he writes strong letters but that in person he is weak and his speech is contemptible.

Against all this, Paul offers the "foolishness" of his own boasting. He appeals to the original effectiveness of the gospel he preached in Corinth, to the fact that he supported himself in Corinth by his trade so as not to be a burden on his converts, and alludes to his own Israelite heritage, as a servant of Christ. Above all, in a "catalogue of sufferings" (11:16–30; cf. 4:8–10), he boasts about his *weakness.* He appeals to the Corinthians' sense of what they owe him and his gospel and to the example of Christ, who was "crucified *in weakness*" (13:4). This is a deliberately ironic contrast to the power in Christ that his opponents claim. Paul claims to live by the power of God. Once again, we see the implications of Paul's theology of the cross.

1:1–2:13; 7:5–16:   *The letter of reconciliation.*   Paul had sent the "tearful letter" to Corinth by the hand of his trusted companion Titus, whom he must have charged with the task of attempting to restore the situation there. The letter and Titus' visit were successful — the Corinthians were probably appalled by the realization of what they had done to the apostle to whom they owed so much — and Paul wrote a letter rejoicing in the resumption of good relations between him and the Corinthian community. In short, Paul's authority at Corinth was confirmed. In the process, Paul proposed that the person who had dishonored him during his tragic second visit be forgiven (2:5–11; 7:12).

The following two letters were probably written in Macedonia.

8:1–24:   *Part of a letter of recommendation for Titus about the collection for the saints in Jerusalem.*   For the discussion that this is part of a separate letter, see Chapter Four.

9:1–15:   *Part of a letter concerning the collection for the saints in Jerusalem.*   For the discussion that this is also part of a separate letter, see Chapter Four. Was it written to a satellite Corinthian church, such as at Cenchreae?

(6:14–7:1:   *A non-Pauline fragment [**interpolation**].*   In terms of ideas and vocabulary, this passage has no claim to come from the apostle Paul. It appears, rather, to reflect the influence of ideas characteristic of the Qumran community. It is not known how it came to be included in a collection of Paul's letters to the Corinthians. One suggestion is that it represented a letter of one of Paul's opponents.)

PHILIPPIANS

The city of Philippi, named for Philip II of Macedon, father of Alexander the Great, was located on the Egnatian Way, the east-west Roman highway that ran across Macedonia eight miles north of the seaport of Neapolis. Rome had conquered Macedonia in the second century B.C.E., and by the first century, Philippi had become a Roman colony. Thus, in addition to Thracians and Greeks, many Romans were there, especially soldiers and bureaucrats. Archeologists have found religious sites associated with Roman and Egyptian deities there.

According to Acts, Philippi was the site of Paul's first European congregation, established in the period before Paul went on to Thessalonica, Athens, and Corinth about 49 C.E. Acts emphasizes the importance of Paul's entering Europe by recording that Paul went to Macedonia in response to a vision (Acts 16:9–10). The author of Luke-Acts tells about the Philippi mission by recording, first, the story of the conversion of a wealthy seller of purple cloth, Lydia; as a result, Lydia's whole household was baptized (16:11–15, 40). Acts then tells about how Paul exorcised a demon from a slave girl who supported her masters with her "spirit of divination" (Acts 16:16; probably she was a possessed girl who could foretell the future through oracles). As a result, Paul and Silas were dragged before the city magistrates and charged by the Philippian Israelites with being anti-Roman, for which they were imprisoned. According to the Acts dramatization, they did not take the opportunity to escape during an earthquake. They then converted their duly impressed jailer and baptized him and his family. Paul was finally released and demanded an apology because he was a Roman citizen (Acts 16:16–39).

Although earthquake and exorcism episodes contain many Lukan and legendary features, certainly Paul's conversion of Philippians is credible. The letter to the Philippians mentions four adherents of the Jesus Movement by name (Phil. 2:25–30, Epaphroditus; 4:2–3, Euodia, Syntyche, and Clement) and other fellow workers "whose names are in the book of life" (4:3). The community was basically Gentile (3:3), and there may have been some local organization (1:1: "bishops" and "deacons," although these terms did not yet quite have the sense of official offices that developed later; thus perhaps a better translation would be "overseers" and "helpers"). There is no certainty that Paul visited Philippi again, although it is very likely that he did (Phil. 2:24; cf. 2 Cor. 13:1; Acts 20:1–6).

Of the undisputed Pauline letters, that to the Philippians was one of Paul's two "prison letters," the other being Philemon (Colossians and Ephesians are also called "prison letters," but we consider them to be deutero-Pauline). Neither letter says *where* Paul was imprisoned. Paul claims to have been imprisoned many times (2 Cor. 11:23), and Acts mentions three such locations: Philippi (16:23–40), Caesarea (23:23–26:32), and Rome (28:16–31). Many commentators have suggested that these letters were written during the Roman imprisonment, thus at or near the end of his life. Evidence for this theory in Philippians is sought in Paul's references to the "imperial guard" (1:13) and the "emperor's household" (4:22). If this theory were correct, Philippians (and Philemon) would have to be placed later in the Pauline chronology, after Romans. However, there are other possibilities. The "imperial guard" (Greek *praitōrion* from Latin *praetorium*) could refer to the guard of a provincial governor, as in Acts 23:35, and the "emperor's household" could include bureaucrats and soldiers in the provinces. In 1 Cor. 15:32, Paul says, "I fought with beasts at Ephesus." Although this statement could be metaphorical, the prison letters assume constant intercourse between the imprisoned Paul and his recipients, a factor difficult to imagine if the distance was so far away as Rome. Speaking for the Ephesus imprisonment is also Paul's comment about facing death in Asia (2 Cor. 1:8–10; cf. his figurative comment in 1 Cor. 15:30–32). Most scholars tend to think that Paul was imprisoned in Ephesus during his long stay there and that Philippians and Philemon originated there. The letters probably date, therefore, from about 54–55 C.E.

As with 2 Corinthians, Philippians has often been thought to contain letter fragments. There are very good reasons. First, Philippians 3:1b ("To write the *same things* to you is not troublesome to me . . .") seems to imply that Paul had corresponded earlier with the Philippians. Second, 3:1a ("Finally, my brethren, rejoice in the Lord") appears to be concluding the letter, but 3:1b suddenly and unexpectedly launches into Paul's sharply worded defense against his opponents. Third, the thanksgiving for the monetary gift comes very late (4:10–12). There are both two- and three-letter hypotheses. In the *two-letter hypothesis,* Paul wrote two letters after Epaphroditus arrived from Philippi with the gift (4:18). One theory is that Paul learned of opponents and responded by sending the angry, defensive Letter B (3:1b–4:20) and then, after Epaphroditus recovered from illness (2:25), sent him back to Philippi (2:25) with Letter A (1:1–3:1a plus 4:21–23), a personal, pastoral letter. Another theory is that Paul wrote the pastoral Letter A first (1:1–3a plus 4:2–7, 10–23), expressing thanks for the gift and Epaphroditus' recovery from illness (2:25), and then wrote the angry Letter B (3:1b–4:1 plus 4:8–9) after he was released from prison. The *three-letter hypothesis* extends the second possibility, but it extracts the thanks for the gift section (4:10–20) as a separate fragment, Letter C, and puts it first; then Paul sends the recovered Epaphroditus with the pastoral Letter A (1:1–3:1a plus 4:4–7, 21–23); and finally, learning of his opponents, Paul dispatches Timothy with the angry Letter B (3:1b–4:3; 4:8–9).

Although these theories make good sense of the break at 3:1b and the late thanksgiving, a strong trend in recent criticism is that the letter is a unity. One reason is that Paul's expression of "friendship," a subject of discussion in ancient philosophical literature, occurs throughout the letter. Moreover, in the friendship discussions, praising friends is often side by side with blaming enemies. Also, the apparent digression about Timothy and Epaphroditus in chapter 2 stresses Paul's desire to have them in Philippi, which can be related to his tirade against enemies in chapter 3. Finally, the postponement of discussion of the monetary gift until chapter 4 could have been part of Paul's rhetorical strategy. He hints at the gift earlier (1:5; 2:25) and then concludes with a theme that conflicts with his usual practice of accepting such gifts. Thus, despite the mixing of thanksgivings, praise, blame, ethical exhortation, and the like—which complicates matters somewhat—in this edition we follow the recent trend to see the letter as a unity and outline the letter as follows:

1:1–2	Pauline salutation
1:3–11	Thanksgiving
1:12–2:11	Body A: Paul's prison circumstances and upcoming trial; the Christological hymn
2:12–2:18	Ethical exhortation
2:19–3:1a	Relationships with Timothy and Epaphroditus
3:1b–4:1	Body B: Warning against opponents and conflict between Euodia and Syntyche
4:2–6	Ethical exhortation
4:7–9	Preliminary conclusion

4:10–20   Thanksgiving for gift

4:21–23   Conclusion: Greetings and benediction

1:1–2: *Pauline salutation, but from both Paul and Timothy.* Paul uses the terms "bishops" (Greek *episcopoi*) and "deacons" (Greek *diakonoi*), but because fixed offices with specific qualifications cannot be documented this early, his meaning is probably less technical; thus some translators prefer "overseers" for bishops and "helpers" for deacons (see further discussion in Chapter Thirteen).

1:3–11: *Thanksgiving* for the concern the Philippians have expressed for Paul, who is now enduring a considerable period of imprisonment.

1:12–2:11: *Body A: Paul's prison circumstances and upcoming trial and his citation of a Christological hymn.* There are hints of opponents in 1:17. The reference to "imperial guard" (1:13) does not rule out Ephesus as Paul's place of imprisonment (see preceding). Paul's desire "to depart and be with Christ" (1:23; cf. 2 Cor. 5:1–9) sounds unusual in relation to the *future* apocalyptic view of the *final* resurrection in 1 Thessalonians; it is not impossible that Paul contemplated suicide; it was not a dishonorable option in Greco-Roman society. "Struggle" in 1:30 comes from athletic competition, which is mentioned several times in this letter (2:16; 3:13–14; 4:3; cf. 1 Cor. 9:24–27; Gal. 2:2; 5:7).

As noted in Chapter Three, Phil. 2:5–11 is a **Christological hymn** that probably portrays the descending-ascending redeemer figure. This figure has a pre-earthly existence ("in the form of God"; "to be equal with God"), takes on an earthly existence ("empties himself"; "in the likeness of men"; "in fashion like a man"; "taking the form of a slave [or servant]"), dies, and is exalted to a postearthly existence where he is glorified and worshipped as a god. If the basics of the hymn existed prior to Paul, as many scholars think, Paul added "the death on the cross" (verse 8b), a phrase that breaks the metrical balance of the hymn and expresses Paul's central theology of the cross (see 1 Cor. 1:18–25).

2:12–2:18: *Ethical exhortation A builds on the Christ hymn:* Christ's obedience should lead to the Philippians' obedience. "Run" in 2:16 is a metaphor drawn from athletic competition (see 2 Cor. 3:13–14; 1 Cor. 9:24–27; Gal. 2:2; 5:7).

2:19–3:1a: *Relationships with Timothy and Epaphroditus.* Timothy is praised; Epaphroditus has been very ill but is now recovered and will be rejoining the Philippians shortly.

3:1b–4:1: *Body B: A sharply polemical section warning the Philippians of the dangers of an enthusiastic "circumcision" party; the conflict between Euodia and Syntyche.* The opponents have traits reminiscent of those in both Galatia (circumcision) and Corinth (enthusiasm). As in Galatians and 2 Corinthians, Paul combats them with an autobiographical statement (3:4–11; 3:5–6). Indeed, Phil. 3:5–6 is his most complete autobiographical statement (see Chapter Four). Paul's characteristic apocalyptic hope is still present (3:20–21). Paul urges two women leaders of the church, Euodia and Syntyche, to resolve their disagreement (4:2–4); this comment indicates again that women had positions of responsibility and leadership in his congregations.

4:2–6: *Moral exhortation.*

4:7–9: *Preliminary conclusion.*

4:10–20: *A thanksgiving to the Philippians* for the revival of their concern for Paul and the gifts sent to him with Epaphroditus. Paul mentions that he accepted money from the Philippians while he was at Thessalonica and that this broke his usual pattern (4:15). The expression "learned the secret" (4; 12) is known from the mystery cults (archeologists have discovered remnants of the mystery cult of Diana at Philippi). Some critics believe that this seemingly out-of-place thanksgiving was the basic impulse for the letter.

4:21–23: *Conclusion: Greetings and benediction.* The greeting mentions "the emperor's household" (4:22), discussed earlier along with the "imperial guard" (1:13).

PHILEMON

At the beginning of this chapter, the little letter of Philemon was used to illustrate how Paul follows the ancient form and rhetoric of the letter, although he gives it his own spin. Here the content of Philemon will be examined more carefully.

Like Philippians, Philemon was a "prison letter" (verses 1, 9, 10, 13, 23). As stated before, the most likely location for this imprisonment was Ephesus, not Rome. Some reasons for this conclusion are discussed earlier in relation to Philippians. The main reason from Philemon is that Paul hoped to visit Philemon (verse 22), and probably this destination was Colossae because eight names—perhaps nine—in Philemon also appear in the letter to the Colossians (Col. 2:19–24; 4:9, 10, 11, 2, 14, 17; only Philemon and Apphia are missing). Colossae is closer than Rome to Ephesus, only about a hundred miles east. However, the intention to visit Philemon in Colossae in the West conflicted with his plans to go westward to Spain after coming to Rome (Rom. 15:22–24). The Ephesians imprisonment suggests that Paul (and Timothy) wrote the letter about 56 C.E.

As noted earlier, most of the letter deals with slavery, specifically the complications that appear when both master and slave in a household become members of a group that has the ideal, "no longer slave or free . . . in Christ Jesus" (Gal. 3:28). It will be helpful, therefore, to recall some generalities about slavery (Bartchy).

Most studies of slavery in Greco-Roman antiquity suggest that it was not the same as slavery in the pre–Civil War period of the United States. Ancient slavery was not based on race, for example. One could become a slave by being born into slavery, captured in war, falling into debt, selling oneself (or family members) into slavery, or being "rescued" from infant exposure and then raised as a slave. Slaves did not constitute a separate social or economic "class." Rather, the status of a slave was based on the status of the master. Indeed, a slave's status was often higher than a free person's status. Moreover, poorer folk sometimes had slaves; even slaves sometimes had slaves! Many slaves, especially those enslaved as a result of war, were more educated than their masters, and they were often encouraged to continue their education in order to benefit their masters. Many slaves held very responsible positions such as teachers, doctors, accountants, secretaries, and property managers. There were responsible slave positions in Caesar's household, indeed quite powerful positions. Slaves could also accumulate property and wealth and buy their freedom, although they normally remained indebted to their former masters, who became their patrons. Female slaves were sometimes set free by their male masters to marry them. Finally, most slaves in Greco-Roman society could expect to be emancipated by the age of thirty, from which masters normally benefited economically.

One might think that slavery was not so bad. However, slaves were slaves, and the previous paragraph relates mainly to domestic or household slaves. There were also slaves who worked on plantations and in mines or who rowed galley ships. Their life was harsh and brutal. Slaves were property (like animals) and did not enjoy the same legal status as free persons. For example, they were sometimes beaten or molested; as witnesses in court they could, in contrast to free Roman citizens, be tortured to obtain testimony. Slaves were not legally married, their families were sometimes broken up, and disreputable masters sometimes sexually abused female and boy slaves. Fugitive slaves had to be returned, and debts were to be paid to their owners by anyone who harbored them. Israelites did not normally enslave other Israelites—when they did, Israelite law limited the time to six years—because their own slavery in Egypt was deeply embedded in their ritual consciousness (*Passover!*). Nonetheless, Israelite law permitted slavery, although treatment of slaves was better. Thus Israelites sometimes had non-Israelite slaves. It is important to see that the Greco-Roman economy was in many respects a slave economy, that is, slaves, not machines, did the heavy labor, which made possible the leisure, thus the culture, of the free. Slavery was an accepted institution. To be sure, there were slave rebellions in the second and first centuries B.C.E., but they were usually led by prisoner-of-war slaves who wanted to go home or make slaves of their masters, not abolish the institution of slavery itself.

Like his contemporaries, Paul accepted slavery as an institution and did not seek to abolish it. Some believers in Paul's congregations were slaves (Rom. 16:10–11), either because their masters became believers (1 Cor. 16:15; cf. Acts 16:15, 31–34) or because of choice (1 Cor. 7:10–11, 21). Probably "Chloe's people" (1 Cor. 1:16) were slaves. It is not surprising, then, that Paul used "slave" as a metaphor for those who believed in, thus obeyed, Jesus as the Christ. As a redeemer, Jesus "emptied himself" and took the form of a slave (e.g., Phil. 2:5–11). So Paul called members of the Jesus Movement "slaves" of Christ (1 Cor. 7:17–24). Yet, in the new fictive family, believers achieved a higher status than household slaves, namely, brothers and sisters. Again, for Paul, the ideal was that in Christ Jesus there would be "no longer slave or free" (Gal. 3:28).

The letter to Philemon contains a complex interplay of authoritarian, friendship, and fictive kin language. It needs to be read and studied carefully.

1:1–3: *Salutation.* Paul, a "prisoner of Christ," and Timothy "our brother," write to a slave owner in the Jesus Movement, Philemon, a "dear friend and co-worker" (verse 1), and to Apphia "our sister" and Archippus "our fellow soldier." Perhaps these latter persons are Philemon's wife and son.

1:4–7: *Thanksgiving.* Paul commends Philemon for his love and faith (verses 5–6) and addresses him as "my brother" (verse 7).

1:8–22: *Body.* Paul is writing on behalf of Philemon's slave, Onesimus. In prison, he has become Onesimus' "father," and Onesimus has become his "child" (verse 10). Paul is very cautious about asserting his authority over Philemon. Philemon is probably a person of some means and a patron of a house-church in Colossae. Although Philemon owes Paul his very "self" or life (verse 19) and Paul as an apostle could *command* him to do his duty (verse 8), Paul appeals to Philemon's free will (verse 14). This delicacy is also reinforced with a bit of humor. Paul puns that the slave Onesimus, whose name in Greek means "Useful," has been "useless" to Philemon, but now he is "useful" to both of them (verse 11). It is possible that there is a second pun involved because another term for "useful" in Greek is *chrēstos,* which would have sounded just like *Christos,* "Christ." Was Paul suggesting that formerly Onesimus had been not only "useless" but "without Christ" (Greek *a-chrēstos*)? Paul puns on Onesimus' name again when he says, "Yes, brother [Philemon], let me have this benefit (Greek *onaimēn*) from you in the Lord" (verse 20). Yet, despite Paul's humor and delicate appeal to Philemon's free will, Paul asserts his authority. He says that Philemon should welcome Onesimus back as "brother" (see verse 17), that Paul will pay any damages that Onesimus might have incurred, and that he is confident of Philemon's "obedience" (verse 21). Paul has said that he has wanted to keep Onesimus with him (verse 13). Now he says that he hopes that Philemon will "do even more than I say" (verse 21). In conclusion, Paul asks him to prepare for his coming, expressing hope for his release.

   1:23–25:   *Conclusion.*   Paul sends greetings from himself, Epaphras, Mark, Aristarchus, Demas, and Luke. Paul concludes with a benediction.

   Not everything in this letter is clear. How did Onesimus come in contact with Paul in prison? Did Paul's mentioning the new "father-child" relationship mean that Paul had baptized Onesimus and that therefore Onesimus had not become a believer earlier when Philemon did? What did Paul really want Philemon to do? Just receive Onesimus back, as he clearly says, or "do more," that is, send him back to Paul, or even free him? Finally, why did Onesimus originally leave Philemon's household? Was Onesimus, whom Paul calls a slave only by implication (verse 16: "no longer a slave"), legally a *fugitive* slave (Latin *fugitivus*)? Had Paul been reflecting on the Israelite law, "Slaves who have escaped to you from their owners shall not be given back to them. They shall reside with you. . . ." (Deut. 23:15–16)?

   There are several different kinds of answers to these questions. One theory is that Philemon and the church at Colossae *sent* Onesimus to Paul; however, the implied problems between Philemon and Onesimus, as well as Paul's appeals to Philemon (cf. verses 11, 15, 18), make this theory difficult to sustain. The most common theory is that Onesimus was a fugitive (*fugitivus*). Various other theories follow. He might have been captured by the authorities and imprisoned with Paul; one of Paul's associates might have brought him to Paul; he might have came freely because of guilt, fear, or inability to provide for himself; or he might have thought that Paul, when freed, would give him asylum.

   A recent alternative and attractive theory is that Paul was being asked by Onesimus to intervene on his behalf as mediator (Lampe [see Harrill]). To understand this "third-party intervention" suggestion, it is important to understand first-century Roman case law about fugitive slaves. This law put the stress on *intentions.* A slave was *not* considered to be a fugitive if he, "having in mind that his master wished physically to chastise him, left to seek a friend whom he persuaded to plead on his behalf" (*Digesta Iustiniani* 21.1.17.4). An example of this possibility was Augustus' rebuke of his friend Pollio, who treated his slave poorly when Augustus was a guest at Pollio's dinner party. Perhaps an even more interesting and relevant example of third-party intervention is Pliny's appeal to Sabinianus, whose former slave, or freedman, asked Pliny to intercede with Sabinianus on his behalf. Because of its importance for the "third-party intervention" theory, it is worth quoting:

> The freedman of yours with whom you said you were angry has been with me, flung himself at my feet, and clung to me as if I were you. He begged my help with many tears, although he left a good deal unsaid; in short, he convinced me of his genuine penitence. I believe he has reformed, because he realizes he did wrong. You are angry, I know, and I know too that your anger was deserved, but mercy wins most praise when there was just cause for anger. You loved the man once, and I hope you will love him again, but it is sufficient for the moment if you allow yourself to be appeased. You can always be angry again if he deserves it, and will have more excuse if you were once placated. Make some concession to his youth, his tears, and your own kind heart, and do not torment him or yourself any longer—anger can only be a torment to your gentle self.
>
> I'm afraid you will think I am using pressure, not persuasion, if I add my prayers to his—but this is what I shall do, and all the more freely and fully because I have given the man a very severe scolding and warned him firmly that I will never make such a request again. This was because he deserved a fright, and is not intended for your ears; for maybe I *shall* make another request and obtain it, as long as it is nothing unsuitable for me to ask and you to grant.
>
> (Pliny *Letters* 9.21)

Sabinianus heeded Pliny's advice because in a subsequent letter Pliny congratulated him for having done so (Pliny *Letters* 9.24).

Perhaps, then, Onesimus wished to be happily restored to Philemon. If so, he was not a fugitive, but rather sought out Paul as a third party—an important friend of Philemon—to plead his case. Thus the letter would be an example of "third-party intervention."

If this is the case, one may wonder why Paul did not mention Onesimus' desire to repent, as did Pliny of the freedman. Perhaps these differences can be explained by the context. Pliny's letter was private, Paul's quasi-public: It was to be read in the house-church, and thus Philemon would have been under public pressure to carry out some reciprocal act to his "father" Paul with honor. Did Paul want to avoid dishonoring Philemon? Despite this difference, the similarities are rather striking. Thus it is not impossible that the letter to Philemon is a "third-party intervention" request by Onesimus; if so, he was probably not a *fugitivus*.

Whatever the exact situation, it should be said again that Paul offered no social program for the emancipation of slaves. He was "a man of his times." Yet, it is equally clear that when both master and slave became believing "brothers," and Paul as "father" asked for a return favor (**reciprocity**), the tension between traditional social values and believers' values surfaced. Finally, it is interesting that in the early second century the Church Father Ignatius of Antioch wrote letters to Asia Minor and mentioned a certain bishop named Onesimus (Ignatius *To the Ephesians* 1.3). Although the time between Paul's letter about Onesimus (50s C.E.) and Bishop Onesimus (110 C.E.) is very great, one is tempted to ask: Was this the same Onesimus?

SUMMARY

In this chapter, the first topic was the Pauline letter and specifically Paul's earliest letters. The letter is one of four genres in the New Testament. Using Paul's most personal letter as a guide, Paul's letters in general followed conventional patterns for ancient letters, although Paul transformed them, first, by changing their introductions and conclusions with typical language and practice in the Jesus Movement and, second, by addressing concerns specific to local congregations. The letter functioned to continue Paul's communication when he was absent, that is, he could thereby clarify his teaching, support a congregation, admonish its deviant members, defend himself against those who challenged his authority, offer advice, and the like. The form of Paul's letters also demonstrated Paul's rhetorical skills, thus indicating that he had at least a secondary-level education. Finally, the letters gave evidence that Paul was well acquainted with many creedal and liturgical traditions, which he occasionally cited, as well as the **Septuagint,** which he often recalled, quoted, and interpreted to demonstrate that his message had the support of the ideas and practices of ancient Israel.

This chapter has offered interpretive outlines and notes on five of Paul's undisputed texts in what is probably their order of composition: 1 Thessalonians, 1 Corinthians, 2 Corinthians, Philippians, and Philemon. In each case we have sketched background about the places and persons to whom Paul writes, noted opponents again, highlighted key issues, and occasionally offered parallels from ancient Israelite and Hellenistic literature. In the process, we have noted that 1 Thessalonians concentrates on thanksgiving, apocalyptic eschatology, and ethics; that 1 Corinthians stresses Paul's responses to key ethical problems; that 2 Corinthians demonstrates Paul's up-and-down relations with the Corinthian church related to opposition; that Philippians is a mixture of pastoral reflection, thanksgiving, anger, and a great Christological hymn; and that Philemon offers a study of slavery that raises as many questions as it answers. In the process, we also noted that 2 Corinthians contains at least five letter fragments and that 1 and 2 Corinthians have interpolations (1 Cor. 14:33b–36; 2 Cor. 6:14–7:1). It is clear from especially 1 Corinthians that although Paul stressed the freedom of members of the Jesus Movement from the Torah, he set the limits of freedom with his focus on love and unity in the community in a case where extremes in behavior were rampant.

We now turn to two letters that, because the questions swirl around the Torah, heighten messages about freedom and salvation: Galatians and Romans.

STUDY QUESTIONS

1. What are the form and function of ancient letters? How does Paul change the usual form of the letter in general, and how is each formally distinctive in particular? What are the historical and social contexts of the five letters in this chapter?

2. 1 Thessalonians: What are the three central themes of this letter?

3. 1 and 2 Corinthians: In what ways is unity in the Corinthian congregation the overarching theme in these letters? How is this question related to religious ideas, social

strata of the groups, pagan and Israelite morality, and religious practice? What are the key problems that Paul addresses, how does he learn about them, and what are his recommended solutions? What is his "theology of the cross?" What is the issue of letter fragments, and what are some approaches to a solution? Who are the "super-apostles" in 2 Cor. 10–13? What does Paul say about "the collection" (cf. Gal. 2:10; 1 Cor. 16: 1–4; Rom. 15:25–29)?

4. Philippians: What is the historical and social context for Philippians? What is Paul's relationship to the Philippians? What is the major teaching of the "Philippians hymn"?

5. Philemon: What is the historical and social context for Philemon? Who is Philemon? Onesimus? How would you describe the ancient institution of slavery? What are Paul's intentions in the letter?

Photo 6.1   A beautiful young woman from a fresco originally in the city of Pompeii, Italy (destroyed by lava from the eruption of Mount Vesuvius in 79 C.E.), now in the National Museum, Naples, Italy. Her apparel shows that she was of the upper social strata. She was presumably educated (she muses over a book). In Paul's churches women of means held authority and seem to have been patrons (e.g., Rom. 16:1–3). Paul's ideal was ". . . no longer male and female . . . in Christ Jesus" (Gal. 3:28); see the summary of Paul's view of women on pp. 249–251.

CHAPTER SIX

GALATIANS AND ROMANS

Most biblical scholars would reject the view that Paul's letter to the Romans is merely a longer version of his letter to the Galatians. The major reason is that in Galatians, Paul formulates his ideas in the heat of controversy and anger, whereas in Romans he writes a more thoughtful, reflective, sophisticated letter. Nonetheless, there would be little disagreement about whether these two books deal with some of the same themes. We shall therefore study them in the same chapter.

Galatians, the shorter of the two, and considered by scholars to be earlier, will be studied first. That strategy will help with the study of Romans, which is the longer, later, and more difficult book. The chapter will conclude with an addendum that summarizes some of Paul's major theological and social-ethical ideas.

GALATIANS

In this little letter, Paul is angry and upset. After Paul left Galatia, other missionaries came into the region. Paul has learned that they are challenging his authority and his message. He responds by sharply defending his authority as an apostle sent by God. He also defends his version of the good news: Having *faith in Christ,* not doing works of the Law as commanded in the Torah, leads to the true meaning of life. For Paul this means that proselytes do not become full members of God's chosen people by undergoing circumcision, the mark of God's covenant with Israel; rather, that happens by believing in Christ. Paul's emphasis was born out of conflict. It had the potential to be divisive—and was. It also had the potential to break down ethnocentric values about Gentiles and gender, as well as social stratification (see 3:28)—matters that can also painfully divide and oppress people. Thus Galatians has been called the "epistle of freedom." Yet, it should be noted that Paul did not totally abandon the Torah and all its laws; indeed, by the end of the letter he had established a few rules of his own!

There are major problems about deciding the letter's destination, recipients, and time of writing. Paul addresses this letter to "the churches of Galatia" (Gal. 1:2). There are two possibilities for this location: (1) the central plateau region of Asia Minor (around modern-day Ankara, Turkey) and (2) the southern coastal region of east-central Asia Minor. Those who defend the northern location take "Galatia" in its old *ethnic sense,* that is, as the region where the Indo-Aryan Celts or Gauls (*Galloi/Galatai,* that is, "Galatians") settled early in the third century B.C.E. This view is called the *North Galatia theory.* Those who defend the southern location take "Galatia" in its larger, *Roman provincial sense.* That region includes the old ethnic region but also extends farther south to the Mediterranean Sea. Rome created this province and called it "Galatia" in 25 C.E. If Paul meant the Roman province of Galatia, he could have been writing to churches in southern Asia Minor. This view is called the *South Galatia theory.*

Arguments can be made for both locations. The South Galatia theory has in its favor the fact that in Acts 13–14 Paul is said to have visited cities in the southern part of central Asia Minor (Perga, Antioch in Pisidia [not in Syria], Iconium, Lystra, Derbe). Acts considers these visits as part of Paul's first missionary journey (cf. also 16:1–5). If this view is correct, Paul sent this letter not long after his visit there. According to the Acts chronology, this would have been fairly early in Paul's letter-writing period, that is, the early 50s. The major weakness of the South Galatia theory is that making three neat missionary journeys in Acts is highly suspect, and thus so are any arguments based on it.

The North Galatian theory has in its favor the fact that, as far as anyone knows, Paul never went back to Galatia. This fact is consistent with two other facts: (1) His failure to return suggests that the letter could be later, and (2) ideas in Galatians and Romans, his latest surviving letter, are very similar, as mentioned earlier. The major weakness of the North Galatia theory is that Acts mentions no major journey to towns in that area. However, once again the Acts chronology cannot be determinative, and the similarity of Galatians and Romans is an impressive argument. The North Galatia theory is more probable, and so Galatians is placed in this chapter with Romans.

The exact place from which Paul wrote the letter to the Galatians is also difficult to decide. If we were to accept the South Galatian theory, he could have written it earlier on his journey back to Antioch or at Antioch. The North Galatian theory suggests that it was written after the latest parts of 2 Corinthians, which were written at Ephesus, but before Romans, written at Corinth. Paul could have written it on his trip from Ephesus to Corinth, thus in Macedonia. If so, a plausible time of writing would have been about 55 or 56 C.E., the period just before he wrote Romans.

The occasion for this letter was developed in Chapter Four. You will recall that there were disturbances in Galatia created by opponents from outside the church. According to Paul, these opponents were like the Israelite conservatives from Judea in demanding circumcision and "the Law"; therefore, many modern scholars have labeled them "Judaizers." However, it has usually been argued that these "Judaizers" were not strict Pharisees like Paul had been because they had some very unusual syncretistic views and seem to have thought that Paul was too dependent on Jerusalem authorities (Gal. 1–2). Some scholars think that Paul was not sure who they were, and so we cannot be sure, either. Whoever they were, they irritated the apostle so much that he defended himself by launching into one of his most vitriolic attacks. In fact, because defenses are often called "apologies," the genre of Galatians might be called an "apologetic" letter (Betz). Moreover, not only does Paul defend himself and his supporters at the end of the letter (6:16), but also he literally curses his opponents (1:8–9). Thus Galatians is also something like a "magical letter." Contemporary studies show that Paul defended himself with all kinds of arguments typical of one who was educated in rhetoric. Finally—this is consistent with Paul's extreme anger—the most striking formal feature of the letter is its omission of the customary "thanksgiving" (see Chapter Five).

In short, the letter to the Galatians is Paul's defense of himself and his gospel, or good news. This leads him to stress that good news: The believer is *justified by faith,* not deeds prescribed by the Torah, and thus the believer is *freed from "the Law."* Justification by faith and freedom from the Law go hand in hand. They will be developed in interpretive summaries later. This view leads Paul to state that "in Christ Jesus" one is free from the restrictions of religion, ethnic identity, social class, and gender (3:28). Paul's gospel in this letter also echoes ideas about sacrifice as a means of atonement from sins. In Paul's view, however, atonement is not related to Jerusalem temple sacrifice but rather takes a more millennial form. It is centered on a faith in Jesus Christ "who gave himself for our sins to deliver us from the present evil age according to the will of our God and Father" (1:4). Paul attempts to defend this new freedom with a kind of rhetorical logic that draws on human experience, scriptural proof, liturgical tradition, past friendship, and indeed the Torah itself.

Here is a brief outline of the letter:

1:1–5	Salutation: Sender, recipients, greeting. No thanksgiving!
1:6–4:31	Body: Paul's polemical defense of his gospel
1:6–10	Polemic against opponents
1:11–2:14	Defense of Paul's gospel
2:15–21	Paul's gospel: Justification by faith
3:1–4:31	Defense of Paul's gospel based on scripture (especially Abraham and Sarah)
5:1–6:10	Ethical exhortation
6:11–16	Summary of gospel in Paul's own hand
6:17–18	Conclusion

1:1–5: *Salutation.* Paul immediately defends himself: He is an "apostle," that is, one sent on a mission (the original background of the Greek term *apostolos* is military). His view of his role is reminiscent of the Cynic philosopher's view: God has ordained the mission. In contrast to the Cynic, Paul thinks that God has ordained his mission *through an intermediary,* Jesus Christ.

Paul does not mention his cosenders by name, as he usually does. His focus, again, is on himself and his role as apostle. The recipients of the letter are "all the churches of Galatia" (verse 2). In the greeting, Paul summarizes the gospel of freedom in millennial terms: It is freedom from the "present evil age" (recall the contrast between the "this [present evil] age" and the "the [good] age to come" in Israelite thought). Paul's gospel is rooted in the forgiveness of sins through Jesus' self-giving death and resurrection as God's will. In contrast to the written Gospels, he does not focus on the life and teaching of Jesus of Nazareth; indeed, he hardly mentions these matters (cf. 4:4, "born of a woman").

1:6–10:   *Amazement, anathema, and transition.*   At this point in his letters, Paul normally offers a thanksgiving for the faith of those who persevere in the community to which he writes. However, Paul is in no mood for a thanksgiving. Rather, he plunges immediately into an attack, expressing amazement at the state of affairs in the churches of Galatia and cursing anyone who preaches a false gospel. To Paul, "Let that one be accursed" (verse 8) can probably be taken literally, as effective magical power.

1:11–2:14:   *A personal and historical defense of Paul's gospel.*   In the first major section of the letter, Paul defines and defends his understanding of the gospel against that of his opponents. This section has three parts: (1) the divine call of Paul to be **apostle;** (2) the **Jerusalem Conference** and the **Jerusalem Compromise;** and (3) the **Antioch Incident.**

1:11–24:   *The divine origin of Paul's message and his call by God to be an apostle.* This invaluable autobiographical account of Paul's "conversion" (call) and early activity as a missionary in the Jesus Movement was the basis for the sketch of Paul's life and work in Chapter Four. Paul tells of his zeal as a persecutor of members of the Jesus Movement. Then, he says, he was recruited directly by God for his mission, that is, he received a "revelation" (Greek *apocalypsis*) of God's Son (cf. 1 Cor. 15:8; 2 Cor. 12:2–4). This revelation for Paul meant that he had no choice in his vocation as an apostle. It was an act of God, predestined before his birth. Paul's view of his destiny reflects scriptural accounts about God's call of the prophets, especially Isaiah (Isa. 49:1–6) and Jeremiah (Jer. 1:5). In short, Paul defends his authority as apostle to the Gentiles by means of his experience that God revealed his Son, Jesus, to him directly (an ASC). Others certainly questioned Paul's legitimacy—for example, Paul's Galatian opponents. In Chapter Four, the theory was suggested that Jerusalem conservatives increasingly opposed Paul. (An Israelite-oriented anti-Pauline movement within the Jesus Movement is also represented by the second-century C.E. *pseudo-Clementine* literature in which the conservative James, brother of Jesus, is highlighted.) The conservatives had a point, and there were competing views within the Jesus Movement. For example, a direct, divine revelation alone would not have passed the criterion to be an apostle later put forward by the author of Luke-Acts. For him, the criterion was having accompanied Jesus from the time of his baptism by John to his ascension to heaven (Acts 1:21–22). Paul did not meet this criterion. Indeed, with the exception of 14:14, Acts does not designate Paul with the term *apostle.*

Paul's autobiographical sketch continues with his three-year period in Arabia (an extensive region south of Damascus, Syria, inhabited by the Nabateans; cf. 2 Cor. 11:32–33; Acts 9:25). Then he mentions his *brief* visit to Cephas (Peter) and James, Jesus' brother (Mark 6:3; Acts 15:13) in Jerusalem. Finally, he notes his move to Syria (Antioch?) and Cilicia (Tarsus?).

2:1–10: *The* **Jerusalem Conference** *and the* **Jerusalem Compromise.** Paul next says that after fourteen years, he attended what many scholars call **the Jerusalem Conference** (see Chapter Four). He says that he was accompanied by Barnabas (2:1; cf. 1 Cor. 9:6) and that he took Titus with him (2:1; cf. 2 Cor. 8:23). Paul emphasizes that he was *not sent* by other apostles, but—using the same term that he had used to legitimate his call—went up "in response to *a revelation*" (2:2). Paul describes the conference as a private affair, a meeting between "the pillars," that is, James, Peter, and John and himself. There seem to have been three, perhaps four, conflicting points of view at the conference, and the leaders, or so-called pillars, seem not to have agreed among themselves. First, there was James (Jesus' brother), who was more conservative and seems to have defended the purity norm that Israelite and Gentile believers should not eat together (2:12). Second, Cephas (or Peter) and John appear to have been more open to Paul's view at this point in time. Third, there was Paul, who argued that Gentile converts did not have to be circumcised. Paul also seems to imply a fourth position that is suggested by his description "false brothers secretly brought in" to spy on them. Presumably these men were an ultra-conservative faction. Perhaps their issue was circumcision because it is never said that James demanded that. Thus there seems to have been a spectrum of viewpoints: ultra-conservatives (required circumcision?), conservatives (separate meals), moderates (compromised with Paul), and Paul (no circumcision; common meals). If Acts can be trusted, earlier there had probably been still another, a fifth, position. There were those who held a position still more radical than Paul's, that of Stephen and the Hellenists (cf. Acts 6–7). They criticized not only certain laws of the Torah, but also the temple itself! However, they had probably been driven out (interpreting Acts 8:2).

From Paul's perspective, the moderate-to-conservative pillars yielded ground to him. From Paul's perspective, the result of the Jerusalem Conference (Apostolic Assembly) was the Jerusalem Compromise: Paul and Barnabas would direct their mission to the Gentiles, who did not have to be circumcised; the conservatives (James) and moderates (Peter [and John?]) would go to "the circumcised," or Torah-observant, ethnic Israelites. In Paul's memory, the only requirement placed on Paul and Barnabas was that they should "remember the poor," which Paul was quite happy to do. It is known from Paul's other letters that he carried out this part of the compromise by undertaking "the collection" of money for the poor at Jerusalem (1 Cor. 16:1–4; 2 Cor. 8, 9; Rom. 15:25–27).

Paul offered two important facts as evidence for this compromise. First, his Gentile companion, Titus, was not compelled to be circumcised (verse 3). Second, the pillars gave Paul and Barnabas the "right hand of fellowship" (verse 9), thus agreeing on the division of labor on the mission field.

In short, Paul in this section is concerned with defending and legitimating his mission to go to the Gentiles, who in his view do not need to be circumcised and thus are free from the commands of the Torah. The leaders of the Jerusalem church, he claims, agreed to a compromise position at the Jerusalem Conference (the Jerusalem Compromise).

Acts 15 has a very different account of what happened at Jerusalem. Paul, Barnabas, and some others are *sent* to Jerusalem. Apostles *and elders* welcome them. Those who demand circumcision of proselytes to the Jesus Movement are also *Pharisees* (like Paul!

cf. Phil. 3:5). At an apparently *large* assembly—not a private meeting—*Peter* gives a speech saying that *he* has been the instrument for the conversion of Gentiles (Acts 15: 7; cf. Acts 10; but cf. Acts 8:26–40; 11:19–26), and in it he also appeals to God's grace. Then *James* (!) agrees with Peter (Acts 15:14), indicating that all this has been foretold in scripture (Amos 9:11–12). Finally, *the agreement has nothing to do with circumcision;* rather, a letter is drafted that requires that the Gentiles observe *three cultic rules about food and one moral rule, all based on scripture* (Lev. 17:8–18:30). They should "abstain only from things polluted by idols and from fornication and from whatever has been strangled and from blood" (Acts 15:20; cf. 15:29; 21:25). Scholars often call these requirements the Apostolic Decree. Paul never mentions such a decree, and, once again, the primary source is Paul's own account in Galatians—even if it should turn out that in his anger (see following) he overstates the agreement about the Gentile mission.

2:11–14: The Antioch Incident.   The Acts version of the so-called Apostolic Decree just mentioned stressed cultic (food) and moral requirements. Although Paul's own account of the Jerusalem Conference stressed the purity issue of circumcision, not food, he nonetheless also had to face the purity issue of food at Antioch. Thus in this passage Paul says that when "people from James" came from Jerusalem to Antioch, Peter, who had been eating with "unclean" Gentiles, stopped this practice. Thus he yielded to the strict Torah-observers' norms. From Paul's perspective, Peter had acted *as if* he accepted the Gentiles, when in fact he had not. Paul took the view (also found among some other Pharisees) that there should be no discrepancy between inner convictions and outward behavior. In effect, he was charging Peter with hypocrisy.

We have only Paul's version of the Peter-Paul conflict at Antioch. Note, however, that Paul eventually moved the center of his activity from Antioch to Ephesus. Thus it is possible that Peter's, not Paul's, authority ultimately prevailed at Antioch. Certainly it appears as if the conservative position was still very powerful there. Had the ultra-conservatives convinced James—hence "men from James"?—that Paul was not Torah-observant enough and that they were right? Had Peter himself never been completely convinced of the Jerusalem Compromise? Or did Peter vacillate at a later time, as Paul says? If Paul was accurate in his recollection about Peter's vacillation in meal practices, was the supposed decision about circumcision, presumably opposed by the ultra-conservatives, still in doubt among certain church leaders?

2:15–21:   *Paul's gospel.*   In reflecting further on the Antioch Incident, Paul is led to one of his great statements on the nature of faith. A main feature of Paul's letter—some think it is the *main* feature—is justification by faith. According to Paul, all people are sinful, thus guilty, and deserve to be punished. God, the powerful Creator and Redeemer, the Great Judge, sits on his judgment seat. Again, however, he is merciful and takes the initiative. His acts are "just" or "righteous" (adjective *dikaios*). He "justifies" or "makes *right*eous" (verb *dikaioō*) persons, not because they do "works of the Law," but rather because *they have faith.* This is the "*right*eousness (noun *dikaiosynē*) of God." This is God's gift, his merciful "grace"; it is the gift of "salvation." Paul has come to believe that obedience to the commands of the Torah (doing "good works"), which includes maintaining purity (circumcision; kosher food), *cannot* earn God's favor because it tends to self-justification. Justification comes only through "grace," or God's freely given gift. It is given to those who believe in Jesus Christ. As one modern theologian has rephrased God's merciful act, believers can now "accept themselves as being accepted in spite of being unacceptable" (Tillich). For Paul, this is salvation.

3:1–4:31: *A defense of Paul's gospel on the basis of God's plan in scripture.* Paul's opponents in Galatia strongly emphasize the necessity of conforming to scripture, especially the Torah command about circumcision. So Paul meets his opponents on their own ground and turns to an argument based on not only the Torah, but also on the scripture as a whole. This second major section of the letter can be divided into six parts, which are basically six "proofs" for Paul's position:

1. The presence of spiritual and miraculous phenomena
2. Jesus Movement members as the true heirs of Abraham, who was justified by faith
3. Baptism as a more inclusive vision
4. The laws of family inheritance
5. The Galatians as Paul's friends and "kin," despite his physical infirmity
6. An allegorical interpretation of Sarah and Hagar

Following the letter, here are some notes on each of these points:

3:1–5: *The gift of the spirit.* Ironically Paul appeals to the very features of Hellenistic religious enthusiasm that had become a major problem for him at Corinth— the gifts of the spirit and miracles. "Who has bewitched you" in Gal. 3:1 should probably be translated "who has afflicted you with the Evil Eye?" The **Evil Eye** is a gaze cast upon innocent people by persons with evil intent (Elliott). It is an evil force, a malicious power associated with envy, miserliness, greed, and the refusal to share wealth with the needy. It is believed to cause pain and misfortune. In the Mediterranean world there were (and still are!) all kinds of amulets, signs, and rituals to help protect persons against the Evil Eye (see Gal. 4:14). Thus Paul seems to say that the Galatians have retreated into their misconceived practices because they have been cursed by the Evil Eye. He continues by saying that the Galatians began with "the spirit" but that they have ended with "the flesh," which for Paul has a double meaning: the lower self attracted to the power of sin and circumcision of the foreskin of the penis. In this different context, spiritual gifts are a validation of the gospel that he preached while he was in Galatia.

3:6–26: *Abraham as the true ancestral "father" of the new family: Justification by faith and freedom from the Law.* Paul offers an interpretation of scripture based on the Greek **Septuagint.** His purpose is to show that God intended to include the Gentiles in his promise of salvation. The interpretation is complicated, involving several double meanings, so let us explore Paul's interpretation carefully.

According to scripture, Abraham *believed* God's promise—trusted in God—and kept the covenant. God rewarded him by making this father of the Israelite people also "the ancestor of a multitude of nations" (Gen. 17:4). From the perspective of a traditional Torah-observant person, Abraham was simply keeping God's law and being an example for other peoples. Paul interprets it very differently.

First, when God promised Abraham that he would become "the ancestor of a multitude of nations," Paul is thinking of the meaning of the Greek term *ethnē,* "nations" or "peoples," which can also mean "Gentiles." Paul capitalizes on this broader meaning: God's promise to Abraham meant that he would become the father (ancestor) of a multitude of *Gentiles* (Gal. 3:8)!

Second, Genesis also says that Abraham "believed the Lord" (Gen. 15:6)—in other words, that he had *faith* in God. Paul has in mind Abraham's trust in God, that God would keep his promise. Paul may also have had in mind the famous "sacrifice of Isaac" story. In that story Abraham trusted God so much that he was willing to obey God's command to sacrifice his (and his wife Sarah's) only son (Gen. 22). Ironically, if he carried out this sacrifice, it would have destroyed the very means by which God's promise about "a multitude of nations" would be carried out! God was testing Abraham's faith, and Abraham remained faithful and obedient. He journeyed to Mount Moriah to sacrifice his son Isaac. Yet, he did not have to carry out the awful act. Just before he plunged the knife into Isaac on the sacrificial altar, God provided a substitute, a sacrificial ram in the thicket. So Abraham's faith was amazing.

Third, Abraham's continuing faith in God was, as Paul quotes the Septuagint, "reckoned to him [by God] as righteousness (*dikaiosynē*)" (Gen. 15:6; Gal. 3:6). Again, Paul uses a word with more than one nuance. The word *dikaiosynē,* usually translated "justification," in his sentence can also be translated "righteousness." God promised that Abraham would be the father of a multitude of *Gentiles.* Abraham through his faith obtained righteousness and thus was justified by his faith. This key theme will be developed at length in Romans.

Fourth, Paul argues that Abraham's justification took place long *before* Moses received the Law on Mount Sinai (Exod. 20)—specifically, as he says, 430 years before (Gal. 3:17; cf. Exod. 12:40–41). Again, Paul uses a Greek word with two meanings, *diathēkē.* It can mean either "covenant" or "will." Thus the *diathēkē* (= covenant) with Abraham preceded the *diathēkē* (= covenant) with Moses, and a *diathēkē* (= will), once ratified, cannot have anything added to it or be nullified (Gal. 3:15). The giving of the Law to Moses does not nullify Abraham's faith.

Fifth, Paul continues with a traditional Israelite method of argument that strings scriptural "proof passages" together. He says that anyone who relies on the Torah must do *all* that the Law commands (cf. Gal. 5:3), a view that can indeed be found in Israelite interpretations of the Torah (*Midrash Sifre on Numbers* 112). If a Torah-observant person does not do *all* that the Torah commands, that person, as the Torah itself says, is under a curse (Deut. 27:26; 28:58). Paul next quotes one of his favorite texts, Hab. 2:4: "the *one who is righteous* will live by *faith*" (Gal. 3:11; cf. Rom. 1:17). This passage is also quoted in the Dead Sea Scrolls where, ironically, "the one who is righteous" refers to anyone who faithfully *observes the Torah,* as well as to those whom God will deliver from judgment because of their suffering and *faith in the Teacher of Righteousness* (1 QpHab 7:17–8:3). For Paul, in stark contrast, the "one who is righteous" has *faith in Christ,* which means *freedom from* the Torah, which cannot give life. Indeed, this text, as interpreted, is probably his favorite text for justification by faith because he quotes it again in Rom. 1:17.

The next quotation, "cursed is everyone who hangs on a tree" (Deut. 21:23), refers in its original scriptural context to the curse on an executed criminal whose corpse after execution is publicly displayed on a tree for all to see (a deterrent to crime). Obviously, such a text can have been easily transferred to anyone publicly executed for capital crimes on a cross (= tree). This interpretation is also found in the Dead Sea Scrolls (4Q 169 PsNah 1.17–18; 11 Q Temple 64:6–13). Because the crucified Jesus is at the very heart of Paul's gospel—recall his "theology of the cross" in 1 Cor. 1:18–25—he finds it necessary to give the embarrassing curse text a different meaning: "Christ redeemed us from the *curse of the law*" (3:13). The term "redeemed," from which the noun *redemption* comes, means "to buy out of slavery." Paul presumably knows that slaves, who cannot legally negotiate contracts, can nonetheless buy their own freedom by a legal fiction. As inscriptions tell us, they can offer the price of their "redemption" to a god at a temple and then have the god purchase them as a slave, which is, in effect, giving them freedom. Thus for Paul "cursed is everyone who hangs on a tree" really means that Christ takes on himself the curse of one hung on a tree by his crucifixion. Like the temple god, Christ "redeems" those who believe in him out of slavery (to the Torah commands), thus setting them free.

In short, God's promise is that he will make Abraham, whose faith justified him, the father of Gentiles. Like Abraham, the Gentiles who believe are justified by having faith, not by doing the commandments, and particularly not by having to be circumcised to be one of God's covenant people (as commanded by the Torah). Thus Christ has transformed the curse of Jesus' death into a means to "redeem" believers from the curse of the Law.

Paul is not yet finished with his argument from scripture. In several passages in Genesis, the promise about the "nations"/"Gentiles" calls Abraham's descendants his "offspring" (e.g., 12:2–3; 15:5; 22:17–18). In one passage it says, "And I will give to you, and to your offspring after you, the land [of Canaan]" (Gen. 17:8). Paul is not interested in the promise of the land of Palestine to Abraham and his descendants. Rather, he is interested in the term "offspring" in relation to the Gentiles becoming a multitude of nations. In the Septuagint, the Greek word for *offspring* is *sperma*, or "seed." As a collective noun it can have a plural meaning, like "seeds" (Greek *spermata*), but *grammatically* it is singular. (The same is true for English.) Now Paul argues that the "seed" or "offspring" of Abraham refers not to *many* descendants but rather, because it is grammatically singular, to *one,* that is, to Christ! Paul's argument here is reminiscent of the view in the **Dead Sea Scrolls** that the "seed of David" in 2 Sam. 7 refers not to his literal descendants (especially Solomon), but rather to the one messianic "Son of David."

The point at issue between Paul and his opponents is the relevance of the Mosaic Torah and especially the commandment about circumcision for Gentiles. Paul argues that the Torah of Moses "was added [to the covenant of Abraham] *because of transgressions*" (3:19). It is debated whether he means that it helps guard against transgressions (because then one knows what they are) or increases them (because although one knows, one cannot do all of them), or both. Whatever he means, he argues that no one can do everything that the law commands (see 3:10). Is the law then useless? No. Between the time of Moses and Christ, the Torah had a function. It was a *paidagōgos* or "disciplinarian" (verse 24). This term refers a slave-guardian who watches over, protects, and instructs schoolboys (from the upper social strata) until they reach puberty and become independent. The Torah is not in itself useless or evil; yet, those who are mature in faith, like mature young men on their own, no longer need this "disciplinarian": They are free from the Law.

3:27–29:   *Baptism into the new family.*   In this passage Paul cites what scholars think are traditional liturgical words used at baptismal initiation into the Jesus Movement. It is therefore a baptismal formula. There is much symbolism behind verse 27: Taking off old clothes means getting rid of the old self, and putting on new clothes means becoming the new self, ideas known from other ancient sources. A similar thought is also attributed to Jesus by the author of the **Gospel of Thomas,** saying 37, which reads:

> His disciples said, "When will you become revealed to us and when shall we see you?"
>
> Jesus said, "When you *disrobe* without being ashamed and take up your garments and place them under your feet like little children and tread on them, then [will you see] the son of the living one, and you will not be afraid."

The central baptismal affirmation in Galatians is in verse 28: "There is no longer Israelite or Greek, there is no longer slave or free, there is no longer male or female; for you are all one in Christ Jesus" (cf. 1 Cor. 12:13; Col. 3:11). The theme in relation to slavery is not totally unique to Paul and other members of the Jesus Movement. Some ancient philosophers held that slavery is contrary to the "natural" state (e.g., Aristotle *Politics* 1, 2.3), and a house inscription from Asia Minor encouraged that free persons and slaves, as well as men and women, should be treated similarly. Nonetheless, Paul's inclusive ideal runs counter to the norm, to *most* ideas and practices in ancient Mediterranean society related to social stratification, ethnicity, and gender. Indeed, Paul himself does not always live up to them. It is probably his Pharisaism that leads him to associate "Greeks" more than Israelites with sexual immorality (1 Thess. 4:5). Despite his hints at manumission, he nonetheless accepts slavery as a social institution (Philemon). He subordinates women in the order of creation as found in the Torah (1 Cor. 11:2–16). Paradoxically there is an element of exclusion in a message centered in weakness and crucifixion: It might be taken as a more virtuous way of life. However, Paul usually lives up to his inclusive family, or fictive kin, ideal and its potential for liberation. For Paul, those baptized into the Jesus Movement as a new family—including lower-status women, slaves, and Gentile outsiders—are collectively the seed/children (plural meaning!) of Abraham through Christ, who is the seed/son/child (singular meaning!) of Abraham (verse 29). They are also the children of God, as is Christ. As adopted children, they are legally heirs, heirs of God through his promise to Abraham. The theme "no longer Israelite or Greek, no longer slave or free, no longer male or female, but one in Christ Jesus" has become central to what modern theologians call "liberation theology," a theology that stresses freeing persons from ethnic, racial, and gender oppression.

4:1–11: *Kinship with God ("children of God").* In this section Paul uses laws about inheritance to develop the new family relation that believers have with God and each other. Just as Christ is the Son of God, so followers of Christ are adopted children of God. However, heirs who are minors (still under the disciplinarian) are those who (at Galatia) have also fallen back into slavery to the "elemental spirits." This is probably a reference to stars and planets personified and understood as powerful magical forces controlling one's life (verse 3; cf. verse 10). In other words, a return to the Law, says Paul, is a return to the "weak and beggarly elemental spirits" and to the observance of a calendar of festivals (verse 10). This passage is our clearest indication that from Paul's perspective (information he had received?), the opponents in Galatia were **syncretistic,** that is, they advocated observance of the Torah and festivals together with a typically Hellenistic admixture of astrology (see Chapter Five).

Two further observations should be made. First, in verse 4 Paul mentions Jesus' "birth by a woman," the only place in his surviving letters where he refers to Jesus' mother (he does not mention her by name). His purpose is to assure his readers that the divine Son of God was a human being. Second, in his use of the language of God as "father"—the cry "Abba! Father!" (verse 6)—Paul seems to demonstrate his awareness of the oral tradition that Jesus taught his disciples to use this name for God in prayer. Does he know the Lord's Prayer or "Our Father" as such?

4:12–20: *Restoring friendship and becoming kin with Paul.*   In this section Paul appeals to the Galatians to restore their friendship. His reference to his "physical infirmity" (verse 13) is mysterious. Many interpretations have been suggested, from malaria to physical weaknesses suggested by "the marks of Jesus branded on my body" (cf. Gal. 6:17). That the Galatians did not "despise me" is literally, in Greek, they did not "spit at me," and spitting was one form of protection against persons believed to have the **Evil Eye** (see earlier). Was Paul suspected to have the Evil Eye because of some physical infirmity (cf. Gal. 3:1), a common idea? He speaks of the Galatians now as *his* children for whom he is in "childbirth," a reference to his suffering (labor pains) before the new creation (birth).

4:21–31: *The **allegory** of Sarah and Hagar: Kinship, law, and freedom.*   Paul's allegory about Sarah and Hagar from scripture is not totally accurate or fully worked out in detail, but its meaning is nonetheless fairly clear. Abraham had two sons. The first was Ishmael by Sarah's slave woman Hagar while Sarah was still barren. The second was Isaac by Sarah in her old age and barrenness—a miraculous birth that fulfilled God's promise to Abraham about his offspring. (This was also the same Isaac whom Abraham, who had faith in God, was later willing to sacrifice, thus risking the fulfillment of God's promise that his offspring would become "a multitude of nations/Gentiles.") Paul argues allegorically that Hagar represents slavery to the covenant of Law symbolized by "the present Jerusalem"; in contrast, Sarah represents the freedom from the Law symbolized by the covenant of promise and "the Jerusalem above." In short, as he as previously argued with respect to Abraham himself, the covenant of promise is prior to—and is superior to—the covenant of Law. Members of the Jesus Movement are allegorically descended from Sarah, the free woman, and are thus children of God's promise. Such children are children of faith and free from the Law, thus *free from the requirement of circumcision*. However, Israelites who do not join the Jesus Movement are children of Hagar, in bondage to the Law.

5:1–6:10: *Moral exhortation.*   In accord with Paul's use of the letter genre—moral exhortation customarily follows theology—Paul now exhorts his readers to preserve and use correctly the freedom they have in Christ. He reiterates that those who are circumcised have to follow the whole law (5:3). Note his metaphor from athletics (verse 7), to which is added a metaphor about leavened bread (verse 9). The castration remark in verse 12, a word-play on circumcision, is Paul's most vicious "cutting" remark against any of his opponents (cf. Phil. 3:2).

In 5:19–24, he again uses a typical form found among Stoic and Cynic philosophers, namely, **vice and virtue catalogues.** Paul coordinates them with his exhortation to live by the Spirit (virtuous living), not the flesh (vice living) (see 1 Cor. 6:9; Rom. 1:28–32 following; also Chapter Five).

The persistent theme in this section is "For in Christ Jesus neither circumcision nor un-circumcision counts for anything; the only thing that counts is faith working through love" (verse 6; see 6:15). That is because ". . . the whole law is summed up in a single command-ment, 'You shall love your neighbor as yourself'" (Lev. 19:18). Lev. 19:15–18 contains Paul's key term "righteousness" and "loving one's neighbor" as a basis for harmony in a commu-nity, as well as "confronting one's 'brother'" as a means of resolving conflict. It was widely used in ancient Israelite texts for group behavior norms and "loving one's neighbor." It is at-tributed to Jesus as the "second" great commandment (cf. Mark 12:28–34), and "con-fronting one's neighbor" is implied by Matthew for conflict resolution (Matt. 18:15–20). Paul also uses it in Romans (Rom. 13:8–10).

6:11–16:   *Summary of his gospel.*   Paul takes the pen from his amanuensis (secretary) and writes with large letters his own summary of his gospel. Even here he cannot avoid one more double-meaning "cutting remark" against his opponents—they want to make a "showing in the flesh" (verse 12). As in the Corinthian correspondence, the theme of boast-ing in the cross of Christ surfaces again (cf. especially 2 Cor. 11:16–33).

6:17–18:   *Conclusion.*   Paul includes a remark about the rigors of his apostleship ("the marks [Greek *stígmata*] of Jesus branded on his body"; cf. 4:13 earlier). (This comment has helped to generate the traditional Roman Catholic belief that certain persons experience the *stigmata,* the awful wounds of Jesus' crucifixion.) Paul ends with his typical benediction.

ROMANS

Paul's letter to the church at Rome, the longest and latest of his surviving letters, was placed first in the Pauline letter collection because of its length. Its primacy is justly deserved. It is unquestionably the most important letter for his religious thought, and its sophistication has made it an important source for theology in the Jesus Movement and historical Christianity. Indeed, Romans has been highly influential in major religious and cultural revolutions in Western civilization. In the fourth century, Saint Augustine, the most important Christian theologian for the next millennium, was converted to Christianity after reading Romans, and, as he says in his *Confessions,* it became the source for his central theological views about God's grace and human freedom. In the thirteenth century, Romans was central to Saint Thomas Aquinas' highly influential views about revealed and natural knowledge of God in his influential *Summa Theologica.* At the outset of the sixteenth-century Reformation, Paul's Letter to the Romans inspired Martin Luther's view of justifi-cation by faith and John Calvin's ideas about predestination. In the seventeenth cen-tury, John Wesley, founder of the Methodist denomination, developed his central view of sanctification ("becoming holy") from Romans. In more recent times, the first major book of Karl Barth, who was probably the most influential Protestant theologian of the twentieth century, was his commentary on Romans. The Letter to the Romans is also critical for a whole host of ethical questions both inside and outside the churches. Examples are Jewish-Christian relations, the status of women, and homosexuality. Thus to read Romans is not only to read an "occasional letter"; it also is to encounter a thoughtful book that wrestles with what became some of the most profound religious and ethical ideas of Western Christendom and, indeed, Western civilization.

Ironically, Paul did not found the church at Rome. Its precise origins are a mystery. The tradition that Peter was martyred in Rome (*1 Clement* 5:2–3; cf. John 21:18–19) may be historically accurate, but there is no evidence that he was the first missionary there. All roads led to Rome, and there were all kinds of travelers on them—religious teachers, philosophers, slaves, soldiers, merchants, and immigrants—and they represented all kinds of beliefs. It is quite possible that one of them was a member of the Jesus Movement.

Both ancient literature and inscriptions show that early first-century Rome contained a large number of Israelite synagogues, mainly Greek speaking, and that from time to time anti-Israelite feelings ran high. The Roman historian Suetonius wrote in his *Life of Claudius* (25.4) that Claudius expelled the Israelites from Rome (ca. 49 C.E.) because of a disturbance that was instigated by a certain "Chrestus." Was Chrestus really his name? Or was this a dispute between Israelites (or Israelites in the Jesus Movement) and Gentiles (or Gentiles in the Jesus Movement) about "Christus" or Christ? Perhaps, then, the church in Rome first took root among Israelites of the Diaspora. At any rate, Acts 18:2 claims that Aquila and his wife Prisca (Priscilla), both of whom had joined the Jesus Movement, were among the expelled *Israelites* (see Chapters Three and Four, the **Edict of Claudius**).

By the time Paul wrote his letter to the Romans, there already seems to have been a sizable community of Christ believers in Rome. The general orientation of the letter (**internal evidence**) suggests to most scholars that the majority of them, although certainly not all, were Gentiles (e.g., 1:5–6, 13–15; 11:13; 15:15–33). The Edict of Claudius (ca. 49 C.E.), which had expelled the Israelites, was rescinded by the emperor Nero (54–68 C.E.). Thus some of those expelled returned to Rome about 54 C.E.. The Letter to the Romans was probably written about two or three years later. If chapter 16 of Romans was not a separate letter fragment, Aquila and Prisca (Priscilla in Acts 18) were among those who came back (16:3; see Chapter Four; also following on Rom. 16). Paul probably wrote the letter from Corinth before departing to Jerusalem with the collection for the poor (Rom. 15:25–26; cf. Acts 20:2–3). In short, by the mid- to late 50s, Paul wrote his most powerful and influential letter from Corinth to an already established church at Rome.

Why did Paul write his Letter to the Romans? It is not easy to give a single answer to this question. Some scholars have suggested that the return of Israelites after 54 C.E. developed (renewed?) tensions between Israelites and Gentiles in the Jesus Movement and that this conflict is represented by tensions between "the weak" and "the strong" in the moral exhortation section of the letter (Rom. 14:1–15:13). In this theory, "the strong" refers to the Gentile majority, and "the weak" refers to the Israelite minority in the Roman Jesus movement. The primary issue in their dispute was, once again, meal practices (14:20–21). This theory suggests that the dispute gave occasion to the letter. A major strength of this theory is that Paul is concerned with Israelites and Gentiles throughout the letter, just as he had been in the letter to the Galatians.

Other interpreters think that Paul wanted to win the approval of the Romans so that Rome could become his next home base for a mission farther west to Spain. This theory derives the purpose of Paul's letter from several scattered statements in Paul's letters, including Romans. Recall that Paul's general principle was *not* to preach the gospel in anyone else's mission territory, a principle he reasserted in

Romans itself (Rom. 15:20; cf. 1 Cor. 3:10; 2 Cor. 10:13–17). In the opening thanksgiving section, Paul writes that he wants to impart to the Roman believers some spiritual gift to strengthen them, but he then quickly adds *with caution,* "that we may be *mutually* encouraged by each other's faith, both yours and mine" (1:12). Further, he wrote, ". . . I am eager to *preach the gospel to you* also who are in Rome" (1:15). Then, near the end of the letter, he says that he wishes to see the Romans "in passing" as he went on to Spain and he wants to receive their encouragement (15:24). If he won their approval, then Rome would be a central place for him, a base from which he could move on and perhaps return, as Antioch and Ephesus had been. Some scholars see this desire for acceptance at Rome as a major reason for his cautious diplomacy. Paul was aware that the controversies in which he had been embroiled in other places might be known at Rome as well and might have led to a false impression of him and his gospel (cf. 3:8).

Still another theory is that Paul did not intend the letter to be read and heard only by those at Rome. One view is that it is a draft, or part of a draft, of what Paul actually wanted to say in his defense when he returned to Jerusalem with the collection of money for the poor (15:25–26). Another common theory is that the letter is a circular letter to *several* churches.

A view that combines some of these theories suggests that Romans is Paul's "last will and testament." Note first that "testament" was another literary genre in antiquity. Testaments were literary creations but were masked as the main ideas and final wishes of some honored worthy on his deathbed, often of a father to his son (for example, *The Testaments of the Twelve Patriarchs*). Paul's letter was not a testament as such, but it did grow out of his anxiety in the face of the dangers that were yet to face him at Jerusalem *and* his views as he had developed them in his previous conflicts at Corinth, Philippi, and Galatia (Bornkamm). His polemical passages were couched in *rhetorical style,* especially the Cynic-Stoic diatribe. Thus his polemical comments might not have been directed at real and specific opponents at Rome. This view tends to be reinforced by observing that there are some strong parallels in Romans with his views already developed in Galatians, Philippians, and Corinthians. Note, for example, the following:

- Justification by faith alone and not by works of the Law (Gal. 3–5; Phil. 3; Rom. 1–4; 9:30–10:4)
- Abraham the father as the type of justification by faith (Gal. 3; Rom. 4)
- Adam as the mythical embodiment of the old humanity and Christ as the head of the new humanity (1 Cor. 15:22–28; Rom. 5:12–21)
- Natural man subject to Law, sin, and death (1 Cor. 15:56–57; Rom. 7:7–25)
- The sending of the Son of God in the flesh for redemption and the testimony of the Spirit that believers are the true children of God (Gal. 4:4–7; Rom. 8)
- The unity of a church described as one body with many members (1 Cor. 12; Rom. 12:4–8)
- The conflict of "weak" and "strong" over food matters (1 Cor. 8, 10; Rom. 14:1–15:13)

The both/and solution of the last will and testament therefore seems like a good compromise.

Before proceeding to an exegetical outline, it is important to address one other well-known and debated issue: the critical question of whether Rom. 16 was added to the letter later. There are several reasons for this theory. First, the chapter begins with what seems to be something new, namely, an independent letter of recommendation for Phoebe, "a deacon of the church at Cenchreae" (16:1–3; Cenchreae, recall, is the southeastern harbor area on the Isthmus of Corinth). Second, Paul uncharacteristically greets twenty-six persons by name, as well as others in families and house-churches (16:4–16); if he has never been to Rome, how does he know personally this many people there? Third, there are personal greetings to Prisca and Aquila, who had been expelled from Rome at the time of the **Edict of Claudius** (ca. 49 C.E.) and had migrated to Corinth, where Paul first met them (Acts 18:1–3), and then to Ephesus, where Paul knew them again (1 Cor. 16:19). Fourth, Epaenetus is called "the first fruits" of *Asia* (16:5), the province where the city of Ephesus is located. Fifth, in Rom. 16:17–19, the opponents (outsiders) do not seem to be the same as those in the earlier part of the chapter (insiders). Sixth, there is a final benediction (16:20) that is not final; it is followed by greetings from the amanuensis and seven friends and coworkers (16:21–23). Seventh, the "final doxology" (16:25–27) does not sound like Paul. Eighth, in some manuscripts this doxology is found at the end of chapter 14 and in other manuscripts at the end of chapter 15! Ninth, some manuscripts of chapter 16 have a concluding benediction *before* the doxology, suggesting that the letter is finished. Because the persons in this chapter are more easily connected with Ephesus than Rome, and Paul lived in Ephesus for about three years, many scholars have plausibly argued that chapter 16 (except the doxology) was written to Ephesus. The original letter probably would have ended at Rom. 15.

These are very weighty arguments, but apart from the diversity of material they represent, they center primarily on questions of Paul's Ephesus connections. The main response to the theory that chapter 16 was written to Ephesus is that when Nero rescinded the Edict of Claudius in 54 C.E., those Israelites and Israelite members of the Jesus Movement who had been expelled from Rome had returned to Rome. If they had, goes the argument, Rom. 16 could have been part of the letter because Paul had met at least some of them elsewhere, such as at Ephesus. This view suggests that Rom. 16 was later omitted in the manuscripts to make the letter less "occasional," that is, to appeal to a wider audience. In other words, omitting Rom. 16 made it relevant for broader use. Originally Paul wanted to show his acquaintance with Roman members of the Jesus Movement rhetorically, even though he had never been there. Possibly he had oral reports about outsider opponents (16:17–20). Or his comments about them could have been Paul's rhetorical generalizations; the expression "such people . . . serve . . . their own appetites [Greek "their own belly"]" (Rom. 16:18) is similar to "their god is their belly," Paul's description of the opponents at Philippi (Phil. 3:19).

The passage illustrates the fact that more recent literary criticism can be in conflict with older literary/historical criticism. In this edition, all of chapter 16 is included as part of Romans except for the "floating" doxology (16:25–27) and the statement about grace in verse 24, which has weak manuscript evidence. The letter is best ended at 16:23.

Outline

Exegetical Survey of Paul's Letter to the Romans

1:1–7:   *Salutation.*   Paul expands his usual salutation into a summary of the gospel. The summary includes a "two-stage" confession about Jesus the Christ (1:3–4), which he probably inherited from others because it is not his usual view. In the first stage, Jesus was a human being descended from the seed of David ("Son of David"). In the second stage, he was declared (by God implied) to be the Son of God by being raised from the dead, that is, at the time of his royal enthronement in heaven (cf. Chapter Three). This "two-stage Christology" echoes the enthronement of the ancient anointed ("messianic") kings of Israel, who were David's descendants, except that the enthronement is in the sky. That the Messiah could be called "Son of God" is also known from the **Dead Sea Scrolls** (4QpsDan Aa = 4Q 246), which contain language much like the Lukan Son of God (Luke 1:32; Acts 2:36). Paul's letter at this point is addressed "to all God's beloved in Rome" (1:7), on which see the preceding discussion of the people who Paul seems to have known at Rome (chapter 16). "Grace" (Greek *charis*) and "peace" (Hebrew/Aramaic ***shalōm***), Paul's characteristic greeting terms, are present.

1:8–15:   *Thanksgiving.*   This thanksgiving, as is usual, sets the tone and indicates at least in part the purpose of the whole letter. Paul is clearly cautious about writing to an influential group of house-churches that he did not himself found and about desiring to preach on someone else's turf, which is not his usual practice. The caution is expressed, for example, in his hope for a *mutual* exchange of faith and the opportunity to preach the gospel. As in Galatians, the gospel focuses on the Son (verse 9).

1:16–17:   *Summary statement of Paul's understanding of the gospel:* **The righteousness of God and justification by faith.**   To grasp Paul's central concept, one should recall his emphasis on justification in Gal. 2:15–21. Moreover, it is helpful to see that it is related to the ancient Roman judicial system. Imagine a judge (such as an emperor or governor) who sits on a *bēma* or "tribunal" (a raised platform with "judgment seat," usually in the *agora* [marketplace] in the center of town). The judge hears cases and has absolute power over life and death. Imagine that the defendants are *all* the members of the human race. They naturally know the identity of this Great Judge, and they know that they have done wrong. Nonetheless, this judge says that those who believe are to be set free. How can this be?

Drawing on language from the legal system, Paul's key concepts, as in Galatians, are the "**righteousness of God**" and "**justification by faith.**" Again, as in Galatians, Paul cites Hab. 2:4: "the *one who is righteous* will live by *faith*" (cf. Gal. 3:11). In line with much Israelite thinking, Paul says that *all* human beings have a "tendency to do evil." The **Dead Sea Scrolls,** for example, say that *all* have sinned and are in need of God's grace (1QS 11:2–22; 1QH 9.14–15). This is also Paul's view. Again, all people are guilty and deserve to be punished. However, God, the Great Judge, is also merciful and righteous. His acts are just and righteous; he justifies or makes people righteous; he "justifies" or "makes (persons) righteous," not because they obey his commandments and are therefore righteous, not because they are obedient and do "works of the Law," but because they have faith. God pardons those who have faith, who believe in Christ, "*the Israelite first* and also the Greek" (verse 16). This is God's gift, his merciful "grace"; it is the gift of "salvation." The act of freeing guilty persons is part of God's righteousness (Greek noun *dikaiosynē*).

In short, using language of the law court, or forensic language, Paul opens his letter essay by summarizing his interlocked ideas of the **righteousness of God** and **justification by faith** (cf. Phil. 3:9; Gal. 3:10–11).

1:18–3:20:   First major section: All have fallen short and are in need of God's mercy, but only those who have faith are justified.

1:18–32:   *The judgment of God is revealed against the sin of humanity.*   Some Israelites in Paul's time would have said that idolatry is the sin that brings about sexual immorality (e.g., *Wisdom of Solomon* 14:21–27). Because Gentile pagans believed in other gods (idols), said such thinkers, they were more easily led to "unnatural" sexual behavior than Israelites (Philo *On the Special Laws* 3.37–39). You will recall that Mediterranean society was a male-dominated society, and, although there were exceptions, it was mostly a few elite males who were educated. The traditional ideal of the beautiful male nude body was also current. Moreover, young boys whose bodies still looked like those of young girls were often considered to be erotic. In earlier periods, some Mediterranean philosophers had considered whether "voluntary" homosexual relations between men and young boys, or pederasty (from Greek "love of boys"), was a "higher" form of love than heterosexual relations. This view was related to cultural ideas about women, that is, women were usually less educated and considered to be inferior intellectual partners (Pseudo-Lucian *Erōtes* 38–43). By Paul's day, however, moral philosophers had come to consider same-sex acts to be "unnatural," thus immoral (e.g., Pseudo-Lucian *Affairs of the Heart* 19–20; cf. Plato *Laws* 836). They judged pederasty to be effeminate, domineering, impermanent, and conducive of jealousy. They singled out as especially disreputable behavior abuse of boy slaves, as well as boy prostitution, that is, call boys. It is important to see that in this (male) philosophical debate such acts were considered to be *willful* behavior resulting from uncontrolled pleasure or lust by heterosexual persons. It was not sexual relations on the part of adult homosexual persons who, in today's language, have different "sexual orientations." In other words, such freely chosen acts were considered to be "contrary to nature."

In line with Israelite thinking, Paul argued that Gentiles have refused to honor God as God, that is, they have committed idolatry. That, in turn, has led to sexual immorality. In line with the moral philosophers of Paul's day, Paul also said that same-sex sex relations are contrary to nature (1:24–27). Some modern scholars think that he had pederasty in mind (cf. 1 Cor. 5:9). In any case, Paul could associate such acts with vices in a vice list (Rom. 1:28–32), as he did in 1 Cor. 6:9 (see Chapter Five).

Perhaps Paul made a shift in his own thought as well. Earlier Paul had written to the Thessalonians that sexual immorality is characteristic of the Gentiles who do *not know* the one true God (1 Thess. 4:1–8). From this perspective, one would logically expect that *ignorance* of God would lead to idolatry and sexual immorality. So Paul seems to think. Here he argues that Gentiles *do* know God but that they still fall short. That is the reason why they, like the Israelites, are on the same footing, that is, without excuse. They have to be held accountable, too. But *how* do Gentiles know God if they have no access to his will in the Torah? Plato, Aristotle, Stoic philosophers, as well as Philo of Alexandria and other Israelites influenced by Hellenistic ideas such as the author of the *Wisdom of Solomon* (13:1–9) held that knowledge of God comes through seeing him in the natural world. Paul, too, argues that Gentiles possess a kind of natural knowledge of God. God can be known in two ways. First, God has revealed his power and deity to all in the works of nature, his creation (1:19–20). Second, Gentiles sometimes follow God's will without knowing the Torah; they thereby show that they have a "law written on their hearts," thus a "conscience" (2:15), which may have been commonly held by his elite contemporaries to be natural (Aristotle *Rhetoric* 1.15.3–8). Again, Gentiles possess a natural knowledge of God. They are therefore without excuse and will be subject to God's judgment on the "day of wrath."

2:1–11: *The Israelites are just as much under the judgment of God as are the Gentiles.* In addressing the Israelite members of the Jesus Movement at Rome, Paul initially changes to the diatribe style (verses 1–5), which involves an imaginary discussion or debate partner. The writer raises questions and then gives answers. In this imaginary "discussion," believing Israelites, too, will receive eternal life on the "day of wrath"; if they "do good," they will have glory and peace. Paul states, "The Israelite *first* and *also* the Greek" (2:9, 10), as in the initial summary (1:16). However, he addresses the Gentile condition first. In chapters 9–11 he thinks that Gentile response to the gospel will trigger Israelite response.

2:12–29: *God judges the Israelites by the standards of the Law of Moses, and the Gentiles by the "law" of their conscience.* The Israelite who has the Torah—he teaches others (the Gentiles) by it—must be wary of not practicing what he teaches. This would be hypocrisy. Nor should the Israelite rely on outward observances; although Torah regulations have value if one follows them, true circumcision is finally a "circumcision of the heart." This view is already found in the Hebrew Bible (Deut. 10:16; Jer. 4:4) and in the Israelite philosopher Philo of Alexandria, who also distinguishes between external and internal circumcision (*Questions and Answers on Exodus* 2.2). For Paul, as noted earlier, the Gentiles often show that they have a "law written on their hearts" and a "conscience."

3:1–8: *The Israelites nonetheless have an advantage.* Again taking up the diatribe style, Paul indicates that God has given the Israelites an advantage by directly revealing his will and purpose to them in their scriptures.

3:9–20: *But all people, Israelites and Gentiles alike, have fallen under the power of sin.* Citing a chain of scriptural passages, Paul shows that the Israelites, of whom he is one, are not any better off than the Gentiles.

3:21–4:25:   Second major section: The nature of God's saving act in Christ and of human appropriation of that act.

3:21–26:   *Restatement of the righteousness of God and justification by faith.*   Having established that the whole world, *both Israelite and Gentile,* is in need of God's grace because it is estranged from God by its sin, Paul now restates his theme in terms of the **righteousness of God** and **justification by faith.** This time he stresses the redemptive power of the cross of Christ. Again, *all* have sinned (Rom. 3:9–20, 23). All are without excuse. But how can it be that the one, all-powerful God of the universe has allowed his Son, the Messiah, to be subject to mere human authorities and thus to suffer a criminal's death on a cross?

Paul must have faced this question many times in his years of attempting to convince others that the crucified Jesus was the Messiah. To the Corinthians he had written, "We preach Christ crucified, a stumbling block (Greek *skandalon*) to Israelites and folly to Gentiles" (1 Cor. 1:23). A crucified redeemer figure was certainly "folly" to the Gentiles. The characteristic redeemers in that society were either gods who came to earth or the heroes/heroines made into ("apotheosized" as) gods and goddesses after their death. In Israelite thought as well there were intermediary angels and figures such as Moses who were venerated. Members of the Jesus Movement had come to venerate— indeed, worship—Jesus in way that advanced beyond what most Israelites were willing to believe. They conceived Jesus as either a descending god or apotheosized hero—or both. Correspondingly, they had to develop a "Passion apologetic," that is, they had to prove to others that the Passion and death of Jesus on a cross, despite the terrible dishonor, despite the embarrassment, were in accord with the will and purpose of God as revealed in the scriptures. However, as time went by, the members of the Jesus Movement came more and more to develop an understanding of the meaning of the cross rather than an apologetic for its necessity. They moved from a defense of Jesus' form of death, or a "Passion apologetic," to an affirmation of the cross as a symbol of God's act of salvation on behalf of humanity by sending his Son to earth. In theological language, this was a "soteriology of the cross" (Greek *sōtēria,* "salvation," from *sōzō,* "I save," "I deliver" and *sōtēr,* "savior"; soteriology, "thinking about how one is saved"). Recall how Paul in Galatians had offered just such an "apologetic" for the scriptural curse about one who hangs on a tree.

Paul played a major role in the development of what theologians call this "soteriology of the cross." He sought to understand how the cross changes forever the relationship between God and human beings. Many, perhaps most, Israelites, as well as members of the Jesus Movement, had come to expect the relationship to be changed by a final act of God yet to occur. Within the movement the form of this expectation was the return of Jesus from heaven as apocalyptic Judge and Redeemer. Then the relationship between God and human beings would be forever changed. In Paul's thinking, this change had *already* begun to be implemented in the cross of Christ. The whole world, Israelite and non-Israelite, was estranged from God by its sin, but the estrangement was not to be eradicated by an act of God *only* in the future. It had *already* been eradicated by an act of God in the past: the cross of Christ.

Paul never seems to tire of this theme. The world is cut off from God because of sin, and something must be done about it. This something is the cross of Christ, and Paul constantly tries to find ways of explaining how the cross of Christ eradicates the estrangement of human beings from God created by their sins. In Rom. 3:25, he focuses on the word *hilastērion* (hill-lah-stáy-ri-on). This language comes from animal sacrifice. In the Septuagint, the unusual term *hilastērion* refers to the actual *place* where the priests sacrifice in the Holy of Holies of the Jerusalem temple: It is the lid of the Ark of the Covenant on which the blood of sacrificial animals is sprinkled on the Day of Atonement. This place is sometimes translated in English as the "mercy seat" (Exod. 25:16ff.; Lev. 16:2, 11–17; see Chapter One). Paul, a Greek-speaking Israelite, seems to say that there is a new place where that takes place, the cross of Christ. But *hilastērion* can *also* refer to the actual *gift* offered to satisfy the angry deity, and Paul also seems to have the sacrificial death of Jesus in mind. The fact is that the English language is insufficient, as the many translations of *hilastērion* show ("propitiation," "expiation," "sacrifice of atonement," and the like). Nonetheless, Paul's fundamental convictions are clear: (1) People are estranged from God and doomed for all eternity because of sin; and (2) God himself has changed this situation through the sacrificial cross of Christ. The need of human beings to atone to God for their sin is paradoxically met by *God's* initiative through the merciful sacrifice of Jesus on the cross. This idea opens up a whole array of difficult concepts about what theologians call "atonement," that is, how human beings make up for their sins, in this case, how they "satisfy" and "appease" an angry God.

For Paul, the act of God that will eradicate human estrangement because of sin is "effective," again, "through faith." Paul reaches this view through reflection and as a result of his controversy with circumcising opponents in Galatia and elsewhere. Whatever God has done in the cross of Christ, it is *effective* for any person who responds by believing. "Faith" (Greek *pistis*) is difficult to describe, and, indeed, the "faith of Christ" is ambiguous in Greek and therefore much debated. At the very least "faith" implies belief, trust, and obedience. For Paul, just as Jesus Christ gave himself totally to God and humanity by accepting the necessity for the cross (he had faith), so must human beings give themselves totally to God-as-revealed-in-Jesus Christ in order to appropriate for themselves the power of that cross. They must have faith or believe in Christ.

In the preceding discussion of justification, a word group in Greek was emphasized. It is based on the root *dikaio-* (di-kai-o-) and is related to the English terms *just* and *right.* This group consists of the verb "to *justify*" or "to make *right*" (*dikaioō* [di-kai-ó-ō]), the noun "*justification*" or "*right*eousness" (*dikaiosynē* [di-kai-o-sú-nay]), and the adjective "*just*" or "*right*eous" (*dikaios* [dí-kai-os]). Again, these terms are juridical, that is, derived from Roman law, and their reference is to a just act of judgment by God. A final point for Paul is the social and ethical implication: God has given humans a standard by which to live—to Israelites a Torah, to Gentiles a conscience and a law written on their hearts—and ultimately they must stand before God and be judged by that standard. No one is innocent of standards or norms. It is no accident that Paul's letters usually end with ethical exhortation—do this, do that! Nonetheless, human beings cannot *earn* salvation. If they have faith, God in his own righteousness will either *declare* them to be "righteous" or possibly *make* them "righteous" (the notion of "imputed righteousness" has a long, much-debated theological history). Again, and paradoxically, God takes the initiative in doing what is necessary to "satisfy" himself. Paul's whole argument is that no one can achieve the necessary righteousness before the Judge on his or her own merit; so God in his bountiful grace has established a new possibility. He will "justify" those— again, declare or make them "righteous"—if they have faith in Christ. This act is a possibility for Israelite and non-Israelite alike. The Israelite has failed to live up to the Torah commandments, and the Gentile has not met the requirements of conscience or the law in his or her heart. However, God in *his* righteousness *nonetheless* declares that they are "righteous." They appropriate this righteousness by their act of faith. Although they are guilty, the merciful Judge says that persons who believe are innocent.

3:27–31: *It is faith and not works of the Law that matters.* Paul's constant controversy with opponents who wanted to circumcise his converts led him to state his position in extremes: *either* gladly accept by the act of faith what God has done in Christ *or* attempt to justify yourself before God by the quality of your own life. It is easy to say that he should have emphasized "both . . . and," but in the heat of controversy contrasting emphases become sharpened to radical opposites, "either . . . or." Paul's argument is that justification must be by faith and not by works. The Israelites have the Law, but the purpose of God is the justification of *all,* Gentiles included. *Everyone* is capable of the act of faith—both circumcised and uncircumcised. Again, however, Paul—paradoxically—did not abandon the Law or ethics!

4:1–25: *Abraham himself was justified by faith and thus is the "father" of all who have faith in the God who raised Jesus from the dead.* As in Galatians, Paul's position here turns on the fact that the Torah says of Abraham, "he *believed* the Lord, and he [the Lord] reckoned it to him as *righteousness*" (Gen. 15:6; cf. Rom. 4:3; cf. Gal. 3:6). Not until Gen. 17—two chapters later!—does God lay on him and his descendants the requirement of circumcision on the eighth day (Gen. 17:11–12). There it is also said of Abraham, "I have made you the father of many *ethnē* ("peoples," "nations,"—or "Gentiles"!)" (Gen. 17:5; Rom. 4:17, 22; cf. Gal. 3:8). Faith is anterior to, prior to, and therefore superior to, circumcision in the drama of being justified before God. Here Paul's interpretation of scripture sounds very "rabbinic." For his earlier formulation in relation to the new family—believers as children of Abraham who are also children of God—see Gal. 3.

5:1–8:39: Third major section: The new life in Christ.

5:1–5: *The consequence of justification by faith: Peace with God and joy in life.* Paul takes up the boasting theme again and formulates his version of why the one, merciful creator God permits human suffering.

5:6–11: *The grounds for the possibility of justification by faith: The cross of Christ.* In one of his most lyrical passages, Paul expresses his fundamental convictions by using two images: the image of **justification,** taken from the language of the law court, and the image of **reconciliation,** taken from the language of personal relationships (cf. 2 Cor. 5:16–21). Both are ways of talking about the plight of human beings before God—the need for justification, the need for reconciliation—and both are ways of talking about the cross of Christ, that is, the means by which God has changed the plight of human beings.

In Phil. 3:10–16, Paul expressed the sharing of Christ's sufferings in relation to Christ's death (past), but sharing of the resurrection remained a goal toward which Paul, like an athlete, was striving (future). Here Paul makes a similar point: The believer *has been* "justified by his [Christ's] blood" or "reconciled by his [Christ's] death"; but the believer who has been so justified or reconciled *will be* further "saved" by his life. The first point is Paul's version of the claim of the Corinthian enthusiasts that they knew *already* the power of the risen Lord, that their life in Christ was *already* the resurrection life. Paul does not *totally* deny this fact; he is willing to claim that members of the Jesus

Movement together share in the power of Jesus' resurrection and that their lives are already transformed by the power of that resurrection. However, there is always for Paul the belief that believers are not yet perfect, that they are "between" what has been accomplished and what is yet to be completed. However much a person knows of the power and quality of the resurrection life *already in the present,* the final resurrection, thus the completion of salvation, still lies *in the future.* However much one is now justified or reconciled, one *still* needs to be "saved from the wrath to come," that is, from the still-outstanding, final judgment of God. There is in Paul a tension between his ability to interpret the faith in terms of Greek religious "passion" *already* achieved and his necessity as an Israelite to think in terms of a Last Judgment *not yet* achieved. Despite his enthusiasm for the effectiveness of the cross of Christ, despite his experience of the present experience of Christ's risen life, he never loses sight of the apocalyptic hope for the coming of Christ as Judge and Redeemer in the future. So in this passage, although believers are *already* "reconciled," they have *not yet* been "saved." Some modern biblical scholars call Paul's reservation about claiming complete salvation already in this life an "eschatological reservation."

Paul will maintain the same "eschatological reservation" in relation to baptism (Rom. 6). In Colossians, however, there will be a major shift on this point, that is, one *already* possesses salvation in the present. Indeed, the different view in Colossians is one of the strongest arguments that it was not written by Paul, but rather by a later follower of Paul. A similar view is developed in Gnostic forms of the Jesus Movement.

5:12–21: The Adam/Christ myth. There were two well-known myths in Mediterranean antiquity. The first is that the First Man "fell" from the world of light above into the world of matter below and then became the inclusive head of the human race. The second is that heavenly Wisdom (Hebrew *hochma;* Greek *sophia*), an extension of God's Wisdom, came to earth through emissaries or emanations (like rays of the sun) in each generation (see Chapter One). She (in Hebrew and Greek the grammatical gender of "wisdom" is feminine) brought to humankind true "knowledge" (Greek *gnōsis*) that would free it from its fallen condition; then she returned to heaven.

Modern scholars hold that Gen. 1–3 also contains two myths: The first is the seven-day creation story (Gen. 1:1–2:4a), and the second is the story of Adam and Eve in the Garden of Eden (Gen. 2:4b–3:24). The ancient Hellenistic Israelite philosopher Philo of Alexandria had an inkling of these two Genesis myths because he correlated both of them with the First Man myth, which he split into two parts (*On the Account of the World's Creation Given by Moses* 134; *Allegorical Interpretation of Genesis* 1.31–32). In this revised, combined myth, the First Man Adam (Hebrew *'Ādām* = "man," that is, "humankind") was created perfect in God's image and thus was the model for all human beings. Philo identified the First Man Adam with divine Wisdom, the "Word," or *Logos* (cf. John 1:1), and "God's Son" (remember that Philo is an Israelite). It was the Second Man (Adam in the Garden of Eden myth), the Adam made of clay, who "fell," that is, sinned. Philo thus developed a two-Adams myth, or a two-humanity myth, the original Perfect Man and the second Fallen Man.

There was in the **Dead Sea Scrolls** an apocalyptic expectation for the *restoration* of the fallen Adam. This restored Adam symbolized the Dead Sea community; thus Adam is the "new humanity" (1QS 4.20–23).

Before looking at Paul in relation to these Adam myths, it is important to note one more interesting idea found in both Hellenistic and Israelite texts: *the link between sin and death.* In the fourth to third century B.C.E., Krantor wrote a letter saying, ". . . even at our birth there is conjoined with us a portion of *evil* in everything. For the very seed of our life, *since it is mortal,* participates in this causation . . ." (*A Letter to Apollonius 6*). Similarly, about 180 B.C.E., Jesus son of Sira, an Israelite wisdom teacher, shifting the burden for sin to the First *Woman,* wrote, "From a woman sin had its beginning, and because of her we all die" (Sir. 25:24). Again, in the late first century C.E., the Israelite author of 4 Ezra laments about the sin of Adam that is passed on to human beings and brings with it death (7:46–50). Thus in both non-Israelite and Israelite texts death was sometimes linked to sin.

These ideas make it possible to understand Paul's fascinating views in Rom. 5:12–21 better. There are hints that Paul may have known the wisdom of ben Sira and, depending on how one interprets the interpolation in 2 Cor. 6:14–7:1 (see Chapter Five), some of the Qumran literature, but there is no evidence that he had ever read Philo. Did he nonetheless have some knowledge of the myth of the two Adams? If he did, he combined and yet in a sense "reversed" the two-Adams myth. For Paul, the First Man is Adam, and his sin resulted in death. Paul apparently did not imagine two Adams in Genesis, a Perfect Man and a Fallen Man, as did Philo, but rather only one. Yet, he did make the common connection between Adam's sin and death. The *second* Adam for Paul, then, is the *Last* Adam, who is Christ. His righteousness resulted in the possibility of the removal of Adam's sin. Whereas the act of the First Man resulted in sin and death, the act of the Last Man resulted in salvation and life. Paul had in view two kinds of humanity: one in Adam (sinful), one in Christ (righteous). In the Dead Sea Scrolls, the restored Adam was the new humanity; for Paul, the new Adam, Christ, symbolized the new humanity. For Paul's earlier, briefer statement of the two-Adams myth, or in Paul's version, the Adam/Christ myth, see 1 Cor. 15:22–28.

6:1–14: *Dying and rising with Christ.* Again Paul uses the characteristic Hellenistic literary device called the diatribe, which formulates questions from an imagined opponent and then gives answers. In Gentile environments where Paul preached, there were a number of the mystery religions (see Chapter One) that stressed the cycles of the seasons. Death was related to the death of vegetation in the autumn, and resurrection was related to the rebirth of vegetation in the spring, so important for an agrarian society, and there were usually fertility rites involved. Most important in this context, their rituals celebrated dying and rising with the mystery cult deity, a god or goddess. Thus it was natural to think that when one was initiated into a hero cult such as that of Serapis or Mithras or a heroine cult such as that of Isis, the initiate, now spiritually reborn, would share in the power and destiny of that cult deity. Although there are differences—Jesus was a recently executed human being, and fertility ideas are only latent—members of the Jesus Movement might have made some connection with the mysteries—or, better, seen their rites in competition with them—because Jesus' death and resurrection were in the spring. (There is a distant parallel in modern celebrations of the Christian Easter in the Northern Hemisphere [flowers, Easter eggs, the Easter Bunny].)

For Paul, the initiate to the Jesus Movement shares in the life and death of Christ through the rite of baptism. However, once again Paul has an eschatological reservation. As in Phil. 3:10–16 and Rom. 5:6–11 the baptized initiate *has already* shared in the *death* of Christ (already)—sins are forgiven—but *shall be* united with Christ in a *resurrection* like his (not yet). Paul then interjects a passage of moral exhortation (verses 12–14), but will continue the theme of sin/death and righteousness/life in the next section. Again, the shift toward present salvation in Colossians and among Gnostics in the Jesus Movement has not yet taken place.

6:15–7:6:   *Two analogies: Slavery and marriage.*   To drive home his point, Paul turns to two analogies: slavery and marriage. A slave is responsible to one master. Similarly, says Paul, a wife is responsible to one husband, as long as he lives. So those who believe in Christ were once slaves to sin and married to the Law. Now, however, they have become slaves of a new master, righteousness, which leads to "sanctification" (being holy). Because the Law (like a deceased husband) is dead for them, they (like a widow) are free and no longer responsible to it. Paul's statement about the Law in this passage was undoubtedly very attractive to second-century Marcionite members of the Jesus Movement because they rejected the Israelite scriptures as authoritative. However, as the next section shows, Paul did not totally reject the Torah.

7:7–25:   *The meaning and function of the Mosaic Law.*   Paul again uses the diatribe to make his point. As a Israelite he inherited the understanding of the Torah as mediated through Moses and as the supreme gift of God's grace, given to human beings that they might know and do the will of God in the world and so inherit the blessings of all eternity.

As a proselyte to the Jesus Movement, Paul had come to see that according to the Torah, Jesus himself was cursed: "cursed be every one who hangs on a tree" (Deut. 21:23; see Gal. 3:13). Perhaps Paul had used this argument in his former days persecuting members of the Jesus Movement. In Galatians, however, he revised this argument—put a "spin" on it—to show that Christ took the curse of the Law upon himself in behalf of those who believe in him (Gal. 3:13). Moreover, according to God's direct revelation to Paul, Jesus was God's own Son. Thus Paul must have begun to question the validity of the Torah on certain issues.

As a preacher convinced of the importance of the death and resurrection of Jesus for salvation, Paul was forced into controversy with his opponents at Galatia and Philippi, and no doubt elsewhere, about the validity of the Law. Underlying this issue was Paul's gospel and freedom (as Paul had come to understand the meaning of that term). So Paul was again forced to question the validity of the Mosaic Torah and indeed to deny its enduring significance for members of the Jesus Movement. In this passage from Romans, he brings his reflections together. Out of his own experience of the crucified Christ and earlier controversies, he fashions his classic statement about the ultimate significance of the Torah. God gave it to the Israelite people as the supreme gift of "grace." Yes, sin brings about death. But the Torah in and of itself is *not* sin; it is "holy and just and good" (7:12). Yet, one who knows the Law knows sin through the Law. Only when one is forbidden to do something by the Law does one become aware that what he does is forbidden. "Apart from the Law sin lies dead . . . but when the commandment came, sin revived and I died" (7:8, 9). So, although the Law was intended to help, it did not; it became a tool of sin and death. For Paul, the Law is spiritual, but humans are carnal. They are "sold under sin," which generates internal conflict. Paul says,

> I do not understand my own actions. For I do not do what I want, but I do the very thing that I hate. . . . Now if I do what I do not want, it is no longer I that do it, but sin which dwells within me.
>
> (7:14–15, 20)

It is sometimes supposed that this Rom. 7 passage is autobiographical, that is, that Paul was reflecting on his own soul-searching as he attempted to fulfill the Law as a Pharisee. Perhaps. However, most modern interpreters think that such an interpretation is too individualistic, too psychological. It seems more likely that the use of the first-person singular is part of his rhetorical strategy, thus a literary device. Although we have no evidence that Paul thought this way about the Torah before his vision of the risen Christ or before his conflicts with the Judaizers, the rhetorical strategy makes it a powerful passage. The ancients had ideas about desiring what is forbidden and the power of pleasure over intellect. For example, the Stoic philosopher Epictetus said, "For since he who is in error does not wish to err, but to be right, it is clear that he is not doing what he wishes" (Epictetus *Discourses* 2.26.1). With more focus on the internal life of the soul as such, Paul says, "The good that I would I do not: but the evil which I would not, that I do" (Rom. 7:19, KJV). And Paul's road to freedom is not to focus on the higher rational, disciplined self, as is common in ancient philosophy, but rather to have faith in God "in the Spirit," as the following passage shows.

8:1–39:   *The new life in Christ and in the Spirit.*   Paul has paused to give his "apology" for the Law (7:7–25). In what is one of his greatest passages, Paul describes the possibilities of new life in Christ. The first section stresses "life in the Spirit," the Spirit that includes freedom from the slavery of sin and death to become, as the rabbis also put life in the Spirit, a slave to God (*Sifre Numbers* Shelah 115, 35a). Through it one cries "Abba! Father!," which is the language of Jesus (verse 15; Mark 14:36; cf. Gal. 4:6). "Life in the Spirit" is also life as future hope for which the whole creation is groaning in labor pains (verse 22), anticipating the new birth. Presently, it is life lived in the love in Christ Jesus, from which nothing can separate the true believer. Some of Paul's favorite and most quoted comments occur in this section: "all things work together for good for those who love God" (verse 28) and "if God is for us, who is against us?" (verse 31).

9:1–11:36:   Fourth major section: The place of Israel in God's plan for the salvation of all humanity ("salvation history").   Nothing disturbed Paul more than the problems posed by his Israelite heritage. He had considered himself an honorable member of the people of God, the "chosen people," to whom God's will and purpose had been revealed directly in the Torah. Indeed, he had undoubtedly boasted of it. Yet, Paul had become convinced that the people of God had rejected God's own Son. Paul spent much of his life arguing with his own people that Jesus was God's Son and that Jesus' life, death, and resurrection were part of God's plan as foretold in the scriptures. Paul also tried to explain to Gentiles how his own people, the chosen people, had not recognized Jesus as the Son of God. Now he was preaching a gospel that claimed that a Gentile could be "justified" not by the Torah but rather on the basis of belief in a recent event—the crucifixion.

What, then, remained of the special calling of the Israelite people to become God's chosen people, the "light of the world"? The most natural answer would have been, "Nothing!," especially when Paul faced the problems created by the conservative Israelite party of believers at Jerusalem who demanded circumcision and adherence to the Torah. Because most Israelites had rejected Jesus, the answer could have been even sharper, "Less than nothing!" Nonetheless, Paul came up with an answer that some scholars discuss under the rubric of the German word *Heilsgeschichte*.

Heilsgeschichte means literally "the story of salvation" and is usually translated "salvation history." However, this story is not simply "secular" history, but rather God working out the divine plan *through* the story of Israel. At crucial points in this story, God revealed the divine will. Although the concept of *Heilsgeschichte* may be too linear in its conception of time, it is nonetheless true that the *story of Israel* is important for understanding the way God works, especially by the writer of Deuteronomy. A major theme of the story was that when Israel had good times, God was rewarding her for her loyalty and obedience to the covenant; when Israel had bad times, God was punishing her for her disobedience. In short, "secular" history became the stage on which the "religious" story of God's relation with his people was told.

Chapters 9–11 take up a crucial problem in Paul's argument: If God now justifies both Israelites *and* non-Israelites on the basis of their faith in Christ, what about his promises to Israel *as a collective people?* What about God's covenant with Abraham, the "father" of this people? The problem is to relate justification by grace through faith to God's plan for, and promises to, his chosen people. We have already encountered this problem in Galatians. In Romans, Paul works out its solution more carefully. He is specifically concerned about how God's plan and promises are being fulfilled when most of those to whom the promises were made have rejected God's Son, the Messiah.

Paul argues that everything that has happened in relation to Christ accords with the original purpose of God and that that purpose is the eventual salvation of *all* humanity, both Israelites and non-Israelites. However, at the moment Israel as a whole has failed to recognize that righteousness is attained only by faith. Israelites have therefore remained stubborn in their insistence that righteousness is attainable by obedience to the Law, "and seeking to establish their own, they did not submit to God's righteousness" (10:3).

Yet, argues Paul, God has *not* rejected the people of Israel outright. Therefore, the Gentile believers should not feel superior to Israelite believers. Paul develops a very rich analogy, the olive tree and its branches. God has broken off branches of a cultivated olive tree (the Israelites who have refused to believe) and grafted on branches of a wild olive shoot (believers, including *Gentiles*). But he reminds the Roman community that if God can do that, then God can just as easily break off the wild branches and graft in the old branches—if they come to believe—especially because they are already natural branches. The rejection of God's Son by "the rest" of Israel has the consequence that the Gentiles have an opportunity to hear the gospel (11:11–12). The word of God to Israel has not failed. After all, he has argued, the promise to Abraham means that his *true* descendants are those who believe, which includes Gentile believers. To be sure, this is not Israel as a whole, *as a nation,* but rather it is *a kind* of Israel. What then of Israel *as a whole,* as a nation? Paul finally decides that there is a mystery here: During the period when the full number of Gentiles comes in, part of Israel will remain outside; nonetheless, in the end all Israel will be saved.

Paul argues all this in much detail and with many references to scripture. Yet, the modern reader cannot help but feel that he is straining too hard. The theme of Rom. 1–8 is one theme, mainly justification by, and reconciliation with, God; the theme of Rom. 9–11 quite another. It is a testimony to the agony of a Pharisee who has come to believe that God's own people *as a whole* have rejected God's own Son, thus God's own good news. Rom. 9–11 is Paul's attempt to accept and to understand this reality.

12:1–15:33:   Fifth major section: Moral exhortation.   The first nine chapters of Romans, the body of the letter, consist of mainly "theology." "Therefore" in Rom. 12:1 introduces the reader or hearer to a new section, the moral exhortation section, of the letter.

What God has done for people in the Jesus Movement (salvation) is followed by what they should do in response (ethics).

In Rom. 12, there are echoes of the "body politic" metaphor also found in 1 Cor. 12, that is, although there are many members with differing spiritual gifts, there is only one body (12:3–8). This is followed by a series of general exhortations about behavior, both with respect to life within the community and to those outside (12:9–21).

Rom. 13 contains Paul's most important political statement—indeed, one of the most important political statements in the New Testament—namely, his recommendation that those in the movement be subject to the governing authorities (see the following summary on Paul and "the state"). You will recall that in 64 C.E., Nero persecuted members of the Jesus Movement in Rome and blamed them for the great fire. Paul was probably martyred at Rome during the time of Nero. One might therefore think that Paul would not have recommended being subject to governing authorities. The Rom. 13 passage, however, was written in the early period of Nero's reign, which was relatively peaceful. It is hard to imagine that Paul in Nero's earlier period would have encouraged the Roman believers, who were in any case a relatively small, insignificant, and powerless group, to oppose the power of Rome on the concrete issue that seems to determine his views here: paying taxes.

Rom. 14:1–15:13 takes up the relation of "the weak" to "the strong," which some scholars think is related to the Israelite and non-Israelite factions in the Roman congregation.

Rom. 15:14–33 speaks of Paul's pride in his mission; it concludes with an itinerary where Paul expresses the hope of going on to Spain and relays his anxiety about taking the collection to Jerusalem. The closing contains an appeal to prayer on Paul's behalf and a benediction (15:33).

Rom. 16:1–23:   This passage has already been discussed. It is a possible addition to Rom. 1–15. It contains a letter of recommendation for Phoebe (16:1–2), greetings to twenty-six people by name and others, and "the kiss" (16:16). Then there is a comment about opponents (17–20), which includes another benediction (verse 20), greetings from Paul and his companions (21–23). As part of the letter, Paul must have known these people personally earlier in his career, probably at Ephesus.

Unknown scribes have added the benediction (verse 24) and doxology (verses 25–27) to the letter (see the earlier discussion).

EPILOGUE: PAUL'S THEOLOGY AND ETHICS, A SUMMARY

From our brief exegetical outlines of Paul's undisputed letters, it will now be helpful to pull together a summary of some of his basic ideas.

As far as anyone knows, Paul had not met the historical Jesus. Yet, as a result of an ASC, a religious experience in which he believed he had seen the crucified and risen Christ, the persecutor of the Jesus Movement abandoned his former life and carried out his "call" to preach the "good news" as apostle to the Gentiles. His surviving letters show that the heart of this good news was *not* what we would call the life and teachings of Jesus. Paul does not emphasize a "Christ-like" moral life in the sense of "following in the steps of Jesus," although he does stress *suffering* modeled on imitation, and he exhorts members of the Jesus Movement to live a life that might be called "Christ-like." Some scholars have argued that Paul, who knew Jesus' brother James, as well as the disciples Peter and John, must have known more about the historical Jesus. That is possible, even probable, but it cannot be proved with certainty. If he did, he chose not to emphasize it. Rather, the center of his message was what theologians have often called "the Christ-event," that is, Jesus' death on the cross and his resurrection from the dead.

For Paul, the "Christ-event" opens up the whole meaning of the divine plan and purpose of the one true God and therefore the whole meaning and purpose of the universe, human history, and human existence. When properly understood, the Christ-event fulfills God's ancient promises. These are that salvation is not only for those who are, and have become part of, God's chosen covenant people as a national entity, Israel, with its religious heritage grounded in the Torah; rather, salvation is ultimately for the whole human race. It is based on belief in the Christ-event itself. Salvation is good news about God, God's purposes, God's relation to humankind, the nature and destiny of humanity, human freedom and ethical responsibility, faith, hope, and love—in short, *all* of reality. The "Christ-event" is what scholars of religion sometimes call a "foundational myth," a creative account that gives meaning and purpose to all of human existence.

This mysterious cross-resurrection event, says Paul, cannot be understood by worldly wisdom. For Paul, this event is an amazingly *powerful* event, signaling that the final period of history has begun, indeed that the end is imminent! Paradoxically, however, God's unlimited power is manifested in *weakness,* symbolized by the cross. It is a power present both in manifestations of the Spirit of God through spiritual gifts (more ASCs!) and in the self-giving love of God who commands that believers respond in the same way. For people in the Jesus Movement, then, spiritual ecstasy and weakness are to be held in balance: Ecstasy without the cross leads to self-seeking pride and "knowledge" (*gnōsis*); yet, the new life in Christ is already manifested by spiritual security and gifts of the Spirit.

At the same time, the "Christ-event" is a gift from God ("grace"). For Paul, the whole person ("body") contains within it a struggle between the "spirit," or the higher self, and the "flesh," or the lower self. The flesh is subject to attack by "sin," which Paul often "personifies" as an evil power. It is sin in the flesh that leads a person to rebel against God, and this rebellion manifests itself in all forms of wickedness and vice. The self cannot overcome this evil power by itself; it therefore cannot overcome evil by "good works"—including those prescribed by the Torah. In fact, an angry God would be justified in rendering the "guilty" verdict on sinful humanity. But God has not done so for those who believe in this act of power. In other words, "the righteousness of God" is the movement of God toward human beings in which, by his free gift of grace ("the Christ-event"), sinners are made just, or "justified," that is, pardoned as innocent on the basis of a trusting belief. This good news is the "power of God for salvation for everyone who has faith" (Rom. 1:16). By this faith the believer departs from an old humanity, symbolized by Adam, and enters a new humanity, symbolized by Christ. He or she becomes part of a new humanity, that is, a new family. She or he is one of the true children of Abraham, who is the prototype of faith. The ritual of baptism means that the believer shares in Christ's death by dying to the old self and by accepting the promise of participating in Christ's resurrection, the new self. This new life in the Spirit is sustained in the group by worship, especially in the common meal, the Lord's Supper, which commemorates Jesus' death. It is also manifested by charismatic gifts and can be characterized as "life" and "peace." Vices associated with the flesh are rejected, and virtues associated with the Spirit are fostered within the new body or community. By God's action "in Christ," then, everyone in the whole world is offered reconciliation with its Creator.

Much more could be added to this brief statement. However, what needs to be stressed is that Paul's view of the good news about Jesus Christ led him into conflict with his own Israelite religious traditions, specifically Pharisaic ones, at the crucial point: the understanding of the Torah and its function among God's elect, covenant people, Israel. It is highly debated whether Paul, as a Hellenistic Greek-speaking Israelite of the **Diaspora,** fully appreciated his religious tradition about the Torah when he spoke of it in terms of "works of the Law." Whether he did or not, one thing is clear: If the sign of God's covenant people is circumcision as stated in the Law, Paul's view that Gentiles could become part of the new community without circumcision and his perspective that Christ is the "end of the Law" led toward a different idea of the community. Eventually this led to a "parting of the ways," as one scholar put it. After the gospel was preached to the Gentiles on this basis, the conflict with those who upheld a more traditional view of the Torah was inevitable. The mature Paul could cite the traditional baptismal formula, "neither Israelite nor Greek . . . in Christ Jesus" (Gal. 3:28), and hope for the ultimate inclusion of the mother, Israel, who had given birth to her children, the Christ believers (Rom. 11). Nonetheless, the way was also prepared for the eventual emergence of a separate and distinct institution, the church.

No matter how or whether one accepts Paul's ideas, he was a profound religious thinker. What, then, about his practical, ethical advice? It is impossible to enter into a full discussion of his ethical teachings, most of which have been briefly noted earlier; it is possible, however, to indicate his general orientation to ethical issues and cite some of the more important examples.

Much of Paul's advice is similar to the conventional morality of his day, which includes both Israelite and Gentile philosophers. Members of the Jesus Movement, like the Israelites in the Diaspora, should settle their disputes outside the pagan courts (1 Cor. 6). Lists or catalogues of vices and virtues reflect popular Hellenistic morality (see Chapter Four). Sources of authority include sacred texts (e.g., 1 Cor. 10), religious tradition (1 Cor. 11:23–25 on the Lord's Supper; 1 Cor. 15:3b–5 on the resurrection), and "words of the Lord" on divorce (1 Cor. 7:10–11) and on the apostolic right to financial support (1 Cor. 9:14). Most liberated persons in the modern West will not accept his views on slavery, women, and same-sex relations. In short, Paul's writings contain conventional, time-bound morality and the appeal to conservative tradition, along with eschatological orientation. His tendency is to put ethical sections—the moral exhortations—near the end of his letters. It is clear from all this that Paul's thought is very cultural and contextual. These features have led some interpreters to suggest that Paul's ethical teachings are so ancient and time-bound that they are a subsidiary, even irrelevant, part of his thinking.

Others have concluded that whatever one thinks of Paul's contextual ethical views on specific subjects, one should not isolate them from his thought as a whole. The form of the letter is sufficiently flexible to permit moral exhortation to occur at almost any place. Indeed, 1 Thessalonians might be called a "moral exhortation letter," and 1 Corinthians is dominated by responses to practical, ethical concerns of the Corinthian church. For Paul himself, at least, the "moral exhortation" is finally part of the message of good news. The ethics grows out of the "Christ-event." As some New Testament theologians put it, the moral imperative—what believers *ought* to do—is rooted in, and therefore inseparable from, the theological indicative—what God *has done* for believers (Bultmann). Thus, although Paul often draws on authority and conventional morality, some of which clearly has a time-bound quality, Paul's theology contains impulses for ethical reflection that go beyond what is typical of his contemporaries.

If Paul's ethical statements are in the service of his message of good news, then they should be coordinated with his view of God's act of power and grace in the Christ-event. For Paul, the final period of human history and society has begun, but the consummation is still forthcoming. Meanwhile, true believers have received a taste of the future in the activity of the Spirit (Rom. 8:23), both in the individual and in the community. This is expressed in *freedom within the bounds of love, especially as developed in imitating the humility of Christ.* When freedom is threatened, especially by strict adherence to the Law, Paul rushes to defend the gospel. At the same time, he checks the abuse of freedom by appeals, first, to love as the highest spiritual gift, at least for relationships within the community; second, to weakness as true strength, with the humility of Christ as a model; and, third, to the "eschatological reservation": Members of the Jesus Movement are not yet perfect. To be sure, Paul is willing to be accommodating (1 Cor. 9:19–23), although he is cautious about this principle. More important, we see him struggling with the issue of freedom and love in his willingness to admit that there is a special wisdom for "the strong." Nonetheless, maturity should never be the occasion for causing "the weak" to stumble (1 Cor. 8, 10; Rom. 14–15). In the last analysis, strength expresses itself in terms of weakness, and believers should imitate the weakness of Paul as he imitates the weakness of Christ. God has acted in Christ to save those who believe; believers must, in turn, respond.

Finally, although the goal might not have been met, it finds one of its best expressions in the traditional baptismal formula of Gal. 3:28:

> There is no longer Israelite nor Greek,
> there is no longer slave nor free,
> there is no longer male nor female;
> for all of you are one in Christ Jesus.

Take a look now at some of Paul's highly debated, concrete ethical concerns.

Sex, Marriage, and Divorce

At Corinth, Paul had to counter two extremes: the libertines and ascetics. The former championed a freewheeling ethic with the slogan, "All things are lawful" (1 Cor. 6:12; 10:23). The latter fought physical, sexual urges with the slogan, "It is well for a man not to touch a woman" (1 Cor. 7:1). Paul took the middle road. He responded to specific questions about sex, marriage, and divorce in 1 Cor. 7 by defending the view that the Corinthians remain as they are because the end of the present social and political order is near, a practical solution geared to service without anxiety. He clearly *preferred* celibacy for the remaining period before the end but considered it nonetheless to be a special "gift" (verse 7), not a proof of superior moral status. He recognized the power of strong sexual desire and did not put marriage down. Drawing on his Pharisaic heritage, he declared that sex belongs in marriage with one partner; indeed, it is a duty. Otherwise, sexual immorality (*porneia*) can result. He said nothing of another major rabbinic argument, that marriage is necessary for the propagation of the race (cf. Gen. 1:28), a view found also in the Hellenistic world. Paul argued that sex is a mutual responsibility of husband and wife as equal partners, conceding the possibility of temporary abstinence for prayer, again a rabbinic recommendation, again by mutual agreement (verse 6).

What, then, of divorce? In Roman law, either partner could divorce the other, and divorce was common. In Israelite religion, the Law of Moses permitted divorce only by the husband if the wife ". . . does not please him because he finds something objectionable about her . . ." (Deut. 24:1). However, in the first century C.E., Israelites did not agree on divorce. The liberal school of Rabbi Hillel interpreted this to mean "any cause," but the conservative school of Rabbi Shammai said that adultery is the only basis for divorce. The Qumran community in effect set aside any Deut. 24–based practice. It interpreted Gen. 1:27 ("male and female he created them") and 2:24 ("they become one flesh") to mean that divorce is not permitted. Paul drew upon a "word of the Lord" forbidding divorce, too, perhaps as a protection for the woman (Mark 10:2–12; Luke 16:18; contrast Matthew's "except for unchastity" [Matt. 5:32; 19:9], probably a reflection of the Shammai position). Yet, Paul did not hold the teachings of Jesus on divorce to be sacrosanct, to be irrefutable laws to be obeyed. In an aside (if it was not interpolated by a scribe!), he admitted that "separations" would occur, that there should not be second marriages, and that if reconciliation between marriage partners is impossible, the wife (and the husband?) should maintain single. Paul recommended that, if possible, the couple stay together because marriage is holy, and so the children of holy marriages are holy. Perhaps he hoped that the nonbelieving spouse would become a proselyte, too; yet, if the nonbelieving spouse wants to separate, he said, the believing spouse is *not* bound to the marriage. In all of this we observe the apostle softening Jesus' views, affirming his own preference for celibacy, yet maintaining a position between the poles of libertine and ascetic ethics, and doing so in the light of his eschatology. This is freedom within the bounds of love.

Women

In assessing Paul's view of women, it should be recalled that the religious and cultural background out of which he came was strongly patriarchal. A woman was subordinate to her father before marriage and to her husband after marriage. In Israel, the woman's main functions were childbearing (preferably a son) and child rearing, being a wife and sexual partner, and cooking and housekeeping. In the Hellenistic world, there was greater freedom, especially for educated women and especially in the Roman sphere. A second point to recall is that in looking at Paul's views one must exclude works of the Pauline School, especially Colossians and Ephesians (late first century C.E.) and the still later Pastorals, or 1, 2 Timothy and Titus (early second century C.E.). This is an important point because these later letters assimilate Paul's views to stricter patriarchal opinions of subordination characteristic of the culture, whether Israelite, Greek, or Roman (Col. 3:18; Eph. 5:24; 1 Tim. 2:9–15). Thus, for example, 1 Timothy argues that women are not to teach or have authority over men (women are to remain silent) because Eve, not Adam, was deceived; indeed, she ". . . will be saved through bearing children, if she continues in faith and love and holiness, with modesty" (2:15). In the light of 1 Cor. 14:33b–36, which has similar language, one might think that this is a fairly accurate representation of Paul's own views. However, the 1 Corinthians passage interrupts the context in such a way that most modern critics conclude it is an interpolation by a later scribe. Probably he was a member of Paul's school that later produced the Pastorals, that is, later copyists brought Paul into line with what they deemed to be Paul's views in 1 Timothy.

In short, 1 Cor. 14:33b–36 is the strongest indication of subordination in Paul's undisputed letters, but it does not come from Paul.

Five important passages remain. In Gal. 3:28, Paul cites the baptism formula, "neither male nor female . . . in Christ Jesus," clearly indicating that in the "new family" old patriarchal gender distinctions should be abolished. We have also seen that in 1 Cor. 7, Paul balances the roles of men and women in marriage (7:2, 3, 4, 10–11, 12–13, 33–34 [twice]). None of these ideas sounds like the patriarchal tradition out of which Paul came or to which his views were later accommodated in 1 Corinthians and in 1 Timothy. Furthermore, there are clear references to women who have achieved prominence as leaders in the churches. Paul says that Euodia and Syntyche "labored side by side" with him at Philippi (Phil. 4:2–3). In Rom. 16:1, Paul commends "our sister Phoebe, a deacon of the church at Cenchreae [the eastern port at Corinth]." The masculine term "deacon" (Greek *diakonos*) implies at least a functional position in the church (Phil. 1:1), and elsewhere Paul uses it of his own role as "servant" or "minister." She is also called a "helper" (Greek *prostatis*), which in Hellenistic literature and inscriptions is clearly a term of authority ranging in meaning from "benefactor" or "patron" to "presiding officer" of a religious cult. Does this one use of the term in the New Testament have the same meaning? Probably. In any case, there follows the long list of greetings to persons among whom are Prisca (Priscilla) and Aquila who are given preeminence, Prisca now being mentioned first (cf. 1 Cor. 16:19 where Aquila is mentioned first, although greetings are given from the church in "their house" in Ephesus). This order of names clearly indicates her importance because it departs from the usual practice of the day (cf. Acts 18:26). There are also other women mentioned in Rom. 16. Although there is a good deal of controversy about how to interpret these passages, it is clear that Paul was not liberated in the modern, Western sense. Yet, women in Paul's communities were not viewed in traditional patriarchal fashion, either. Indeed, on occasion they could hold positions of status and authority.

By modern liberationist standards, Paul's most chauvinistic-sounding passage is 1 Cor. 11:2–16, the passage about women's appearance in the house-church assembly. As we saw in Chapter Five, this passage is exceedingly difficult to interpret. Here Paul insists that women should wear a head covering (or long hair?) when they pray and prophesy in worship, and he gives several arguments to support this view. First, he appears to establish a hierarchy of subordination: God is the "head" (*kephalē*) of Christ, Christ is the "head" of man/husband, and man/husband is the "head" of woman/wife. He uses a play on words: "Any man who prays or prophesies with his head covered dishonors his head [= Christ], but any woman who prays or prophesies with her head uncovered dishonors her head [= man/husband]." In part, he has the sequence of creation in Genesis in mind because in verses 7–9 he states that a man may worship with a bare head because he is "the image and glory of God" (Gen. 1:26). The woman, however, should be veiled because she is the glory (image is absent) of man (cf. Gen. 2:18–23). Does "head" refer to a subordinationist hierarchy, or is it simply a metaphor for the order of creation? If the latter view holds, Paul does not appear *quite* as chauvinistic as he might otherwise be, although he certainly does not sound as liberated as he does in some passages.

These problems of interpretation are compounded by another: The woman should wear a head covering "because of the angels" (1 Cor. 11:10). What does this mean? Demonic angels who lust for human women (cf. Gen. 6:2, the basis for the Israelite tradition of the fall of the angels)? Angels who also participate in worship? No one knows. Yet, the following comment is clear: "in the Lord" men and women have equal status because if originally woman came from man, man is now born from woman, "and all things are from God" (verses 11–12). This comment sounds a good deal more like Paul's balancing of men and women in 1 Cor. 7. In 1 Cor. 11, his final comments on the issue of head coverings indicate his frustration: For a woman to pray without her head covered is improper, against nature, and against Paul's rule in the churches! What lies behind this contrived argument appears to be this: Equal status at Corinth has led to a denial of sexual differentiation. In other words, freedom has led to potential abuse. Did women who "let their hair down" distract men from serious worship? The matter is not clear. In the process it is clear that Paul attempts to reassert his Gal. 3:28 point of view (verses 11–12, "no longer male or female") and that women do in fact speak in church insofar as they pray and prophesy. Paul's ethical premise of freedom within the bounds of love prevails, but he certainly has difficulty with it this time.

Slavery

As we have seen, slavery was an accepted social and economic institution in Greco-Roman society (see Chapter Five, section on Philemon). One could become a slave through defeat in war, kidnapping, debt, sale of one's self (or children), and breeding of female slaves. Although slaves were often permitted common law marriages, they could not be legally married, and they had no legal rights or obligations over their spouses or children. Neither could they participate in local government. They could, however, join a social club or burial society, and they were exempt from paying taxes and military conscription. A slave could be manumitted, in which case he or she became a freedman or freedwoman. This took place either formally (usually by a master's legal will or by a magistrate, if eligible) or informally (by letter, permission to recline at table with one's master, the witnessing of friends, or by asking one's heir to manumit slaves at one's death). The freed person gained certain civil rights and the possibility of becoming a Roman citizen, but he or she owed his or her former master, also his or her patron, certain continuing obligations such as labor and professional services. Due to manumission and subsequent marrying, perhaps five-sixths of the population of Rome by the end of the first century was servile or had a servile background.

From this cultural perspective, it is not surprising that slavery is an accepted institution in the New Testament. A number of well-known "pet" names for slaves are known in the culture, one of which is Onesimus ("useful") in the letter to Philemon. The "master"- "slave" terminology is frequently found, both literally and metaphorically. Paul, who understands the slave system of his culture, reflects widespread notions of "internal" as compared with "external" slavery when he writes:

> Were you a [real] slave when called? Do not be concerned about it. Even if you can gain your [real] freedom, make use of your present condition now more than ever [this clause could be translated as "by all means, (as a freedman/woman) live according to (God's calling)"]. For whoever was called in the Lord as a [real] slave is [metaphorically] a freed person belonging to the Lord, just as whoever was [really] free when called is [metaphorically] a slave of Christ. [As a real slave is bought with a price so] you were [metaphorically] bought with a price; do not [metaphorically] become slaves of human masters.
>
> (1 Cor. 7:21–23)

As in the case of Philemon and Onesimus, Paul did not attempt to overturn the institution of slavery; he did, however, appeal to Philemon to accept back, and perhaps to manumit, Onesimus, or even to return him to Paul. The final appeal, however, was directed to Philemon's free decision.

Same-Sex Relations

Once again, concerning same-sex relations, the Hellenistic cultural background should be kept in mind. Greco-Roman society, and especially public life, was male dominated. Males sought out other males for companionship and intellectual stimulation. Nudity in athletics was common. The ideal of beauty was physical and youthful, and female-looking boys were by Hellenistic times considered most attractive, even seductive. Bisexual relationships were common.

With these ethical and aesthetic values in place, so-called voluntary pederasty ("love of boys") was common and socially acceptable in some circles, especially in an earlier period. Sometimes such relationships were physical, the older partner normally taking the active sexual role. Sometimes the relationships were not sexual, at least explicitly. Some philosophers came to distinguish between noble pederasty and base pederasty. Noble pederasty was considered to be masculine, thought to aid military education, and believed to foster the teacher-pupil relationship as the pupil moved toward wisdom. In an earlier age, Plato considered pederasty a higher form of love ("platonic love," the "platonic relationship"). Pederasty was common, and similar relationships were sometimes admired among women and girls. Sappho, a sixth-century B.C.E. poet, was head of a community of girls on the island of Lesbos, from which the term *lesbian* derives.

These supposedly voluntary homosexual relationships were distinguished from involuntary homosexual relationships, for example, slave boys who were made to perform sexual favors for their masters and their companions. Slave boy prostitutes populated the public brothels. Some boys were castrated to preserve their "effeminate" appearances. In Rome homosexual prostitutes were taxed, and boy prostitutes were given a legal holiday.

Voluntary pederasty—boys freely selling their sexual services as "effeminate call boys"—was often distinguished from involuntary pederasty, which was especially condemned. Moreover, there emerged a counter philosophical point of view that opposed pederasty as such. It was seen as seductive, domineering, impermanent, productive of jealousy, not as pleasurable as male-female relationships, associated with lust and debauchery, and *contrary to nature*. In the middle of the first century, the Roman philosopher Seneca deplored the exploitation of boy slaves. Slightly later, Plutarch and Dio Chrysostom had similar warnings. Laws against rape and abuse were enacted, and there were careful regulations to protect boys at school.

When considering comments about same-sex relations in the Torah, it is important, as usual, to examine the literary context. In these texts, male same-sex relationships were seen as typical of foreigners or Gentile outsiders ("pagans"). Thus within Israel, same-sex relationships were condemned as "unholy," and the penalty for both partners was death (Lev. 20:13; cf. 18:22). However, in context the text really opposes *religious practices* of outsiders like the Egyptians and Canaanites. They are not what modern people would call consensual same-sex relations by adult gays and lesbians. Most scholars say that the famous story of Sodom (Gen. 19) was not about consensual homosexuality at all, at least as normally defined in the modern world. It was about *hospitality* and *homosexual rape*. At the time of the New Testament, homosexuality was apparently not condoned in Israelite society; it was viewed as a revolting Gentile vice and contrary to nature (Josephus *Antiquities* 15.2.6 par. 27–29; *Against Apion* 2.199; Philo *On Abraham* 135–136). The rabbinic literature extends the Torah prohibition to female homosexual practices. Again, none of this literature is aware of modern views of "sexual orientation."

It is important to note that Paul does not appear preoccupied with homosexual practices. What he does say is in line with his Israelite background and Hellenistic moral philosophy, which condemned abuses. In his attempts to preserve the purity of the group, Paul denounced same-sex practices and sexual abuses. In 1 Cor. 6:9 the difficult term *malakoi*, "(those who are) soft, weak, effeminate," occurs in a traditional "catalogue of vices" (see Chapter Five). Because that list includes other sexual sins ("adulterers"), it is probably a term of innuendo referring to pederasty and would conjure up an image of the "call boys." The second term in the catalogue is *arsenokoitai*, which comes from two words, *arsen*, "male," and *koitē*, "bed" (see English *coitus*). The term has sexual overtones. The word *arsenokoitai* is so rare that it may be Paul's translation of the Torah expression in the previously noted Levitical prohibition against homosexuality, *mishkav zakur*, "lying with a male" (referring to the active, rather than the passive, partner). In Paul's vice-list context, however, two terms seem to refer to the active and passive partners in pederasty.

A second major Pauline passage is Rom. 1:26–27. Here both male and female homosexual practices are viewed as the consequential activity of those who refused to acknowledge the one true God. Such practices, then, are associated with idolatry, that is, idolatry leads to "unnatural" sexual acts, and for ancients these acts included same-sex relations between persons who are really heterosexual. Thus it is a matter of lack of self-control (self-control was a major philosophical virtue) by heterosexuals. It was lust, not what moderns call "sexual orientation." Because Paul discusses no certain instance of homosexuality—some think that the head dress passage could be a veiled issue of homosexuality—it is uncertain how he would have reacted to a specific case. What would he have said in relation to his ethic of "freedom within the bounds of love"? The theological context of Romans as a whole shows his major point: *All*—Israelites and Gentiles—have sinned and are in need of the gift of God's grace and salvation (Rom. 1:16–3:31).

"The State"

In Greco-Roman antiquity, there were no carefully bounded nation-states comparable to those in the modern world. Yet, there was the Roman Empire and its provinces on the one hand and regions associated with traditional ethnic groups or peoples and languages on the other. (You will recall that "peoples" had very strong stereotypes about other "peoples.") Nonetheless, Paul's political perspective has often been used in discussions of "the state."

Rom. 13:1–7 is Paul's chief comment on this theme, and it has been the source of much church-state reflection down through the centuries. In this passage, God has instituted the governing authorities, and every person should be subject to them. Usually this view has been interpreted in a pacific sense, namely, pacifism. This interpretation seems to be reinforced by Paul's appeal to conscience (verse 5). Nonetheless, the total context points to a very specific issue—paying taxes. Moreover, when Paul wrote this letter there was as yet no major persecution of Jesus Movement members at Rome. Also, a tiny religious movement that had as yet had no major conflict with mighty Rome would naturally pick up this widespread position in relation to the empire. Finally, Paul's eschatology may have offered a rationale: God would ultimately destroy earthly powers anyhow.

SUMMARY

In this chapter, exegetical outlines of two of Paul's letters, Galatians and Romans, have been presented. These are at the heart of Paul's views on a series of key ideas: justification, the Law, sin, salvation, Christ, the Spirit, and the church and its relation to Israel. The chapter concluded with a summary of Paul's theology and ethics, which can serve as a summary to this chapter.

ANOTHER EPILOGUE: THE IMPACT OF THE APOSTLE PAUL

It is impossible to overestimate the importance of the apostle Paul to the New Testament in particular and Christendom in general. His vision of the nature of faith in Jesus Christ came at the crucial moment when circumstances were beginning to transform the Jesus Movement from an apocalyptic sect within the Israelite religion into a separate missionary religion within Greco-Roman society and beyond that into an established institutional religion. In this process, Paul came to play a major part. He was not only a leader in the movement; he blended ideologies and their corresponding behaviors from three contexts—Israelite, Hellenistic, and Jesus Movement—into a new whole.

Paul's vision of the nature of faith became normative. However, competing interpretations of it arose. Paul trained followers who not only served the church during his lifetime, but who also lived to provide leadership in the next generation. The very existence of 2 Thessalonians, Colossians, Ephesians, and the Pastorals, not to mention Gnostic interpreters of Paul, is eloquent testimony to his continuing influence. Although Paul's letters are difficult to understand, as the author of 2 Peter put it (2 Pet. 3:15–16), he had a tremendous influence on later thinkers noted at the outset: Augustine, Thomas Aquinas, Luther, Calvin, Wesley, and Barth.

Finally, Paul's letter writing provided the impetus toward the formation of the New Testament itself. The first step in establishing the New Testament as a distinctive body of literature was taken when his letters to individual churches were recognized as being important to all churches and were copied, placed in collections, and circulated. For Paul himself, "scripture" consisted of certain books now in the Septuagint version of what Christians now call the "Old Testament," but it is in no small part due to him that there is a New Testament.

STUDY QUESTIONS

1. What are the historical and social contexts for Galatians? What and where is Galatia? Who are the so-called Judaizers? Why is Paul so angry in this letter? Why does he begin with a defense of his role as apostle in the first two chapters? Why are Abraham and Sarah so central to this letter? What is "justification by faith"? What did Paul think about the role of the Torah for members of the Jesus Movement? Why is Paul so upset about circumcision? What does he say about Gentiles, women, and slaves? How does he use adoption and family analogies? What does he mean by "Spirit" and "flesh," and how does he develop the contrast between them? What are virtue and vice lists?

2. What is the historical and social context for Romans? What are Paul's views about sin and salvation? Revelation? Law and gospel? Israelite and Gentile? Adam and Christ? Baptism? Human struggle to "do good"? Justification by faith? The relation between Israel and the church? Rulers and "the state"? Women's roles in the church?

3. How would you summarize Paul's major theological and social-ethical ideas?

Photo 7.1 Title page of the book *Thomas the Contender,* one of the texts discovered at Nag Hammadi, Egypt, most of which are Gnostic. Especially important for New Testament study is the *Gospel of Thomas* from Nag Hammadi (see Chapters Three and Fourteen and Appendix Three).

CHAPTER SEVEN

THE DEUTERO-PAULINE LETTERS AND THE LETTER TO THE HEBREWS

Two phenomena in antiquity that sometimes disturb modern readers are **anonymity** and **pseudonymity.** The term *anonymity* means "to have no name" (from Greek *a-*, "without," "no," and *onoma*, "name"). An anonymous writing is a writing whose author is not known; it literally has no name. The term *pseudonymity* means "to have a false name" (from Greek *pseud-*, "false," and *onoma*, "name," thus "under a false name"). A pseudonymous writing is a writing that is falsely attributed to a person, usually well known, venerated, or famous; it literally has a false name.

Modern readers are quite familiar with the notions of plagiarism and copyright, which are moral and legal issues. (Debates about downloading copyrighted music from the Internet and cheating on exams easily illustrate the problem.) Although many ideas believed to be original have been thought before, and there are many cases of literary and musical creativity that use earlier work, it is nonetheless also true that some ideas are, or at least appear to be, new. Today a writer's ideas are said to belong to that writer. They are "intellectual property." No serious modern writer would normally think of being intentionally anonymous or pseudonymous.

Attitudes were different in the ancient Mediterranean world. Ancient peoples did not have the same notion of intellectual property. To be sure, there were cases of forgery for personal financial gain, and there were numerous condemnations of forgery. Yet, it is also true that writers wrote in others' names without motives of personal gain. Sometimes writings were anonymous because they were a prophet's or a visionary's report of what she or he experienced in an ASC and thus not considered that person's own. Writings could be associated with an another's *opinion*. Writings could have been innocently but falsely *believed* to have been written by an author and so attributed to that author. Writings could have been given authorship with the conscious intention to give them authority or to counteract some opinion thought to be false. In some cases it is difficult to be sure which reasons apply. In other cases there may have been several motives: conscious attribution to an author, belief that the author wrote, and association with the author's opinions. Indeed, in some cases—for example, the attempt to correct false beliefs—an author might compose a letter, falsely attribute it to someone in authority, and then give warnings about false writings! In this case, pseudonymity does indeed approximate modern forgery. However, it is important to realize that many ancient schools of learning existed to perpetuate the ideas of influential persons such as rabbis and philosophers (see Chapter One). Later disciples of Plato imitated his lifestyle, formed schools, and wrote books in his name. They are now called "pseudo-Socratic" and "pseudo-Platonic." Such works functioned to foster the views, newly interpreted to be sure, of their founders and to offer a particular interpretation of the founder's life. In a later chapter on historical writing, it will be important to note that ancient writers also created speeches on the basis of what they supposed or imagined should have been said on a particular occasion.

Much of the literature of the Hebrew scriptures is pseudonymous. For example, Moses was believed to have written the Pentateuch, King David is supposed to have written the Psalms, and Solomon was credited with the Proverbs. None of these views is accurate. Modern scholars hold that there were at least three Isaiah authors in the book of Isaiah, each from a different period in history. You will also recall that apocalypses written in the period before, during, and just after the rise of the Jesus Movement were attributed to ancient ancestors such as Abraham, Moses, Enoch, Daniel, and Ezra (Chapter Three). Several different genres can be attributed to the same famous person from the past, for example, the *Psalms of Solomon, the Wisdom of Solomon,* and *The Testament of Solomon.* There was also "Pseudo-Philo," an imitation of the Israelite philosopher Philo of Alexandria.

Obviously, then, there was some attempt to foster certain views and attribute them to some ancient worthy to give them authority. Pseudonymity was thus a complex phenomenon. Often writers and groups of writers revered or venerated the persons in whose names they wrote. In many cases, terms like *plagiarism* and *forgery* with their attendant notions of intellectual property do not easily fit all of these nuances of pseudonymity.

Given widespread anonymous and pseudonymous works in antiquity, it is not surprising that members of the Jesus Movement wrote anonymous and pseudonymous books. Scholars think that writings such as the *Gospel of Thomas* and the *Gospel of Peter* were initially pseudonymous, that is, attributed *by their authors* to disciples. Other gospels were initially anonymous and only subsequently ascribed to an ancient worthy. Modern scholars often collect noncanonical pseudonymous works in collections called "Pseudepigrapha" (*pseud:* "false"; *epigraphos:* "inscription"), for example, the Old Testament Pseudepigrapha. New Testament Pseudepigrapha are normally collected in what is called the **New Testament Apocrypha.**

It is well known that letters were written in Paul's name. Examples are the letters to the Laodiceans (cf. Col. 4:16) and to the Alexandrians (noted in the **Muratorian Canon**). There is a famous instance a couple of centuries later in which an Asian "presbyter" or "elder" confessed to having written forged accounts of Paul's life "out of love for Paul" (Tertullian *On Baptism* 17). In the New Testament, six letters attributed to Paul are probably pseudonymous. "Probably" because, as observed in Chapter Four, modern New Testament scholars are not in agreement about some of them. The so-called Pastoral Letters—1 Timothy, 2 Timothy, Titus—are judged by almost all scholars to be pseudonymous, Ephesians by most, but Colossians and 2 Thessalonians only by some. Although there is difference of opinion, especially in the case of 2 Thessalonians, this textbook will treat all six as pseudonymous and give reasons for this judgment in relation to each book. The three in this chapter will be considered as "deutero," that is, "secondary." Here, again, is the basic dating list on which such judgments are made.

Pauline (50–60)	Non-Pauline (70–100)	(100–125)	(70–100)
1 Thessalonians	2 Thessalonians	1 Timothy	Hebrews
1 Corinthians	Colossians	2 Timothy	
2 Corinthians	Ephesians	Titus	
Philippians			
Philemon			
Galatians			
Romans			

This chapter will take up the deutero-Pauline letters in the second column, namely, 2 Thessalonians, Colossians, and Ephesians. It will add to them the Letter to the Hebrews. Strictly speaking, Hebrews does not belong here. It does not claim to have been written by Paul, but rather was attributed to him later in the church. Its content is very different from that of the Pauline School. It is included here because it is usually thought to come from the same general period as those in the second column, and it is not quite long enough for a single chapter. We are leaving the three Pastoral Letters in the third column until a later chapter, largely because of content and chronology (see Chapter Thirteen).

SECOND THESSALONIANS

Historical Criticism of 2 Thessalonians

You will recall that 1 Thessalonians was Paul's earliest, most apocalyptic letter. He wrote it to give thanks and encouragement to the persecuted members of the Jesus Movement at the port city of Thessalonica, the capital of Macedonia. He promised them that departed brothers and sisters would join living brothers and sisters to meet the Lord in the air at the coming of the Lord.

2 Thessalonians is strikingly like 1 Thessalonians. Verbal similarities begin with the first verse and continue throughout; the same is true of stylistic peculiarities. Both letters are structurally alike, and both are heavily millennial. These facts, plus the unusual claim—indeed, the very strong emphasis—that Paul himself signed the letter in 2 Thess. 3:17 (cf. 1 Cor. 16:21; Gal. 6:11), have led some scholars to

conclude with church tradition that Paul himself wrote it. Occasionally a scholar will argue that 2 Thessalonians was written *before* 1 Thessalonians or to another place, such as Philippi.

Nonetheless, there are some very real differences between the two letters. At the level of vocabulary and style, 2 Thessalonians contains many cliches and phrases not characteristic of the letters in column 1 preceding. It omits Paul's characteristic tendency to state matters in threes. The close similarity in structure leads to the possibility of imitation. This argument becomes more convincing when it is observed that the letter even includes an expanded thanksgiving like 1 Thess. 2:13–16, which some scholars think was interpolated. The claim that Paul signed the final greeting in his own hand (3:17) cannot be determinative because such claims were also made by known pseudonymous writers; indeed, Colossians also contains one (Col. 4:18), and Colossians is even more likely pseudonymous. Pseudonymity is thus a strong possibility.

This theory is so far based on form. It gathers a little more steam when one notes that the letter's view of the coming of Christ—that it will be *delayed* until certain events happen—is quite different that that found in 1 Thessalonians. In 1 Thessalonians, the *parousia,* or coming of Jesus from heaven as apocalyptic judge and redeemer, will be soon. The end is imminent. When Paul speaks of "we who are alive, who are left until the coming of the Lord" (1 Thess. 4:15; cf. 4:17; 5:1–15), he clearly expects something to happen in his own lifetime. However, 2 Thess. 2:1–12 sets out an elaborate apocalyptic scenario of what must happen *before* that event can occur, namely, the appearance of the Anti-Christ, the apostasy, and "what restrains." Nowhere else does Paul speak this way. Not only has the apocalyptic imagery changed, but also the whole tenor and content of the expectation are different: The end is *no longer imminent.* Yet, Paul's presumably later correspondence, especially 1 Corinthians, maintains much of the eschatological perspective of the imminence of the end found in 1 Thessalonians. Would Paul have written a letter so soon after 1 Thessalonians, yet so different in his ideas about the end, and then gone back to his earlier ideas in later letters?

A notably *non-Pauline* feature of the letter is the idea that the judgment of God will result in a *reward for the persecuted members of the Jesus Movement and punishment for the persecutors* (1:5–10). To be sure, this idea is quite common in apocalyptic literature; for example, it is poetically expressed in Rev. 16:5–7 and 19:2. Yet, it is not typical of the Apostle Paul. Furthermore, 2 Thessalonians ascribes to Jesus attributes and functions that Paul himself reserves for God. This tendency was a natural result of a developing veneration of Jesus within the Jesus Movement. Thus Paul says, "Now may our God and Father himself and our Lord Jesus direct our way to you. And may the Lord make you increase and abound in love to one another . . . so that he may establish your hearts unblamable in holiness before our God and Father . . ." (1 Thess. 3:11–13). In 2 Thessalonians, Jesus Christ is put first: "our Lord Jesus Christ himself and God our Father, who loved us and through grace gave us . . ." (2:16). We also find the prayer, "May the Lord direct your hearts to the love of God and to the steadfastness of Christ" (3:5). The two types of statements are close enough together to be related, but in 2 Thessalonians, the Christology represents a slight advance in the honor and dignity of Jesus. Although the latest possible date is about 110 c.e., when Polycarp, bishop of Smyrna, quotes it (Polycarp *To the Philippians* 11:4), more likely it comes from the generation after Paul.

There is also an oral report and another letter purporting to be from Paul (2:2, 15; cf. 3:14, 17) saying that the *parousia* has already come. Because such a letter cannot be 1 Thessalonians, which expects it to be in the future, it probably represents the view of opponents. Perhaps they have interpreted the persecutions that the Thessalonians are suffering as the "day of the Lord" (2:2). Some of the Thessalonians have stopped working and are living in idleness. Do the letter and the oral report come from an alternative, rival Pauline school? In any case, a Paulinist writes 2 Thessalonians using 1 Thessalonians as a model. *The best understanding of 2 Thessalonians, therefore, is to see it as a deliberate imitation of 1 Thessalonians, most probably by a member of a Pauline school.*

Exegetical Survey

The Paulinist exhorts the community to keep the Pauline traditions, warning against opponents who teach that the *parousia* has already come. He admonishes certain members of the church not to be idle and tells them to work and earn their own living. In so doing, the author stresses a delay of the *parousia* in a way that goes beyond anything Paul himself envisages. He reveals a situation of persecution and the response to it reaching the stage we know from the Book of Revelation, a text from near the end of the first century c.e. His veneration of Jesus is a slight advance on that of 1 Thessalonians. The letter is apocalyptic and, like other millennial pieces, is meant to be a source of encouragement and hope for those who are in crisis and suffering persecution. However, the persecution context fits the generation after Paul better (see 2:1–12 following). Nonetheless, our author is clearly in the Pauline tradition and immensely dedicated to the apostle.

1:1–2: *Salutation,* a repetitive imitation of 1 Thess. 1:1.

1:3–12: *Thanksgiving,* with the awareness of persecution and the expectation that God will reward the persecuted and punish the persecutors. Paul's "faith, hope, and love" (1 Thess. 1:3; 1 Cor. 13) is missing.

2:1–12: *The problem of the delay of the parousia* is dealt with by developing what must come first: "the rebellion," the revelation of "the lawless one, . . . the one destined for destruction. He opposes and exalts himself above every so-called god or object of worship, so that he takes his seat in the temple of God, declaring himself to be God" (2:4). Satan will be involved, but someone or something "restrains" him (cf. Rev. 20:1–3), and there will be feigned signs and wonders. Such references sound like a recollection of events associated with the destruction of Jerusalem and the temple in 70 c.e., on which see Chapter One. See also Rev. 13.

2:13–3:5: *Thanksgiving and moral exhortation.* The church must hold fast to the Pauline traditions ("the things that we command," 3:4). The pattern of thanksgiving, admonition, and benediction occurs twice (2:13–16; 3:1–5).

3:6–16: *Closing appeals, rebukes, and prayer.* Considering the delayed *parousia,* the Paulinist warns: "Anyone unwilling to work should not eat."

3:17–18:   *Autobiographical   conclusion.*   Paul   wrote   autobiographical   conclusions (1 Cor. 16:21; Philem. 19; Gal. 6:11), and there is also one in Col. 4:18. However, the very strong defense here is unusual; thus it seems likely that this note may be based on Gal. 6:11.

COLOSSIANS

Church Tradition about Colossians

Statements within the Letter to the Colossians claim that the Apostle Paul wrote it (1:1; 4:18) to a Greek-speaking church (1:2, 21; 2:13) while he was in prison (4:3, 18; cf. 1:24) with several companions. These companions are named as Epaphras (4:12; 1:7), Aristarchus (4:10), Mark (4:10), Luke (4:14), and Demas (4:14; cf. Philem. 23). Thus church tradition has counted this letter among Paul's "prison letters," along with Philippians, Philemon, and Ephesians. As early as Marcion (ca. 150 C.E.), it was included as one of Paul's ten letters, and by the time of the Muratorian Canon, which most historians date about 200 C.E., it was in the canonical lists.

Historical Criticism

Among modern scholars, the authorship of the Letter to the Colossians is much debated. Many who review the evidence and arguments decide for authenticity; many decide against authenticity. The data on which the issue has to be decided are not in dispute; only the interpretation of that data is in dispute. The data and the questions they raise may be summarized as follows.

Arguments about Language and Style

The vocabulary of Colossians is not precisely like that of the seven undisputed Pauline letters. There are twenty-five words not found elsewhere in Paul and thirty-four not found elsewhere in the New Testament; the vocabulary is, to say the least, distinctive.

The awkward style of the letter is not like Paul's style elsewhere. The author overloads sentences with words, dependent clauses, synonyms, and various Greek constructions. Col. 1:9–20 (eleven verses) is only one sentence! Col. 2:9–15 (six verses) is another example.

These linguistic and stylistic features initially suggest that Paul did not write this letter.

However, several expressions and stylistic peculiarities in Colossians are found elsewhere in the New Testament only in the genuine Pauline letters. Thus some scholars argue that the non-Pauline language and style occur because the author intentionally uses the opponents' vocabulary and style (see following). More argumentation is therefore needed.

A second argument used in favor of Pauline authorship is that the extensive use of traditional material in this letter—hymns, confessions, lists of virtues, household codes, and the like—can account for most of the differences in vocabulary and style. Yet, such an extensive use of traditional material is itself not typically Pauline.

In Phil. 2:6–11, Paul does quote a hymn, and in Rom. 1:3–4, he cites a traditional liturgical formula, and so on. However, never does he quote such material to the extent that we find in Colossians. So the arguments from language and style appear to be inconclusive.

The Argument about the Absence of Typical Pauline Concepts

Several of the important concepts particularly characteristic of Paul—righteousness, justification, law, salvation, revelation, the language of "brothers" and "sisters" (besides the greeting)—are noticeably absent from Colossians. Of course, *some* of them are missing from other undisputed Pauline letters; nevertheless, the absence of these central Pauline themes in Colossians is particularly high.

The Presence of Central Ideas Not Found in the Earlier Letters

Colossians has a whole series of concepts that is either new in the Pauline corpus or a significant development over anything in the earlier letters. The most important of these concepts are the following.

1. Christology. The Christology of Col. 1:15–23 is an advance on anything found in Paul's undisputed letters. In 2 Cor. 4:4 (NEB), Christ is the "image" of God, and in Rom. 8:29, God predestines members of the Jesus Movement "to be conformed to the image of his Son, in order that he might be the firstborn within a large family." However, in Col. 1:15, "He is the image of the invisible God, the firstborn of all creation." Thus no longer does Christ reflect a likeness to which others can be conformed; rather, he is now a *true representation of God,* making visible what was invisible. He is no longer the firstborn among the believers who in part share that new birth at their baptism and will share it completely at their resurrection, but rather the *firstborn of all creation.* In 1 Cor. 8:6, *God* is the goal of creation, "from whom are all things and for whom we exist." In Colossians, *Christ* is now the goal of all creation, "all things have been created through him and for him" (Col. 1:16). In the undisputed letters Paul never reaches the pancosmic thinking of Colossians, even though in Rom. 8:19–23, he is on the way to it. If we argue that these developments in Colossians occur because the author is quoting a Christological hymn, as indeed he is, it is still true that he accepts what he quotes and that is more "divine" than anything found in Romans or the Corinthian correspondence.

2. The church as the body of Christ. In Romans (7:4; 12:5) and 1 Corinthians (12:12–31), the body, an ancient political metaphor, the gathered "body politic" of free citizens, is transformed into a religious metaphor, the body of mutually interdependent believers in the church. However, in Colossians the body of the church sounds more cosmic (1:18, 24; 2:19; 3:15), and Christ is its "head." Again, the author quotes a hymn in 1:15–20, but he accepts its distinctive view (1:24; 2:19; 3:15). The cosmic dimensions continue in Ephesians.

3. "Reconciliation." A further development from the earlier letters also applies to both Colossians and Ephesians: It is the verb that expresses the reconciling activity of Christ. "In Christ God was reconciling the world to himself" (2 Cor. 5:19) is the starting point for the developments in Col. 1:19–20 ("to reconcile to himself all things") and in Eph. 2:16 ("reconcile us both [Israelite and Gentile] to God in one body

through the cross"). However, 2 Cor. 5:19 uses *katallassein* for "to reconcile," as the earlier letters uniformly do; in contrast, Colossians and Ephesians uniformly use a different verb, *apokatallassein.*

4. Forgiveness of sins. In the undisputed letters, Paul often speaks of "sin" in the singular and usually personified with reference to a demonic power (e.g., Rom. 5–8). Colossians, however, speaks of the "forgiveness of sins" in the plural (1:14; 2:13; 3:13).

5. Eschatology. When Paul speaks of baptism in Rom. 6, he emphasizes the "eschatological reservation" (see Chapter Six), that is, the believer does not yet share the full benefits of the resurrected state. Thus, although members of the Jesus Movement have symbolically died with Christ, their symbolic resurrection with Christ is still *future:*

> we *have been* united with him in a death like his,
>   we *will* certainly *be* united with him *in a resurrection like his.*
>   (Rom. 6:5)

However, contrast Col. 2:12–13:

> you *were* buried with him in baptism in which
>   you *were* also *raised* with him through faith in the power of God,
>   who raised him from the dead. 13) And when you
> were dead in trespasses and the uncircumcision of your flesh, God *made you*
>   *alive together with him,*
>   when he forgave us all our trespasses.

A similar statement occurs in Col. 3:1: "So if you *have been raised* with Christ, seek the things that are above, where Christ is, seated at the right hand of God." Here, a subtle but very significant shift has occurred: Those who have faith and have been baptized have been incorporated into a new community with its attendant benefits: resurrection to new life.

Ethics

In Galatians, Paul's ethical ideal "in Christ Jesus" is expressed:

> no longer Israelite nor Greek,
> no longer slave nor free,
> no longer male nor female.
>   (Gal. 3:28)

Although Paul does not always maintain these norms in specific situations, he hints that the slave Onesimus should be set free (Philemon). He also balances the mutual relationship between men and women in marriage (1 Cor. 7) and supports women who had authoritative roles in his churches (Phil. 4:2–3; Rom. 16:1–3).

In contrast, Colossians and Ephesians draw on traditional "household rules" or **"household codes."** Such codes had been formulated by Aristotle and become common as guides for family relations, especially among the Stoic and neo-Pythagorean philosophers. They are also found in the writings of Josephus and Philo. "Family values" were considered to be the basis of the social and political order—just as they are today—except that their basis was dominance over submissiveness. Thus, although parents, not just fathers, were often cited, and women could be slave owners, the most common tradition from Aristotle onward stressed three family relationships that suggest more strongly male dominance: husbands over wives, parents over children, and masters over slaves:

> Wives, be subject to husbands . . . ,
> Children, obey your parents . . . ,
> Slaves, obey your earthly masters . . .

In the literature of the Jesus Movement, household codes are first found in the late first and early second centuries, that is, *in the generations after Paul.* Such literature includes the Church Fathers (1 21:6–9; Polycarp *To the Philippians* 4:1–6:3; Ignatius *To Polycarp* 4:1–6:1; *Didachē* 4:9–11; *Barnabas* 19:5–7), as well as canonical literature (Col. 3:18–4:1; Eph. 5:22–6:9; 1 Pet. 2:13–3:7; Titus 2:1–10).

Steps toward the Church as an Organized Social Institution

The most important developments in Colossians are not so much those *from* as those *toward:* developments toward the kind of thinking characteristic of the church becoming a *more routine, structured social institution.* Institutional structures are more developed in the Pastoral Letters of the early second century C.E. (see Chapter Thirteen) but are not found in the freer, more charismatic days reflected in the undisputed Pauline letters in the 50s.

1. The *diakonos* (translations: "minister," "servant," "deacon"). This term first occurs in references to Epaphras as "a faithful *minister* of Christ on your behalf" to the gospel of which "I, Paul, became a *servant*" (Col. 1:23; cf. 1:25) and finally of Tychicus, "a beloved brother and faithful *minister* and fellow servant in the Lord" (4:7). These references are a step beyond the use of the same Greek word, *diakonos,* in any of the early Pauline letters and perhaps all of the undisputed letters. In 1 Cor. 3:5, 2 Cor. 6:4, and 11:23 it is used of Paul and others as "ministers" or "servants" of God or of Christ. In two of these last three instances, the New Revised Standard Version uniformly uses the English word "servant" rather than "minister." In Rom. 13:4, 5, the word is used of the worldly governing authorities. In Rom. 15:8, it is used of Christ as a "servant" to the circumcision. In 2 Cor. 3:6, which the RSV and NRSV translate, "[God] who has made us competent to be ministers of a new covenant," the usage is closer to Colossians. In Phil. 1:1 (RSV, NRSV: "deacons") and Rom. 16:1 (RSV, NRSV: "deacon"), Paul *might* have a specific local office in view, but it is not likely, and some translators prefer "minister." However, the word in 1 Tim. 3:8–13 and 4:6 from the early second century clearly describes a specific role (office?) with specific moral and managerial qualifications. Thus the use in Colossians is on a trajectory *from* the earlier Pauline letters, perhaps through the later letters (Phil. 1:1; Rom. 16:1), *toward* the use in the second-century Pastorals.

2. Authoritative tradition. A further step away from the earlier letters and toward the Pastorals is the understanding of "Christ Jesus" as the subject of the authoritative tradition believers "received" and in which they "continue to live your lives" (Col. 2:6). Here there is an understanding of *faith as accepting authoritative tradition* as the basis for living. All this is characteristic of the literature of the Jesus Movement as it begins to develop into an institutional church. However, it is foreign to Paul himself. To be sure,

Paul accepts this role of tradition in connection with certain moral issues (1 Cor. 7:10) or liturgical practices (1 Cor. 11:23–26), but never is it the very essence of faith.

3. Baptism as circumcision. In the undisputed Pauline letters, circumcision is a rite now abandoned by members of the Jesus Movement (Rom. 2:25–29; 3:1; 3:30; 4:9–12), and baptism is the dynamic means of entrance into a new and different life (Rom. 6:3–11). In Col. 2:11, however, baptism is "spiritual circumcision." As such it formally signifies membership in the community. Although Col. 2:11–14 uses the baptismal language of Rom. 6:3–5, baptism has become more formal and does not have the "eschatological reservation" of Paul in Rom. 6. In Colossians, therefore, one can see the trajectory on the way toward 1 Peter, which says, "Baptism . . . *now* saves you, not as a removal of dirt from the body but as an appeal to God for a clear conscience, through the resurrection of Jesus Christ" (1 Pet. 3:21). Note also that the baptismal formula in Gal. 3:28, "There is no longer Israelite or Greek, there is no longer slave or free, *there is no longer male and female . . . ,*" omits the last pairing (see Col. 3:11), and thus it conforms to the male dominance of the "household codes" of the post-Pauline period.

Scholars do not always agree on all these interpretations, but the cumulative weight of the evidence is impressive and suggests pseudonymity.

The Opponents at Colossae (the "Colossians Heresy")

The city of Colossae was located in the Lycus River valley in Phrygia (the interior region of western Asia Minor [modern Turkey], about one hundred miles east of Ephesus). It was not far from Laodicea and Hierapolis, where there were also churches (Col. 4:13–17). As far as we know, Paul himself had never been there, although it was in his general area of mission activity. The letter suggests that the church at Colossae was a Gentile church (1:21, 27; 2:13).

Paul's opponents at Colossae are a subject of special interest that has generated much literature. Col. 2:16–23 portrays them as a "philosophy" in which adherents accept the "elements of the universe" (Greek *stoicheia* [cf. Gal. 4:3]) and which seems to demand "worship of angels" and Israelite cultic practices (food, drink, festivals, new moons, and sabbaths). How different from the Pauline belief about the crucified Lord who *reigns over* all the "principalities and powers" (1:16; 2:15)! This philosophy also stresses ascetic rigor of devotion, self-abasement and severity of the body, and regulations such as "Do not handle, do not taste, do not touch." We also hear of "wisdom" and "knowledge" (2:3).

What is this "philosophy"? Who held it? Who are the Colossian opponents? To complicate matters, a phrase in the Greek of Col. 2:18 is difficult to translate. It might be translated "taking his (the opponent's) stand on visions" (RSV), "dwelling on visions" (NRSV), or even "which he has seen, upon entering." The Apollo shrine at Claros, a mystery cult shrine not far from Colossae, has language like the latter translation. The term "entering" in this translation has frequently been held to refer to entering the secret sanctuary of just such a mystery cult. If this is right, the initiate might have had an ecstatic vision of the cosmos during the rite of initiation, having already been instructed in proper beliefs, especially angel worship. Another theory is that "worship of angels" in Col. 2:18 refers to a revelatory vision of entering into heaven in a mystical trance state, thus an experience in an altered state of consciousness (ASC). In other words, the initiate has an experience of worshiping with the angels in heaven.

In view of the difficulty of precisely identifying these references, it is not surprising to find a number of theories about the identity of the "Colossians heresy" and the opponents who held it. Some have suggested that the cultic regulations point to a sectarian group like that at Qumran. Others, probably more accurately, have noted parallels in the "Wisdom" speculation of the Israelite **Diaspora** or in Pythagorean philosophy. A very widespread view based on distinctive language ("wisdom," "knowledge," "fullness"), the boasting and arrogance of adherents, and the connection with the redeemer myth in the Colossians hymn (1:15–20) is that the "philosophy" is an early, undeveloped form of Gnosticism (see Chapter One). You will recall that Gnostics despaired of this world because it is believed to be under control of evil and hostile powers that have imprisoned one's true spiritual self in a material body. Gnostics sought release in the form of a true "knowledge" (*gnōsis*). This enabled the Gnostic to "know" of his or her origins from the God of Light above, his or her present status as "an alien" who is "thrown" into this world, and his or her destiny in returning to the world from which he or she originally came. Later Gnosticism developed a Gnostic redeemer myth that stated that the redeemer brought the requisite knowledge necessary for salvation. Such developed views cannot be proved as early as New Testament times. Nonetheless, many scholars think that early forms of Gnosticism existed ("proto-Gnosticism," "pre-Gnosticism"), and it will be illuminating to point to some passages from a second-century Gnostic text, the *Gospel of Truth:*

> The gospel of truth is joy for those who have received from the Father of truth the grace of knowing him, through the power of the Word that came forth from the *plērōma* (Greek *plērōma,* "fullness"), the one who is in the thought and mind of the Father, that is, the one who is addressed as the Savior, (that) being the name of the work which he is to perform for the redemption of those who were ignorant of the Father, while in the name [of] the gospel is the proclamation of hope, being discovery for those who search for him.
>
> . . . .
>
> Then, if anyone has *knowledge,* he receives what are his own and draws them to himself. For he who is ignorant is in need, and what he lacks is great, since he lacks that which will make him perfect. Since the perfection of the totality is in the Father and it is necessary for the totality to ascend to him and for each one to receive what are his own, he enrolled them in advance, having prepared them to give to those who came forth from him.
>
> . . . .
>
> Therefore, if anyone has *knowledge,* he is from above. If he is called, he hears, he answers, and he turns to him who is calling him, and *ascends* to him. And he knows in what way he is called. Having knowledge he does the will of the one who called him, he wishes to be pleasing to him, he receives rest.
>
> . . . .
>
> About the place each one came from he will speak, and to the region where he received his establishment he will hasten to return again and to take from that

place—the place where he stood—receiving a taste from that place and receiving nourishment, receiving growth. And his own resting-place is his *plēroma*.

> (*The Gospel of Truth* I, 16:31–17:4; 21:10b–25a; 22:2; 41:3b–14a [trans. Attridge and MacRae in Robinson, ed.])

It may be that the "Colossians heresy" held by the opponents was a form of syncretism that combined an early form of Gnosticism with Israelite views, for example, dietary laws, observances of religious festivals, and the Sabbath (Col. 2:16–17). As such, it would have accepted the idea of "elemental spirits (Greek *stoicheia*) of the universe." These were considered to be supernatural intermediaries between God and the world. They had to be pacified because they controlled the world and human destiny. One had to know what days were favorable or unfavorable; what was under the control of malevolent supernatural beings and therefore taboo; and what was under the control of beneficent beings and therefore permitted to the person of "knowledge" (Col. 2:20–23).

The author of Colossians counters the opponents by claiming that Christ is superior to supernatural beings because the salvation he offers is superior to that offered by Gnostic "knowledge." The author rebukes those falling into the false beliefs because they disqualify themselves from enjoying the true riches available in Christ. If the opponents' view is a form of proto-Gnosticism, the author counters by blending Pauline and proto-Gnostic ideas.

Exegetical Survey of the Letter to the Colossians

1:1–14:   *Salutation, thanksgiving, and intercession.*

1:1–2:   *Salutation,* somewhat shorter than usual.

1:3–14:   *Thanksgiving and intercession.*   In Paul's letters, and now in the Pauline School, the thanksgiving often anticipates the concerns of the letter. In verse 7, Epaphras is strongly and emphatically supported in his position in the Colossian church. Nowhere in the undisputed letters does Paul show such esteem for a fellow or sister worker as is here shown for Epaphras. The intercession fades over into the hymn venerating Christ (1:15–20). For all the periods and paragraphs in the English translations, in the Greek, 1:9–20 is one long sentence, which is not characteristic of Paul.

1:15–23:   *Belief about Christ and moral exhortation.*

1:15–20:   *The Christ hymn.*   An analysis of the structure of this hymn is found in Chapter Three. Many scholars think that originally it was not a hymn to Christ, but rather to some other redeemer figure in the Mediterranean world. Certainly the language is characteristic of the ancient biblical Wisdom myth (Prov. 8:27–30) that was taken over in certain circles of the Jesus Movement (e.g., John 1:1–3) and developed in later Gnosticism. One theory is that the hymn is an early form of the Gnostic Redeemer myth (see Chapter One). This does not mean that the language and ideas are foreign to the Jesus Movement. It simply means that the movement was eclectic, as eclectic as any other religious movement in the Mediterranean world. Thus it adopted and adapted material offered to it by its cultural environment.

The social and religious setting of this hymn is suggested by verses 12–14, which contain reminiscences of the baptism of Jesus ("beloved Son," cf. Mark 1:11) and of texts relating to baptism elsewhere in the New Testament. The dynamics of the Jesus Movement in the late first century C.E. are illustrated by a church that adapted a known hymn to a redeemer figure to express faith in Christ as *the* Redeemer and used it in baptismal rites. It is likely that the author of Colossians, wishing to focus attention on Christ as *the* Redeemer, took up such a hymn and used it in his letter.

The hymn contains many of the themes discussed earlier, that is, an exalted view of Christ (image of God, firstborn of creation, participation in creation, head of the body, firstborn of the dead, one in whom fullness dwells), as well as the important theme of reconciliation.

1:21–23: *Moral exhortation.* The Christological hymn is followed by an exhortation to the readers based on it. This concludes on the note of Paul as a "servant" (*diakonos*) of this gospel, which leads into the next section.

1:24–2:5: *The apostolic role.* As noted, Colossians has a somewhat more advanced concept of *diakonos* than we find in the undisputed Pauline letters (see earlier). This points to a higher level of formal church organization. Also in this section the Paulinist is more formal than Paul, but he continues to emphasize Paul's preparedness to suffer in and for the ministry of the church (cf. 2 Cor. 1:5–6; 4:10). Moreover, there appear to be some characteristic Hellenistic ideas. The word of God is the hidden "mystery" now made manifest; the believer knows "the riches of the glory of this mystery"; is warned and taught "in wisdom"; and becomes "mature." Although "mystery" turns up in the Dead Sea Scrolls, it is more characteristic of Hellenistic religion in general and is used to interpret Jesus' parables in Mark 4:10–11. Yet, new emphases characteristic of the Jesus Movement are also to be found: "the word of God," "the energy that he (Christ) powerfully inspires within me," and "faith in Christ." This passage is a good example of how different religious traditions came together in the period after Paul.

2:6–23: *Warning against the false teaching.*

2:6–7: *The nature of faith.* In Col. 2:6, the Paulinist takes up an Israelite technical term, the verb "he walks," "he goes" (Hebrew *hālak*). This is the Hebrew verb from which the scribes in Greco-Roman Israel took their term for the way one *ought* to walk or behave, that is, legally binding rules or decisions (Hebrew *halākāh*). Paul is using a technical term when he says, "As you therefore have received Christ Jesus the Lord, so *walk* (NRSV note 1) in him." "Christ Jesus" has become the subject of tradition handed on formally in the church and received as authoritative by the church member. There is here a transition from the notion of tradition found in the undisputed Pauline letters (1 Cor. 11:23; 15:3: "receiving," "delivering") to the notion of faith as the acceptance of the *authoritative* tradition about Jesus Christ. Thus faith is the guide, the way in which the follower of Christ should "walk." The letter thus moves toward a more fixed morality, a sort of *halākāh* for a developing Jesus Movement.

2:8–15: *Warning against the false teaching as doctrine.* The central element in true faith is "Christ Jesus" as the subject of authoritative tradition. Thus the Paulinist must claim that Christ Jesus as correctly understood is superior to the spiritual powers and beings who figure so prominently in various Hellenistic religions. This he does by contrasting the "human tradition" concerning "elemental spirits of the universe" with the concept of Christ as the supreme spiritual being. In Christ "the whole fullness (*plērōma*) of the deity dwells bodily." He "is the head of every ruler and authority." He has proven successful in making available to those who believe in him a salvation infinitely superior to anything offered by the "rulers and authorities" over whom Christ triumphed on his cross.

An interesting aspect of this section, again, is its syncretism, that is, the dynamic blend of developments of Pauline ideas (which the author clearly knows well) with ideas taken from Hellenistic religions. The term *plērōma*, a key word in the Christology of this passage, is a technical term in later Gnosticism. Furthermore, Col. 2:11–14 must be contrasted with Rom. 6:4–11. The differences in the two passages are sufficiently great for us to regard the Colossians passage as written by a Paulinist rather than by Paul himself. Yet, the author has understood Paul and is legitimately developing his insights to meet the needs of a later generation. Similarly, Col. 2:15 develops for still another situation a metaphor Paul uses in 2 Cor. 2:14.

2:16–23: *Warning against the false teaching as practice.* The Paulinist now argues against the religious and ethical practices encouraged by the false teaching at Colossae. He opposes Israelite dietary laws, festivals, and Sabbath-day observances that the false teaching encourages: "These are only a shadow of what is to come, but the substance belongs to Christ" (2:17). This statement is a further example of the syncretistic blending of Hellenistic and Israelite ideas in the deutero-Pauline Jesus Movement. The distinction between shadow and substance (with the worldly being the shadow and the eternal being the substance) is Hellenistic and indeed Platonic. However, the reference to "what is to come" sounds like a note from traditional Israelite apocalyptic hopes. The Paulinist further argues against "visions" and the "worship of angels" by claiming that they are not proper to the church that is the body of Christ and wholly dependent on its head. Here the church's need for an integrated structure and a disciplined organization comes to the fore and necessarily pushes out the charismatic freedom of an earlier day typified by Paul and his revelatory visions. Finally, in this section the author again takes his point of departure from Paul's idea of dying with Christ in baptism. He holds that entrance into the community sets the initiate to the Jesus Movement free from service to those very same elemental spirits to which Christ died. Thus he appropriates Paul's view that through baptism the believer dies to the Israelite Law and its demands (Gal. 2:19–21; Rom. 6) and applies it to a later and different set of circumstances.

3:1–4:6: *Moral exhortation.* There now follows a long section of moral exhortations. Col. 3:1–4 accepts the claim characteristic of religious fervor that sometimes surfaced in the Hellenistic wing of the Jesus Movement (and apparently a part of the false teaching at Colossae), namely, that the enjoyment of the power of the resurrection life *already in the present.* Paul rejected this view (1 Cor. 15; Rom. 6:5: the "eschatological reservation"). Yet, the Pauline follower maintains that there is still something that will be known only in the future: "When Christ who is your life is revealed, then you also will be revealed with him in glory" (3:4). A similar note of traditional Pauline eschatology is sounded in 3:6, "the wrath of God (the final judgment) is coming."

Col. 3:5 and 8 are traditional vice lists common in Hellenistic moral literature and in Paul (cf. Gal. 5:19–21; Rom. 1:29–31). Taking off old and putting on new clothes, here used in ethical exhortation, are also common metaphors in baptismal contexts (*GTh* 37) and found in Paul's letters (Gal. 3:27; Rom. 13:14). However, the Paulinist's comment in 3:11, "no longer Greek and Israelite, circumcised and uncircumcised . . ." takes up only two of the three lines of the Gal. 3:28 baptism formula (cf. 1 Cor. 12:13). The missing part, "no longer male and female," is consistent with the patriarchal norm of the household code in the following section, 3:18–4:1.

Col. 3:18–4:1 is a "**household code,**" a literary form typical in Hellenistic moral instruction. Household codes stressed three pairs: Women must be subordinate and obedient to men, children must be subordinate and obedient to fathers, and slaves must be subordinate and obedient to masters. These codes were taken up and adapted in the deutero-Pauline literature and illustrate the emergent institutional church (see earlier discussion). However, they are not found in Paul's undisputed letters and present a clear contrast to Paul's view of women in Gal. 3:28, as just noted in connection with Col. 3:11. The Colossians household code is the earliest and most precise version in the New Testament. This version is especially concerned about the obedience of slaves to masters, the longest of the pairs. Except for the references to "the Lord" and the "Master in heaven," it has no elements unique to the Jesus Movement. If we accept the view that such codes do not represent Paul's view of women and the family, and perhaps slavery, they become evidence of assimilation in the movement to the dominant norms of its culture.

4:7–18:   *Final greetings and benediction.*   Note the references to Onesimus (Philemon), Mark (4:10), and "Luke the beloved physician" (4:14).

EPHESIANS

Church Tradition about Ephesians

The Letter to the Ephesians is attributed to Paul (1:1; 3:1), who says that he is "a prisoner for Christ Jesus" (3:1). Church tradition thus assigned Ephesians to Paul's "prison letters," along with Philippians, Philemon, and Colossians (see earlier). About 150 C.E., Marcion included this letter as one of Paul's ten letters, but he thought that it was written to the Laodiceans (mentioned in Col. 4:16), perhaps because the words "in Ephesus" were not in some of the earliest manuscripts of Ephesians (see following discussion). Yet, it is also found in the **Muratorian Canon,** which most historians still date as early as 200 C.E.

Historical Criticism

2 Thessalonians and Colossians are attributed to Paul. Although the preceding discussion favors pseudonymity, scholars still debate whether Paul wrote them. In the case of Ephesians, however, the difficulties with Pauline authorship are more widely acknowledged. Here are some key problems.

Language and Style

More than ninety words in Ephesians do not occur elsewhere in the Pauline corpus. Many of them appear in later New Testament writings and in the literature of the Christ-believing communities immediately following the New Testament period.

Where typical Pauline terms do appear, they are often used in different combinations and with different shades of meaning than in the undisputed Pauline letters. Further, synonyms are clustered together in an un-Pauline manner. Eph. 1:19, for example, has four separate words for "power." There is also a passion for long, involved sentences, going far beyond anything even in Colossians. Examples are Eph. 1:15–23 (nine verses), 3:1–7 (seven verses), and 4:11–16 (six verses). These sentences are so complex that some modern English translations have broken them up and made several sentences out of them. In general, the style of Ephesians is not terse, but slow and somewhat tedious, thus unlike that of Paul.

Relationship to Colossians

Ephesians constantly quotes and develops Colossians, as a couple of statistics show. About one-third of the words in Colossians are found in Ephesians. Of 155 verses in Ephesians, 73 have verbal parallels in Colossians; indeed, only short, connected passages from Ephesians have no parallel in Colossians (e.g., Eph. 2:6–9; 4:5–13; 5:29–33). In Chapter Three, one of the clearest examples of Colossians as a source for Ephesians was illustrated, Col. 4:7–8 and Eph. 6:21–22. Here are two more examples:

Col. 3:12–13

As God's chosen ones, holy and beloved, clothe yourselves with compassion, kindness, *humility, meekness*, and *patience*, 13) *bearing with one another* and, if anyone has a complaint against another, forgive each other; . . .

Eph. 4:1–2

I therefore, the prisoner in the Lord, beg you to lead a life worthy of the calling to which you have been called, 2) with all *humility* and *meekness,* with *patience, bearing with one another* in love. . . .

Col. 3:16–17

Let the word of Christ dwell in you richly; teach and admonish *one another in* all wisdom, and with gratitude *in your hearts* sing *psalms and hymns and spiritual songs to God.* 17) And whatever you do, in word or deed, do *everything in the name of* the *Lord Jesus, giving thanks to God the Father* through him.

Eph. 5:19–20

. . . addressing *one another in psalms and hymns and spiritual songs,* singing and making melody to the Lord *in your hearts,* 20) *giving thanks to God the Father* at all times and *for everything in the name of* our *Lord Jesus* Christ

This dependence on a previous letter is unparalleled in the Pauline corpus. It is reinforced by observing that Ephesians depends verbally on *other* Pauline letters, except 2 Thessalonians. Of course, the same person could have written the two letters, Colossians and Ephesians, in much the same language within a short time; this is the usual way of arguing for the Pauline authorship of Ephesians. However, it is highly unlikely that Paul would have reached back into his memory for constant reminiscences of earlier letters written to meet quite different needs. Thus the dependence argues for pseudonymity.

Theology

Ephesians contains the familiar Pauline theme of justification by faith (2:5, 8–9). In many respects, however, the ideas in Ephesians are simply not like those of Paul. That is so even if Colossians were to be counted among the genuine Pauline letters, which is unlikely.

1. Eph. 2:19–22, where members of the Jesus Movement are called ". . . members of the household of God, built upon the *foundation of the apostles and prophets,* with Christ Jesus himself as the cornerstone . . . ," is inconceivable as a statement of the apostle, even if Col. 2:7 were to be included among the Pauline letters, and much more so if it is not.

2. The reference to the "holy apostles" as recipients of special insights into "the mystery of Christ" in Eph. 3:4–5 is not Pauline. Paul never distinguishes apostles in this way and never regards them as "holy" in a way that other members of the Jesus Movement are not.

3. Ephesians uses the word "church" (*ekklēsia*) for the *universal church* (Eph. 1:22; 3:10, 21; 5:24, 25, 27), whereas in the undisputed Pauline letters and even in Colossians (4:16), the term is used for the local congregation meeting in a house-church. Indeed, in Ephesians there is a striking movement toward understanding the church as the "Great Church" very characteristic of later centuries but not typical of Paul.

4. In Eph. 3:4–6, the "mystery of Christ" is already *the unity of Israelites and Gentiles* in the body of Christ. In the undisputed letters, Paul was still fighting for this synthesis. Moreover, the idea of "church" (ecclesiology) engulfs the view of Christ (Christology). Paul of the undisputed letters does not think this way.

5. In Eph. 2:16, *Christ* is the subject of the verb "to reconcile," whereas in Col. 1:20, *God* is the subject. In Eph. 4:11, *Christ* appoints the apostles and prophets, whereas in 1 Cor. 12:28, *God* does this. In general, Paul's emphasis on the death of Christ is not central; what replaces it is an emphasis on the exalted Christ.

6. With respect to eschatology, Ephesians never mentions the *parousia* of Jesus or final judgment, as does Paul, and *believers are,* as in Col. 3:1, *already resurrected* (Eph. 2:6), in contrast to Paul (Rom. 6:1–5; 1 Cor. 15).

Literary Character of Ephesians

Finally, Ephesians is not really a letter in the usual Pauline sense. Observe the distinction made in the discussion of "Paul as a writer of letters," that the letters are written because of some *particular* conflict or set of problems, or at least an occasion in Paul's life (Romans). All of the concrete, localized features are missing in the Letter to the Ephesians, even though Paul had clearly made Ephesus a kind of "mission headquarters" and had spent considerable time there.

Much more could be said—see also the lack of address following—but this is enough to show why on literary, source, and theological grounds, even scholars who accept Colossians as Paul's letter regard Ephesians as pseudonymous. For those who accept Colossians as pseudonymous, this conclusion is all the more likely.

The Occasion for the Writing of Ephesians

If Ephesians was *not* Paul's letter, it must now be determined, if possible, why it was written. Two factors related to pseudonymity are very important.

The Lack of an Address

Although the opening salutation sounds like a typical address, the oldest and best manuscripts (P46, B, etc.), the text of Marcion, and some of the late second-century Fathers, *omit any reference to Ephesus* in the first verse. As noted, Marcion said the letter was written to the Laodiceans. The conclusion of Text Critics is that a scribe added the words "at Ephesus" later during the course of the transmission of the text. Thus modern Greek editions and most translations of the book also omit "at Ephesus" in the first verse. Because titles of the letters such as "To the Romans" or "To the Ephesians" come from the period when Paul's letters were collected, these titles (superscriptions) cannot be used to argue for the destinations of the letters. In relation to the omission of "at Ephesus" in the first verse, a point about Greek is important. In Greek, the word *kai* can mean either "and" or "also." The original address might have read, "To the saints who are *also* (*kai*) faithful in Christ Jesus" (no place name). However, because "who are" in Paul's letters is normally followed by a place name, readers to assembled members of house-churches could have understood this first verse to mean, "To the saints who are . . . [fill in the blank] *and* (*kai*) faithful in Christ Jesus." If so, they would have supplied the place name before *kai*: "To the saints who are [at X] *and* faithful in Christ Jesus." Another related possibility is that the letter was *intended* to be a general letter in which the reader supplied the place name. In other words, it would have been an "open letter" addressed to any church. Either way, the original appears to have had no specific address, a phenomenon that is very uncharacteristic of Paul. Because some later manuscripts do have "at Ephesus," it may be that someone wrote "at Ephesus" in the margin, and it was then thought to be part of the text.

Relationship of Ephesians to Other Letters Attributed to Paul

It is possible to carry the "open letter" possibility further. We have already indicated that Ephesians knows and makes extensive use of Colossians. In addition, Ephesians shows familiarity with all the other letters attributed to Paul except 2 Thessalonians. Particularly interesting parallels are:

Eph. 1:4–5	=	Rom. 8:29
Eph. 1:10	=	Gal. 4:4
Eph. 1:11	=	Rom. 8:28
Eph. 1:13	=	2 Cor. 1:22 (cf. also Eph. 4:30)
Eph. 3:81	=	1 Cor. 15:9–10

Eph. 4:11	=	1 Cor. 12:28
Eph. 4:28	=	1 Cor. 4:12
Eph. 5:2	=	Gal. 2:20 (cf. also Eph. 5:25)
Eph. 5:15	=	1 Cor. 6:9–10
Eph. 5:23	=	1 Cor. 11:3

These parallels—there are many more—combined with the problems of verse 1 suggest the further theory that Ephesians might have been written as a general *introductory summary* of Paul's letters when they were first brought together into a collection. Again, this would have happened sometime in the last quarter of the first century. Although this theory is not universally accepted, it gets some reinforcement by three facts: The other letter elements in Ephesians are very formal, not personal; this letter contains no greetings to or from individuals; and there are statements that sound as if the writing was not written to people who knew Paul personally (1:15: "I have heard of your faith . . ."; 3:2: "for surely you have already heard"). The theory of a "circular letter" that introduces Paul's views should not be ruled out. In any case, it is hardly likely that Ephesians was written by Paul to a location that had become his headquarters.

Exegetical Survey of Ephesians

1:1–23: *Salutation, thanksgiving, and intercession.*

1:1–2: *Open salutation.* This is typically Pauline, but, as just noted, it lacks the usual addressee, which might have been supplied.

1:3–14: *Blessing.* In Greek, this whole section is one long sentence with an amazing conglomeration of interesting expressions, all of which results in a great variety of English translations. Yet, the thanksgiving does make clear the general concern of the "letter," the unity of the whole cosmos in Christ, an anticipation of which is the church.

1:15–23: *Thanksgiving.* All persons everywhere should grasp the magnitude of the hope that awaits them in the church of which Christ is the head. The myth of the world as the body of the "cosmic man" has been transferred to the body of the church, with the resurrected Christ in heaven as the head.

2:1–3:21: *The glory of the one holy church.*

2:1–10: *By grace members of the Jesus Movement are saved through faith.* The basis for the glory of the church is that all persons, including the writer and his readers, are brought into it because they are saved by grace through faith. As in Colossians (3:1), believers already participate in the resurrection.

2:11–22: *Israelite and Gentile are reconciled in Christ.* The readers were once Gentiles, "without Christ, being aliens from the commonwealth of Israel, and strangers to the covenants of promise, having no hope and without God in the world," but now they are included. The rhetoric of this section, which develops the idea that members of the Jesus Movement are citizens in a great city-state, the church, is magnificent. They have been reconciled and brought into the one body of the church by the work of Christ.

In this section there is probably a Christological hymn that has been reworked. A possible translation is:

[For]
he is our peace,
who has made both one
and has broken down the dividing wall of the fence
[the enmity],
in order to make the two into one new man in him
[making peace]
and to reconcile both in one body to God
[through the cross].

The poetic arrangement has been lost in the text itself because the author is both quoting and interpreting. One interpretation is that the words we have put in brackets were added. This method of interpretation by addition is also found in Paul. For example, he interprets the phrase "became obedient unto death" of the hymn in Phil. 2 by adding another phrase, "even death on a cross" (see Chapter Three). It is possible that the hymn in Eph. 2 originally had a first stanza celebrating the redeemer's participation in creation, as does the hymn in Col. 1:15–20. The stanza that is in fact quoted deals with reconciliation, a major theme in the deutero-Pauline phase of the movement. Christ has broken down the dividing wall between Israelites and members of the Jesus Movement (the wall that separates Israelites and non-Israelites in the temple precincts at Jerusalem? The proto-Gnostic barrier between heaven and earth? Now it refers to the Law.). Thus one man is created out of two. In a series of images the church is viewed as a holy temple of the Spirit.

3:1–21:   *Intercession and doxology.*   The basic structure of this passage is a prayer-style intercession (interceding with God for people) begun in 3:1, broken off at 3:2, resumed in 3:14–19. The intercession is a prayer for the Gentile members of the church, that they may know all the riches that accrue to the believer. Eph. 3:2–13 is a parenthetical interruption concerning Paul's mission to the Gentiles, and it testifies to the importance of Paul's work among the Gentiles to a later generation, as the Acts of the Apostles also does. The section concludes with a doxology, or concluding praise of God, in 3:20–21.

4:1–6:20:   *Ethical exhortation.*   Now comes the characteristic element of exhortation.

4:1–16:   *The unity of the faith and of the church.*   As in 1 Cor. 12 and Rom. 12, there is mention of gifts of the Spirit in the church; however, the church is again viewed as the body of which Christ is the head (cf. 1:22–23).

4:7–32:   *The necessity to put off the old and to put on the new.*   Again, this language suggests transformation to a new life in the rite of baptism.

5:1–20:   *Instruction to shun immorality and impurity.*   This section develops negatively from a "vice catalogue" (verses 3–7) and then positively from a "virtue catalogue" (verses 8–20). Such lists of vices and virtues are, like the household codes, characteristic of Hellenistic moral philosophy (see Chapter Three; see 1 Cor. 6:9–11; Gal. 5:19–23; Col. 3:18–4:1).

5:21–6:9: *The **household code.*** This passage is a household code such as that found in Col. 3:18–4:6, but it is more developed. The major theme of unity, expressed as peace and unity between Israelites and members of the Jesus Movement, leads to unity and mutuality within the household of God, which is the Paulinist's chief metaphor for the community. Thus Paul's metaphor of the church as Christ's body and the image of the church as the bride of Christ (5:31–33) are combined with the cultural norms of the household code. However, the author's interpretation interprets these norms "theologically." In other words, "reverence for Christ" (verse 21) means obedience to Christ; then, obedience to Christ becomes the model for obedience of wives, children, and slaves to husbands, parents, and masters. With respect to husbands and wives, this obedience is somewhat softened by Jesus' command to love your neighbor as yourself (Lev. 19:18) and Christ's self-giving love. Nonetheless, unity and obedience go together, and obedience is still the norm. Social practice has its theological justification.

6:10–20: *The "panoply passage": The armor of God and warfare images.* "Putting on" armor might recall the putting on/taking off of clothing in baptism in 4:7–32.

6:21–24: *Closing reference to Tychicus and benediction.*

SOCIAL-HISTORICAL FACTORS: THE DEUTERO-PAULINE LITERATURE AS REPRESENTATIVE OF A DEVELOPING JESUS MOVEMENT

Jesus lived during the first third of the first century; Paul lived out his adult years and wrote during the middle third of the first century; and the deutero-Paulines were written in the last third of the century. These documents clearly show the continuing influence of the apostle in the churches he founded and influenced, but also they hint at the beginnings of an institutional church that was advancing beyond Paul.

The problems of the Paulinists in the last third of the first century were engrossing, and so were the ways in which they were solved. From 2 Thessalonians, a major problem was the *delay of the parousia.* Jesus should have already come on the clouds of heaven to judge the world by now, but he had not done so. The Paulinist who wrote 2 Thessalonians met this problem by virtually repeating what Paul wrote in 1 Thessalonians, which he clearly knew well and obviously regarded as a tract for his own time but also as an answer to the new problems he and his group were now facing. The Paulinist tried to make sense of this delay—other events must happen first. In the meantime, it is necessary to live and work in the world.

A second problem came to the fore in Colossians, namely, *the increasing challenge of ideas that became characteristic of second-century Gnosticism.* At this early stage, the church did not meet these Gnostic ideas head on, but freely adapted them. The church sought to meet the early Gnostic challenge by claiming that "anything you can do we can do better." Later the conflict grew more intense, and the church developed more specific responses: canon, creed, apostolic succession, and monarchial episcopate.

A further insight into the situation of the generation after Paul also can be gained from 2 Thessalonians. The church now had to come to terms with *the increasing possibility of persecution,* especially with the awareness that its distinctive teachings might bring it into conflict with stricter forms of Israelite faith, a legal religion in the empire. Historically, the first *major* persecution of the Jesus Movement was localized at Rome when the emperor Nero in 64 C.E. blamed its adherents for the fire. However, the movement began to face other threats, real and imagined, down to the period of its legal acceptance in the early fourth century C.E. We catch a glimpse of this already in 2 Thessalonians.

Another insight in the last third of the century is continuing reflection about *the more-than-human nature of Jesus as Messiah (Christology).* The Paulinist of 2 Thessalonians attributes to Jesus what the previous generation had attributed only to God. The Paulinist of Colossians develops particularly the idea of Christ as active in creation, as embodying in himself the fullness (*plērōma*) of the godhead, and as reconciling everything unto himself as the head of the body, the church. The Paulinist of Ephesians develops further the theme of Christ as reconciler and head of the body, the church.

Directly related to this advance is the notion that *Christ is the head of the body, the church.* When Paul speaks of the church as the body of Christ (Rom. 12:5; 1 Cor. 12:12–26), the expression is a metaphor for the mutual interdependence of brothers and sisters in the church. In contrast, when Col. 1:18 and Eph. 1:23 and 5:23 claim that the church is the body of Christ, that Christ is its head. It is a "cosmic" theme. The social implication of this claim is the move toward all-encompassing reality, a claim that implies great power.

Yet, related to the notion of Christ as head of the body is *the theme and language of reconciliation.* Christ as reconciler is already a major theme in Paul's undisputed letters (Rom. 5:10; 2 Cor. 5:18–19). 2 Cor. 5:19 says, "in Christ God was reconciling the world to himself, not counting their trespasses against them." Colossians and Ephesians develop this insight. Col. 1:19–20 says, "For in him all the fullness of God was pleased to dwell, and through him *to reconcile* to himself all things, whether on earth or in heaven . . ." Eph. 2:16 states, "[that he] might *reconcile us* both to God in one body through the cross." In Colossians and Ephesians, reconciliation advanced beyond a metaphor to an expression of expectation of what is possible in the real world.

Another development is the *increasing adaptation to Hellenistic religious and philosophical literary themes.* Paul uses Hellenistic literary forms and metaphors; indeed, the Philippians hymn may be a Hellenistic hymn that Paul interprets for the Hellenistic Christ believers of the Jesus Movement. The hymn in Col. 1:15–20 appears to be a literary product adapted in the Jesus Movement as well. However, in Colossians and Ephesians as a whole, the influence of Hellenistic religious myth is much more pervasive.

Still another development is that *ethical reflection in the deutero-Paulines* shows signs of cultural assimilation. Paul's undisputed letters never cite a household code with its model of husband/parent/master dominance. His own statements about slaves and women often do not correspond to cultural norms about the family and often must have caused tension in traditional households. In contrast, both Colossians and Ephesians emphasize household codes. Thus the movement is making adjustments that have political implications. It accepts the norm that a well-ordered house is crucial for a well-ordered society, and by accepting this norm it implies accepting the necessity of outsiders' views about socio-political norms as such.

The more-developed themes of the cosmic body and reconciliation lead to the major theme of Ephesians: *the one universal church.* Paul normally uses the word *church* to refer to a house-church at a particular place; only secondarily is it linked to churches at other locations. For example, in the Corinthian correspondence he addresses "the church of God that is *in Corinth . . . together with* all those who in every place call on the name of our Lord Jesus Christ" (1 Cor. 1:2; cf. 2 Cor. 1:1). For the author of Ephesians, "church" refers primarily to the cosmic church. It speaks of ". . . the church, which is his body, the fullness (*plērōma*) of him who fills all in all" (1:22–23). The Jesus Movement is no longer perceived as simply small, localized groups meeting in house-churches, but rather as the one all-encompassing social unit that represents God to all peoples and by means of which all peoples come to God. In Ephesians, it is possible to *begin* thinking about an institutional church, that is, the Church with a capital *C* (see Chapter Thirteen). A major theme of Ephesians is the one body of Christ. This self-understanding was to characterize and sustain the church through the long centuries of the Middle Ages.

The preceding discussion of Ephesians calls attention to the rhetoric of Eph. 2: 11–22. It is important not only because the author polishes his phrases, but also because it is at the heart of his concern: the unity of Israelite and Gentile in the church of God. Jerusalem has now fallen to the Romans, the temple is no more, there is no longer a Jerusalem community from which emissaries can come arguing that the Christ believers must also be Israelites. The circumstances that lead to Paul's battles in Galatia, Philippi, and elsewhere are no more, and the author of Ephesians can celebrate in sonorous phrases the unity of Israelite and Gentile in the one church of God. Yet, even here we catch a glimpse of a major concern of the Jesus Movement in the post-70 developing period: *the necessity to come to terms with the destruction of the Jerusalem temple.* The section concludes:

> So then you are no longer strangers and aliens, but you are citizens with the saints and also members of the household of God, built upon the foundation of the apostles and prophets, with Christ Jesus himself as the cornerstone. In him the whole structure is joined together and grows into a holy temple in the Lord; in whom you also are built together in the Spirit into a dwelling place for God.
> (Eph. 2:19–22)

This passage illustrates what will become so important in the future. It shows that *the church is "built upon the foundation of the apostles and prophets."* Christ Jesus is "the cornerstone." The days of the free, charismatic "enthusiasm" that provided the dynamism for the beginning of the churches are past. We have the first glimpse of the firm and careful structure that enabled the church to survive and, indeed, to mold the centuries that were to come in the West.

THE LETTER TO THE HEBREWS

We have studied the seven undisputed letters and the three deutero-Pauline letters. The three Pastorals will be considered in Chapter Thirteen.

The fourteenth and final "letter" that church tradition later came to associate with Paul was called simply "To the Hebrews." Curiously, however, it was not a letter in the usual sense and was probably not sent simply "to the Hebrews," that is, Israelite members of the Jesus Movement. Indeed, "Hebrews," as it is often called, is not easily related to the rest of the Jesus Movement. Like the scriptural figure Melchizedek of whom it speaks, it is "without father, without mother, without genealogy" (Heb. 7:3; cf. Ps. 110:4) and virtually also "without offspring." In the New Testament, it has neither antecedents nor descendants and is not part of any other known movement. Yet, it is a text of great excellence and, when the church eventually associated it with Paul, it made its way into the canon of the New Testament, although with great difficulty.

Early Traditions about Hebrews

The earliest traditions about the book called "To the Hebrews" come from the very late second and early third centuries C.E. Clement of Alexandria (ca. 150–215 C.E.), head of a catechetical school in Alexandria, Egypt, argued that Paul wrote "To the Hebrews" in the Hebrew language but did not mention his own name because its recipients, conservative Israelite believers, were hostile to "the apostle to the Gentiles." He proposed that Luke translated Hebrews and published it in Greek for the Greeks, thus giving it its fine, Lukan-like Greek style (Eusebius *Ecclesiastical History* 6.14.2–4). The second Alexandrian authority, Origen (185–253 C.E.), head of the same catechetical school, argued that Hebrews was Pauline but also acknowledged that its style and composition were more "Greek-like" than Paul's. He also noted that some critics believed that it was written by another Clement, a bishop at Rome, who first quotes it (*1 Clement*). Other ancient writers said that Luke composed it. Origen offered what has become the most famous statement about Hebrews from antiquity, "But who wrote the letter, God really knows" (cf. Eusebius *Ecclesiastical History* 6.25.11–14). Despite the hesitation of these great Alexandrian critics, however, the view that Paul himself wrote it gradually gained ground in the churches of the East. Thus Hebrews is found after Romans in the important third-century Egyptian papyrus of Paul's letters, P⁴⁶. When Bishop Athanasius of Alexandria circulated his famous Easter Letter of 367, he included Hebrews among the twenty-seven books of the New Testament canon (see Chapter Two and Appendix Two).

Meanwhile, Church Fathers in the West remained skeptical. Hebrews was not included in New Testament lists of Irenaeus of Lyons and the Roman presbyter Gaius. It was also missing from the list of books used in worship at Rome about 200 C.E., the **Muratorian Canon.** At Carthage in northern Africa, Tertullian (155–220 C.E.), the "father of (Western) Latin theology," suggested that it was written by Paul's early companion, Barnabas (Tertullian *On Modesty* 20). It did not begin to be generally accepted as Paul's until the late fourth century, when the great Augustine supported the canon of the eastern bishop Athanasius, and the famous Vulgate translator Jerome added his assent. In the following century, Pope Innocent I concurred (405 C.E.). In short, the battle for Hebrews was won in the West only after three centuries of doubt. Once established, the common opinion of East and West persisted until the sixteenth century, at which time Martin Luther surmised that Hebrews might have been written by the learned Alexandrian apostle Apollos (1 Cor. 1:12; 3:4–6, 21; Acts 18:24–28), a view that has been attractive to some modern scholars.

General Historical Criticism about Hebrews: Author, Date, Place

As the ancients discerned, there are many reasons to doubt that Paul wrote this book. First, the author is never mentioned by name in the book, which is not at all typical of Paul or even deutero-Pauline letters. In those books, Paul is mentioned as the sender or cosender in the salutation. Hebrews does mention "our brother Timothy," but "Timothy" is a common name, and it occurs in a closing that seems intended to make the book look more letter like (13:22–25), so much so that this closing has sometimes been considered an addition to the book. Second, as the ancients realized, the very carefully composed and studied Greek of Hebrews is not Paul's spontaneous, volatile, contextual Greek. Third, Hebrews has been traditionally grouped with the New Testament letters, and it certainly closes like a letter. However, it has no salutation, greeting, or thanksgiving. Rather, it alternates theological (Christological) and ethical exhortations in a manner quite unlike Paul. Thus, it is not formally a letter. Fourth, the author of Hebrews considers himself the recipient of apostolic tradition in a way Paul scarcely would have done (2:3). Fifth, and most important, the content of Hebrews is totally different from the content of Paul's letters and even the other letters of the Pauline School. Not only does it lack Paul's important ideas of justification, the body of Christ, and the like; but also, its major theme, Jesus as the great heavenly High Priest who himself is a sacrifice, is never found in the other Pauline letters, disputed or not. Indeed, the theme is unique to the whole New Testament. In short, the ancient Alexandrian Origen was no doubt correct: The person who wrote Hebrews is known only to God. It is safe to call it anonymous.

Anything else we know about the person or persons from whom the book was sent or those to whom the book was addressed must be inferred by literary analysis of the book itself (**internal evidence**), and there are many theories about these matters. The writer of Hebrews speaks very frequently of the Israelite sacrificial system. Yet, he thinks about it in terms of substance and shadow, of reality and copy of reality, which are thoroughly Greek ideas stemming ultimately from Plato and typical of Philo of Alexandria. For example, Heb. 9:1–5 describes the "earthly sanctuary . . . a tent," but 9:11 says that "the greater and more perfect tent not made with hands, that is, not of this creation," appears with Christ. Heb. 9:23–24 speaks of "the heavenly things" and the "copies of the heavenly things," of "a sanctuary made with hands, a copy of the true one." Such ideas suggest that the author of Hebrews should be regarded as an Israelite in the Diaspora, like Philo, but one who has joined the Jesus Movement. Apparently his Hellenistic Greek way of thinking about his Israelite heritage has prepared him to interpret that faith as the revelation of the reality of which Israelite faith was always a copy.

The letter-like conclusion to Hebrews contains greetings from "those from Italy" (13:24). The phrase is debated. Some interpreters have concluded that the book was written *from* Italy and, because it also contains material about the Jerusalem temple, that it was written to Jerusalem. Yet, it has often been concluded that the phrase "those from Italy" refers to Italians who were living someplace else and were writing home, in which case Hebrews was written *to* Italy, perhaps Rome, from some unknown location. This solution gains some support from the fact that Clement of Rome wrote a letter from Rome to the church in Corinth in 96 C.E., and in it he cited passages from Hebrews (*1 Clement* 17:1 [Heb. 11:37]; 36:2–5 [Heb. 1:3, 4, 5]). Yet, we also recall that this book had great problems at Rome being accepted as having been written by Paul. Did the Romans have a tradition that it was not Paul's work?

The title "To the Hebrews," as noted, was present when the best manuscript of Paul's letters, P[46], was copied in the third century; thus the book was current by about 200 C.E. Although the term *Hebrews* is the old term for Israelites who spoke Hebrew (or Aramaic?), the book was clearly written to members of the Jesus Movement (6:1–3) who practiced baptism (10:22) and who were thought to be in danger of falling away from their faith (e.g., 6:1–12; 10:23–32). "Hebrews" could therefore have meant Hebrew- or Aramaic-speaking Israelite members of the Jesus Movement who remained loyal to worship in the Jerusalem temple. This meaning would correspond to the term *Hebrews* in Acts 6 where it refers to those who came into conflict with the more radical "Hellenists," Greek-speaking Israelites who rejected temple worship, like Stephen. It would also correspond with Paul's use of the term *Hebrew* in Phil. 3:5 and 2 Cor. 11:22.

Correspondingly, two views attempt to explain the superscription or title for this book. The first view is that it was added to an anonymous book because a Hellenist like Stephen sought to correct certain Hebrew beliefs (cf. e.g., 2:1), in which case the book might well have been written to exhort more traditional Israelite members of the Jesus Movement. This view is especially interesting because Hebrews contains certain themes that are similar to Stephen's ideas as portrayed by the author of Acts, especially the wandering people of God (Acts 6–7). The second view is that, given the likelihood that the recipients of "To the Hebrews" included Gentiles, the title was added in the early church because the subject matter of the book is concerned throughout with Israelite ritual. The latter seems more likely, but either way, the title seems to have been added to the book.

As for date, Hebrews must have been written before 96 C.E. because in that year Clement, bishop of Rome, referred to passages from it (*1 Clement* 17:1; 36:2–6). The other end of the temporal spectrum has been debated. Some scholars have argued that Hebrews must have been written before 70 C.E. because its concentration on the sacrificial system implies that the Jerusalem temple (destroyed in 70 C.E.) was still standing. Although this suggestion would push it back to a date closer to Paul, it nonetheless seems unlikely in the light of internal evidence in the text. Heb. 2:3 speaks of the message of salvation as being "declared at first by the Lord, and . . . attested to us by those who heard him," and Heb. 13:7–8 implies that "those who spoke to you the word of God" had died some time ago. Such references, similar to those found in Luke 1:1–4, suggest that the writer belonged to the generation of the author of Luke-Acts, about 85–90 C.E.

Other internal factors reinforce this view. At some earlier time the recipients had experienced persecution (10:32–35; cf. 12:3–13), which might be a reference to the Neronian persecution at Rome in 64 C.E.—especially if it was written to Rome. Moreover, comments about the sacrificial cults do not refer to the *actual* Jerusalem temple, but rather to its very ancient predecessor, the movable tent sanctuary, or tabernacle, which the Hebrew scriptures place in the time of Moses (cf. Exod. 25:9; 33:7). In fact, a case can be made that the author's argument was derived wholly from scripture, not a knowledge of the actual Jerusalem temple still standing in his own day. Moreover, as we noted, the discussion of the tent sanctuary is in terms of a heavenly reality and of an earthly copy of that reality, of heavenly substance and earthly shadow (9:1–5, 11). This kind of thinking is characteristic of Hebrews, and it shows that the author is not concerned with the physical fact of the temple, but rather with the spiritual reality of which the Old Testament tabernacle was always only a shadow and copy. Pattern and copy are, again, Platonic- and Philonic-sounding associations. In short, it is likely that Hebrews should be dated sometime between 70 and 96 C.E.

In general, it is likely that "To the Hebrews" was an anonymous writing by a Israelite of the **Diaspora.** It was probably written to a community that contained both Israelite and non-Israelite members of the Jesus Movement, perhaps at Rome. Its aim was to correct some of the views of that community. It is likely that the book was written sometime after 70 but before 96 C.E.; in the lists of this textbook, it is dated in the 70–100 C.E. period.

Social-Historical Context of Hebrews

The social-historical context of Hebrews is difficult to determine because references are quite vague and general. The recipients of Hebrews can recall earlier preaching; some of their leaders have died; thus they seem to have been members of the Jesus Movement for some time (2:4; 13:7). In days gone by, the community was marked by love and charismatic miracle working (2:4). It has also suffered, and some are still in prison (10:32–34), although there have been as yet no martyrs

(12:4). Yet, believers in the Jesus Movement appear to be in danger of tiring of their faith (5:11–14; 12:3). They are tempted to unbelief (3:2–14), and some appear to have renounced their faith altogether (6:4–6; 10:26–31; 12:15–17). To the author, they are clearly in need of exhortation, guidance, and comfort, and that is precisely what they receive:

> "Take care, brothers and sisters, that none of you may have an evil, unbelieving heart that turns away from the living God. But exhort one another every day . . ." (3:12–13a).
>   ". . . let us go on toward perfection . . ." (6:1).
>   "Let us hold fast to the confession of our hope without wavering . . ." (10:23).
>   ". . . let us consider how to provoke one another to love and good deeds, not neglecting to meet together, as is the habit of some, but encouraging one another . . ." (10:24–25b).
>   ". . . be made perfect" (11:40b).
>   "Endure trials for the sake of discipline" (12:7).
>   "Pursue peace with everyone, and the holiness without which no one will see the Lord" (12:14).
>   "Let mutual love continue" (13:1).
>   "Do not neglect to show hospitality to strangers . . ." (13:2).
>   "Remember those who are in prison, as though you were in prison with them; those who are being tortured, as though you yourselves were being tortured" (13:3).
>   "Let marriage be held in honor by all, and let the marriage bed be kept undefiled . . ." (13:4).
>   "Keep yourselves free from the love of money, and be content with what you have . . ." (13:5).
>   "Remember your leaders . . . and imitate their faith" (13:7).
>   "Do not be carried away by all kinds of strange teachings . . . by regulations about food" (13:9).
>   "Obey your leaders and submit to them . . ." (13:17).

Such sayings represent general ethical exhortation backed by the ideal of Christ's purity or perfection. Thus, as Christ is perfect and the leaders have faith to be imitated, so the followers are encouraged to go on to perfection. Clearly, there is also a group dimension to the sayings, especially those that exhort the community to peace, love, good deeds, hospitality, and obedience to leaders. Finally, as in many Christ-believing communities, the tendency to desire riches is decried.

Language, Style, and Form of Hebrews

Hebrews is known as a letter but, as already indicated, its only formal letter-like characteristic is its conclusion, which contains a benediction, final remarks, and greeting (13:22–25). Hebrews is better understood as a homily or sermon deeply rooted in scripture. Some recent study has suggested that it might be a "homiletic midrash" (a special Israelite sermonic interpretation) on the Old Testament Ps. 110.

This psalm contains one of the two instances where the high priest Melchizedek, a key figure in the book, is mentioned in the scriptures (Ps. 110:4; cf. Gen. 14:17–20; see following). Although this midrash theory may go too far, it is an intriguing suggestion. The reason is that Melchizedek is mentioned in the **Dead Sea Scrolls,** especially in an eschatological midrash on Lev. 5:9–13, which claims that Melchizedek is "the priest of the Most High" and is a heavenly angelic being (11Q Melch [11Q 13]). In Hebrews, the sermon alternates what God has done in Christ with moral exhortation, and it represents the kind of discourse the church was developing to meet the needs of its members. It is not a missionary sermon written to convert nonmembers of the Jesus Movement; rather, it is directed to believers who are in need of guidance and comfort.

Intellectual Environment and Thought of Hebrews

Hebrews uses the Greek **Septuagint,** although it contains some variants from the Septuagint text types that have survived. The book contains many explicit quotations, especially from the Psalms, notably Ps. 2 and 8 and especially Ps. 110. It also alludes to scripture frequently. All of this is done without great concern for the original contexts of the passages, which was not unusual in antiquity. What counts are the author's new interpretations. We may also note the famous "praise" passage in chapter 11. It refers to many heroes in scripture. We shall note further uses of scripture later.

The importance of scripture, especially ideas about the tabernacle and the priesthood and sacrifice, points to Israel; yet, Hebrews uses the **Septuagint,** and its notion of heavenly pattern and earthly example sounds very Platonic and thus Greek. A wide variety of opinion exists about its intellectual environment. Some scholars suggest that the heavenly/earthly dualism of Hebrews, along with its Melchizedek theme, is reminiscent of the **Dead Sea Scrolls,** which has the midrash on Melchizedek; if so, the book sounds Israelite. Others emphasize connections with the philosophy of Plato. Still others have looked at the very Platonically oriented Hellenistic Israelite philosopher, Philo of Alexandria, and still others have gone further and seen in Hebrews an early form of Gnosticism. One area of connection is the view of the Hellenists who, as represented by Stephen, held that the ancient nomadic Hebrews worshipped a God who could be moved about in a tent or tabernacle, who therefore should not be confined to a temple "made with hands" (Acts 6–7). Still others have noted that the opposition to the Jerusalem temple and certain other themes point to connections with the Samaritans, who had a competing temple on Mount Gerizîm!

There is no simple explanation for the intellectual environment of Hebrews. Ideas about dualism and Melchizedek are similar to some of those found in the Dead Sea Scrolls, but many other features of belief found in the scrolls are not present in Hebrews. Platonic and Philonic ideas are clearly present but do not easily fit with Hebrews' eschatology. Contacts with Samaritan and Israelite themes of the Hellenist Stephen type are present as well. What becomes obvious is that the environment represents a very syncretistic Diaspora Israelite form of the Jesus Movement.

The heart of the theology of Hebrews is its fascinating view that Jesus as the Christ is the preexistent, exalted, Son and also the great heavenly High Priest according to the priesthood of Melchizedek, one who is "without father, without mother, without genealogy" (Heb. 7:3; cf. Ps. 110:4). This Christology is not always systematic and logical. Heb. 1 opens with the affirmation that the Son of God is preexistent and functions as the divine agent in the creation of the earth. The passage proceeds with what is probably a traditional Christological hymn (1:3; see Chapter Four):

> Who, being the reflection of God's glory and
> the exact imprint of God's very being,
> Sustaining all things by his powerful word,
> Having made purification for sins,
> Sat down on the right hand of the
> Majesty on high.

The hymn is based in part on the widespread Israelite myth of the descent from heaven to earth and reascent to heaven of God's divine Wisdom (see Chapter Three). Thus terms like "reflection" and "exact imprint" are known from Wisdom literature and from Philo of Alexandria; they describe Wisdom's, or the Son's, or the Logos' close relation to the Deity (e.g., Wisd. 7:26; Philo *On Special Laws* 3.161; cf. John 1:1–16; Phil. 2:5–11, etc.). The "purification for sins" describes the work of Christ in Heb. 9 and 10 and is closely related to the dominant sacrificial themes and the heavenly High Priest in the book. Thus some scholars think that this theme might have been added to an already existing hymn by the author of Hebrews.

The one who "sat down on the right hand of the Majesty on high" describes Christ's exaltation and is derived from Ps. 110:1:

> The Lord says to my lord,
> Sit at my right hand,
> Until I make your enemies your footstool.

This verse is quoted in 1:13 at the end of a string of scriptural quotations (1:5–13). Ps. 110:1, the most quoted passage in the Jesus Movement (cf. e.g., Mark 12:35–37; Acts 2:34–35), provides the imagery for the position of power of the resurrected and exalted Messiah/Son/Lord: sitting at God's right hand (e.g., Mark 14:62; Acts 2:34–36). Its imagery is implied again in 8:1, 10:12–13, and 12:2, and in every instance the author of Hebrews links it with Jesus' death (12:2), which is interpreted as a sacrificial purification for sins (8:1; 10:12).

Verse 4 of this same psalm is one of the two scriptural sources for Hebrews' central theme that Christ is the great heavenly High Priest according to the order of Melchizedek:

> The Lord has sworn and will not change his mind,
> "You are a priest forever according to the order of Melchizedek."

In Gen. 14:17–24, the second place where Melchizedek is mentioned in the scriptures, he appears to Abram the Hebrew (Gen. 14:13). Melchizedek is also called "King of Salem" and priest of the "God Most High" (Hebrew *ēl-elyōn* [Gen. 14:18]; "God Most High" is now known to have been a name for a Canaanite deity). He is thus a "priest-king." In the account, Abraham has been victorious in regaining the possessions of Lot in war; so Melchizedek produces bread and wine and blesses Abraham, whereupon Abraham offers him a tenth of the possessions. When Melchizedek says he does not want possessions, but only the persons, Abraham then swears an oath to God, now also called by Melchizedek's God's name, "God Most High," that he does not want the tenth of possessions either, lest Melchizedek think that he is greedy.

Six points are important for understanding Hebrews' interpretation of this figure. First, the name "Melchi-zedek" in the Hebrew language can mean either "My king (*melchi*) is righteous (*zedek*)" or "King of Righteousness." Second, the Hebrew consonants of the town of S(h)alem in "King of S(h)alem" are *S(h)-l-m*. However, these are the same consonants of the Hebrew term *shalōm*, "peace." Because the Hebrew vowels were not written in this period, and the letter for the "s" sound was at that time also the letter for the "sh" sound, the *written* consonants *S(h)-l-m* could be mean either *Salem* or *shalōm*. The author of Hebrews takes up the second meaning. He points out that the "King of Righteousness" ("Melchi-zedek") is also the "King of *Peace*" (7:2). Third, even though it is absolutely imperative in Israel for the priest's parentage and genealogy to be known—purity has to be maintained (see Chapter One)—nothing is said in the two Melchizedek passages of the Hebrew scriptures about his genealogy; Melchizedek suddenly appears and disappears. This point is also not lost on the author of Hebrews. Fourth, you will recall that a major function of priests was to sacrifice to atone for the sins of the people.

The fifth point is especially important from a historical and religious perspective. In 11Q Melchizedek in the **Dead Sea Scrolls,** Melchizedek is presented as a heavenly being of exalted status who appears in the last stage of history as a warrior and chief of the heavenly armies. He is also a judge and high priest who acts on God's behalf as his viceroy. He will overcome the evil powers, free the human "sons of light" from the evil Beliel, execute final judgment, and function as high priest in the **Day of Atonement** ritual. His role parallels the role of the archangel Michael and also the high priest. Thus he is the most important angel, a viceroy of God. It should be noted that there are expressions of Melchizedek as a heavenly figure in other ancient Israelite texts (especially 2 Enoch 71–72), a Nag Hammadi text called *Melchizedek* (*NHC* 9, 1), and it continues in Israelite and Christ-believing traditions.

Although the parallels are not exact, there are enough to suggest that the author of Hebrews shares various Melchizedek traditions and puts many of them together in a very special way. In Heb. 1, messianic passages are cited to show that Jesus is God's Son who is higher than the angels. Ps. 2:7 ("You are my son . . .") comes first (1:5a). This psalm verse is quoted in the synoptic gospels as God's words to Jesus identifying him as his Son at the baptism and transfiguration (cf. Mark 1:11; 9:7). Ps. 2:7 is also combined with 2 Sam. 7:14 ("I will be a father to him and he shall be a son to me"), Hebrews' second quotation (1:5b), in another text of the Dead Sea Scrolls (4Q174 [4QFlor]). Both are further combined with Ps. 110:1, Hebrews' last quotation (1:13), in Luke-Acts; there it also identifies the resurrected and exalted Lord (Acts 2:33–35) or Son (13:33) at God's right hand in heaven. The third passage, Deut. 32:43, is cited to show that the angels worship the Son (1:6). The fourth, the Septuagint of Ps. 104:4, shows the impermanence of the angels, in contrast to the fifth, Ps. 45:7–8, which shows the permanence of *God's* throne, thus implying an identification of the Father with the Son (1:8–9). The sixth, Ps. 102:26–28, stresses that the creation is impermanent in contrast to the Creator, again implying the Son's agency in creation. The seventh returns to Ps. 110:1, quoted in full. Thus the Son is superior to all the angels, and all the heavenly beings must serve him.

In Heb. 2, the argument is continued with Ps. 8: The Son of Man was temporarily made lower than the angels (Ps. 8:6a) but was then crowned with glory (Ps. 8:6b). Thus he became like "his brothers" and was tested by the devil, but he defeated him (cf. Melchizedek's defeat of Beliel in 11 QMelch). Thus he became the merciful and faithful High Priest before God "to make a sacrifice of atonement for the sins of the people" (2:17). This theme is developed in Heb. 4:14–5:10 by reference, again, to Ps. 2:7, Ps. 110:1, and Melchizedek, but the climactic passage is Heb. 7, where the main elements of the Gen. 14 account are given, including the meanings of his name, "King of Righteousness," and "King of Peace." With hints of Ps. 110:4 in the last line, Heb. 7:3 reads like a hymn about Melchizedek:

> Without father, without mother, without genealogy,
> having neither beginning of days nor end of life,
> but resembling the Son of God,
> he remains a priest forever.
> (Heb. 7:3)

His permanence is highlighted; because of it, this new priesthood is superior to the old Levitical and Aaronic priesthoods, as well as the Moses who in Philo is also a high priest (cf. 3:1–6). According to Ps. 110:4, God has sworn it by an oath (7:17, 20). Moreover, as heavenly Son of God, he is superior also to Melchizedek, who was a type of the Christ, but not yet the Christ himself. It is this priest whose sacrificial death and purifying blood are "once for all" (7:27; 9:12, 26; 10), yet he perpetually atones for the sins of humankind. He does so in the heavenly temple. It establishes a new and lasting covenant between God and his people (Heb. 8–10; cf. Jer. 31:31).

The Structure of Hebrews

A major structural feature of Hebrews is the careful alternation between its message about Christ and ethical exhortation. It has a distinctively sermonic form. It has no introduction, but rather plunges immediately into its Christ message. A simplified structure is as follows:

Christ message	Jesus as Son of God and savior, 1:1–3:6
Ethical exhortation	3:7–4:13

Christ message	Jesus as High Priest, first statement of the theme, 4:14–5:10
Ethical exhortation	5:11–6:20
Christ message	Jesus as High Priest, development of the theme, 7:1–10:18
Ethical exhortation	10:19–39
Christ message	Jesus as the pioneer and perfecter of faith, 11:1–39
Ethical exhortation	12:1–13:17
Closing benediction and greetings	13:18–25

Exegetical Survey of Hebrews

1:1–3:6: *First aspect of the Christ message: Jesus as Son of God and savior of all.* The preacher dwells on Jesus as Son of God and as savior of all, and, further, as the merciful and faithful High Priest who has expiated the sins of the people. Yet, human beings are flesh and blood, and so Jesus had to share their nature. Sharing human nature and sufferings, he has not only redeemed human beings but also can help them because he understands their temptations.

Here the Christology of Hebrews is highlighted. On the one hand, Jesus is the heavenly High Priest, making the true sacrifice for the sins of the people; on the other hand, he is of the same flesh and blood as those he sanctifies (2:5–18). In Israel, the high priest represented the people before God; this he could do because he was one with them. Yet, he also represented God before the people. Thus he came to be thought of as partaking in some way in the aura of divinity, especially when he came out of the most holy precinct of the temple, the Holy of Holies. He and he alone might enter this most sacred area and even then only one day in the year, the Day of Atonement. Against this background it is easy to see how the writer of Hebrews, who regards Jesus as fulfilling both functions perfectly as compared to the imperfect fulfillment in the person of the Israelite high priest, came to use the language he does.

Heb. 2:1–4 contains a short section of exhortation. Note also the warning against falling away from the faith in 2:1, a theme repeated many times in Hebrews. Heb. 2:3–4 implies that the author is not from the first generation of the Jesus Movement.

3:7–4:13: *First major section of ethical exhortation.* This section is built around Ps. 95:7b–11. Verses 7b–10 are concerned with the journey of the Israelites through the wilderness, or what has been called by some modern scholars "the wandering people of God." The section interprets it as God's test of this people. The people failed this test by rebelling against Moses, hence their failure to reach the perfect "rest" of God (verse 11). People in the Jesus Movement must not similarly fail, and if they can but endure, if they persist in their belief, they will inherit the promised "rest," in which they will share the glory of God's own Sabbath when God rested after the creation (cf. Gen. 1:1–2:4). The priesthood of Melchizedek in Ps. 110:4 is cited in 5:6, 10.

4:14–5:10: *Second aspect of the Christ message: Jesus as High Priest* (first major statement of the theme).

5:11–6:20:   *Second section of ethical exhortation: The new maturity.*   Chapter 6 may be based on a traditional catechism for the Jesus Movement.

7:1–10:18:   *Third aspect of the Christ message: Jesus as High Priest*   (the major development of the theme). The major Christological theme of Jesus as High Priest is now developed in various ways, each designed to exhibit the superiority of the high priesthood of Jesus over what it superseded.

7:1–28:   *Jesus is High Priest after the order of Melchizedek.*   The shadowy figure of the priest-king Melchizedek blesses Abraham the father of the Israelite people in Gen. 14, and this is interpreted as indicating that his order is superior to that of any Israelite priesthood. A special emphasis is on God's oath in Ps. 110:4 (see earlier).

8:1–6:   *Jesus has made the one perfect sacrifice.*   It is eternal and takes place in the heavenly sanctuary.

8:7–13:   *He is the mediator of the new covenant that replaces the old, obsolete one.*

9:1–14:   *The priesthood of Jesus is the pure perfection of which the Levitical priesthood had been only the promise.*   The Day of Atonement ritual is mentioned in verse 7, thus leading to the sacrificial blood of Christ (9:11–14, especially verse 12).

9:15–22:   *The new covenant is superior to the old because the death that ratified it is a death redeeming human beings from their transgressions under the old.*

9:23–10:18:   *Shadow and substance in regard to the sanctuary and the sacrifice.*

10:19–39   *Third section of ethical exhortation.*   Because of Christ, members of the Jesus Movement can enter the Holy Place purified and should encourage each other to love and good works.

11:1–39:   *Fourth aspect of the Christ message: Jesus as the pioneer and perfecter of faith.* The writer's definition of faith indicates his Diaspora Israelite heritage. Faith as "the assurance of things hoped for" reflects the Israelite model of promise and fulfillment, and faith as "the conviction of things not seen" reflects the Greek model of appearance and reality. The idea of listing the heroes of the faith is Israelite. In ben Sira 44:1, we read, "Let us now praise famous men, and our fathers in their generations," and there follows a list from Enoch to Simon the high priest (Sir 44:16–50:21). The heroes listed in Heb. 11 were all faithful to God, but they did not receive the promise. God had reserved the promise for believers in the Jesus Movement.

12:1–13:17:   *Fourth section of ethical exhortation.*

13:18–25:   *Benediction and greetings.*

STUDY QUESTIONS

1. What is pseudonymity? What are some of the similarities and differences between 1 Thessalonians and 2 Thessalonians? What is the major problem in 2 Thessalonians? What is its author's advice about it? What are some of the major reasons why Paul probably did not write Colossians? Is this letter as "liberating" as, say, Gal. 3:28? What are household codes, and how do they relate to the developments of the church? Who were the opponents in Colossians? How does the "Colossians hymn" portray Jesus?

2. What are some of the main features of the deutero-Pauline phase of the Jesus Movement in general?

3. Why does the Letter to the Hebrews have that name? Why is it difficult to imagine that Paul wrote it? When was it written? What are some of the issues about its language, style, and especially intellectual environment? How does the author use scripture? Who was Melchizedek? Why does the author use him? What is Hebrews' view of Christ as the heavenly High Priest?

Wadsworth/Thomson Learning

Photo 8.1   The western wall in Jerusalem. The larger stones remain from the western wall of the first-century Herodian Temple; the smaller stones come from Moslem additions beginning in the seventh century. Jews return to this site to mourn the Temple's destruction by the Romans in 70 C.E. and pray for its restoration (note the separation of men and women). The synoptic gospels, including the Gospel of Mark, are usually dated in part by the Roman destruction of the Temple (Mark 13:14; see also Matt. 24:15; 22:7; Luke 21:20, 24b; 19:43–44). The mount above is a holy site for Jews, Christians, and Moslems.

CHAPTER EIGHT

THE GOSPEL OF MARK: A MYSTERIOUS APOCALYPTIC DRAMA

THE GOSPEL

In Chapter Two, it was observed that in broad terms there are four kinds of literary genres in the New Testament: the gospel, the letter, the chronicle or ancient "history," and the apocalypse. Chapters Four to Seven focused on the second of those genres, the letter, in connection with the Apostle Paul and his successors (along with Hebrews). This chapter focuses on the first genre, the gospel.

First, it will be helpful to discuss the word. The English word *gospel* comes from the Old English *godspell,* "good news." *Godspell* was a translation of Latin *evangelium,* which was a translation of Greek *euangelion,* the term for "good news" in the New Testament. The Greek for "good" is *eu* (as in *euphoria,* "a good feeling"), and the verb *euangelizomai* is "I announce" (from which English gets the word *angel*). Where did the members of the Jesus Movement get this word? Two major answers have been proposed.

The first answer is that it comes from the **Septuagint (LXX).** In the Septuagint there are references to the oral proclamation of good news about Yahweh's (God's) liberating rule of peace. Especially pertinent is the following verse from the prophecy attributed to Isaiah (actually from deutero-Isaiah, or Isa. 40–55):

How beautiful upon the mountains
are the feet of the messenger *who announces* (LXX: *euangelizomenou*) peace,
who *brings* good *news* (LXX: *euanglizomenos*),
    who announces salvation
    who says to Zion, "Your God reigns."
               (Isa. 52:7)

The first members of the Jesus Movement were Israelites who proclaimed the message about Jesus the Messiah as the "good news" of salvation. The prophecies about the coming royal Messiah, attributed to Isaiah, were extremely important. One possible source for the noun *gospel* came from these sacred books, particularly this passage, which uses the verb and follows it with the proclamation of the reign of God, also the central teaching of Jesus (see Chapter Fourteen).

The second answer is also plausible. Not long before the birth of Jesus, the Greek term for *gospel* was being used in Roman inscriptions for the proclamation of good news of a new age of peace brought by the rule of the emperor. The following example is the **Calendar Inscription of Priene** (in Asia Minor), ca. 9 B.C.E.

> Whereas the Providence which has guided our whole existence and which has shown such care and liberality, has brought our life to the peak of perfection in giving to us *Augustus Caesar,* whom it [Providence] fills with virtue for the welfare of mankind, and who, being sent to us and to our descendants as a *savior,* has put an end to war and has set all things in order; and whereas, having become visible [as a God], Caesar has fulfilled the hopes of all earlier times . . . not only in surpassing all the *benefactors* who proceeded him but also in leaving to his successors no hope of surpassing him; and whereas, finally, that the birthday of the god [i.e., Caesar Augustus] has been for the whole world the beginning of *the gospel* (Greek *euangelion*) concerning him; (therefore, let all reckon a new era beginning from the date of his birth, and let his birthday mark the beginning of the new year).

In this inscription the term *gospel* is associated with the most powerful ruler on earth, the emperor, believed by many of his subjects to be divine. Thus he is called "god," "savior," and the greatest of all benefactors, or patrons, of his subjects (**patron/client** relations). He ends war and social chaos and brings peace on earth. His birthday marks the new age. The social, political, and religious implications of this inscription are enormous. Beliefs about a divine god-savior-ruler-benefactor and peace-bringer in the emperor cult (see Chapter One) might have suggested the term *gospel* to early Christ believers. By implication, Jesus would have been a competitor with the emperor himself!

Staying with the *word* for a moment, a related question is how *gospel* was used in the Jesus Movement. In much of the New Testament, it refers primarily to the *oral* proclamation of the good news of salvation. For the author of the Gospel of Matthew, it refers to Jesus' oral preaching. In the letters of Paul, it refers to Paul's oral message about Jesus' death and resurrection. Was this oral usage of the term then transferred to the *written* story of Jesus? The matter was probably a little more complicated.

You may recall from Chapter Two that in the second century C.E. superscriptions were inserted into the manuscripts of gospel collections to separate and distinguish one gospel from another. They read only "According to Matthew," "According to Mark," and the like. Thus the term *gospel* was not part of these superscriptions; modern translators added it. To be sure, the very first verse of Mark reads, "The beginning of the *gospel* [Greek *euangelion*] of Jesus Christ, Son of God." However, that verse does not easily solve the problem. Some scholars hold that a later copyist inserted it to mark off the Markan story from the previous story of

Matthew before the superscriptions were added. The argument makes some sense because no other New Testament gospel is actually *called* a "gospel," but there is no manuscript evidence that the verse was added. Yet, a problem *still* exists. Some scholars think that the expression "the *beginning* of the gospel" requires the verse to refer only to the first story, the story about John the Baptizer. Furthermore, the first known instance of calling these books "gospels" *outside* the New Testament was not until the middle of the second century C.E., when Justin Martyr wrote, "For the apostles in the memoirs composed by them, which are called *gospels* . . ." (Justin Martyr *Apology* 1, 67). In short, it may be that "gospel" was *never* the title for written stories about Jesus' life until the second century when the superscriptions were added in relation to then-current beliefs about their authorship.

Nonetheless, the custom of calling Mark, as well as Matthew, Luke, and John "gospels" is not likely to change. This textbook continues to call these books by their traditional name "gospel." But what sort of literature it is?

WHAT IS A "GOSPEL"?

It is always helpful for understanding any piece of literature to know its genre. For example, if one interprets satire as serious drama, misunderstanding will inevitably result (for this point in relation to **Form Criticism,** see Chapter Two). Similarly, if a gospel is interpreted as, for example, a modern historical biography, misunderstanding will inevitably result. Second, genres tend to function in particular ways in historical and social settings. Understanding the genre, then, is a step toward understanding a historical and social setting—and vice versa! Form, function, and social-historical context go together. This point was already made in Chapter Four by observing that Paul modified the typical letter genre to express his own point of view as a Christ believer in the Jesus Movement. In Chapters Ten and Twelve, similar observations will be made about the "history" and "apocalypse" genres. Thus it will be imperative here to ask about the gospel genre and its social function.

What is a "gospel"? Apocalypses, but especially letters and histories, were well known and widely used genres in the ancient world; those who could write in the Jesus Movement simply developed variants of them. The gospel as a narrative story about Jesus, however, seems to be different.

Perhaps it is wise to begin with a theoretical dimension, the nature of classification itself. With respect to literature, does a set of similar writings have enough similarity in structure, content, length, and emotional tone to be classified as a common type? If you like to focus on what is common, you will be more likely to see a genre. However, if you like to focus on what is different, you will be more likely to deny that there is a genre. In relation to the stories about Jesus, the Gospel of John is rather different from **the synoptic gospels.** Does it really conform to the genre? Redaction Critics like to point out that each of the three synoptic gospels has different emphases. Should they be classified together? Finally, are there other accounts of heroes and heroines outside of the New Testament. Do all of these accounts conform to a common genre? Or are they a new and unique creation of the Jesus Movement?

As you might deduce, the question about the gospel genre has a history. In the nineteenth and early twentieth centuries, the Gospel of Mark was usually classified as an ancient "biography" (Greek *bios*) comparable to the lives of Socrates or Apollonius of Tyana. Modern biographies usually have highly interwoven plots, complicated characters, and character development. The ancient writers did not write this sort of biography; indeed, they seem to have had little interest in character development. Yet, they did compose biographies about gods and heroes (Greek *bios*), and often they are full of miracles like the gospels. Is the "gospel" an example of this genre of ancient literature?

In the 1920s, Form Critics challenged the *bios* view. They continued to claim that the Gospel of Mark is "unique" but judged that it is mainly a collection of oral traditions strung together like pearls on a string. In the past few decades, many Redaction and Literary Critics have modified this view by arguing that the gospel authors were not just oral tradition collectors, but rather creative authors who totally remolded their oral and written traditions. Yet, again, the gospel seemed to be unique in comparison with other ancient writings. However, the pendulum has swung again. The view has recently gained ground that gospel writers included various subgenres (e.g., miracle collections, sayings collections, and infancy gospels) and that they must have adapted *some* known forms of communication for their story to communicate (**Historical, Genre, and Social Science Criticism**). Thus the quest for some ancient genre prototype for the gospel has resurfaced, especially in relation to the Gospel of Mark.

Here, in brief, are a few theories. One is that the Gospel of Mark looks like an *"aretalogy,"* that is, an account in which a hero is characterized by a life of "virtue" (Greek *aretē*), especially marked by wise teachings, miracle working, and martyrdom at the hands of a tyrant. However, some scholars question whether this genre really existed, especially because no ancient narrative text is called an "aretalogy." Another theory is that Mark seems to be a variant of *Greek tragedy* because it dramatically moves from complication (blindness of the disciples; conflict) to crisis (messiahship; opposition) to resolution (death; resurrection). Yet, the gospel's portrait of a miracle-working Galilean who debates with opponents, as well as its tone, does not quite fit the Greek tragedy. Similarly *"tragicomedy"*—a tragedy that actually has a good-newsish, hopeful ending—has also been found wanting. The Hellenistic *"romance"* novel, which mixes history and myth, sounds interesting, but it has weird and fanciful elements not characteristic of the gospels. *Martyrologies*— stories of the martyrdom of some brave person or persons—seem to have a very different tone, too. *Midrash,* a type of Israelite commentary that interprets sacred scripture (the Old Testament), seems too narrow to describe Mark. The possibility that the gospel was a *lectionary* of readings for a church calendar is fascinating but exceedingly difficult to demonstrate. Another recent theory, that Mark is developing a "biography of the prophets," perhaps with the aid of biographies about Roman officials ("office biography"), is also interesting but has not yet gained credence. Mark as parable is suggested because of its mysterious revelation and open-ended conclusion, "for they were afraid"; however, its narrative is too long, and the story implies what the outcome *should* be, at least in the future.

Another attempt, Mark as apocalyptic myth, requires a little definition. *Myth* usually refers to a narrative story that takes place in some distant time and place, a story that expresses the origins of the world and the social order, as well as fundamental human experiences, in difficult-to-understand, but symbolically rich, language. *Apocalyptic,* as you recall, refers to experiences (ASCs), movements, and literatures dealing with revelations from the other world about a transformation of society, indeed, the whole world, thus holding out a better life for those who labor under persecution and oppression. If myths of origin imagine a "paradise," apocalyptic myths transfer the paradise to the future. They draw their symbolism from the realm of impending social disruption and cosmic catastrophe, which gives expression to the hope for a better social life and a new world for the oppressed.

Is the Gospel of Mark an apocalyptic myth? It is not an apocalypse in the sense of the Book of Revelation. However, it does contain a "little apocalypse" (Mark 13) and, in the light of that chapter, as well as certain passages—for example, the coming Kingdom of God and Son of Man—it contains some very powerful apocalyptic images. If the Markan author was not clumsy (this theory has also been suggested!), we must conclude at this point that the he used the literary techniques of apocalyptic writers but that he combined them with elements of other genres to create the gospel. To a degree, it is "apocalyptic." But is it a myth? Certainly the story has language about evil, sin, suffering, alienation, failure, hope, and much more in symbolically rich and meaningful ways and in narrative form. It lays a foundation for truth, morals, and being a true disciple. Those features sound like myth. Yet, it is not rooted in just some dim and distant past or future; it is about a historical person and is also rooted in *recent* "historical" events. In some respects it is like a drama in three acts. In Markan language, each act involves people who "preach" and who are "delivered up."

1. John the Baptizer "preaches" and is "delivered up" (Mark 1:7, 14).
2. Jesus "preaches" and is "delivered up" (Mark 1:14; 9:31; 10:33).
3. The members of the Jesus Movement "preach" and are to be "delivered up" (Mark 13:9–13).

When the third act is complete, the drama will reach its climax in the coming of Jesus as Son of Man (13:26).

In short, the Gospel of Mark combines elements of *bios,* aretalogy, encomium, and prophecy; its heroic element is highly ironic and expresses the tragic, even though its hope can be simply seen; it interprets ancient texts, but it is not simply a commentary on them; it represents customs and practices from an ancient, alien world; it is parabolic in its mystery, yet mythic in its foundational significance for telling the truth and revealing the future in symbolically rich language for its readers. It is not an apocalypse, but it is nonetheless very apocalyptic, and millennial dreams and visions are central to its ethos.

Is, then, the Markan gospel "unique"? The word *unique* is probably too strong both in genre theory and as a historical description. In many respects this gospel is still a *type* of ancient "biography" (*bios*). Yet, it is a distinctive mixture and eclectic combination as well. This solution is less than satisfying at the formal level of genre, but perhaps the key to the prototype for the genre of the Gospel of Mark has not yet been found. Decide for yourself!

EARLY CHURCH TRADITION ABOUT THE GOSPEL OF MARK

The earliest surviving tradition about the Gospel of Mark is preserved in the writings of a fourth-century church historian named Eusebius. He records what is now called "the **Papias tradition.**" Eusebius says that a certain bishop of the mid-second century named Papias of Hierapolis (in Asia Minor) claimed that he had received an oral tradition about "Mark" from a certain, otherwise unidentifiable "elder" or "presbyter" (Greek *presbyteros*), who was a person of some local authority in the movement.

> And this the Presbyter used to say: Mark indeed, because he was the interpreter (*hermēneutēs*) of Peter, wrote accurately, but not in order, the things either said or done by the Lord, as much as he remembered.
>
> For he neither heard the Lord nor followed Him, but afterwards, as I have said, [heard and followed] Peter, who fitted his discourses to the needs [of his hearers] but not as if making a narrative of the Lord's sayings; consequently, Mark, writing some things just as he remembered, erred in nothing; for he was careful of one thing — not to omit anything of the things he had heard or to falsify anything in them.
>
> (Eusebius *Ecclesiastical History* 3.39.15)

The heart of this tradition is the first paragraph. It affirms that "Mark" was the "interpreter" — or perhaps "translator" (Greek *hermēneutēs*) — of Peter. Furthermore, it says that the gospel is based on what Mark *remembered* about what Peter said, that it was not in order, but that nonetheless it was accurate. The second paragraph may be Eusebius' interpretation. In any case, this so-called Papias tradition needs to be examined a little more closely.

Although the name "Mark" was common in the ancient world, Papias was most likely referring to a follower and companion of Paul in the Pauline and deutero-Pauline materials and in 1 Peter. In the Acts of the Apostles, this same Mark is called "*John* Mark" (not to be confused with anyone else called John in the New Testament). Acts also says a community of believers met in Mark's mother's house in Jerusalem. This Mark accompanied Paul and Barnabas on a missionary journey to Asia Minor but then left them and returned to Jerusalem. Finally, Acts says that Paul did not welcome Mark on his next missionary journey and that he instead accompanied Barnabas on a mission to Cyprus (Acts 12:12, 25; 13:5, 13; 15:37–40).

In Paul's undisputed letters, Mark is mentioned as well. Paul's letter to Philemon states that when Paul was in prison (probably Ephesus), he sent greetings from "Mark" (Philem. 24). If he was referring to the Mark of Acts, some reconciliation between Paul and Mark must have taken place.

A third kind of reference is found in the deutero-Pauline literature. A Paulinist writing in Paul's name from the latter third of the first century also associated Mark with Paul (Col. 4:10). A still later Paulinist placed Paul and Mark together in prison, apparently in Rome (2 Tim. 4:11; 1:17).

In short, three kinds of references—Acts, a Pauline letter, and later letters from the Pauline School—connected Mark with *Paul* and, somewhat less securely, *Rome.* This is the dominant New Testament tradition.

There is still another New Testament reference, however. It is found in 1 Peter, a pseudonymous work probably from the late first century C.E. (see Chapter Thirteen). 1 Peter concludes with supposed greetings from its author and "my son Mark" (1 Pet. 5:13). In other words, *Peter,* not Paul, is being associated with Mark, as in the Papias tradition. A possible similarity with the Pauline literature, however, is that the greetings are sent from "Babylon" (1 Pet. 5:13). In apocalyptic literature of the late first century, "Babylon" symbolized *Rome* because both cities were remembered for destroying Jerusalem (Babylon in 587 B.C.E., Rome in 70 C.E.). In short, a *Peter*-Mark-Rome connection in 1 Peter parallels the *Paul*-Mark-Rome connection in the Pauline and Acts sources. In this regard, note that there were late first- and early second-century traditions that Peter and Paul were martyred at Rome (John 21:18–19?; Rev. 11:3–4?; cf. *1 Clement* 5; Ignatius *To the Romans* 4:3). A recently discovered document says that Mark wrote the first draft of his gospel in Rome (the *Secret Gospel of Mark*).

In short, sometime late in the first half of the second century C.E., certain circles in the Jesus Movement accepted the view that the shortest gospel was written by "(John) Mark," who from time to time had been an interpreter ("translator"?) of Peter and a follower of Paul. The place of composition was widely thought to have been Rome, the location where, it was believed, Peter and Paul had been martyred. By the later second century, these conclusions about the origins of the Gospel of Mark were taken for granted (Irenaeus *Against Heresies* 3.1.1, ca. 185 C.E.).

GENERAL HISTORICAL CRITICISM: AUTHOR, DATE, PLACE

General Historical Criticism analyzes ancient literature in relation to external events (see Chapter Two). From this critical perspective, the Papias tradition may contain some accurate history. First, if the name "Mark" was chosen by second-century members of the Jesus Movement for this gospel in order to give it authority, why did they choose a follower of Paul rather than a disciple of Jesus? This is especially noteworthy when it is recalled that the names of other followers of Jesus were attached to anonymous writings. Second, the emphasis on Peter in the Papias tradition corresponds to the fact that Peter is the most frequently mentioned and prominent disciple in the gospel (e.g., 1:16–18, 29–31; 8:27–9:1; 9:2–8; 14).

The focus on the origin of the gospel at Rome, often suggested by those who defend the Papias tradition, also has some support. First, although written in Greek, Mark contains a number of "Latinisms" (e.g., 4:21; 5:9, 15), that is, words taken over or derived from Latin, the language of native Romans. (A Latinism in English is *et cetera*.) Second, terms from the Aramaic language, Jesus' language, are explained (5:41; 7:34; 10:46; 14:36; 15:34), suggesting that intended readers did not speak Aramaic, thus perhaps were Romans. Third, the Markan gospel reckons time in the Roman manner (6:48; 13:35). Fourth, Israelite customs are interpreted (7:3–4; 10:12), sometimes inaccurately (14:1). Fifth, the gospel is imprecise about Palestinian geography (e.g., 5:1; 6:45, 53; 7:31). These considerations might reinforce the suggestion that this gospel was composed at Rome. If Rome is correct, the "**abomination that makes desolate**" (13:14) could have symbolized that famous persecutor of members of the Jesus Movement at Rome: the emperor Nero. Thus modern scholars who have accepted the Papias tradition, at least in part, have usually dated the gospel to about the time of the Neronian persecution at Rome, 64 C.E., or soon thereafter.

Yet, there are problems with the Papias tradition as well. The description of "Mark" in Papias sounds suspiciously defensive. Consider, for example, the expressions "accurately," "nor in order," "erred in nothing," "not to omit . . . or falsify." Although the last two phrases might have been additions by Eusebius, the first two are in the core tradition. Either way, there appears to be an attempt to give the gospel legitimacy. Moreover, although the person "Mark" is not Jesus' disciple, he is connected with a disciple of Jesus in the tradition, namely, Peter. In other words, there is a "chain of tradition" established:

Jesus → Peter (disciple/apostle) → Mark (disciple of disciple/apostle) → the Presbyter → Papias himself

Finally, some critics think that the gospel's apparent geographical imprecision about Palestine is odd if, as some Roman-origin defenders suggest, the author was the Jerusalem-based John Mark of Acts. (However, that analysis competes with the view that the ancient author did not have modern perceptions of Palestinian geography or—this is especially prevalent among literary critics—the Markan geography is purely symbolic!).

Suspicions about the accuracy of the Papias tradition combined with no explicit statement in Mark about its composition have led scholars to comb the gospel for the slightest hints about matters of authorship and time and place of writing (**internal evidence**). They have usually turned to the apocalyptic speech attributed to Jesus in Mark 13. Mark 13:14:

"But when you see the '**abomination that makes desolate**' standing where it ought not to be (let the *reader* understand), then let those who are in Judea flee to the mountains . . ."

In Chapter Two we noted that the expression "**the abomination that makes desolate**" or "**the desolating sacrilege**" was derived from the apocalyptic book Daniel (11:31; 12:11; cf. 9:27; 8:13–14; cf. also 1 Macc. 1:54), as the Matthean writer makes clear (Matt. 24:15). In Daniel, it refers to the act of setting up an altar to the Greek god Zeus in the Jerusalem temple by Seleucid Greeks in 168 B.C.E. (for the history, see Chapter One). This act was considered offensive, disgusting, and defiling. It was an act of pollution. In the first century, it was probably connected with a similar polluting act, the presence of the Roman general Titus in the temple in 70 C.E. Titus' presence in the temple was not only an "sacrilege" in the temple; it symbolized the destruction or "desolation" of the temple. It was another "desolating sacrilege."

The identification of this allusion with an event related to the destruction of Jerusalem, although occasionally questioned, is the opinion of most scholars. It gains some support from a prophecy of the destruction of the temple attributed to Jesus in Mark 13:2. This prophecy suggests either that that tragic event is about to happen or, more likely, that it has just happened because apocalyptic writers often portrayed their characters as predicting events that had already happened (for more on Mark as an apocalyptic writer, see following).

Thus there are plenty of reasons to be suspicious of the Papias tradition. The most important reason for questioning it, however, is modern critical theory about the formation of the gospels. The Papias view of a chain of authoritative tradition simply does not fit the form and redaction critical view that the gospel authors created their gospels and modified anonymous, long since interpreted, Jesus traditions. Thus Papias' view of Mark's recording of Peter's personal reminiscences, as though he were taking notes, is not easy to coordinate with the dominant position in modern critical theory.

If an unknown writer composed the gospel shortly after the destruction of Jerusalem and the temple in 70 C.E., was it nonetheless composed at Rome? As noted, Rome seems to fit some of the internal evidence and remains a strong contender. Yet, a location in some eastern Roman province is also possible. The Greek of this gospel is unsophisticated and, although it contains Latinisms, some of them were in general usage, and others could have come from Romans in the East. Moreover, the gospel also contains Semitic (Hebrew or Aramaic) language influences. The work's Israelite flavor, its accuracy about matters such as housing and taxation, and its interest in peasant, village, and rural agricultural life might suggest Galilee. The perpetual problem with Galilee is that the gospel is thought to be inaccurate about Galilean geography, although there are some ingenious explanations of this supposed inaccuracy. Even if Jesus' Galilean movements have mainly symbolic meaning, and even if the Markan writer has an unusual perception of place, it is still difficult to imagine that he was intimately familiar with Galilee. Some scholars have therefore offered a third alternative: the region north of Galilee, rural Syria.

In short, the evidence about author, time, and place of Mark is very mixed and difficult to establish critically. A cautious conclusion is that the gospel is pseudonymous and that it was written soon after the destruction of the Jerusalem temple in 70 C.E. Southern Syria is possible for a place of composition, but Rome cannot be ruled out. For the sake of convenience, the author will be called "Mark."

SOCIAL-HISTORICAL CONTEXT

If the precise genre is difficult to determine, it is correspondingly difficult to isolate the precise groups from which and to which the author of Mark wrote. From time to time in the gospel, the author seems to hint at something about his intended readers. Many interpreters think that "disciples" in Mark's story shade off into disciples in general, including the intended readers and hearers some forty years after Jesus' death. For example, Jesus tells the disciples that after his death he would "lead" (NRSV: "go before") them back to Galilee (Mark 14:28). These words could refer to those who later heard the story of Jesus, like the women at the tomb to whom the words were repeated (16:7); in this view such persons should go back to Galilee and await the *parousia* (9:9). However, this theory is helpful only in a limited and general way.

More important for the question of the writer and his recipients is the little apocalypse in Mark 13:3–37. In the story context, Jesus *speaks* these words to the disciples on the Mount of Olives in Jerusalem. However, when Jesus refers to the **"abomination that makes desolate"** (13:14) discussed earlier, the text cryptically says in an aside, "Let *the reader* understand" (13:14). If this phrase was not added later (there is no manuscript evidence that it was [**Textual Criticism**]), it implies that the discourse is addressed not only to those in the story, Jesus' twelve disciples, but also to an *intended reader* of the gospel. Such a reader could have been an individual, but because most people could not read, he could have been the one expected to read or recite the gospel to illiterate listeners. Thus the apocalyptic context in the speech might refer to potential signs and events in the period of writing, reading, and hearing. As the gospel says, false Christs are leading "the disciples" astray (verses 5–7). The disciples are undergoing tribulation and persecution (verses 8–13). They are seeing "the **abomination that makes desolate** set up where it ought not to be" (verse 14). There is more tribulation and an increase in the activity of false Christs and false prophets (verses 19–23). Yet, the end is near. The Son of Man will soon be seen "coming in clouds with great power and glory" (verse 26). One must now "Take heed, watch" (verses 33–37). If the **"abomination that makes desolate"** in Mark 13:14 implies the destruction of the temple by the Roman general Titus in 70 C.E., this shattering event would have brought forth apocalyptic fervor and expectation to a fever pitch. Such an event *had to be* at least the beginning of the end. From this perspective, "Mark" wrote to encourage his readers to wait and hope and to instruct them that as Jesus himself had to go through his Passion to his glory, they had to be prepared for discipleship that involves suffering.

In short, "Mark" and the readers of this gospel are living in a period when apocalyptic expectations are heightened, a period of millennial dreams, visions, and hopes: The *parousia* is thought to be imminent, and "false Christs" and "false prophets" are leading some members of the Jesus Movement astray. We do not know who these so-called charlatans were, but 13:5b–6 suggests that some were claiming to be the risen Jesus himself, that is, claiming that he had already returned.

Still—again—who were the intended readers? Were they *Palestinian* readers? This theory, which some interpreters connect with the question about the place of composition, has some merit. Two places in Palestine have been suggested: Galilee and Judea.

In favor of Galilee is the very strong emphasis on Galilee in the gospel. Rural and peasant Galilee is the scene of Jesus' early activity: the gathering of disciples, exorcisms, healings, and the like. It is also the location for the awaited return of Jesus, the *parousia* (14:28; 16:7). A problem with Galilee, however, is that "Galilee" was a district of marked ethnic mixing and could have been symbolic for the work of God in the whole world. We cannot be certain that the emphasis on Galilee in the gospel means that it was intended for Galileans in particular. Indeed, the opposite argument could be, and has been, made: Because Galilee is symbolic, the gospel was *not* written to the people who actually lived in Galilee.

Alternatively, Mark 13:14 says, "let those who are in Judea flee to the mountains." If one dates the gospel in connection with the crisis of 70 C.E., when Jerusalem and the temple were destroyed, does the reference to Judea have some geographical import? If it does, the false prophets and false Messiahs are in Judea, and the author is warning *Judean members of the Jesus Movement* and offering them hope that although the end is not yet, still it is not far off. As a result of these possibilities, some critics have concluded that the ancient tradition that the Jerusalem members of the Jesus Movement fled to Pella across the Jordan at the outbreak of the war between the Israelites and Rome (Eusebius *Ecclesiastical History* 3.5.3) is not historically accurate.

In short, Palestine, especially Judea, remains a real possibility for the intended recipients, but there can be no absolute certainty. It is much more certain that Mark writes with an apocalyptic/millennial bent and gives warning and hope to those experiencing oppression and persecution—wherever it might have been.

The Markan gospel is a document produced at a time of crisis and is dominated by apocalyptic eschatology, probably in a millennial movement. Millennial movements emerge among peoples who experience alienation from the dominant social and religious powers, especially in times of catastrophe and persecution. Such was the experience with Israelites and members of the Jesus Movement in the late first century C.E. The Markan gospel fits this social context when it warns readers to beware of false prophecy, encourages them to hold on to their hope in the imminent return of Jesus (the *parousia*), and teaches them that discipleship involves suffering in the face of persecution.

Some modern social-scientific interpreters would say that Mark came out of, and wrote for, a faction of the Jesus Movement that was becoming a millennial "sect." In the Markan story, Jesus often appears as an apocalyptic prophet, preacher, and healer: characteristics typical of charismatic leaders of millennial sects. Similarly, the disciples are called to become preachers and healers (1:39; 3:14–15; 6:13). They are *somewhat* like the Cynic-Stoic wandering philosophers in that they are asked to abandon everything (10:28) and take on their mission only the bare essentials (6:8–9: "a staff; no bread, no bag, no money . . . sandals . . . ," one tunic). However, throughout the gospel, the field of activity is not in the cities, but rather in the villages, both inland and around the Sea (Lake) of Galilee. Furthermore, the disciples must be prepared to abandon and be rejected by their families and villages (6:1–6) and join together with the true "mother, brothers, and sisters" (3:20–21, 31–35). This new family—social-scientific interpreters refer to these nonbiological stand-in, surrogate family members as "fictive kin"—seems to be composed primarily of people who are "marginal" in the sense that they are being denied access to the forces that control their lives (structural marginality). This "family" includes women (1:31; 10:30; 15:41) and children (9:33–37; 10:13, 16), the unclean and dispossessed, the poor and outcast (6:34–41; 8:2). Riches can be an obstacle (10:17–27). Both Israelites and Gentiles are welcome (4:35–8:21; cf. 15:39). Jesus' proclamation of the Kingdom brought into being an apocalyptically oriented community for which John and Jesus are models: As they "preach" and are "delivered up," so the followers "preach" and are "delivered up." But discipleship in the millennial community, for all its trials and sufferings, at least for those who understand and are faithful, has its reward: eternal life in the age to come (10:31).

To this millennial view of the social context of the Markan gospel, which has as its focus politics and economics, one should add social stratification and the portrayal of Jesus' social status (Rohrbaugh). The infancy stories of Matthew and Luke, each in their own way, trace Jesus' lineage to King David, the "father" of all the Messianic kings, and to Abraham, the patriarchal "father" of the whole Israelite people. Moreover, in both gospels, Jesus' birthplace is Bethlehem, the prophesied birthplace of the King Messiah descended from David (Mic. 5:2 [5:1]; see Chapters Nine and Ten). For these writers, Jesus has the "right" family tree, the right pedigree, and is therefore an honorable person by virtue of his birth (**ascribed honor**). Later in their stories, Jesus gets more honor in debate with opponents such as Pharisees, Sadducees, and Herodians (**acquired honor**). The Markan Jesus, by contrast, gains honor only in the latter way, by besting his opponents in debate (e.g., Mark 12). The author is silent about Jesus' supposed birth at Bethlehem, and Jesus' father is not mentioned. Indeed, it is possible that the author questions whether the Davidic descent of Messiah is necessary (Mark 12:35–37). Moreover, nothing is said about Jesus' physical attributes, native intelligence, education, and other aspects of honorable status in antiquity. What he does mention—Jesus' trade as an artisan and his way of poverty and homelessness—would not be honorable, except perhaps for a few deviant prophets or philosophers. In short, the Markan Jesus does not seem to have the proper credentials, at least to the upper strata of Greco-Roman society. Was the gospel, therefore, written to give hope primarily to the lower strata of society, perhaps in Palestine, or specifically in Judea?

THE SOURCES USED BY THE MARKAN WRITER

You will recall that the **Synoptic Problem** is solved for the majority of New Testament scholars by the **Two-Source Theory,** that is, Mark and Q are important written sources for Matthew and Luke. A byproduct of this theory is the **priority of Mark,** that is, that Mark comes chronologically first. We have just seen that the probable date of the Markan gospel is about 70 C.E., probably soon after the destruction of Jerusalem and the temple. Recall also that Form Critics argue that the author had at his disposal oral traditions in the form of sayings of Jesus and stories about him, some created by prophets and storytellers of the Jesus Movement. A number of these sayings and stories had been gathered into collections and put into writing. Here we shall briefly note again some important pre-Markan materials, especially these collections (see Chapter Three).

Many scholars in the past thought that the most extensive pre-Markan unit was a connected **Passion Story,** that is, an account of the arrest, trial, and crucifixion of Jesus in Jerusalem (Mark 14–15 par.; John 18–19). The reason for this theory is that this story is linked together by numerous and specific time references (the days of "Holy Week" or the hours on the day of crucifixion) and place (specific sites in and about Jerusalem). Certainly the Passion Story gives the *impression* of a realistic, connected account. More recent studies of the Passion Story in Mark's gospel, however, have tried to argue that the Markan author put the Passion Story together out of a number of isolated oral traditions about Jesus' last days in Jerusalem. If so, he created the framework of the story, just as he created the framework of the other oral traditions and collections in the gospel. Yet, those who hold this view do not deny that many of the individual episodes were early and perhaps rooted in some historical event.

There are other suggestions for pre-Markan collections of sayings and stories (see Chapter Three). Mark 2:1–3:6 contains a healing story and several **anecdotes** revolving around Jesus' controversies with opponents about forgiveness of sins, eating with tax collectors and sinners, fasting, and keeping the Sabbath. Jesus' controversies with Israelite leaders in the temple precincts in Jerusalem (Mark 12:13–37a) may have been put together as a written collection and then placed at this location to heighten Jesus' conflicts with his Jerusalem opponents leading to his death. A fourth possibility—a very plausible one—is that behind Mark 4 is a little parable collection around the theme "seed" (Mark 4:3–8 [Sower], 26–29 [Seed Growing Secretly], 30–32 [Mustard Seed]).

A fifth possible pre-Markan source is worth considering in more detail. The theory is that the source contained *parallel* "cycles" of miracle stories and that each contained a sea miracle, healings, and a feeding miracle:

Cycle 1 (Mark 4:35–6:44)	Cycle 2 (Mark 6:45–8:26)
4:35–41 Stilling of the Storm	6:45–51 Jesus Walks on the Sea
5:1–20 Gerasene Demoniac	**8:22–26 Blind Man of Bethsaida**
5:25–34 Woman with a Hemorrhage	7:24b–30 Syrophoenician Woman
5:21–23, 35–43 Jairus' Daughter	7:32–37 Deaf Mute
6:34–44, 53 Feeding of 5,000	8:1–10 Feeding of 4,000

These miracle stories portray Jesus as exhibiting the powerful traits of a combined Israelite hero and a Hellenistic miracle-working hero or "Divine Man" (see Chapter One). They suggest that some group in the Jesus Movement who admired Jesus in this way collected them and put them together. Some scholars hold that the parallel sequences were actually longer, that is, after the feeding miracle there was (1) a crossing of the lake, (2) a controversy with Pharisees, and (3) teaching concerning bread. This is because the Gospel of John, which is generally very unlike the synoptic gospels in sequence, has in this case a similar sequence:

Mark 8:1–21	John 6:1–51
8:1–10 Feeding of 4,000	6:1–15 Feeding of 5,000 and attempt to make Jesus a king
8:10 Crossing the "sea"	6:16–21 Crossing the sea
8:11–13 Dispute with Pharisees	6:22–24 Transition: coming of people
8:14–21 Incident of "no bread"; discourse about the leaven of the Pharisees	6:25–51 Discourse on bread

Possibly Mark inherited two versions of the same cycle of tradition—the feeding of the five thousand and four thousand are especially symmetrical—and *some* of this sequence was also known to the author of John from his miracle source (the "**Signs Source**"). If so, the Markan author has taken the story of the Blind Man out of its original position in the collection (boldface and italics in the first list) and positioned it later in the account (after *both* sequences) at 8:22–26. It is not difficult to find a rationale for this repositioning. The Markan writer has a major theme, "the blindness of the disciples." The disciples are blind to Jesus' identity and mission, as well as their own (see following). Thus, if the Markan author received a miracle collection, he took the blindness miracle out of its position there and put it at the end of the sequence to highlight the blindness of the disciples. In this position, it forms the beginning of the turning point in the story, the transitional section of the gospel in which the disciples' blindness is emphasized:

8:22–26	Blindness miracle
8:27–10:45	Transitional section (major theme: blindness of disciples)
10:46–52	Blindness miracle

In short, the theory is that he lifted the blindness miracle out of its context in the miracle collection he received and put it last as an introduction to his major theme of the blindness of the disciples in the following section.

A sixth and last possible source is the apocalyptic discourse now in Mark 13. It may have been developed from pre-Markan Israelite apocalyptic materials developed in conjunction with the emperor Gaius Caligula's attempt to set up his statue in the Jerusalem temple and then remolded in an earlier phase of the Jesus Movement. If so, the author of Mark appears to have totally reworked it. This is especially clear not only from Markan vocabulary and style (cf. especially 13:5b–27), but also from specific historical allusions (13:5b–6, 14, 21–22; cf. 13:2), such as the "**abomination that makes desolate**" (13:14), now used to date the gospel.

Several scholars add other units or collections to these six; others do not accept all of these six. Nonetheless, scholars agree that *some such list* of sources came to Mark.

Apart from written collections, Form Critics think that many small or isolated units of oral tradition also came to the Markan writer, and Redaction Critics agree that the Markan author organized these oral traditions, as well as the written collections, into an integrated whole. It is precisely this perspective that raises the most important questions about **the Papias tradition** (see earlier). It should be noted in this regard that some collections of Jesus' sayings, miracles, and anecdotes were not included. The "sayings gospel" **Q,** for example, is missing. Thus the four canonical gospels have a perspective that is dominated by the Passion story, that is, the arrest, trial, suffering, execution, and death of Jesus. Teachings and miracle stories, although acceptable in some quarters, were accepted in the emergent orthodox churches only in the larger Passion-oriented genre. Do we see here a Pauline-type emphasis on Jesus' death and resurrection?

Before attempting to outline Mark's structure, we need to look at several emphases and techniques that contribute to isolating this structure.

STYLISTIC, LITERARY, AND STRUCTURAL FEATURES OF MARK

Modern **Literary Critics** are usually more interested in how Mark's story is told than in the sources he used or the historical and social context of the gospel. Often their focus is on what is called "rhetoric." For example, the Markan story is not told from the perspective of one of its characters, like Holden Caulfield in *Catcher in the Rye* or a "voiceover" in a film, but rather by a third party, one who takes a position outside and above the story. This storyteller is able to move his readers imaginatively from one place to another in space and over time or to tell what will happen (some literary critics therefore call him an "omniscient narrator"). He has a particular ideological "point of view" from which, like the director of a film, he leads his readers and hearers. The intent is to let them make the right judgments about the events he narrates. Sometimes he tells them what the characters are thinking. Almost always this is an *unstated* perspective in narratives, one of which readers or listeners are unconscious. In Mark, however, it is interrupted when the narrator says in an aside to the reader, "let the reader understand" (13:14).

From this sort of literary critical perspective, the "hidden" narrator tells the story in the third person in simple, terse, pictorial, and imaginative language (see Chapter One on **Literary Criticism**). The story moves rapidly from scene to scene. Action dominates. A dramatic sense of urgency is present. The author also uses a number of stereotypical words and phrases. If you read through the story, you will see heavy use of "and" (Greek *kai*) and "immediately" (Greek *euthus*), sometimes in combination, to link sections (grammarians call this "parataxis"). Such stereotypical words and phrases are often found in the little introductions and conclusions to the smaller units that came from oral tradition, and on linguistic grounds many of these links give every indication of having been composed by the evangelist himself as links between the episodes. An especially well-known Markan example is the repetitive phrase, "And he said to them . . ." Narrative techniques such as these help analysts to spot places where the author is weaving together his traditional sayings and narratives, and thus it is possible to see him at work in structuring his narrative.

In considering his overall structure, we shall note especially the introductions to the apocalyptic discourse and the Passion narrative (13:1–5a and 14:1–2, 10–12).

The introductions and conclusions to Mark's episodes also contain *local* geographical settings for episodes in his story, although some almost certainly came to Mark connected with the oral or written traditions. In Mark's storytelling, they often take on some symbolic significance. Thus, again, the Sea of Galilee is a "place" where Jesus teaches. Similarly, the wilderness represents a "place" of temptation. Houses are often "places" for private teaching to the disciples. The synagogue and temple are "places" of opposition to Jesus. The mountain and sea are "places" of revelation. Gentile areas are "places" where Jesus' compassion to outsiders is demonstrated. All of these places are usually filled with complications or conflicts and move the plot along.

The author of the Markan gospel also uses a number of structuring techniques. For example, he likes the number "three." Often there are three people (e.g., 3:35:

brother, sister, mother; 5:37, 9:2, 14:33: Peter, James, and John; see also 8:31, 11:27, 14:43, 14:53, 15:1). There are also three *types* of characters (chief priests, scribes, and elders). There are three Passion predictions (8:31; 9:31; 10:33–34). The disciples fall asleep and are rebuked by Jesus three times (14:32–42). Peter denies Jesus three times (14:66–72). In many instances, the author develops his account by units of three, each building on those that have gone before (Robbins calls this "three-step progression").

Another technique is called the Markan "sandwich" or "**intercalation.**" In this case, one story (the meat of the sandwich) is placed *inside* another story (the beginning and end are the slices of bread). For example, the statement of Jesus' identity as Son of Man with authority to forgive sins (Mark 2:5b–10) is sandwiched inside a miracle story, the healing of the paralytic (Mark 2:1–5a, 11–12). The interruption of the story is clearly marked by "he said to the paralytic" (2:5a), which is then repeated when, after the insertion, the healing story resumes (2:10b). In this example, the second "he said to the paralytic" breaks the syntax of the sentence. Modern editors, aware of this interruption, mark off these words in 2:5b and 2:10b by dashes in English translations. Another example is the insertion of the cleansing of the temple (11:15–19) into the cursing of the fig tree and its meaning (11:12–14, 20–25). Still another is the woman with a hemorrhage (5:25–34) sandwiched into the healing of Jairus' daughter (5:21–24, 35–43). In some of these intercalations, one kind of material interprets the other; for example, the cursing of the fig tree and the cleansing of (curse on?) the temple seem to interpret each other.

The gospel as a whole is a large "sandwich" in which the "bread" is 1:1 to 8:26 and 11:1 to 16:8 and the meat is 8:27–10:45. In the middle section, Jesus predicts his Passion three times and each time tries to make his disciples see the necessity for his suffering and its significance for discipleship. This transitional section is sandwiched between two blindness or "giving of sight" miracle stories. The first is the blind man at Bethsaida (8:22–26), noted earlier as repositioned to this location, and the last is blind Bartimaeus (10:46–52). These miracle stories clearly have a more-than-literal sense: Blind people with faith truly "see," but disciples who physically see remain "blind" because of their lack of understanding of Jesus' teaching and mission. This, again, is Mark's theme of the blindness of the disciples.

Finally, we come to two of the most important structural features of the gospel: the overall geographical movement of the story and the summaries of Jesus' teaching and activity along the way. With respect to geography, Galilee predominates in the first half of the gospel and Jerusalem in the second half. More specifically, from 1:14 to 6:13, the story takes place in Galilee; from 6:14 to 8:26, beyond Galilee; from 8:27 to 10:52, moving from Caesarea Philippi to Jerusalem; and from 11:1 to 16:8, in Jerusalem. This movement from Galilee to Jerusalem gradually funnels the plot to the scene of *ironic tragedy:* Jesus' Passion and death on the cross and his return to Galilee at the *parousia* (14:28; 16:7). If we had *only* the Galilean story, Jesus would appear primarily as a miracle-working hero or "Divine Man" who occasionally teaches.

The second major feature is a set of summary reports about Jesus' teaching and healing activity. These reports occur at 1:14–15, 21–22, 39; 2:13; 3:7–12; 5:21; 6:6b, 12–13, 30–33, 53–56; 10:1. They mark transitions in the narrative and thus point both backward and forward.

There is no clear consensus about the structure or outline of the Markan gospel. Suggestions range from "clumsy construction" to quite elaborate outlines. Our outline will be simple. We stress the three-stage geographical movement of Jesus—from Galilee to Caesarea Philippi to Jerusalem—and combine it with the Markan summaries, occasionally adding other literary, stylistic, and structural features discussed earlier. This will give Mark's structure as follows:

1:1–13	Introduction
1:14–15	*Transitional Markan summary*

Galilee

1:16–3:6	**First major section**: The authority of Jesus exhibited in word and deed
3:7–12	*Transitional Markan summary*
3:13–6:6a	**Second major section:** Jesus as Son of God and as rejected by his own people
6:6b	*Transitional Markan summary*
6:7–8:21	**Third major section:** Jesus as Son of God but misunderstood by his own disciples

Transition: Caesarea Philippi

8:22–26	*Transitional giving-of-sight story (blindness miracle)*
8:27–10:45	**Fourth major section:** Christology and Christian discipleship in light of the Passion (blindness of the disciples)
10:46–52	*Transitional giving-of-sight story (blindness miracle)*

Jerusalem

11:1–12:44	**Fifth major section:** The days in Jerusalem prior to the Passion
13:1–5a	*Introduction to the apocalyptic discourse*
13:5b–37	**Sixth major section:** Apocalyptic discourse
14:1–12	*Introduction to the Passion narrative* with intercalation, verses 3–9
14:13–16:8	**Seventh major section:** Passion narrative

EXEGETICAL SURVEY OF THE GOSPEL OF MARK

1:1–13: *Introduction.* The best manuscripts of Mark that we possess begin with the words, "the beginning of the good news (*gospel*) of Jesus Christ [the Son of God]" (1:1). If the author of Mark wrote these words, and if they characterize the whole writing, he was announcing the "good news" of a divine-human drama in which Jesus Christ as the Son of God is the chief protagonist. However, it is often thought that these words refer only to the *beginning* of good news, which refers to the story of John the Baptizer (see the earlier discussion). If so, it continues with Jesus' coming into Galilee preaching the gospel of God, the preaching of the gospel of Jesus Christ, the Son of God.

A necessary preliminary to the story is the mission of John the Baptizer. In the Hebrew Scriptures, the prophet Elijah, dressed in haircloth with a leather belt around his waist (2 Kings 1:8; cf. Zech. 13:4), did not die a natural death, but rather was taken up to heaven by a chariot in a whirlwind (2 Kings 2:10–11). He was then expected to return as forerunner of God at the time of final judgment (Mal. 4:5–6 [3:23–24]). By his description of John's dress, the Markan writer identifies John with the returning Elijah. Isa. 40:3 says, "*A voice cries out*: '*In the wilderness* prepare the way of the Lord, make straight in the desert a highway for our God.'" In the **Dead Sea Scrolls,** this verse is interpreted literally as a command that God's elect people should go out into the wilderness/desert to prepare for the end by the "way" of Torah study (Community Rule 8:12–16). The Markan account reads the prophecy quite differently: "*A voice cries out in the wilderness:* 'Prepare the way of the Lord. . . .'" Now the verse is not a command about what to do to prepare for the end, but rather a prophecy about the end. The one in the wilderness is the Baptizer, not a group, and the "Lord" is Jesus, not God.

The historian Josephus recognized that John the Baptizer was an eloquent, good, and pious man (Josephus *Antiquities* 18.116–119). For Mark, John is extremely important, but he is also relegated to a secondary role in comparison with Jesus, that is, the role of prophet and forerunner of the Messiah. The writer pictures John as describing himself as a slave unworthy to tie Jesus' sandals. Mark's account of the Baptizer carefully leads up to the scene in which John baptizes Jesus and the voice of God from heaven (the Israelite *bath qôl,* "daughter voice") reveals him to be his Son in the words of Ps. 2:7, Isa. 42:1 and 44:2 (1:11; cf. 1:1). Mark thinks that Jesus has an initial religious experience at the beginning of his public activity. Mark will place the all-important "Son of God" title at other crucial turning points in the story: when Jesus is so identified by demons (1:24; 3:11; 5:7); when he is transfigured on a mountain (9:11); when he identifies himself at his "trial" before the high priest (14:61–62); and—take note that this is the only identification as Son of God by *humans*—by the Gentile (!) centurion (15:39).

The Temptation of Jesus by Satan is brief in Mark (1:12–13), but it sets the stage for the cosmic battle between good and evil.

1:14–15:   *Transitional summary.*   The drama begins. As John is "delivered up" (NRSV: "arrested"; see 6:17), so Jesus will be "delivered up" (14:46). John the forerunner foreshadows Jesus. This summary by the gospel writer stresses the "gospel" (cf. 1:1) and points forward to Jesus' central Kingdom preaching (e.g., Mark 4). The inaugural scene and teaching summary look in the main apocalyptic.

1:16–3:6:   First major section: *The authority of Jesus exhibited in word and deed.* Jesus' authority dominates this whole section, as its two summaries emphasize (1:32–34, 39). Jesus recruits fishermen Simon and Andrew, as well as James and John, who immediately leave their father Zebedee to follow him (1:16–20). He exhibits his authority in Capernaum in teaching and healing (1:21–34); he cleanses a leper (1:40–45); he heals a paralytic at Capernaum (2:1–12); he calls another disciple who immediately leaves everything to follow him (2:13–14).

Mark 2:15–3:6 is a series of **anecdotes** exhibiting the authority of Jesus in various ways: He rejects convention by eating with the outcast "tax collectors and sinners"; he disregards fasting regulations, thus challenging purity laws; he breaks the Sabbath law in both working and healing on the Sabbath. The rubric for this section as provided by the evangelist himself is found in 1:27. "What is this? A new teaching! With authority he commands even the unclean spirits, and they obey him."

This section on the authority of Jesus includes two Son of Man sayings both emphasizing the earthly authority of Jesus as Son of Man, first, to forgive sins (2:10) and, second, to abrogate the Sabbath law (2:28). It will be remembered that in 1:11 the divine voice at his baptism identified Jesus as Son of God. Now he is being identified in his full authority as Son of Man.

In this section there are also a number of miracle stories, perhaps from a miracle source:

1:21–28	The man with an unclean spirit
1:29–31	Simon's mother-in-law
1:32–34	A summary report of many healings
1:40–45	The leper
2:1–12	The paralytic at Capernaum
3:1–5	The man with the withered hand

For Mark, these stories have a definitive function: to exhibit the power and authority of Jesus in deeds, just as his teaching and his calling of disciples exhibit it in words. Especially prominent is the image of Jesus as healer and exorcist, which fits the context of folk medicine.

These miracle stories also introduce a major Markan theme that will be developed throughout the gospel until it reaches a climax in 14:62: the theme of the "**Messianic Secret**" (see the section on this theme at the end of this chapter). This theme is introduced in a summary report: "he would not permit the demons to speak, because they knew him" (1:32–34). It is certainly formulated by Mark himself; so evidently the theme of the demons "knowing Jesus," that is, knowing the secret of his identity as Son of God (see 3:11–12) and being commanded to keep silent about it is Mark's concern. What he intends to achieve by it will become evident as we trace the theme through the gospel to its climax.

The section ends on a note anticipating the Passion, the plot to destroy Jesus (3:6).

3:7–12:   *Transitional summary.*   This is the longest of the summary reports composed by the evangelist, and it marks the transition from the first to the second major section of the gospel. The summary points both backward and forward to familiar themes: the spread of Jesus' fame, Jesus' activity by the sea, miraculous exorcisms and healings, the designation of Jesus as "Son of God," and the **Messianic Secret.**

3:13–6:6a: Second major section: *Jesus as Son of God and as rejected by his own people in Galilee.*   Two themes dominate this section. The first is the power of Jesus as Son of God exhibited through miracles, as in the following references.

4:35–41	"even wind and sea obey him"
5:1–20	the Gerasene demoniac: "What have you to do with me, Jesus, Son of the Most High God?"
5:21–24a, 35–43	Jairus' daughter: "they were overcome with amazement."
5:24b–34	the woman with the hemorrhage: "And Jesus, perceiving in himself that power had gone forth from him . . ."

These miracle stories are longer and more elaborate than in the first section of the gospel, and the emphasis on the superhuman in Jesus' power is more marked. He is shown as a charismatic healer and miracle-working hero, with power over wind and sea and with power to raise the dead, as one who is openly confessed as Son of God, the touch of whose garments has the power to heal. There are major questions of the origin of these stories and of the use to which Mark is putting them. These are best discussed after observing the very similar stories in the next section of the gospel.

The second theme dominating this section is Jesus' being misunderstood and rejected. His friends misunderstand him (3:21); he is considered to be crazy and he is in tension with his family (3:21, 31–35); and finally, people in his own village reject him (6:1–6a). This final rejection anticipates the Passion Story.

In the middle of this secrecy, growing misunderstanding, and opposition Mark inserts his parable chapter (4:1–34). Probably Mark inherited a "seed" parable collection from either oral tradition or, more likely, as a written unit. If so, he inserts it here because it enables him to begin a theme that becomes prominent in the next section (6:7–8:21) and dominant in the fourth (8:27–10:45): the theme of the disciples and discipleship.

The disciples appear originally in the first major section of the gospel, where their immediate response to Jesus' call is to follow him, an aspect of the presentation of Jesus' authority. In this second section, they figure more prominently, and characteristic Markan ideas and themes appear in connection with them. The section begins with an account of their formal appointment as a group (3:13–19), and in the parable chapter Mark makes a special point about them. They are among those privileged few to whom are revealed "the secret (Greek: *mystērion*, "mystery") of the Kingdom of God." In other words they are insiders in an especially privileged position compared to "those outside." In a summary report (4:33–34), again composed by Mark, their privileged position is further emphasized: ". . . he explained everything in private to his disciples." Yet, never in this gospel do they understand Jesus. He develops the misunderstanding or blindness of the disciples more and more strongly in later sections of the gospel. It reaches a climax when the disciples desert Jesus (14:50) and Peter denies him (14:66–72).

Note again the use of titles of honor. The introduction established Jesus as "Son of God" (1:1 and 1:11), accompanied by the special revelatory circumstances of the heavens opening and the divine voice speaking out of a cloud. The first major section had two occurrences of "Son of Man" (2:10 and 2:28), and these are now balanced by two occurrences of "Son of God" (3:11 and 5:7). This placement of titles is one means whereby Mark presents his "Christological" teaching about Jesus. Yet, the disciples do not understand.

6:6b: *Transitional summary.* This is the shortest of the transitional summaries in Mark's gospel, but the shift in emphasis between the second and third sections of the gospel is not great.

6:7–8:21:   Third major section: *Jesus as Son of God and as misunderstood by his own disciples.* This section does not move as smoothly as do the others, probably because Mark is reproducing two different versions of the same cycle of tradition and finding it difficult to fit them into the overall movement of his narrative. Nonetheless, the two overall themes of the section are clear; indeed, if we accept the thesis that Mark is using a duplicated cycle of tradition, the second, the misunderstanding of the disciples, becomes even clearer.

The first theme of this section is a continuation of the presentation of Jesus as Son of God by reason of his miracles:

6:30–44   The feeding of the five thousand

6:45–52   Jesus walks on the sea, portrayed as an ASC—"He meant to pass them by" (verse 48)

6:54–56	A summary report emphasizing that Jesus' garments have the power to heal (cf. 5:28)
7:24–30	The Syrophoenician woman's daughter, healed at a distance
7:31–37	The deaf man with a speech impediment. This is much more in the spirit of the stories in the first section (compare 7:37 with 1:27). But Mark can and does link the stories together in the various sections by returning to former emphases (compare 1:27 with 4:41 and 7:37).
8:1–9	The feeding of the four thousand

Although these stories continue the theme of Jesus as Son of God (e.g., in the deliberate link between 6:56 and 5:28), the title "Son of God" does not occur explicitly. Having balanced the two "Son of Man" references in 2:10 and 28 with the "Son of God" references in 3:11 and 5:7, Mark does not use another title until the "Christ" of 8:29.

The Markan author is undoubtedly reinterpreting the miracle stories he presents in these two sections of his gospel. In the form in which he received them they seem to have presented Jesus as a miracle-working hero. Mark preserves the traits by which they do this. However, he then introduces the note of secrecy (3:11; 5:43; 7:36, although not in the Gerasene demoniac, see 5:19). This element of secrecy would strike his readers as startling because the purpose of such stories is normally precisely to proclaim the power and authority of the hero, a tendency that Mark preserves unaltered in the story of the Gerasene demoniac. Mark goes a step further by his use of the Christological titles, whereby Son of Man seems to interpret Son of God. He also interprets by his narrative structure, which subordinates everything to the upcoming Passion.

The second theme of this third major section of the gospel is that of the disciples and their misunderstanding of Jesus. The section begins with an account of the mission of "the Twelve" (6:7–13) and of their return (6:30), into which is sandwiched or intercalated the account of the death of John the Baptizer (6:14–29). Mark does not report this mission of the disciples as a success. He cannot do so, of course, because he is developing the theme of the misunderstanding and failure of the disciples that comes to a climax in chapter 8:

6:52:	"they did not *understand* . . . , but their *hearts were hardened*"
7:18:	". . . are you also without *understanding?*"
8:15, 21:	"Do you not yet perceive or *understand?* Are your *hearts hardened?*" . . . "Do you not yet *understand?*"

8:22–26: *Transitional giving-of-sight story.* Mark moves from the third section to the fourth, as he does from the fourth to the fifth, with a story of Jesus giving sight to a blind man (8:22–26; 10:46–52). The metaphorical meaning is that the blind see. These stories enclose or frame the fourth section of the gospel (8:27–10:45), in which Jesus attempts to lead his disciples to sight (i.e., understanding) and fails to do so. Metaphorically, the supposedly sighted do not see. From the perspective of geographical structure, the story moves Jesus out of Galilee to Caesarea Philippi.

8:27–10:45: Fourth major section: *Christology and Christian discipleship in light of the Passion.* This is the most homogeneous and carefully constructed of all the sections in the gospel. It begins geographically at Caesarea Philippi to the north of Galilee and has the external form of a journey from there to Jerusalem. The stages of the journey are clearly marked by further geographical references: 9:30, Galilee; 9:33, Capernaum; 10:1, Judea and beyond Jordan (10:1 is also a summary report, the last such in the gospel); 10:32, the road to Jerusalem. The section is built very carefully around three Passion prediction units about the suffering Son of Man, which have a fixed pattern:

- Prediction of the Passion and resurrection by Jesus
- Misunderstanding by the disciples
- Teaching by Jesus concerning discipleship

Each of these units occurs at a different geographical location. The section indicates that true discipleship means "following" Jesus "on the way" to the Passion, that is, the potential for suffering and death.

Geographical Location	Suffering Son of Man Prediction	Disciples' Misunderstanding	Discipleship Teaching
8:27 (Caesarea Philippi)	8:31	8:32−33	8:34−9:1
9:30 (Galilee)	9:31	9:32, 33−34	9:35−37
10:32 (near Jerusalem)	10:33−34	10:35−41	10:42−45

In more detail, the section, framed by the two "giving of sight" miracles (blindness theme), has the following structure:

8:22−26	*Bethsaida transitional giving-of-sight (blindness) story*
8:27	Caesarea Philippi
8:27−30	Fundamental narrative of Peter's confession
8:31−9:1	**First suffering Son of Man prediction unit**
	Prediction, 8:31
	Misunderstanding (blindness), 8:32−33
	Teaching about discipleship, 8:34−9:1
9:2	"After six days . . ."
9:2−8	Transfiguration
9:9−13	Elijah as forerunner
9:14−29	Appended incident and teaching on discipleship
	Disciples and boy with the dumb spirit, 9:14−27
	Teaching to disciples, 9:28−29
9:30	Galilee (9:33, Capernaum)
9:30−37	**Second suffering Son of Man prediction unit**
	Prediction, 9:31
	Misunderstanding (blindness), 9:32
	Teaching about discipleship, 9:33−37

9:38–50	Appended incident and teaching on discipleship
	Nondisciple practicing exorcism, 9:38–40
	Teaching to disciples, 9:41–50
10:1	Judea and beyond Jordan. Intercalated units of incident and teaching to disciples
10:2–12	Divorce
	The Pharisees and divorce, 10:2–9
	Teaching to disciples, 10:10–12
10:13–16	Receiving the Kingdom of God
	The presentation of the children, 10:13
	Teaching to disciples, 10:14–16
10:17–31	Entering the Kingdom of God
	The man with the question, 10:17–22
	Teaching to disciples, 10:23–31
10:32	The road to Jerusalem
10:33–45	**Third suffering Son of Man prediction unit**
	Prediction, 10:33–34
	Misunderstanding (blindness), 10:35–41
	Teaching about discipleship, 10:42–45
10:46–52	*Jericho transitional giving-of-sight (blindness) story*

The three prediction units are extraordinarily interesting and in many respects provide the key to the Markan story. The first summarizes the divine necessity for the Passion and is entirely in the present tense. The second is transitional in that the first part anticipates Jesus being delivered into the hands of his enemies but still uses the present tense, "is to be betrayed," and then puts the second half of the prediction into the future tense, "they will kill . . ." The third puts the whole prediction into the future and introduces specific references to Jerusalem and the details of the Passion itself.

This composition provides an element of movement to the plot of the gospel. In this central section, readers and hearers can look back over what has happened to make the Passion necessary (the plots, rejections, misunderstanding, all foreseen by God); they can pause for these solemn moments of insightful teaching and then move forward to Jerusalem and the Passion itself.

The predictions and the prediction units not only provide the framework for this section of the gospel, but also are the main thrust of the teaching on Mark's interpretation of Jesus and what it means to follow him in the gospel as such. The first prediction follows Peter's confession of Jesus as "the Messiah" (8:29). In the first and second sections of the gospel, the Markan pattern of interpretation was to coordinate authoritative titles for Jesus; here the same pattern is followed. There is a spin. Peter's confession is correct only if "the Messiah" is understood as the Son of Man who "must suffer," and Peter's reaction indicates that his confession (politically victorious?) was in fact false. The second and third prediction units continue the development of this true meaning of Jesus' Messiahship by using "Son of Man"; they also implicitly continue the pattern of correcting Peter's confession of Jesus as the Christ.

These units provide the key elements to the teaching on discipleship in light of the necessity for the Passion: as the Teacher went, so must the disciple be prepared to go. The first unit stresses the need to take up the cross in following Jesus (8:34–37); the second, the necessity for servanthood (9:35); and the third defines servanthood in terms of the cross (10:45). There is, further, more general teaching on discipleship between 10:1 and the third prediction unit, probably introduced here in a general context of teaching to disciples.

The first and second prediction units each have appended to them an incident and teaching to the disciples, and the incidents are curiously related. In the first (9:14–27), the disciples are failures as exorcists, whereas in the second (9:38–40), a nondisciple who uses the name of Jesus is successful. In this way Mark pursues dramatically his theme of the misunderstanding and failure of the disciples. Indeed, insiders seem to be moving toward the outside, and certain outsiders seem to be moving toward the inside. The third prediction unit has no such appendix; the servant/ransom saying in 10:45 is the climax of the whole section. It functions as its summary, and so as its climax.

The one unit in the section not yet discussed is the **transfiguration** account in which God's voice from a cloud again identifies Jesus as his Son (9:2–13). The author again portrays Jesus as having an ASC experience. It is also likely that Mark viewed the transfiguration as an anticipation of the *parousia* because 9:9 says that the meaning of the event should remain secret "until the Son of Man should be risen from the dead" (**Messianic Secret**). This Son of Man reference suggests that the event symbolized by the transfiguration will be of special importance after the resurrection, thus at the *parousia*. The same point is made by a literary-redactional connection. Mark contrasts "after six days" used of the transfiguration (9:2) with "after three days" of Jesus' prophecy about his resurrection (8:31; 9:31; 10:34).

The transfiguration seems to be a literary foreshadowing, that is, an anticipation of the *parousia,* and its link to the first prediction of the Passion and resurrection prepares readers and hearers of the story to appreciate their own position. Like the original disciples, those who read or hear the story stand between the past Passion and resurrection and the imminent *parousia.* The transfiguration unit also furthers Mark's purpose by a characteristic linking of titles for Jesus. Having presented a confession of Jesus as the Messiah, Mark now says that God identifies Jesus as the Son of God (9:7). Again, however, the implication is that the "Son of God title" can be clarified by the Son of Man. Mark will make this point more explicit when Jesus himself links the two titles in his response to the high priest in the climactic "trial" scene (14:61–62).

The discussion of Elijah is also added at this point (9:11–13), apparently because of the reference to Elijah in 9:4. It is a convenient moment for Mark to present the early *Christian* understanding of John the Baptizer as Elijah, the forerunner of the Messiah, an understanding of the role of the Baptizer that he shares (see 1:6).

Finally, the motif of the Messianic Secret is continued through this section (8:30–9:9).

10:46–52:   *Transitional giving-of-sight story.*   Bartimaeus "sees" and follows "on the way."

11:1–12:44:   **Fifth major section:** *The days in Jerusalem prior to the Passion.*   The entry (11:1–10) presents all kinds of problems at the level of the historical life of Jesus, but Mark's purpose in presenting the narrative is clear. Although not explicitly quoted, as it is in the gospel of Matthew, it fulfills Zech. 9:9:

Lo, your king comes to you;
triumphant and victorious is he,
humble and riding on a donkey,
on a colt, the foal of a donkey.

In the Hebrew Scriptures, this text originally referred to the triumphant king's entry into Jerusalem in a humble manner to demonstrate his peaceful intentions. It contains what scholars call "poetic parallelism," that is, the second line repeats the first with different words, and the fourth line repeats the third with different words. In later Israelite interpretation of the passage, the irony of the king coming in such a humble fashion is highlighted. The Babylonian Talmud preserves such a traditional interpretation. It claims that if Israel is worthy, the Messiah will come in might "upon the clouds of heaven" (i.e., in fulfillment of the coming of the Son of Man in Dan. 7:13). If it is not worthy, he will come "lowly, and riding on an ass" (i.e., in fulfillment of this text, Zech. 9:9). Did the Markan writer know this tradition? If he did, he implied that Israel was unworthy, and so the Messiah—in his view, Jesus—entered Jerusalem in this way.

Mark 11:11–25 contains the sandwich noted in the preceding discussion of the Markan literary techniques. Mark interprets the cleansing of the temple (11:15–19) by intercalating it into, or setting it inside, the account of the cursing of the fig tree (11:12–14, 20–25). Mark thus comes to terms with the catastrophe of the destruction of the temple by understanding it as the judgment of God on a place become unworthy and by seeing the tradition of Jesus' cleansing the temple as anticipating that judgment.

The remainder of the section offers a series of units relevant to the situation of Jesus in Jerusalem immediately before the Passion. First, there is a parable interpreting the fate of Jesus (12:1–12); then comes a series of three controversy **anecdotes,** the first two featuring adamantly hostile authorities and the third an individual who can be swayed and become sympathetic (12:13–17, 18–27, 28–34). The section may have a controversy source behind it. Then there follow two incidents featuring scribes, a denial that the Messiah must necessarily be understood in terms of a Son of David, presumably a warrior leader in the tradition of David (12:35–37), and despite the "good scribe" in the previous passage (12:32–34), a denunciation of scribes (12:38–40). The section closes on the widow's sacrifice, which anticipates the sacrifice of Jesus.

13:1–37:   *The apocalyptic discourse.*   After 12:44, there are no more summaries and no more transitional units or stories. Rather, two important sections, an apocalyptic discourse (Mark 13) and the Passion narrative (Mark 14–16), are developed. Each has an introduction composed by Mark (13:1–5a; 14:1–2, 10–11). These passages are important indicators of Mark's intended structure. The content of this millennial speech has been discussed in Chapter Three—which should be reviewed—and earlier the social and historical context of the gospel was developed in relation to this discourse. The concluding ethical exhortation (13:28–37) is most probably a Markan addition. Certainly this ethical section reflects Mark's message to his readers. Similarly, the juxtaposition of the apocalyptic discourse with the Passion narrative reflects the author's attempt to have his readers see their situation as they watch for the *parousia* as necessarily and profoundly affected by the Passion of Jesus.

14:1–16:8:   **The Passion narrative.**   This section—the most unified of all of the Markan sections—will be discussed unit by unit.

14:1–11: *The introduction.* Here Mark takes a traditional account of an anointing of Jesus by an unknown woman at Bethany and intercalates it into the introduction to the Passion narrative. The intercalation has the ironic effect of juxtaposing the plots of the authorities and the connivance of Judas Iscariot with an anointing of Jesus as the Messiah ("anointed one").

14:12–25: *Jesus' last meal with his disciples.* The parallel in 1 Cor. 11:23–26 indicates that Mark is using a traditional account of the Last Supper. However, the emphasis on the betrayal is a characteristically Markan emphasis, as is the language in Mark 14:21 ("is betrayed" is *paradidotai* from *paradidonai,* the verb used in the Passion predictions, 9:31 and 10:33). Members of the Jesus Movement traditionally used this language in describing the Passion of Jesus, and the author of Mark follows this precedent, especially by using it in the predictions. For Mark, in contrast to the author of the Fourth Gospel (and probably Paul), Jesus' last meal with his disciples was a Passover meal (there are many historical problems about identifying this meal with the **Passover,** however).

14:26–31: *Prediction of the flight of the disciples and the betrayal by Peter.* Again, Mark is moving his readers carefully to the climax of themes very important to him: the suffering and death of the Messiah and the misunderstanding of the disciples. Note that 14:28 predicts the movement toward the anticipated *parousia* in "Galilee," a prediction that will be recalled in 16:7.

14:32–52: *The betrayal and the arrest.* This narrative represents Markan redaction of a traditional narrative and reflects the Markan emphasis on the disciples' failures: They do not watch as they were commanded to do, but rather fall asleep three times (14:37, 38), and they flee from the scene of Jesus' arrest (14:50). In 14:41, it further reflects the traditional language used of the Passion of Jesus, "the Son of Man is betrayed (*paradidotai*) . . ." The young man who fled naked is a quite mysterious reference (see discussions of the *Secret Gospel of Mark*).

14:53–72: *The betrayal by Peter and an intercalated account of the night "trial" before the Sanhedrin.* First, there is the intercalated account of the night trial before the Sanhedrin (14:55–65), but is "trial" the correct term? The Mishnah tractate *Sanhedrin,* although the source is somewhat later than Mark, says that court proceedings cannot be held on the Sabbath or holy days and that capital cases cannot be tried at night. It appears that Mark composed this narrative. It functions to humiliate Jesus (like a "status degradation ritual" [Neyrey]). It brings his views of Jesus to a climax. When the high priest challenges whether Jesus is "the Messiah, the Son of the Blessed One," i.e., Son of God (14:61), the two titles that have been separately juxtaposed with "Son of Man" earlier in the gospel are brought together. This linking was anticipated in the transfiguration story (9:2–8). Here Jesus publicly accepts the titles (14:62). Thus Mark's Jesus formally abandons the **Messianic Secret** by using "I am"—a formula of self-identification for deities, heroes or heroines, and redeemers in the Hellenistic world, and indeed in the ancient Near East at a much earlier period (Exod. 3:14–15; much used in the gospel of John). Jesus himself uses such a formula earlier in Mark (6:50; cf. Mark 13:6). Then Jesus goes on to interpret both Christ and Son of God in terms of Son of Man, the last such reinterpretation in the gospel. The Messianic Secret *is now revealed:* Jesus is both Christ and Son of God, but as such he has to be understood in light of the emphases associated with Son of Man.

The betrayal by Peter is also a climax, a climax to the presentation of Peter as representative disciple typifying in himself the promise and failure of discipleship as such: the confession (8:29); the misunderstanding (8:32); the leader at the transfiguration (9:5); the responsible person at Gethsemane (14:37). Here he betrays Jesus, as had been predicted after the Last Supper (14:30–31) and then collapses (14:72) in a scene that Aristotle would have recognized as "cathartic."

15:1–47:   *The trial before Pilate and the crucifixion.*   This section is probably in the main from pre-Markan tradition. It heavily quotes or alludes to the scriptures, especially in the crucifixion scene itself where 15:23 = Ps. 69:21; 15:24 – Ps. 22:18; 15:29 = Ps. 22:7; 15:34 = Ps. 22:1; 15:36 = Ps. 69:21. Thus details in this section have probably been added through constant retelling and recollection of what members of the Jesus Movement believed were prophecies about the crucifixion.

An incident of particular importance, in view of earlier elements in the gospel, is the rending of the temple curtain (15:38). The curtain separated the innermost part of the Jerusalem temple, the Holy of Holies, which only the high priest might enter and where God was particularly to be experienced, from the remainder of the temple. Its rending probably symbolizes traditional Christian interpretation of the death of Jesus as removing the last barrier between God and man. However, in Mark's gospel it seems to allude to the cleansing of the temple by means of the fig tree incident (11:13–25) and emphasizes that the temple not only no longer exists, but also is no longer needed (it is cursed like the fig tree?). In other words, it is most likely part of Mark's attempt to come to terms with the catastrophe of the temple destruction in 70 c.e.

The next verse (15:39) is also very important because the centurion's confession of Jesus as Son of God is the climax of Mark's view of the identity of Jesus. It is the first and only statement about Jesus' identity by a human being in the gospel that is not immediately corrected or reinterpreted. The reason is that after 14:62 the reinterpretation of a confession of Jesus as Christ or Son of God by a use of "Son of Man" is complete, the **Messianic Secret** is finally revealed, and such a correct confession is now possible. That a Roman centurion makes the confession symbolizes Mark's concern for the Gentiles, also to be seen in his reference to Galilee (14:28 and 16:7).

16:1–8:   *The Resurrection.*   A major problem for **Text Criticism** is whether 16:8 was the real ending of the gospel. The variant manuscript endings are shown in this list of the four endings of Mark:

1. **Shortest Ending:** 16:8 So they (the women) went out and fled from the tomb, for terror and amazement had seized them; and they said nothing to anyone, for they were afraid.

2. **Shorter Ending:** 16:9 And all that had been commanded them they told briefly to those around Peter. And afterward Jesus himself sent out through them, from east to west, the sacred and imperishable proclamation of eternal salvation.

3. **Longer Ending:** 16:9 Now after he rose early on the first day of the week, he appeared first to Mary Magdalene, from whom he had cast out seven demons. (10) She went out and told those who had been with him, while they were mourning and weeping. (11) But when they heard that he was alive and had been seen by her, they would not believe it. (12) After this he appeared in another form to two of them, as they were walking into the country. (13) And they went back and told the

rest, but they did not believe them. (14) Later he appeared to the eleven themselves as they were sitting at the table; and he upbraided them for their lack of faith and stubbornness, because they had not believed those who saw him after he had risen. * (15) And he said to them, "Go into all the world and proclaim the good news to the whole creation. (16) The one who believes and is baptized will be saved; but the one who does not believe will be condemned. (17) And these signs will accompany those who believe: by using my name they will cast out demons; they will speak in new tongues; (18) they will pick up snakes in their hands, and if they drink any deadly thing, it will not hurt them; they will lay their hands on the sick, and they will recover." (19) So then the Lord Jesus, after he had spoken to them, was taken up into heaven and sat down at the right hand of God. (20) And they went out and proclaimed the good news everywhere, while the Lord worked with them and confirmed the message by the signs that accompanied it.

4. **Longest Ending** (*Manuscript W has the longer ending plus the following words after verse 14): And they excused themselves, saying, "This age of lawlessness and unbelief is under Satan, who does not allow the truth and power of God to prevail over the unclean things of the spirits. Therefore reveal your righteousness now"— thus they spoke to Christ. And Christ replied to them, "The term of years of Satan's power has been fulfilled, but other terrible things draw near. And for those who have sinned I was handed over to death, that they may return to the truth and sin no more, that they may inherit the spiritual and imperishable glory of righteousness that is in heaven."

"For they were afraid," the shortest ending (no. 1), seems abrupt. Most Text Critics think that early church manuscript copyists tried to "correct" it by adding two new, smoother endings: a shorter ending after verse 8 (no. 2) and a longer ending that the old King James Version has as verses 9–20 (no. 3). In addition to these three endings, one manuscript (W) of the longer ending adds another verse, which really makes it a fourth, or longest, ending (no. 4). It is clearly an attempt to explain the disciples' blindness in the Markan story as the work of the devil. All modern translations relegate the shorter, longer, and longest endings to the footnotes and print the shortest ending as 16:8.

This shortest ending is odd. It is even odder in Greek because the Greek sentence "for they were afraid" (Greek *kai ephobounto gar*) ends with the coordinating conjunction "for" (Greek *gar*), which obviously does not coordinate or link anything. Some scholars speculate that the text of the gospel was accidentally mutilated, that is, that the original ending was lost. Other scholars think that the ending as it stands in 16:8, despite its unusual nature, is appropriate to the gospel's consistent thrust through the Passion to the *parousia* and its view of the readers as standing between those events. Thus some **Literary Critics** think that the author wanted to leave the readers/hearers "up in the air" anticipating the Messiah's return. This point is especially pertinent for those who think of the gospel as parable.

Mark 16:1–8 sounds especially like the author of the gospel. First, the author portrays this whole experience in terms of ASC phenomena, and in that respect it is similar to his baptism, walking on the sea, and transfiguration stories. Second, Mark 16:7 recalls Jesus' earlier command for the disciples to go to Galilee after his resurrection

(14:28). It thus seems to be an emphasis that the *parousia* will occur in Galilee. A third Markan feature is the presence of the women. Recall that **anecdotes** about women earlier in story serve as models of faith (5:24–34; 7:25–30; 12:41–44; 14:3–9). This is significant because the male disciples have not been good models of faith. Yet, fourth, 16:7, "tell his disciples *and Peter,*" should be read in the light of Jesus' prophecy about Peter's denials in 14:72. In that verse, Peter cried for having denied Jesus, that is, the verse implies that Peter was repentant and would be restored. It is possible to see it as the author's hope for a similar happy ending out of the problems afflicting the readers/hearers whom Peter represents in his narratives.

FURTHER OBSERVATIONS

Further observations on some of the points touched on in the preceding discussion can now be made.

Esoteric Secrecy and Mysterious Revelation: The Messianic Secret and the Markan Christology

As noted in the preceding exegetical outline, a major motif in the Gospel of Mark is what scholars call the **Messianic Secret.** Jesus' identity as Messiah is very dominant, but it is part of the more subtle motif about esoteric secrecy and mysterious revelation that pervades the Markan gospel as a whole. Scholars interpret this motif, usually expressed in the words of Jesus in the narrative, as the special and intentional emphasis of the writer. In other words, it was not a secret and self-revelation emanating from the historical Jesus, but rather "*Mark's*" motif about secrecy and revelation.

Here are some of the most explicit references about secrecy in Mark.

The Kingdom of God

4:11: "And [when he was alone] he said to them [the twelve disciples and a few others around him]: 'To you has been given *the secret* of the Kingdom of God, but for those outside everything is in parables; so that they may indeed see but not perceive, and may indeed hear but not understand; lest they should turn again and be forgiven.'"

Exorcisms

1:34: "[Jesus] would not permit the demons to speak because they knew him."
3:12: "[Jesus] strictly ordered them [the demons] not to make him known."

Healings

1:44: "See that you say nothing to anyone" (cleansing of the "leper").
5:43: "And he [Jesus] strictly charged them [the people] that no one should know this . . ." (resuscitation of the synagogue leader's daughter).

7:36: "Then Jesus ordered them [the people] to tell no one; but the more he ordered them, the more they zealously proclaimed it" (healing of the deaf man).

8:26: "And he sent him away to his home, saying, 'Do not even go into the village'" (healing of the blind man).

Disciples

8:30: "(Peter:) 'You are the Messiah.' And he [Jesus] sternly ordered them not to tell anyone about him."

9:9: ". . . he ordered them to tell no one what they had seen [on the mount of transfiguration], until after the Son of Man had risen from the dead."

The first category (Mark 4:11–12) shows that for Mark, Jesus' parables were interpreted as riddles meant to be understood only by a select few. Scholars think that parables originally told by the historical Jesus to tease the imagination of hearers became for the Markan writer esoteric wisdom for insiders, especially the twelve disciples. However, their privileged insider position, as the development of the story shows, was not maintained (see the "Blindness of the Disciples" following).

The other three categories focus on Jesus' hidden identity as Messiah. The author of the gospel apparently wants to show that Jesus is not a messiah *simply* because he performs acts of miraculous power like other ancient miracle-working heroes. Indeed, he stresses that those who are healed already come to Jesus with faith. Nonetheless, the miracles still play a role because the people sometimes do not heed his commands to remain silent about his miracle-working identity. In the larger picture, however, Jesus' messianic identity is unveiled in mysterious and unexpected ways, especially through his suffering and death. This Markan perspective leads the author to reinterpret well-known traditional titles of social status and honor about messianic dignity, usually called "Christological titles." This point needs a little clarification.

We have studied what scholars sometimes call "Christological hymns." They are found in the Pauline literature and elsewhere (see especially Chapter Three). These poetic passages make confessions about Jesus' remarkable origins from God and his tremendous honor. In Mark, however, the identity of Jesus is gradually unveiled in *narrative* form. Some scholars call this a "narrative Christology." In the Gospel of Mark, the narrative focuses on the suffering and crucified one, as in Paul, but does it in story form. Yet, within the story there are also messianic or Christological titles that capture images of a variety of "messianic" expectations in Israel. These titles identify and crystallize specific cultural roles of status and honor in antiquity: "Son of David" (Israelite king descended from David), "Son of Man" (heavenly apocalyptic/millennial figure), "Son of God" (Hellenistic emperor, Israelite king, and/or miracle worker), "Lord" (emperor; a title for God in the Hebrew Scriptures), and "Messiah" ("anointed," usually in reference to kings). There are also other cultural roles less associated with titles: prophet, teacher, exorcist, healer, and martyr. The point is that Mark reinterprets and remolds these roles in relation to his portrayal of Jesus as the suffering, crucified, and resurrected one.

This point is easy to illustrate. As noted in the exegetical outlines, Jesus is "Son of God," a title for kings, emperors, and miracle workers. The title is found in key revelatory scenes: at Jesus' baptism by God (1:11), at the transfiguration by God (9:7), at the trial in Jesus' own words (14:61–2), and at the cross by a centurion (15:39). He is also so identified by demons (3:11; 5:7). "Son of God" is certainly an important role for Jesus. Superhuman beings and a single human, a Gentile, identify him correctly. Thus the "Son of God" title was probably present in the author's initial statement, despite some textual variants (1:1; see preceding and following). However, this title seems to be interpreted and interrelated with reference to other titles, especially the "Son of Man." There are two occurrences of Daniel's title for the heavenly apocalyptic figure in the first section (2:10, 28). They are balanced by two uses of "Son of God" in relation to Jesus' miracle working in the second (3:11; 5:7).

Again, the titles "Christ" and "Son of Man" are juxtaposed in the story of the confession of Peter at Caesarea Philippi (8:27–34) and are immediately followed by the use of "Son of God" at the transfiguration (9:7). Further, "Christ," "Son of God," and "Son of Man" are juxtaposed at the trial before the Sanhedrin (14:55–65), and "Son of God" is the title in the climactic confession by the centurion (15:39). Thus Mark seems to use "Son of Man" to interpret what he considers to be an inadequate understanding of Christ and the Son of God prevalent in his day. Moreover, "Son of Man" has a threefold emphasis: authority on earth (2:10, 28), apocalyptic authority at the final judgment (8:38; 13:26), and necessary suffering (8:31; 9:31; 10:33–34, the Passion predictions). Some interpreters think that these last three suffering "Son of Man" sayings are Mark's answer to a *false* Christology he is combating.

The "Blindness" of Jesus' Disciples and His True "Following"

In Mark's parable interpretation (4:11–12), the disciples are insiders who receive special instruction in esoteric wisdom (cf. 4:13–34). Outsiders see and hear but do not *really* see and hear, that is, perceive and understand. Moreover, as Jesus' companions they should begin to understand the mysterious Messiah, like the true "disciples" (= readers/hearers of this story who are let in on the secret!). Yet, as Mark tells his story, the twelve disciples persistently, even increasingly, fail to "see" and understand. In contrast, outsiders are recipients of Jesus' compassion. Thus the insiders begin to look like outsiders, and some outsiders begin to look like insiders. Such role reversals are highlighted in the transitional section: Two blind men receive their sight (8:22–26; 10:46–52), but ironically the disciples, who have already been described as having "hardened hearts" (6:52; 7:18; 8:15, 21), misunderstand Jesus and his mission as the suffering martyr/Son of Man, as well as the true nature of their discipleship (8:32–33; 9:32–34; 10:35–37). They will not really "follow" Jesus "on the way" to his Passion and death. Ultimately, one of them betrays him, the rest abandon him, and at the end he is crucified alone. Again, if anyone is consistently loyal in the story, it is the Galilean women who look on his crucifixion from a distance (15:40–41) and come to bury him (16:1–8). Although burial of an unclean corpse would be "women's work," this role of the women seems consistent with **anecdotes** about women as models of faith earlier in the story (5:24–34; 7:25–30; 12:41–44; 14:3–9). Thus, as Mark would have it, the twelve (male) disciples never receive Jesus' final message that he would lead them back to Galilee, where the *parousia* will occur (16:8).

To what extent is Mark still thinking about "disciples" *in general?* Some modern interpreters argue that the "blindness of the disciples" should be seen as a polemic against certain disciples, for example, Peter, and thus that it symbolizes the writer's opposition to "church authority," that is, in *Mark's* day. In other words, Mark engages in "disciple bashing" because he thinks that the church leaders in his time, symbolized by Peter and the other disciples, do not understand the real nature of Jesus and discipleship. That is the reason why they do not get the final message of Jesus about going to Galilee for the *parousia*. Why else would they be portrayed so negatively?

Yet, other modern interpreters have argued that this theory paints the disciples too negatively. Thus, as noted, Peter seems to be rehabilitated in 16:1–8 (see earlier). From this perspective, Mark is simply addressing the fact that any disciple who wishes to follow Jesus is in danger of not understanding the significance of Jesus and commitment to follow him. The true disciple must be prepared to endure suffering and martyrdom. If these latter interpreters are correct, Mark would be warning about the potential misunderstanding of *any* disciple. Although this position is more attractive in relation to other New Testament literature that portrays Peter and the disciples as important church leaders in the interim between Jesus' death and writing of the gospels, it cannot be denied that the Gospel of Mark is very hard on the disciples. Thus the former interpretation may be more probable, but it does not totally cancel out the latter interpretation.

In either case, the authors of the gospels of Matthew and Luke (like the later copyists of Mark!) were not happy with the Markan portrait of Peter and the disciples. Following the **Two-Source Theory** and **Redaction Criticism,** we can see that they changed it by portraying them more favorably.

The Passion of Jesus

It has often been said that the Gospel of Mark is "a Passion narrative with an extended introduction." In other words, the drive of this gospel is toward Jesus' suffering and martyrdom, with such a fate possible for those who follow him. Structural analysis bears this out. Every major section of the gospel ends on a note looking toward the Passion, and the central section, 8:27–10:45, is concerned with interpreting it:

3:6	The plot "to destroy" Jesus
6:6	The unbelief of the people of "his own country"
8:21	The misunderstanding of the disciples
10:45	The cross as a "ransom for many"
12:44	The widow's sacrifice, which anticipates Jesus' sacrifice

All through the gospel, the Passion and the *parousia* of Jesus stand in a certain tension with each other. For example, the apocalyptic discourse of Mark 13, in which the *parousia* is the central concern, is parallel to the Passion narrative of 14:1–16:8. They both have introductions—neither one is subordinated to the other—and there is an element of parallelism in that the events predicted for members of the Jesus Movement in 13:9 are exactly what happens to Jesus in the Passion narrative. Furthermore, as noted, there is a relationship between the uniform "after three days" of the prediction of the resurrection in 8:31 (and 9:31; 10:34) and the "after six days" of the transfiguration in 9:2. If the transfiguration anticipates the *parousia,* the sequence would seem to be: after three days, the resurrection; after six days, the *parousia.* Moreover, 9:9 indicates that the event represented by the transfiguration comes after the resurrection and will be of concern to the disciples then: "he ordered them to tell no one about what they had seen, until after the Son of Man had risen from the dead." Finally, there are the two references to Galilee in 14:28, "*after* I am raised up, I will go before you into Galilee," and in 16:7, "he is going before you into Galilee; there you will see him." These appear to refer to the anticipated *parousia.* They are, therefore, a final indication of a consistent movement in the gospel through the Passion, including the resurrection, to the *parousia.* Mark is addressing people in a situation like that of the women at the tomb, aware of the resurrection and awaiting the *parousia* in "trembling and astonishment" (16:8).

THE INTERPRETATION OF THE GOSPEL OF MARK

From the very beginning, the Gospel of Mark presented problems to its interpreters because of tensions within the gospel itself. There is a tension between the purpose of the evangelist and the actual needs of the church within a generation of the writing. There is a further tension between the evangelist's purpose and the literary form he chose to express that purpose. These two points need to be clarified.

It seems likely that the Markan evangelist followed an apocalyptic purpose, writing within the circumstances of the resurgence of apocalyptic thought during and immediately after the war with Rome, 66–70 C.E. Nevertheless, for all the resurgence of millennialism at that time (and at subsequent times of persecution or catastrophe), apocalyptic itself was on the verge of an inevitable decline in the churches of the Jesus Movement. Its members were faced with the necessity not only of coming to terms with the delay of the *parousia,* but also with finding a way of living out their faith in a world that continued to exist despite all their hopes, expectations, and prayers to the contrary. The gospel story became something like a foundational myth from which members of the Jesus Movement lived, as the Israelites lived from the myths of Creation and the Exodus. However, its "myth" was not conservative because it was millennial; its symbolism was a symbolism of suffering and death with the promise of new life.

A second element of tension was that between the purpose of the evangelist and the literary form through which he expressed that purpose, between his apocalyptic purpose and his narrative story about Jesus. There is no doubt that the narratives of Mark sound literal. That is why the gospel has often been considered to be personal reminiscence of an eyewitness (for example, from Peter). However, the preceding discussion has shown that the personal reminiscence is only a shadow, if indeed there is any personal reminiscence at all. Yet, the narratives *sound* realistic. With the decline of millennialism in some churches, the apocalyptic purpose of Mark became less clear, and what remained was the realistic nature of the narratives. As Gnosticism grew and spread, it preferred gospels expressing its teaching in the "secret" words of Jesus to his disciples, or in post-resurrection revelatory discourses. The more "orthodox" churches combated the Gnostic Christian movement by emphasizing the apostolic authority of *its* gospels, and under these circumstances a tradition developed that the Gospel of Mark was built up largely of the reminiscences of Peter.

This realism offers the first clue to the interpretation of Mark's gospel: The narratives are meant to be understood. The evangelist himself takes pains to help his readers and hearers by explaining the value of coins (12:42) and by giving the Roman equivalent for the name of a place (15:16). Readers and hearers should appreciate the significance of the charge of blasphemy in 2:7. The forgiveness of sins was not only reserved to God, it was reserved to God at the end of time. The force of the plot in 3:6—Pharisees and Herodians plot against Jesus—has political implications. The interpreter needs to know enough about the references and allusions in these narratives for them to become realistic to us and not strange or foreign.

A second clue lies in the fact that the narrative functions in a certain way: It draws its readers and hearers into the story. When the one who took up his Cross challenges the disciples to be prepared to take up theirs (8:34), or as he who gave his life interprets the giving as a "ransom for many" (10:45), readers and hearers are *there,* like a disciple challenged. Similarly, in the dark hours of the Passion when Peter protests that he is loyal (14:26–31) but ultimately abandons Jesus, readers and hearers share the catharsis of Peter's breakdown in the courtyard (14:72) and wonder whether they will also abandon the Messiah in a time of crisis. The natural function of narrative is to help the readers/hearers understand the voices, take part in the action, get involved in the plot, identify with the characters. The effectiveness of the evangelist Mark as a preacher is that he has cast his message in a realistic narrative rather than in the direct discourse of a letter or a homily. The realism of Mark's narratives is significant because it enables those who read and hear to be caught up into the narrative as a participant.

From this perspective, it is possible to appreciate the affinities and differences between the apocalyptic Mark and the Book of Revelation. Their social context was quite different. Both were written in a period of turmoil and an accompanying resurgence of millennial fervor; one because of the war between Rome and Israel and the other because of fears about persecution of Christ adherents in the last decade of the century. Both address their readers directly out of their narrative: Mark by a parabolic discourse, sections of teaching on discipleship, an apocalyptic discourse, and so on; John of Patmos by letters to the churches and interpretations of his visions. Both have essentially the same purpose: to prepare their readers for the imminent *parousia.* But there is an extremely important difference between them. Mark's narratives are more realistic; John's more symbolic. The one captures the imagination of his readers and hearers by drawing them into his narrative as participants in a story, the other by the sheer power of symbols to challenge, evoke, and sustain.

Like all writings that contain millennial dreams and visions, the Gospel of Mark needs to be interpreted in its own time before it can be interpreted in general. Millennial dreams and visions are usually the stuff of those who experience oppression. For modern Western readers, the Jesus who comes on the clouds of heaven as Son of Man must be symbolic. These readers can allow Mark to catch them up into his narratives as participants and to challenge them with the teaching and example of that Jesus.

STUDY QUESTIONS

1. Who was John Mark? What is "the Papias tradition"? What are some problems with the tradition?

2. What do modern scholars say about authorship, date, and place of this gospel? Why do they make these conclusions? What is the gospel's social context? What are some possibilities for Mark's use of oral and written tradition? How did Mark compose his story? How does he use numbers?

3. What are summaries? "Sandwiches"? What is the role of "geography" and topography in Mark? How does this gospel treat John the Baptizer? What is the central role of miracles in Mark? Mystery and secrecy?

4. Who are some of the main characters in the story? What is the role of the disciples? The crowds? The scribes? The Pharisees? The priests? The Romans? What are some of the important Christological titles, especially the "Son of God" and the "Son of Man"?

Photo 9.1 A scribe at work in a way that has not changed through the centuries. Only in the Gospel of Matthew does Jesus refer to a "scribe . . . trained for the kingdom of heaven" (13:52), usually considered by modern scholars to be an apt description of the anonymous author of this gospel. See the medieval scribe at the beginning of Chapter One.

CHAPTER NINE

THE GOSPEL OF MATTHEW: OBEDIENCE TO THE NEW REVELATION

The Gospel of Matthew was placed first among the four gospels because it was believed in the late second century to have been the first gospel written (Irenaeus *Against Heresies* 3.1.1–2). It had become influential in Israelite forms of the Jesus Movement and was fast becoming the most important gospel among all the Jesus movements in general. Its stories about Jesus' miraculous birth; its representation of Jesus' moral discourses; its potential for liturgy (e.g., the Lord's Prayer, the Last Supper); its views of church discipline, law, and discipleship; its stress on Jesus' presence with believers until his return—all made it destined to become the pre-eminent gospel. By the third century c.e., the Roman bishops argued that Jesus' grant of honor to Peter in Matt. 16:17–19, combined with Peter's burial place in Rome, legitimated their claim to be the true heirs of Peter, their primacy among the bishops, and thus their authority as popes. Ultimately, then, Matthew became very special to the Western Roman branch of Christendom.

EARLY TRADITIONS ABOUT MATTHEW

The earliest explicit reference to "Matthew" outside the New Testament comes from the same author who also is the first to mention "Mark," namely, **Papias,** bishop of Hierapolis in Asia Minor, who wrote in the first half of the second century c.e. As recorded by the fourth-century historian Eusebius, the Papias tradition about Matthew states:

> Then Matthew put together [text variant: wrote] the sayings (*logia*) in the Hebrew (*Hebraiois*) dialect (*dialectō*) and each one translated (*hērmēneusen*) them as he was able.
>
> (Eusebius *Ecclesiastical History* 3.39.16)

The Papias tradition about Matthew opens up a couple of problems. The first is that Papias referred only to a *person* "Matthew." Was he then describing a *gospel?* The usual view is that Papias probably had the gospel in mind because he had just described how "Mark" came to be written (see Chapter Eight).

The second problem is this: How should the italicized Greek words be translated? If Papias meant that Matthew originally wrote in the *Hebrew* language, others had to *translate* his gospel into Greek. However, the gospel we have, experts agree, was originally written in Greek. One solution is to say that Papias meant that Matthew originally wrote in the Hebrew *manner* (not dialect) and that each *interpreted* (not translated) as he was able. Translation was not necessary. However, this solution does not accord with ancient scholars' understanding of Papias' meaning. They thought he meant *language* (Irenaeus *Against Heresies* 31.1–2; Eusebius *Ecclesiastical History* 3.24.5). Most modern scholars agree, although many think that Papias meant by "Hebrew" the *Aramaic* language (see John 20:16). If Papias did in fact mean a Semitic (either Hebrew or Aramaic) language, he must also have meant "translated," and the dilemma that our Matthew is not a translation remains.

In short, the most common scholarly view of the **Papias tradition** is that Papias was referring to a Semitic language document, probably Aramaic; that he was indeed referring to a gospel, and that *logia* meant "sayings," its usual meaning. Papias meant that Matthew wrote a gospel of sayings in the Aramaic language and that it had to be translated. But is this our Gospel of Matthew? Before answering this question, recall some facts about "Matthew."

The Name "Matthew"

The name "Matthew" in English comes from the Greek *Matthaios,* which is a translation of the Hebrew *Mattiyah,* "gift of God." Although the name was common in antiquity, the Papias tradition, as well as others based on it (e.g., Irenaeus *Against Heresies* 3.1.1), is no doubt referring to Jesus' disciple "Matthew." However, there was some confusion about this disciple. The name "Matthew" is found in all four of the lists of the twelve disciples/apostles (Mark 3:18; Matt. 10:3; Luke 6:15; Acts 1:13). However, the only writer to identify this Matthew as "the toll collector" (Greek *telōnēs*) is author of the Gospel of Matthew (10:3). In Mark, Jesus called a toll collector to be his disciple, but he was named "Levi son of Alphaeus" (Mark 2:14). Luke accepts the view of his Markan source (Luke 5:27). However, Levi is not in any of the disciple lists. Further, Mark identifies Levi as the "son of Alphaeus" (Mark 2:14; cf. *GPet* 60); curiously, a textual variant of Mark describes a certain *James* as the "son of Alphaeus," and this James the son of Alphaeus is in the twelve disciple lists!

Why did the Gospel of Matthew call the toll collector "Matthew" and in contrast to Luke not follow his source? A traditional view is that Levi and Matthew were one and the same (Jerome *Prologue to Matthew*). However, there is no evidence for a name change of this sort. The simplest explanation is that the author of the Gospel of Matthew, like the later copyist of Mark 2:14 who changed "Levi" to "James," sought to replace an unknown person (Levi) with one known from the disciple lists (Matthew). In short, following the **Two-Source Theory,** the author of the Gospel of Matthew changed "Levi" in Mark 2:14 to "Matthew" sitting at the "toll booth" (9:9) because "Matthew" was in his traditional disciple list. Then he inserted "the toll collector" after "Matthew" in the disciple list (10:3) to show that it was the same Matthew. (The later copyist made the same move by calling the toll collector "James son of Alphaeus.") Luke, however, simply retained Mark's "Levi" in the toll booth story and "Matthew" in the disciple lists.

Why did the author of the Gospel of Matthew not choose some other disciple? There are several interesting theories (**Redaction Criticism**). First, "Matthew" was in the disciple lists. Second, certain circles no doubt honored Matthew. A third theory is that the word "disciple" (*mathētēs*) and the command "learn!" (*mathete*), an idea prevalent in the Matthean Gospel, suggested the name *Matthias* as the representative of learning and discipleship. Fourth, perhaps the author considered that the name "Matthew" ("gift of Yahweh") symbolized God's acceptance of "toll collectors and sinners." Whatever the precise explanation—some combination is possible—*only the Gospel of Matthew claims that the Apostle Matthew in the lists is the Capernaum toll collector* (9:9; 10:3). Papias undoubtedly meant this Matthew.

GENERAL HISTORICAL CRITICISM: AUTHOR, DATE, PLACE

The **Papias tradition** presents a number of historical problems. The first is, as noted, that language experts do not think that Greek Matthew is a translation from a Semitic language, although they recognize Semitic influences. Moreover, it makes very extensive use of the Greek Gospel of Mark. It is likely that a bilingual, perhaps trilingual, person composed our Gospel of Matthew in *Greek*. That does not accord with what Papias meant.

The second problem is that our Gospel of Matthew is not simply a collection of "sayings," the usual meaning of *logia*. Indeed, Papias' description of Matthew sounds more like an Aramaic form of **Q**! Was Papias referring to some tradition about Q and confusing it with Matthew? No one knows. The conclusion is inescapable: Papias' description does not seem to refer to the Gospel of Matthew as we know it.

Papias' statement about Matthew is also difficult to accept on the basis of other historical factors. Ancient writers concluded from Papias that Mark was written sometime in the early 60s. Correspondingly they deduced that the Gospel of Matthew, supposedly written by a disciple, must have been composed earlier than the 60s (Irenaeus *Against Heresies* 3.1.1–2; Eusebius *Ecclesiastical History* 5.8.2). However, modern scholars date Mark shortly after 70 C.E. because the "**abomination that makes desolate**" referred to the desecration of the temple by Titus at the time of the destruction of Jerusalem (Mark 13:14). The Matthean author probably understood the "abomination that makes desolate" the same way (Matt. 24:15–18; 22:7; cf. 21:41). Combining all this with the **Two-Source Theory,** the Gospel of Matthew also must have been written sometime after 70 C.E.

If the author of 1 Peter knew the gospel (especially 1 Pet. 2:12 [Matt. 5:16]; 1 Pet. 3:14 [Matt. 5:10]), the latest possible date for the Matthean Gospel might be established by the dating of 1 Peter—perhaps late first century C.E.—but it is possible that they shared only common oral tradition. Thus scholars usually established the latest possible date for Matthew by arguing that Ignatius of Antioch (Syria), an early bishop and martyr, seems to know Matt. 3:15, "that all righteousness might be fulfilled by him" (Ignatius *To the Smyrnaeans* 1.1; cf. also *To the Philadelphians* 3:1 [Matt. 15:13]). These words, say Redaction Critics, were not oral tradition, but rather composed by the author of Matthew (see following). Modern critics place the period of Ignatius' letter writing in the early second century (fourth-century Eusebius, who dated Ignatius' martyrdom in the reign of the Roman emperor Trajan, 98–117 C.E.; see *Ecclesiastical History* 3.21–22). Thus the gospel would likely have been written before 110 C.E.

Is it possible to be more precise than sometime between 70 and 110 C.E.? Two factors are very important. First, one generation after Mark would place the composition of Matthew about midway between 70 and 110, or about 90 C.E. Second, the conflict with Pharisees is heightened in the gospel, and this fact fits the period when the Pharisees of the **Jamnia (Yavneh) Academy** were asserting their power over the Israelites, that is, about 80–90 C.E. Thus several considerations converge to conclude that the Gospel of Matthew was written about 80–90 C.E. This late date adds difficulty to its having been written by a disciple of Jesus. Again, the composition of the First Gospel by "Matthew the toll collector" is highly unlikely.

Finally, *where* was the Gospel of Matthew written? The Church Fathers, following Papias, deduced that Jesus' disciple wrote for his own people in Judea (Jerome *Commentary on Matthew*; Monarchian *Prologue to Matthew*). A few recent interpreters have tried to make a case for Palestine, too. Because the gospel has hints of having been written in an urban area, some city with Greek-speaking Israelite members in the Jesus Movement is usually sought. One suggestion is Jerusalem, although it is not very likely after its destruction in 70 C.E. Another is the "Roman capital" of Palestine, Caesarea Maritima (see Chapter One), but the Israelites there were massacred in 66 C.E., and apparently very few of those who escaped returned. Also, the ancient **Church Father** Eusebius of Caesarea never mentions the Gospel of Matthew. Another possibility is suggested by comments that Galilee and Judea lie "beyond the Jordan" (Matt. 19:1; 4:15). Thus a few scholars have suggested a city *east* of the Jordan River, for example, Pella, where, tradition says, members of the Jesus Movement fled at the outbreak of the wars with Rome in 70. Still others, however, suggest Alexandria, Egypt, or Edessa, Syria, but they have not won many adherents. Some city in southern Syria just north of Palestine is possible, but speculative.

Most modern interpreters have therefore returned to Antioch in Syria as the place of composition. It was important for Gentile missions, but it also contained a sizable Israelite population. Peter, the most important disciple in the gospel, had been important there (see Chapters Three, Four, and Six [the Antioch Incident]). Syria was not far from Palestine, and the gospel contains possible links with Palestine, for example, millennial thought and a strong Israelite flavor. Thus a city in Syria meets the conditions of the gospel. This suggestion is reinforced by the probability that Ignatius of Antioch referred to the gospel, as mentioned earlier. Thus Antioch is a plausible choice.

In summary, the First Gospel was anonymous and presumably circulated anonymously at first. It was written about 80–90 C.E., perhaps in Antioch of Syria. The ascription of the gospel to "Matthew the toll collector," disciple of Jesus and eyewitness to his life, is probably a second-century attempt to give special authority to what was becoming the most important gospel. It was likely that the super-scription "According to Matthew" was inserted at the same time and thus that Papias wrote that "Matthew" collected the sayings of Jesus in the "Hebrew language" because Jesus and his followers spoke Aramaic. For convenience the author will be called "Matthew."

MATTHEW AND GENRE

"Matthew" rarely uses the word *gospel,* and when he does, it refers to what Jesus says orally (cf. e.g., 4:23; 9:35). He does not call his whole work a "gospel," as *might* be thought if he knew Mark 1:1 (see Chapter Eight for the theory that the term might not have been in Mark yet). Does he call it anything?

Matthew opens with these words: "An account of the genealogy of Jesus Christ, the Son of David, the Son of Abraham" (Matt. 1:1 NRSV). The English word "account" is literally "book" (Greek *biblos*), and the words "of the genealogy" are literally "of the origin" (Greek *geneseōs*). "Book of the origin of Jesus Christ . . ." has suggested to some modern interpreters that he might be referring to his whole composition. This is unlikely. Although "origin" could refer to the infancy story (Matt. 1–2), "an account of the genealogy" is supported by the fact that these very same words refer to a genealogy in Gen. 5:1, and the Matthean genealogy stresses the line of Abraham and David.

Yet, there is some notion in the First Gospel that the whole story is a new beginning. The Markan apocalyptic drama collapses past, present, and future. Although past, present, and future in some respects flow together in Matthew—much of the story is transparent for the author's own time—the time of Jesus in the past is more sharply focused. It is a special time, the time of fulfillment and revelation, a sacred time. The "church" is constituted on the basis of this sacred time. The sacred time of Jesus is the time of beginnings. As such, the gospel functions something like a "foundation myth": a myth of origins to which a later group relates by careful study and interpretation. Thus the gospel is often said to be "transparent," that is, you can see through it to understand the time when it was written.

Does this observation lead to more specificity about the genre of Matthew? In Chapter Eight, it was suggested that the precise nature of the Markan genre has features of a Hellenistic "biography" (Greek *bios*) but is finally difficult to determine. In the Matthean revision of Mark, the story now contains the birth and infancy, more explicit ethical teachings, and the moral example of Jesus himself. There is here a step toward "salvation history" in that Jesus' "pastness" is more fully developed as a model for the author's present. Further, the story begins with the credentials for a messiah descended from Abraham and David (1:2–17) and then from God (1:18–25). Great honor is being ascribed to Jesus by virtue of his birth. Thus the Gospel of Matthew is moving a step closer to the genre of Hellenistic "biography" (*bios*). One scholar has called it an *encomium* ("praise") biography. Yet, its Israelite qualities—genealogies, references to Scripture, fulfillment, and the like—are distinctive. Thus, by a narrower definition, it, like Mark, does not easily fit any known genre; however, by a broad notion of genre, the Gospel of Matthew is something like an Israelite *bios.*

SOCIAL-HISTORICAL CONTEXT

Genre functions in a historical and social context. To understand the Gospel of Matthew better, it will be helpful to recall some major developments in Israel in the period from about 70–100 C.E., the period of its composition.

You will recall that prior to 70 C.E., Palestine was a minor temple state, a colony subject to imperial Rome. The destruction of Jerusalem and its temple in 70 was catastrophic. It meant the destruction of Israel's social system, political organization, and economic order. Religiously, the holy temple and its sacrificial rituals were no longer available as a way of knowing God and experiencing forgiveness of sins. The holy city was no longer the center of pilgrimage for the great religious festivals.

There emerged a shift in the balance of power, status, and influence of the various Israelite parties, sects, and movements that existed before the war. The Sadducees, who were the aristocratic, primarily priestly, ruling elite of Jerusalem, lost their influence. The Essenes, a priestly anti-Sadducee sect along the Dead Sea, were overrun. More radical messianic, millennial "freedom fighters"—Josephus' "fourth philosophy"—provided some of the leadership for the final resistance to Rome, but their influence seems to have declined after the war. Josephus claims that the Sicarii committed suicide at Masada rather than be taken captive.

Of the major "philosophies" mentioned by Josephus, the **Pharisees** were left in an advantageous position after the war. They devoted themselves to applying the laws of purity to everyday life. They set up a new school at Yavneh (Jamnia) in the remote northwest of the ancient territory of Judah. Although the later rabbinic traditions about the **Academy** are difficult to use as sources of history, it appears that the aim of the Pharisees was to form a united Israel under their leadership and thus to bring an end to whatever Israelite factions and sects remained. Archeological evidence shows that synagogue buildings were being built in Palestine in this period, and the synagogue was the special province of the Pharisees. They seem to have introduced into the synagogue prayers the "**Prayer against the Heretics**" aimed at any sort of deviants, and they increasingly banned from the synagogues factions who did not agree with them. The process of settling the canon and text of the Hebrew Scriptures was probably begun. They were concerned particularly with the Torah, God's fundamental revelation of his will to his people, and its interpretation.

It is highly likely that the Matthean author wrote his gospel in the period when the Pharisees made their move to consolidate Israelite religion. Indeed, although the Yavneh Academy is not mentioned in the gospel, it is plausible that the author was in sharp opposition to Yavneh-influenced synagogues in some Gentile city with a strong Israelite element in its population, perhaps Antioch. Listen to the gospel's attitude about the Pharisees. On the one hand, "The scribes and the Pharisees sit on Moses' seat; so practice and observe whatever they *tell* you" (Matt. 23:2–3). On the other, "But not what they *do;* for they preach, but do not practice." Indeed, the condemnation becomes vitriolic. Six times comes the refrain: "Woe to you, scribes and Pharisees, hypocrites!" (23:13, 15, 23, 25, 27, 29), which is joined by "Woe to you blind guides" (23:16). Of them it is said, "So you also outwardly appear righteous to men, but within you are full of hypocrisy and iniquity" (23:28). In other words, Matthew honors the activity of the Pharisees and "their scribes" in interpreting the authoritative tradition; his quarrel with them is about the details of their interpretation, their quality of observance, and especially their public display of their alms-giving, prayer, and fasting (6:1–18).

The conflict with Pharisaism also seems apparent from Matt. 23:8–10. Here Matthew attributes to Jesus the view that his community should not use the titles of honor known to have great importance among the Pharisees (and some members of the Matthean community?):

> (8) ". . . you are not to be called *rabbi,* for you have one teacher and you are all students [Greek "brothers"].
>
> (9) And call no one your *father* on earth, for you have one Father—the one in heaven.
>
> (10) Nor are you to be called *instructors,* for you have one instructor, the Messiah."

The opposition to these titles betrays a distinct group whose leaders think of themselves as being in competition with the Pharisees, their leaders, and their interpretation of the Torah.

It is clear that the Matthean objection to Pharisaic leadership is expressed chiefly in a clash over the right interpretation of the Torah and its proper observance. For Matthew, Jesus is *the* instructor, *the* teacher, but more: the very fulfillment of the Torah and the prophets. He is the new Moses. Indeed, he is the new revelation. There remains, therefore, the further interpretation of his teaching by the Matthean equivalent of "scribes and Pharisees." In a key passage found only in the Gospel of Matthew, 5:17–20, Matthew's Jesus says,

> (17) "Do not think that I have come to abolish the law or the prophets; I have come not to abolish but to fulfil. (18) For truly I tell you, until heaven and earth pass away, not one letter, not one stroke of a letter, will pass from the law until all is accomplished. (19) Therefore, whoever breaks one of the least of these commandments, and *teaches* others to do the same, will be called least in the kingdom of heaven; but whoever does them and *teaches* them will be called great in the kingdom of heaven. (20) For I tell you, unless your righteousness exceeds that of the scribes and Pharisees, you will never enter the kingdom of heaven."

Thus it is necessary to practice a "higher righteousness," that is, an obedience to the Torah that exceeds that of the scribes and Pharisees (Matt. 5:17–20). Jesus' interpretation is the right interpretation; he teaches the famous Sermon on the Mount (Matt. 5–7), from which this emphasis is taken. Even more, *he is the new revelation and is to be obeyed.*

It is clear that the main external opponents of the Matthean community were the Pharisees. However, there were also conflicts *within* the Matthean group. Jesus' parables (13:24–30; 22:1–14; 25:1–13) and statements about the Son of Man (13:41; 16:28) indicate that the Matthean author considered his church to contain a mixture of both good and evil. The group was disturbed by false prophets (7:15–20) and "antinomians" ("opposed to the law," from Greek *nomos,* "law"; 5:17–20; 7:15–20). Some scholars surmise that they were in some way related to Paul, who had come to think that the Torah was not sufficient for salvation. There was also some internal discord about a Matthean faction called the "little ones" (e.g., 18:6).

No one in the Matthean context should be called "rabbi," "father," and "instructor," says the author (Matt. 23:8–10). Yet, there were leadership roles in the community. Prophets were highly valued (e.g., 10:41; 23:34) and warnings against false prophets were issued (7:15–23; cf. 24:11–12, 23–24; cf. *Didachē* 11–13). Some scribes were seen in a positive light (13:52; 23:34), and there were "wise men" who are sent out, perhaps to satellite groups in the region (23:34). Perhaps "righteous men" were also a distinct group of leaders (especially 10:41–42; 13:17; 23:29).

In order to protect against external opponents and internal factions, the Matthean writer stresses "law and order." In this connection, the Gospel of Matthew is the only one of the four gospels to use the word "**church**" (Greek *ekklēsia*). The term is found in two places. The first of them alters Peter's confession in Mark, first, by adding the title "Son of God" and then by inserting the so-called blessing of Peter and the "church" saying. Together they are called the "**praise of Peter.**" The following list puts his insertion in boldface:

Mark	Matthew	Passage
8:27–29	16:13–16	Peter confesses Jesus as Messiah, Son of God
—	**16:17**	**Jesus honors Peter by giving him his blessing**
—	**16:18–19**	**Jesus honors Peter as a church leader/founder with (teaching?) authority**
8:30	16:20	Jesus' command to secrecy (Messianic Secret)
8:31	16:21	Jesus' first Passion prediction
8:32–33	16:22–23	Peter's misunderstanding and Jesus' rebuke
8:34–9:1	16:24–28	Teaching on discipleship

The boldface insertion reads:

> (17) And Jesus answered him, "Blessed are you, Simon son of Jonah!
> For flesh and blood has not revealed this to you,
> but my Father in heaven.
> (18) And I tell you, you are 'Peter' (Greek *Petros,* Aramaic *Kēphas:* literally
>   "Rocky"),
> and on this rock (Greek *petra,* Aramaic *kēpha:* "rock") I will build *my church,*
> and the gates of Hades will not prevail against it.
> (19) I will give you the keys of the kingdom of heaven,
> and whatever *you* (sg.) bind on earth shall be bound in heaven,
> and whatever *you* (sg.) loose on earth shall be loosed in heaven."

This tradition singles out Simon son of Jonah, gives him a new name, "Peter," and makes a symbolic play on the name (Greek *Petros/petra;* Aramaic *Kēphas/kēpha;* English Rocky/rock). It then emphasizes the authority of the "church" or community on earth and stresses that Jesus ascribes honor and authority to Peter (singular tense) in the church. Most critics have taken the "power of the keys" and the "binding and loosing" statements to refer to honor and authority as it is found in scriptural (cf. Isa. 22:22b) and rabbinic texts. Several meanings are possible, but the most probable is authority to teach. The passage thus offers clear evidence for a group or networked collection of regional groups who sharply defined their boundaries and their leadership in contrast to Pharisaic groups and their leadership.

The second place where the Gospel of Matthew refers to the word *ekklēsia* is in Jesus' long discourse in 18:1–35. This time the term occurs twice (18:17). The discourse has a core taken from Mark 9:42–50, but Matthew expands and develops it. Part of what he has added to the section, 18:17, reads:

> 17) If the member [the one who sins against "his brother," verse 15a] refuses to listen to them [two or three witnesses, verse 16], tell it to *the church;* and if the offender refuses to listen even to the *church,* let such a one be to you as a Gentile and a tax collector.

This section offers an embryonic order for regulating the life of the group, apparently a process for including or excluding "a brother" who has sinned. Matthew then adds a version of the binding and loosing saying found in the preceding Petrine passage, this time in the plural tense:

> (18) Truly I tell you (pl.), whatever you (pl.) bind on earth shall be bound in heaven, and whatever you (pl.) loose on earth shall be loosed in heaven.

In this case, the plurals show that the authority to "bind and loose" previously invested in Peter is now given to an assembled group, the composition of which remains unclear. Although the general point of the literary context is forgiveness, the specific point is nonetheless clear: The community should self-consciously define itself, now in terms of certain moral norms, and if the offender does not conform, he should be banned. Thus what appears to be a judicial process similar to that in the Qumran community (although not as developed) is in place. Again, emerging institutional structures go beyond anything we find in the Gospel of Mark.

There are other aspects of the Matthean community. Note that the preceding "praise of Peter" corresponds to a major change in Matthew's attitude toward the disciples. Whereas in the Markan Gospel they are without understanding, there are numerous instances in Matthew where they do understand (e.g., 13:51; cf. the omission in 14:32 [Mark 6:52]; 17:23 [9:32]), although they are also "men of little faith" (6:30; 8:26; 14:31; 16:8). Matthew's "rehabilitation" of the disciples is also found in the climax of the gospel, called the **Great Commission** (28:16–20). Here the risen Jesus commands his disciples to "make disciples of all nations, teaching them all that I have commanded you" (28:19). The disciples are to undertake this mission and are given the authority—for the first time in the gospel!—to teach.

Were the Matthean "churches" still within Israel, or had they separated from Israel? Even if we hold that Israelites were included in the Matthean mission, it is nonetheless clear that the polemic against certain Israelite leaders and specifically the Pharisees is very strong (Matt. 23). The Matthean writer speaks of "their synagogues" (4:23; 9:35; cf. 10:7; 28:20) and "their scribes" (7:29). Finally, it is clear that the Matthean writer emphasizes the Gentile Pilate's confession of innocence (27:24) and follows it with a statement that has left an unspeakable mark on subsequent Jewish-Christian relations: "Then the people as a whole answered, 'His blood be on us and on our children!'" (27:25). It is possible that such ideas can come from a context of sectarian disputes within Israel of the post-70 period, but they also seem to suggest an indictment of Israel itself.

A final comment is in order. What has been said so far, plus elements of language, style, and organization that follow, suggests that that author may have been a scribe. If so, he was like the scribe he describes, that is, "trained [literally "discipled"] for the Kingdom" and "like a master of a household who brings out of his treasure what is new and what is old" (13:52). He is an Israelite scribe of the Jesus Movement who opposes competing Pharisaic scribes but who is also interested in the mission to all peoples. One scholar (Stanton) has suggested that the First Gospel may have circulated as a "foundation document" in a cluster of Israelite Christ-believing communities in Syria and that the gospel offered "legitimizing answers" for a "new people." Probably an evangelist knew of other Jesus movements within a particular region. As a literate scribe, he may have composed his version of the gospel to be read to members of various congregations, perhaps piecemeal, and as such it would have been used as a means of educating certain members, perhaps other scribes, of the Jesus Movement.

LANGUAGE, STYLE, AND LITERARY FEATURES OF MATTHEW

The Greek of the First Gospel has been called "synagogue Greek." It is a more polished Greek than the Greek of Mark or **Q**, but it is nonetheless "semitizing," or Semitic sounding. This writer uses Hebrew/Aramaic idioms. He likes parallelisms characteristic of Hebrew poetry. He stresses the numbers "two" (e.g., many instances of two versions of the same story ["doublets"]), "four" (e.g., four parables about the church [21:28–22:11]), and "seven" (e.g., 3 × 14 names in genealogy [1:1–16]; seven parables [13]; seven "woes" [23]). He often repeats key words (e.g., "angel of the Lord" [1:18–2:23]; "righteousness" [5–7]) and emphasizes key passages (e.g., law [5:17–20]; behavior [12:35–40]). Similarly, he lumps materials with a common theme together (e.g., ten miracles in 8–9; parables about Israel and the "church" in 21:28–22:14; the Pharisees in 23; see the five discourses following). Most of his quotations from (what were becoming) the Israelite Scriptures seem to be from the Greek Septuagint, and it has influenced his language, although not his style. His style is meant for teaching: It is very tightly focused and is characterized by formulae, leading words, leading and concluding verses or sections that frame his materials, and "chiasms" (as in certain forms of poetry, A, B, C, C′, B′, A′, approximating the letter *chi*, which looks like the English letter *X*). In general "Matthew" likes to anticipate themes that are only gradually developed (e.g., 1–4: Jesus is Son of David, Son of God; righteousness; Gentiles). "Framing," or "inclusion," that is, leading and concluding sentences that summarize the material that falls between them, also occur (see following on structure).

Formula Quotations

Matthew's view that Jesus' life and teaching fulfill the scriptures is well represented by a series of what scholars call "**formula quotations**." These are quotations from the scriptures and are always preceded by a formula that stresses fulfillment, for example, "all this took place to fulfill what the Lord had spoken by the prophet." They are carefully placed in the story to show that events are in accord with the plan of God as foretold in the ancient prophecies. They interrupt the story (called "asides" in **Literary Criticism**) and are usually addressed directly to the readers or hearers by the writer (exceptions are 2:5–6, spoken by chief priests and scribes; 13:14–15, spoken by Jesus). They are always preceded or followed by the narration of an incident from the life of Jesus that fulfills the scriptural quotation. With the exception of one formula quotation cited by a person in the story, they could be removed and the story would flow quite nicely without them. Here is a list of these important formula quotations and the incidents to which they refer:

Matthew	Israelite Scripture	Incident from the Life of Jesus
1:22–23	Isa. 7:14	The virgin birth
(2:5b–6)	Mic. 5:1(2); 2 Sam. 5:2	The birth in Bethlehem
2:15b	Hos. 11:1	The flight to Egypt
2:17–18	Jer. 31:15	The massacre of the innocents
2:23b	Unknown; Isa. 11:1?	Jesus dwells in Nazareth
3:3	Isa. 40:3	John the Baptizer
4:14–16	Isa. 9:1–2	Jesus moves to Capernaum
8:17	Isa. 53:4	The healing ministry of Jesus
12:17–21	Isa. 42:1–4	The healing ministry of Jesus
13:14–15	Isa. 6:9–10	Jesus' reason for parables
13.35	Psa. 78:2	Jesus' teaching in parables
21:4–5	Isa. 62:11; Zech. 9:9	Jesus' entry into Jerusalem
27:9–10	Zech. 11:12–13; Jer. 18:1–13	The fate of Judas

Most of Matthew's other quotations and allusions to scripture seem to come from the Greek **Septuagint.** That is not the case for most of these formula quotations. This observation has led to the question of whether they come from some special source used by members of the Jesus Movement—specifically scribes in the Matthean group—to authenticate their story of Jesus; if they do, they could be discussed in the following section on sources. If they do not, they may be the result of the author's own knowledge of scripture and linguistic capabilities. Whatever the origin of the scriptural quotations themselves, vocabulary and style of the opening formulae strongly suggest that the Matthean author wrote them and, at the very least, that he probably has worked over the quotations.

SOURCES AND STRUCTURE OF MATTHEW

Following the **Two-Source Theory,** much material in the Gospel of Matthew comes from three sources: the Gospel of Mark, the sayings source **Q**, and other oral and written material (**Special M**). However, this material has been remolded by the author himself.

As one might expect from the use of language in this gospel, many subsections are tightly structured. One of the most impressive structures uses the framing technique, that is, an almost exact matching introduction and conclusion (the frame) that summarize the intervening content (RSV):

Frame: 4:23 (–25): *And* he *went about all* Galilee,
    teaching *in their synagogues and*
    preaching *the gospel of the kingdom, and*
    healing *every disease and every infirmity* among the people.

Content:
    5–7: **teaching and preaching** (the Sermon on the Mount)
    8–9: **healing** (the ten-miracle collection)

Frame: 9:35: *And* Jesus *went about all* the cities and villages,
    teaching *in their synagogues and*
    preaching *the gospel of the kingdom, and*
    healing *every disease and every infirmity.*

Almost all critics think that Matthew created a teaching section, the **Sermon on the Mount** (Matt. 5–7), largely from **Q** and **Special M,** and placed Jesus on a mountain to teach it. Then he assembled together scattered miracle stories from Mark, sometimes creating doublets in order to arrive at the number ten (Matt. 8–9). His object may have been to suggest that Jesus was the new Moses. As Moses received God's Law (the Ten Commandments) from the mountain, so Jesus teaches the new Law on the mountain (sitting, as do teachers of the Law); and as Moses performed the ten miracles in Egypt (the ten plagues), so Jesus performs ten miracles. He then introduced and concluded the section with what is essentially the same teaching, preaching, and healing summary (the frame).

There are other examples of tight structuring in the gospel. The author clearly likes the number "seven" (seven spirits [12:45]; seven loaves [15:34; 16:10]; forgiveness seventy times seven [18:21]; seven brothers [22:25]). It influences his structure when he turns Mark's four parables (Mark 4) into seven (Matt. 13) and develops seven woes against the "scribes and Pharisees" (Matt. 23). He also likes the number "two" (two brothers [1:2; 4:18; 4:2; 20:24]; two masters [6:24]; two demoniacs [8:28]; two blind men [9:27; 20:30]; two tunics [10:10]; two sparrows [10:29]; two fish [14:17, 19]; two hands and two feet [18:8]; two eyes [18:9]; two witnesses [18:16, 19, 20]; two sons [20:21; 21:28]; two disciples [21:1]; two key commandments [22:40]; two men [24:40] and two women [24:41]; two talents [25:15, 17]). He doubles accounts (e.g., two blind men twice [9:27–31]). The number "three" is also important (three days and nights [12:40; 13:52]; three measures of flour [13:33]; three denials [26:34]; rebuilding the temple in three days [26:75]; resurrection after three days [27:63]). D. Allison thinks that the author's penchant in the gospel is to organize many subsections into triads. Consider the **Sermon on the Mount** in Matt. 5–7 (two sets of three antitheses [5:21–48]; three religious practices [6:1–18]; three "Thou" and three "we" petitions in the Lord's Prayer [6:9c–13]; moths, rust, and thieves [6:19–24]; two sets of triads about social issues [6:19–34; 7:1–12]; three warnings [7:13–27]). If one collapses two of the ten miracles that are one unit

Table 9.1 Discourse Endings

Matthew	Subject of Discourse	Formula Ending	
5:1–7:27	Sermon on the Mount	7:28	And when Jesus finished these sayings
10:5–42	Missionary discourse	11:1	And when Jesus had finished instructing his twelve disciples
13:1–52	Teaching in parables	13:53	And when Jesus had finished these parables
18:1–35	Community regulations	19:1	Now when Jesus finished these sayings
24:3–25:46	Millennial discourse	26:1	When Jesus had finished all these sayings

in Matt. 9:18–26, the collection of ten miracles in Matt. 8–9 becomes three sets of three (8:1–22; 8:23–9:17; 9:18–38). The threes disappear beginning in chapter 14:1, where the author resumes following much more closely the outline of the Gospel of Mark (as he had in chapters 3:1–4:11). Indeed, Robert Gundry and others have wondered whether the author began to experience "literary fatigue" in the latter half of the gospel, a possibility that late-night writers of term papers will appreciate!

One conclusion for the total structure of the gospel is that in general the Matthean author follows the outline (largely geographical) of Mark: Galilee → Caesarea Philippi transition → Jerusalem. He prefaces it with a prologue (1:1–2:23), joins Mark with the baptism and temptation stories (3:1–4:11), and then begins most of his creative triadic restructuring with Jesus' ministry in Galilee down to chapter 14 (4:12–13:58). Most of his **Q** material is put in these sections, especially in Jesus' long discourses (5–7; 10; 13). However, he follows Mark much more carefully again in his accounts of Jesus and his opponents in Galilee, his movement toward Jerusalem (14:1–20:34), and his last days in Jerusalem (21:1–28:20).

The one structural feature mentioned, but not yet described, is that he clearly intended to create five large discourses. Two of them are expansions of the major Markan discourses (Mark 4, parables, expanded as Matt. 13; Mark 13, "Little Apocalypse," expanded as Matt. 24–25). The other three are developed mainly from Q and Special M (Matt. 5–7, Sermon on the Mount; Matt. 10, missionary discourse; Matt. 18, community regulations). The author clearly calls attention to these five discourses by ending each discourse with a formula, "when Jesus finished these sayings," or the like, as in Table 9.1 (RSV).

The creation of five discourses recalls the five books of the Torah, and many scholars since B. W. Bacon (1930) have accepted the hypothesis that the author of Matthew wants to portray Jesus as teaching a new Torah. For Matthew, the new revelation fulfills, yet supersedes, the old. There are numerous Moses themes in the gospel, such as the slaying of the boy babies (2:16–18), Jesus' exodus from Egypt (2:13–15), Jesus' revelation on a mountain (5–7), the ten miracles (8–9; ten plagues in Egypt). In this case Jesus would again appear to be the new Moses. As Moses taught the old Torah (recall that Moses was thought to have *written* the five-book Torah [Pentateuch], and it was called "the book of Moses"), so Jesus taught the *new* Torah. In short, this structure emphasizes Jesus as the teaching Messiah who teaches like, indeed in a manner superior to, Moses.

Table 9.2   Chiastic Structure

Matthew		Content
1–2	A Prologue	Infancy
3–4	B Narrative	First appearance in Galilee
5–7	C *Discourse 1*	*Sermon on the Mount*
8–9	D Narrative	Ten miracle stories
10	E *Discourse 2*	*Mission of the Twelve*
11–12	F Narrative	Growing opposition
13	G *Discourse 3*	*Parables*
14–17	F' Narrative	Miracles and discipleship
18	E' *Discourse 4*	*Community order and discipline*
19–23	D' Narrative	Journey to, first days in, Jerusalem
24–25	C' *Discourse 5*	*Little Apocalypse*
26–27	B' Narrative	Passion story
28	A' Epilogue	Resurrection; Great Commission

Matthew's creation of the five great discourses and his tendency to develop **"chiastic" patterns** (from the Greek letter *chi* [X]) or "ring structures" (A, B, C, B', A', etc.) have led to the well-known "five-book" structure. Building on the influential work of B. W. Bacon, C. H. Lohr developed the structure in Table 9.2.

This "chiastic" structure emphasizes alternating discourses and narratives. It suggests that the Matthean author developed the Markan "geographical" outline by prefacing it with his infancy/prologue and developing speeches with **Q** and **Special M** material. The restructuring is especially clear in chapters 5–13. Again, concluding formulae clearly mark the five speeches. The total construction is balanced—indeed, discourses 1 and 5 are longer, discourses 2 and 4 are shorter (almost the same in length), and discourse 3, the parables discourse (Matt. 13), is in the center. It highlights the five-book notion that Jesus taught a new Torah or Pentateuch, as well as Jesus' role as teacher (the new Moses). It corresponds to many themes in the gospel and fits social-historical context nicely indeed. In short, it has much to commend it and has been widely held by scholars. It is favored in this textbook.

Yet, this chiastic structure theory has some problems. It is perhaps a bit too neat, especially given that Matthew does not follow his structural reordering as much in the latter part of the gospel when he is following Mark. Also, Matt. 11 and 23 are not really "narratives" as such, but rather discourses, and there are other minor speeches in narrative sections (e.g., 12:25–45; 21:18–22:14). Although there are clear Moses parallels in Matthew, one wonders why the author did not make the Moses typology explicit.

Dissatisfaction with the "five-book" Moses hypothesis has naturally led to alternative hypotheses. One structure is based on the saying, "from that time on, Jesus began . . ." in Matt. 4:17 and 16:21. If the gospel is divided on the basis of this "formula," it looks like this (Kingsbury):

1. 1:1–4:16   The Person of Jesus Messiah

2. 4:17–16:20   The Proclamation of Jesus Messiah

3. 16:21–28:20   The Suffering, Death, and Resurrection of Jesus Messiah

From this perspective, Matt. 1:1, "the book of the origin of Jesus Messiah," is a title to the first section, and "from that time on Jesus began . . ." is a title to the second and third sections. Correspondingly, chapters 1–2 (the infancy) are continued directly into chapters 3–4 (baptism, temptation, first appearance in Galilee). The direct flow into chapters 3–4 means that the "Son of God" title in the baptism (3:17) and temptation stories (4:3, 6) becomes more dominant in the first section. The second section develops the proclamation about the Kingdom of Heaven, and the third section develops the Passion.

This structure, which is more congenial to Christology, has also gained a number of adherents, partly because of the literary analysis of the gospel as a continuous, unified story, or narrative. However, there are also weaknesses with this theory. The formula "from that time on Jesus began . . ." is not nearly as prominent as the discourse-ending formulae of the five-discourse theory; it does not seem to make the crucial break in the narrative that such a structure demands. Also, if Matthew is a redaction of Mark, which has no infancy, seeing the infancy (Matt. 1–2) as a new section that prefaces the Markan outline is reasonable, and this creates the necessary break (Matt. 3:1: "In those days"). This theory, however, denies that break, a denial that is weak.

Given all the difficulties, but recognizing the stress in the story on Jesus as teaching the new revelation, indeed *being* the new revelation, the following outline attempts to maintain something of the general geographical outline taken from Mark but will also focus on the five discourses that alternate with narratives. Thus it is admittedly a little artificial, but it is offered as a guide for reading the book:

1. Introduction: Jesus as the new revelation of God, 1:1–4:22

     1:1–2:23   Prologue: The infancy story

     3:1–4:22   Narrative: John and Jesus in Galilee

2. The new revelation: The ministry of Jesus to Israel in Galilee, 4:23–13:58

     4:23–7:29   **Discourse 1:** Sermon on the Mount

     8:1–9:38   Narrative: Ten miracles

     10:1–11:1   **Discourse 2:** The missionary discourse

     11:2–12:50   Narrative: Growing opposition of leaders

     13:1–58   **Discourse 3:** Parables speech to Israel and disciples

3. The ministry of Jesus to his disciples in Galilee and on the way to Jerusalem, 14:1–20:34

     14:1–17:27   Narrative: Miracles, confession, transfiguration, and discipleship

     18:1–18:35   **Discourse 4:** Community order and discipline

     19:1–20:34   Narrative: Households and discipleship

4. Jesus in Jerusalem, 21:1–25:46

   21:1–23:39   Narrative: The final clash between Jesus and the
                     Israelite leaders

   24:1–25:46   **Discourse 5:** The millennial discourse

5. The Passion in Jerusalem and the return to Galilee, 26:1–28:20

   26:1–27:66   Narrative: Passion story

   28:1–20   Epilogue: The resurrection and Great Commission

EXEGETICAL SURVEY OF THE GOSPEL OF MATTHEW

1. Introduction: Jesus as the
New Revelation of God, 1:1–4:22

1:1–2:23: Prologue: The infancy story.

1:1–17:   *Genealogy.*   "An account of the genealogy (Greek *genesis*) of Jesus the
Messiah, the son of David, the son of Abraham," is the opening of the first section, but
especially the genealogy (see Gen. 5:1 **LXX**). The author thinks of this section as Jesus'
first *genesis,* which is human. The second, superhuman *genesis* will come in verse 18. In
the *Psalms of Solomon* 17 (ca. 63 B.C.E.) and among the later rabbis, the title "Son of
David" became a favorite title for the expected Messiah. It emphasized the Messiah's descent from David and his coming as fulfilling God's promise to David in 2 Sam. 7. Interestingly, it had political overtones. Matthew, in dialogue with Pharisee-led Israel, uses
the title more frequently than Mark (1:1; 9:27; 12:23; 15:22; 20:30; 21:9, 15; 22:42, 45),
but usually doing so in relation to Jesus' marvelous deeds.

The genealogy traces the descent of Jesus from Abraham, the father of the Israelite
people, to whom was also given the promise of becoming the father of many peoples
(Gen. 17:4). It also stresses the royal line of King David. It is divided into three divisions of fourteen names (the numerical value of the Hebrew consonants of David's name
is fourteen [$D = 4$; $V = 6$; $D = 4$]). Matthew stresses Jesus' significance as the fulfillment of the Israelite heritage and anticipates the **Great Commission** of Jesus to the disciples to go to *all* peoples (28:19). The line of males, however, is broken in verse 16, and
the next section, the second *genesis,* explains why.

1:18–25:   *The birth story.*   The word "birth" here is *genesis,* translated "genealogy"
in 1:1; this is a second *genesis.* The episodes in this section fulfill scripture (virgin birth
[LXX Isa. 7:14]; Bethlehem birth [Mic. 5:2; 2 Sam. 5:2]; flight into and return from
Egypt [Hos. 11:1]; weeping over slaying of infants [Jer. 31:15]; the residence in Nazareth
["He shall be called a Nazorean," a prophecy not explicitly found in the Israelite scriptures; cf. Isa. 11:1; Judg. 13]). This section provides the heaviest concentration of "**formula quotations**" in the gospel. The virgin birth story portrays Jesus' second "origin"
(Greek *genesis*), this time from God through a virgin. The formula quotation from Isa.
7:14 is from the Greek LXX (Hebrew has "young woman").

2:1–12:   *Bethlehem and Magoi from the East.*

2:3–15:   *Flight to Egypt.*   This story allows the evangelist to stress the exodus
theme and Jesus' connection with Moses, but he does it through a **formula quotation:**

As God's son Israel had come out of Egypt (Hos. 11:1; "Out of Egypt I have called my son"), so now God's son Jesus comes out of Egypt. The "Son of God" title is central to the gospel, especially in the upcoming baptism and temptation stories and Peter's confession.

2:16–18:   *Massacre of the infants.*

Nazareth.   The killing of infant boy babies also recalls the stories about the attempt to kill the infant boy Moses (Exod. 1:15–22). The fifth formula quotation about Nazareth is not a literal quotation in any surviving manuscripts of the Hebrew Bible.

3:1–4:25:   Narrative: John and Jesus in Galilee.

3:1–17:   *John the Baptizer and Jesus' baptism.*

3:1–6:   *John the Baptizer in the wilderness* (= Mark 1:1–6; Q 3:2–4 [in part]?). Matthew brings John the Baptizer into close contact with Jesus, giving him exactly the same message as Jesus (3:2 = 4:17) and making his ministry a fulfillment of prophecy in his sixth formula quotation. As Jesus' immediate precursor, he shares in the act of fulfillment. In the Israelite scriptures, the prophet Elijah did not die a natural death and according to the prophet Malachi was expected to return before the day of judgment (Mal. 4:5). John's clothing shows that he is Elijah (2 Kings 1:8), and Matthew's Jesus makes this identification explicit (Matt. 11:10).

3:7–10:   *John's warning to Pharisees and Sadducees* (= Q 3:7–9).   Matthew often depicts the leaders of Israel as a united front opposed to Jesus; in this passage they are opposed to John, but John's language here is echoed by Jesus later (7:16–20; 12:33).

3:11–12:   *John predicts the coming of Jesus* (= Mark 1:7–8).   These verses reflect the belief by members of the Jesus Movement that their baptism supercedes John's. The idea of the separation of the good from the evil at the last judgment is dominant in Jesus' eschatological teaching in Matthew, especially chapters 24–25.

3:13–17:   *The baptism of Jesus* (= Mark 1:9–11; Q 3:21–22?).   Although Matthew carefully parallels John the Baptizer and Jesus in several ways, he also carefully subordinates John to Jesus by adding verses 14–15, which have no parallel in his source, the Gospel of Mark. They explain why the inferior baptizes the superior. "Righteousness," a favorite term of Matthew (cf. especially 5:17–20), is introduced; the theme of Jesus as God's son is further expressed through a combination of words from Ps. 2:7 and Isa. 42:1.

4:1–25:   *Temptation, preaching, and call of first disciples.*

4:1–11:   *The temptation of Jesus* (= Mark 1:12–13).   Mark simply mentions the temptation of Jesus in the wilderness, but both Matthew and Luke share a **Q** tradition (Q 4:1–13) in which Jesus meets three temptations by quoting Deuteronomy (Matt. 4:4 = Q 4:4: Deut. 8:3; Matt. 4:7 = Q 4:12: Deut. 6:16; Matt. 4:10 = Q 4:8: Deut. 6:13). The passages in Deuteronomy reflect an interpretation of the people of Israel journeying through the wilderness, which is a testing by God to determine their fitness to inherit the Promised Land (Deut. 8:2–3). Again, Jesus, like Israel before him, is identified as Son of God (4:3, 6).

4:12–16:   *Jesus goes to Galilee and begins to preach* (= Mark 1:14).   Verse 14 introduces Matthew's seventh formula quotation (Isa. 9:12), which identifies Galilee as "Galilee of the Gentiles," perhaps anticipating the disciples' mission to *all* peoples (28:16–20).

4:17:   *Jesus' central Kingdom proclamation and revelation* (= Mark 1:15).   "From that time on . . ." (RSV) marks a modest temporal division (see 16:21 RSV). Jesus takes up the message that John had proclaimed (3:2).

4:18–22: *The call of the four fishermen* (= Mark 1:16–20). The ministry begins with the challenge to "follow" Jesus, as it will end on the note of "Go therefore and make disciples . . ." (28:19). Note that Matthew does not call them "disciples" until 5:1, when they begin to listen to the teaching.

2. The New Revelation: The Ministry of Jesus to Israel, 4:23–13:58

4:23–7:29: **Discourse 1: The Sermon on the Mount.**

4:23–25: *Summary of the characteristic activity of the ministry* (= Mark 1:39). As noted earlier, verse 23 is a framing summary stressing teaching, preaching the good news of the Kingdom, and healing every disease and infirmity. After a section on teaching (5–7) and healing (8–9), Matthew repeats essentially the same summary (9:35). This section introduces the **Sermon on the Mount.**

5:1–7:29: *The first book of the new revelation: the Sermon on the Mount.* This takes place on a mountain, whereas the comparable discourse in Luke is on a "level place" (cf. Luke 6:17, 20–49). Matthew is stressing the parallel to Moses receiving the Torah on a mountain, the previous revelation now being superseded (Exod. 19:36). The first book of the new revelation concerns the personal aspects of the new piety and behavior.

5:1–2: *Introduction.* Jesus sits (like a rabbi?) to teach.

5:3–12: *The Beatitudes* (= Q 6:20b–23). "Blessed" in the sense used here refers to the fortunate, happy condition of a person honored by God. The reference is to the conditions that will obtain after Jesus has returned as Son of Man. These are therefore eschatological blessings, and Matthew is using them to set the whole teaching in the context of eschatological expectation.

5:13–16: *Salt and light: The disciples' special status* (= Q 14:34–35; 11:33).

5:17–20: *The essential nature of faith in the Matthean form of the Jesus Movement: Obedience to the new revelation.* This is a key passage found only in Matthew's gospel; it expresses the evangelist's understanding of the essence of faith: obedience to the new revelation as it is interpreted by the equivalent of "scribes and Pharisees" in the Matthean wing of the Jesus Movement. In Israel, obedience to the revelation in the Torah was expressed by the concept of "righteousness." Righteousness was the quality of obedience one must have achieved to be able to stand before God, and "the righteous" are those who have achieved it. For Matthew, the quality of the believer's obedience to the new revelation by and through Jesus must exceed that of the rival "scribes and Pharisees" to the old revelation. By this means the true followers will "enter the Kingdom of Heaven," that is, enter into that realm Jesus will establish for the "righteous" when he comes as Son of Man. There are, however, political, social, and economic implications for the present (see the parable of the Last Judgment in Matt. 25).

5:21–48: *The antitheses* (partial parallels only in Mark and Luke; Q 6:27–38). In a series of six antitheses (two sets of three), Matthew expresses aspects of the new revelation in contrast to the old. In each instance, the new is an intensifying or radicalizing of the old.

6:1–18: *Instruction on almsgiving, prayer, and fasting* (Matt. 6:9–13 = Q 11:2–4). Almsgiving, prayer, and fasting are three forms of Israelite piety independent of the temple. Even while the temple stood, the Pharisees emphasized them, and after its destruction they developed them still further. Matthew is here in dialogue with the Pharisees, and his hostile tone indicates its intensity. Note his constant condemnation of "hypocrites," which occurs as a refrain throughout the denunciation of the "scribes and Pharisees" in Matt. 23. For an analysis of the **Lord's Prayer** (Matt. 6:9–13 = Q 11:2–4), see Chapter Two.

6:19–34: *Various images describing the truly righteous person.*

7:1–12: *Various maxims illustrating the new righteousness.*

7:13–27: *Warnings designed to stress the necessity for obedience to the new revelation.* These warnings constitute the ending to the sermon. They end it on a note of eschatology as the Beatitudes had begun it on a similar note.

7:28–29 **contains the formula ending the first book of the new revelation.**

8:1–9:38: Narrative: Ten miracles (the Messiah of deed). Matthew follows his first revelatory discourse with a block of ten miracle stories interwoven with teaching on discipleship. In 4:23 and 9:35, the summaries of the characteristic activity of Jesus' ministry stress healing, and nine of the ten miracles are healing miracles. This pulling together of ten miracles that are scattered in Mark perhaps recalls the ten plagues of Moses in Egypt (Exod. 7:8–11:10); if so, it is a Moses theme. In general, Matthew shortens the Markan miracle stories but reinterprets them with dialogues and honors for Jesus (Christology).

8:1–17: *The first three healings: The leper, the centurion's servant, and Peter's mother-in-law.* In Matt. 8:17, the eighth formula quotation from Isa. 53:4 (Hebrew) shows that Jesus' healing fulfills scripture. The faith of the centurion, a Gentile, is emphasized.

8:18–22: First discipleship section: Sayings on "following" Jesus as a disciple (Matt. 8:19–21 = Q 9:57–59).

8:23–9:8: *The second three miracles: The stilling of the storm, the healing of the demoniac, and the cure of the paralytic.* Matthew's source for the stilling of the storm is Mark 4:35–41, and it is instructive to observe his redaction. In Mark, the story takes the natural form of a nature miracle: Jesus and his disciples embark in a boat, accompanied by other boats; a great storm arises; the disciples appeal to Jesus, and he calms the storm. The following dialogue in Mark ends on a note of wonder. In Matthew, the story is still a miracle, but it contains more dialogue and Christology and is finally a teaching about the difficulty of being a disciple in the church. There is no mention of any other boats. "Following" Jesus from the previous section becomes central. The dialogue takes place *before* the storm is calmed, and Jesus is addressed as "Lord" (Mark: "teacher"); he in turn addresses the disciples as "men of little faith," a frequent reproach by Jesus in this gospel (6:30; 8:26; 14:31; 16:8) and only in this gospel. The one boat is the little ship of the church, beset by the storms of persecution, and the disciples are the members of the church who fail because of their "little faith" and need the presence of their Lord to help them, which presence they have. Again, Matthew has interpreted Mark's traditional miracle story to make it an allegory about the difficulty of following Jesus.

9:9–17: *Second section on discipleship: The call of Matthew, eating with "tax collectors and sinners," fasting.* "Tax collectors and sinners" in Palestine were ostracized and treated as *Gentiles;* thus eating with them would be unclean, an issue of purity. Because table fellowship between Israelites and Gentiles was also a major problem in the mission of the Jesus Movement, Jesus' attitude toward "tax collectors and sinners" was for Matthew an important aspect of teaching on discipleship. Fasting was also important because it was a form of piety stressed by the Pharisees.

9:18–34:   *The last four miracles: The ruler's daughter and the woman with a hemorrhage, the two blind men, the dumb man.*   Note that healing the two blind men recasts a similar story taken from Mark later in the gospel, thus an instance of doubling (cf. Matt. 20:29–34 = Mark 10:46–52).

9:35–38:   *Summary of the characteristic activity of the ministry* (9:35a = Mark 6:6b; 9:35b = Mark 6:34; 9:37–38 = Q 10:2).   Matthew reflects on Mark 6:6b–11, an account of a teaching journey by Jesus followed by the commissioning of "the Twelve" for a missionary journey. He reformed the section. Matt. 9:35 is a concluding framing summary that encapsulates the activities characteristic of Jesus' ministry—preaching, teaching, and healing. It reproduces the first framing summary, 4:23, almost verbatim.

10:1–10:42:   Discourse 2: The missionary discourse.

The commissioning of "the Twelve" (10:1–4) becomes the occasion for the second revelatory discourse (10:5–42), which Matthew derives mainly from originally disparate elements (Mark 6:7; 3:16–19; 6:8–11; 13:9–13; Q 10:3, 6–9, 12; 12:2–9, 51–53; 14:26–27; 17:33). The discourse instructs about the mission to the Israelites, but it also has elements both similar to and different from the Cynic wandering beggar-philosopher. Perhaps Matt. 10:9–16 comes from a development from some traditional "handbook" for the missionaries because Luke incorporates this material for his Gentile mission (Luke 10:1, 4–12). In 10:7, Matthew gives to the disciples the exact proclamation of Jesus (4:17) and John the Baptizer (3:2). All are the succession of the new revelation. Notice, however, that the disciples are *not* commissioned to teach, as they are when the revelation is complete (Matt. 28:20).

11:1   contains the formula ending to the second book of the new revelation.
11:2–12:50:   Growing opposition of leaders.

11:2–6:   *John the Baptizer's question* (= Q 7:18–23).   Jesus is the Christ (Messiah), as his ministry testifies.

11:7–15:   *Jesus' testimony to John* (= Q 7:24–28; 16:16).   John is the Elijah expected by the Israelites to come as the forerunner to the Messiah.

11:16–19:   *Parable of the Children in the Marketplace* (= Q 7:31–35).   Neither the strict John nor the banqueting Jesus has been recognized or accepted by "this generation" (cf. 12:38–39).

11:20–24:   *Woes on the Galilean cities* (= Q 10:13–15).   The cities that have rejected Jesus will be judged accordingly.

11:25–30:   *The "thunderbolt from the Johannine sky"* (= Q 10:21–22).   These verses are striking because their style sounds more like that found in the Gospel of John than Matthew. Yet, they represent a major Matthean Christological statement: Jesus is the revealer of knowledge of God, a knowledge that he reveals to his intimates. "Yoke" is a metaphor much used by the Israelite rabbis of obedience to the Law, the "yoke of the Torah," which paradoxically is a joy. However, in Matt. 11:25–30, there is a contrast between the burden of the old yoke and the ease and joy of the new.

12:1–14:   *Jesus in controversy with Pharisees* (= Mark 2:23–28; 3:1–6).   Matthew here gives two stories of Jesus in controversy with Pharisees, taken from a collection of five such stories in Mark 2:1–3:6. He had given the other three earlier (9:1–8, 11–13, 16–17), interpreting them as dealing mainly with discipleship.

12:15–21: *Jesus as servant of God.* Jesus' role as God's chosen servant and beloved is shown by the ninth formula quotation (Isa. 41:1–4).

12:22–24: *A healing and two reactions* (= Mark 3:19b–22). A healing evokes two reactions: The crowd raises the question of whether Jesus might not be the Son of David; the Pharisees denounce him as an agent of Beelzebub, ruler of the demons (cf. 9:34).

12:25–37: *Jesus denounces the Pharisees* (= Mark 3:23–30). The opposition between Jesus and the Pharisees sharpens. Matthew expands and intensifies the tone of his Markan source.

12:38–42: *The sign of Jonah* (= Q 11:29–32). Jesus rejects a Pharisaic request for a "sign" that would vindicate his authority and denounces "this evil and adulterous generation." The sign will be the sign of Jonah, that is, Jesus' resurrection will be his vindication over "this generation" that rejected him.

12:43–45: *Further denunciation of "this generation"* (= Q 11:24–26).

12:46–50: *The true family of Jesus* (= Q 8:19–21). Matthew stresses, in contrast to the crowds' misunderstanding, that the true family of Jesus consists of those like the disciples who accepted him and his revelation.

13:1–52: Discourse 3: The parables of the Kingdom.

In creating this parable discourse, Matthew revises and expands Mark's parable collection (Mark 4). He removes the Seed Growing Secretly (Mark 4:26–29) but adds the Leaven from **Q** (13:33 = Q 13:20–21) and four other parables: the Weeds (13:24–30), the Treasure (13:44), the Pearl (13:45), and the Net (13:47–50), thus increasing the number of the collection from four to seven. He accepts Mark's allegorical interpretation of the Sower and then offers an allegorical interpretation of his additional parable, the Weeds (13:36–43).

A further word about the Matthean structure is in order. Just before the chapter 13 passage, the Matthean writer stresses the true family of Jesus as those "who do the will of my Father in heaven" (from Mark 3:31–35) but inserts a specific application of the true family to *the disciples* (verse 49). In the parable chapter, he follows Mark in seeing Jesus as speaking to "the crowds" (13:1–33) and as giving his allegorical explanation to the disciples (13:10–15). After a formula quotation (13:34–35), he has Jesus turn again to his disciples. The effect is that in contrast to Mark, but in concert with the preceding passage, *they* seem to be his true family. Then he gives them the explanation of the Weeds—again, an allegory, this time applied to "the righteous" versus "all evil-doers." Then he offers the parables of the Treasure, the Pearl, and the Net, the latter again allegorically interpreted in terms of "the righteous" and "the evil." It is easy to see from these interpretations, as well as his interpretation of the calming of the sea miracle, his more consistent tendency to interpret the parables as allegories, which will become very important in later chapters. The section concludes with one of the most important Matthean emphases about the disciples who understand and the scribe who brings out of his treasure what is new and what is old (13:51–52).

13:1–35: *The Sower, Weeds, Mustard Seed, and Leaven.* The Sower with its allegorical interpretation from Mark (13:1–9 = Mark 4:1–9; 13:18–23 = Mark 4:13–20) interprets the ministry of Jesus as rejection and acceptance. By inserting a verse from Mark's later context (13:12 = Mark 4:25) and changing Mark's "so that" to "because" (13:10–11, 13 = Mark 4:10–12), Matthew views the purpose of Jesus' speaking in parables as a contrast between those who do and do not see, hear, or understand him. Then he adds his tenth formula quotation about faulty seeing, hearing, and understanding

(Isa. 6:9–10). The parable of the Weeds (13:24–30) continues the theme of acceptance and rejection, this time in the context of the coming "harvest," which the allegory will explain in terms of the Last Judgment. The parables of the Mustard Seed (13:31–32 = Mark 4:30–32) and the Leaven (13:33 = Luke 13:20–21) in Matthew's context are means of interpreting the rejection of Jesus and of holding out the hope of ultimate acceptance, if not by all Israelites, then certainly by the peoples at large. Matt. 13:34–35 adds the eleventh formula quotation as a second way to view Jesus' emphasis on parables, that is, as revealing what has been hidden (Ps. 78:12).

13:36–50:   *Allegorical interpretation of the Weeds; the Treasure, the Pearl, and the Net.*   Notice that Matthew shifts from the crowds (13:2) to the disciples (13:36). In this new context, the parable of the Weeds is interpreted as an allegory of the earthly ministry of Jesus as Son of Man and of his coming apocalyptic judgment. Notice also the Matthean promise of blessing to "the righteous" in verse 43, and compare it with 5:20. In the Matthean context, the parables of the Treasure in the Field and the Pearl refer to the blessing that awaits the "righteous," those who accept Jesus' revelation and obey it. The parable of the Net is a restatement of Matthew's characteristic view of the judgment that will separate the evil from the righteous. It is also interpreted allegorically (13:49).

13:51–52:   *The scribe in the Matthean form of the Jesus Movement.*   As a climax to his parable chapter, Matthew adds this description of the ideal of acceptance and obedience, the scribe "trained for the kingdom of heaven" who is "like a householder who brings out of his treasure what is new and what is old." The literate scribe is an excellent description of the author of Matthew's gospel. The new and the old are an excellent way to view not only Jesus and his teaching, but also the Matthean author/scribe and his teaching.

13:53   **contains the formula ending of the third book of the new revelation.**

13:54–58:   *The climactic rejection.*   Matthew ends his third revelatory discourse with the theme that Jesus is not honored "in his own country and in his own house," and because of lack of belief, he is not able to work many miracles.

3. The Ministry of Jesus to His Disciples: Galilee and the Way to Jerusalem, 14:1–20:34

The ministry to Israel now having reached the climax in the inability of Jesus to find faith among "his own," Matthew turns to the second stage of the new revelation: the relationship between Jesus and his disciples.

14:1–17:27:   **Narrative: Miracles, confession, transfiguration, and discipleship.**   In this section, Matthew begins to follow his narrative source, the Gospel of Mark, more carefully. At the same time, he pays less attention to structural detail.

14:1–12:   *The death of John the Baptizer* (= Mark 6:14–29).   Matthew abbreviates the story as it occurs in Mark, and he subordinates other elements in the story to his theme of John's death being the occasion for the withdrawal of Jesus with his disciples.

14:13–21:   *The withdrawal of Jesus and the feeding of the five thousand* (= Mark 6:30–44).   Matthew is still abbreviating Mark's narrative in the interest of his withdrawal theme. Jesus, having compassion on the crowds, heals them and feeds them. In

Matt. 14:19, the disciples play more of an intermediary role than they do in Mark 6:41; are they becoming the church that mediates the sacraments?

14:22–33: *The walking on the "sea"* (= Mark 6:45–52). Again Matthew is abbreviating Mark, in this instance to make room for the redactional insertion of the incident of Peter also walking on the sea (Matt. 14:28–31), described as a typical ASC experience—until Peter sinks. Metaphorically Peter becomes a paradigm of the "disciple" who has "little faith" and so needs the help of his "Lord"; compare 8:23–27, another sea miracle. Matthew ends the account with a formal confession of Jesus as the Son of God (verse 33). In Matthew's thinking, the story has become a paradigm of the relationship between Jesus and his followers in Matthew's day.

14:34–36: *Healings at Genneseret* (= Mark 6:53–56).

15:1–20: *Dispute with "scribes and Pharisees" about the tradition of the elders* (= Mark 7:1–23). In the dispute with the scribes and Pharisees, Matthew is following Mark, but he uses his source as a starting point for instruction of the disciples.

15:21–39: A group of three miracles in Mark (= Mark 7:24–8:10) becomes *two miracles and a summary.* Matthew is still following Mark's language closely, shortening somewhat as he goes. Jesus claims he was sent only to the lost sheep of the house of Israel (cf. 10:6), but he nevertheless heals a Gentile woman because of her faith (cf. 8:10, the centurion). The crowds glorify the God of Israel in response to Jesus' healing, that is, Matthew has created a summary (15:29–31) from Mark's healing of the deaf mute (7:31–37). Jesus has compassion on the crowds and feeds the four thousand, the disciples again acting as intermediaries (cf. 14:13–21). The one real change is that a healing of a deaf mute in Mark 7:31–37 is generalized into a healing of many sick persons in Matt. 15:29–31.

16:1–4: *The sign of Jonah* (= Mark 8:11–13). This is another version of the passage found earlier in the gospel (12.38–40). Matthew has added verses 2–3, taken from Q (Q 12:54–56), and the reference to Jonah. He also has the request coming from "Pharisees and Sadducees" (Mark: "Pharisees"), indicating further opposition from the Israelite leaders (cf. 3:7).

16:5–12: *Warning against the teaching of Pharisees and Sadducees* (= Mark 8:14–21). Again from Mark, with "Pharisees and Sadducees" substituted for Mark's "Pharisees and Herod."

16:13–20:34: *The predictions of the Passion and resurrection and instruction on life in the community.* This section is Matthew's equivalent of Mark 8:27–10:52 (he omits 8:22–26). In general, he follows Mark but adds considerable material, and the additions transform Mark's teaching on discipleship into instruction on life in the community.

16:13–28: *Caesarea Philippi* (= Mark 8:27–9:1). The most important change is Matthew's insertion of verses 17–19, the blessing and commissioning of Peter. Certainly the Matthean writer viewed Jesus as transferring authority to the chief apostle (ascribed honor), most likely in relation to teaching (see earlier discussion). Further changes are the addition of "and then he will repay everyone for what he has done" (verse 27) and the modification of Mark's "before they see the Kingdom of God come with power" to "before they see the Son of Man coming in his Kingdom." These changes transform the Markan understanding of discipleship as preparedness to accept suffering, as one followed Jesus to his Cross and awaited the *parousia,* into the Matthean understanding of discipleship as living the life of obedience to the new revelation in the church until the coming of Jesus as Son of Man. Note the temporal marker, "From that time on Jesus began . . ." (16:21) discussed earlier (cf. 4:17).

17:1–8:   *The transfiguration* (= Mark 9:2–8).   This reproduces Mark with the significant addition of verses 6–7, where Jesus reassures the disciples who are afraid. We saw in 8:23–27 and 14:22–33 that this is a very important theme to Matthew, representing his understanding of the reality of life in his own day. Matthew keeps Mark's theme that Jesus is Son of God, an important emphasis of his own (cf. e.g., 3:17).

17:9–13:   *The coming of Elijah* (= Mark 9:9–13).   Matthew adds his verse 13 to Mark's narrative, stressing the identification of John the Baptizer and Elijah.

17:14–20:   *The healing of the epileptic boy* (Mark 9:14–29).   Matthew shortens Mark's narrative, most probably to make room for verse 20, which introduces another of his favorite themes: the disciple in the church as a person of "little faith" (see also 6:30; 8:26; 14:31; 16:8).

17:22–23:   *The second prediction* (= Mark 9:30–32).   Matthew abbreviates the prediction and then breaks up the carefully structured Markan prediction unit by introducing his fourth revelatory discourse.

17:24–27:   *The temple tax.*   A legend, reproduced here by Matthew because it features the prominence of Peter, the foundation stone of the church, in verse 24. Because the temple had been destroyed and the Romans had confiscated the tax for the temple of Jupiter Capitolinus in Rome, the passage may have political implications.

18:1–35:   Discourse 4: Community order and discipline.
In this discourse, Matthew follows Mark in part, but he adds material from Q and special material of his own to make the whole a revelatory discourse.

18:1–5:   *Greatness in the Kingdom* (= Mark 9:33–36; 10:15; 9:37).   Matthew uses the latter part of Mark's second prediction unit to introduce the discourse.

18:6–9:   *On temptations* (= Mark 9:42–48).

18:10–14:   *The parable of the Lost Sheep.*   Matthew seems to interpret the "little ones" of Mark 9:42 as a special group within his churches and then uses the parable of the Lost Sheep to reassure them that God will take care of them. The parable has a more universal application in Luke 15:3–7.

18:15–22:   *Two community regulations.*   In verses 15–20, Matthew greatly expands a saying from **Q** (Q 17:3) by adding references to the need for witnesses to the church, to the authority of the church (18:18; cf. 16:19), and to the promise of the presence of the risen Lord in the church. The passage is built on the community regulation of the necessity of reproving one's offensive "brother" (cf. Lev. 19:15–18), a theme with a long tradition in Israel. The regulation sounds like a three-stage judicial process for handling offensive persons in the Christ-believing communities of his own day, leading to—if necessary—banishment. Yet, all is set within the context of unending forgiveness—seventy-seven times, based on Q (Q 17:4)—as the following parable also shows.

18:23–35:   *The parable of the Unmerciful Servant.*   Matthew brings his discourse to a close by using the parable of the Unmerciful Servant to reinforce the regulation concerning the necessity for reconciliation within the community. Note the characteristic emphasis on the eschatological judgment in verse 35.

19:1a   contains the formula ending of the fourth book of the new revelation.
19:1–20:34:   Narrative: Households and discipleship.

After concluding his revelatory discourse, Matthew resumes the Markan outline as he portrays the journey of Jesus from Galilee to Jerusalem. As in Mark, the journey features teaching on discipleship, and the differences reflect the different understandings of discipleship by Matthew and Mark.

19:1–12: *Marriage and divorce* (= Mark 10:1–12; cf. Matt. 5:31–32). Matthew goes on to shorten, then extend, a passage from Mark as a community regulation on marriage and divorce. Note the addition of "except for unchastity" in verse 9, which brings the teaching into line with that of the strictest Israelite rabbi of the period (Rabbi Shammai). Note also the addition of verses 10–12, the famous "eunuch" saying that illustrates that it is better to remain single if you cannot divorce. (The later church used this passage as an argument for celibacy.)

19:13–15: *The blessing of the children* (= Mark 10:13–16).

19:16–30: *The rich young man* (= Mark 10:17–31). The Markan incident is made into a community regulation by the addition of verse 28, which introduces the eschatological promise for those who will accept the challenge to leave everything to follow Jesus, the key to discipleship.

20:1–16: *The parable of the Laborers in the Vineyard.* Matthew inserts this parable into the Markan narrative to illustrate the theme of the reversal of values in the coming Kingdom of the Son of Man (verse 16). However, the parable fits that purpose uneasily; thus it is an excellent example of a parable of Jesus resisting an attempt to serve a later and different context.

20:17–28: *The third prediction unit: Prediction-misunderstanding-teaching* (= Mark 10:32–45). This essentially reproduces Mark's third prediction unit. In Mark, the three prediction units are carefully structured (Mark 8:27–9:1; 9:32–37; 10:32–45): prediction-misunderstanding-teaching on discipleship. Matthew breaks up the first two by various insertions, but he leaves this third practically intact. Even in Mark, the third unit has what are to all intents and purposes community regulations (Mark 10:42–44); so the narrative easily serves Matthew's particular purpose.

20:29–34: *The healing at Jericho* (= Mark 10:46–52). In Mark, this is a transitional giving-of-sight passage. Matthew simply reproduces it with a characteristic doubling of the healing: Mark's blind Bartimaeus becomes *two* blind men, a miracle already duplicated in 9:27–31. Matthew is fond of healings in pairs (8:28–34; 9:27–31). Furthermore, he expands the title "Son of David" not only in reference to descent (1:1; 1:20; cf. 22:42 = Mark 12:25), but also in reference to healing (9:27; 12:23; 15:22; 21:9, 15), and here doubled (20:30, 31; cf. Mark 10:47).

4. Jesus in Jerusalem, 21:1–25:46

This section narrates Jesus' activity in Jerusalem before the beginning of the Passion itself. For the most part, Matthew follows Mark 11:1–13:37 but with some very significant changes and additions.

21:1–23:39: **Narrative: The final clash between Jesus and the Israelite leaders.**

21:1–11: *The entry* (= Mark 11:1–10). Matthew follows Mark in the main, but he adds the twelfth formula quotation in verses 4–5 and changes one animal to two, apparently to make the narration agree exactly with his own understanding of the quotation.

21:12–17:   *Jesus in the temple* (= Mark 11:11a, 15–17, 11b).   Mark intercalates the cleansing of the temple into the fig tree incident, probably to interpret the cleansing by means of the fig tree. Matthew has no such purpose, so he restores what was most likely the original unity of the cleansing: Jesus going directly into the temple. Verses 14–16 have no parallel in Mark; they represent Matthew's characteristic emphasis on the healing ministry of Jesus. The children respond to Jesus' healing with the same cry as that found in the entry scene, "Hosanna to the Son of David!" This arouses official indignation.

21:18–22:   *The fig tree incident* (= Mark 11:12–14, 20–25).   What in Mark had been a testimony to the judgment of God on the temple and a way of coming to terms with the fact of its destruction becomes in Matthew an example of the power of faith.

21:23–27:   *The question of Jesus' authority* (= Mark 11:27–33).   This follows Mark in narrating a clash between Jesus and the Israelite authorities.

21:28–32:   *The parable of the Two Sons.*   Matthew develops four parables with essentially the same theme: rejection of Israel's leaders and warning against self-righteous arrogance. In the Two Sons, the true son of God is he who accepts Jesus as his revelation, and marginal people do that (Matt. 21:31–32 = Q 7:29–30).

21:33–46:   *The parable of the Wicked Tenants* (= Mark 12:1–12).   In the main, this follows Mark, but the addition of verse 43 stresses that the true followers of Jesus and not the Israelite leaders are now the heirs of God.

22:1–10:   *The parable of the Marriage Feast* (= Q 14:16–24).   Matthew interprets the parable as testimony that after the Israelites rejected Jesus and killed him, their heritage passed to those who follow Jesus.

22:11–14:   *The parable of the Wedding Garment.*   But even the true follower must have the wedding garment of true obedience, without which rejection will occur. Note the allegorical reference to the destruction of Jerusalem in 70 C.E. as a punishment (22:7).

22:15–46:   *Four questions in the dispute between Jesus and his opponents* (= Mark 12:13–37).   Matthew now follows Mark in narrating four questions that cause disputes between Jesus and the Israelite leaders: tribute to Caesar, the resurrection, the Great Commandment, and David's son. Because his source already had a strong element of conflict between Jesus and his Israelite opponents, Matthew engages in no extensive redaction, except that he carefully omits the sympathetic answer of the scribe and Jesus' praise of him in Mark 12:32–34. He then places the concluding remark at the end of the question about David's son (22:46) and thereby formally brings to an end all debate between Jesus and his opponents. The rejection is complete and the conflict over; there remains now only the working out of the consequences.

23:1–36:   *The woes against the Pharisees.*   Mark 12:38–40 has a warning against the scribes; in Matthew, it becomes a carefully organized diatribe of seven woes against his opponents, the Pharisees and their scribes, that is, certain Israelite leaders and their influence. It is not their *function* he opposes—very much to the contrary—but their practice. Thus hypocrisy is the objection.

23:37–39:   *The lament over Jerusalem* (= Q 13:34–35).   This is a lament over Jerusalem that interprets its destruction as the judgment of God for its rejection of his true envoys. It anticipates a restoration at the *parousia.* A saying developed in the church to help members of the Jesus Movement come to terms with the destruction of Jerusalem is used by both Matthew and Luke.

24:1–25:46: **Discourse 5: The millennial discourse.**

The apocalyptic discourse proper, Matt. 24:1–36, is an expansion of Mark's "Little Apocalypse," 13:1–32. However, the writer of Matthew omits Mark's ending of the discourse and goes on to add millennial teaching that he takes from Q (Matt. 24:37–51 = Q 17: 26–27, 34–35; 12:39–40, 42–46) and then a series of allegorical parables (the Ten Maidens [Special M], Talents [Q 19:12–27], Last Judgment [Special M]). As the Matthean author interprets them, the first two are concerned with the coming of the Son of Man and his judgment (25:13, 29–30), and the third directly describes that judgment. The third parable, the Last Judgment parable, is the last element of the teaching of Jesus in the gospel. It sums up many prominent themes: the need for "righteousness" to enter the Kingdom; righteousness consisting of obedience expressed in deeds. The Son of Man will repay everyone according to his or her deeds, stressing mercy, especially to those who are hungry, thirsty, a stranger, naked, sick, and imprisoned. Here is one of the strongest social and religious messages in the gospel, and it may have political implications for the Kingdom. It is a fitting climax to Matthew's presentation of the teaching of Jesus.

26:1 contains the formula ending of the fifth book of the new revelation.

5. The Passion, Resurrection, and Great Commission, 26:1–28:20

26:1–27:66: **The Passion and death of Jesus.**

In his account of the Passion and death of Jesus, Matthew follows Mark closely, with only occasional redactional changes; the divisions are therefore essentially those found in the Markan narrative.

26:1–5: *The Introduction: The plot on Jesus' life* (= Mark 14:1–2). An important change here is the introduction of a fourth Passion prediction in verse 2, which links the narrative more closely to the previous teaching of Jesus.

26:6–16: *The anointing at Bethany* (= Mark 14:3–11). Matthew essentially follows Mark; however, he replaces Mark's "the gospel" with "this gospel" (see 24:14).

26:17–29: *Jesus' last meal with his disciples* (= Mark 14:12–25). Mark does not identify the betrayer by name until the Gethsemane scene (14:43); Matthew indicates it here (26:25). In the supper scene itself, Matthew adds the drink command (26:27) and the forgiveness of sins (26:28) and changes Mark's Kingdom of God to "my Father's kingdom."

26:30–35: *Prediction of the flight of the disciples and the betrayal by Peter* (= Mark 14:26–31).

26:36–56: *The betrayal and the arrest* (= Mark 14:32–52). Matthew adds the pacifist statement about the sword and heightens the theme that Jesus' betrayal and arrest are part of God's plan as found in Scripture. Similarly, he rewrites verse 56 (= Mark 14:49b) to read, "But all this has taken place, so that the scriptures of the prophets may be fulfilled."

26:57–75: *Betrayal by Peter and intercalated account of the night trial before the Sanhedrin* (= Mark 14:53–72). The only significant change is that Matthew edits the dialogue between Jesus and the high priest to make it a formal statement of the person of Jesus before the spiritual leader of Israel: "I put you under oath before the living God, tell us . . . You have said so . . ." (verses 63–64).

27:1–2:   *Jesus is delivered to Pilate* (= Mark 15:1).

27:3–10:   *The fate of Judas.*   Only Matthew has this narrative of the suicide of Judas. The thirty pieces of silver recalls 26:15 and is the price of a slave (Exod. 21:32), but the story also fulfills Scripture, Matthew's thirteenth formula quotation (Zech. 11: 12–13). Suicide by hanging does not correspond with the "gutsier" tradition of how Judas died in Acts 1:15–20.

27:11–66:   *The trial before Pilate and the crucifixion* (= Mark 15:2–47). Matthew introduces several editorial changes in this narrative. In 27:19, he adds Pilate's wife's dream and her comment that Pilate should have nothing to do with "that righteous man," thus suggesting Jesus' innocence. In verses 24–25, he continues Pilate's innocence and stresses the guilt of all Israel. With Mark, the crucifixion scene has several allusions to suffering in Ps. 22 and 69 (27:32–44). In verse 40, he adds the bystanders' mocking reference to the Son of God, then in verse 43 he adds Ps. 22:9 and the charge that he claimed to be the "Son of God." He changes Mark's Aramaic for "my God" (*Eloi*) in Ps. 22:1 to Hebrew (*Eli*) in order to make the mistaken view of the bystanders that he was calling out to "*Eli*-jah" clearer. In verses 52–53, he inserts a series of events, including a temporary resurrection of "the saints" to stress the fact that God is at work in these events and that new life will emerge from the death of Jesus. Finally, in verses 62–66, he adds the incident of the guard at the tomb, anticipating their fear in 28:4. This is a late composition, very probably by Matthew himself, designed to forestall a possible claim that the resurrection was a fraud because the disciples had stolen the body of Jesus. It anticipates the report of the guard in 28:11–20.

28:1–20:   Epilogue: The resurrection and Great Commission.
Mark has no account of the resurrection, but only of the women at the empty tomb. Matthew changes this ending dramatically.

28:1–10:   *The empty tomb* (= Mark 16:18).   The first major change is that additional verse 24 further emphasizes the "supernatural" nature of these events—the earthquake, the appearance of an angel, the fear of the guards. In verse 8, the women, in contrast to Mark, *do* deliver the message to the Eleven that he is going before them to Galilee, as he had promised (Matt. 26:32 = Mark 14:28). In verses 9–10, Matthew provides an appearance of Jesus to the women and another indication, this time a command by the risen Lord, that the disciples should go into Galilee.

28:11–15:   *The report of the guard.*   This addition recalls the Matthean posting of the guard at the tomb in 27:62–66, the purpose of which is clearly to forestall the objection that the disciples stole Jesus' body.

28:16–20:   *The Great Commission.*   This is the climax to the Gospel of Matthew. It tells intended readers and hearers what the gospel has narrated. Jesus has given the new revelation to his disciples, and it is now their responsibility to go into the world and make new disciples. Thus those who read and hear the story become heirs to the new revelation. Some must interpret it, and all must obey it. Further, the commission implies a mission—to make further disciples of all peoples. In this way, readers and hearers appropriate the revelation and locate their place in the scheme of things. During the interval between the Passion and the *parousia,* followers are to accept, interpret, and obey the revelation and at the same time persuade others to do the same. They will not be alone in this task; always the risen Lord will be with them to the close of the age.

The narrative is not so much a resurrection appearance story as an account of the risen and exalted Lord commissioning the disciples. Certainly it represents the message of the evangelist Matthew because it reveals the convictions that inspired his writing of the gospel. Jesus is the medium of the new revelation that fulfills and decisively reinterprets the old; disciples are recipients of the revelation and are to obey so that the quality of obedience exceeds that of the Pharisees and their scribes. These themes have been central to the gospel. But now new elements are added. In language recalling the Son of Man vision in Dan. 7:14, Jesus explicitly claims the authority that had before been his only implicitly (verse 18). Now, for the first time, certain disciples are commissioned to "*teach*," to interpret the revelation. Now also the church is given the baptismal confession (verse 19). Finally, the gospel ends on a note sounded earlier (8:25–26; 14:27; 18:20): The distinguishing mark of the church and the source of its power and authority are the presence of the risen Lord.

FURTHER OBSERVATIONS

The Matthean View of Jesus:
The New Revelation Requiring Interpretation

Matthew's five major discourses, themes related to Egypt and the exodus, Jesus' temptation of forty days and forty nights, and several revelations on mountains have sometimes suggested to scholars that Matthew thinks of Jesus as a new Moses who teaches a new Torah. If this is correct, the theme is more implicit than explicit. At the very least, Matthew presents the teaching of Jesus as the correct interpretation of "the Torah and the prophets" in major discourses. This perspective leads to the recognition that for Matthew, as for the Pharisees, revelation requires authoritative interpretation with changing times and circumstances.

Matthew goes further: Jesus not only *teaches* the new revelation, but also he himself *is* the new revelation, the very fulfillment of "the law and the prophets." The new revelation is, to be sure, related to the old revelation. This is reinforced by Matthew's use of titles for Jesus. In the genealogy, not only is Jesus descended from Abraham, the father of the Israelite people and the one to whom a promise was given to the peoples/nations; but also he is descended from the first great king of Israel, King David and his royal line. This ascribed **honor** by descent gives him the proper credentials to be a royal messianic king—the Son of David—and he can enter Jerusalem as such (21:5, 9). Matthew further develops Jesus' role as the Son of David in the miracle stories (9:27; 12:23; 15:22; 20:30; 21:9, 15; 22:42, 45); indeed, even the daughter of a Gentile woman who addresses Jesus as Son of David is healed (15:22).

Related to the title "Son of David" is the title "Son of God," also a title for the messianic king of Israel (e.g., Ps. 2:7). We noted that one attempt to see Matthew's overall structure stresses the expression "from that time on, Jesus began . . ." (4:17; 16:21) and the title "Son of God." Son of God is very important to him. Jesus' birth from the virgin Mary is exceptional; he is Immanuel, which in Hebrew means "God is with us" (1:23). Like Israel, he has been called out of Egypt as God's Son (2:15 [Hos. 11:1]). As in Mark, God himself in the voice at the baptism and the transfiguration declares, "This is my son, the Beloved, with whom I am well pleased (listen to him)" (3:17; 17:5; cf. Ps. 2:7; Isa. 42:1). As in Q, he is tempted as the Son of God (4:3, 6). Peter's messianic confession in Matthew adds "Son of God" to Jesus' identity as the Messiah (16:16), and we find it added in other places, such as in the crucifixion scene (27:39).

Although the Moses themes and the titles "Messiah," "Son of David," and "Son of God" are crucial for relating the new revelation to the old, Matthew also emphasizes Jesus' messianic role with the titles "**Son of Man**" and "Lord." As in Mark and **Q,** the "Son of Man" title encompasses authority on earth (e.g., 9:6; 12:8; 8:20), necessary suffering (16:21; 17:22; 20:18–19, the Passion predictions), and apocalyptic authority at the final judgment (e.g., 16:27; 24:27, 30). Although, as in Mark, Son of God and Son of Man are coordinated, Matthew's particular interest is the third, or apocalyptic, category, to which he adds the most sayings (six). Thus Matthew is strongly interested in Jesus as Son of Man at his *parousia,* where his role is particularly associated with judgment of outsiders, that is, Israel and "the nations." He will suddenly come at the end with his angels on the clouds of heaven with power and glory; standing before the world as a king before his kingdom (13:37–38), he will judge (e.g., 25:31–46).

Finally, Jesus is "Lord." This term can mean "sir" in certain contexts, but often it has Christological meaning associated with worship, although not yet "*the* Lord God" of the Scriptures. Matthew employs the title not only in relation to the miracle-working Son of David (e.g., 22:41–46) and one who is frequently addressed as such by the disciples who worship him (8:25; 17:4; 20:33), but also especially in Jesus' return as Son of Man (cf. 7:21–22; 24:42; 25:11, 37, 44).

The Disciples in Matthew

Emphasis on titles of honor drawn from the culture of the times is one way to look at the "new revelation." Yet, one can, as with Mark, also look at the total drive of the story, a story that in contrast to Mark ends with a more upbeat note about the disciples, their mission to the peoples, and the resurrected Lord's presence with them until the end.

In contrast to Mark, who portrays the disciples as those who misunderstand Jesus, Matthew portrays them as sometimes having "little faith" but as nonetheless growing in understanding and ultimately to be entrusted with the new revelation. So when Matthew is thinking of disciples, he is probably thinking of those who hear and believe the story of Jesus. He does not object to the *function* of "scribes and Pharisees" as interpreters of "the book of Moses." On the contrary, at one point he applauds it (23:2–3a). The need is for scribes "trained for the kingdom of heaven" (13:52) as more or less official interpreters of the revelation as fulfilled in Jesus Christ. Peter is given a special role, and the Matthean disciples themselves (in contrast to the Markan) are said to "understand" and are charged to teach.

An interesting aspect of his presentation is that he avoids any mention that the disciples of Jesus *teach*—until the very end of the story. In the Gospel of Matthew, only Jesus teaches, and that teaching is the new Torah, the fulfilled revelation. But after the revelation is complete, and the situation has become such that the revelation now needs authoritative interpretation, he commands the Eleven: "Go therefore and make disciples of all nations, baptizing them . . . *teaching them to obey every-*

thing that I have commanded you; and remember, I am with you always, to the end of the age" (Matt. 28:19–20, the Great Commission). The commandment sums up the major emphasis of the Gospel of Matthew: The teaching of Jesus is the new revelation, and it requires the authoritative interpretation of disciples who have a special role in Matthew's "church."

The Kingdom of Heaven, Ethics, and the Church

Whereas the Gospel of Mark refers to Jesus' preaching the Kingdom of *God,* the Gospel of Matthew prefers Jesus' preaching the Kingdom of *Heaven,* a way of speaking about God indirectly. Statistics indicate the importance of Jesus' "Kingdom of Heaven" references in Matthew: Mark has fourteen references, Q has at least nine references, but Matthew has a striking thirty-eight references plus sixteen references to "Kingdom," all attributed to Jesus but one (3:2: John the Baptizer). The "gospel of the Kingdom" is primarily what Jesus preaches in "their synagogues" (4:23; 9:35; cf. 10:7; 28:20), but it implies the presence of Jesus himself—"repent, for the Kingdom of Heaven is at hand" (4:17; cf. 3:2)—and might even refer to what Matthew writes (13:19; cf. 4:15).

The Kingdom of God/Heaven, never precisely defined in the gospels, has a number of dimensions in Israelite and Greco-Roman texts (Duling). It includes political, economic, and religious dimensions. Whatever the Kingdom meant to Jesus (Chapter Fourteen), in Q, and in Mark (Chapter eight), for Matthew, the Kingdom of Heaven seems to be primarily something forthcoming. A number of sayings emphasize that "the righteous" will "enter" the Kingdom in the future (e.g., 5:20; 7:21). Nonetheless, there are implications for ethical behavior in the present, as the pervasive repentance theme indicates. Those who are "righteous" are those who are "like children" (18:3–4; 19:13–15), who "bear fruit" (7:16–21), and although there are positive hints about the (urban) rich (5:3), the political-economic-social dimension seems to be present when he says that "a rich person" will have difficulty "entering" (19:23–24). One also gains the impression that for Matthew the Kingdom of Heaven is anticipated in his present community, the "church," which, as some of the parables show (13:24–30; 22:1–14; 25:1–13), contains both good and evil until the final judgment. A parallel theme seems to be the Kingdom of the coming Son of Man (e.g., 13:41; 16:28), a kind of provisional Kingdom of both righteous and unrighteous, ultimately to be replaced by the Kingdom of the Father (13:41–43a), which will include only "the righteous."

The Idea of "Salvation History"

In the Bible, authors often think in terms of cycles, for example, the agricultural seasons and the great seasonal festivals. Yet, they will sometimes think in broader temporal terms, that is, of past, present, and future. Millennial thinkers write not only in spatial but also in temporal fashion, with their sights fixed on the present and near future; so do ancient biblical "historians," with their focus on what God has done, is doing, and will do.

However, the history that an ancient person sees is not simply the factual recounting of events. In the sacred texts of Israel, it is the history "of the world" in which God may be known, a history that is both a history of a chosen people and their own affairs and at the same time a history of God's affairs with his chosen people. As the history of God's affairs with Israel, of God's activity on behalf of his people, it is "*salvation* history," the story of the deliverance of Israel by God. There is then a "secular history," a history of kings, queens, prophets, priests, war, peace, and the like, but there is also a salvation history, a history of God operating in that everyday world to save his chosen people.

The New Testament writer who has most often been thought to have an idea of salvation history is the author of Luke and Acts, the only "history" genre in the New Testament. Yet, there are also indications that the author of the Gospel of Matthew had some idea of salvation history. He mentions the temporal division "from that time on" (4:17; 16:21). There are other temporal expressions (e.g., "then," some ninety times; "in those days," 3:1, cf. 24:3, 19, 22 [twice], 29; "at that time," 11:25; 12:1; 14:1; ". . . to the close of the age," 28:20; cf. 24:3). A major theme throughout Matthew is the fulfillment of "the old" by "the new," especially in the formula quotations. The author of Matthew claims that Jesus' own mission was to the "lost sheep of the house of Israel" (10:5; 15:24). Yet, the Great Commission of the resurrected Messiah at the end of the gospel stresses a mission to "all the peoples" (28:19), and Matthew's story notes Gentiles of great faith (e.g., the magi in 2:1–12; the centurion in 8:5–13).

Clearly Matthew's view of the new revelation in Jesus Christ suggests a mild distinction between a "period of Israel" and a "period of Jesus" beginning with John the Baptizer (cf. the temporal references and Kingdom proclamation in 3:1 and 4:17). A more difficult question is whether these two phases should be extended to three, that is, whether "period of Jesus" and "period of the post-Jesus 'church'" should be distinguished and, if so, when the latter begins. On the one hand, he lets the story of Jesus, the disciples, and their opponents speak directly to his own day. This tends to blur any distinction between the period of Jesus and the period of the church. Yet, the author thinks of the "church" as a socio-religious entity with leadership roles, especially that of Peter, and a mission to all peoples, and he certainly places central significance on the Great Commission in that regard (28:16–20). The gospel ends with the promise of the risen Lord to the disciples: "and remember, I am with you always, to the end of the age" (28:20). Moreover, in the discourse on community regulations there is a quasi-judicial discipline for the group, and a similar note is sounded: "For where two or three are gathered in my name, I am there among them" (18:20). Such passages seem to point to a distinction between Jesus and the church. If so, there are three phases: Israel, Jesus, and the church. Thus, although Matthew has not yet developed a salvation history to the extent of Luke-Acts, he tends to favor a move *toward* a three-phase view, the period of Israel, the period of Jesus, and the period of the church.

THE INTERPRETATION OF THE GOSPEL OF MATTHEW

The evangelist Matthew has distinctive ideas. The ideas of the fulfillment of a previous promise, of a revelation authoritatively interpreted, of a carefully organized and structured community of believers—for all of these Matthew is indebted to his

Israelite heritage. His main conflict centers around the growing influence of the Pharisees in what some scholars call "formative Judaism." It is possibly symbolized by the innovations at the **Jamnia Academy.** Yet, Israel at this point in history was already showing influences of the wider Greco-Roman world. Most of Matthew's scriptures are from the Greek **Septuagint,** and in some respects his church discipline section in 18:15–20 looks like the discipline of a Hellenistic voluntary association. Israelite rabbis were to come to speak of the "presence" (Hebrew *shekînāh*) of God, formerly in the Jerusalem temple, wherever two or three gathered to study the Torah. The Matthean view of the risen Lord who is present in the church, helping, sustaining, and guiding the "disciples," has its roots in the Hellenistic religious concept of the presence of the Lord in the cultic worship of the community and perhaps a proto-rabbinic idea about Torah study. Again, Matthew stands between worlds.

By the intent of its author, the Gospel of Matthew cries out for the interpretation it has in fact received through the centuries: as a text enshrining a revelation subject to authoritative interpretation within the Jesus Movement. More than that, this is what happened to the whole of the New Testament of which Matthew became the first book. The centuries have treated it as the embodiment of revelation and authoritatively interpreted it within the church, which would undoubtedly have delighted the evangelist himself.

STUDY QUESTIONS

1. Who was the person "Matthew" in the New Testament? What does the Papias tradition say about the gospel? What do modern scholars think about author, date, place, and social context of this gospel? How do the rise of the Pharisees and the Academy at Yavneh (Jamnia) relate to these questions?

2. In what way is Matthew more structured than Mark, and what are some theories about this structure? What is the Sermon on the Mount (chapters 5–7)? Why might Matthew have bunched Mark's miracles in chapters 8–9? How does the author portray Jesus in the mission discourse (chapter 10)? How does Matthew develop Mark's parable chapter in the third discourse (chapter 13)? What are some community regulations in the fourth discourse (chapter 18)? How does Matthew handle the eschatological discourse (chapters 24–25) found in Mark 13? What does Matthew add at the end of the story, and what is its significance? What is the genre of Matthew?

3. How is the church portrayed in Matthew? How and why does the Matthean author transform the "confession of Peter" at Caesarea Philippi? In contrast to Mark, how do the disciples look in the Gospel of Matthew? Why was this gospel put first in the New Testament canon?

4. What is the importance of Torah and scripture in Matthew? What are some special features of the Matthean infancy? What is the importance of Moses and the "Son of God" title for this gospel? What is the new revelation requiring interpretation? What is Matthew's view of "Salvation History"?

Photo 10.1 Detail from *The Liberation of St. Peter* by Raphael (1483–1520), Vatican Stanze, Rome. Peter's cell is illuminated by the light of an angel who miraculously helps him escape (Acts 12:1–10). The story is typical of the Lukan view that God guides his chosen people through history, or "salvation history."

CHAPTER TEN

THE GOSPEL OF LUKE AND THE ACTS OF THE APOSTLES: THE IDEA AND ETHICS OF SALVATION HISTORY

Very early in the history of the Jesus Movement, as the ancient manuscripts show, the four gospels sometimes circulated together. When larger collections of New Testament texts were assembled, the four gospels remained together as a distinct group in the order Matthew, Mark, Luke, and John. This arrangement was unfortunate for modern study because the Gospel of John came between the Gospel of Luke and the Acts of the Apostles. However, the author of Luke and Acts clearly wrote them to be read together, as Book I and Book II in sequence. That is clear from the reference to Theophilus at the beginning of each book (Luke 1:3: ". . . to write an orderly account for you, *most excellent Theophilus* . . ."; Acts 1:1: "In the first book, *Theophilus,* I wrote about all that Jesus did and taught . . ."). The separation of Acts from Luke also led to the title "According to Luke" being given to the first volume and "Acts of the Apostles" to the second volume sometime in the second century C.E. As far as we know, the author did not title his two-volume work, although he does refer to it as "a *narrative* of the things which have been accomplished among us" (Luke 1:1) and an *"orderly account."* Here it will be treated as the two-volume work, and it will often be called, as it is by most modern scholars, "Luke-Acts."

EARLY TRADITION ABOUT THE COMPOSITION OF LUKE-ACTS

Writers of the Jesus Movement in the latter second century C.E. recognized that the same person wrote the Gospel of Luke and the Acts of the Apostles, despite their separation. They believed that that person was Luke the physician, a companion and follower of the Apostle Paul. After offering comments about Matthew and Mark that sound like the second-century Papias tradition, the Church Father

Irenaeus, bishop of Lyons (said fourth-century Eusebius), wrote about Luke and Acts. Of the gospel he wrote:

> Luke also, the follower of Paul, put down in a book (Greek *biblō*) a gospel (Greek *euangelion*) preached by that one.
>
> (Irenaeus Against Heresies 3.1.2 in Eusebius Ecclesiastical History 5.8.2.)

His view of Acts shows that some ancient writers, like modern critical scholars, were well aware of issues posed by first-person plural sentences ("we") in sections of the Acts travel narrative:

> *Now, that this Luke was inseparable from Paul and his fellow worker in the Gospel, he himself made clear,* not vaunting, but guided by truth itself. For when both Barnabas and John, who was called Mark, had departed from Paul and had sailed to [the island of] Cyprus (Acts 15:39), he says, "*We* arrived at Troas [in northwestern Turkey]" (Acts 16:8 [the verse reads, "they went down to Troas" (NRSV)]). And when Paul had seen a Macedonian man in a dream saying: "Come over into Macedonia [northern Greece] and help us, Paul," he says: "Immediately *we* sought to proceed into Macedonia, knowing that the Lord had called us to proclaim the Gospel to them. So *we* set sail from Troas and steered *our* course toward Samothrace" (Acts 16:9–11). . . .
>
> (Irenaeus Against Heresies 3.14.1)

Irenaeus continues with other examples, but enough is quoted to see that he deduced from the first-person plural that the narrator of the story, who he believes was Luke, was referring to himself as a close traveling companion of Paul. Contemporary scholars call these first-person plural statements "**we passages**," and they still pose interesting questions about authorship (see following).

A second tradition about Luke-Acts is found in a late second-century Greek prologue to the gospel, which some have thought was "anti-Marcionite" (for the "heretic" Marcion, see Chapters Two and Seven and Appendix Two). This prologue reads:

> Luke was a Syrian of Antioch, a physician by profession, a disciple of the apostles, and later a follower of Paul until his martyrdom. He served the Lord without distraction, without a wife, and without children. He died at the age of eighty-four in Boeotia, full of the Holy Spirit.

The prologue continues by claiming that the gospel was composed in Achaia (southern Greece) for Gentile converts and that Acts was composed after the gospel.

A third tradition is found in the "**Muratorian Canon**" (named for its discoverer), a list of authoritative books that almost all scholars think represents the Roman church's list of inspired books in the late second century C.E. It has the following statement:

> The third book of the Gospel [is that] according to Luke. Luke, the physician, after the ascension of Christ, when Paul had taken him with him as a companion of his traveling, [and after he had made] an investigation, wrote in his own name—but

neither did he see the Lord in the flesh—and thus, as he was able to investigate (Luke 1:3), so he also begins to tell the story [starting] from the nativity of John.

All these traditions are from the late second century C.E. Our earliest, best manuscripts of the Third Gospel are from the late third and fourth centuries C.E., and they follow this tradition when they call the gospel "According to Luke."

Summarizing, the preceding late second-century accounts about the author of the Gospel of Luke and the Acts of the Apostles claim that he is "Luke the beloved physician" and companion of Paul, who at an old age wrote the gospel for Gentiles in Greece and then wrote Acts.

A Person Named "Luke" in the New Testament

A person named "Luke" (Greek *Loukas*) is mentioned three times in the New Testament. In Paul's prison letter to the slave owner Philemon (see Chapter Five), Paul extends greetings to Philemon from "Mark, Aristarchus, Demas, and, *Luke,* my fellow workers" (Philem. 24). Colossians, considered in this book to be deutero-Pauline, also associates Luke with Paul. It says, "*Luke, the beloved physician,* and Demas greet you" (Col. 4:14) and implies that he was most probably a Gentile (cf. 4:11). In a still-later deutero-Pauline letter called "1 Timothy," attributed to Paul by the church, the author states, "Only *Luke* is with me" (2 Tim. 4:11). In short, the source of the view that the author of the Third Gospel is Luke the physician, a companion of Paul, is the New Testament view that Paul had a fellow worker and traveling companion, Luke the physician.

GENERAL HISTORICAL CRITICISM: AUTHOR, DATE, AND PLACE

Modern scholars have examined the late second-century view that the author of Luke-Acts was Luke, the beloved physician and companion of Paul. There are several interesting critical questions related to this tradition.

First, is it possible to discern in Luke-Acts a specialized medical language typical of ancient physicians? In the late nineteenth century, the answer to this question was a decisive "Yes!" Scholars pointed to expressions such as "suffering from a very high fever" (Luke 4:38) or "paralyzed" (Luke 5:18, 24) as specialized medical language. However, twentieth-century scholars have come to realize that Luke's supposed medical terms were in fact commonly used by educated writers of the times and thus not unique to physicians. Thus it is impossible to prove that the medical language in Luke-Acts is from a specialized medical person.

Second, if the author of Acts was a companion of Paul, he would portray Paul's life in accord with what Paul himself says. Does he? This question has already been answered in Chapters Three and Four (see discussions of "Acts of the Apostles" as a source for history). Although Acts is in some cases valuable for the movements of Paul, it is also often quite legendary, and its details often conflict with what Paul says about himself. Thus Acts can be used for Paul's life only with great caution, a conclusion that does not add to our confidence that its author was a close companion of Paul.

Third, do the *speeches of Paul* in Acts correspond with *Paul's thought* as known in the letters? Studies have shown that Paul's speeches in Acts differ in important respects. For example, the Acts version of Paul's speech in Athens (Acts 17:22–31) attributes to the Gentiles a natural knowledge of God. Romans 1 also says that the Gentiles have a natural, innate knowledge of God. However, although the Acts speech emphasizes humanity's enlightened quest for and natural kinship with God (especially verses 26–31), Romans says that the Gentiles' knowledge of God is insufficient to overcome their idolatry and immorality and that their immoral acts are condemned as inexcusable and sinful (Rom. 1:18–21). Both writings seem to have been influenced by Stoicism, but the tone of Acts is much more philosophically open than Paul's tone is in Romans.

Another example is Paul's speech in Antioch of Pisidia (central Asia Minor; Acts 13:16–41). This speech sketches the story of Israel and the Israelites' misunderstanding of the messianic prophecies about Jesus. However, it sounds familiar, much like other Acts speeches of Peter and Stephen (cf. Acts 2; 4; 7). Indeed, in Paul's speeches in Acts, we fail to find the great Pauline themes: the emphasis on the cross, justification by faith, freedom from the Law, and the expectation that Christ will return soon. In this regard, recall that the ancient historical writers wrote speeches for their heroes based on what they thought was appropriate for the occasion and that such speeches were designed to teach virtues. Most analysts conclude that the author of Acts also composed speeches for his hero Paul, based on what he thought was important for the occasion but in line with key themes in the other speeches. An analysis of the Lukan writer as a historian will reinforce this point (see following). Again, the differences between the Acts speeches and what Paul himself says do not easily lead to confidence that their author was Paul's close companion.

Finally, did Paul's companion write the famous "**we passages**" (Acts 16:10–17; 20:5–15; 21:1–18; 27:1–28:16) because he was with Paul on his journeys? Second-century writers like Irenaeus thought so. Some modern interpreters have concluded that the "we passages" came directly from a companion of Paul. Others have offered the alternative that they come from a lost *diary* of Paul's companion. Both solutions would support the view that Acts is based on eyewitness sources. Yet, there are complications. The introduction of each of these "we passages" occurs at the beginning of a sea voyage. The study of ancient sea voyage narratives shows that they are a subgenre in which their composers often shifted into the first-person style; in sea voyages, it was common literary convention. Thus it is impossible to conclude with certainty that the person writing was *actually* present on the voyage. Today most critics conclude that the "we passages" *cannot* prove without doubt that their author was present with Paul on his voyages.

Internal analysis—medical language, comparison of Paul's life and thought in the letters and the Acts speeches, and the "we passages"—does not offer convincing proof that the author of Luke-Acts was Luke the physician. Interestingly, the author of Acts did not stress—indeed, may have not even mentioned—that Paul was an "apostle" because he required that apostles had to have accompanied Jesus (cf. Acts 1:21–22; but cf. 14:4, 14 [textual variants in verse 14!]). Yet, Paul called himself an apostle. Most critics favor the view that the Gospel of Luke, like the gospels of

Matthew and Mark, was anonymous and that the same goes for Acts. They were only later attributed to Luke the physician. For convenience, the traditional name "Luke" is retained. To discover who this person was, however, the deciding factor, as with "Mark," "Matthew," and "John," will be internal evidence. First, however, consider the problems of date and place.

As with Mark and Matthew, a date for Luke-Acts must be fixed by external and internal evidence. Late second-century Christ believers clearly knew about the Third Gospel, as the preceding early church traditions show. Additionally, Dionysius of Corinth cited Acts in a letter to a certain Soter of Rome about 170 C.E. (Eusebius *Ecclesiastical History* 4.23.3). Earlier references from the middle of the second century are possible but uncertain (e.g., Justin Martyr *Dialogue with Trypho* 105 [Luke 23:46]). Marcion seems to have known Luke or some version of Luke. Thus the latest date of composition would probably be about 150 C.E.

At the early end of the dating spectrum, the author of the Gospel of Luke clearly states that other accounts were written before his (1:1–4). He was thus not from the first generation of the Jesus Movement. According to the **Two-Source Theory,** Luke knows and uses the Gospel of Mark, which we have dated shortly after the destruction of Jerusalem in 70 C.E. This post-70 dating is very strong because Luke interprets Mark's "desolating sacrilege" (Mark 3:14) with the words, "When you see Jerusalem surrounded by armies . . ." (Luke 21:20). Earlier he had had Jesus prophesy of Jerusalem, "when your enemies will set up ramparts [or cast up a bank] around you and surround you" (Luke 19:43; cf. verses 39–44). These descriptions correspond well to Josephus' description of the Romans' siege of Jerusalem (e.g., Josephus *Wars* 5.11.4 [446]–5.12.4 [526]).

In short, the outside dates for the composition of Luke-Acts are between 70 and 150 C.E. Because other themes in Luke are characteristic of the late first century C.E., most interpreters date it in the generation following the fall of Jerusalem. So a date of about **80–90 C.E.,** about the time of Matthew, is appropriate.

The preceding located composition in Achaia, or southern Greece, although other ancients placed it in Boeotia, the traditional place of Luke's death, or Rome, where the story of Paul in Acts ends (Acts 28). The Lukan view of Palestinian geography is not very good, suggesting some place outside of Palestine. Probably any city where Greek was spoken would be possible (Caesarea Maritima is one guess).

In summary, the gospel attributed to Luke was anonymous and circulated anonymously. It was written about 80–90 C.E., probably in some city where Greek was spoken, Caesarea Maritima having often been suggested. The ascription of the gospel to the physician and companion of Paul cannot be demonstrated by internal analysis. Perhaps it was an inference from clear indications of the "we passages," as in Irenaeus. Its vocabulary and style are characteristic of a well-educated Greek (see following).

SOCIAL-HISTORICAL CONTEXT

As noted at the beginning of this chapter, both volumes of Luke-Acts are addressed to "**Theophilus.**" The name is Greek, although it is commonly found among both Israelites and Greeks. It means "lover of God" (*theos,* "God," plus the root *phil-,* "love"), and it is prefaced by "most excellent," meaning something like "Your Excellency." A person named Theophilus is otherwise unknown in the Jesus Movement. These facts have led interpreters to suggest two solutions about his identity. The first is general, that is, *any* "God-loving" Greek-speaking person of high rank and status, for example, a member of the ruling strata. The second is an unknown, wealthy, high-status person who has recently been initiated into the Jesus Movement. Recently it has been suggested that such a person might be a patron of the Lukan churches. Either way, the author probably intended his books to be read and heard by those of higher status in Greco-Roman society.

Luke's broader social context can be illustrated by his themes. One is boundary-breaking inclusiveness, often called "*universalism.*" In the new household of God, the old social, economic, ethnic, religious, and sexual barriers are broken down. Only in the Gospel of Luke does the genealogy begin with Jesus and move backward beyond Abraham (Matthew's first person) to Adam, who is considered to be the *first* Son of God. Adam, of course, was believed to be the First Man, the representative of the whole human race; in Hebrew, his name means "man" in the generic sense, or better, "humanity" (Luke 3:23–28). Only in the Gospel of Luke does Jesus send *seventy* disciples on a mission, the number "seventy" being symbolic for the number of nations/peoples of the world (Luke 10:1–20). Luke's second volume, Acts, shows how the gospel spread by guidance of the Spirit from Jerusalem, through Judea, to Samaria and Gentile lands (Acts 1:8). Luke's world is cosmopolitan, universal. Thus salvation is extended to everyone: women, sinners, the poor, Israelites, Samaritans, and Gentiles, among them especially the Romans.

Women are very prominent in Luke's two volumes. Whereas in Matthew, Joseph dominates the infancy story, in Luke, Elizabeth, the mother of the Baptizer, and her relative Mary, the mother of Jesus, hold center stage (Luke 1–2). Found only in Luke are these key passages: Mary's being blessed for bearing Jesus (11:27–28); a sinful woman who shows Jesus hospitality (Luke 7:36–50; [cf. Mark 14:3–9]); the praise of Mary of Bethany, who listens to Jesus' teaching (Luke 10:38–42); and Jesus' healing of the crippled woman (Luke 10:13–17). Special to Luke are also women of means who support Jesus' ministry (Luke 8:1–3) and the "great number" of women present at the crucifixion (Luke 23:27). In Acts, the wealthy purple cloth merchant, Lydia, extends hospitality to Paul (16:11–15); so do Aquila and Priscilla (Prisca) at Corinth (18:1–3, 18) and Philip's four daughters, who are prophetesses (21:9). When it is recalled that most women in the ancient world were subordinate to men, that Israelite women were considered unclean a significant part of their lives, and that women in most social contexts were near the bottom of the social ladder, Luke's accounts of women are rather remarkable. Indeed, the question has been raised whether the author is a well-educated Gentile woman. In any case, there must have been many women converts in the Lukan communities.

Luke also has a special concern for *sinners,* or "the lost." In addition to the woman who was a sinner (7:36–50), Luke has the story of the rich tax collector Zacchaeus, "a sinner" (19:7), and another tax collector who cries out, "God, be merciful to me, a sinner!" (Luke 18:9–14). Only in Luke is paradise promised to the sinful, but penitent, thief on his cross (Luke 23:43). The theme of sinning is especially prevalent in the Lost Sheep, the Lost Coin, and the Lost (or Prodigal) Son (Luke 15).

Luke-Acts is also distinctive because of its heightened interest in *the poor*. As in **Q,** Jesus says, ". . . where your treasure is, there will your heart be also" (12:34). Jesus proclaims good news to the poor (Luke 4:16–20; 7:22), blesses the literal poor (6:20; contrast Matt. 5:3), tells parables in behalf of the poor (e.g., 12:13–21; 16:19–31), condemns the Pharisees as lovers of money (16:14), and says that it is impossible to serve both God and money (16:13). Only in Luke does the poor widow successfully importune an unjust judge (Luke 18:1–8). Only this author has the parable of the Rich Fool, in which Jesus comments, "one's life does not consist in the abundance of possessions" (Luke 12:15). In Acts, Peter is poor (Acts 3:6), yet his miraculous powers are not for sale (Acts 8:18–24). Cornelius the Gentile convert is praised for his almsgiving (Acts 10:2), and Paul observes the same practice (24:17). In short, in a society where a very high percentage of the population consists of poor peasants and urban poor living at a subsistence level, Luke stresses the honor code especially found among the poor: hospitality, redistribution of the wealth, and almsgiving. Scholars have often suggested that there seem to have been a number of rich among those to whom Luke writes; if it is not always necessary to sell everything (19:8), the message of the Kingdom brings with it concern for the poor and destitute. In other words, Luke may be telling his patron and others that those in the upper strata of society, the rich, powerful, and prestigious, should support the lower strata, the peasants and other marginal people.

Luke's inclusive "universalism" includes many ethnic groups, especially the *Samaritans,* who are the regional rivals of Palestinian Israelites. Only the Gospel of Luke contains a parable in which a hated Samaritan is "good" (Luke 10:29–37) and the miracle of the healing of the ten lepers in which the only one to return to thank him is a Samaritan (Luke 17:11–19 [verse 16]). In Acts, Luke also tells the story of the spread of the Jesus Movement to the Samaritans (8:4–8, 14–17). This interest in Samaritans is illustrated by the spread of the gospel from Jerusalem to "all Judea *and Samaria* . . ." (Acts 1:8).

Luke says that the Jesus Movement passed beyond Samaria to the "ends of the earth" (1:8), and Acts portrays this movement to Rome. In this regard, note that Luke-Acts is very *pro-Roman*. To be sure, Jesus is subservient to Rome, and the Roman governor Pontius Pilate yields to the Israelite leaders' charges that Jesus stirs up and perverts the people (Luke 23:2, 5, 14). Yet, Pilate yields only after declaring three times that Jesus is innocent (Luke 23:4, 14–15, 22). Only Luke has the Israelites commend the Roman centurion whose slave is healed (Q 7:1–10); ". . . he loves our nation, and it is he who built our synagogue for us" (Luke 7:5). In Acts, the very first Gentile to be converted to the Jesus Movement is a Roman centurion (Acts 10:1–33). In Cyprus, the Roman proconsul "believes" on the basis of Paul's message (Acts 13:12). In Achaia (Greece), the Roman proconsul Gallio takes Paul's side against the Israelites (Acts 18:14–15). Paul is a Roman citizen (Acts 16:37–38; 22:25–29; 23:27), and in general, Roman authorities treat him with respect.

Can this pro-Roman stance be explained? In the latter third of the first century C.E., many members of the Jesus Movement had to adjust to their success among the Gentiles. Part of this story was the ever-present possibility of persecution by the Romans. Yet, members of the Jesus Movement also had Israelite roots. In Luke-Acts, the Jesus Movement is consistently represented as descended from Israel and as the proper fulfillment of Israelite prophecy (e.g., 13:16–41). Thus one explanation for Luke's pro-Roman stance has been that he wanted believers in Jesus as the Messiah to be able to share the Israelites' special privileges in the Roman Empire. These included a degree of political freedom and religious toleration (see Chapter One). If so, the author attempted to present the members of the Jesus Movement as nonthreatening to Roman authorities and perhaps also vice versa. Perhaps there were a number of Romans in the Lukan community (was Theophilus a Roman with a Greek name?). If so, Luke may have wanted to show that, despite Jesus' death by crucifixion, the usual punishment for crimes against the Roman state, being a member of the Jesus Movement and being Roman were not really mutually exclusive. In short, it is plausible that the Lukan author wanted to legitimate the Jesus Movement for political reasons.

There is a debated question in this regard: Does the pro-Gentile, and especially pro-Roman, emphasis in Luke-Acts allow room for *the Israelites* to be included in God's plan of salvation? In discussing the Gospel of Matthew, we found this question difficult to answer but answered it positively; the question is all the more difficult to answer in the Lukan writings.

The early part of Acts claims that many Israelites "were persuaded" by the Jesus Movement (e.g., 4:4; 6:1–6; 9:26–28). The inclusion of the Israelites seems to persist (e.g., 12:24; 17:10–12; 19:17–26) even down to the final scene at Rome where the imprisoned Paul is still attempting to prove to Israelite leaders there that Jesus is the Messiah. Near the end of Acts, Paul, during his voyage to Rome as a prisoner, says in reference to his Roman citizenship and rightful appeal to be tried by Caesar, "since it is *for the sake of Israel* that I am bound with this chain" (28:20; cf. 26:7). *Some* Israelite leaders were then "convinced," that is, "persuaded" (28:24).

Yet, the main difficulties for the Jesus Movement, according to Luke, come from the plotting of Israelite leaders who misunderstand the prophecies (e.g., Luke 23:1–2; Acts 2:23). Clearly the Israelite authorities rather than the Israelite people as a whole are blamed for Jesus' death. Also, there are recurring statements that Paul "turns to the Gentiles" only when the Israelites oppose him, become violent or incite violence, and reject his message (e.g., 13:43–48; 18:6). Nonetheless, there are very volatile statements in the speech of Stephen, said to have been martyred by Israelites in Jerusalem:

> You stiff-necked people, uncircumcised in heart and ears, you are forever opposing the Holy Spirit, just as your ancestors used to do. Which of the prophets did your ancestors not persecute? They killed those who foretold the coming of the Righteous One, and now you have become his betrayers and murderers.
> (Acts 7:51–52)

Such words represent the Lukan author's views. Finally, at the end of Acts, Paul's "further statement" is added in reference to those Israelite leaders who were *not* "persuaded." Their lack of understanding is said to fulfill scripture:

> "The Holy Spirit was right in saying to your ancestors through the prophet Isaiah,
> 'Go to this people and say,

> You will indeed listen, but never understand,
> and you will indeed look, but never perceive.
> For this people's heart has grown dull,
> and their ears are hard of hearing,
> and they have shut their eyes;
> so that they might not look with their eyes,
> and listen with their ears,
> and understand with their heart and turn—
> and I would heal them.'"
>
> (Acts 28:25–27 [Isa. 6:9–10])

Paul then claims that salvation "has been sent to the Gentiles; they will listen" (28:28).

What, finally, is Luke's position about the Israelites? Luke's view is that the Jesus Movement fulfills scripture and is truly Israel. This, along with his universalism, suggests that despite the tragic rejection of Jesus, the door of salvation remains open, however slightly, probably because there are Israelite members of the Jesus Movement in the Lukan communities. Yet, the constant Israelite opposition, especially of the Israelite leaders and mobs, combined with the dramatic reception of the Gentiles, especially the Romans, indicates that in Lukan circles the Jesus Movement has now become virtually Gentile. Thus it is difficult not to conclude that despite the door's being slightly ajar, it is still difficult to open further.

Another social aspect of the Jesus Movement portrayed especially in Acts is growing *institutionalization*. Luke is well known for portraying a smooth and almost noncontroversial internal development from Jesus to Peter and the apostles, then to Paul, and finally to Paul's mission to the Gentiles. Twelve apostles bear witness to the life of Jesus beginning with Jesus' baptism (1:21–26), and the number "twelve" represents Israel. Institutions require leaders, and Peter emerges as the leader of the Jerusalem church (2–5; 8–10; 15). Moreover, people are now commanded and missionaries are sent, which is a sign of authority. The Holy Spirit is received in connection with the rite of "laying on of hands," which means that persons transfer spiritual power (e.g., 8:17; 9:17; 19:6). Seven deacons (6:1–6) are appointed, and there are elders (e.g., 14:23). "Apostles and elders" seem to be in charge, and Paul seems to entrust the elders of Ephesus with pastoral authority (20:28–35). Such passages seem to suggest that "**apostolic succession**"—the transfer of authority from the apostles to their successors—is in its infancy.

There is more evidence for communal life in Luke-Acts. Meal practices symbolize the life of a group (Chapters One, Three, and Fourteen). More than any other gospel, Luke speaks of *meals and meal practices*. There are eating and drinking together, there are parables about meals, and Jesus banquets with all sorts of people (e.g., Luke 11:37–41; 14:7–24; 16:19–31), especially "the poor, the maimed and blind and lame" (14:13, 21). In Acts, there is distribution of food to widows (6:1–6).

Finally, there is also evidence for *meditative and liturgical life* in the Lukan communities. Some practices merge with meals, as in the Last Supper (Luke 22:14–38). Luke's Jesus is the Jesus of prayer, and Jesus prays before every major event: the baptism (3:21), the choice of the Twelve (6:12), Peter's messianic confession (9:18), the transfiguration (9:28), the teaching about the Lord's Prayer (11:1), and Jesus' last hours in Jerusalem in the Garden of Gethsemane (22:4). Baptism is also a major motif throughout Luke-Acts, and it is often connected with the gift of the Holy Spirit (e.g., Luke 3:16; Acts 1:5; 10:47; 11:16). One should also mention the laying on of hands in this context.

LANGUAGE, STYLE, AND LITERARY FEATURES OF LUKE-ACTS

Among the four evangelists, Luke has always been recognized as the most sophisticated writer. He composes speeches and writes Paul's sea voyages in the typical first-person plural style. Three further points can be made. First, the prologue of Luke-Acts (1:1–4) is written in a very elegant and formal Greek style called "Atticistic Greek," that is, it imitates the Greek Attic prose and poetry writers of the fifth-century B.C.E. Hellenic period. Second, scholars have compiled lists of the numerous ways in which Luke improves the Greek of his sources, especially Mark, and of many terms not otherwise found in the New Testament. Often Luke's style is recognizable in English, for example, his replacement of Mark's repetitious "and" (parataxis) with more complicated constructions. Third, Luke is fond of repeating words, but he varies their form and bunches them together in particular contexts. Finally, he can imitate Hebraicized Greek found in the **Septuagint** (Septuagintisms).

Luke's Use of Scripture

Luke does not stress **formula quotations**, as does Matthew (Chapter Nine), but he nonetheless shows that events fulfill scripture. He uses the **Septuagint,** especially at the beginning and end of his gospel and in the Acts speeches. For example, he models the song of Mary, the "Magnificat" (Luke 1:46–55), on the Song of Hannah in the Israelite scriptures (1 Sam. 2:1–10). He also composes other poetic-type materials in the infancy story from words and phrases in the Greek Septuagint (e.g., Luke 1:14–17, 32–34, 68–79; 2:29–32).

Extremely crucial for understanding Luke's use of scripture is his view that God carries out his foreordained plan as prophesied, especially in Isaiah. Two crucial examples will suffice. First, Luke repositions the scene of Jesus' teaching in the synagogue at Nazareth (Mark 6:1–6) to the beginning of Jesus' public preaching (Luke 4:16–30), where it sets the stage for the particular Lukan accent on Jesus. Jesus first claims to fulfill the Isaiah prophecy about preaching good news to the poor and healing by an anointed, Spirit-filled prophet (Isa. 61:1–2). Then the rejection of Jesus by his own people in his hometown anticipates rejection of Jesus by the Israelite leaders and to an extent by the Israelite people. Ultimately, they misunderstand him, just as they do at the end of Acts (Acts 28:25–28 [Isa. 6:9–10]; see earlier). Similarly, stories about a Gentile man and a Gentile women (note the male-female pair) by the prophets Elijah and Elisha in scripture anticipate the pro-Gentile stance of Luke and the movement of the good news to Gentiles, as well as his concern about women. A similar point is made in the Acts speeches when speakers cite prophecies about David and his descendant and link these to other "prophecies" by David as found in "his" psalms (e.g., Ps. 2:7; 16:10; 89; 110:1; 132:10–12). All this shows how Jesus' life, death, resurrection, and ascension fulfill prophecy (Acts 2:14–36; 7:1–53; 13:16–41).

SOURCES AND STRUCTURE OF LUKE-ACTS

According to the **Two-Source Theory,** the author of Luke-Acts takes up and interprets three major sources: the Gospel of Mark, **Q,** and **Special L.** However, Luke omits more of Mark—about three-tenths—than does Matthew. This allows him to include a higher proportion of his special material, Special L, which makes up about one-third of the gospel. Whereas Matthew combines Q and Special M to form large blocks of teaching material—the five discourses—Luke *alternates* non-Markan (Q and Special L) with Markan material in blocks something like Figure 10.1.

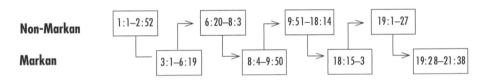

Figure 10.1 Alternating Blocks in Luke

This schema is oversimplified. Nonetheless, it is generally accurate. Beginning at 9:17, Luke omits large chunks of Mark (Mark 6:30–44; 8:1–10; cf. 8:14–21), in part, no doubt, because Mark duplicates some stories. Scholars call this "**the Great Omission.**" This allows him to insert most of his Q material in the second and third (non-Markan) blocks, Luke 6:20–8:3, which scholars call "**the Lesser Insertion,**" and Luke 9:51–18:14, which scholars call "**the Greater Insertion.**" Finally, Q and Special L are mixed in such a way that a few scholars have argued that this combination occurred first and that only later did he insert Mark into it. This source theory is called "**Proto-Luke.**" Although some interpreters still think that Luke had a separate Passion source—Proto-Luke works best in the Passion Story (note again 22:14–24:12)—"Proto-Luke" seems to have fallen out of favor. Most hold that it is more likely that Luke himself composed the distinctive Passion Story (**Redaction Criticism**).

The result of the preceding analysis is that in relation to Mark's structure, there are five major changes:

1. **The infancy narrative** (1–2)

2. "**The Lesser Insertion**" (6:20–8:3), which includes Luke's counterpart to Matthew's Sermon on the Mount, called the "Sermon on the Plain" (6:20–49), almost all Q

3. **"The Great Omission"** (at 9:17) of a portion of Mark (6:45–8:26), consisting primarily of miracles, parts of which are duplicated by Mark elsewhere

4. **"The Greater Insertion"** (9:51–18:14), a much-extended journey to Jerusalem, containing much Q and Special L

5. **The resurrection and ascension** (24:13–53) accounts at the end

More must be said about "the Greater Insertion" (no. 4). It makes up most of Luke's long, rambling "travel narrative," which takes Jesus to Jerusalem (18:15–19:28 [Mark 10:13–11:1]). Luke places much Q material in this section, and about one-third of his gospel is Special L, much of which is in this section as well. Of five distinctively Lukan miracles, three are in the travel narrative (13:11–14; 14:2–4; 17:12–19). Even more impressive, of Luke's seventeen distinctive parables, sixteen are in the travel narrative! These parables stress many of the distinctive Lukan themes about rich and poor, lost and saved, women, and the like, and they include the famous Good Samaritan (10:30–37) and Prodigal Son (15:11–32) parables.

Two interlocking purposes for the travel narrative stand out. First, there is a widespread tradition based on scripture that prophets are martyred in Jerusalem; for Luke, Jesus is just such a messianic prophet who must meet his fate there, and from there the church will spread. So Luke has a *Jerusalem* fulcrum in his story. Second, there was also a widespread belief based on scripture that some of God's special prophets did not die a natural death, but rather ascended directly to heaven (e.g., Enoch, Elijah, and Isaiah). Luke relates the death of Jesus as a natural one—he is a martyr-prophet—but he nonetheless says in contrast to Mark and Matthew that *Jesus ascended to God's right hand in heaven (Ps. 110:1) in an event separate and distinct from the resurrection.* So Luke has an **ascension** theme. The following passages with Luke's words for the ascension transliterated in the left margin and *prophet(s)* and *Jerusalem* in italics will easily make the point about the ascension of the prophet-Messiah at Jerusalem:

exodon	Luke 9:31: "[Moses and Elijah] . . . were speaking of his *departure,* which he was about to accomplish at Jerusalem."
analēmseōs	Luke 9:51: "When the days drew near for him to be *taken up,* he set his face to go to *Jerusalem.*"
	Luke 9:53: "but they [the Samaritans] did not receive him, because his face was set toward *Jerusalem.*"
	Luke 13:33b: ". . . because it is impossible for a *prophet* to be killed outside of *Jerusalem*" (cf. Acts 7:52 quoted earlier at Jerusalem: "Which of the *prophets* did your ancestors not persecute?")
anaphereto	Luke 24:51: "[at *Jerusalem*] . . . he withdrew from them and was *carried up* into heaven."
analēmphthē	Acts 1:2: " . . . first book . . . all that Jesus did and taught until the day when he was *taken up* to heaven [at *Jerusalem*]
epērthē	Acts 1:9: "[at *Jerusalem*] . . . he was *lifted up,* and a cloud took him out of their sight."

In short, Luke' Jesus is destined, like the prophets of old, to go to Jerusalem, to be martyred there like certain prophets, and finally, to ascend to heaven. The gospel clearly focuses on the martyrdom and ascension of its prophet-hero at Jerusalem.

Jerusalem is also an important structural and thematic feature in Acts. The story of the church begins in Jerusalem (Acts 1–7). The three accounts of Paul's experience of the risen Jesus on the Damascus Road (his so-called conversion; see Chapter Four) say that he immediately began his witnessing in Jerusalem (9:1–30; 22:3–21; 26:9–23). Like the gospel, Acts has a long travel narrative that begins with a statement of intent, ". . . Paul resolved in the Spirit to go through Macedonia and Achaia, and then to go on to Jerusalem" (19:21), and then Paul said, "After I have gone there, I must also see Rome!" Thus Jerusalem is in the center of a two-volume work: Galilee, Jerusalem, and Rome. Indeed, the Lukan author has a special spelling of Jerusalem (*Ierousalēm,* sixty-three times in Luke-Acts; *Ierosolyma,* from Mark, occurs only twice, 13:22 [= Mark 10:32] and 19:28 [= Mark 11:1]).

Two other points can be made about the Lukan structure. First, at critical junctures in the geographical progression of Acts, there are vague, generalizing, formula-like summaries. An example is 19:20: "So the word of the Lord grew mightily and prevailed" (cf. also 2:43–47; 5:42; 9:31; 12:24; 15:35). They provide clues to the structure of the narrative. Second, Luke loves parallelism (the "law of duality"). Most obvious, Acts has parallels to the gospel. There are similar introductions to each volume (Luke 1:1–4; Acts 1:1–5) and the parallelism in the journeys of Jesus to Jerusalem and Paul to Rome. There are a baptism and descent of the Spirit in each volume. Other examples are parallels between the healing activities of Jesus and the apostles (e.g., Luke 8:40–42, 49–56; Acts 9:36–42) and between the trials of Jesus and Paul (Luke 23:1–25; Acts 25–26). There are many other parallels of detail, but these make the point.

All of these structural features play a role in Luke-Acts and will contribute to an understanding of the author's overall perspective and purpose. Before developing that, consider one other very dominant feature of Luke-Acts: the delay of the *parousia.*

THE DELAY OF THE *PAROUSIA*

Like all the Jesus Movement authors of the post-70 C.E. period, the author of Luke-Acts must deal with "the delay of the *parousia.*" By now Jesus should have returned on the clouds of heaven to complete the final eschatological drama. To be sure, certain Lukan passages say that the *parousia* is near (cf. Luke 3:9, 17; 10:9; 21:32), and the author can even add to them (Luke 10:11; 18:7–8). Yet, the more dominant Lukan view is that the *parousia* will take place in some *indefinite* future.

There are numerous examples. Mark 1:14–15 has Jesus coming into Galilee and proclaiming, "The time is fulfilled, and the Kingdom of God has come near," an announcement intended to express the expectation that the End is coming soon. In contrast, Luke 4:14 simply says, "Then Jesus, filled with the power of the Spirit, returned to Galilee . . ." and then comments about his growing fame and teaching.

The key point is not the impending *parousia,* but rather Jesus' teaching in the synagogue at Nazareth (Luke 4:16–30). As noted, this relocation of the scene at Nazareth stresses the key Lukan points that Jesus fulfills Isaiah's prophecies about preaching good news to the poor, as well as healing by an anointed, Spirit-filled prophet, and it anticipates the importance of the mission to the Gentiles. The element of imminent expectation has been replaced by a focus on the past ministry of the Savior of all and the church's continuing mission activity.

An important illustration of the delay of the *parousia* is Luke's reworking of the synoptic apocalypse (Mark 13 = Luke 21). Mark says that the *parousia* will come soon after the destruction of Jerusalem and warns about false prophets who say that the immediate *parousia* is to be identified with the destruction of Jerusalem (Mark 13:5b, 14 21–23), but he nonetheless adds that it will be *soon thereafter* (Mark 13:24). Luke, however, severs the connection of the *parousia* with the destruction of Jerusalem (21:20, 24a), omits the false prophets (cf. 17:20–23), and adds a note that it will not occur ". . . until the times of the Gentiles are fulfilled" (21:24b). He thereby lengthens the interval between the earthly signs in relation to the destruction (21:7–24) and the cosmic signs of the *parousia* of the Son of Man (21:25–28), and he emphasizes events that must happen first (21:8–9, 32). The implication is that the *parousia* is indefinitely delayed.

The author of Luke-Acts also makes sense of the extended interim period; it is the period of the mission to the Gentiles, called the "witness" of the church, and its story is told in Acts. This is very clear in the words of the resurrected Jesus to the disciples noted earlier: "You shall be my witnesses in Jerusalem and all Judea and Samaria and to the end of the earth" (Acts 1:8).

"SALVATION HISTORY" IN LUKE-ACTS

Apocalyptic writers portray historical periods by means of symbols. Several biblical writers think in terms of the theme of "salvation history" (taken from German *Heilsgeschichte*), that is, the view that God is working out his will for his people through a series of historical events. Among the evangelists, the one most dominated by the idea of salvation history is the author of Luke-Acts (Conzelmann). Indeed, Luke has sometimes been called "Luke the historian." To place Luke-Acts' particular view of salvation history in proper perspective, it will be important to recall first the general nature of historical writing as such in the ancient world.

Ancient Greek historians tended to focus on key events and personalities, especially from their own time, for several reasons. Such events illustrated the human drama of political life. They were important to instruct and exhort people in proper moral behavior. History telling could also be used to enculturate the young with patriotic ideas about the destinies of their people. For some, history—storytelling—could be entertaining. Finally, ancient historians created speeches for their heroes, not only to show what might have been said on a particular occasion, but also to give an impression of some of the great ideas of the age.

Historians writing in Greek and Latin generally followed these precedents. Lucian of Samosata in *How to Write History* stressed that the task of the historian is not entertainment, but rather description of things as they actually happened. Nonetheless, Lucian chose to describe only what he thought were the most important matters, such as political events and wars, and very important people, such as generals, politicians, or poets. Moreover, he freely created programmatic speeches in their mouths on subjects that he considered appropriate for the occasion. In his *Annals of the Roman People,* Livy combined history and legend in order to write "inspiring history." He stated his rationale clearly: to perpetuate the memory of "the first people in the world" and to hold before the reader models of moral behavior. Even Tacitus, one of the most accurate Roman historians of the period, chose his material with a political prejudice and freely wrote the speeches of the Roman emperors.

In ancient Israelite history writing, the "Court History of David" (2 Sam. 9: 1–20:26; 1 Kings 1–2) appears on the surface to have an almost eyewitness character. However, underlying it is the ideology of the "Deuteronomic historian" who attempts to show how God is carrying out his plan to fulfill his promises to David that his descendants, as royal "sons of God," would reign on the throne forever (2 Sam. 7). "Real" history is not just a sequence of cause-and-effect empirical events in time; rather, God carries out his purposes for the salvation of his people through it. It is the "story of salvation," or "salvation history." Closer to New Testament times, 1 Maccabees (late second, early first century B.C.E.) develops fairly accurate Israelite history. However, its author, like Greek and Roman historians, inserts speeches and prayers into the mouths of his heroes. Finally, Josephus, an Israelite historian contemporary with the author of Luke-Acts, writes to glorify his national heritage and to defend his participation in the Israelite wars with Rome. He, too, follows the usual practice of composing appropriate speeches. To grasp the point one need only read the masterfully written speech of the zealot Eleazar atop the mesa Masada just before the Israelites committed suicide rather than be taken by the Romans (Josephus *Wars* 7.8.6 [323–336]).

In this light, the speeches in Acts by Peter, Stephen, and Paul often tell of God's plan for Jesus' life in relation to the history of Israel, thus offering a salvation historical sketch. They stress the following themes:

1. Jesus was born of the seed of King David.

2. He died in accord with prophecies in the scriptures, thus bringing forgiveness of sins and salvation to his followers.

3. He was buried.

4. He rose on the third day according to the prophecies in the scriptures.

5. He is exalted at the right hand of God, as Messiah Son of God and Lord.

6. He will come again as judge and savior.

Finally, observe that the introductions to Luke and Acts are composed in the manner of introductions to ancient books of *history,* that is, the Lukan author refers to other sources and dedicates his book (see following exegetical notes on Luke 1: 1–4 and Acts 1:1).

The preceding discussion indicates that Luke was an ancient historian, but an ancient historian of a particular kind, because he was also a "religious writer" and a "gospel" writer. Recall that ancient Greco-Roman biography was not like modern biography. On one end of the spectrum it often contained rather loose collections of sayings and anecdotes; at the other end it was similar to the Hellenistic "romance" calculated to evoke praise of the hero's virtues. With this observation, one is back to the controversial question of to what extent the gospels in general, and the Third Gospel in particular, are like ancient romantic biographies of especially endowed human beings (see Chapters Eight and Nine). It would be generally agreed that of the four New Testament gospels, Luke's story comes closest to the popular biographies of the period.

In summary, when thinking of Luke-Acts as historical writing, four points should be kept in mind: (1) the character and aims of ancient Greek, Roman, and Israelite historical writing, especially in relation to the Acts of the Apostles and its speeches; (2) the character and diversity of the Greco-Roman biography (Greek *bios*), especially in connection with the gospel; (3) the tradition of salvation historical writing in the Old Testament (especially Deuteronomy), with prophecy and fulfillment as major themes; and (4) the modification by the Lukan author of his source Mark, a special example of which is Luke's reorientation of Mark's apocalyptic.

As history, then, Luke-Acts is not modern history, but rather ancient historical writing, and a special example of that. It puts in sequence a particular form of an ancient *bios,* or "biography" (the gospel) and an ancient "history" (Acts), the latter of which is guided by the biblical, especially Deuteronomic, idea of "salvation history." It hints at a distant past, the time of the creation of the first human (taking the genealogy of Jesus back to Adam, Luke 3:38), and has in view a distant future, the time of the *parousia,* now delayed. Within these outer limits lies everyday history, or "world history," a story of everyday events, of emperors, governors, kings, and high priests, of taxation and censuses (Luke 2:1; 3:1–2). Yet, this story is also a story in which the plan of God is being worked out, the promises of God are fulfilled, the word of God is proclaimed, and the message of salvation is made known to the world. For Luke, the Spirit of God is operating in "world history," especially in the story of Jesus and the church. But salvation history is also beyond world history because it is the history from which the Spirit of God comes to and to which Jesus ascends after his resurrection.

One way to think of Luke-Acts is that its author thinks of history as divided into a series of three periods or epochs lying between creation and the *parousia*. At least two of the three epochs are indicated by Luke 16:16: "The law and the prophets were in effect until John came; since then the good news of the kingdom of God is proclaimed, and everyone tries to enter it by force." The *first era* is the era of "the law and the prophets" down to John the Baptizer. Then comes an *interim period* represented by the birth and infancy stories of John and Jesus and the activity of John as forerunner. The *second era* is the era of "the proclamation of the Kingdom of God," the time of Jesus (Luke 16:16; Acts 28:31). This middle period, the period of Jesus, is further subdivided into three periods based on the Markan geographical outline: Galilee, journey to Jerusalem, and Jerusalem. Then comes a second *interim period* in which Jesus is raised from the dead, appears and speaks to the disciples,

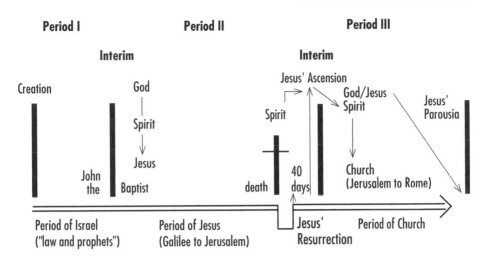

Figure 10.2   The Lukan Three-Stage Salvation History.

and ascends to heaven (Luke 24:51; Acts 1:1–11). This is followed by the *third era,* the period of the church. This era will end with the *parousia* (Luke 21:25–28), which will be at some indefinite point in the future (Luke 9:27; 17:20–21; 19:11; 21:8–9; cf. Acts 1:7). Luke's "salvation history" can be outlined as follows:

First period: The time of "the law and the prophets," from Adam to John the Baptizer

Interim period: The time of the birth and infancy of John and Jesus and of the ministry of the forerunner John

Second period: The time of the proclamation of the Kingdom of God by Jesus, from the descent of the Spirit on Jesus to the return of the Spirit to the Father at the cross. Following the Markan outline, this period can be further subdivided into gathering of witnesses in Galilee (beginning Luke 3:21) → journey to Jerusalem (beginning Luke 9:51) → and Passion in Jerusalem (beginning Luke 19:27).

Interim period: The time of the resurrection, appearances, revelatory teaching to the disciples by the risen Jesus, and the ascension

Third period: The time of the proclamation of the Kingdom of God by the church, from the descent of the Spirit at Pentecost to the *parousia*

Graphically, the whole conception of the Lukan salvation history may be represented as in Figure 10.2.

In this overall view, the "law of duality" is at work between Periods II and III. As Jesus goes from Galilee to Jerusalem in Period II, so the church expands from Jerusalem to Rome in Period III. As the Spirit descends on Jesus at his baptism in Period II, so the Spirit descends on the church at Pentecost (a new baptism, Acts 1:5) in Period III. As Jesus gathers witnesses and preaches the Kingdom in Period II, so Paul recruits members of the Jesus Movement and preaches the Kingdom "with all boldness and without hindrance" in Rome (Acts 28:31) in Period III. As Jesus performs miraculous acts in Period II, so the apostles perform miraculous acts in the early church in Period III.

Let us now fill in the gaps a little.

The Time of "the Law and the Prophets" (Luke 16:16)

The time of the law and the prophets (Luke) is most characterized by prophecy. The Lukan author of Luke-Acts sees the events of salvation history in the first period as fulfilled in the succeeding periods of Jesus and the church.

The Interim Period of the Birth and Infancy of John and Jesus and of the Ministry of the Forerunner John

John the Baptizer in Luke's schema ("since then") is a transitional figure between Israel and Jesus. His place is structurally analogous to the transitional events between Jesus and the church. John does not preach "the good news of the Kingdom of God" (contrast Matt. 3:2), and Luke brings forward his imprisonment to a time *before* Jesus' public ministry begins (3:20; cf. Mark 6:17–18). In this way, he accents the tradition of John's subordination to Jesus (3:15–16; Acts 13:25). Yet, Luke 1–2 shows a parallelism and overlap between John's birth and Jesus' birth. John's is announced in prophetic fashion by the old age of his parents (1:7). He is "prophet of the Most High" who will "prepare his ways" and "give knowledge of salvation to his people by the forgiveness of their sins" (1:76–77). His exhortations are viewed as preaching the good news (Luke 3:18). Thus Luke's ambiguous "since then" (16:16) seems to see John as a transitional figure who, although clearly subordinate, prepares the way for the time of proclamation of the Kingdom of God by Jesus. He represents, then, an interim period.

The Time of the Proclamation of the Kingdom of God by Jesus

The descent of the Holy Spirit on Jesus at his baptism (3:21–22) marks a time when "the good news of the Kingdom of God is proclaimed." This time will be continued in the third major epoch, the time of the church, which is also given the Spirit (at Pentecost, Acts 2). Luke stresses the activity of the Spirit in each epoch. In the gospel, God identifies Jesus as his Son at the descent of the Holy Spirit; he is "full of the Holy Spirit" and "led by the Spirit" (4:1). Next Satan tests or tempts the Spirit-filled Son of God in the wilderness (4:3, 9). (Luke adds that the devil then "departed from him until an opportune time" [Luke 4:13; cf. Matt. 4:11].) That opportune time does not come until Jesus is in Jerusalem, where "Satan entered into Judas called Iscariot, who was one the twelve" (Luke 22:3). Thus, during most of the "time of Jesus," Satan does not directly hinder Jesus. Satan returns during the tragic Passion events in Jerusalem, which also fulfill prophecy. Although the activity of Satan lies behind the sick and possessed whom Jesus heals (cf. 10:18; 11:16–18; 13:16), Jesus *himself* is free from Satan's evil power.

After the testing of God's Son in the wilderness, the theme of the Spirit resumes. Jesus returns to Galilee in the "power of the Spirit." Then comes the programmatic scene in the synagogue at Nazareth (4:16–30; moved backward from Mark 6:1–6), where Luke adds his key prophecy about the Spirit-filled Messiah who brings liberation and healing (Isa. 61), which Jesus fulfills "today." The Spirit is with Jesus during his ministry until he commits it to God in the crucifixion scene in Jerusalem (Luke 23:46).

Hans Conzelmann called the time of Jesus in Luke-Acts "the center of time." The meaning of both the past and the future is revealed in this time. Thus one epoch in history, the time of Jesus, is also the decisive epoch in salvation history, the time when the good news of God's activity on behalf of human salvation is proclaimed in the world.

The Interim Period of Jesus' Resurrection, Appearances, Revelatory Teaching to the Disciples, and Ascension

Between Jesus' act on the cross of committing his spirit to God (Luke 23:46) and the return of the Spirit to the church at Pentecost (Acts 2), there is an interim period of resurrection, appearances, teaching, and ascension. Mark has no resurrection appearances at all (16:1–8). Matthew has one (28:9–10) and then the commissioning scene (28:16–20). Luke, in contrast, places appearances on the Emmaus road (24:13–35) and in Jerusalem (24:36–43), and he also mentions an appearance to Peter (24:34). Further, the risen Jesus teaches the disciples (Luke 24:44–49; Acts 1:6–8). Then comes the ascension (Luke 24:51; Acts 1.9). Although various prophets had ascended directly into heaven, the author of Luke-Acts was, as far as anyone knows, the first person in the Jesus Movement to conceive of the ascension of the martyred Jesus as separate from the resurrection. Perhaps he separates the ascension from the resurrection in order to have a place to put his various traditions of Jesus' appearances. Indeed, in the death of Jesus on the cross (Luke 24:44–49) and in his appearances after death (Luke 24:12–53; Acts 1:4–8), some of Luke's key understandings are revealed. Here is clarified the necessity for repentance and forgiveness of sins to be preached by the disciples (23:43), who in Acts are "witnesses." Here is the necessity of Jesus' suffering death and entry to heaven according to scriptural prophecies (24:26–27). Here is the "beginning from Jerusalem" and the moving "to the end of the earth." Here, finally, is Jesus' committing the Spirit that was on him to God, which makes baptism of the Spirit at Pentecost possible.

The Time of the Proclamation of the Kingdom of God by the Church, from Jerusalem to Rome

The *time of Jesus,* the center of time, is the time of the work of the Spirit through Jesus, the time of preaching the good news of the Kingdom of God, and the time of witnessing from Galilee to Jerusalem. The *time of the church* is the time of the work of the Spirit through the *church,* the time of the proclamation of the Kingdom of

God in the form of the church preaching repentance and the forgiveness of sins, and the time of witnessing from Jerusalem to Rome. This time of the church will continue until the *parousia*. It is the time of the author of Luke-Acts and his readers, and beyond.

THE STRUCTURE OF LUKE-ACTS

Drawing these themes together, the following structure suggests itself for the two-volume work:

The Gospel of Luke: The Ministry of the Spirit through Jesus

Introduction to the two volumes, 1:1–4

Introduction of the ministry of the Spirit through Jesus, 1:5–4:15

The ministry in Galilee, 4:16–9:50

The journey of Jesus to Jerusalem, 9:51–19:27

Jesus in Jerusalem, 19:28–21:38

The Passion narrative, 22:1–23:49

Burial, resurrection, teachings, ascension, 23:50–24:53

Acts of the Apostles: The Ministry of the Spirit through the Church

Introduction to the second volume relating it to the first volume, 1:1–5

Introduction to the ministry of the Spirit through the church, 1:6–26

The descent of the Spirit on the church, 2:1–42

　　Summary, 2:43–47

The church in Jerusalem, 3:1–5:41

　　Summary, 5:42

The movement into Judea and Samaria, 6:1–9:30

　　Summary, 9:31

The movement into the Gentile world, 9:32–12:23

　　Summary, 12:24

To the end of the earth: (1) Paul's first missionary journey and its consequence, the Conference at Jerusalem, 12:25–15:33

　　Summary, 15:35

To the end of the earth: (2) Paul's second missionary journey, the movement into Europe and the decision to go to Rome, 15:36–19:19

Summary, 19:20

The journey of Paul to Rome, 19:21–28:16

Paul in Rome, 28:17–31

EXEGETICAL SURVEY OF LUKE-ACTS

Because of the length of both volumes—the Lukan Gospel is very long, and Acts makes up about one-fourth of the New Testament!—it will be possible to call attention only to particular emphases of the author. Parallels to Mark or Matthew are given where they are close.

Book 1—The Gospel of Luke:
The Ministry of the Spirit through Jesus

Introduction to the Two-Volume Work, Luke 1:1–4

The well-written Greek introduction is couched in the conventional language and style known from other, similar prologues in the ancient world, especially histories (e.g., Josephus *War*, Preface 1.1.1–3). It indicates that the Lukan author is attempting to compose a better literary work than his predecessors composed. He bases it on eyewitness (oral?) accounts and written sources. Note also that he desires to write "an orderly account" (in contrast to Mark?). He also says that the events he records are the fulfillment of scripture. For Luke the historian and salvation history, see earlier. Theophilus could be any "lover of God" or a real person of prominence ("most excellent"), such as a patron (see Acts 1:1).

Introduction to the Ministry
of the Spirit through Jesus, 1:5–4:13

1:5–80: *The birth of John the Baptizer and the announcement of the birth of Jesus.* This introduction is written in a Greek characteristic of the **Septuagint.** John's annunciation and birth (1:5–25, 57–80) are parallel in structure to Jesus' annunciation and birth (1:26–38; 2:1–20); the two are dovetailed by the pregnant Mary's visit to the pregnant Elizabeth (1:39–56). Note the importance, yet subordination, of John. He is a prophet (1:39–45) who will announce salvation and forgiveness of sins (1:77); he is of priestly descent. Jesus, however, will be called "Son of the Most High" (1:32), a clear reference to the "Son of God" descended from King David (2 Sam. 7:13–16; Ps. 89:26–29; cf. Luke 3:23–28). Mary's prominent role—Joseph is more prominent in Matthew—is highlighted in the anticipation of Jesus' supernatural birth (1:25–56). Mary's hymn of praise (2:46–55, the *Magnificat*) is modeled on Hannah's song at Samson's birth [1 Sam. 2:1–10]). Zechariah's prophecy (1:68–79, the *Benedictus*) echoes several psalms.

2:1–52: *The birth and infancy of Jesus.* Luke attempts to set the historical context by referring to Augustus the emperor and Quirinius the governor of Syria, who had ultimate rule over Israel. History becomes the arena for salvation history. The "registration" (census), which would have been the basis for taxation and political control, cannot be shown to have happened at this time; perhaps Luke recalled a census that modern historians think was later (Acts 5:37). In any case, Luke used it to get Mary and Joseph to Bethlehem, the place of David's and the expected Messiah's birth. In Matthew, the family was *originally* from Bethlehem, and, in line with Matthew's focus on formula quotations, the Bethlehem prophecy about the Messiah, Mic. 5:2, is quoted. In contrast, Luke more subtly shows Jesus' descent from King David and future promise. His infancy stories are designed to interpret the "center of time" of salvation history in advance (e.g., 2:30–32, 34). The Spirit inspires prophecy (2:29–32, the *Nunc Dimittis*). Mary and Elizabeth hold center stage; Luke follows his tendency to balance a story about a male (here the prophet Simeon) with a female (here the prophetess Anna) (2:22–38).

3:1–18: *Activity of John the Baptizer* (= Mark 1:1–8 = Matt. 3:1–12). This section picks up the Markan order. Mark quotes Isa. 40:3, and Luke extends the Isaiah quotation to verse 40:5a because it includes the comment, "all flesh shall see the salvation of God" (universalism). He tones down the note of apocalyptic urgency in John's proclamation, partly from **Q** (verses 7–9), and adds some general ethical teaching from **Special L** (verses 10–14). He omits Mark's reference to the scriptural prophecy about the forerunner in reference to John (Mal. 3:1 in Mark 1:2) but picks it up in 7:27.

3:19–20: *The imprisonment of the Baptizer.* In relation to his understanding of the three periods of salvation history, Luke tells the story of Antipas' "shutting up" John in prison *before* the "baptism" of Jesus.

3:21–22: *The descent of the Spirit on Jesus* (= Mark 1:9–11; Matt. 3:13–17). What in the other gospels is an account of the baptism of Jesus becomes in Luke focused on the descent of the Spirit on one who has *already* been baptized. Luke also introduces Jesus at prayer ("and was praying") in verse 21. This addition is characteristic of Luke, who places Jesus at prayer at critical turning points in his story (3:21 [baptism]; 6:12 [choice of the Twelve]; 9:18 [Peter's confession]; 9:28 [transfiguration]; 11:1 [Lord's Prayer]; 22:41 [on the Mount of Olives]). Jesus also teaches his disciples, "the church," to pray (6:28; 10:2; 11:1–3; 18:1–8; 21:36). Luke, like Mark and Matthew, in his own way thinks of Jesus as the Son of God (verse 22).

3:23–28: *The genealogy of Jesus* (= Matt. 1:1–16). The descent of Jesus is traced back past Abraham to Adam, the first human and son of God, and not, as in Matthew, just to Abraham. Jesus is the Son of God. A second implication is that because *Adam* means "humanity," his origins are from the father of the human race, and thus his salvation is for all (universalism).

4:1–13: *The testing of God's Son* (= Mark 1:12–13; Matt. 4:1–11). Jesus, full of the Holy Spirit, is led by the Spirit and tempted as the Son of God. The *three* temptations are from Q. The devil, unsuccessful, departs "until an opportune time" (see Luke 22:3).

The Ministry in Galilee, 4:14–9:50

4:14–15: *The first preaching in Galilee* (= Mark 1:14–15). Luke omits the apparent apocalyptic content of Jesus' Kingdom preaching in Mark (see preceding discussion); he is much more concerned to develop the following section.

4:16–30: *The synagogue scene at Nazareth* (= Mark 6:1–6). An account of the rejection of Jesus by "his own" in Galilee, which is later in Mark (Mark 6:1–6), is moved up to this location and elaborated by Luke to become an inaugural scene for the whole ministry of Jesus. Jesus reads the prophecy from Isaiah about the Spirit-filled Messiah who brings good news to the poor, release to the captives, healing of the blind, freedom of the oppressed, all at the time of "Year of Jubilee," or "Year of Liberty" (Isa. 61:1–11). In the Torah, the Jubilee Year is every fiftieth (forty-ninth?) year, when in theory ancestral lands, apparently sold in bad economic times, were to be returned to the family and Israelite slaves were to be released (Lev. 25:8–55, especially verses 10, 23, 39–41). The former part of the law was meant to protect one's ancestral lands from being taken over by a few wealthy and powerful because in reality it was God's land and thus a sacred trust; the latter was also to maintain equality. Although in principle the Jubilee Year was noble, in practice it probably never really took place. Nonetheless, Luke's Jesus claims that "today" the Isaiah text is fulfilled. Moreover, when Jesus mentions two accounts about *Gentiles* who receive one of the benefits, healing, the Israelites in his village want to kill him by mob action (see preceding on Israelites and Romans in Luke-Acts). In these Elijah/Elisha healing miracles about Gentiles, Luke shows that Jesus is rejected because he implies that it is God's will that his offer of salvation go to the Gentiles (1 Kings 17:1–16; 2 Kings 5:1–14). The Nazareth inaugural scene presents the reader or hearer with an announcement ahead of time of subsequent events, a typical literary technique of Luke. Thereby he understands the time of Jesus as a time when prophecy is fulfilled, specifically Isa. 61:1–2 (cf. also Isa. 58:6). Luke sees these great themes—the Spirit, messianic anointing, good news to the poor, release of prisoners of war, healing, freedom from slavery and oppression, land redistribution—as a summary of the presentation of the time of Jesus (see preceding). By putting an account here that occurs later in the Markan sequence, Luke creates a sequential anachronism: He refers to Jesus' miracles that had taken place at Capernaum (4:23), but *in Luke,* in contrast to Mark, Jesus does not go to Capernaum until the following story (4:31).

    4:31–41: *The Sabbath day at Capernaum* (= Mark 1:21–34). Luke omits the call of the first disciples (Mark 1:16–20); it comes as the miraculous catch of fish later in 5:1–11, which has a broader meaning. This literary change makes possible a direct transition from the great themes of the previous passage to Jesus' fulfillment of them in exorcising and healing at Capernaum.

    4:42–44: *A preaching journey* (= Mark 1:35–39). Verse 43 represents Luke's view of the ministry.

    5:1–6:11: *Incidents of the ministry in Galilee* (= Mark 1:40–3:6). With the exception of the miraculous catch of fish, which is a hint forward to the worldwide mission of the church (5:1–11), Luke mainly follows Mark: healing of a leper, healing of a paralytic, call of Levi the tax collector, question about fasting, plucking grain on the Sabbath, and the man with a withered hand.

    6:12–16: *The call of the Twelve* (= Mark 3:13–19). Luke adds his characteristic emphasis on Jesus' spending the night in prayer before a major event (6:12).

    6:17–19: *Jesus heals the multitudes* (= Mark 3:7–12).

    6:20–49: *The Sermon on the Plain.* Luke 6:20–8:3 deviates from the Markan order and combines **Q** and **Special L ("the Lesser Insertion").** The sermon is analogous to Matthew's **Sermon on the Mount,** but much shorter. Like Matthew, Luke opens the sermon with beatitudes (6:20–23). Luke has only four (not nine) beatitudes, but he balances them with four woes. In line with his social concerns, these stress the poor (6:24–26). The remainder of the sermon is Q material, probably in the Q order.

7:1–8:3: *Further incidents of the ministry in Galilee.* There follows a series of incidents that reflects Luke's interests. The healing of the Centurion's Servant from **Q** emphasizes the faith of a Gentile (7:1–10). The resuscitation from the dead of the Widow's Son at Nain (only in Luke, although similar stories about other heroes were well known) shows that Jesus is concerned about women who no longer have the protection of men (7:11–17). The Baptizer's Question from Q (7:18–23 = Matt. 11:2–6) echoes the keynote of the Nazareth synagogue scene in 4:16–30, that is, Jesus' healing and proclaiming good news to the poor; thus it also echoes the Jubilee prophecy, Isa. 61:1. Jesus' testimony to John from Q stresses John's preparatory role in the story of salvation (7:24–35 = Matt. 11:7–19; cf. 1:76–77). The quotation of Mal. 3:1 [Mark 1:2] had been omitted in Luke 3:4. The Woman with the Ointment could be a version of the anointing at Bethany (Mark 14:3–9; see Luke 22:3–6), but here it highlights Jesus' concern for women and sinners (7:36–50), and the Ministering Woman emphasizes his preparedness to help and be helped by women (8:1–3). Some parts have parallels in Matthew, thus Q (Luke 7:18–35 = Matt. 11:2–19).

8:4–18: *The parable of the Sower and the purpose of parables* (= Mark 4:1–29).

After **the Lesser Insertion,** Luke returns to the Markan order. He omits Mark's parable of the Seed Growing Secretly (Mark 4:26–29) and transposes the Mustard Seed to a different setting (Luke 13:18–19). Also, the three sayings in 8:16–18 come from Mark 4:21–25, but Luke has doublets of them (11:33; 12:2; 19:26), each time with a Matthean parallel. Different versions of these sayings must have been known to both Mark and to the Q community. Luke 8:16 has a small, but interesting, variant. Mark 4:21 has a saying about a lamp not being put under the bushel basket, or under the bed, or on a lampstand. In Matt. 5:15, the lamp on the lampstand "gives light to all in the house," illustrating "You are the light of the world" (5:14). It concludes with, "Let your light so shine before others, so that they may see your good works and give glory to your Father in heaven" (5:16). The Lukan writer has, "so that people who enter can find their way by the light," suggesting the Roman custom that a lamp is often found in the vestibule of a house and implying the moral of finding one's way.

8:19–21: *Jesus' true relatives* (= Mark 3:31–35).

8:22–25: *The stilling of the storm* (= Mark 4:35–41).

8:26–39: *The Gerasene demoniac* (= Mark 5:1–20).

8:40–56: *Jairus' daughter and the woman with the hemorrhage* (= Mark 5:21–43).

9:1–6: *The mission of the Twelve* (= Mark 6:6b–13).

9:7–9: *Herod thinks Jesus is John, risen* (= Mark 6:14–16).

9:10–17: *The return of the Twelve and the feeding of the five thousand* (= Mark 6:30–44). Luke is in the main following Mark, with some transpositions of order. His omission of the beheading of the Baptizer is striking (Mark 6:17–29). Perhaps he does so because he locates John in prison before the baptism of Jesus.

9:18–27: *Caesarea Philippi* (= Mark 8:27–9:1). Like Matthew, Luke omits the healing of the blind man at Bethsaida (Mark 8:22–26). But it is left out along with other, preceding material, the whole block being called "**the Great Omission**" (Mark 6:45–8:26). The reason is probably because Mark duplicates some stories (Mark 6:30–44; 8:1–10; cf. 8:14–21). Luke's version of Mark's first Passion prediction unit (Mark 8:27–9:1) in 9:18–22 introduces Luke's typical emphasis on Jesus at prayer, in this case in connection with Peter's confession (9:18). Moreover, he omits the misunderstanding and rebuke of Peter, perhaps in the interest of honoring a hero of the church. Finally, the eschatological note of Mark 9:1 ("has come with power") is minimized (9:27), and the addition of the word "daily" after taking up one's cross (9:23) implies that cross bearing is a daily matter, thus that the life of the community goes on because the *parousia* is delayed.

9:28–36: *The **transfiguration*** (= Mark 9:2–8). Luke follows Mark but omits the eschatological reference to the coming of Elijah in Mark 9:9–13 and—again—places Jesus at prayer for this major event in salvation history. Note Luke's first remark in 9:31 about Jesus' **ascension** at Jerusalem (see preceding discussion and comment on 9:51).

9:37–43a: *The healing of the epileptic boy* (= Mark 9:14–29). Luke omits Mark's identification of John the Baptizer with Elijah (Mark 9:9–13; cf. 7:24–35; 8:19–21), who was expected to return at the end. Therefore, he is fairly consistent in his view that Elijah themes are related to Jesus himself and that the *parousia* is delayed. His special use of Jesus at prayer will probably explain its omission in an exorcism context (cf. Mark 9:29).

9:43b–48: *The second prediction unit* (= Mark 9:30–37). Luke greatly abbreviates Mark at this point, almost obliterating the Passion prediction.

9:49–50: *The strange exorcist* (= Mark 9:38–41). This story abbreviates Mark.

The Journey to Jerusalem, 9:51–19:27

Luke begins this section with a key verse: "When the days drew near for him *to be taken up,* he set his face to go to *Jerusalem*" (9:51). This refers to the **ascension** to which he had added a reference in 9:31. It is even more important here because from this point forward the gospel moves toward Jerusalem. Luke 9:51–18:14 is a long, rambling, loosely organized section about the journey to Jerusalem. At 18:15, Luke follows Mark's narrative again (Mark 10:13). The material in this journey section is Luke's longest non-Markan block ("**the Greater Insertion**"), being derived partly from Q and partly from Luke's own special traditions. Sixteen of Luke's seventeen special parables fall in this section! We call attention to only some special features that represent the concerns of this gospel.

10:1–20: *Following and the mission of the seventy.* From Q, Luke derives the section on the difficulty of following the itinerant Son of Man. However, only Luke has a mission of the Seventy, created from Mark's mission of the Twelve (cf. 9:1–6 = Mark 6:6b–13) and Q (Matt. 9:37–38; 10:9–16). It is probably a symbolic anticipation of the church's mission to the Gentiles because in Israelite thinking "seventy" is a traditional number for "the nations."

10:25–37: *The parable of the Good Samaritan and its introduction.* This famous parable is found only in Luke. It reflects the writer's interest in ethnic outcasts because Israelites regarded Samaritans with hostility (cf. 9:51–56). Luke has created the introduction to the parable from a later Jerusalem debate in Mark about the greatest commandment (Mark 12:28–31). However, in Mark it is not a lawyer's question about inheriting eternal life, but rather a scribe's question about the first commandment, which is a more Israelite-sounding question. Luke wishes to appeal to his Gentile audience. Note that the lawyer's question is not really answered.

10:38–42:   *Mary and Martha.*   This passage is usually considered to be a good illustration of the characteristic Lukan approach to women. The woman disciple who sits at the feet of the teacher listening to his teaching—not a woman's usual role—is praised; the woman domestic who serves—a woman's usual role—and complains about her sister's action is chided.

11:1–13:   *Prayer.*   Again Luke portrays Jesus at prayer (11:1), this time as a prelude to Jesus' teaching about prayer to the disciples. The Lord's Prayer (11:1–4), which emphasizes the literal poor, is followed by a parable (11:5–7) and a series of sayings about persistence and God's willingness to give the Holy Spirit, all interpreted by Luke as prayer teaching (contrast Matt. 7:7–11 in Matthew's Sermon on the Mount). For a very detailed analysis of the Lord's Prayer, see Chapter Two.

11:27–28:   *True blessedness.*   Only Luke has this saying about Mary.

12:2–53:   *Teaching to the disciples.*   Jesus stresses the risks of discipleship and the importance of devotion to his way. Note especially the parable of the Rich Fool (12:13–21), found only in Luke. It introduces Jesus' Q teaching about anxiety (12:22–34), which for Luke is really about wealth; the theme of the Holy Spirit, also taken from Q (12:10, 12); and the notation about the delay of the *parousia* (12:45).

13:22, 31–35:   *Jerusalem themes.*   In 13:22, Luke reminds his readers of the journey to Jerusalem already mentioned in 9:31 and 9:51; in sayings of Jesus he stresses that a prophet must be martyred in Jerusalem (13:33) and inserts from Q a lament over Jerusalem, which kills its prophets (13:34–35).

14:7–24:   *Luke's banquet theme and teaching on humility.*   The Lukan interest in issues about wealth and concern for the poor and outcast, associated with the Kingdom, is expressed by inviting the uninvited: "the poor, the crippled, the lame, and the blind" (14:13). This leads to his interpretation of the parable of the Great Dinner in which the rejected invitation is extended to just such persons (14:21).

15:1–32:   *The Lost Sheep, the Lost Coin, and the Lost Son.*   This is one of the most impressive chapters in the New Testament. Luke's meal and ethical themes are first stressed by Jesus' banqueting with the outcast tax collectors and sinners (15:1). Then, in three parables, Luke presents Jesus' concern for "the lost" and joy for "the found," that is, on sin and salvation. The sheep is lost from the flock, the coin from the woman's meager house, the boy from the land and standards of his father. However, all are found again, and there is much joy. These stories are symbols of God's love and concern for the lost and the outcast as epitomized by Jesus' life, which is an ethical model for the believer.

16:1–31:   *Wealth and the Kingdom.*   The parable of the Unjust Judge, told to the disciples, becomes the occasion for sayings culminating in the theme, "You cannot serve God and wealth" (16:13). Only Luke says that the Pharisees, who observed Jesus' banquet with sinners (15:2), are "lovers of money" (16:14–15). Luke 16:16 is a key text for understanding the Lukan salvation history. It contrasts the era of the law and prophets with the era of proclaiming the good news about the Kingdom of God (see earlier). The parable of the Rich Man and Lazarus (16:19–31) continues the theme of wealth and poverty.

17:11–19:   *The faith of the Samaritan leper.*   Ten lepers are cleansed "on the way to Jerusalem . . . between Samaria and Galilee." Only the Samaritan praises God and gives thanks. Jesus notes that the faith of "this foreigner" has healed him. Recall Jesus' acceptance of outsider Samaritans, as in the famous parable that uses a Good Samaritan as the model for ethical behavior.

17:20–21: *The Kingdom of God and the day of the Son of Man.* The Pharisees' question of "when" the Kingdom will come is answered with a denial of signs and denial of place; it is "among you" (17:21). Luke 17:22–25 reflects the delay of the *parousia*.

18:1–14: *The parables of the Widow and the Tax Collector.* Luke emphasizes piety in the form of prayer by having Jesus tell stories about a poor widow who successfully pesters an unjust judge and a tax collector who successfully prays for mercy.

18:15–43: *Jesus draws near to Jerusalem (= Mark 10:13–52).* At 18:15, Luke begins to follow Mark's gospel again. Mark's story about the blessing of the children (18:15–17 = Mark 10:13–16) would obviously appeal to Luke, as would the story of the rich ruler who cannot distribute his wealth to the poor and follow Jesus (18:18–30 = Mark 10:17–31). Luke 18:31–34 has the third prediction of the Passion, and 18:35–43 has the healing of the blind man, both with only minor variations from Mark.

19:1–27: Zacchaeus *and the parable of the Pounds.* Only Luke has the story of Zacchaeus (19:1–10), a tax collector praised for giving to the poor, thus a lost person who is saved—all key Lukan themes. The parable of the Pounds from Q (19:11–27 = Matt. 25:14–30) is told "because he was near Jerusalem, and because they [wrongly] supposed that the Kingdom of God was to appear immediately" (19:11).

Jesus in Jerusalem, 19:28–21:38

This section mostly follows Mark 11:1–13:37. Luke 19:39–44 adds a prediction of the destruction of Jerusalem, which interprets that catastrophe as a judgment on the city, "because you did not recognize the time of your visitation from God" (19:44). He retains the apocalyptic discourse of Mark 13 because he accepts the *parousia* (Luke 21:25–38) but adds an emphasis on the universal nature of the event (Luke 21:34–36). He also edits the chapter to separate the destruction of Jerusalem (21:20–24) from the more remote *parousia* (21:25–36), the "times of the Gentiles" falling between (21:24; cf. 21:8–9). Note also that his description of the destruction generally conforms to that of Josephus.

The Passion Narrative, 22:1–23:49

Luke's Passion narrative is somewhat different from Mark 14:1–16:8. Some scholars have suggested that Luke may be following another source. However, the general framework of his narrative seems to be from Mark. The divergences can probably be explained partly by his use of special material and partly by a particular interpretation of the Passion.

One important reorientation is that Luke understands the Passion of Jesus as a legal murder by the Israelite authorities who are joined by the Israelite people. This view is achieved despite a favorable attitude to Jesus by the Roman and Herodian authorities. The Israelites alone—especially the Israelite leaders—bear the guilt for the death of Jesus. A second major change from Mark is that Luke does not regard the cross as atonement for sin. In Jesus' words at the Last Supper, it is an act of service, not as Mark's "ransom for many" (Mark 10:45). There is even doubt as to whether the words of interpretation of the bread and wine at the Last Supper—a body "given for you" and blood "poured out for you"—belong in the original text of the gospel (Luke 22:19b–20).

22:1–2: *The conspiracy against Jesus* (= Mark 14:1–2).

22:3–6: *Satan returns to the scene* (= Mark 14:10–11).   Luke's account of Judas Iscariot's agreement to betray Jesus stresses the reappearance of Satan, who has been absent from Luke's narrative since the temptation (4:13). He omits the anointing at Bethany (Mark 14:3–9), although his earlier account of the woman who anoints Jesus in 7:36–50 may be a variant of it.

22:7–13: *Preparation for the Last Supper* (= Mark 14:12–16).

22:14–38: *The Last Supper* (= Mark 14:17–25, but with significant variations).   Luke begins his account of the Last Supper with the institution of the Eucharist and follows it with the announcement of the traitor, an inversion of the Markan order. More important, Luke places eating in the Kingdom before, rather than after, the words of institution (22:15–16; 2:17–19a [?19b–20]). Does he thereby wish to place more stress on the Kingdom? Only Luke places the "dispute about greatness" in the context of the betrayal by Judas in Jerusalem (22:24–27; cf. Mark 10:42–45). Moreover, the two versions seem to have developed separately in the oral tradition, and Luke may be choosing his version because it avoids Jesus' death as a ransom (Mark 10:45), which is not in accord with his views. Verses 28–30 seem to be from **Q.** Luke has special traditions about Peter's denial (verses 31–34), and the purse, bag, and sword sayings (verses 35–38) are also special Lukan tradition (cf. Luke 10:4 [Q]).

22:39–53: *Jesus on the Mount of Olives* (= Mark 14:26–52).   Abbreviating Mark, Luke omits Jesus' prediction that he will go Galilee after his resurrection (Mark 14:28); for Luke, Jerusalem remains the focus.

22:54–71: *The trial before the Sanhedrin and Peter's denial* (= Mark 14:53–72).   Luke finishes the account of the denial *before* beginning the trial, whereas Mark inserts the trial into the denial story.

23:1–5: *Jesus before Pilate* (= Mark 15:1–5).   This and following sections present Luke's striking emphases on the innocence of Jesus, the guilt of the Israelite leaders, and the positive view of the Roman Pilate. The latter does not easily accord with the historical Pilate.

23:6–12: *Jesus before Herod.*   Only Luke has a hearing before Herod.

23:13–25: *The sentencing of Jesus* (= Mark 15:6–15).   The added verses (13–16) stress again Jesus' innocence, the guilt of the Israelite leaders and the people, and Pilate's capitulation.

23:26–32: *The road to Golgotha.*   Luke adds verses 27–31, the lamenting of the women of Jerusalem, to Mark 15:21.

23:33–43: *The crucifixion* (= Mark 15:22–32).   Particular Lukan emphases are the prayer for forgiveness (verse 34) and the Penitent Thief (verses 39–43).

23:44–49: *The return of the Spirit to the Father* (= Mark 15:33–41).   Luke rewrites the account of the death of Jesus in accordance with his concept of the role of the Spirit in salvation history. The centurion's confession becomes still another declaration of Jesus' innocence (verse 47), rather than a confession of his status as Son of God (so Mark 15:39).

Burial, Resurrection, Ascension, 23:50–24:53

23:50–24:11: *The burial of Jesus and the empty tomb:*   Basically follows Mark 15:42–47; 16:1–8.

24:13–35: *The road to Emmaus.*   This is the first of the postresurrection appearances of Jesus. Verses 19–21 represent Luke's view of Jesus as a miracle-working prophet. Emmaus is located a few miles from Jerusalem (24:13). The story stresses that the suffering and exaltation of Jesus fulfill "Moses and the prophets" (24:27). The "breaking of bread" (24:30) seems to contain an echo of the eucharistic meal. The appearance of Jesus to Peter is a very early tradition (see 1 Cor. 15:5), but Luke does not narrate it as a story (does it compete with the first appearances to the women in 24:1–12?).

24:36–49:   *The risen Christ appears in Jerusalem.*   This is Luke's gospel version of the risen Jesus' teaching to his disciples. The Acts version is in Acts 1:6–11. These slightly different duplicate versions develop two sets of teaching, which stress the fulfillment of prophecy, the reception of the Spirit, repentance and forgiveness, and the mission of the disciples-witnesses to the ends of the earth (Rome). They are the keys to the Lukan salvation history. Most scholars think that Luke seems concerned to stress the physical reality of the resurrection by the disciples' touching his wounds and eating (24:36–43; cf. 24:30; 8:55); yet, others view eating as a typical part of ASC experiences (Pilch).

24:50–53:   *The ascension.*   In accordance with 9:31, 9:51 (cf. Acts 1:2, 1:9), the reference to the ascension in verse 51b should not be relegated to a manuscript variant in the Revised Standard Version.

Book 2—Acts of the Apostles:
The Ministry of the Spirit through the Church

Introduction to Volume 2 (Acts of the Apostles), Acts 1:1–5

The introduction to Volume 2 mentions the recipient Theophilus again, thus looking back to the introduction to Volume 1 (Luke 1:1–4). There are parallel introductions in ancient histories, for example, Josephus' *Antiquities.* The water baptism of Jesus by John (with its descent of the Spirit) is duplicated by the Holy Spirit baptism of the church (1:5).

Introduction to the Ministry of the Spirit
through the Church: The Risen Lord
and His Disciples, 1:6–26

1:6–26:   *The risen Lord with his disciples and the replacement of Judas.*   This is Luke's second account of the interim period (compare Luke 24:36–39). Note the emphasis on the power of the Holy Spirit to guide the church, the work of witnessing, and the geographical progression of the mission from Jerusalem to the end of the earth (Rome). These verses lay the groundwork for developments in Acts. The expectation of the *parousia* is still maintained (verse 11). The author of Luke-Acts seems to think of the early Jerusalem church as an organized institution like that of his own day; thus Judas must be replaced so that it can be headed by a formal group of twelve apostles (twelve symbolism = twelve tribes of Israel). Note two other Lukan emphases. First, an apostle is "defined" as an eyewitness of Jesus' ministry from John's baptism until the ascension and a witness to the resurrection (1:22–23). Second, there is an emphasis on prayer (1:24). This latter looks back to Jesus at prayer before the appointment of the Twelve in the gospel (Luke 6:12) and looks forward to the church at prayer in Acts (e.g., 2:42; 6:4–6; 10:9; 13:3; 28:8). Contrast a very different tradition about Judas' suicide by hanging in the Gospel of Matthew (Matt. 27:3–10).

The Descent of the Spirit on the Church, 2:1–42

The descent of the Spirit in this story, which has already been interpreted as a "baptism" in 1:5, parallels the descent of the Spirit on Jesus at his baptism. The gift of speaking in other languages is not the well-known gift of "speaking in tongues" (*glossolalia;* see discussion of 1 Cor. 14:1–25 in Chapter Five); rather, it is (mis)interpreted as speaking so that other ethnic-language groups of Israelites understand (2:4, 11). It symbolizes the mission to Israelites from the Diaspora and thus the beginning phases of the worldwide mission of the church.

Ancient historians composed speeches for their heroes. Peter's speech in this section (verses 14–36 and 38–39) is the first of the author's composition of speeches in Acts. Other such speeches are Acts 3:11–26 (Peter); 4:8–12 (Peter); 5:29–32 (Peter); 7:51–53 (Stephen); Acts 10:34–43 (Peter); 13:16b–37 (Paul); 17:22–31 (Paul). Common themes about Jesus occur in most of them: fulfillment of scripture, descent from David, powerful deeds, crucifixion by the Israelites, resurrection and heavenly exaltation at God's right hand, return, and repentance, baptism, and forgiveness of sins. In this speech, note especially Luke's emphasis on the humanness of Jesus (verse 22); the guilt of the Israelites (verse 23); the death, resurrection, and present status of Jesus as the fulfillment of scripture (Ps. 16:8–11; 132:10–11; 110:1); the witness of the church (verse 32); the subordination of Jesus as heavenly "Lord" and "Messiah" to God (verse 36); and repentance and the forgiveness of sins (verse 38). The method of interpreting scripture is similar to that found in the **Dead Sea Scrolls** (Hebrew *pesher,* "interpretation"). The section closes with a summary, 2:43–47.

The Church in Jerusalem, 3:1–5:41

The witness of the church begins in Jerusalem in accord with the plan of Acts 1:8. Luke may be drawing on early traditions about the church in Jerusalem. For the most part, they are legends about the early days of the church, developed in the church for the edification of the believers. Luke gives them his own interpretation, especially in the speeches, in this section 3:12–26 (Peter at Solomon's Porch), and 4:8–12 and 5:29–32 (Peter before the Sanhedrin). Here, for example, Jesus is understood as a prophet (3:22); there is also an emphasis on the resurrection (3:26; 5:30) and on the guilt of the Israelites (4:11; 5:30).

The section closes with a summary, 5:42.

The Movement into Judea and Samaria, 6:1–9:30

Following the plan in Acts 1:8—Jerusalem, Judea, Samaria, the ends of the earth (Rome)—the witness of the church now moves outward to Judea, the territory immediately surrounding Jerusalem, and farther to Samaria, north of Judea. It is likely that this material echoes the history of the early church as distinct from the earlier chapters that interpret legends about it. For example, behind the narrative of the dispute between "Hebrews" and "Hellenists" in Jerusalem (6:1–6) and the persecution of the church in Jerusalem (8:1), there seems to lie a memory of some real factional conflict in the early church and the persecution of one part of it. This section of Acts may also echo the historical origins of the early mission.

Stephen's speech (7:2–53) is another key speech in Acts. It is the longest and is probably an example of the interpretation of scripture and the events by which the Jesus Movement justified its break with Israel. The parallels between the passion of Stephen, the proto-martyr, and that of Jesus are well known (see preceding discussion).

In 8:1, Paul appears for the first time in Acts. There can be no doubt that he did in fact persecute the church, as Acts says (see e.g., 1 Cor. 15:9; Gal. 1:13–14). Acts 8:4–24 is a collection of legends about the origin of the mission, remarkable in that it associates Peter firmly with that movement and presents both Philip and Peter as Hellenistic heroes.

Acts 8:25 is a summary reflecting a division in the narrative, although it is not a major one (it is not associated with a geographical shift). Acts 8:40 is another summary, Philip's further activity (8:40). In between these two summaries is the incident of Philip and the Ethiopian Eunuch (8:26–39). Two points are striking. First, strict Israelites would have considered a eunuch as unclean and therefore not worthy of being a proselyte; in contrast, Philip witnesses to him about Jesus. Second, the passage contains a quotation from the Servant of God passage in Isa. 53, which, however, carefully avoids any interpretation of the death of Jesus as atonement for sin. Both are distinctive Lukan themes. Thus the author of Luke-Acts has formulated these summaries, and it is probable that he has inserted the story of the Ethiopian Eunuch between them, which illustrates his interest in outcasts and his view of Jesus' death.

Luke 9:1–30 is the first of the three accounts narrating Paul's experience of the risen Jesus on the Damascus Road ("conversion") in Acts (see also 22:3–21; 26:9–23). This ASC experience has already been discussed (see Chapter Four). That this event is narrated three times indicates its importance to the author. The account is formulated in line with the plan of Acts 1:8—Jerusalem, Judea, Samaria, the ends of the earth (Rome)—even though Paul's witness did not begin in Jerusalem. The purpose of the story is overtaking the "history"!

The section closes with a summary, 9:31.

The Movement into the Gentile World, 9:32–12:23

Still following the guiding statement of Acts 1:8—Jerusalem, Judea, Samaria, the ends of the earth—the narrative now moves toward the spread of the gospel to a Gentile form of the movement. The author of Luke-Acts continues to emphasize the role of Peter in this new stage of the mission. Paul stresses his conflict with Peter at Antioch of Syria (Gal. 2:11–21; cf. 1 Cor. 1:12–13; 9:5). In Acts, however, that conflict virtually disappears. Instead, the author develops a positive parallelism between Peter and Paul, the two great heroes of the early movement. Peter dominates the first stage at Jerusalem; Paul dominates the second stage in the movement to Rome. Moreover, Peter's miracle-working activity parallels that of Jesus. Peter witnesses—performs miracles—in Lydda and Joppa, Gentile regions along the Mediterranean coast. Then he moves to the Roman district capital, Caesarea, also along the coast. Very important for the Lukan author is the detailed account about an Italian centurion named Cornelius at Caesarea (Acts 10). In an ASC, God tells

Peter to eat unclean food, which prepares for Peter's participation in Cornelius' affiliation with the Jesus Movement. He is described as "a devout man who feared God" ("God-fearer").

Characteristically Lukan themes occur in Peter's speech (10:34–43) after Cornelius' "conversion" and in the account of the founding of the church at Antioch (11:19–21). The latter marks the true beginning of the mission to the Gentile world, and Acts says that "in Antioch the disciples were first called 'Christ-ies'" (11:26), which may be historically correct. In any case the remark expresses the importance of this moment in the Lukan history of the early church. The story of the "famine relief" sent from Antioch to Jerusalem (11:27–30) illustrates Luke's view of the close connection between the Jerusalem church and mission churches around the Mediterranean. The martyrdom of James son of Zebedee (Acts 12:2), a disciple of Jesus—not to be confused with the martyrdom of James the brother of Jesus (Josephus *Antiquities* 20.9 197–203; Eusebius *Church History* 2.23–4–18; see Chapter Thirteen)—may also be implied by Mark 10:38 (the "baptism" of death?).

The section closes with a summary, 12:24.

The Movement to the "End of the Earth": (1) Paul's First Missionary Journey and Its Consequence; the Conference at Jerusalem, 12:25–15:33

According to Acts, Paul undertook three missionary journeys. No one doubts that Paul traveled to many of the regions described in Acts because undisputed letters to Galatia, Philippi, Thessalonica, Corinth, and Rome survive. The question is whether he undertook *three* missionary journeys in the neatly developed fashion found in Acts. The fondness of the Lukan author for journeys—the extended journey of Jesus to Jerusalem and Paul's extended journey to Rome—suggests to many scholars that the three journeys are a stylized literary device, a way of organizing Paul's movements to these regions and cities. If this theory is correct, it does not totally destroy the importance of Acts as a source, especially where Acts overlaps with what Paul himself says.

The first missionary journey (Acts 13:13–14:28) takes Paul from Antioch in Syria, west by boat to the island of Cyprus, north to southern Galatia, and back to Antioch. Narrating Paul's activities at key towns in these regions (Cyprus: Salamis and Paphos; Galatia: Iconium, Lystra, Derbe, "Pisidian" Antioch [not Antioch in Syria]), Paul's first journey centers on his first major speech in Acts, the speech at Antioch in Pisidia (13:16–41). The speech rehearses typical Luke-Acts themes: God's saving acts in salvation history, the Messiah, Son of God from the line of David, John the Baptizer, Jesus' death and resurrection as the fulfillment of scriptures, the complicity of Israelite leaders, Jesus' appearances, and the forgiveness of sins. The speech appears to represent themes of the author of Luke-Acts in the various speeches more than it does Paul's distinctive ideas (see preceding).

The Council at Jerusalem should be termed the **Jerusalem Conference** (there was no major, ecumenical church council until the Council of Nicaea in 325 C.E.). The conference as described in Acts 15 took place *after* the first of Paul's three missionary journeys in Acts 13–14. Scholars call the solution reached in Acts the "**Apos-**

tolic **Decree**" (Acts 15:29). It says that Gentiles should refrain from food sacrificed to idols, blood, what is strangled, and fornication. Such a decree could have represented a solution to problems that Paul encountered in Gentile churches. However, historians are often suspicious of the Acts version because it is not exactly like what is in Galatians 2:1–10. On the one hand, the key issue in Galatians, circumcision, was not even mentioned in the Apostolic Decree. On the other, Paul himself never mentioned the decree, a solution that would have been to his advantage, had he known it. More likely, the compromise reached in Gal. 2:9–10—the pillars would go to the circumcised, whereas Paul and his companions would go to the Gentiles—is more accurate. More likely, this compromise would have taken place *prior* to Paul's missionary journeys because it would have provided an agreed-upon basis for Paul's Gentile mission. In short, Luke probably created a version of the Jerusalem Conference on the basis of experiences typical of missionaries in the Jesus Movement, not on what precisely happened.

This section ends with a summary, 15:35.

The Movement to the "Ends of the Earth": (2) Paul's Second Missionary Journey, the Journey into Europe, and the Decision to Go to Rome, 15:36–19:19

This section of Acts is dominated by Paul's decision to carry the new message about the Christ from Asia into Europe, presented as a direct consequence of the activity of the Spirit. It ultimately leads to Rome (19:21). In Acts, it structurally parallels Jesus' journey to Jerusalem in the gospel, beginning in Luke 9:51. This section of Acts has the famous dream vision, an invitation to Paul to enter Macedonia (16:6–10) used by Martin Luther King Jr. to defend his activities as an outsider in the cities of the southern United States. The account also contains the story of Lydia's affiliation with the Jesus Movement; the first of the "we passages" (Acts 16:10–17); legends of Paul's imprisonment at Philippi; the attack on Paul's host Jason at Thessalonica; Paul's exit from there by night; and the move to Athens, where hearers scoffed at Paul's preaching of the resurrection. Paul's experiences as presented in this section must have been very like those of many missionaries in the Jesus Movement. Although his speech at Athens (17:22–31) shares much with the patterned speeches of Peter and Stephen, it sounds more typically like an appeal to the Hellenistic world. Yet, as noted earlier, it does not conform precisely to Paul's own emphases. Note also the characteristic Lukan themes of the favor of the Roman authorities toward the Jesus Movement and the guilt of the Israelites (18:14–17). The section ends with a summary, 19:20.

The Final Journey of Paul to Jerusalem and Then to Rome, 19:21–28:16

As Jesus' resolve to go to Jerusalem in Luke 9:51 begins a long, rambling travel narrative that ends there, Paul's resolve to go Jerusalem in Acts 19:21 begins a long, rambling travel narrative that ends there provisionally, but ultimately in Rome. The narrative is composed of a mixture of traditions and legends about the work of the Apostle Paul that are interpreted by the author of Luke-Acts. Examples are the second and third accounts of the "conversion" of Paul (22:3–21; 26:9–23), where Paul's witness always begins in Jerusalem and ends with proclaiming the gospel to the Gentiles, implying Rome.

In the story, the apostle arrives at Jerusalem, where, after meeting with James and going through a rite of purification at the temple to show that he observes the law, he becomes the victim of accusations by Israelites of the Diaspora. He lands in jail and is then brought before the Sanhedrin, where he defends himself. A plot on his life by "the Israelites," discovered by his otherwise unmentioned nephew (23:16), leads to his being sent to Caesarea, where he first comes before the Roman governor Felix, and then his successor, Festus. Claiming to be a citizen of Roman, Paul appeals his case to Nero, the emperor (25:11, 21). He is then brought before King Herod Agrippa II of Palestine, famous for his incestuous relationship with his sister Bernice, who is mentioned in passing (25:13, 23), and in this context the Lukan author offers his third account of Paul's experience with the risen Jesus (26:4–23). He is then sent to Rome, and after a precarious sea voyage he arrives there. In this section of Acts, there are more "we passages" (20:5–15; 21:1–18; 27:1–28:16). The Lukan author emphasizes Paul's innocence (e.g., 26:31), education (26:24), and especially his high social status because, although those with Roman citizenship had the right of appeal to Caesar, only those of such status could actually carry such an appeal forward.

Paul in Rome, 28:17–31

This is the climax of the Luke-Acts narrative that begins in Jerusalem and ends with the establishment of Paul and his mission in Rome (Acts 1:8). The account stresses Paul's preaching the gospel about the Gentiles "with all boldness and without hindrance" and doing so to the Roman *Israelites!* We have already discussed the complex issue it raises for the position of Luke on the salvation of the Israelites (see earlier).

FURTHER OBSERVATIONS

Jesus as the Prophet, Servant-Messiah, the "Divine Man" Hero, and the Benefactor of All Humanity

In Luke-Acts, Jesus is the "middle of time," the center of salvation history. He is portrayed, on the one hand, as the fulfillment of Old Testament prophecies (Luke 16:29, 31), especially as the Spirit-filled, anointed Servant-Messiah descended from David and prophet who brings salvation, especially by preaching to the poor and outcast and by healing (Luke 4:16–43; 24:19, 27, 41). He is said to also fulfill the prophecies when he is rejected by the Pharisees, is condemned by the Israelites, and is martyred at Jerusalem, the city where the prophets were killed (Luke 7:16, 39; 11:47–50; 13:34–35). Finally, he fulfills the prophecies and the psalms when he is vindicated as Christ, Lord, and Son of God in his resurrection and ascension to the right hand of God (Luke 24:25–26, 44–53; Acts 2:33, 36; 13:26–41).

On the other hand, Jesus is portrayed as a Son of God by a human mother and by divine agency. He is full of the Holy Spirit. He appears after death and ascends to heaven; he is a savior who offers peace and salvation to the whole world. Luke's Jesus is thus the great benefactor of all humanity.

Such an account read by any high-ranking Gentile or Gentile group would have indicated that the Israelite Messiah who fulfilled the scriptures shared much in common with all kinds of savior figures throughout the eastern Mediterranean. He was like the miracle workers and wandering philosophers, whose disciples learned and passed on their teacher's teaching and total way of life; but he was also like the emperors whose inscriptions proclaimed peace and salvation to the world. Indeed, he was like the gods.

These overall views in Luke-Acts contrast with dominant Son of Man and Son of God of the Gospel of Mark. Mark wants to present Jesus as Christ and Son of God and to interpret those designations by a careful and systematic use of the apoc-alyptic Son of Man. Thus he leads up to the climactic admission of Jesus that he is the Son of Man in 14:62 and the climactic confession of him as Son of God by the centurion in 15:39. In Luke, however, the confession of the centurion in Luke 23:47—"Certainly this man was innocent"—becomes simply a declaration of Jesus as the innocent victim. The acceptance of the titles "Christ" and "Son of God" by Jesus from Mark 14:61–62 becomes in Luke 22:67–70 quite general and lacks the sensitivity to the nuances of these titles. The author of Luke-Acts does not have the same Christological concerns as the evangelist Mark.

It is also interesting to consider Luke's interpretation of Mark's three predictions of the Passion, death, and resurrection (Mark 8:31; 9:31; 10:33–34) in Luke (Luke 9:22; 9:44; 18:31–33). Mark stresses the power and authority of Jesus. Jesus is said to "rise again" or "rise." In Luke 9:22, the verb goes into the passive voice, that is, Jesus will "be raised" (by God). In this case, Luke emphasizes that the resurrection is the act of God on behalf of the man Jesus. To be sure, Jesus "rises" in Luke 18:33, but the concern of the author elsewhere is to subordinate Jesus to God and to stress the resurrection as an act of *God's* power, as in Acts 2:33,36; 4:10; 5:30.

Much can be learned about Luke's understanding of Jesus' Passion by examin-ing his interpretation of Mark's Passion predictions. For Mark, the Passion and death of Jesus are the means of human salvation. Jesus comes "to give his life as a ransom for many" (Mark 10:45), and Jesus' cross is a sacrifice in which his blood is "poured out for many" (Mark 14:24). None of this sort of atonement for sin survives in Luke-Acts. For Luke, Jesus' cross is simply the sacrificial act of one who serves (Luke 22:27), not the means of human salvation. Similarly, Luke's ac-count of the Last Supper omits the word of interpretation of the wine (Luke 22:19b–20 has little claim to be part of the original text of the Gospel of Luke [**Textual Criticism**]). Moreover, the Markan understanding of the cross was reached in the Jesus Movement by interpreting it in terms of the great servant of God passage of Isa. 53, to which Mark 10:45 and 14:24 certainly allude. However, when this passage comes up in Acts 8:32–33, it is not used to interpret the death of Jesus as atonement for sin.

In short, for Mark, the death of Jesus is the means of human salvation, and the cross of Jesus has made this salvation possible. For the author of Luke-Acts, in contrast, the death of Jesus is an act of legal murder by the Israelites, and the gospel as preached by Jesus and the church is a claim that if people will repent and turn to God they will receive the forgiveness of their sins. The death of Jesus does not have the central saving effect in Luke-Acts that it has in the Gospel of Mark. In Luke-Acts, being a disciple means witnessing to the resurrection of Jesus rather than following Jesus to the way of the cross. As the Gospel of Luke puts it, one bears one's cross "daily" (9:23). Thus the Jesus of the Gospel of Luke is not the Israelite Messiah whose death ransoms people from the power of sin. He is the one who lives out of the power of the Spirit of God in the world and provides a model for behavior of believers in an ongoing church.

It is also interesting to compare and contrast reinterpretations of the Gospel of Mark by the evangelists "Matthew" and "Luke." One similarity is that both evangelists separate the time of Jesus from all preceding or succeeding times. Matthew does so by birth stories at the beginning and the commissioning scene at the end; Luke does so by the descent of the Spirit on Jesus at the beginning and Jesus' ascension to heaven at the end. For both, the time of Jesus is the time of fulfillment. However, Matthew does this by means of formula quotations, whereas Luke does this by making Satan absent between the temptation of Jesus and the plot to betray him. Therefore, both Matthew and Luke transform the apocalyptic drama of Mark into a "foundation myth" of the origins of a new religion. For Luke, this possibility becomes most evident in Jesus as the center of time in salvation history, a view that is clearly more evident in Luke than in Matthew.

The Apostles and Apostleship in Luke-Acts

If Matthew and Luke both transform the apocalypse of Mark into a "foundation myth," they offer very different ways in portraying how their readers may relate to it. Matthew presents an authoritative interpretation of the teaching that occurred in the sacred time of Jesus. Luke stresses imitating the Jesus of the sacred time. Although Jesus and the disciples in Matthew are in subtle ways transparent examples of behavior at the time their authors wrote, Luke much more clearly sees Jesus as a past example to be imitated and the past heroes of the church carrying this example forward.

Thus the Gospel of Luke more explicitly presents both Jesus and the apostles as models and norms of behavior. By presenting Peter as one whose rebuke can bring Ananias to death (Acts 5:3–5) and Simon to penitence (8:14–24), or by presenting Paul as one whose garments have the power to heal and whose name has power over demons (19:11–15), Luke presents his heroes as especially endowed human beings. They are models of behavior for the Jesus Movement. Peter is its supporter, Paul is its hero, and Jesus is its savior; all three have the aura of divinity, are human and yet more than human. Such dual beings are common in the Hellenistic world.

One very striking parallel between Jesus and the apostles in Acts—illustrating the "law of duality"—is the parallel between Jesus' and Stephen's martyrdom. In the trial of Jesus, Luke makes no reference to the false witnesses found in Mark (Luke 22:66–71; cf. Mark 14:56–64). However, in Acts 6:13–14, the false witnesses appear at Stephen's trial with the testimony that Mark has them give at the trial of Jesus! Another example is that Jesus cried from his cross, "Father, forgive them; for they do not know what they are doing" (Luke 23:34), and Stephen cries with a loud voice at his stoning, "Lord, do not hold this sin against them" (Acts 7:60).

The author of Luke-Acts, in portraying many parallels between Jesus and the apostles, wants the readers and hearers of Luke-Acts to identify with them. He tones down the Markan view of the Christ and avoids a focus on the cross as necessary for salvation. Again, Jesus and the apostles are models, or examples, of behavior for believers. As Jesus and the apostles are empowered by the Spirit, so might be any member of the Jesus Movement, and as they pray and attend worship regularly, so should any member of the Jesus Movement. Again, the death of Jesus is not "a ransom for many"; rather, Jesus is "one who serves" (Luke 22:27; cf. Mark 10:45). Correspondingly, the author of Luke-Acts consistently plays down the differences between Jesus and the apostles. A good example is the reply to the question of the high priest in Mark 14:62. Jesus accepts the titles of "Christ" and "Son of the living God" by using the formula "I am." But in Luke 22:70, when Jesus is asked if he is the Son of God, he replies, "You say that I am."

The effect of these parallels between the time of Jesus and that of the church, and between Jesus and the apostles, is to make it possible for any believer—such as Theophilus and those like him—to relate directly to the time of Jesus and to Jesus himself. The author of Luke-Acts is carefully providing his reader(s) and hearer(s) with an understanding of their place in salvation history and of their role in the world.

The Kingdom of God, Ethics, and the Church

In the Lukan salvation history, the time of the proclamation of the Kingdom of God takes place since the transitional time of John the Baptizer, that is, during the time of Jesus and the time of the church. Note again that the Kingdom in Luke-Acts for the most part has not "come near," as in the future apocalyptic emphases of Mark and Matthew (cf. Luke 4:43). To be sure, Luke does not totally abandon the future element found in his sources (e.g., Luke 21:27 [Mark 13:24], 31–33; cf. 11:2 [Q]). Nonetheless, striking statements claim that the Kingdom is "among you" (17:21; cf. 19:11), or present in Jesus' exorcisms (Luke 11:20), or near in Jesus' and the disciples' healing (Luke 9:2, 11; 10:9). Other sayings stress "seeking" his Kingdom (12:31 [Q]), or "receiving" or "entering" the Kingdom like a child (18:16 [Mark 10:14]; 18:24 [Mark 10:15].

In short, the Kingdom points to the past time of Jesus and the present time of the church. The Lukan ethical approach is based on the examples of the great heroes, Jesus, Peter, and Paul. Luke's key passage discussed at the outset (4:16–30) points to the inclusion of Gentiles, Romans, Samaritans, women, the poor, sinners, the sick, and the like. This emphasis points preeminently to the life of the church and its inclusive ethical ideals.

THE GENRE OF LUKE-ACTS

As with the other gospels, there has been an extensive discussion about the genre of the Gospel of Luke and the Acts of the Apostles. The main features of this discussion have already been noted; here a brief summary will suffice.

Although there have been various proposals, the discussion of Israelite, Greek, and Roman history, as well as "Luke the historian" and author of salvation history, naturally suggests a genre closely related to ancient history. To be sure, the Gospel of Luke of all the canonical gospels comes closest to the *bios,* or ancient biography, discussed in the previous two chapters. Given Luke's penchant for Isaiah and prophecy, much can be said for the story of Jesus as a "prophetic biography." Acts, too, features its heroes Peter and Paul, and in some ways it is like biography. Strong cases have also been made for Luke-Acts in relation to biographies of philosophers and their schools, or the historical romance. However, given the introductions to both the gospel and Acts, and other emphases just discussed, it would appear more likely that the biographical gospel has been set within the ancient history genre. Luke seems to have combined the *bios* with ancient historical writing.

THE INTERPRETATION OF LUKE-ACTS

The author of Luke-Acts is the forerunner of all presentations of the life of Jesus whereby Jesus becomes a moral example to be emulated. Similarly, the early church is a challenge to, and exemplar of, what is expected of members of the Jesus Movement in their daily lives and of what members of the Jesus Movement may expect in their daily lives. The author presents Jesus and the heroes of the early church as models of the challenge and possibilities of what it means to be a Christ believer. Whereas the evangelist Matthew encouraged the interpretation of the gospel as a teaching to be authoritatively interpreted, the author of Luke-Acts encourages the interpretation of Jesus, Peter, Stephen, and Paul as norms for being and living as disciples. It is no accident that the Gospel of Luke has functioned in historical Christianity, especially in the late nineteenth and early twentieth centuries, as a basis for the "social gospel," that is, the attempt to reform society by helping the poor, outcasts, the ill, and the like. More recently, it has become the gospel of political and social liberation, that is, the liberation of those politically oppressed, minorities, and women.

STUDY QUESTIONS

1. Who was the person named "Luke" in the New Testament? Who was Theophilus? How are the Gospel of Luke and the Acts of the Apostles related? What is the early church view about Luke-Acts (Irenaeus)?

2. What do modern historical critics say about authorship, date, and place of composition for Luke-Acts? What are the issues related to medical language, the speeches in Acts, and the "we passages"? What is the Lukan portrait of Jesus, and how does it differ from that of Mark and Matthew?

3. What are some of Luke's social interests and concerns? How does Luke use scripture? Why does the author of Luke-Acts stress the delay of the *parousia?* What is the Luke-Acts view of "salvation history"? How would you characterize the early church according to Acts?

4. How does Acts view the following in relation to Jesus: the apostles in the early church? The church? The Kingdom of God? Ethics? The Israelites? The Gentiles? What two genres seem to be best represented in the Gospel of Luke and the Acts of the Apostles?

Photo 11.1 Rylands Greek Papyrus 457, a fragment of John 18. Known also as P[52], it is the oldest surviving New Testament text fragment, and shows that the Gospel of John could not have been written later than its date (ca. 125–130 C.E.). For a discussion of ancient manuscripts, see Chapters Two and Three.

CHAPTER ELEVEN

THE GOSPEL AND LETTERS OF JOHN: THE LITERATURE OF THE JOHANNINE SCHOOL

Traditionally, five of the books in the New Testament are regarded as having been written by the Apostle John: the Fourth Gospel, the three letters of John, and the Book of Revelation. The last, however, has at best only a tenuous relationship to the others and is so representative of the style and thought of apocalyptic kinds of believers that it cannot easily claim a place in the "Johannine **corpus.**" We shall consider it in the following chapter. The other four books, however, exhibit a unity of style and thought that immediately shows that they came from the same person or group of persons, whatever the details of their origins may turn out to have been.

EARLY TRADITION ABOUT THE JOHANNINE LITERATURE

One of the earliest surviving traditions about the Gospel of John comes from Irenaeus, a bishop of Lyons (modern France), about 185 C.E. In a passage about the four gospels, he writes:

> Afterwards John, the disciple of the Lord who also *leaned upon his chest,* he, too, published a gospel while residing in Ephesus.
>
> (Irenaeus *Against Heresies* 3.1.1)

Irenaeus is referring to John 21:20–24, which says that "the disciple who is testifying to these things and has *written them*" is also the "one who had *leaned upon Jesus' chest*" (NRSV verse 24: "reclined next to Jesus at the supper"). He had said, "Lord, who is it that is going to betray you?" (21:20). John 21:20–24 refers back to an earlier passage in the gospel, John 13:23, where at the Last Supper a disciple, "the one whom Jesus loved," "*leaned upon his (Jesus') chest*" (NRSV: "was reclining next to him"). The verse means that the disciple whom Jesus loved was leaning on his left elbow, in typical Mediterranean banquet style, next to Jesus, his head coming close to Jesus' chest. It was the place of honor. (Western paintings that portray the Last Supper with Jesus *sitting at a table,* however beautiful [such as Raphael's famous rendition], are historically and culturally inaccurate.) The Gospel of John does not identify the disciple whom Jesus loved by name. Irenaeus, however, identifies him with Jesus' disciple, the fisherman John, son of Zebedee. Elsewhere Irenaeus states that John moved from Jerusalem to Ephesus, that he wrote all five Johannine writings there, that he lived to an old age, that he died in Ephesus, and that the gospel was written in opposition to certain Gnostics, especially Cerinthus (*Against Heresies* 3.3.4; 3.11.7; 5.33.4).

From about the same time several other Church Fathers offer these same or similar views. The Latin anti-Marcionite Prologue, perhaps as early as 200 C.E. (some scholars date it later), also claims that this John dictated his gospel to Papias, who records the traditions about the gospels of Matthew and Mark. Clement of Alexandria (ca. 150–203 C.E.) adds in a now-famous statement that in contrast to the other three gospels, John wrote "a spiritual gospel" (Clement of Alexandria, *Outlines;* cf. Eusebius *Ecclesiastical History* 6.14.5). Finally, there is the **Muratorian Canon,** or canonical list of the New Testament (perhaps Rome, ca. 200 C.E.), which states that the Fourth Gospel was written by the disciple John from the revelation he received after fasting three days and that the other apostles checked it.

In sum, the late second-century church tradition says that the Gospel of John was a spiritual gospel written by a disciple who in the Johannine account of the Last Supper "was reclining next to him [Jesus]" (John 13:23). It identifies this unnamed person as "John." It claims that the gospel was written in Ephesus, a major city on the coast of western Asia Minor, a city also associated with Paul and the Book of Revelation. No date is given; however, it is judged to be the fourth of the four gospels and thus had to be written in John's old age.

Irenaeus attributes 1 and 2 John to this same John (*Against Heresies* 3.15.5, 8). It is striking that there is no mention of 3 John in the first or second century. By the third century, Origen says that John *might* have written a second and third letter, but not everybody admits that they are genuine (*In John* 5.3). By the fourth century, Eusebius puts 2 and 3 John in his list of "disputed books" (*Ecclesiastical History* 3.25.3), although he says that they may have been written by *another* John. A little later Jerome builds on all these traditions but identifies the author of 2 and 3 John as a certain "John the *Presbyteros* ("Presbyter"; NRSV: "Elder") and says that he has a separate grave at Ephesus (Jerome *Illustrious Men* 9). This corresponds with what the author of 2 John and 3 John says about himself (2 John 1:1; 3 John 1:1).

John in the New Testament

The Israelite name "John" (Hebrew: *Yōhānān;* Greek: *Iōannēs*) was common in the first century C.E. Indeed, there are a number of persons in the New Testament with that name: John the Baptizer; John son of Zebedee, the disciple of Jesus; John Mark, follower of Paul; John, father of Peter (John 1:42; 21:15–17); and an unknown John (Acts 4:6).

It is highly likely that Irenaeus and the other second-century members of the Jesus Movement meant to refer to Jesus' disciple John. He is mentioned in the gospels of Matthew, Mark, and Luke (but not in the original Gospel of John!) as the son of Zebedee and brother of James, all of whom were fishermen on the Sea of Galilee (Mark 1:19–20 = Matt. 4:21–22). Luke adds the comment that James and John were partners with Peter, whose brother was Andrew (Luke 5:10). At Jesus' summons, all four left their nets (James and John left their father!) and followed Jesus.

In the first three gospels, this John is often honored along with his brother James and Peter as Jesus' inner circle. "The Three" are not only found (along with Andrew, Peter's brother) first in the disciple lists (e.g., Mark 3:17), but also they occur together as those closest to Jesus (e.g., Mark 5:37; 9:2; 14:33). In one story John joins in rebuking a man who has been casting out demons in Jesus' name, for which he in turn is rebuked by Jesus (Mark 9:38 par.). Mark says that John and his brother James requested that Jesus give them special positions of power in the future kingdom (Mark 10:35–41 [Matt. 20:24 attributes the request to their mother!]). The brothers were also nicknamed "Sons of Thunder" (Mark 3:17), perhaps—this is a guess—a reference to their stormy personalities.

This John is also mentioned once in Paul and three times in the Acts of the Apostles. Paul considers him one of those acknowledged "pillars" at the **Jerusalem Conference,** the other two being Peter and James, the brother of Jesus (*not* the brother of John; cf. Gal. 2:9). In Acts, John follows Peter in the list of disciples (Acts 1:13). He accompanies Peter when Peter goes to the Jerusalem temple and heals the lame beggar; the two are subsequently arrested and imprisoned and then released (Acts 3–4). He also accompanies Peter on Peter's mission to Samaria (8:14–25). He is portrayed as subordinate to Peter. The martyrdom of John's brother James under Herod Agrippa I is recorded (Acts 12:2), and this would have been prior to 44 C.E. John is not mentioned in this connection. However, a hint of John's death is given by way of a tradition that Jesus predicted the martyrdom of *both* brothers (Mark 10:35–40; Matt. 20:20–23). This prediction probably represents a historical event after the fact because, among other things, Mark and Matthew were written long after 44 C.E.

GENERAL HISTORICAL CRITICISM: AUTHOR, DATE, PLACE

There are, as might be expected, problems with this traditional view that the beloved disciple at Jesus' Last Supper was the author of these five books. First, the notion that John wrote the Fourth Gospel was from early times questioned. The *Alogoi,* who opposed the ideas of the Logos prologue-hymn in John 1:1–18 (see Chapter Three and following), said that this gospel was written by the Gnostic Cerinthus. Although the *Alogoi*'s view could have been prejudicial—John was indeed a favorite gospel of the Gnostics—the Cerinthus identification was also held by the Roman presbyter Gaius in the early third century. In any case, the tradition about John as author was not unanimous.

Second, the chief early witness, Irenaeus, was not always accurate, and there is a good deal of confusion about "Johns." He claimed that he got his information from the elderly Polycarp "when I was still a boy" and that Polycarp had had an "association with John and others who had seen the Lord" (Irenaeus, *Letter to Florinus*). This remark suggests a "chain of tradition": Jesus → John (in his old age) → Polycarp (in his old age) → Irenaeus (still a boy). However, the ancient historian Eusebius says that Irenaeus was not always a reliable witness. For example, Irenaeus said that *Papias* was also a "hearer of John," but according to Eusebius, Papias said only that he had questioned *followers* of the *presbyters* (or "elders"), who in turn were respected *disciples of the first disciples,* including John (Eusebius *Ecclesiastical History* 3.39.1–7). In other words, there was a much longer chain of tradition: Jesus → Jesus' disciple John → John's disciples → presbyters → followers of the presbyters → Papias, who is still a couple of generations earlier than Irenaeus. One of those presbyters was also named John. To complicate matters, it will be recalled that the author of 2 John and 3 John identifies himself simply as "the presbyter" ("elder," cf. 2 John 1:1; 3 John 1:1). If Irenaeus misconstrued what Papias, whom he apparently did not know, said about a certain presbyter/elder John, it is also possible that Irenaeus' evidence about Polycarp's information about John was inaccurate! This is especially the case if John was martyred at an earlier age (as Jesus' prophecy in Mark 10:39 seems to imply) and Irenaeus' memory comes from his childhood.

Finally, as noted, the author of the Fourth Gospel never explicitly identifies himself as John in the gospel itself.

In short, scholars conclude that authorship by Jesus' disciple John was most probably a deduction from comments both within and outside the gospel. Within the gospel, the one who "leaned on Jesus' chest" at Jesus' last meal is also called "the one whom Jesus loved" (13:23). This "Beloved Disciple" (as scholars call him) is mentioned later in the story as one known to the high priest and present at Jesus' trial before him (18:15–16). He is also the one to whom Jesus, while on the cross, entrusted his mother (19:26–27). Lastly, he is linked with Peter (18:15; 21:7); indeed, he is "the other disciple" who outruns Peter to the tomb but enters the tomb only after Peter (20:2–8). As noted at the outset, John 21:20–24 says that the author of the gospel, or at least, "the one who caused these things to be written," is the "one who had reclined next to Jesus at the supper" (21:20). If you read this passage carefully you will see that it seems to suggest that the Beloved Disciple is dead or about to die. Its main point is to correct a false impression or rumor that Jesus had prophesied that the disciple whom Jesus loved would still be alive at Jesus' *parousia.* In other words, it attempts to correct the rumor that Jesus had made a false prophecy about when he would return—before the death of the Beloved Disciple. Yet, the testimony of the one who "caused these things to be written" is said to be "true" (21:24). If 19:35 also refers to him—"he who saw this has testified . . . and *his testimony is true*"—then he is also said to have been an eyewitness to Jesus' death.

Note also that these verses are in chapter 21. Scholars hold for a variety of reasons that John 21 was added to the first twenty chapters of the gospel at a later date (see following). This judgment would not have concerned second-century readers.

Finally, observe that in the Fourth Gospel there is also a mysterious, unnamed disciple present when the brothers Andrew and Peter, along with Philip and Nathaniel (the latter is not mentioned in the first three gospels), are called to become Jesus' disciples (John 1:35–40). In the first three gospels, *James and John* are called at the same time as Peter and Andrew, and John was one of Jesus' inner circle, "the Three," among "the Twelve." Because the Beloved Disciple leaned on Jesus' chest, the place of honor, it would have been logical for second-century **Church Fathers** to deduce that the unnamed disciple, the Beloved Disciple, was John.

Summarizing, the Beloved Disciple, who in the first twenty chapters of the gospel was honored at Jesus' last meal and was so close to Jesus that Jesus entrusted his mother to him, was said to have authored the gospel, or at least have "caused it to be written." A natural inference would have been that this was a disciple who in the synoptic gospels was from Jesus' inner circle, namely, John. Like John son of Zebedee in the synoptics, this disciple was called in the early part of the story (John 1:35–40). He was thought to be the mysterious disciple who loved Jesus and thus the author of the Fourth Gospel. Yet, the gospel never identifies him as such and maintains the enigma. At the very least, then, both external evidence and internal evidence pose a very knotty problem about the identity of the author(s) of the gospel.

How do critical historians deal with this knotty problem? The latest possible date of the Fourth Gospel can be established by a very interesting piece of external evidence. You will recall that the earliest manuscript fragment we have of any part of the New Testament is a papyrus fragment containing parts of John 18:31–33, 37–38, discovered in Egypt (**P**[52]). Scholars consider it to have been written about 125 C.E. Because this fragment comes from a copy, the gospel must have been written early enough to circulate in Egypt in the first decade or two of the second century C.E.

As for the earliest possible date, John's gospel, like the synoptics, seems to allude to the destruction of Jerusalem in 70 C.E. Jesus' opponents, the chief priests and Pharisees, say, "If we let him go on like this (performing miracles), everyone will believe in him, and *the Romans will come and destroy both our holy place and our nation*" (11:48). Such a date would be possible if John wrote in his old age. Of course, it does not correspond with the possibility that John was martyred before 44 C.E., as might be implied from Mark 10:39 and Acts 12:2 (see preceding). The post-70 date is suggested by other internal factors, especially, as in the case of the Gospel of Matthew, Jesus' conflict with the Israelite synagogue leaders in John 9 (see following).

In short, the reference to the destruction of Jerusalem and the conflict between Jesus (= the Johannine members of the Jesus Movement) and the Israelite synagogue leaders, on the one hand, and **P**[52] on the other end, point to a date in the late first or early second century C.E. Most scholars hold to a date about 90–100 C.E.

Finally, the place of composition in the second-century church traditions is Ephesus in Asia Minor. Although that location is connected to the belief that the author of the Fourth Gospel was "John of Patmos," who wrote Revelation on the island of Patmos off the coast of Asia Minor (Rev. 1:7), Asia Minor has remained one possibility for the location for the gospel. Nonetheless, many other suggestions have been offered, especially some city in Syria. We cannot be certain about the place of origin, but Ephesus is probably as good a place as any. At least some of the Johannine oral traditions and sources came from Palestine.

Questions of authorship, date, and place of the Johannine literature have often been correlated with certain source questions and the history of the Johannine community. To those we now turn.

TEXTUAL, ORAL TRADITIONAL, AND SOURCE QUESTIONS IN THE GOSPEL OF JOHN

The Gospel of John has many fascinating literary puzzles, sometimes called "the Johannine riddle" or "the Johannine problem." They result in part from *aporias* (Greek: "difficulties" in passing), that is, breaks or interruptions in the flow of the narrative, such as sudden shifts in geographical location, time, theme, language, or style. These breaks, plus various theories about oral traditions and written sources, have led scholars to a variety of positions about the Johannine problem. Here we can touch only on some of the more important problems and a few of the proposed solutions.

The Text of the Gospel: Chapter 21

No extant, complete manuscript of the gospel omits chapter 21. Yet, scholars recognize that that chapter was added to the first twenty chapters at a later time. There are several reasons for this consensus. First, the last verses in the *previous* chapter (20:30–31) read like the original ending. Second, there are some important differences between the Greek of chapter 21 and that of chapters 1–20. Third, in 21:2 "the sons of Zebedee," who are missing in chapters 1–20, suddenly appear. Fourth, whereas in chapter 20 Jesus' resurrection appearances are located in Jerusalem, as in Luke-Acts, in chapter 21 they take place in Galilee, as in Matthew; thus there is an attempt here to supplement Jerusalem appearance traditions with Galilean resurrection appearance traditions. Finally, as noted, John 21:24 seems designed mainly to identify the Beloved Disciple as the author of what goes before in the gospel, probably the first twenty chapters, but perhaps everything up to that point. Thus it seems indisputable that chapter 21 was added to the original chapters 1–20 of the gospel but before the text of the gospel had actually circulated beyond those who were certifying it (21:24: "we").

If this virtual consensus is correct, who added chapter 21 to the Gospel of John? Note first that the account of the woman taken in adultery, the famous "let among you who is without sin be the first to throw a stone at her" story (7:53–8:11), is *not found in the earliest manuscripts.* The usual scholarly view is that it was also added to the Johannine text. There are other examples. These phenomena suggest a "Johannine School," which clearly affects our judgment about authorship. We shall consider this possibility later; at this point we shall note several other well-known problems in the gospel that lead in this direction.

Geographical, Temporal, and Content Problems in John 1–20

There seem to be a number of geographical, temporal, and content interruptions or dislocations in the flow of the gospel. We cannot cite all these *aporias,* but here are some of the more interesting ones. In chapter 5, Jesus, who has been in Galilee, is suddenly in Jerusalem; in chapter 6, he is back in Galilee; and in chapter 7, he is back in Jerusalem again. A more logical order would be chapters 6, 5, and 7. In chapter 3, Jesus is in Judea; yet, 3:22 says that he came into Judea. At the Last Supper, Peter asks Jesus where he is going (13:36); yet, later, Jesus complains that no one has asked him that (16:5). In 14:31, Jesus says, "Rise, let us be on our way," but Jesus' farewell discourse, which takes up three chapters, follows! Jesus performs his first sign in Cana at 2:11, and 2:23 says he worked many miracles ("signs") there; yet, 4:54 says that his *second* miracle was at Cana as if no intervening miracles had taken place. John 7:3–5 speaks as if Jesus has performed no signs in Judea, but he has (5:1–9). There are also some clear interruptions about John the Baptizer in the prologue to the gospel (1:1–18; see following). Finally, there seem to be two conclusions to Jesus' public activity (10:40–42; 12:37–43).

Modern critics have offered two major solutions to these fascinating problems. First, there was some accidental misplacement of manuscript pages or parts thereof. Second, and more plausibly, the writer or writers were loosely merging several traditions or sources, perhaps over a long period of time by a series of redactions.

Differences and Similarities between John and the Synoptics

There are some major differences and similarities between John and the synoptic gospels. This will help prepare us further for the problems about traditions and/or sources.

Differences

1. *The chronological and geographical framework.* The synoptics have Jesus begin his ministry after John is imprisoned; it lasts one year, includes only one visit to Jerusalem, and Jesus' last meal is a Passover meal. The Fourth Gospel has Jesus begin his ministry while John the Baptizer is still active; it lasts two to three years, includes several trips to Jerusalem (the temple cleansing occurs in chapter 2!), and the last meal is not a Passover meal. Curiously, from the perspective of archeology, Palestinian sites are more accurately placed in John.

2. *Jesus' teaching: Style.* In the synoptics, Jesus teaches in aphorisms, short discourses, and parables. In John, Jesus teaches in long, rambling discourses—complex monologues and dialogues and a lengthy farewell discourse and prayer (John 13–17)—and there are no developed parables.

3. *Jesus' teaching: Content.* In the synoptics, Jesus' central teaching is the Kingdom of God. The Gospel of John has no Kingdom of God sayings, but rather symbolic themes such as "light" and "life."

4. *Unique incidents,* including four "signs" (the last four incidents)

> Nicodemus, who came to Jesus "by night" (3:1–21)
>
> The Samaritan woman at the well (4:7–42)
>
> Changing water into wine at the wedding at Cana (2:1–11)
>
> The Sabbath healing at the pool of Bethzatha (5:1–9)
>
> The healing of the man born blind (9:1–12)
>
> The raising of Lazarus (11:1–44)

5. *Miracles: No exorcisms.* In the synoptics, especially Mark, Jesus' folk healing is dominated by exorcisms. John has no exorcisms whatever. Rather, there are "signs," John's term for miracles, some of which, as noted earlier, are unique.

6. *Jesus' opponents.* In the synoptics, Jesus' opponents are distinct groups, even though they are not always historically accurate (scribes, Pharisees, Sadducees). John usually prefers an undifferentiated group called "the Israelites" (NRSV: "the Jews").

Similarities

1. Common incidents

> Call of disciples (1:35–51)
>
> Peter's confession (6:66–70)
>
> Triumphal entry into Jerusalem (12:12–15)
>
> Cleansing of the temple (2:13–22)
>
> Anointing at Bethany (12:1–8)
>
> Last Supper with a prophecy of betrayal (13:1–11)
>
> General story of the Passion itself

2. Common miracle stories

> Healing of the official's son (4:46–53)
>
> Feeding (6:1–15)
>
> Sea miracle (6:16–21)

3. Exact verbal similarities

Mark	John	Words or Phrases
2:11	5:8	"Stand up, take your mat and walk."
6:37	6:7	"two hundred denarii worth of bread" (*denarius* = coin, about a day's wage)
14:3	12:3	"costly perfume made of pure nard"
14:5	12:5	"300 denarii"
14:54, 67	18:18, 25	Peter "warming [*thermainomenos*] himself"
14:54	18:15	Peter goes "into" the courtyard
15:14	19:15	they cry "crucify him" in the Greek imperative case
15:17	19:2, 5	the purple cloak
15:42	19:15	mention of the Day of Preparation

Three areas of discussion have arisen to address these differences and similarities: (1) John's possible literary relationship to the synoptic gospels; (2) John's special sources; and (3) the history of the Johannine community.

The Relation of the Gospel of John to the Synoptic Gospels

Do the similarities suggest that the author of the Gospel of John knew any or all of the synoptic gospels, or are they based on a common oral tradition? There is no consensus. Recently, theories of *indirect* dependence of John on the synoptics have gained favor, that is, John and the synoptics shared some *oral traditions*. Part of the argument is that the few verbal parallels in the preceding columns are of the type that would be preserved in oral tradition.

Others, however, say that the differences are not enough grounds for denying the Johannine author's knowledge of one or more of the synoptic gospels. In the first part of the gospel (John 1–12), the author simply did not *choose* to follow the Markan order but rather built his account around his "Signs [miracles] Source" (discussed later; see also Chapter Three). In the second section (John 13–17), he developed thematic discourses and a prayer; and in the Passion Story (John 18–20), which seems to show familiarity with Mark and Luke, he decided to go his own way. Finally—this is an impressive argument—the *Markan* author often places one account inside another ("intercalation"; see Chapter Eight). The author of John appears to follow this Markan literary technique in John 18:15–27:

	Mark	John
Peter's denial	14:54	18:15–18
Hearing	14:55–65	18:19–24
Peter's denial	14:66–72	18:25–27

To illustrate the debate further, look at a passage that is similar in John and the synoptics, John 12:25–26 and Mark 8:34–35.

John 12:25-26	Mark 8:34-35
He who loves his life loses it, and he who hates his life in this world will keep it for eternal life. If anyone serves me he must follow me; and where I am, there shall my servant be also; if any one serves me the Father will honor him.	If any man would come after me, let him deny himself and take up his cross and follow me. For whoever would save his life will lose it; and whoever loses his life for my sake and the gospel's will save it.

The theme of following Jesus and losing and saving one's life indicates some relationship between the two. Was it indirect (common oral tradition that had developed in different directions) or direct ("John" knew and interpreted "Mark")? Do the verbal similarities noted earlier reinforce literary dependence, or are they just the sort of thing that might be remembered in *oral* tradition?

With respect to the relationship between John and *Luke,* an important example is the story of the woman who anoints Jesus (John 12:3–8 = Luke 7:36–50; cf. Luke 10:38–42). In Mark 14:3–9 and Matt. 26:6–13, the woman anoints Jesus' *head,* and there is no mention of her hair. In Luke, the woman *wipes Jesus' feet* with her *hair* and then anoints them. In John, Mary anoints Jesus' *feet* and wipes them with her *hair.* Does this similarity between Luke and John mean that John knew the Lukan account, or did they simply share an oral tradition?

Some scholars mediate by suggesting that the author of the Gospel of John had *at one time* read the Gospel of Mark and perhaps also of the Gospel of Luke. Yet, there seems to be a growing opinion that John's knowledge of the synoptics is *indirect,* if not from common oral tradition, then perhaps through John's special sources—or some combination of the two. This solution requires a consideration of special written sources in the Gospel of John.

The Gospel of John and Special Written Sources

In addition to the prologue (John 1:1–18), the Gospel of John contains three obvious complexes of material (see Chapter Three):

1. "Signs" or miracle stories
2. Long discourses centered around great symbolic themes
3. Passion, death, and resurrection stories

One of the things for which the twentieth-century critic Rudolf Bultmann is famous is his argument that these complexes represent three sources:

1. A "**Signs Source**"
2. A discourse source derived from Gnostic revelation discourses
3. A Passion Story source

Bultmann argued that the author of the Fourth Gospel combined these three sources and edited them. Later, the gospel was reworked further by an "ecclesiastical redactor" who added apocalyptic (5:28–29; 12:48) and sacramental themes (e.g., 3:6 [baptism]; 6:51–58 ["Eucharist"]).

Bultmann's second source, the Gnostic revelation discourse source, is the most difficult to establish. There are three important reasons. The first is that the discourses contain what is usually thought to be the most distinctive ideas of the author himself, making a previous source hard to isolate. The second is that in the Johannine context many of the discourses are so closely connected to miracle stories that they often look like author's interpretations of them; thus again, a separate source is extremely difficult to isolate. A third, quite different, reason is that since the discovery of the **Dead Sea Scrolls** in 1947, increasing numbers of scholars have related the background of John to dualistic Israelite thought; some of these scholars are not convinced that this Israelite thought was influenced by Gnosticism. Similar arguments are made about the Johannine Prologue (see Chapter Three). Because of these complications, the theory of a Gnostic discourse source has not received the same support in recent scholarship as has the miracle source and Passion source.

Of Bultmann's three supposed sources, the first, miracle source, or **Signs Source,** has received the most support (see Chapter Three). Its name comes from "sign" as the special Johannine word for *miracle* (2:11; 2:23; 4:54; 12:37; 20:30–31). In John 1–20, there are seven signs, the three that are paralleled in the synoptics (4:46–53; 6:1–15; 6:16–21) and the four that are unique to the Fourth Gospel (2:1–11; 5:1–9; 9:1–12; 11:1–14). In addition there is the miraculous catch of fish in the non-Johannine chapter (21:1–14). Robert Fortna's attempt to reconstruct the Signs Source behind John was noted in Chapter Three. Here is the reconstructed source again:

Unit	Passage
The Opening	
1. John's testimony	1:6–7, 19–23, 26b–27, (33d), 29–34
2. First disciples find the Messiah	1:35, 37, (38a), 38b, 39–42, 43b–47, 49

The Signs of Jesus
Galilee

3. Water to wine	2: 1–3a, 5b–11a, (11b [himself]), 11c
4. The official's son restored to life	2: 12a; 4: 46b, (47), 49b, 50a–c, 51–52, (53), 54
5. The catch of fish	21: (1), 2–4, 6–7, 8b, 11, 14
6. Feeding the multitude	6: 1, (3), 5, 7–11, (12–13a), 13b–14, 15c, 17–20, 21b, (22, 25)

Jerusalem

7. Lazarus resuscitated from death	11: 1, 2c–3, 7, 11, 15c, 17, 32–34, 38–39a, 41, 43b–45
8. A blind man sees	9: 1, 6–7, (8)
9. A crippled man walks	5: 2–3, 5–9

Bultmann also held that the synoptic gospels and the Gospel of John are indebted to a *written Passion source.* This possibility has received mixed reviews. Fortna went on to suggest that *before* the Gospel of John was written a Passion source had already been joined to the **Signs Source** to make a narrative gospel, the "Signs Gospel." J. D. Crossan argued that a written Passion source he calls the "Cross Gospel" lies behind all four canonical gospels and the apocryphal *Gospel of Peter.* Such interesting theories would make it possible to explain many of the similarities between John and the synoptics in the Passion Story.

In short, of Bultmann's three major source proposals, the Signs Source has received the most positive response, and there is also some support for an earlier Signs Gospel. However, there is no consensus about sources behind John. This is in sharp contrast to the majority opinion about the **Two-Source Theory** in synoptic studies. There is, moreover, a third option that attempts to solve the Johannine problem.

The History of the Johannine Communities

The third option for dealing with the Johannine problem is the attempt to see various stages of development in the history of an independent Johannine community. An influential perspective is that of the American scholar Raymond Brown who, reading between the lines of the gospel, finds hints of a development of the Johannine community related to its developing Christology, which increasingly brought it into conflict with more conservative Israelite groups. The following six-stage development is based on Brown's reconstruction. The first three stages are before the writing of the gospel; the last two stages come after its composition.

Stage 1

Reflected in John 1:35–41, Stage 1 reflects *an original group of Palestinian Israelites.* It included followers of John the Baptizer, and it held an essentially Israelite view of Jesus as Messiah. It also had views similar to views found in the **Dead Sea Scrolls** (the dualism of good versus evil, light versus darkness, etc.). According to this early, relatively "low" (human) Christology, Jesus was descended from David, fulfilled the

Law and the prophets, worked miracles (like Moses or Elijah), and would soon return. This group began to collect some synoptic-like sayings and miracle stories (like the "Signs Source"). One of this original group was a disciple of Jesus (1:35–40), who was perhaps a former follower of the Baptizer, the "disciple whom Jesus loved," or as scholars say, "the Beloved Disciple."

Stage 2

Jesus' Samaritan journey and encounter with the woman at the well in Samaria (John 4:4–42) hint at a further stage (Stage 2) of development. The story says that the Israelites worship God on Mount Zion in Jerusalem, whereas the Samaritans worship him on Mount Gerizîm in Samaria, but God really resides in neither place because he is a spirit. This implies that the community included members of the Jesus Movement who opposed the temple (cf. Acts 6–7) and that they are carrying out a mission to the Samaritans (Acts 8). In the process, the community assimilates some Samaritan ideas, especially the Samaritan hope for a messianic figure as a new Moses, the *Taheb* (cf. Deut. 18:18). This new Moses would be a Law bringer, teacher, and revealer who would restore his people. The story also suggests that like Moses, Jesus is believed to have seen God and to be descended from him— and more: He is the "Savior of the world" (John 4:42). Thus the inclusion of the Samaritans becomes a catalyst for a "higher" Christology, the view that Jesus is the "Man from Heaven" or "Man from the Sky." More traditional Israelite monotheists, including former adherents of the Baptizer, could not tolerate such a development because it implied a challenge with monotheism; thus began conflicts with traditionalists. In this stage, there is a decline in the expectation of the return of Jesus ("delay of the *parousia*"), leading ultimately to the Johannine focus on the mysterious *presence* of Jesus. The disciple who shepherds the community through this period of conflict is the Beloved Disciple.

Stage 3

According to Brown, Stage 3 is marked by the inclusion of the Gentiles and thus a more universalistic outlook (John 12:20–23, 37–42). It may be that at this time the Johannine members of the Jesus Movement migrated from Palestine to the regions of Ephesus or some other city, perhaps in Syria (cf. John 7:35). In any case, the higher Christology and possible inclusion of Gentiles lead these Israelite members of the Jesus Movement to be expelled from the synagogue (12:42; see following).

Stage 4

In Stage 4, someone writes the Johannine Gospel, about 90 C.E. At this stage seven groups can be distinguished. There are three groups of *outsiders* with whom the Johannine group has increasing conflict, three groups of *sympathizers* whose faith is nonetheless inadequate, and the *Johannine members of the Jesus Movement* themselves. The first group of *outsiders* is implied by the expression "the world" in the gospel (e.g., 9:39; 12:31, 35–36). It suggests a society more inclusive than, yet sometimes identified with, the second outsider group, "the [undifferentiated] Israelites" (NRSV: "the Jews"), among whom are especially "the chief priests and scribes" and the Pharisees at Yavneh, who are behind exclusion of members of the Jesus Movement from the synagogues (see following). The third group consists of the continuing followers of John the Baptizer (3:2–26).

There are also three groups of *sympathizers, although the Johannine author thinks that their beliefs are inadequate.* The first of these consists of Israelites who secretly believe in Jesus—in today's jargon they might be called "closet believers"—but fear being expelled from the synagogues (9:28; 12:42–43). The second consists of members of the Jesus Movement whose faith is inadequate (6:60–66; 7:3–5; 8:31; 10:12). The last group consists of Christ believers in other than Johannine churches. In the Johannine story, Peter represents this group, and so he is often seen as competing with the Beloved Disciple, who represents the Johannine believers (e.g., 6:60–69; 20:1–10).

Finally, there are *Johannine members of the Jesus Movement themselves.*

Stage 5

About 100 C.E. or so, someone writes the Johannine letters. In the same period, someone adds chapter 21 (and perhaps 7:53–8:11, the adulterous woman) to the gospel. The leaders of the community become something of a "Johannine School." The letters in part show believers how to read the gospel. They stress that it is necessary both to believe that Jesus came "in the flesh" and to keep the commandments; those who do not are said to be of the devil and the Antichrist. Once again we find a factional conflict about Christology. Some factions take "high" Christology too far, that is, the Man from Heaven's humanity is of little importance for salvation; others—including the writer—believe in the importance of stressing that "the Word became flesh."

Stage 6

In Stage 6, the Johannine community splits into two factions: The majority denies that the human Jesus "in the flesh" is necessary for its message about "Christ." This view sounds like emergent Gnosticism. A minority follows the interpretation found in 1 John, namely, that the true view of the Man from the Sky requires Jesus "in the flesh." This view sounds anti-Gnostic. It paves the way for the acceptance of the gospel and the letters into the "orthodox" canon in the late second century. Ironically, a "high (divine) Christology" that led to the conflict with conservative monotheistic Israelite believers and dominated the more "orthodox" creeds was a major component of what those same believers thought was the Gnostic heresy!

THE GOSPEL, THE LETTERS, AND THE "JOHANNINE SCHOOL"

We now take up the question of the literary relationship between the gospel and the letters (Stages 4 and 5 earlier). Are they by the same author? In antiquity the author of 2 and 3 John was called "the Presbyter" ("Elder"). Thus Jerome claimed that the author of the gospel and 1 John was not the author of 2 and 3 John. A complication is that in the late second century, 1 and 2 John were known, but evidence for 3 John is lacking. Yet, all four were eventually attributed to the same person.

Modern critics agree that the gospel and the letters have a similar style, tone, and thought. That commonality suggests that the same person wrote all four. However, careful examination reveals a more limited vocabulary and style, as well as a few differences in thought, in the first letter as compared to the gospel, and some scholars have suggested that the gospel was made to conform with the letters. Despite 1 John's nonmillennial thrust (e.g., 3:16–21, 36), the letter occasionally maintains the traditional hope for the *parousia* (e.g., 2:17–28; 3:2–3). It also hints at an interest in the sacraments (2:12–27; 3:9; 5:1–6). The gospel stresses that people become believers in the present (3:31–36), but it has a few sayings scattered about that express the traditional millennial hope (5:27–29; 6:39–40, 44b, 54; 12:48). Similarly, the gospel has little interest in rites; yet, there are sacramental allusions. One example is that the words "water and" in 3:5 and allusions in 19:34b-35, which interrupt the narrative, unmistakably refer to baptism. Another is that references to eating flesh and drinking blood in the discourse on the bread of life, 6:51b–58, sound "sacramental."

Bultmann once argued that the gospel was edited to conform to the letter, that is, a future *parousia* hope and concern for the sacramental life have been introduced into the gospel by the author of the first letter. If so, the main text of the gospel (John 1–20) is by one author and the first letter by another. Is either of these authors the "Presbyter" who is mentioned as the author of the second and third letters? Is this the person who added chapter 21 and perhaps the story of the woman taken into adultery? Although such questions are impossible to answer with certainty, it seems likely that at least two authors are involved in the gospels and letters of John, and perhaps three.

Multiple authors and editions suggest that these writings come from a literate leadership of the Johannine community that may have formed a "school." Schools were a common feature of the environment of the New Testament, from the rabbinical schools and schools of scribes such as those at Qumran to the many schools of the philosophers of the Greco-Roman world (see Chapter One). A school hypothesis suggested itself in relation to Paul and the deutero-Pauline letters. Similarly, the hypothesis of a Johannine School seems likely, and the literary features of the gospel and letters of John make it virtually certain.

LANGUAGE AND STYLE: JOHANNINE "ANTILANGUAGE"

Some scholars who specialize in the meaning of language in its social context, called "sociolinguists," say that there are three main modes of meaning in communication: (1) *what* one says (ideational), (2) *with whom* one speaks (interpersonal), (3) and *how* one speaks (textual). We begin with the last, *how* the author of the Johannine literature "speaks," that is, writes. This requires consideration of his language.

The Greek of the Johannine literature is easy, very well-written Greek. Nonetheless, it is notoriously difficult to translate. Why? The major answer is that the author uses wordplay, symbol, irony, repetition, and the like. Note his creation of double meanings, one literal, another metaphorical. An interesting illustration is John 3:3. Jesus says that one must be "born *anōthen.*" *Anōthen* in Greek means literally "again" (recall that Greek is not Jesus' native tongue; it is the gospel writer's). However, the term can also mean "from above" (Jesus comes "from above" in the gospel), and metaphorically it can mean born "again" in the sense of spiritual rebirth (like being born "of God" in the prologue to the gospel). In the story, a Pharisee Nicodemus takes *anōthen* literally, but he totally misunderstands it and looks foolish. Readers and hearers of the gospel are led to understand its deeper meaning; indeed, the writer has Jesus speak so that they will understand. Again, his words are overloaded with metaphorical, symbolic, and spiritual meanings. He uses old words in a new way (relexicalization). Thus they are difficult to translate.

A feature of his style is similar. He repeats a major theme over and again but uses different words for it (overlexicalization). This is especially the case with dualistic oppositions. Examples are light versus darkness, life versus death, above versus below, freedom versus slavery, and the like. The terms on the plus or positive tend to point to the same reality, whereas terms on the minus or negative tend to point to a different reality.

With respect to the "how" of Johannine language, the writer also uses antitheses, **sandwiches,** irony, and "**chiasms**" (A-B-C-B′-A′; see Chapter Nine). Again, in his story, various interlocutors, especially opponents of Jesus, cannot understand Jesus' language or, indeed, who Jesus is, but the readers/hearers of the story do.

Using words metaphorically in a new way, using different words for the same concept, wordplay, symbol, irony, repetition, antitheses, sandwiches, and chiasms are all dimensions of the textual mode. However, what kind of odd language is this? Some scholars call it "**antilanguage**" (Malina and Rohrbaugh). Antilanguage is type of language used by groups who are "marginal" with respect to the larger society, which in the most general sense is Mediterranean society but in a more restricted sense is more traditional Israelite society. The key in this case is the choice of believers to live in opposition to "this world" and "the Israelites" (NRSV: "the Jews"). Their "antilanguage" is thus an expression of their "antisociety" stance.

SOCIAL-HISTORICAL CONTEXT:
THE JOHANNINE "ANTISOCIETY"

The second mode of meaning noted earlier is *with whom one speaks* (the interpersonal mode). Insider antilanguage of the gospel has a parallel in sharp opposition to three kinds of outsiders previously suggested by Brown: (1) "the world," or the values of Mediterranean society, (2) "the Israelites" (NRSV: "the Jews"), or the values of traditional Torah observers, and to a much lesser extent, (3) the followers of the Baptizer, who are competitors. The Johannine group has turned inward (ideological marginality [Duling]; "introversionist sect" [B. Wilson]). It has become a conscious alternative to "the world," "the Israelites," and the followers of the Baptizer. In the jargon of sociolinguistics used here, it is an **antisociety.** In short, antilanguage is the insider language of an antisociety.

A little more needs to be said about the outsiders. There are seventy-nine references to "the world" in the gospel, of which the following are typical. God created the world through the agency of the divine Word/Jesus (1:10). God loves the world (3:16) and wants to save the world (3:17), as does Jesus (12:47). However, it is temporarily under the control of "the ruler of this world" (12:31; 14:30) and is characterized by darkness (12:46), sin (1:29), and blasphemy (10:36). Jesus does not come from the world (16:28), does not belong to the world (17:16), and will depart from this world (13:1). His kingdom is not from this world (18:36). The world does not know God (17:25) or Jesus (1:10); indeed, the world hates Jesus (7:7). Neither he nor his followers belong to the world (15:19). The world persecutes them, but ultimately Jesus conquers the world (16:33).

The Johannine antisociety also opposes the Israelites (NRSV: "the Jews"). The gospel claims that believers have been put out of the synagogue (9:22, 34; 12:42; 16:2a). The most illuminating example is found in the story of the Sabbath healing of the man born blind in chapter 9 (Martyn). When brought before the Pharisees, the man who now "sees" calls Jesus a prophet, and later in the story he claims that Jesus must be from God or else Jesus cannot have healed him. He is promptly thrown out. His parents do not want to discuss the miraculous healing because the Israelites "had already agreed that anyone who confessed Jesus to be the Messiah would be put out of the synagogue" (9:22). These Israelites regard Jesus as a sinner, not the one sent from God (9:24, 29).

You will recall from previous chapters that by about 80–90 C.E., the Pharisees at the Yavneh Academy were attempting to consolidate Judaism under their authority and influence. According to rabbinic tradition (*Berakoth* 28b), they introduced a prayer against the *Minîm* ("heretics") into their synagogue prayers. Part of it said: "may they perish immediately. Speedily may they be erased from the Book of the Life. . . ." This "**Prayer against the Heretics**" (*Birkat ha-Minîm*) was aimed at dissenters. One must be cautious about making a direct connection between the Prayer against the Heretics and the ban from the synagogue mentioned in the Fourth Gospel. The gospel does not explicitly link the two, and the new prayer may not have been fixed in form. Indeed, some scholars have argued that the explicit reference to "Nazoreans" (*Nōzrîm*) in the prayer may have been added in the early second century C.E. Yet, there may be an indirect connection. Certainly the Gospel of John contributes to the history of the "parting of the ways" between Israelites and the Jesus Movement.

All that suggests that the gospel was written in an Israelite environment. As evidence, there are parallels with Aramaic paraphrases of the Old Testament (the **Targums**). There is interpretation of the Old Testament typical of rabbinic "midrash" (e.g., John 6). There is a Christology deeply indebted to the myth of a descending and ascending figure reminiscent of the Wisdom myth (see Chapter One and following). There are miracle-working figures such as Moses (the ten plagues, which in the Scriptures are "signs") and Elijah. There is influence of the Greek **Septuagint,** with fourteen direct scriptural quotations, seven from the prophets. There are also famous Johannine "I AM" sayings, which, among other things, suggest scriptural statements about Yahweh, whose name can mean "I AM WHO I AM" (e.g., Isa. 45:18; Exod. 3:14). John's dualism is similar to the light-and-darkness dualism of the Dead Sea Scrolls. This points to an Israelite environment.

Yet, the language of the gospel is Greek. Apocalyptic is not a characteristic feature. Moreover, there are other ideas that suggest contact with the far-flung Hellenistic mystery religions—"I AM" is also found in the Isis cult—and perhaps the dualism shades off into some very early from Gnosticism.

In short, Johannine antilanguage and antisociety point to a marginal group within Israelite society much affected by Hellenistic society—the "world"—at large.

JOHANNINE IDEATION

Antilanguage (textual mode) and antisociety (interpersonal mode) dominate the Johannine Gospel. Yet, there is a related ideation: what is said. It is traditionally called "theology." The Johannine theological ideas can be outlined as follows.

Christology

The Gospel of John has a "high" Christology. Jesus fulfills all the Old Testament messianic expectations—Lamb of God, Chosen One of God, Messiah, King of Israel, the new Elijah—and in all of these, he is vastly superior to John the Baptizer (1:19–51). However, the center of John's Christology is that Jesus is the mysterious "Man from Heaven," the Son of Man, or simply Son (of the Father). He is not the synoptics' apocalyptic Son of Man derived from Daniel. Rather, he originates from his Father in heaven, *descends* to earth as one "sent" as an envoy from his Father (8:42) or as one who "came" from God, stays for a period (7:33), and *ascends* to his Father again (e.g., 3:13–15; 16:28), only to reappear to his disciples in ASCs. He is as close to the Father as one can imagine (10:30), and yet he is subordinate to the Father (14:28) and is the Father's representative dispensing judgment (5:22, 27) and "eternal life" (3:13–15; 6:27; 6:53). He reveals God's "glory" (13:31). His ascent is also his being "lifted up," which is given a double meaning in relation to his being "lifted up" on the cross (3:13–15; 8:28; 13:34–36). He is God's *only* son (3:16,18), and responding to Jesus is equivalent to responding to the Father. "The Israelites" (NRSV: "The Jews)" and a disciple do not understand his origins (6:41–42; 3:11–13). Ultimately, he is a stranger from another world (8:23).

Wayne Meeks once proposed that the Johannine Jesus, the Man from Heaven, is an enigma, a stranger to "the world" and "the Israelites." Meeks realized that John's gospel was for insiders, those who "love *one another*" as Jesus loved them. (Contrast the synoptics' stress on loving God, neighbor, *and enemy*.) Antilanguage, antisociety, and "otherworldly" Christology are mutually reinforcing. Those who are alienated believe in the Alien Man from the Sky, and the Alien Man from the Sky symbolizes those who are alienated.

It was also noted that the revelation discourses contain some of John's most characteristic ideas. One of them is "I AM." Sometimes it has a predicate, sometimes it has an implied predicate, sometimes it has an explicit predicate (6:35: "I am the bread of life"; 8:12: "I am the light of the world"; 10:11, 14: "I am the good shepherd," and the like). Scholars suggest especially two important backgrounds for the "I AM" sayings: one Israelite, the other Hellenistic.

The sayings with no predicate seem to have a background in the Old Testament. In Exodus, God tells Moses to explain to the Israelites that God's name is "I AM WHO I AM," or perhaps "I AM WHAT I AM" or "I WILL BE WHAT I WILL BE" (Exod. 3:14). This name comes from the Hebrew root "to be" (*h-y-h*), but this root is also related to the Divine Name, "Yahweh" (*Y-h-w-h*), that is, "the Lord"—indeed, it appears to be a pun on Yahweh. The text continues, "Thus you shall say to the Israelites, 'I AM (*y-h-w-h*) has sent me to you.'" It says further, "This is my name forever . . ." (3:15b). In modern idiom, God "is there" for the Israelites!

The sayings with a predicate are more like those known from various Hellenistic religions in antiquity (the Coptic Gnostic texts; the Hermetic literature; the Mandaean literature; literature about the Isis mystery cult). One example comes from the Hermetic literature in connection with the revealer Poimandres:

> [The revealer appears to the speaker in a vision] "Who are you?" I said. "*I am Poimandres*," said he, "*the Mind of the* Sovereignty. I know what you wish, and *I am with you Everywhere*. . . . Keep in mind the things you wish to learn and I will teach you."

Clearly, the "I AM" sayings are intended to signal the revelation of a god.

Note also the concept of the *Logos,* or "Word," the preexistent mythical Wisdom figure who participates in the act of creation, a figure from the realm of Light. This idea, well known in Israelite thought of the **Diaspora** (see Chapter Three), will be discussed in connection with the Johannine Prologue (1:1–18).

Dualism

As noted earlier in connection with antilanguage, the Fourth Gospel is characterized by a set of symbolic opposites: light/darkness; life/death; God/Satan; above/below; heaven/earth; spirit/flesh; truth/falsehood; (true) Israel/"the Israelites"; belief/unbelief. This "overlexicalized" dualism is not simply the *temporal,* or horizontal, dualism, which contrasts "this world" and "the world to come" as known in apocalyptic. It may have roots in this type of thinking, but it has become much more "cosmic" (Greek *kosmos* = "world"), or *vertical.* Temporal dualism has become spatial dualism, a contrast between the heavenly world above and the earthly world below. But this dualism also has a human, personal dimension, that is, the way of the world is a sinful, inauthentic existence contrary to God's plan. In short, the world has become so corrupted by Satan (12:31) that it falls on the negative, earthly side of darkness (8:12) and is in need of redemption by a loving God who sends the Man from another world (3:16), the world of light. Clearly, a document that is so negative about "the world" implies that it—as in apocalyptic literature—proceeds out of an antisociety, a community that has experienced alienation from the dominant political and religious structures. This observation corresponds with the possibility that the Johannine members of the Jesus Movement represent a sect that has been expelled from the synagogue, and thus the gospel's sharp judgment of "the Israelites."

Signs and Faith

Earlier it was also suggested that the evangelist reinterprets a "**Signs Source,**" which originally presented Jesus as a hero or "Divine Man" whose miracles induce faith. "Signs" become the basis for the first part of his work (2:1–12:50), that is, they become actions around which Jesus' monologues and dialogues are constructed. With regard to specific signs, one's first impression is that the evangelist uses them in the same manner as his **Signs Source,** that is, they lead disciples and others to faith (e.g., 2:11, 25; 12:37), and they prove Jesus' messiahship (2:18). An example is 20:30–31: "Now Jesus did many other *signs* in the presence of the disciples, which are not written in this book. But these are written *that you may come to believe. . . .*"

This view is not the synoptic view of miracles. In the synoptics, the persons healed already have faith when they come to Jesus (e.g., Mark 6:5–6). In John, the signs induce faith. However, this faith-inducing function is not consistently emphasized. In 2:23–25 and 4:48, Jesus *repudiates* the kind of faith induced by signs. Likewise, the conversation with Nicodemus contrasts miracle-induced faith unfavorably with rebirth "from above" and "of the spirit" (3:2, 3, 5–6). These passages make it very probable that the author of the Gospel of John *reinterprets* the Signs Source: Faith induced by signs is not enough. Yet, "seeing" a sign can mean *more* than understanding Jesus as a wonder-working hero miraculously capable of providing basic needs, such as food (6:26); moreover, some do *not* respond to signs with faith (12:37). These subtleties about the impact of signs seem to be reinforced by 4:48, where Jesus responds to the request of the Capernaum official's son for healing by what appears on the surface to be a criticism: "Unless you see signs and wonders you will not believe" (4:48).

In short, the evangelist understands the relation of signs to faith in a complex manner:

1. Not all who see signs *truly* "see" and believe

2. Some "see" and do believe, or perhaps "see" *because* they are open to faith

3. Some "see" more than the mere performance of a sign, that is, they "see" spiritually, beyond material needs

4. Some may not need signs at all: "Blessed are those who have not seen and yet have come to believe" (20:29)

There seem, then, to be different levels of perception of "signs" and some qualitative difference among them. Did the author have some notion of the maturation of faith? Perhaps. In any case, he sees a multilevel, dynamic interaction between signs and faith; or to put it another way, between religious experience and religious knowledge. This view can be correlated with his subtle view of faith and knowledge throughout the gospel.

Eschatology

The eschatology of the fourth evangelist is rooted in his Christology. In traditional Israelite thinking, events about to happen—the coming of the Messiah, resurrection, judgment, eternal life—are already *present* for the believer in ASC encounters with Jesus. It is one way of responding to the *parousia* that is in abeyance, or delayed. To be sure, the expectation of events about to happen is not totally lacking (cf. e.g., 5:28–29; 6:39–40, 44, 54; 12:48). Bultmann once suggested that such features might have come from a member of the Johannine School who later redacted the gospel to bring it more into line with traditional apocalyptic hopes and expectations. There may also be a *type* of *parousia* that suggests that Jesus will return and take the Christ believer to his heavenly home, perhaps at death (14:2–3). The most characteristic view of the evangelist, however, is suggested by 5:24: "Very truly, I tell you, anyone who hears my word and believes in him who sent me has eternal life, and does not come under judgment, but has passed from death to life."

Spirit, Church, and Sacraments

The stress on the present in John's "eschatology" is matched by his view of the presence of the Spirit among believers. The special term for the Spirit in John 14–16 is "Paraclete" (Greek *paraklētos;* cf. 14:15–17, 25–26; 15:26–27; 16:5–11, 12–15). Literally, it means "the one called beside," but it can mean (1) "Advocate" or "Intercessor," that is, something like a defense attorney before God in behalf of the Johannine believers; (2) "Comforter" or "Counselor" to such believers; and (3) "Exhorter" or "Proclaimer." Like the Stranger from heaven, the Paraclete comes from the Father at the request of Jesus, or in Jesus' name after Jesus departs; alternatively the departed Jesus himself sends the Paraclete. The Paraclete represents, then, the continued and recognized "presence" of the Christ in the community. He is a prophet teaching Jesus' followers and bearing witness and glorifying Christ, recalling all that Jesus said. In fact, Jesus is viewed as the first Paraclete in relation to "*another* Paraclete" (14:16). Like Jesus, the Paraclete is rejected by the world; it does not recognize him. However, the Paraclete convicts the world of sin because it does not believe in Jesus.

The fourth evangelist, unlike Matthew and Luke-Acts (or the deutero-Pauline letters), seems to have no interest in any organized institutional church. He mentions no church officials, and he normally refers simply to "the disciples." In fact, Peter's role (and the apostolic church related to him) is devalued in contrast to the role of the Beloved Disciple. The writer seems more concerned with all believers. As Christ is one with the Father and manifests his glory, so believers are one in Christ and manifest his glory (17:22–23). As God loved the world and gave his Son (3:16), so the Son loves his brothers and sisters, and they are to love one another (15:17). It would appear that John shares an important characteristic with apocalypticism in the Jesus Movement: His group's expulsion from the synagogue seems to have contributed to a sectarian, "free," antisociety.

Finally, the fourth evangelist does not lay emphasis on sacramental rites, either. True, as we saw earlier, there are hints of *possible* sacramental language (3:5: "water and"; eating flesh and drinking blood in 6:51–58). However, scholars do not agree about their meaning, and in any case they may be the product of a redactor in the Johannine School wishing to be more explicit about such matters. In summary, the major Johannine ideas may be stated: The world below has become dominated by sin so that God the Father in his love sends his preexistent Son, an alien Man from Heaven. He descends, works signs, reveals himself in revelatory discourses, undergoes a Passion, ascends, and reappears to his followers. His Spirit-Paraclete is an advocate and comforter of these believers who, without necessity of church structures and sacraments, already experience resurrection and eternal life now, in the present. As God loved the world and gave his Son, so his Son loved them, and so they are to love one another.

STRUCTURE AND PLOT OF THE GOSPEL OF JOHN

You will recall that the redaction critical approach attempts to determine the main emphases of a gospel writer and how that writer modifies and interprets traditions and sources. It also attempts to learn about the writer's intentions by the way the material as a whole is structured. Finding the structure is especially complicated in this particular instance, especially because of the many possible *aporias* noted earlier. Moreover, in a book as reflective and meditative in character as the Gospel of John, narrative consistency is not to be expected. Displacements within and sources behind the text only mildly affect general understanding, with a few exceptions, for example, the relation of the Signs Source to faith.

In this connection, a comment must be made about the "plot" of the gospel. The goal of the story is the glorification of Jesus at his "hour," a symbolic time when Jesus on the cross will be "lifted up," that is, will return to his Father. This theme is anticipated by Jesus' references to "the hour" ("My hour has not yet come" [2:4]; "an hour is coming . . ." [4:21, 23; 5:25, 28–29; 16:2, 25, 32] or "has come" [12:23; 17:1]; cf. 12:27; 13:1). Thus, although Jesus periodically faces opposition and misunderstanding by outsiders and others, ultimately he arrives at this goal.

Given the preceding analysis and due caution, the Gospel of John nonetheless falls naturally into five main parts:

1. Introduction: Prologue and testimony, 1:1–51
2. The "Book of Signs," 2:1–12:50
3. Farewell discourses and prayer for the church, 13:1–17:26
4. Passion narrative, 18:1–20:30
5. Epilogue: The appearance in Galilee, 21:1–25

Long ago C. H. Dodd observed that there is a characteristic Johannine pattern of narration. Usually it looks something like this:

Action → dialogue → monologue → appendix Here are some examples.

Action ("sign"): 5:1–9 (healing at Bethzatha)

Dialogue: 5:10–18 (Sabbath healing)

Monologue: 5:19–40

Appendix: 5:41–47

Or it can be, as in chapter 6:

Action ("sign") plus dialogue: 6:1–23 (feeding of the multitude)

Dialogue tending to monologue: 6:24–59 (bread of life)

Two brief concluding dialogues: 6:60–65, 66–71

Or it can be, as in chapters 9 and 10:

Action ("sign"): 9:1–7 (healing at Siloam)

Dialogue: 9:8–41 (trial scene and two brief colloquies)

Monologue: 10:1–18

Brief concluding dialogue: 10:19–21

Appendix: 10:22–39

The farewell discourses and prayer follow this pattern, except that in this instance we have the action, the Passion narrative, coming last and not first.

Opening dramatic scene: 13:1–30

Dialogue: 13:31–14:31 (on Christ's departure and return)

Monologue: 15:1–16:15 (on Christ and his church)

Concluding dialogue: 16:16–33

Appendix: 17:1–26 (the prayer for the church)

Action: 18:1–20:31 (the Passion narrative; anticipated in 13:1–3)

This is a very important structural observation. It, along with the preceding simplified outline, will be taken seriously in the following exegetical survey of the gospel.

EXEGETICAL SURVEY OF THE GOSPEL OF JOHN

Introduction: Prologue and Testimony, 1:1–51

Prologue, 1:1–18

The prologue consists of the famous Logos hymn (see Chapter Three) with comments. As reconstructed and translated by R. E. Brown, the hymn reads as follows:

> 1 In the beginning was the Word;
>   the Word was in God's presence,
>   and the Word was God.
> 2 He was present with God in the beginning.
> 3 Through him all things came into being,
>   and apart from him not a thing came to be.
> 4 That which had come to be in him was life,
>   and this life was the light of men.
> 5 The light shines in darkness,
>   for the darkness did not overcome it.
> 10 He was in the world,
>   and the world was made by him;
>   Yet the world did not recognize him.
> 11 To his own he came;
>   Yet his own people did not accept him.
> 12 But all those who did accept him
>   he empowered to become God's children.
> 14 And the Word became flesh
>   and made his dwelling among us.
>   And we have seen his glory,
>   the glory of an only Son coming from the Father,
>   filled with enduring love.
> 16 And of his fullness
>   we have all had a share—
>   love in place of love.

This reconstruction omits several verses that break up the formal pattern of the hymn. These verses refer to the testimony of John the Baptizer (verses 6–9), a reference to being born "of God" (verse 13), further testimony of the Baptizer (verse

15), and the evangelist's climactic summary (verses 17–18). The interruptions are important verses, and their ideas are further developed in the gospel (1:19–42 [testimony of the Baptizer]; 3:1–15, being born of God [the dialogue with Nicodemus]). Most scholars think that they are the evangelist's later insertion into the hymn. Similarly, verses 17–18, which are a summary of the whole gospel, also represent the evangelist's point of view. However, the remaining verses—the hymn itself—contain some ideas that are *not* characteristic of the rest of the gospel. Jesus as the Logos and the phrase "enduring love" (literally, "grace and truth") are never found in the gospel again—although the presentation of Jesus as the preexistent Redeemer who manifested his glory in the world matches well the major aspects of the gospel's presentation of Jesus. In its presentation of Jesus as the Redeemer who descends to the world the hymn shares the emphasis of the other Christological hymns discussed in Chapter One. In short, it is likely that the writer took over an early Christological hymn and modified it with some of his own themes.

The word *Logos,* "Word," is the key term in this hymn ("In the beginning was the Word. . . ."). Yet, the *Logos* as Rational Principle in the cosmos, known from ancient Greek philosophy, cannot be meant. Most recent scholars have therefore suggested that the *Logos* represents the "wisdom" and that the ancient Israelite **Wisdom myth** lies in the background. The theory is that the author of the hymn used *Logos,* which is masculine in gender, instead of "wisdom," which is feminine in gender in both Hebrew (*hōchma*) and Greek (*sophia*). In these Wisdom speculations Wisdom exists with God, descends, and ascends. Indeed, a version of the myth found in Ben Sira (ca. 180 B.C.E.) says that Wisdom "tented" among her people (24:8–10), like the moveable tabernacle shrine in the Hebrew Scriptures. This is the language of the famous verse 14, here translated by Brown, "made his dwelling." The first-century Israelite philosopher Philo of Alexandria identified this Wisdom with God's Word and Son. Perhaps such cosmological Wisdom speculation was known in the Johannine group.

Testimony, 1:19–51; 3:22–30

The theme of testimony, prominent in the comments on the hymn in the prologue, is now developed in relation to John the Baptizer (verses 19–34) and some of John's disciples who shift allegiance to Jesus (verses 35–51). Although Philip (verses 43–46) occurs in the disciple lists of the synoptics, he plays no role there, as he does here. Nathaniel (verses 45–51) is found in only in the Gospel of John (cf. 21:2). This chapter, with its "low Christology," is the source for Brown's idea that this section represents the earliest stage of the Johannine community. Originally, 3:22–30 followed 1:51. It has been (accidentally?) displaced.

The Book of Signs, 2:1–12:50

The first major section of the gospel, the Book of Signs, is built on the skeleton framework of seven "signs," or miracle stories, probably from a **Signs Source** (see earlier discussion). These seven "signs" are as follows:

Changing water into wine at Cana (2:1–11)

Healing the official's son at Cana (4:46–54)

Healing the lame man at Bethzatha (5:1–15)

Miraculous feeding in Galilee (6:1–15)

Walking on the "sea" (6:16–21)

Healing the blind man in Jerusalem (9)

Raising of Lazarus in Bethany (11)

In addition, there are three thematic concerns:

1. From Cana to Cana—Jesus manifests his glory in various ways and elicits various responses (2:1–4:42)

2. Jesus and the principal feasts of the Israelites (5:1–10:39)

3. Jesus moves toward the "hour" of his glorification (11:1–12:50)

    With help from C. H. Dodd's observations about patterns, here is an exegetical survey of the Book of Signs.

Manifestation and Response, 2:1–4:42

ACTION

    2:1–11:   *The first sign: The miracle at Cana.*   It is explicitly stated that this is the first of the signs through which Jesus manifested his glory and that it elicited the response of faith (verse 11). As previously observed, the view that miracles produce faith is very different from the synoptic approach to the miracle stories; there, faith precedes the miracle. This miracle does not occur in the synoptics. The symbolic "hour" (verse 4 and used six more times) is known from the scriptures and Hellenistic religions; here it points forward to Jesus' death and exaltation in glory (13:1; 17:1). Jesus' relationship with Mary is probably respectful but nevertheless distant (cf. Mark 3:31–35).

    2:12:   *Transition.*

    2:13–22:   *The anticipation of the final sign: The cleansing of the temple in Jerusalem.* In the synoptics, Jesus goes to Jerusalem only once, and the "cleansing of the temple" scene occurs at that time and thus near the end of the story (Mark 11:15–19). In John, however, Jesus makes several trips to Jerusalem. The cleansing is not a sign, but it anticipates the climactic sign, the resurrection. In turn, the resurrection elicits the response of faith (verse 22).

    2:23–25:   *Transitional summary.*

DIALOGUE

    3:1–15:   *Jesus and Nicodemus.*   The notion of spiritual rebirth was common in ancient religions. It is used of proselytes to Judaism (*b. Yebamoth* 48B). It is characteristic of the mystery religions, an example being the so-called Mithras Liturgy:

O Lord, while being born again, I am passing away;
While growing and having grown, I am dying;
While being born from a life-generating birth,
    I am passing on, released to death—
as you have founded,

as you have decreed,
and have established the mystery.

(from A Mithras Liturgy; trans. M. Meyer)

Spiritual rebirth is a major theme among the Gnostics as well (see Chapter One).

The Johannine author develops rebirth by the use of irony. As noted earlier in relation to antilanguage, the dialogue is built around double entendres, that is, words with double meanings. In 3:3, Jesus says that one must be "born *anōthen*," that is, either "born from above" (Jesus' place of origin) or "born anew," in the sense of spiritual rebirth, or being "born again." The Pharisee Nicodemus, however, takes it literally. The Johannine Jesus then explains its spiritual meaning with a second double entendre because the word *pneuma* can mean either "wind" or "spirit." Like the invisible "wind," to be born *anōthen* also means to be born "*of the Spirit.*" Then he goes on to speak of the Son of Man who descends from *above*, from heaven. This Son of Man saying (verses 14–15) is not the synoptic apocalyptic version, but the Johannine "Man from Heaven," and it contains the symbolism of Jesus' being "lifted up" on the cross (verse 14). There is no explicit reference to baptism in the passage, but verse 5 hints at baptism when it speaks of being born "*of water and* the Spirit." Because the passage otherwise speaks only of the Spirit, did a later redactor add this "sacramental" interpretation (so Bultmann)? For a dialogue on "living water," see 4:7–21, and for the view that Jesus did not baptize, see 4:2.

MONOLOGUE

3:16–21:   *The power of the Son to give eternal life to the believer.*   John 3:16, one of the most famous verses in the New Testament, is a development of the theme of the Son's power to give eternal life to the believer, stated in the preceding verse. Traditional eschatology oriented more to the future has now been replaced by an eschatology paradoxically realized in the present (realized eschatology), a major Johannine theme: "This is the judgment . . ." (verse 19). The farewell discourses parallel the same theme (12:46–48), where, however, the more traditional eschatology has been restored ("the word that I have spoken will be his judge on the last day," 12:48).

3:31–36:   *A displaced section of monologue.*   John 3:22–30 seems originally to have belonged after 1:51. But what about 3:31–36, obviously part of a monologue by the Johannine Jesus on the theme of witness, testimony, and belief? It does not fit well after 3:21; it fits better after 3:15.

ACTION

4:1–6:   *Jesus moves to Samaria.*

DIALOGUE

4:7–21:   *Jesus with the woman at the well.*   Irony and symbolism pervade the dialogue, which turns on two themes: "living water" and worship "in spirit and truth." Water is a symbol with many meanings (a condensed symbol), for example, cleansing and purity, baptism, resurrection, and new life. Worship is a universal religious practice. The Johannine writer develops them dualistically by contrasting "this" water/false worship and "living" water/true worship. In another reference to the symbolic "hour" (verse 21; cf. 13:1; 17:1), the Johannine Jesus stresses that God is a spirit and will finally be worshipped spiritually, on *no* holy mountain—either the sacred mountain in Jerusalem (Mount Zion) or the sacred mountain of the Samaritans in Samaria (Mount Gerizîm). Purity is spiritual. Compare criticism of temple worship in Acts 7:44–50, implied in 1 Cor. 3:16–17, 6:19, and Heb. 8:5–7.

MONOLOGUE

4:22–26:   *The coming of the true worship.*   The second theme of the dialogue now develops in a short but characteristic monologue. It is significant that Jesus reveals himself as the Messiah to the strange Samaritan woman in the first "I AM" saying (4:25–26). The messianic hope for a "prophet like Moses" (3:6; 4:12) is derived from Deut. 18:15. It is found in the expectations of the **Dead Sea Scrolls.** The Samaritans called the prophet like Moses the *Taheb* (see the *Memar Marqah*). The "living water" theme will come up later.

APPENDIX

4:27–42:   *Further dialogue and testimony in Samaria.*   As a result of the woman's witness, the Samaritans accept Jesus as "Savior of the world" (4:41–42).

4:43–45:   *Transition to Galilee.*

4:46–54:   *The second sign: The official's son in Capernaum.*   In Cana, Jesus heals an official's son from a distance. A variant of this miracle is found in **Q** (Matt. 8:5–13; Luke 7:1–10). In the Gospel of John, this second sign in Cana marks the end of the first section of the Book of Signs.

Jesus and the Israelite Festivals, 5:1–10:39

The second section of the Book of Signs explores the significance of Jesus as understood in the symbolism and meaning of the great Israelite religious festivals and observances.

5:1–47:   *Jesus and the Sabbath.*   The Sabbath is a weekly observance, a sacred time built on Gen. 2:3: "So God blessed the seventh day and hallowed it, because on it God rested from all his work, which he had done in creation." The Israelites observed, and Jews still observe, this sacred day of the week by refraining from secular work, thus linking themselves ever more closely with God. Sabbath day observance led to the legal question of what was to be considered work, which is the background for many synoptic controversy stories. In the Fourth Gospel, however, this aspect of controversy has been transformed into a meditation on the fact that Jesus "works" as God "works," to give life to the dead and to judge.

5:1:   *Transitional verse.*   This verse speaks of a feast, that is, a religious festival, but the term is used broadly because the concern is not with an annual religious observance but rather with the Sabbath.

ACTION

5:2–9:   *Jesus heals a lame man at Bethzatha on the Sabbath.*   This is Jesus' third sign. The exact word parallelism between the command to this paralytic (5:8) and the command to a paralytic in Capernaum in Mark 2:9 is striking; it is one of the bases for arguing that John knew the Gospel of Mark (see Mark 2:1–12). All the miracle stories in the Book of Signs have been so transformed into vehicles for meditation on the significance of Jesus for the believer that historical questions about them are all but impossible to answer.

DIALOGUE

5:10–18:   *A series of dialogues between the Israelites, the man, and Jesus.*   By means of these dialogues, the evangelist introduces the theme of the relationship between Jesus and God. Jesus is the Son of the Father and equal with God.

MONOLOGUE

5:19–47:   *Jesus' relation to God.*   This monologue explores the relationship of Jesus and God. Jesus is the Son of God, and as such his actions are identical with those of God: He judges, and he gives life to the dead.

6:1–71:   *Jesus and the Passover.*   The **Passover** is another sacred time, eight days celebrating the deliverance of the Israelites from Egypt. It is observed annually and includes a meal in which the food eaten and the wine drunk symbolize this deliverance and anticipate the final deliverance. In the synoptics, Jesus' last meal is a Passover meal, and some other forms of the Jesus Movement use much of the same symbolism. In the Gospel of John, Jesus' last meal is the night *before* Passover (19:31). Nonetheless, the evangelist explores the significance of Jesus in terms of Passover and eucharistic symbols.

ACTION

6:1–14:   *The feeding of the multitude.*   This is Jesus' fourth sign, which has parallels in the synoptic gospels (e.g., Mark 6:32–44; 8:1–10).

6:15:   *Transitional verse.*

6:16–21:   *The walking on the water.*   This is Jesus' fifth sign. The fourth and fifth signs, a miraculous feeding and a sea miracle, are in Mark in exactly the same sequence: Mark 6:30–44 (feeding); 6:45–51 (walking on the water). In John's gospel, both have parallels in the narrative of the deliverance from Egypt: The Israelites miraculously crossed the sea (Exod. 14:21–25) and were equally miraculously fed in the wilderness (Exod. 16:13–16, "He gave them bread from heaven to eat" [6:31]. In Exod. 16:31, this bread is called *manna.*).

DIALOGUE

6:22–34:   *A dialogue between Jesus and the Israelites on the bread that God gives to humans.*   John follows his usual pattern of beginning with a dialogue that turns into a monologue. The theme is the "bread of life." It evokes the manna that fed the Israelites in the wilderness and the bread of the Eucharist.

MONOLOGUE

6:35–40:   *Jesus as the bread of life.*

DIALOGUE

6:41–59:   *The bread of life is the flesh of Jesus, the bread of the Eucharist.*   The theme of Jesus as the "bread of life" is developed in a monologue, which in turn is followed by a dramatic dialogue. The manna that the Israelites ate in the wilderness is transformed into a symbol of the life-giving power of God to his people, which is now fulfilled forever in Jesus. The life-giving power of Jesus is in turn symbolized in the bread of the Eucharist.

APPENDIX

6:60–70:   *Jesus and his disciples.*   In its theme, this passage is strikingly reminiscent of the misunderstanding and confession in Mark 8:14–21.

7:1–13:   *Transition to the Feast of Booths.*   Jesus is now to be considered in light of the symbolism of a further major Israelite festival, the Feast of Booths.

Jesus and the Feast of Booths, 7:14–10:21

The Feast of Booths, a seven-day pilgrim festival named for the huts in which grape pickers lived during the grape harvest, was held at the end of the agricultural season in the autumn (see Chapter One). It was originally an agricultural festival celebrating the vintage harvest, but in the course of time it came also to celebrate the wilderness wanderings (Lev. 23:43) and the constant renewal of the covenant between God and his people. This latter fact makes it natural to take up here the theme of Jesus as the one who fulfills the old covenant as the Israelite Messiah. So in this section the evangelist explores the messianic claims of Jesus and also makes extensive use of the literary device of dramatic dialogues between Jesus and his Israelite opponents about those claims.

ACTION

7:14:   *Jesus in the temple during the Feast of Booths.*

DIALOGUE

7:15–36:   *The claim of Jesus to be the Christ.*   This is a series of three dramatic dialogues. The first (verses 15–24) concerns the authority of Jesus to heal on the Sabbath; the second (verses 25–31) deals with the claim of Jesus to be the Christ by the signs he has done; the third (verses 32–36) introduces the theme of the death of Jesus. This last will loom larger and larger from this point on in the gospel, until it dominates everything else as the theme of the farewell discourses.

ACTION

7:37–39: *Jesus makes a personal claim to be the Living Water.* At the Feast of Booths in Jerusalem, water was ceremoniously carried from the Pool of Siloam to the temple as a reminder of the water miraculously supplied in the wilderness (Num. 20:2–13) and as a symbol of the coming of the Messiah as the "water of life" (Isa. 12:3). The evangelist has the opportunity to return to the theme of Jesus as the water of life, which he had first stated in the dialogue between Jesus and the woman of Samaria in John 4.

DIALOGUE

7:40–52: *The Israelites dispute among themselves concerning the claim of Jesus to be the Messiah descended from David.* Unlike the previous dialogues, these do not feature Jesus at all but rather present the Israelites in dispute among themselves concerning the validity of his claims.

(The adulteress story, 7:53–8:11, is not part of the original text of the gospel.)

ACTION

8:12: *Jesus makes a personal claim to be the Light of the World.* A further feature of the symbolism of the Feast of Booths was the ceremonious lighting of lamps in the temple court. The evangelist can return to the theme of Jesus as the "Light of the World," a theme first stated in the prologue (1:4–5, 9).

DIALOGUE

8:13–20: *The validity of Jesus' claims.* The Israelites are presented as disputing with Jesus the validity of the claims he is making. This dialogue concludes on a further note of anticipation of the Passion (verse 20).

ACTION

8:21: *Jesus condemns the Israelites.* The theme of the death of Jesus understood as his going where he cannot be followed (i.e., back to the heavenly region he came from) is developed at length in the farewell discourses (13:31–14:7). Here is its first statement in the context of a condemnation of the Israelites (NRSV: "the Jews"), who cannot follow him. Later the disciples are promised that they will be able to be with him (cf. 13:36; 14:1–3).

DIALOGUE

8:22–30: *Jesus and the Israelites who do not believe in him.* Jesus is here presented as debating vigorously with, and condemning, the Israelites who did not believe in him.

ACTION

8:31–32: *Jesus and the Israelites who did believe in him.* Jesus is now presented as making promises to the Israelites who did believe in him.

DIALOGUE

8:33–59:   *Jesus and the natural claims of the Israelites on God.*   This dialogue begins with the Israelites who did believe in Jesus and ends with those same Israelites taking up stones to throw at him. Here the evangelist is wrestling with the problem of the Israelite rejection of Jesus. Jesus himself had some success in his mission to the Israelite people—he had attracted disciples—yet the Israelite leaders had finally engineered his crucifixion. Similarly, the members of the Jesus Movement had some success in their mission to the Israelites, especially among the Greek-speaking Israelites of the **Diaspora,** yet the Israelites at Yavneh had finally produced the benediction that drove the Israelites who believed that Jesus was the Messiah out of the Israelite community. The evangelist anguishes over this tragic pattern in the literary form of a dialogue between Jesus and his Israelite contemporaries.

ACTION

9:1–7:   *Jesus gives sight to a man born blind.*   This is Jesus' sixth sign. Continuing the theme of Jesus as the Light of the World, the evangelist now presents an account of Jesus giving sight to a man born blind, a typical example of folk healing.

DIALOGUE(S)

9:8–41:   *The fate of Jesus and his followers in the Israelite community.*   What is at issue here in this series of dialogues is the fate of Jesus and his followers in the Israelite community.

The first dialogue is between the previously blind man and his neighbors (verses 8–12). It reflects the original impact of Jesus on his Israelite contemporaries and the questions to which it gave rise.

The second dialogue is between the man and the Pharisees (verses 13–17). Here the Pharisees represent not only the Israelite authorities who finally condemned Jesus, but also perhaps those Pharisees at Yavneh who produced the **Prayer against the Heretics** (see the discussion earlier). Perhaps it was this prayer that made it uncomfortable for the Israelites who had beliefs about Jesus of the Johannine type to remain in the synagogue. Perhaps the ban is implied in this passage.

The third dialogue is between the Israelites and the man's parents (verses 18–23). It reflects the problems and divisions within the Israelite community produced by Christology. As we indicated, verse 22 might refer to the ban.

The fourth dialogue concerns the man himself and his fate at the hands of the Israelite authorities (verses 24–34). It reflects the fate of the Israelite convert to the Jesus Movement as the evangelist knows it, perhaps even the fate of the evangelist himself.

The fifth dialogue mirrors the further fate of the man who, now banned by the Israelite community, finds his new home in the community of those who come to faith in Jesus (verses 35–41). The members of this antisociety reject the community out of which they came, as they reject "the world" (see earlier discussion). These dialogues perhaps reveal the actual situation of the evangelist and his readers/hearers, just as Mark 13 revealed the situation of the evangelist Mark and his readers/hearers.

CONCLUDING MONOLOGUE

10:1–18: *Jesus as the shepherd and the sheepgate.*   The evangelist closes this section with a monologue and a dialogue on the messianic claims of Jesus and the response of the Israelites. The monologue concerns Jesus as the shepherd and the sheepgate. The discourse is an involved allegory in which various images on the care of sheep appear in connection with Jesus. In verses 1–6, Jesus is the shepherd responsible for the sheep and to whom the sheep are responsive. In verses 7–10, he is the gate through which sheep enter and leave their fold. Verses 11–15 introduce the theme of Jesus as the good shepherd prepared to die for his sheep, and Jesus is contrasted in this respect with other shepherds. Finally, in verses 16–18 Jesus refers to "other sheep"; some scholars think that these may be the Gentiles. In any case, the shepherd lays down his life for his flock.

CONCLUDING DIALOGUE

10:19–21:   *The Israelites disagree with the claims of Jesus.*   The section concludes with a dialogue on the varied responses of the Israelites (NRSV: "the Jews") to Jesus. This dialogue probably reflects the experience of the evangelist as he affiliated with the Jesus Movement.

10:22–39:   *Jesus and the Feast of Dedication.*   The term "dedication" translates the Hebrew word *hanukkah*. The **Feast of Hanukkah** celebrated the rededication of the temple in 164 B.C.E. after its desecration by Antiochus IV Epiphanes, who erected an altar to the Greek god Zeus in the Jerusalem temple (see Chapter One). This is the "**abomination that makes desolate**" to which such frequent reference is made in apocalyptic texts (e.g., Mark 13:14). Because the festival celebrated a major victory of the people of God against their enemies and was seen as a renewal of the covenant between God and his people, it becomes a suitable occasion for the evangelist to return to his theme of the messianic claims of Jesus.

ACTION

10:22–23:   *Jesus at the Feast of Dedication.*

DIALOGUE

10:24–39:   *The climactic claims of Jesus and the response of the Israelites to them.*   In this dialogue the evangelist presents Jesus as summarizing the claims he has already made for himself. He is the shepherd and the giver of life; he and the Father are one. At the same time a new note is introduced in accordance with the symbolism of the rededication of the temple, which lies behind the Feast of Dedication: Jesus is the one consecrated by God and sent into the world (verse 36). Similarly, the negative response of the Israelites is also summarized and presented as reaching a climax. The Israelites attempt to stone Jesus (verse 31) as they had before in 8:59; they also attempt to arrest him (verse 39) as they had before in 7:30, 32, 44; 8:20. Do these events represent fear of local persecutions in the Johannine community?

Transition: The End of the Public Ministry of Jesus, 10:40–42

The evangelist is now directing attention to the cross. The last section of his Book of Signs deals with the meaning of the death of Jesus. So this transitional passage marks the end of the public ministry of Jesus; from this point forward the writer is concerned only with the death of Jesus and its meaning. However, the evangelist thinks in a spiral manner. We pointed out that the first part of the Book of Signs began and ended in Cana. Similarly, Jesus appeared on the scene for the first time in this gospel at the place where John was baptizing (1:29–34), and his public ministry must end at that same place, as it does in these transitional verses.

Jesus Moves toward the Hour of His Glorification, 11:1–12:50

This is the last section of the Book of Signs. Jesus is still presented as working and teaching in public, but in the mind of the evangelist the public ministry is over, and now the cross dominates everything. In this section, therefore, the evangelist begins the meditation on the death of Jesus and its meaning.

ACTION

11:1–44:   *The raising of Lazarus.*   This is Jesus' seventh and last sign in chapters 1–20. For the reader who comes to the Gospel of John after a reading of the synoptics, this miracle is most startling. It is a major miracle of Jesus about which the synoptic gospels appear to know nothing. (If the *Secret Gospel of Mark* exists, there is a parallel to the Lazarus story there, and the Martha and Mary of this story appear also in Luke 10:38–42, where, however, there is absolutely no mention of Lazarus.) The historical problems in connection with the story are all but insurmountable. Most scholars suggest that the evangelist John is meditating upon a Jesus Movement tradition otherwise lost to us. At this level the story comes alive as a dramatic presentation of Jesus as the resurrection and the life to those who believe in him. Note Martha's full confession of faith, probably representing true Johannine believers.

REACTION

11:45–53:   *The Israelite authorities condemn Jesus to death.*   The normal pattern of the Johannine literary construction is shattered by the nearness of the cross. So here we have the reaction of the Israelite authorities to the raising of Lazarus rather than the dialogue and monologue that would normally follow the action.

11:54–57:   *Transition: Will Jesus come to Jerusalem for the Passover?*   The evangelist dramatically heightens the tension of his narrative in this transitional section.

ACTION

12:1–8:   *The anointing at Bethany.*   This has a parallel in Mark 14:3–9, which in turn is related to Luke 7:36–38, the anointing of Jesus by the disreputable woman in Galilee (see preceding source analysis). In the Gospel of John, as in Mark, the anointing anticipates the burial of Jesus. Jesus defends Mary's actions.

12:9–11:   *Transition: The tension in Jerusalem heightens.*

ACTION

12:12–19: *Jesus enters Jerusalem in triumph.* This parallels the synoptic gospel accounts of the same incident (Mark 11:1–10; Matt. 21:1–9; Luke 19:28–38). In John, however, the incident is interpreted as an anticipation of Jesus' glorification (verse 16).

ACTION

12:20–22: *The Greeks come to Jesus.* The evangelist has been concerned thus far in his story with Jesus and the Israelites, which perhaps reflects his personal position as an Israelite who joined the Jesus Movement. However, now he turns to Jesus and the Greeks in an incident referring to his being a Christ believer in a Greek city and preaching the gospel to Greeks.

DIALOGUE

12:23–36: *The meaning of the cross.* The evangelist now returns to his favorite literary device and explores the meaning of the cross in dialogue between Jesus and the voice from heaven and between Jesus and the crowd.

12:37–50: *The ending of the Book of Signs.* The evangelist brings his Book of Signs to an end with a summary of the meaning of the signs of Jesus, meditating on their meeting with the reactions of both nonbelief and belief.

Farewell Discourses and Prayer for the Church, 13:1–17:26

In this third major section of the gospel the evangelist explores the meaning of Christ for the believer in a series of discourses and a prayer by Jesus at the Last Supper. Some scholars think that they may have originated as a series of meditations at the celebration of the Eucharist.

OPENING DRAMATIC SCENE

13:1–30: *The Last Supper.* Last Supper narratives are also found in 1 Cor. 11:23–26; Mark 14:17–25; Matt. 26:20–29; Luke 22:14–38. Unlike the synoptic Last Supper, the meal is not a Passover meal. Moreover, the fourth evangelist includes the incident of foot washing and omits the "Eucharistic words," or words of interpretation spoken by Jesus over the bread or the wine. With respect to the latter, we have no idea why they are missing. Earlier it was suggested that the evangelist seemed to have no concern for the sacraments and puts his emphasis elsewhere ("spiritual" water and bread). Did he omit them because of this general trend? Did he regard them as linked with the Passover meal even though Jesus and the disciples did not celebrate it? These words were especially sacred to believers in other circles. Did the evangelist regard this aspect of the narrative as *too* sacred to be written down?

The matter of the washing of the feet lends itself more readily to an explanation. The evangelist casts his thought in the imagery of incident and dramatic dialogue. He dramatizes the sacrifice of Jesus and its significance by means of an acted parable of humility and service, like a slave. The humility of the action is the more striking in light of the evangelist's concentration on the Passion of Jesus as his glorification. This section contains the first reference to the disciple whom Jesus loved (Beloved Disciple) who "was reclining next to him" (13:23, 25). There are five references to the Beloved Disciple. In 13:23–26, the disciple whom Jesus loved is intimately close to Jesus at the Last Supper. In 19:25–27, Jesus from the cross commits his mother to the care of the Beloved Disciple. In 21:7, "that disciple whom Jesus loved" recognizes the resurrected Jesus, and in 21:20–23, there is a dialogue between the risen Jesus and Peter about "the disciple whom Jesus loved, who had reclined next to Jesus at the supper." Finally, in 21:24, this disciple is identified as the ultimate source for the tradition in the Gospel of John: "This is the disciple who is testifying to these things, and who has written them, and we know that his testimony is true." See preceding for further interpretation about his identity and importance for the Johannine community.

13:31–14:31:   *Christ's departure and return.*   In this dialogue between Jesus and his disciples, the evangelist explores the glory of the relationship between the believer and the glorified Christ. 14:31, "Rise, let us be on our way," is one of the more obvious *aporias* noted earlier; they do not depart until 18:1.

MONOLOGUE

15:1–16:15:   *Christ and the believer.*   The evangelist now turns to the pattern of the believer's life in the world. The believer *abides* in Jesus (15:1–11); he enters into a relationship of *love* with the fellow believer (15:12–17); and he *separates* himself from the world (15:18–27). This section also introduces a particular Johannine conception: the *paraklētos,* the Paraclete (15:26: RSV, "Counselor"; NEB and NRSV, "Advocate"; TEV, "Helper"). In John's thinking it represents the thought that the risen Lord is spiritually present to the believer.

DIALOGUE

16:16–33:   *Jesus and his disciples.*   Turning now from monologue to dialogue, the evangelist explores the relationship of the risen Lord with those who believe in him. As is uniformly the case in these discourses, the Lord who speaks is the Jesus who died and rose again from the dead, who came from the Father and returned to him, and whose mysterious presence can now be known by the believer in the world.

MONOLOGUE

17:1–26:   *Christ's prayer for his church.*   This is the evangelist's climactic statement of the significance of Jesus for the believer. It falls naturally into three parts. In part 1 (verses 1–5), the prayer is concerned with Jesus himself, with his death as his glorification, and with his power to give eternal life to those who believe in him. In part 2 (verses 6–19), the thought turns to the believer who is still in the world. Jesus is now glorified, but the believer still has to live out his life in the world and to represent Christ in the world. Finally, part 3 (verses 20–26) considers the corporate body of believers, and the prayer is that they may know the in-dwelling love of God as it fulfills its mission in the world of leading that world to belief in God.

The Passion Narrative, 18:1–20:31

The fourth major section of the Gospel of John is the Passion narrative. In general, John covers the same ground as the synoptic gospels. Parallels between John and Mark, and a few between John and Luke, have already been noted. Theories of sources and gospel interrelationships abound. Yet, no one doubts that the narrative in John has its own particular emphases. First, there is a stronger pro-Gentile slant, that is, only the Israelites are presented as the villains of the plot, whereas Pilate is portrayed as sympathetic to Jesus and interested in his welfare. Second, the Jesus of the Johannine Passion narrative is not merely a victim, but also a sovereign figure, a superhuman being who could, if he wished, cause the whole process to cease.

18:1–11 (cf. Mark 14:32–48): *The betrayal in the garden.*   See 14:31. John omits any reference to the prayer of Jesus, perhaps because he has just completed Jesus' great prayer.

18:12–27 (cf. Mark 14:53–72): *Jesus before the high priest and Peter's denial.*   The narrative has the same structure as Mark, even to the extent of intercalating the trial scene into the account of the denial by Peter. Did they share a common source, or had he once read Mark (see preceding)? However, compared with the Markan narrative there are some new elements. There is the informal appearance before Annas (18:12–14), which has the effect of bringing Jesus before *two* high priests: "then the high priest questioned Jesus . . ." (verse 19) and "Annas then sent him bound to Caiaphas the high priest" (verse 24). The historical evidence suggests that Annas was deposed from the high priesthood by the Romans in 15 C.E. However, he remained enormously influential, and it may well have been that the Israelites continued to grant him the courtesy of the title, if only as a protest against the Roman power to appoint and depose the high priest. It may be that John has access to a tradition about the appearance of Jesus before Israelite authorities that is otherwise lost. At the same time, however, it is obvious from the comment in verse 14 that John's interest is in the symbolic significance of the high priest as the chief representative of the people before God. With dramatic irony he puts on the lips of Caiaphas the key to understanding the meaning of the death of Jesus. Another new element in the Johannine narrative is the appearance of "another disciple" who was known to the high priest (verses 15–16). Note that he appears again in 20:2–10, where Mary Magdalene runs to Peter "and the other disciple" to tell them that Jesus' body is not in the tomb. In that context the "other disciple" is identified as "the one whom Jesus loved" (20:2; cf. 13:23 and preceding discussion).

18:28–19:16 (cf. Mark 15:1–15): *Jesus before Pilate.*   This narrative portrays Pilate as a sympathetic figure earnestly interested in Jesus' welfare and the Israelites as the real villains of the plot. One gets a very strong impression that the author is himself an Israelite reacting bitterly to the treatment of Jesus by his own people. The bitter note of rejection in John 19:15 is an echo of that found in Matthew's gospel (Matt. 27:25). There is no evidence that John knows the Gospel of Matthew; probably both John and Matthew react equally strongly to a situation in which they feel themselves, as Israelites, personally involved.

19:17–37 (cf. Mark 15:22–41 and Luke 23:33–49): *The crucifixion.*   This narrative is close to Mark's with the exception of the mention of "the disciple whom he loved," who is entrusted with Jesus' mother and the reference to the giving up of the spirit (verse 30), which is reminiscent of Luke 23:46.

19:38–42 (cf. Mark 15:42–47): *The burial.*   All the gospels stress the role of Joseph of Arimathea in the burial of Jesus (Mark 15:43; Matt. 27:57; Luke 23:50), but John is alone in introducing the figure of Nicodemus, whom he carefully identifies as the one who had come to Jesus by night (verse 39; cf. 3:1–15; 7:50–52).

20:1–10 (cf. Mark 16:1–8): *The discovery of the empty tomb.*   All the gospel narratives diverge dramatically after the point at which Mark ends: the discovery of the empty tomb and the astonishment of the women. In Matthew, the women run to tell the disciples and are met by the risen Jesus on the way (Matt. 28:9–10); then the risen Lord appears to the disciples in Galilee. In Luke, the women tell of their discovery of the empty tomb, but they are not believed until a series of resurrection appearances in and around Jerusalem convinces the disciples that "The Lord has risen indeed" (Luke 24:34). In John's gospel, Mary Magdalene tells Peter and the "other disciple" of the empty tomb, and Jesus appears to her and to the disciples both in Jerusalem (20:19–23, 26–29) and in Galilee (21:1–14).

20:11–18:   *The appearance to Mary Magdalene.*   The Gospel of John puts a major emphasis on the mysterious presence of Jesus with the believer, which is typical of ASC experiences. Both in 6:62–63 and 16:7 the evangelist emphasizes the return of Jesus to the sky from which he came and the consequent possibility of his presence with the believer. Here he returns to this note in the story of the appearance to Mary Magdalene as Jesus tells her that he is about to ascend to the Father. That will make possible his presence with the believer, and the promise of that presence is the point of the next story.

20:19–23:   *The appearance to the disciples as a group.*   The evangelist dramatizes the possibility of the mysterious presence of Christ with the believer through this story of the risen Lord appearing to his disciples and breathing on them. Both in Hebrew and Greek the word for *spirit* is the same as the word for *breath* (see 3:8).

20:24–29:   *The appearance to Thomas.*   Thomas traditions and gospels have been discussed in Chapter Three. In this Thomas story the evangelist brings his gospel to a climax by dramatizing doubt so as to highlight the possibility of belief. Thomas' coming to faith becomes a model for everyone everywhere to reach the point of saying to the risen Jesus, "My Lord and my God" (20:28), a saying that contains honorific titles also known in the emperor cult.

20:30–31:   *The purpose of the gospel.*   The evangelist climaxes his work with a statement of its purpose: to bring the reader to belief in Jesus and to the life that belief makes possible. The natural conclusion to the gospel is in verse 21.

Epilogue: The Appearance in Galilee, 21:1–23

Another writer, presumably of the Johannine School, has added Chapter 21 as an epilogue. The language is not quite the same as the evangelist's; yet the epilogue certainly echoes his concerns. It emphasizes the role of Peter, it uses the imagery of shepherd and sheep, and it features the Beloved Disciple. In some respects it is like the prologue to the gospel (1:1–18), which also shares the concerns of the gospel and yet at the same time differs in language from the text of the gospel itself. R. E. Brown makes the interesting suggestion that both the prologue and the epilogue may have been added to the main text of the gospel by the same redactor.

The author stresses four important matters in the epilogue. First, he knows a tradition of a resurrection appearance to the disciples in Galilee as they were fishing, and he preserves it as a supplement to the accounts of the appearances in Jerusalem (verses 1–8). Second, he has an interest in the community's sacred meal, and he presents here an account of a meal between the risen Lord and his disciples (verses 9–14), which echoes the Eucharist (Jesus takes the bread and gives it to the disciples in a solemn manner, verse 13). Third, there is the restoration of Peter after his denial of Jesus (verses 15–19). The Gospel of Mark already hinted at the restoration of Peter and a resurrection appearance to him: "But go, tell his disciples *and Peter* that he is going ahead of you to Galilee; there you will see him. . . ." (Mark 16:7). The epilogue to the Gospel of John develops the theme further. Finally, the "disciple whom Jesus loved" is identified as the ultimate "author" of the gospel—or at least its ultimate source. Is this disciple a historical or an ideal figure?

THE FIRST LETTER OF JOHN

Discussions about 1 John already made at various places in this chapter need to be brought together. Although there are many similarities with the gospel—for example, its spiral structure and its dualism—it is probably not from the same author as John 1–20. We have noted its more limited vocabulary and style and some differences of thought—for example, eschatology and the sacraments—as compared to the gospel. Yet, it is also possible that the author of 1 John redacted the main text of the gospel, especially in the case of chapter 21.

A few points need to be emphasized. The author of 1 John does not mention his name (or a name with a title). A probable date will be a few years after the gospel (ca. 100–110 C.E.?), the major reason being that the attention has shifted from *external* opponents ("the world"; "the Israelites") to false teachers *within* the community. What do they teach? Mainly a view of Jesus that denies that he is the Christ, the Son of God (2:22–23), and especially *that he came "in the flesh"* (4:2–3), a view that, the author is convinced, resulted in immoral behavior. How might this supposed false teaching have arisen?

In the Christology of the Gospel of John, Jesus as the Son of God comes into the world to empower and "glorify" those who accept him. This Christology contains dualism, that is, the contrast between above and below, light and dark, good and evil, the spirit and the flesh, and the like. Members of the Jesus Movement who held dualistic views like those in the gospel could also have held the view that "the world" and "the flesh" are essentially evil. If so, how could the Man from Heaven have come "in the flesh," that is, have taken the form of real, evil matter? Some concluded that he maintained his heavenly nature and only seemed to be in the flesh, or human, as in an ASC. After all, such experiences were really real. Indeed, his continuing mysterious presence with them was the way it had always been. This way of thinking was common in the larger Mediterranean world, and it was especially characteristic of Gnosticism. Gnostics also claimed that Jesus was mysteriously present to them; they also had experiences. However, many other members of the Jesus Movement could not accept the further tendency to deny that Jesus had once had a physical presence as well. They rejected the view that Jesus had only *seemed* to be physically present. Later they labeled it "docetism" (Greek *dokeō:* "I seem") and considered it to be "heresy." Clearly, a schism over true and false views of Jesus arose within the Johannine wing of the Jesus Movement. For the author of 1 John, the "docetic" view of the Man from Heaven led to moral deviance: disobeying the commandments, hating one's brother, and telling lies.

Formally, 1 John is not so much a letter as it is an ideological tract or sermon. It is written with obvious love and concern for the spiritual welfare of its recipients. Some scholars have supposed that there is also a source behind 1 John and have tried to reconstruct it. Here it will suffice to take 1 John as it is and outline it on the basis of alternating declarations and exhortations:

1:1–4: *Declaration.* The eternal life has been made manifest through the Son.

1:5–2:17: *Exhortation.* Right behavior is walking according to the light and keeping the commandments. It depends on true knowledge of God and renunciation of the world.

2:18–27: *Declaration.* True knowledge of God depends on recognizing that Jesus is the true and only Son of God. He rewards with eternal life those who abide in him now. The dissidents are those who deny Jesus in the flesh; they are deceivers (2:26).

2:28–3:24: *Exhortation.* Those who abide in him now and exhibit the love of one another that naturally flows from that relationship avoid sin and have no need to fear his *parousia*.

4:1–6: *Declaration.* Jesus Christ actually came in the flesh as the Son of God; those who do not believe this belong to the world or to the spirit of the Antichrist.

4:7–5:5: *Exhortation.* To abide in God is to be "of God," and to be "of God" is to exhibit love in the world. "We love because he first loved us" (4:19).

5:6–12: *Declaration.* Jesus Christ is the Son of God, and acceptance of him is the means to eternal life.

THE SECOND AND THIRD LETTERS OF JOHN

In contrast to 1 John, 2 and 3 John are true letters. They were written by a member of the Johannine School who calls himself the "Presbyter" or "Elder" (Greek *presbyteros*). About 100 C.E. this term was coming to refer to a specific office in the church (1 Tim. 5:17: "Let the elders who rule well. . . ."). Probably, then, the author calls himself by such a title used in the Johannine community.

One interesting question is the kind and extent of authority the author exercises over the churches to which he writes. It seems to have been moral or even spiritual rather than formal (cf. 3 John 9–12). If so, this fact, together with the very nature of the gospel and letters of John themselves, suggests that the writer's authority may have come from his role and function as a preacher in the Johannine community. Perhaps, then, he was a much-loved leader of worship in the Johannine wing of the Jesus Movement. He celebrates the Eucharist and attempts to extend his influence into matters of belief and organization.

The second letter of John is notable for its reference to Johannine groups as "the elect lady" and the "elect sister" and to the members of these communities as "her children" (2 John 1, 13). The letter also continues the theme of loving one another and the argument against docetism (2 John 7–11).

The third letter of John is a letter from "the Elder" (Greek *presbyteros*) to a certain Gaius commending him for his earlier hospitality. The author recommends that Gaius now receive Demetrius in hospitality. (Possibly Demetrius also brought the letter.) It clearly implies that a certain Diotrephes has refused such hospitality for the presbyter's emissaries. In the letter the Elder attempts to exert his moral or spiritual authority (3 John 13; cf. 2 John 12). A natural inference is that Diotrephes has seen the Elder as a threat to his local authority. Did Diotrephes also hold docetic views? The letter also testifies that members of the Jesus Movement should recognize that they have a definite responsibility to receive members of the Jesus Movement who come to them from another place (3 John 5–8). This **hospitality** to other members of the Jesus Movement was to become an important social factor in the development of the movement.

STUDY QUESTIONS

1. What is the Johannine literature? Who was the person "John"? What is the early church tradition about this literature? What are some problems with this tradition? Who is "the Beloved Disciple"? What is the importance of John 21 for these questions?

2. What seems to be the relation between the Gospel of John and the synoptic gospels? What are some of the special sources behind the gospel? How is the Johannine literature related to Gnosticism? How did the discovery of the Dead Sea Scrolls affect the interpretation of John?

3. What do some scholars see as the distinctive history the Johannine community? What was the Johannine School like? In what sense might the Johannine community be described as an antisociety?

4. What are some major ideas of the Gospel of John? What kind of Jesus is portrayed in the Johannine Prologue? How does the first major section of the gospel seem to be organized around "signs"? What are some of the main literary techniques used by the evangelist? What seem to be some of his key symbolic themes in the discourses? What is the author's view of the world and human beings? What are some of the main themes of the farewell discourses and prayer for the community? Who is the "Paraclete"?

5. From where does Jesus come? Where is he going? How is he present? How are the Johannine letters related to the Johannine gospel? What is their emphasis on ethics like? What is the importance of loving one another? Who is the "Elder"? What is his controversy with Diotrephes? What is "docetism," and what does the author say about it?

Photo 12.1 This manuscript portrays Jesus as the lamb standing on Mt. Zion, surrounded by the 144,000 redeemed (holding lutes). See Revelation 14:1–5, 7:1–8.

CHAPTER TWELVE

REVELATION

The Book of Revelation—also called the Apocalypse—is the only complete *literary* **apocalypse** in the New Testament. It has been interpreted many ways throughout Christian history. Christians who have been relatively well integrated into the larger society have usually found its otherworldly Messiah and array of beasts, numbers, colors, and the like difficult to understand, even disturbing. In contrast, politically persecuted Christians have often identified with its message about salvation and encouragement for martyrs. Fundamentalist Christians have seen in it literal prophecies of modern events. Political and religious revolutionaries have drawn on its political, antiestablishment rhetoric. Literary figures and artists have found in its bizarre images a source of great inspiration. Some students during the turbulent 1960s wondered whether its author knew about psychedelic drugs. Other students, educated in myth and symbolism, have found much intellectual stimulation in Revelation. Some social-scientific interpreters have stressed the ancient sky voyager's astronomical-astrological attempt to read the meanings of the stars. There are have been a variety of interpretations, but it would be generally agreed among scholars that historical, literary/symbolic, and social-scientific approaches provide the best avenues to unlock its secrets.

REVELATION AND THE GENRE APOCALYPSE

An apocalypse is a written book or part thereof that records visual and auditory revelations to one who knows how to read the meanings of the sky world and who has special revelations of that world in an altered state of consciousness or ASC ("in the Spirit") (see Chapter One). Sometimes this "seer" has visions, especially dream visions that are interpreted through an otherworldly medium such as an angel. When recorded, the visions are normally prefaced by and concluded by narrative. With respect to content, these visions usually stress two dimensions. First, there are *spatial matters* such as astronomical/astrological lore, heavenly regions, and celestial star-beings that dwell in the sky (constellations, gods, angels, and demons, the cosmic Son of Man). Second, there are *temporal matters* such as world origins, past history, contemporary or future crises, wars and persecutions, resurrection of the dead, final judgment, salvation of the elect, the afterlife. Such matters are revealed to the seer, who witnesses them in a state of trance. (S)he experiences a journey into the sky ("soul flight"), where (s)he is overwhelmed by what (s)he sees but receives assurance. The revelation is then recorded in highly symbolic terms and is usually informed by images from the sacred scriptures, especially the prophets. It usually concludes with the seer's return to a "normal" state of consciousness. The seer may also receive instructions about concealing or publishing what (s)he has seen. Written apocalypses are normally attributed to some very important person from the remote past, such as Abraham, Moses, or David, who is then said to have prophesied the future. Thus apocalypses are, like many other genres, **pseudonymous** (from "false name"). Finally, apocalypses are genres that contain apocalyptic ideas and probably represent apocalyptic or "millennial" movements, although, of course, literate scribes write them.

Revelation is in two respects strikingly different from the many apocalyptic texts of Israel in the period before, during, and after the New Testament. First, it is *not* **pseudonymous**—the name of its author is clearly stated as John (1:1)—and, second, it contains features of letters, especially the beginning (1:4–5a) and ending (22:21), and edicts (chapters 2–3). So striking are these characteristics that one might ask whether the book that gives its name to this genre of literature is really an apocalypse! On the other hand, it can scarcely be doubted that the Book of Revelation is completely absorbed with apocalyptic eschatology and no doubt illustrates a millennial movement that experiences a great threat of persecution, whether real or imagined.

CHURCH TRADITION ABOUT REVELATION

An early tradition about Revelation comes from a Church Father named Justin Martyr, about 155 C.E.:

> And further, there was a certain man, even with us, whose name was *John, one of the Apostles of Christ,* who prophesied in a revelation which came to him that those who believed in our Christ will spend a thousand years in Jerusalem, and after that, the general and, in short, the eternal resurrection and judgment of all will come to pass at one and the same time.
>
> (Justin Martyr *Dialogue with Trypho* 81.4)

Justin's references to the thousand-year reign of Christ (the millennium) and the final resurrection for judgment are clearly from the Book of Revelation (Rev. 20). Moreover, its author is identified as "John, one of the apostles of Christ," that is, Jesus' disciple John son of Zebedee. About 185 C.E. Irenaeus claims that this person wrote both the gospel and Revelation (*Against Heresies* 3.1.1–3; 4.20.11). Irenaeus adds that John was still living at the time of Trajan (98–117 C.E.), that his vision was "seen" at the end of Domitian's reign (81–96 C.E.; *Against Heresies* 5.30.3), and that he died in Ephesus (*Against Heresies* 2.22.5). The first canonical list, the Muratorian Fragment at Rome (ca. 200 C.E.), implies Johannine authorship. These views were generally accepted in the churches of the western Roman Empire despite the objections of the *Alogoi* in Asia Minor and Gaius at Rome. "John" was thought to have written it on Patmos (Rev. 1:9), an island in the Aegean Sea off the coast of Asia Minor (about 150 miles southeast of Athens). Jerome summarized the fully developed tradition in the late fourth century C.E.:

> Therefore, in the fourteenth year [of his reign as emperor], when Domitian began the second persecution after [the emperor] Nero, when he [John] had been banished to the island of Patmos, he wrote the Apocalypse, which Justin Martyr and Irenaeus interpret[ed]. But when Domitian had been killed and his decree rescinded by the Senate because of excessive cruelty, he [John] returned to Ephesus under Nerva [96–98 C.E.] and, continuing there even until [the time of] the Emperor Trajan [98–117 C.E.], he established and directed all the churches of Asia, and, weakened with age he died in the sixty-eighth [year] after the passion of the Lord. He was buried near the same city.
>
> (Jerome *Illustrious Men* 9)

In the East, Revelation was accepted into the canon by the Alexandrian scholar Clement (ca. 150–215 C.E.) and his successor Origen (185–253 C.E.). Origen, who traveled widely, put it in his list of "uncontested" books; he himself accepted it as written by John son of Zebedee. However, about 250 C.E. Dionysius of Alexandria analyzed the vocabulary and style of Revelation and concluded that it could not have been written by the author of the Fourth Gospel and 1 John (cf. Eusebius *Ecclesiastical History* 7.24–25). Thereafter, ancient scholars in the East, including a number of prominent bishops, doubted that the son of Zebedee wrote Revelation, and so they excluded it. Although Athanasius' Easter Letter of 367 C.E. included it, doubts persisted in the East. Indeed, some Syriac churches did not include it until the sixth century, and other Syriac churches have never accepted it! Although the Greek Orthodox churches followed the trend in the West, they have generally ignored it.

GENERAL HISTORICAL CRITICISM OF REVELATION: AUTHOR, DATE, AND PLACE

Information about John son of Zebedee was presented in Chapter Eleven and need not be repeated here. Rather, we shall look more closely at external and internal evidence.

As just noted, Israelite apocalypses of the Greco-Roman period were usually **pseudonymous,** being attributed to some famous person from the past. A number of them held that this ancient worthy prophesied historical events down to and including the present and near future. This form of pseudonymity was an attempt to show that the events of history took place according to the plan of God and that the ancient prophets were correct in their predictions about the rapidly approaching end. In contrast, the author of Revelation explicitly identifies himself as John (Rev. 1:1, 4, 9; 22:8) and claims to be a contemporary of the events about which he is writing.

Authority comes directly from Jesus, whose martyrdom launched the final period of history and provided understanding of potential martyrdom in the present.

You will recall that many groups in the Jesus Movement believed that prophecy had broken out among them (Chapter Three). John of Patmos implies that he is a *prophet, too.* He writes that he was exiled "because of the word of God and the testimony of Jesus" (Rev. 1:9), which is "the spirit of prophecy" (19:10). He states that he was told to prophesy after eating what is certainly a prophetic scroll (Rev. 10:11; cf. Ezek. 1–3; *Shepherd of Hermas* 1:3–4, here a heavenly book of prophecy). He describes his work as "the words of prophecy" (Rev. 1:3; 22:7). His apocalypse also contains many traditional prophetic forms and acts, although they are often colored by apocalyptic. Examples are judgment pronouncements (Rev. 2–3); symbolic actions like eating the scroll (Rev. 10:8–11); seven beatitudes (Rev. 16:15; 19:9; 22:7); words and promises of God (Rev. 16:5; 21:5–8); and interpretations of visions by intermediaries or the prophet himself (e.g., Rev. 7:13–17; 17:7–18). He describes his altered state of consciousness as an ecstatic vision that qualifies him: "I was in the Spirit on the Lord's day . . ." (1:10). This language is reminiscent of the classical Hebrew prophets, and the vision that follows is an interesting example of the kind of ASC those prophets used to validate their message (Isa. 6). We may think of this book as a combination of prophecy and apocalyptic and its author as an apocalyptic prophet. Because of the predominance of astrology in his visions, he might also be termed an "astral prophet" (Malina and Pilch).

Was this apocalyptic prophet, as tradition claims, a disciple of Jesus, John the son of Zebedee? His mother tongue was a Semitic language, probably Aramaic (see following). This might imply that he was a Palestinian. Yet, he never identifies himself as the son of Zebedee or as a disciple or an apostle. After Dionysius wrote, ancient scholars of the eastern Mediterranean doubted that the author of the gospel and the letters was the same person who wrote the Apocalypse. Modern scholars add that although Revelation has some of the same words as the gospel, they do not mean the same thing. It also uses different words for the same thing. They point out that the Gospel of John is the least apocalyptic of the Gospels, but Revelation is the most apocalyptic writing in the New Testament. In short, vocabulary, style, and content lead modern scholars to agree with Dionysius that the person or persons who produced the Johannine Gospel and letters did not write the Apocalypse. At best, Revelation might have been composed within the Johannine School, but even that solution does not seem very likely.

If this literary critical view is correct, in theory it would still be possible that John son of Zebedee wrote Revelation because, in the modern view, he did not write the gospel and letters! However, this theory also has difficulties. Some critics think that the Apocalypse was not an immediate transcription of visions just experienced, but rather falls within a *literary* apocalyptic tradition that builds on other written apocalypses, as well as oral and other written sources. This does not necessarily deny the possibility of a seer's recent vision in the process; it does, however, suggest that composition of the Apocalypse was complex, not the sort of thing one would expect from a Galilean peasant-fisherman.

In short, it has become customary among scholars to refer to the author of Revelation as "John of Patmos" and *not* to think of him as Jesus' disciple, John son of Zebedee.

The earliest possible date, which is related to authorship, was probably after 70 C.E. Although it is true that Rev. 11:1–13 implies that the Jerusalem temple, destroyed along with the city in 70, is still standing, most scholars think that this passage contains pre-70 traditions that have not been assimilated or updated; the passage thus represents an earlier time. More importantly, John of Patmos refers to "Babylon" six times (e.g., Rev. 14:8; 16:19; 17:5). "Babylon" is most likely a symbol for Rome. Both Babylon and Rome destroyed Jerusalem and the temple. The former took place in 587 B.C.E., the latter in 70 C.E. The connection between these two destructions was a known symbol in Israelite apocalyptic texts in the post-70 period (*IV Ezra; Apocalypse of Baruch; Sibylline Oracles* 5). The connection is also made in 1 Pet. 5:13. Dan. 9:26 assumes that the destruction of Jerusalem was a sign that the end was near. Thus, in referring to "Babylon," the author seems to know of the destruction of Jerusalem and the temple in 70 C.E. In short, a date sometime after 70 C.E. is most likely.

The latest possible date is more difficult to establish. Irenaeus claimed that John "saw" his visions near the end of the reign of Domitian, assassinated in 96 C.E. This comment (see preceding) might imply that they were written some years later, but that is not so stated. Probably Irenaeus implies writing about that time, as well. This dating raises a number of issues, most important of which is the question of the so-called Domitian persecution. A few comments are in order.

Even the casual reader of the Book of Revelation cannot doubt that John of Patmos thinks that the members of the Jesus Movement in his region, Asia (western Asia Minor), faced an imminent and terrible crisis. He speaks of a past persecution of the movement, and he expects more persecution. The following "persecution passages" will illustrate this point:

1:9 "I John, your brother, who share with you in Jesus *the persecution and the kingdom and the patient endurance,* was on the island called Patmos because of the word of God and the testimony of Jesus."

2:10 (Jesus speaks through John to the city of Smyrna): "Do not fear what you are *about to suffer.* Beware, the devil *is about to throw some of you into prison,* so that you may be tested, and for ten days you will have *affliction.* Be faithful unto *death,* and I will give you the crown of life."

2:13 (Jesus speaks through John to the city of Pergamum): ". . . you did not deny your faith in me even in the days of *Antipas my witness* (= *martyr*), my faithful one, *who was killed among you, where Satan lives.*"

3:10 (Jesus speaks through John to the city of Philadelphia): "Because you have kept my word of patient endurance, I will keep you from the *hour of trial which is coming* on the whole world, to test the inhabitants of the earth."

6:9–11 "When he opened the fifth seal, I saw under the altar the souls of *those who had been slaughtered* for the word of God and for the testimony they had given; 10) they cried out with a loud voice, 'Sovereign Lord, holy and true, how long will it be before you *judge and avenge our blood* on the inhabitants of the earth?' 11) They were each given a white robe and told to rest a little longer, until the number would be complete both of their fellow servants and their brothers and sisters, *who were soon to be killed as they themselves had been.*"

16:6a "For they shed *the blood of saints and prophets . . .*"

17:6a "And I saw the woman was drunk with the *blood of the saints* and the *blood of the witnesses* to Jesus."

18:24 "And in you was found the *blood of prophets and of saints,* and of *all who have been slaughtered on earth.*"

What kind of persecution of the Jesus Movement is in view? Various passages in the New Testament point to both Israelite and Gentile mistreatment of members of the Jesus Movement. Some Israelite communities tended to have sharp boundaries and a strict discipline and authority over their own members. Paul says, "five times I have received from the Israelites the forty lashes minus one" (2 Cor. 11:24), a Israelite punishment, balanced by "three times I was beaten with rods" (2 Cor. 11:25), a Roman one. Similarly, Mark 13:9 anticipates Christ followers being "beaten in synagogues," a Israelite context, and standing "before governors and kings because of me," a Gentile context. There is also general oppression of the Jesus Movement in 1 Peter and Hebrews. No one doubts that members of the Jesus Movement were persecuted; however, the preceding quotations leave the impression that maltreatment was sporadic, local, and spontaneous, not some widespread, well-organized persecution.

However, the preceding quotations also suggest at least *fears* of a Roman persecution of major proportions, and the last four seem to imply actual persecutions. Is this an accurate impression? By way of background, recall that the Roman government was generally tolerant of local religions if they were loyal to the empire. This was a polytheistic society, and many religions presented no political problems. Local inhabitants were simply asked to acknowledge formally the gods of Rome and sacrifice to the Roman emperor, and having done so, they were free to continue their local religious beliefs and practices. The Israelites, however, were an exception because they were strict monotheists. The Romans recognized their special position legally. Israelites did not have to keep the requirement about the gods and the emperor. They had to pay their taxes, of course. After 70 C.E., the Romans collected what had been "the Israelite tax" for the temple and used it for the temple of Jupiter Capitolinus in Rome (the *fiscus iudaicus;* Josephus *Jewish Wars* 7.6.6 par. 218; Suetonius *The Twelve Caesars,* "Domitian" 12). This transference was part of the penalty for Israelite rebellion. Taxes were to be paid. On the whole, however, Israelite privileges with respect to the Roman gods and the emperor continued.

As members of the Jesus Movement became increasingly distinct from other Israelites, the traditional Roman protection of Israelite religion was no longer theirs. A local Roman official could demand that they acknowledge the gods of Rome. They would have to either recant or refuse. If they refused, they would be liable to banishment, torture, or even execution. This ever-present possibility hung over the Jesus Movement wherever it became recognized as distinct and separate.

A similar circumstance existed with respect to worshipping the Roman emperor as a god (see Chapter One). Recall that the emperor cult took its inspiration from the monarchies of the eastern Mediterranean, where pharaohs and kings were considered gods or sons of gods. Although the Roman Senate resisted such veneration of the emperor and most Roman emperors deplored the practice, it was allowed to flourish in the provinces in order to promote political unity. Moreover, in some provincial settings it seems to have been taken quite seriously. That appears to have been the case in Asia (western Asia Minor), where it is supposed that Revelation was written. Moreover, despite strong resistance, a few Roman emperors in the first century demanded that they be worshipped as gods. Similarly, some local Roman authorities pressed for it. As in the case of worshipping Roman gods, the Israelites were in a privileged position. Again, members of the Jesus Movement increasingly could not share this privilege.

The first known persecution of the Jesus Movement by Romans took place at Rome under the emperor Nero (ruled 54–68 C.E.). In listing what he considered to be Nero's vile, scandalous, and depraved deeds, the ancient Roman historian Suetonius remarks, "Punishments were also inflicted on the Christ-ies, a sect professing a new and mischievous religious belief . . ." (Suetonius *The Twelve Caesars,* "Nero" 16). The Roman historian, Tacitus, is more explicit. He tells about the terrible fire that destroyed a quarter of Rome in 64 C.E. and says that when the rumor persisted that Nero himself had ordered the fire started to make space for his building operations, he found his scapegoat in the Jesus Movement:

> But all human efforts, all the lavish gifts of the emperor, and the propitiations of the gods did not banish the sinister belief that the conflagration [fire] was the result of an order [by Nero]. Consequently, to get rid of the report, Nero fastened the guilt and inflected the most exquisite *tortures* on a class hated for their abominations, called "Christ-ies" by the populace. Accordingly, an arrest was first made of all who pleaded guilty; then, upon their information, an immense multitude was convicted, not so much of the crime of firing the city, as of hatred against mankind. *Mockery* of every sort was added to their *deaths. Covered with the skins of beasts, they were torn by dogs and perished, or were nailed to crosses, or were doomed to the flames and burnt, to serve as a nightly illumination when daylight had expired.* Nero offered his gardens for the spectacle, and was exhibiting a show in the circus, while he mingled with the people in the dress of a charioteer or stood aloft on a car. Hence, even for criminals who deserve extreme and exemplary punishment, there arose a feeling of compassion; for it was not, as it seemed, for the public good, but to glut one man's cruelty, that they were being destroyed.
>
> (Tacitus *Annals* 15.44)

Almost a half-century later, about 112 C.E., the precarious situation of the Jesus Movement in Asia Minor is documented in the correspondence between Pliny, the governor of Bithynia in northern Asia Minor, and Trajan, the Roman emperor (98–117 C.E.). Pliny writes to Trajan:

> It is my rule, Sire, to refer to you in matters where I am uncertain. For who can better direct my hesitation or instruct my ignorance? I was never present at any trial of Christ-ies; therefore I do not know what are the customary penalties or investigations, and what limits are observed. I have hesitated a great deal on the question whether there should be any distinction of ages; whether the weak should have the same treatment as the more robust; whether those who recant should be pardoned, or whether a man who has ever been a Christ-ie should gain nothing by ceasing to be such; whether the name itself, even if innocent of crime, should be punished, or only the crimes attaching to that name.
>
> Meanwhile, this is the course that I have adopted in the case of those brought before me as "Christ-ies." *I ask them if they are Christ-ies. If they admit it I repeat the*

question a second and a third time, threatening capital punishment; if they persist I sentence them to death. For I do not doubt that, whatever kind of crime it may be to which they have confessed, their pertinacity and inflexible obstinacy should certainly be punished. There were others who displayed a like madness and whom I reserved to be sent to Rome, since they were Roman citizens.

Thereupon the usual result followed, the very fact of my dealing with the question led to a wider spread of the charge, and a great variety of cases were brought before me. An anonymous pamphlet was issued, containing many names. *All who denied that they were or had been Christ-ies I considered should be discharged, because they called upon the gods at my dictation and did reverence, with incense and wine, to your image which I had ordered to be brought forward for this purpose, together with the statues of the deities; and especially because they cursed Christ, a thing which, it is said, genuine Christ-ies cannot be induced to do.* Others named by the informer first said that they were Christ-ies and then denied it; declaring that they had been but were so no longer, some having recanted three years or more before and one or two as long ago as twenty years. They all worshiped your image and the statues of the gods and cursed Christ. But they declared that the sum of their guilt or error had amounted only to this, that on an appointed day they had been accustomed to meet before daybreak, and to recite a hymn antiphonally to Christ, as to a god, and to bind themselves by an oath not for the commission of any crime but to abstain from theft, robbery, adultery, and breach of faith, and not to deny a deposit when it was claimed. After the conclusion of this ceremony it was their custom to depart and meet again to take food; but it was ordinary and harmless food, and they had ceased this practice after my edict in which, in accordance with your orders, I had forbidden secret societies. I thought it the more necessary, therefore, to find out what truth there was in this by applying *torture to two maidservants, who were called deaconesses.* But I found nothing but a depraved and extravagant superstition, and I therefore postponed my examination and had recourse to you for consultation.

The matter seemed to me to justify my consulting you, especially on account of the number of those imperiled; for *many persons of all ages and classes and of both sexes are being put in peril by accusation,* and this will go on. The contagion of this superstition has spread not only in the cities, but in the villages and rural districts as well; yet it seems capable of being checked and set right. There is no shadow of doubt that the temples, which have been almost deserted, are beginning to be frequented once more, that the sacred rites which have been long neglected are being renewed, and that sacrificial victims are for sale everywhere, whereas, till recently a buyer was rarely to be found. From this it is easy to imagine what a host of men could be set right, were they given a chance of recantation.

Trajan responds:

You have taken the right line, my dear Pliny, in examining the cases of those denounced to you as Christ-ies, for no hard and fast rule can be laid down, of universal application. They are not to be sought out; if they are informed against, and the charge is proved, they are to be punished, with this reservation, *that if anyone denies that he is a Christ-ie, and actually proves it, that is by worshiping our gods,* he shall be pardoned as a result of his recantation, however suspect he may have been with respect to the past. Pamphlets published anonymously should carry no weight in any charge whatsoever. They constitute a very bad precedent, and are also out of keeping with this age.

> (Translation Bettenson [replacing "Christian" with "Christ-ie"], *Documents of the Christian Church,* p. 10)

The internal evidence of the Book of Revelation suggests that its author believed that persecution was imminent. The persecution would come from the Romans and would be sparked by demand for emperor worship (13:4, 12–17; 16:2; 19:20), which those who believed in Christ would have to refuse (14:9–12). When would such a fear have arisen?

The question is not easy to answer from internal evidence. Rev. 17:10 refers to a series of seven heads or kings. Five have fallen, but there is also one *"who is"* (*the sixth*) and a seventh who is to come. Many scholars think that this refers to a sequence of seven Roman emperors. The writer implies that he lives during the reign of the sixth, the one "who is." If we begin with Julius Caesar prior to the empire, the sixth is Nero (54–68 C.E.). Some scholars prefer this option. The number of the beast, 666, in Rev. 13:18 symbolizes Nero, and members of the Jesus Movement certainly lived with the memory of sudden persecution in Rome in 64 C.E. under the emperor Nero. Church tradition says that both Peter and Paul were martyred under Nero (e.g., *1 Clement* 5). However, because the Neronian persecution was limited to Rome and the issue was not emperor worship, other scholars think that the number "666" refers *not* to Nero himself, but rather to a Nero *redivivus,* that is, a new Nero. This theory is related to the ancient belief that Nero would come back to life and invade the empire from the East, a theme also found in Revelation (cf. Rev. 13:3, 12, 14; 17:8, 11). Nero committed suicide in 68 C.E.; if the "666" reference is to a Nero *redivivus,* the author could have written the book in the post-70 period based on the Babylon/Rome correlation noted earlier.

If the six Roman emperors begin with the first emperor, Augustus, and if the three short reigns of 68–70 are omitted, the sixth would be Vespasian, the emperor from 70 to 79 C.E. The problem is that Vespasian was not known for demanding worship of himself as a god, and there is no knowledge of a persecution of the Jesus Movement in Asia Minor during his reign. The conditions implied by the book simply do not fit.

A third suggestion for the identity of 666 is that the first five rulers or emperors are those who were deified by the Roman Senate after their deaths (Julius Caesar, Augustus, Claudius, Vespasian, and Titus). The sixth, or one "who is," would then be Domitian, who did indeed demand divine honors of himself. An alternative possibility would be to start with the ruler who encouraged the emperor cult, Gaius Caligula (37–41 C.E.; see Chapters One, Three, and Eight). In this case Domitian would again be the sixth.

Was, then, Domitian considered to be a Nero *redivivus?* Was Irenaeus correct in placing Revelation in the last years of Domitian's reign (81–96 C.E.)?

The crucial historical question boils down to this: Did Domitian undertake a major persecution of the Jesus Movement in Asia Minor as a matter of imperial policy, as Nero did at Rome in 64 C.E.? Church traditions certainly held this view in the latter second century, and Eusebius mentions others who held it thereafter (Eusebius *Ecclesiastical History* 4.26). Jerome's statement quoted earlier is a good fourth-century summary of it. Also, a number of second-century Roman writers were very critical of Domitian's policies. However, some modern historians of Rome think that these Roman writers were biased in their opposition to Domitian. Thus, when Suetonius claimed that Domitian demanded to be addressed as "our Lord and our God" (e.g., Suetonius *The Twelve Caesars*, "Domitian" 13.1–2), the address was actually used by persons who wished to flatter the emperor, not required by Domitian himself. Also, it is well known that when he defended the Jesus Movement to the emperor Marcus Aurelius (*To Antonius*), he told the emperor what he wanted to hear, namely, "bad" emperors were those who persecuted the movement.

This modern revisionist view of Domitian, when combined with the lack of hard evidence for imperial persecutions of members of the Jesus Movement in this period and positive evidence that Domitian was sensitive to the needs of provincials, suggests two options. One is that Revelation was written later, at the time of the Pliny and Trajan correspondence (ca. 112 C.E.), when there is clear evidence for actual persecution in Asia Minor. The other is that the author of Revelation, perhaps concerned about local enthusiasm for the emperor cult in western Asia Minor, feared a persecution that was local or regional. The latter is more probable. Indeed, Pliny's letter to Trajan (quoted earlier) implies some previous persecution in Asia Minor ("I was never present at any trial of Christ-ies; therefore I do not know what are the customary penalties or investigations, and what limits are observed"). There are also a number of minor details in the Apocalypse that can be interpreted to refer to the time of Domitian. Rev. 6:6 possibly alludes to an edict by Domitian in 92 C.E. Both Domitian and Jesus are compared with the morning star (2:28). Problems of poverty may have been intensified by a famine in Asia Minor in 93 C.E. Tensions between Israelites and members of the Jesus Movement (2:9; 3:9) may have been intensified by the **Prayer against the Heretics** about 80–90 C.E. (see Chapters Nine and Eleven; Ignatius *To the Philadelphians* 8.2).

In short, there is no absolute certainty. The traditional viewpoint is as good as any. Thus most date the Book of Revelation about 95–96 C.E.

The place of composition is one of the lesser problems connected with Revelation. The writer says that his first vision took place on the island of Patmos (1:9), a small rocky island in the Aegean Sea about forty miles west of the coast of Asia Minor (modern Turkey) and thus not far from the seven churches to which he writes (Rev. 1–3). (See Figure 12.1.) He states that he himself was "on the island called Patmos because of the word of God and the testimony of Jesus," suggesting that he might indeed have been exiled. In any case, the ancients drew that conclusion, and, as already indicated, modern scholars call him simply "John of Patmos," in part to distinguish him from the writers of the other Johannine literature.

SOCIAL-HISTORICAL CONTEXT OF REVELATION

Whether there was a full-scale "Domitian persecution" of the Jesus Movement or not, a number of things seem clear from the persecution quotations listed earlier. John has been exiled on the island of Patmos. He expects the persecution, imprisonment, and possible martyrdom of members of the Jesus Movement at Smyrna. Antipas has already been martyred at Pergamum. John is preoccupied with martyr-

Figure 12.1 The seven cities of the Roman Province of Asia mentioned in Revelation 2–3. To the church in each city, a certain John writing from the island of Patmos addressed a letter.

dom in relation to the emperor cult that is known to have been thriving in the cities of western Asia Minor. In short, he perceives an impending political crisis in western Asia Minor.

Revelation also implies that there are conflicts with the local synagogue. In the vision message to Smyrna, John refers to those who "say that they are Israelites and are not, but are a synagogue of Satan. Do not fear what you are about to suffer . . . ," and thereafter come statements about imprisonment and potential death (2:9–11). Similarly the vision message about Philadelphia refers to a "synagogue of Satan who say that they are Israelites and are not, but are lying" (3:9). This negative labeling suggests conflicts between Israelites and Christ believers, each group considering itself to be the true Israel. Perhaps this split was intensified by the "Prayer against the Heretics" (see Chapters Nine and Eleven; Ignatius *To the Philadelphians* 8.2); or perhaps there was collaboration between Israelites and Gentiles against the Jesus Movement.

Additionally, nonbiblical sources who say that there was a sharp conflict between rich and poor in western Asia Minor seem to be confirmed by statements about wealth in Revelation. The Laodiceans who say, "I am rich, I have prospered, and I need nothing" (3:17) are warned to repent. "Babylon," presumably Rome, is attacked for its lavish display of wealth and luxury and its crass commercialism (17–18).

Poverty is related to famine and inflation (6:6). These texts indicate social stratification and conflict on the basis of economics, which would have been widespread in most social relations in the ancient world.

Political, social, and economic conflicts led John of Patmos to advocate exclusivism and rejection of the ways of the world. John's attack on the Nicolaitans (2:6, 15), "Balaam" (2:14), and "Jezebel" (2:20) is an attack on eating meat sacrificed to idols (2:14, 20) and those who "practice fornication" (2:14, 20–23). These acts were often considered by Israelites and members of the Jesus Movement to be idolatrous Gentile practices to which lax Christ believers were accommodating themselves, or apostasy (cf. 1 Cor. 8, 10). Such marginality, sometimes accompanied by what moderns think to be bizarre behavior, is typical of groups who consider themselves to be oppressed. More needs to be said about this phenomenon in our conclusion to this chapter.

The seven edicts to the seven churches are written to "brothers" (1:9) who are also "prophets" (22:9; cf. 19:10). This suggests that the book was written for leaders in a network of churches in Asia. These leaders may have been fellow seers who claimed to know the astronomical/astrological secrets of the cosmos and the prophetic and apocalyptic literature of the Israelites.

LANGUAGE, STYLE, AND FORMAL FEATURES OF REVELATION

Language and Literary Features

The Book of Revelation is written in Greek, but it has numerous grammatical errors in it. This feature suggests that its author's mother tongue was not Greek, but rather a Semitic language, probably **Aramaic.** It also contains a number of interesting literary features. There are not only apocalyptic and prophetic, but also liturgical, mythical, and parenetic materials and forms. There are antiphonal hymns (4:1–11; 5:9–12, etc.), the so-called *trishagion* ("Holy, Holy, Holy," 4:8c), doxologies (1:6; 4:9; 5:13b–14; 7:12); acclamations of worth (4:11; 5:9b–10, 12); a thanksgiving formula (11:17–18); the *amen* and responses (22:20; 19:1); a woe oracle (12:12b); the lament or dirge (18:1–24); the curse (22:18–20); and others. The world is viewed as heaven above, earth in the middle, and hell below, and great portents occur in the sky, which is inhabited by constellations, specifically, star-gods, angels, demons, beasts, and the Son of Man. Animals speak and act in this book. It also contains a number of traditional myths. One is the birth and attempted destruction of the divine child (12:1–6). Another is the sacred marriage (19:6–10: Christ, the Lamb, and his bride). In the combat myth, the good angel (Michael) and his followers are victorious over the primeval dragon and his angels. There is a divine warrior who is portrayed as a martyred Lamb who overcomes and rules the universe from his glorious throne (cf. especially chapter 12; 19:11–22:9). Finally, there is the theme of the divine, heavenly city (21:9–22:5). Exhortations are found not only in the prophetic commands, but also in virtue and vice lists (e.g. 9:20–21; 13:4–8; 14:4–5). All of these features come from oral traditions and written sources, but continuity of language, style, and imagery also suggests a unified composition.

Symbolism

Apocalyptic prophets in ASCs express their dream visions in the symbolic language and concepts of their culture, and other apocalypses give expression to such language and conceptuality. Similarly, literary apocalypses among the Israelites echo the symbolic language of the ancient prophetic literature, primarily Ezekiel, and apocalyptic literature, primarily Daniel. Literary critics emphasize that such symbolism is part of the prophet's quest for a total, all-encompassing vision of reality.

Several kinds of symbols are worth noting. Sacred, symbolic numbers are especially prominent in Revelation. Consider the numbers "four," "twelve," and "seven" in the ancient world (Malina and Pilch). The number "four" represented the four cardinal directions (points of the compass) as divisions of the created order. The number "twelve" was the astrological number of the zodiac as well as the symbol for Israel (the twelve tribes). The number "seven" was the number of the "wandering stars" (the planets, which are gods: Jupiter, Pluto, etc.), the Greater and Lesser Bear constellations, the *Pleiades,* and much more. One-fourth of the days between full moons is seven, hence the seven days of the week. The ancient Babylonian astrologers organized their whole calendar around seven and seven times seven. In Israelite tradition, the seventh day of the week was a holy day of rest. Thus the number "seven" came to symbolize perfection, completeness, totality, and fullness, whereas "six" was the opposite.

In light of extensive cosmic symbolism of "four," "twelve," and "seven," consider Rev. 7:1–8. In 7:1–3, the seer has a vision of four angels standing at the four corners of the earth holding back the four winds (which cause plagues, cf. Dan. 7:2–3). A fifth angel ascends from the rising of the sun with God's seal and orders the other four to hold back the four winds until the servants(martyrs, cf. 6:11) should be sealed as a form of supernatural protection (cf. Isa. 44:5; Ezek. 9:1–8). In 7:4–8, the number of the sealed is 144,000, that is, 12,000 from each of the twelve tribes of Israel. These are also the believer-martyrs from all nations (5:9; 7:9) and presumably the true Israel. There are seven stars (1:13), seven edicts to seven churches (2–3), seven seals (6:1–1, 8:1), seven trumpets (8:7–9:21, 11:15–19), seven bowls of wrath (16:1–12, 17–21), and seven heads, which are seven kings (17:9–15). So important is the number "seven"—it occurs fifty-four times—that the outline of the Book of Revelation can be developed by groups of seven (see following).

A final example of numbers symbolism is the famous number of the beast. It symbolizes the Roman Empire and its imperial line, as well as the Antichrist. He forced all the people to place a number on their right hands or foreheads, a number standing for the emperor-beast's name (Rev. 13:18). In most manuscripts, the number is 666; in one fifth-century manuscript, the number is 616, which was also known by Irenaeus in the late second century. Who is the mysterious emperor-beast 666 (616)? Many theories have been suggested, but most historical critics agree that the number symbolizes Nero. The letters of the Hebrew alphabet are also numbers (A = 1, β [B] = 2, etc.), and "Neron Caesar" transliterated from Hebrew as $N\text{-}R\bar{O}N$ $C\text{-}S\text{-}R$ adds up to 666, whereas "Nero Caesar" (without the final "N") spells "616."

N =	50	N =	50
R =	200	R =	200

Ō =	6	Ō =	6
N =	50		
C =	100	C =	100
S =	60	S =	60
R =	200	R =	200
	666		616

Color symbolism is also common in the Apocalypse. An excellent example is the "four horsemen of the Apocalypse" (once used to describe a famous Notre Dame backfield!), each of whom rides a horse of a different color (6:1–8). Thus white = victory (not purity; contrast 19:8); red = violence and war; black = famine and suffering; and pale green = decomposition and death. As is typical in apocalyptic, white also symbolizes the brilliance of the divine glory (6:11; 7:9, 13–14; 22:14).

There are many animals and beasts in Revelation. The lamb and the lion represent the sacrificial martyrdom and royal kingship of Jesus, respectively. Beasts are satanic figures, for example, the Roman emperor symbolized by 666. Horns represent power (6:6; 12:3), and wings symbolize mobility (4:8; 12:14). Other symbols include a woman = a people or a city (12:1–6; 17); eyes = knowledge (e.g., 1:14; 2:18); the sharp sword = judging and punishing word of God (e.g., 1:16; 2:12, 16); crowns = rule and kingship (e.g., 2:10; 3:11); and the sea = chaos and evil (13:1; 21:1).

Son of Man symbolism from Dan. 7:13 also occurs in Rev. 1:7, 12–16, as it does in some other New Testament apocalyptic texts, for example, **Q** and Mark 13. When one gets to a certain level of experience or expectation, the normal structure of language is simply shattered; certainly ASC experiences and millennial hopes can be best expressed in symbolic language, often in archetypal symbols that have deep roots in the human consciousness. This is certainly the case with the consciousness of evil, sin, and guilt. For example, sin is said to be the result of the rebellion of the First Man, Adam. Paul says, "as one man's trespass led to condemnation for all (Adam), so one man's act of righteousness leads to justification and life for all (Christ)" (Rom. 5:18). In the language of apocalyptic symbolism, the same natural consequence is the idea of the coming of a redeemer figure "like a Son of Man," a figure human yet more than human. Certainly this propensity of the human mind to think in such terms helps to account for the prominence of Son of Man symbolism in apocalyptic texts.

STRUCTURE AND OUTLINE OF REVELATION

Revelation contains apocalyptic eschatology, prophetic forms, and liturgical materials. There is also a whole set of compositional techniques in the work such as the distribution of symbols and images over the whole work, announcements that are developed later, cross-references, contrasts, numerical structures, interludes of material, insertions (**intercalations**), and various combinations of these techniques. Finally, as we have just seen, the writer incorporates letter-like features and edicts, and the structure of his writing as a whole takes the form of a letter. Perhaps the most unusual feature of Revelation is its seven edicts from the heavenly Son of Man (ultimately from God) to the messengers or "guardian angels" of the seven churches in Asia Minor: Ephesus, Smyrna, Pergamum, Thyatira, Sardis, Philadelphia, and Laodicea (Rev. 2–3). John of Patmos mediates them. This feature is unparalleled in apocalyptic writing. The seven edicts have a common pattern of five parts:

- Address and command from the sky, or angel, to write to the angel/messenger of a church
- A prophetic messenger introduced with the formula, "Then says . . ." (sometimes translated with "These are the words of . . ." [NRSV])
- A section about the individual church that begins "I know . . ." containing praises and/or warnings and concluding with an exhortation
- A formula call to hear the message ("Let anyone who has an ear listen to what the Spirit is saying to the churches")
- A prophetic promise to the martyr as one "who overcomes" or "conquers"

That Revelation has the outward form of a letter (see Chapter Five) helps one to understand the book. It begins with a salutation in the Pauline style: "To him who loves us and freed us from our sins by his blood and made us a kingdom, priests to his God and Father, to him be glory and dominion forever and ever. Amen" (Rev. 1:5b–6; cf. Gal. 1:3–5). Similarly, there is a closing benediction, "The grace of the Lord Jesus be with all the saints. Amen" (22:21), preceded by a prayer for the coming of the Lord, "*Our Lord, come!*" (22:20), which Paul used at the end of a letter (1 Cor. 16:22).

The natural question that arises from these considerations is this: Is it possible to develop an exact analysis and a precise outline of a work as complex as this? It is also important to recall that many symbolic features of the book were commonly understood in antiquity. It was a high-context society that, in contrast to our low-context society, preferred indirect symbolic and poetic language to direct detailed descriptions and explanations. Other references seem to have flourished among a core of apocalyptic prophets. All of this makes logical structural analysis difficult. Nonetheless, frequent attempts have been made, many of them revolving around the book's clear references to the symbolic number "seven." A simplified outline based on two cycles of visions with three series of seven in each cycle would look like this (cf. Yarbro Collins 1984, 1990):

I. Prologue		1:1–8
	Preface	1:1–3
	Letter framework	1:4–8
II. First cycle of visions		1:9–11:19
	Seven edicts to seven churches	1:9–3:22
	Seven seals	4:1–8:5
	Seven trumpets	8:2–11:19
III. Second cycle of visions		12:1–22:5
	Seven unnumbered visions	12:1–15:4
	Seven bowls	15:1–16:21
	Babylonian appendix	17:1–19:10
	Seven unnumbered visions	19:11–21:8
	Jerusalem appendix	21:9–22:5

EXEGETICAL SURVEY OF REVELATION

Prologue, 1:1–8

1:1–3: *Preface: Descriptive introduction and beatitude.*   Christ reveals God's word to his "servant" John through the mediation of an angel. The reader and hearers (probably in a house-church) are blessed (cf. beatitudes also in 14:13; 16:15; 19:9; 20:6; 22:7, 14).

1:4–8: *Letter framework.*   John greets the seven churches off the coast of Asia Minor. The greeting to a redeemed priesthood is from God, the seven spirits, and the resurrected King of kings, who is pictured in the imagery of the coming Son of Man (Dan. 7:14; Zech. 12:10). Verse 6 contains a doxology.

First Cycle of Visions, 1:9–11:19

1:9–3:22: *Seven edicts to seven churches.*   After an inaugural vision of the heavenly Son of Man come seven prophetic messages from John to his prophetic brothers. They take the form of ancient edicts, but they are from the heavenly Christ to the angels/messengers of seven churches in seven cities and thus finally to the churches. They have a common form. Because the seven cities were on a major highway, perhaps Revelation was meant to be a circular document read to a house-church in each city.

1:9–20: *Inaugural vision: The cosmic Son of Man.*   John, "your brother," exiled on Patmos, shares the "persecution" and receives the prophetic spirit "on the Lord's day" (Sunday!). In an ASC, he is commanded to write on a scroll to the seven churches, symbolized by seven lampstands. He has a vision of the heavenly Son of Man expressed in the language of Dan. 7:9–14, which is rooted in ancient Canaanite myth and is also similar to descriptions of astral deities, for example, those in the astrological manual *Salmeschoiniaka* or the Greek magical *Testament of Solomon*. The seven stars that are seven angels of the churches may be symbols with multiple meanings (condensed symbols), perhaps suggesting a constellation and universal rule, as in the Persian mystery religion Mithraism (see Chapter One).

2:1–7: *The edict to the angel of Ephesus.*   Ephesus was the prosperous capital of the Roman province of Asia (cf. Acts 2:9; 18, 19; 1 Cor. 16:8; the deutero-Pauline Ephesians; Chapter Seven). The famous temple of the goddess Artemis (Roman Diana), goddess of the hunt and women's fertility, was there, as Paul's conflict illustrates (Acts 19:23–40), and so was a temple to Domitian, suggesting a revival of the emperor cult. The Ephesians are praised for their works. They have tested and exposed wandering missionaries (cf. **Q;** *Didachē* 11–13; 2 Cor. 10–13; Chapter Five) and have endured suffering. They are blamed for allowing their love to grow cold. They must repent or else lose their standing. On the Nicolaitans, see verses 14–15. "Everyone who conquers" in Rev. 2:7 is the first occurrence of a formula that refers to the Christ believer who, like the Christ himself, is martyred for his faith but rewarded in heaven (2:7, 11, 26–28; 3:5, 12, 21; 5:5; 21:7; cf. 1:7–8; 12:10–11; 13:7; 15:2; 17:14).

2:8–11: *The edict to the angel of Smyrna.* Smyrna was a beautiful commercial city about forty miles north of Ephesus. Like Ephesus, it was a center of the emperor cult. The church there suffers, apparently persecuted by members of the large Israelite community (2:9; cf. 3:9), and is materially poor, although praised for being spiritually rich. "Whoever conquers" (see comment on 2:1–7) will not be harmed by the "second death," an eternal punishment for the wicked (20:6, 14; 21:8).

2:12–17: *The edict to the angel of Pergamum.* Pergamum, forty-five miles north of Smyrna and ten miles from the Aegean coast, was a major Hellenistic and Roman granite citadel-hill city and the original capital of Asia. It remained politically influential and had a famous library. It was also known for its many religions. The "Satan's throne" (2:13) may refer to such religions, and especially to the emperor cult because Pergamum had temples to both Rome and Augustus. Jesus Movement members at Pergamum are praised for remaining loyal, even when Antipas (?) was martyred but are blamed for following Balaam, probably a symbolic reference to idolatry, apostasy, and sexual immorality (Num. 25:1–3; cf. 2 Pet. 2:15; Jude 11), and the Nicolaitans, that is, accommodating themselves to their environment. They are exhorted to repent.

2:18–29: *The edict to the angel of Thyatira.* Thyatira was a small town about forty miles southeast of Pergamum. The church is praised for its love, faith, and works but is blamed for tolerating the mysterious prophetess "Jezebel," who in the Hebrew Scriptures led King Ahab into idolatry (1 Kings 19:1–2; 21:1–14; 2 Kings 9:22, 30–34). Here "Jezebel" leads the believers to accommodation, interpreted as apostasy, perhaps in connection with the cult meals of Thyatira's trade guilds. The "morning star" symbolizes the Davidic Messiah (Num. 24:17), who is Christ (cf. Matt. 2:2, 10; Luke 1:78).

3:1–6: *The edict to the angel of Sardis.* Sardis was about thirty miles southeast of Thyatira, was once the capital of ancient Lydia, then a Seleucid kingdom, and had a Israelite community. A few Christ believers are praised, and it is said that they will have their names inscribed in the "book of life" (3:5), perhaps recalling citizen-registers of antiquity. Had they had their names removed from the synagogue register? For the apocalyptic image of Christ returning unexpectedly "like a thief in the night," see 1 Thess. 5:2; Matt. 24:42–44; Luke 12:39–40; 2 Pet. 3:10.

3:7–13: *The edict to the angel of Philadelphia.* The church group at Philadelphia, about thirty miles southeast of Sardis, is modestly praised for its endurance under persecution from the Israelite community (3:9–10). The "key of David" (3:7) from Isa. 22:22 suggests Christ's power to include or excommunicate (cf. Matt. 16:17–19; 18:18). For the "new Jerusalem," see Rev. 21:10–22:5.

3:14–22: *The edict to the angel of Laodicea.* Laodicea, the last city in the circuit, was about forty miles southeast of Philadelphia and due west of the first city, Ephesus, about one hundred miles. It was a very wealthy commercial city, its citizens having had the funds to rebuild the city after an earthquake in about 60/61 C.E. Jesus Movement members there are blamed for being "lukewarm" (3:16) and complacently wealthy (3:17), but they are spiritually poor. The "one who conquers" (see 2:1–7) in this passage is enthroned with Christ in the sky, as Christ is enthroned with God (Ps. 110:1; Acts 2:34–35; Rev. 22:1, 3). There are several visions of the heavenly throne room in Revelation, the first in the following chapter (4:1–11).

4:1–8:1: *Seven seals.* The vision in chapter 4 portrays the worship of God sitting on his throne in the sky (4:10), and that in chapter 5 notes that in his right hand is a scroll sealed with seven seals (5:1). These two visions introduce the visions of the seven seals in chapter 6 and two supplementary visions in chapter 7.

4:1–11: *The heavenly worship of God.* "In the spirit," the seer is invited to enter the opening in the sky to view the world from that perspective, a common theme in apocalyptic, astrological, and magical texts. Indeed, there is a throne constellation. The seer sees God seated on his throne in the sky reigning over the cosmos, an image derived in part from Ezek. 1 and 10 and Isa. 6 but also common to other religions of the period. The twenty-four elders seated on twenty-four thrones, who with the four living creatures also worship God, may have been suggested by the notion of *decans,* star-gods, each of whom rules ten degrees of the zodiac (hence, usually thirty-six, not twenty-four). Perhaps also in mind is the imagery of the emperor cult, the twelve tribes of Israel, and the twelve apostles (cf. Matt. 19:28). The four living creatures are described in Ezek. 1:5–21. In Ezek. 10:20–22, 14–15, they are cherubim. For their six wings, see Isa. 6:2.

5:1–14: *The scroll and the Lamb.* The scroll in God's right hand, which contains forthcoming events, has seven seals; no one can open it (inaugurate the events of the end), but "the Lion of the tribe of Judah, the Root of David" (5:5), that is, the Davidic Messiah (Isa. 11:1, 10; cf. Rev. 22:16), "has conquered" (see note on 2:1–7). In the sky the "lion" is the constellation Leo. The sacrificial Lamb has seven horns (power) and seven eyes (knowledge); a very frequent image in Revelation, it represents the exalted Christ who is also worshipped. The Lamb, of course, has Passover associations. It is also related to the sacrificial cult in Jerusalem and therefore suggests that the blood of Christ is now the means of atonement. In the sky, the cosmic Lamb is the constellation Aries. As the seer can see from the sky, he can also hear the cosmic chorus in the presence of God's throne (5:8–14).

6:1: *The opening of the seals by the Lamb.* This symbolizes what must happen before the end. When the first four seals are broken, the famous four horsemen who bring punishment to the world are revealed. The horses, colors, and bow are related to constellations, comets, and the visions in Zech. 1 and 6.

6:2: *The first seal.* A white horse from the east symbolizes victory. The Parthian armies are probably implied by the rider with a bow (cf. Rev. 17), but comet-stars in the sky are also horses. Whiteness and the crown may suggest the star-god Jupiter.

6:3–4: *The second seal.* A red horse from the south symbolizes war on the battlefield. There may be an allusion to the red planet Mars, god of war.

6:5–6: *The third seal.* A black horse from the north symbolizes famine. Black and the balance may suggest the star-god Mercury.

6:7–8: *The fourth seal.* A pale green horse from the west symbolizes death in the form of sword, famine, and flood. It may suggest the star-god Venus.

6:9–11: *The fifth seal.* This seal reveals the faithful martyrs. The altar in the sky may suggest the Milky Way.

6:12–17: *The sixth seal.* This seal reveals the apocalyptic cataclysm (cf. Mark 13:5–37 = Matt. 24:4–36 = Luke 21:8–36).

7:1–17: *Two supplementary visions.* In the first vision (7:1–8), there are four winds from the four corners of the earth (Ezek. 37:9; Dan. 7:2; Mark 13:27). The 144,000 elect (12,000 from each of the twelve tribes; see earlier) are sealed on their foreheads (cf. Ezek. 9; 14:1–5). They are before God's sky-throne. In the second (7:9–17), a great multitude of the elect are from "every nation, from all tribes and peoples and languages" (7:9; cf. 10:11; 13:7; 14:6; 17:15). They will survive the final tribulation.

8:1: *The seventh seal.* The seventh seal is a transition to the seven trumpets.

8:2–11:19: *Seven trumpets.* There are trumpet-shaped comets in the sky. Each trumpet blast announces a cosmic catastrophe (2 Enoch 30:8; cf. Matt. 24:31; 1 Thess. 4:16). The catastrophes are based on the plagues of Egypt (Exod. 7–10).

8:2–5: *The heavenly throne room.*

8:6: *The angels prepare to blow the trumpets.*

8:7: *The first trumpet.* Hail and fire are mixed with blood (Exod. 9:22–26).

8:8–9: *The second trumpet.* One-third of the sea becomes blood (Exod. 7:14–24).

8:10–11: *The third trumpet.* One-third of the fresh waters becomes bitter wormwood (cf. Jer. 9:15–16).

8:12: *The fourth trumpet.* One-third of the sun, moon, and stars are darkened (cf. Exod. 10:21–23).

8:13: *The three woes.* Each woe represents one of the next three trumpets or catastrophes (Rev. 9:12; 11:14).

9:1–12: *The fifth trumpet (first woe).* Like heaven, hell had an entrance. A star-demon falls to earth, and he opens up the abyss (Rev. 20:1–3, 7–10) and lets loose a plague of locusts (Exod. 10:4–20) with scorpion-like stingers, led by "Abaddon" (Aramaic: "Destruction") or Apollyon (Greek: "Destroyer").

9:13–21: *The sixth trumpet (second woe).* This trumpet probably heralds an invasion from the east, suggested by verse 14, which mentions the Euphrates River. It may be the Parthian invaders from the east, enemies of the Romans (cf. the sixth bowl, 16:12–16); however, the Euphrates River was also said to be in the sky.

10:1–11:14: *Two supplementary visions.* These two visions point ahead to the second cycle of visions (12:1–22:5). In the first supplementary vision (Rev. 10), "another mighty angel" (cf. 5:2) descends with a little open scroll (cf. 5:1) and announces that when the seventh trumpet is blown, there will be no more delay; the plan of God will be revealed (10:7). John is commanded to eat the scroll (Ezek. 2:8–3:3), which is sour (suffering) and yet sweet as honey (salvation of the elect), and then to prophesy about many peoples, nations, tongues, and kings (10:11; cf. 7:9; 13:7; 14:6; 17:15). In the second vision (Rev. 11:1–14), two mysterious witnesses prophesy that the time of woes will be limited to three and one-half years (11:2–3; cf. Dan. 7:25; 12:7; Rev. 12:6, 14; 13:5). The beast from the abyss (cf. 9:1–12) may be the Roman emperor or Antichrist (cf. 13:1–10; 17:8).

11:15–19: *The seventh trumpet (third woe).* This trumpet marks the final woes, resurrection of the dead for judgment, and salvation of the elect who are ruled over by the Lord and his anointed.

Second Cycle of Visions, 12:1–22:5

12:1–15:4: *Seven unnumbered visions.* The visions are usually marked by the formula "And I saw" (13:1, 11; 14:1, 6, 14; 15:1, 2). The main theme in this series is persecution.

12:1–18: *First vision.* The myth of a sky goddess who is pregnant with a savior and pursued by the many-headed monster of the abyss, or Leviathan (12:1–6), is well known in the religions of antiquity (Babylonian and Canaanite myths; the birth of Apollo; the Isis cult; Ps. 74:12–14; 1 Enoch 48:10). It is sometimes related to the constellation Virgo. Here the woman is also the heavenly Israel, which is the heavenly church. Her male child is the Davidic Messiah, who is also the heavenly Son of Man. The archangel Michael defeats the serpent, the monster, or the Devil, who is expelled from heaven (12:9); the woman is aided in her escape by the great eagle (12:14).

13:1–10:   *Second vision.*   The beast from the sea may be related to the constellation Cetus. It has ten horns (power) and seven heads (cf. Dan. 7:2–28). Although seven heads can be found in sky beings, most scholars think that it symbolizes the Roman Empire (cf. 7:9; 10:11; 14:6; 17:15; see further 17:10–14). The head that is mortally wounded and then healed (13:3) may refer to the Nero *redivivus* in the following vision.

13:11–18:   *Third vision.*   The second beast is from the earth; elsewhere it is identified with false prophets and false messiahs (e.g., 16:13; 19:20; cf. Mark 13:22). Its authority (13:12) may refer to emperor cult functionaries. Its miracle working is reminiscent of the lawless one (2 Thess. 2:9). Most scholars think that the number "666" (13:18) refers to a Nero *redivivus,* mostly likely Domitian, although this is much debated (see preceding discussion). An astrological explanation would be related to the constellation *therion* ("the Beast," that is, Lupus, the Wolf).

14:1–5:   *Fourth vision.*   The vision of the Lamb and his followers on Mount Zion in Jerusalem contrasts with that of the beast. For the 144,000 (14:1), see 7:1–8; they are the first fruits of the resurrection of the dead, presumably the martyrs of the first resurrection (20:4–6).

14:6–13:   *Fifth vision.*   Of the three angels, the first announces good news to all (cf. 7:9; 10:11; 13:7), the second announces the fall of Babylon (probably Rome; see preceding), and the third announces divine judgment on all.

14:14–20:   *Sixth vision.*   In Joel 4:13 and Isa. 63:3, the harvest and vintage images symbolize victory of the divine warrior and angry judgment on the nations. Here the harvest represents the salvation of the elect by the Son of Man (14:14; cf. Matt. 13:24–30), and the vintage represents the judgment of wicked (14:14). Compare Rev. 19:13, 15.

15:2–4:   *Seventh vision.*   The victors sing the song of Moses, recalling the victorious hymn of Moses and the escaping Israelites in Exod. 15.

15:1; 15:5–16:21:   *Seven bowls.*   The main theme in this series is judgment, and the opponents of God are more specific. Several parallels are in 2 Enoch 30.

15:1; 15:5–16:1:   *Seven angels; the last seven plagues = seven bowls.*   Rev. 15:1 introduces 15:5–19:10.

16:2:   *The first bowl.*   Sores come on those who have the mark of the beast (13:18; cf. Exod. 9:8–12).

16:3:   *The second bowl.*   The sea becomes blood (cf. Exod. 15:1–18).

16:4–7:   *The third bowl.*   The rivers and springs also turn to blood.

16:8–9:   *The fourth bowl.*   The sun burns people.

16:10–11:   *The fifth bowl.*   The kingdom of the throne of the beast turns into darkness (cf. Exod. 10:21–23).

16:12–16:   *The sixth bowl.*   This bowl is linked to the sixth trumpet (9:13–21) via the Euphrates. The battle in the sky has its earthly counterpart, and again the kings of the east are probably the Parthians (9:13–21). For the frogs, see Exod. 7:25–8:15; for the thief, see Matt. 24:43–44; Luke 12:39–40; 1 Thess. 5:2, 4; 2 Pet. 3:10. Hebrew *Harmageddon* means "Mountain of Megiddo." The plain before the ancient Israelite city of Megiddo was the site of many ancient battles.

16:17–21:   *The seventh bowl.*   God judges "Babylon" (probably Rome) and rains hailstones on it (Exod. 9:23–24). See the following Babylonian appendix.

17:1–19:10:   *Babylonian appendix.*   The punishment of "Babylon" = Rome is now detailed.

17:1–18:   *The great whore of Babylon (Rome).*   Ancient cities are always pictured as women. Although the expression "many waters" suggests Babylon (Jer. 51:13), the expression "seven mountains" in 17:9 suggests Rome, which is situated on seven hills. She is the great whore (see Isa. 1:21; 23:16–17) who has intercourse with the kings of the earth. She sits on a beast with ten horns and seven heads (see 13:1–10). In 17:12–16, the ten horns, or ten kings from the East, will leave the beast desolate, but in a great battle she will be defeated by the Lamb (17:14). 17:16 may allude to the Nero *redivivus* and the Parthian armies. From the perspective of astrology, the description best suits Venus.

18:1–24:   *A dirge about the fall of "Babylon."*

19:1–5:   *Responses in the heavenly throne room to Rome's fall.*

19:6–10:   *A victory song.*   This song celebrates the marriage of the Lamb (the groom) to the elect (the bride) (see 21:2, 9; 22:17; 2 Cor. 11:2; Eph. 5:25–33).

19:11–21:8:   *Seven unnumbered visions.*   These visions reveal the destruction of Satan's evil age (the devolution, decline, or running down of the world), then the millennial interim, then God's eternal age, and, finally, the divine city. They echo the ancient combat myth (see Rev. 12).

19:11–16:   *The first vision.*   The seer has a vision of heaven open and the heavenly Christ, called the Word of God and wearing a robe dipped in blood, astride a white horse. Following him are the heavenly armies clad in white linen, also astride white horses. All this is reminiscent of the holy war (2 Macc. 10:29–31). The heavenly Christ is once again "King of kings and Lord of lords" (19:16; cf. 17:14).

19:17–18:   *The second vision.*   God's banquet anticipates the following battle. Both visions recall Ezek. 39:4, 17–20.

19:19–21:   *The third vision.*   Opposing this army are the Antichrist (the beast 666, cf. Rev. 13:1–10, 18) and the kings of the earth with their armies, along with the false prophet (the second beast, cf. Rev. 13:11–17), that is, a miracle-working helper, a pseudo-Christ. The Antichrist and the false prophet are caught and thrown into the lake of fire, a place of eternal damnation and punishment, and the rest are slain with a two-edged sword issuing from the mouth of the heavenly Christ. So ends the reign of idolatrous Rome and the Antichrist!

20:1–3:   *The fourth vision.*   An angel descends from the sky, binds Satan, who is the mythical dragon, and locks him in the bottomless pit.

20:4–10:   *The fifth vision.*   The martyrs for Christ are now raised (the first resurrection) and reign with Christ as priestly judges for one thousand years (the millennium). However, all is not ended. After the millennium, Satan is released to deceive the enemy nations, called "Gog and Magog" (Ezek. 38–39). In the *Babylonian Talmud* these terms represent Israel's enemies (*Berakoth* 7b and *Sanhedrin* 97b). Here the Gog and Magog surround the martyrs and Christ in Jerusalem, but fire comes down from the sky and destroys them, once and for all. Now the devil is thrown into the lake of fire with the Antichrist and the false prophet, and there they are tormented forever.

20:11–15: *The sixth vision.* John "sees" God on his great white throne, and from God's presence heaven and earth disappear. The dead (except the martyrs) are raised for judgment (the second resurrection), and Death and Hades, along with those evil ones whose names are not written in the book of life, are also cast into the lake of fire.

21:1–8: *The seventh vision.* Next the seer has a vision of a new creation, a new heaven and new earth (cf. Isa. 65:17; *Baruch* 32:6; 48:50; 51:3; *1 Enoch* 45:4–5), and a new Jerusalem descends to earth, prepared as a bride adorned for her husband. The new age has begun! God and Christ now join the saints in the New Jerusalem in eternal joy and bliss.

21:9–22:5: *Jerusalem appendix.* Finally the seer is transported by one of the seven angels to a high mountain, where he is shown the divine city. It is a square-shaped Jerusalem (cf. Ezek. 40–48; 11QTemple in the **Dead Sea Scrolls**), the city is the bride of the Lamb (cf. 19:7), and it descends from the sky in all of its magnificent glory.

Epilogue, 22:6–21

22:6–20: *Sayings, epistolary authentication.* It includes the *Maranatha,* "Come, Lord Jesus!" (1 Cor. 16:21).

22:21: *Letter-like benediction.*

THE ENDURING INFLUENCE OF APOCALYPTIC

The most obvious influence of apocalyptic from the early churches is the persistence of millennial movements in the Christian churches. Throughout Christian history, believers have fed their hopes on New Testament millennial visions and calculated the date of the coming of Jesus as Son of Man. Many groups still do. Similarly, the beast whose number is "666" (Rev. 13:18) has been identified with most every tyrant in Western history, including Hitler and Stalin.

The Apocalypse has influenced worldwide millennial movements that have come in contact with Christianity. A vivid example is the Native American movement related to the great vision of Black Elk, a holy man of the Oglala Sioux, as reported by him to John G. Neihardt. Here is a scene taken at random from that vision:

> And as I looked and wept, I saw that there stood on the north side of the starving camp a sacred man who was painted red all over his body, and he held a spear as he walked into the center of the people, and there he lay down and rolled. And when he got up, it was a fat bison standing there, and where the tree had been in the center of the nation's hoop. The herb grew and bore four blossoms on a single stem while I was looking—a blue, a white, a scarlet, and a yellow—and the bright rays of these flashed to the heavens. I know now what this meant, that the bison were the gift of a good spirit and were our strength, but we should lose them, and from the same good spirit we must find another strength.
>
> (J. Neihardt, *Black Elk Speaks,* p. 32)

Like John of Patmos, Black Elk speaks for his oppressed people. Recalling the past, he hopes for a day when the white man will be gone and the bison will return. Such hopes were prominent in the Ghost Dance Movement that lay in the background of one of the most tragic events in American history, the massacre of Native Americans at Wounded Knee, South Dakota, in 1890.

In the modern period many liberal Christians have not been attracted to Revelation because it is a major source book for Fundamentalism, and many feminists have been disturbed by its images of women. Yet, as noted at the outset, poets and artists have found it an unending source of inspiration precisely because it uses images of immense evocative power. It has also been helpful to peoples undergoing oppression or crisis. The human mind's fundamental propensity to embrace myth or symbol when attempting to approach the ultimates of human experience or expectation is found in Amos Wilder's poetic expression of his experience in the First World War.

> There we marched out on haunted battleground,
> There smelled the strife of gods, were brushed against
> By higher beings, and were wrapped around
> With passions not of earth, all dimly sensed.
> > There saw we demons fighting in the sky
> > And battles in aerial mirage,
> > The feverish very lights proclaimed them by,
> > Their tramplings woke our panting, fierce barrage.
> Their tide of battle, hither, thither, driven
> Filled earth and sky with cataclysmic throes,
> Our strife was but the mimicry of heaven's
> And we the shadows of celestial foes.

The Book of Revelation is pervaded with the human mind thinking at a level of ultimate meaning. At that level it turns naturally to the use of myth and symbol as they related to both the sky and the earth. In the apocalyptic literature of Greco-Roman Israel and the Jesus Movement, ultimate meaning came from the belief that the devolution of the cosmos and the oppressive course of human history were not the final answer to those who had an absolute trust in the final purposes of God.

STUDY QUESTIONS

1. What is the church tradition about Revelation? Who was John of Patmos? What do most modern scholars say about author, date, and place?

2. What is the importance of numbers symbolism and the numbers "four," "twelve," and "seven"? How does the number "666" relate to time and place?

3. What is the social-historical context of Revelation? In what sense is Revelation prophecy or apocalyptic? How and why is the author so preoccupied with the sky? Where were the seven churches, and why does John complain about them? Who were the 144,000? What are the beast and the whore of Babylon symbols? What is the millennium in Revelation? Is the Book of Revelation a book of hope? How?

Photo 13.1   The Eucharistic Meal mural in the catacombs of Callistus in Rome, second century C.E. The reclining position at meals was usual. By the time the Christian literature in Chapter Thirteen was written, Jesus' last meal (1 Cor 11:11–23–24; Mark 14:22–25; Matt 26:26–29; Luke 22:15–20; John 13; 6:11) was becoming a sacred rite separate from a meal (1 Cor 11:27–34; *Didachē* 9, 10; Ignatius *Letter to the Smyrneans* 6; Justin Martyr *Apology* 1.65–67). The fish became a "condensed symbol" for Christianity itself ("fish" = Greek *ICHTHYS,* an acrostic: *I* = *Iēsous* [Jesus]; *CH* = *CHristos* ["Christ"; *TH* = *THeou* ["God's"]; *YS* = *YioS* ["Son"], or "Jesus Christ God's Son").

THE BEGINNINGS OF INSTITUTIONALISM: 1 PETER, JAMES, 1 AND 2 TIMOTHY, TITUS, JUDE, 2 PETER

Traditionally the letters in the New Testament are divided into two groups: the "Pauline Epistles" (including 1 and 2 Timothy and Titus, called the "Pastoral Epistles") and the "Catholic Epistles" (James; 1 and 2 Peter; Jude; and 1, 2, and 3 John). The latter group was called "Catholic" ("universal") Epistles because the letters are addressed to the church in general rather than to a particular individual or congregation. Today these letters are usually grouped according to literary and historical criteria. We have discussed seven undisputed (Chapters Five and Six) and four disputed Pauline letters (Chapter Seven), and we have taken up 1, 2, and 3 John in connection with the Gospel of John (Chapter Eleven). This chapter concerns itself with the remaining seven letters.

In the period of roughly 90–125 C.E., new problems and possibilities faced the churches. Although Revelation demonstrates that millennialism could resurface, many, perhaps most, Christ believers thought that the *parousia* was no longer near. They were learning to adjust to the destruction of Jerusalem and the temple, and they sought to develop social relations with Israelites, Greeks, Romans, and others in more "acceptable" ways. Religious movements that survive usually have to settle down to the process of determining their relationship to the rest of society, to sufficiently assimilate to cultural norms, values, and beliefs. At the same time, they draw boundaries, that is, they develop more formalized sets of beliefs to determine who "we" are, as contrasted with who "they" are. Members of the Jesus Movement descending from the house of Israel, which was forming its canon, began to be conscious that they needed their own authoritative texts. Some of Paul's letters, as well as three attributed to him, probably had become a collection. No doubt gospels were beginning to become authoritative, as well. Moreover, the churches began to develop their own formal institutions, organizational structures, and decision-making boards. Authoritative roles and their corresponding functions were beginning to look like formalized offices, especially at the local level. The churches at the end of the New Testament period were beginning to establish a creed, a canon, a liturgy, and an organized ordained ministry. This is institutionalization. It would reach a more unified self-definition as "Christianity" in the fourth century C.E.

The New Testament canon was a *choice* of books that was only *eventually* accepted by certain church leaders. Some smaller genres of literature—sayings collections, parable collections, miracle collections—survived by being incorporated into other, larger genres. Some documents, for example, the *Gospel of Thomas* or *The Acts of Paul and Thecla,* were in use by groups in the Jesus Movement but were ultimately rejected by the growing majority of believers. Still other documents now collected as the **Church Fathers** were almost accepted (e.g., *1 Clement*). There was no unanimity on the Book of Revelation in the East. Hebrews had its difficulties in the West. Manuscripts from the third century show that some books ultimately rejected were included and that some books ultimately included were not yet accepted. From a strictly historical perspective, all known books in use in the early second century should be considered alongside the canonical books. This chapter, however, will discuss only the New Testament texts and in this order: 1 Peter, James, the Pastorals, Jude, and 2 Peter. Then will come the characteristics of emerging institutionalism and some remarks on the interpretation of its literature.

1 PETER AND THE PETRINE CIRCLE

1 Peter claims to be a letter written by Peter and his companions in Babylon ". . . to the exiles [resident aliens] of the Dispersion in Pontus, Galatia, Cappadocia, Asia, and Bithynia. . . ." (1:1; 5:12–13; cf. James 1:1). It will be important to look more closely at these references.

Peter, Babylon, and the Dispersion in Asia Minor

We have encountered Peter before. "Peter" is one of four names given to the same person. The other three are "Symeon" (Acts 15:14; 2 Pet. 1:1); "Simon," the Greek equivalent of "Symeon" (many times, especially in the Gospels and Acts); and "Cephas," a transliteration of the Aramaic word for "rock" (Gospel of John [once], 1 Corinthians [four times], Galatians [four times]). The English "Peter" is derived from the Greek *Petros,* which also means "rock" and translates the Aramaic "Cephas." It occurs by far most frequently, largely in the Gospels and Acts. According to the Gospel of Matthew, the name *Petros* was the name bestowed by Jesus on Symeon/Simon: "Blessed are you, Simon son of Jonah . . . You are Peter (Greek *Petros* [Aramaic *Kēphas,* or Cephas]) and on this rock (*petra;* Aramaic *kēpha*) I will build my church" (Matt. 16:17).

Here is a summary of information about Peter. Peter was the "son of Jonah" (Aramaic *bar-Jonah*), married (Mark 1:30 = Matt. 8:14 = Luke 4:38; 1 Cor. 9:5), and had a brother Andrew, who also became Jesus' disciple (Mark 1:16–20 = Matt.

4:18–22). They and another set of brothers, James and John, sons of Zebedee, were fishermen on the northwestern corner of the Sea of Galilee near Capernaum, where Peter lived. Some archeologists think they have identified Peter's house there. The synoptic gospels portray Peter as the leading and representative disciple, usually the spokesman for the other disciples. In John, the Beloved Disciple rivals him (John 20). Despite his denial of Jesus, Peter is said by Paul to have been the first to see the resurrected Jesus (1 Cor. 15:3; cf. Luke 24:34). In Acts, he is the first major leader of the Jerusalem church (Acts 1–5). Paul says he was a "pillar" at Jerusalem and an apostle to the Israelites (Gal. 2:9). Tradition places his death in Rome under Nero (*1 Clement* 5).

"Babylon," claimed to be the location of the writing of 1 Peter (5:13), probably refers to Rome (see Chapter Twelve). The author of 1 Peter says that it was written to "exiled" members of the Jesus Movement in five Roman provinces in central and northern Asia Minor. The exiles are said to be facing various kinds of trials and sufferings (e.g., 2:19–20; 4:12–16).

Church Tradition about 1 Peter

1 Peter was accepted as the composition of Jesus' disciple Peter by the late second century C.E. (Irenaeus *Against Heresies* 4.9.2). Probably the belief in Petrine authorship was current earlier. A **Church Father,** Polycarp (ca. 70–156 C.E.), was said to have quoted from "the former epistle of Peter" (Eusebius *Church History* 4.14.9). This tradition appears to be confirmed by Polycarp's letter *To the Philippians,* written before 140 C.E., because he often refers to 1 Peter (*To the Philippians* 1:3 [1 Pet. 1:8]; 2:1 [1 Pet. 1:15, 21]; 6:3 [1 Pet. 3:13]; etc.). 1 Peter sends greetings from "my son Mark" (5:13) who, said Papias (ca. 135–140 C.E.), was the "interpreter of Peter" (Eusebius *Church History* 3.39.15). Whether historical or not, this shows that Mark was believed to be an associate of Peter. Thus Peter's name was linked to the writing we call "1 Peter" by the second quarter of the second century.

Historical Criticism

There is no scholarly consensus about the dating of 1 Peter. Very important with respect to dating is the sudden shift in tone at 4:12. The references to suffering and persecution earlier (e.g., 1:6; 3:14; 4:1), as well as to "trials," suffering "for righteousness' sake," and "abuse," are very general. In 4:12, however, the readers are said to endure some "fiery ordeal," and in 5:8 they are warned, "like a roaring lion, your adversary the devil prowls around, looking for someone to devour." These latter references appear to be more specific. Do they imply an actual persecution? One common theory is that 1:1 to 4:11 deals with the general possibility of suffering but that after 4:11 there is reference to an actual persecution.

If one accepts this theory, there are three known possibilities. The first is the persecution by Romans at Rome under Nero about 64 C.E., accepted as the occasion for Peter's martyrdom. The second is some local persecution in western Asia Minor under Domitian in the 90s, the time usually suggested for the Book of Revelation.

The third is a persecution in Asia Minor in the early second century under the emperor Trajan (98–117 C.E.; see Chapter Twelve). Those who have tried to defend actual Petrine authorship with a secretary hypothesis have defended the earliest date. Some scholars have favored the latest date. Bithynia in northern Asia Minor is one known location of persecution (Pliny-Trajan correspondence, Chapter Twelve), and Bithynia is mentioned in 1 Pet. 1:1. Recent scholarship, however, noting the absence of any official, empire-wide Roman persecution of the Jesus Movement prior to 251 C.E., sees the suffering mentioned in 1 Peter as the result of sporadic, localized, native harassment of Jesus Movement members. Accordingly, the date of the letter must be determined on other grounds, such as its reflection of a social situation subsequent to Paul and the letter's existence prior to either *1 Clement* (ca. 96 C.E.), which appears at points to echo 1 Peter, or the Pliny-Trajan correspondence (ca. 111–112 C.E.). The position adopted here is the second position, from the latter period of the first century. This date does not require an *actual* Roman political persecution under Domitian (81–96 C.E.). Rather, it is built on local, sporadic oppression of Christ-believer minorities in native environments, which fits certain conditions in the book (see following).

Did Jesus' disciple Peter, who was martyred about 64–67 C.E., write 1 Peter? It is very unlikely. The question is related to disputed issues: literacy and literary style, genre, traditions, developed theological ideas, date, place, and addressees. Briefly, the literary style of 1 Peter is characterized by sophisticated Hellenistic Greek rhetorical devices: the play on words ("perishable/imperishable" [*phthartēs/aphthartou*], 1:23); carefully paralleled clauses ("whoever . . . ; whoever . . . ," 4:11); the series of similar compound words ("imperishable, undefiled and unfading," 1:4); and others. It is written in excellent Greek, and all quotations from and allusions to the scriptures come from the Greek **Septuagint.** It is not likely that such Greek would have been written by a Galilean fisherman who was illiterate or at best possessed of "craftsman's literacy" and whose native tongue was Aramaic. Modern scholars who have defended Petrine authorship have usually suggested that its style came from Silvanus (5:12) functioning as Peter's secretary. Most scholars, however, do not accept this view because of an accumulation of other problems, especially those involving the letter's traditions and ideas. Here are some examples.

First, the author of 1 Peter knows Jesus traditions (1:13 [Luke 12:35]; 2:12c [Matt. 5:16]; 3:9 [Matt. 5:44]; 3:14 [Matt. 5:10]; 4:14 [Luke 6:22]), but he does not attribute them to Jesus! Would Jesus' leading disciple have done that? 1 Peter also incorporates a variety of developed ideas, including remnants of preaching formulas or perhaps fragments of a Christological hymn in 1 Pet. 3:18–19, 22 (discussed in Chapter Three). Would an intimate peasant disciple in Jesus' network have thought about Jesus this way? 1 Pet. 1:3 speaks of "new birth into a living hope" and an explicit mention of baptism in 3:21. This reflects the use of language and imagery associated with baptismal tradition. Similarly, the author stresses the saving significance of Jesus' Resurrection to God's right hand, a widespread belief in the Jesus Movement that interprets Ps. 110:1 (e.g., Acts 2:33–36).

If Babylon (1:1) symbolized Rome, as it did in apocalyptic literature, including Revelation (e.g., 18:2, 10, 21), 1 Peter could have come from a Petrine circle at

Rome. Peter had been very influential there and according to tradition was martyred there. The book stresses persons known to have been associated with Paul, that is, Silvanus (1 Pet. 5:12 [Acts 15:22, 27 (= Silas)]), John Mark (1 Pet. 5:13 [Philem. 23; Col. 4:10], and certain ideas related to Paul's letter to the Romans (e.g., 1 Pet. 3:21–22 [Rom. 4:24; 8:34; 6:11]).

Social-Historical Factors

1 Peter is addressed to "exiles [resident aliens] of the Dispersion in Pontus, Galatia, Cappadocia, Asia, and Bithynia. . . ." (1:1; cf. 5:12–13) in Asia Minor. The term "Dispersion" refers to the Israelite **Diaspora;** thus members of the Jesus Movement were being compared to Israelites who no longer lived in their homeland. They are said to have an "alien residence" (1:17) or to be "aliens and exiles [visiting strangers]" "among the Gentiles" (2:11). "Resident alien" is a single word in Greek, *paroikos,* and it had a technical meaning (Elliott). It referred to a registered, displaced person living abroad, a "foreigner" with certain political, economic, legal, and social restrictions. *Paroikos* is used in the **Septuagint** and other Greek literature to refer to displaced Israelites of the Diaspora. Such persons were beneath the status of full citizens, on the one hand, but above the status of mere "transients" (Greek: *xenoi,* "strangers"), freedmen, and slaves, on the other. Longer residence at one location could naturally change one's status from "transient" to "resident alien." In exceptional cases, freedmen and slaves were also granted the "resident alien" status.

Yet, *paroikos* could also have symbolic significance. It could refer to someone who was not "at home" in the environment. Although it has such overtones in 1 Peter, it is not simply symbolic and spiritual. Rather, the term "resident aliens" in 1 Peter refers in the first place to members of a group of Christ believers, an oppressed minority who was being exhorted to maintain its purity in a "pagan," sometimes hostile environment. There is a clear attempt to show outsiders—nonbelieving families of believers, Romans, and the like—that the movement was not subversive. Although *some* members of the community were of Israelite background, *most* were converted Gentiles. Perhaps the group included newly relocated rural villagers. In any case, the members of the group were not "at home" in their social environment. Symbolic overtones associated with the term are grounded in social reality.

A key term related to *paroikos* by etymology and social context is *oikos,* or "house." *Oikos* is used as a metaphor in 1 Peter. The term describes its recipients: They are a "spiritual house(hold)" (2:5) and the "house(hold) of God" (4:17). Yet, the term is also grounded in social reality. When the head of the household converted and was baptized, so usually were the members of his household. In such houses the *paterfamilias* had absolute authority over his wife, children, and servants. Well-ordered household management (Greek: *oikonomia*) was thought to be the foundation of the well-ordered society. This was expressed in the traditional household management tradition sometimes called a **"household code"** (Chapters Three and Seven). 1 Peter makes use of this tradition (2:13–3:9; cf. 5:1–5a). Moreover, the "household" is a way of referring to the believing community. Thus the *oikos,* or household of God, was composed of actual *paroikoi,* or "resident aliens," who experienced *paroikia,* or "homelessness." This "household" symbolized the community. A byproduct of this social analysis is that the possibility of an actual *political* persecution becomes less certain.

A Letter or a Sermon about Baptism?

1 Peter has the formal features of a letter. It has a prescript that mentions the author as Peter, the recipients, and a prayer (1:1–2) and it concludes with a postscript containing final greetings, the kiss, and the peace wish (5:12–14). Its letter body (1:3–5:11) is filled with ethical exhortation, common in the letters of the Jesus Movement. The salutation contains no personal greetings, and there are no personal relations developed between author and recipients. Yet, the postscript contains personal greetings. The book contains the language of baptism, for example, "new birth into a living hope" (1 Pet. 1:3), being "born anew" (1:23). 1 Pet. 2:2 states, "Like newborn infants, long for the pure, spiritual milk, so that by it you may grow into salvation. . . ." 1 Pet. 3:21 reads, "And baptism, which this [the eight persons who in the days of Noah were saved from the flood waters] prefigured, now saves you—not as a removal of dirt from the body, but as an appeal to God for a good conscience, through the resurrection of Jesus Christ. . . ." These terms and phrases about water, rebirth, and infancy are the language of baptism, that is, of entering the state of childlike innocence and growing in faith. Some earlier scholars have therefore suggested that 1 Pet. 1:3–4:11 is a reworked baptismal homily or sermonette. This hypothesis, however, finds little support among more recent scholars, who generally regard 1 Peter as a genuine letter. Perhaps in a time of oppression or persecution the author used baptism to remind his readers of the spirit in which they first affiliated with the Jesus Movement, in which case 4:12–5:11 points to the specific historical situation of the recipients in Asia Minor.

Summary

1 Peter is probably best understood as a pseudonymous letter written about 80–90 C.E. at Rome by a member of the Petrine circle of the Jesus Movement. He used the pseudonym of the apostle to encourage and exhort oppressed members of the Jesus Movement in central and northern Asia Minor. Perhaps persons in the communities addressed had been recruited to the Jesus Movement by followers of Peter. In any case, the purpose of 1 Peter was to express concern for, solidarity with, and encouragement of, believers at a time when the Roman church was growing in importance (cf. *1 Clement;* letters of Ignatius *Romans*).

Structure

Here is a tentative outline:

1:1–2	Opening greeting
1:3–4:11	Sermonette, possibly based on a sermon about baptism

4:12–5:11   An exhortation to stand fast in the face of oppression

5:12–14   Closing greetings

Exegetical Survey

1:1–2:   *Opening greetings.*   The author claims to be Peter writing to "strangers of the Dispersion."

1:3–4:11:   *The first section, perhaps based on a sermon about baptism.*

1:3–9:   *An opening blessing.*   It was (and is) customary in Israelite worship to bless God for saving humanity. Here we may have a development of that liturgical practice. The language of "rebirth" occurs in 1:3. Note how the author moves from "him" to "us" to "you" as his thought moves from God to Christ believers in general and then to the group he is addressing.

1:10–12:   *Salvation as the fulfillment of prophecy.*

1:13–2:10:   *An exhortation to be God's holy people.*   This is an ethical exhortation based upon key biblical passages for holiness ("[You shall] be holy, for I am holy" [Lev. 11:44–45] and related to rebirth [2:2, 22–23]). Interwoven with the exhortation is reflection upon the identity of the believers and the significance of Christ: He is foreknown; he is the Lamb of God; he is the elect, precious cornerstone. The first theme may come from a Christological hymn (see preceding and Chapter Three). The latter two are metaphors developed from passages in the Hebrew Bible much used in the New Testament, the Lamb from Isa. 53 and the stone set in Zion (Isa. 28:16; Ps. 118:22; Isa. 8:14), which has led to other scriptural passages mentioning stones. The community is also a "spiritual house" (2:5; cf. 4:17) and a "holy priestly community" (see Hebrews, Chapter Seven).

2:11–3:12:   *An exhortation on honorable conduct among outsiders.*   This is a long parenetical section dealing with the relation of believers as strangers and resident aliens to the outside Gentile world. It begins with an emphasis on maintaining good conduct among the outsiders (2:11–12) and moves to the necessity for accepting the authority of earthly rulers (2:13–17). In this latter passage we see the practical necessity for Christ believers to adjust to the realities of their social context (insofar as commitment to God is not compromised). As the author of Luke-Acts addresses the subject of the believer's relationship to the empire, so the author of 1 Peter finds it necessary to speak to the believer's relationship to institutions of authority. Next the writer turns to the domestic realm ("a household code"), treating the responsibilities of domestic slaves, wives, and husbands (2:18–25; 3:1–6).

A feature of this development is the use of Isa. 53. Let us compare 1 Pet. 2:21–25 with Isa. 53.

Isaiah 53	Peter 2:21–25
(4) . . . Surely he has borne our infirmities . . .	(21) . . . (Christ) also suffered for you, leaving you an example, so that that you should follow his steps.
(9) . . . although he had done no violence, and there was no deceit in his mouth.	(22) He committed no sin, neither was guile found in his mouth.
(7) He was oppressed, and he was	(23) When he was abused,

afflicted,
yet he did not open his mouth;
like a lamb that is led to the slaughter,
and like a sheep that before its shearers
is silent . . . ,
so he did not open his mouth.
(11d) He shall bear their iniquities
(cf. 4 – 6)
(5d) by his bruise we were healed.
(6) All we like sheep have gone astray;

he did not return abuse; when he
suffered, he did not threaten; but he
entrusted himself to the one that
judges justly;
(24) He himself bore our sins in his
body upon the cross, so that, free
from sins, we might live for
righteousness;
by his wound you have been healed.
(25) For you were going astray like
sheep. . . .

The parallels are too close to be accidental. In 1 Pet. 2:21–25 the suffering servant of Isa. 53 has provided the language and model for describing to household servants the crucified Jesus as God's suffering servant.

3:13 – 4:6: *Further exhortation and exposition.* This passage deals in general with Christ believers preparing to suffer for their faith and in their prospective suffering to follow the example of Jesus' martyrdom. It reflects the suffering servant of Isaiah as well. Verses 3:18–22 (see also 4:1–6) claim that Christ, made alive in the Spirit, preached to the spirits in prison, that is, the disobedient angels/spirits of primordial time (Gen. 6:1–4) and Noah's day. There is a strong possibility that there are fragments of Christological hymns and confessions in this section.

4:7–11: *With the end at hand, support one another.* The section climaxes on the note of anticipation of the *parousia,* providing motivation for the exhortation that follows.

4:12–5:11: *Suffering.* The general suffering in the last part of the book looks more specific, raising the possibility that the author has in mind real suffering. The writer exhorts his readers to stand fast and reiterates many themes.

5:12–14: *Commendation of Silvanus and closing greetings* from the brotherhood in Babylon/Rome and Mark.

THE LETTER OF JAMES

Traditions about James

"James" (Greek: *Iakōbus*) was a common, apparently popular, name in the first century C.E. In this letter, James is described as "a servant of God and of the Lord Jesus Christ" writing "to the twelve tribes in the Dispersion" (1:1). Who was this James?

Several people in the New Testament were named James. One was the son of Zebedee, the disciple of Jesus (Mark 1:19). Another was the son of Alphaeus, also a disciple of Jesus (Mark 3:18). Still another was the son of Mary (Mark 15:40). The father of Judas was also a certain James (Luke 6:16; Acts 1:13). Finally, there is the brother of Jesus (Mark 6:3), who after Jesus' death became the leader of the church at Jerusalem (e.g., Gal. 2:9, 12; 1 Cor. 15:7; Acts 15:13).

Were any of these persons the author of the Book of James? Later church tradition said, "yes." It identified him with the brother of Jesus in Mark 6:3. Recall that Jesus' brother James was also the conservative "pillar" of the early Jerusalem church (cf. Gal. 2:1–10; Hegisippus in Eusebius *Church History* 2.23.4). This tradition is easy to reconcile with the focus on the Law in the writing. Especially Christ believers with Israelite background called this James "James the Just"; the same view is found in the *Gospel of Thomas* 12. In the late first century, Josephus wrote that the high priest Ananus had James executed by stoning (*Antiquities* 20.9.197–203). In the late second century, Hegisippus claimed that the Pharisees and Sadducees had him hurled from the pinnacle of the Jerusalem temple, whereupon he was stoned and clubbed to death (Eusebius *Church History* 2.23.4–18). What was the purpose of this later church identification, and how might it have been found plausible?

Historical Criticism

The book called "The Letter of James" begins with greetings (1:1) and contains a number of direct addresses (1:2–5, etc.), but formally it lacks certain features of a genuine letter, such as an epistolary postscript. It consists mostly of ethical exhortation or encouragement. Indeed, half of its 108 verses contain verbs of command!

Moral exhortation (scholars call it *parenesis*) is common in the literature of the ancient world. Proverbs and practical wisdom were borrowed from the Israelites. You will recall that moral instruction on household management (**household codes**) was presented by Hellenistic moral philosophers and was taken over and modified in the Jesus Movement. In the New Testament writings there are collections of ethical teachings ascribed to Jesus (especially Matthew's Sermon on the Mount) and the exhortations in the Pauline and deutero-Pauline letters. It is obvious that there was a strong tradition of moral teaching in the social environment, as well as within the Jesus Movement that borrowed from it, although it also developed its own distinctive forms.

The existence of a lively hortatory tradition (exhortations) in the Jesus Movement is important for understanding James. One consequence is that verbal similarities between James and other New Testament writings do not mean that James necessarily knows them; they may have come from a common oral tradition.

The Book of James contains sayings that are ascribed to Jesus in the Gospels, especially in the Matthean Sermon on the Mount. It is striking that in James they are not ascribed to Jesus. Compare the following examples.

James	Gospels
James 1:22: But be doers of the word, and not merely hearers who deceive themselves.	**Matt. 7:24–27:** "Everyone then who *hears these words of mine and acts on them* will be like a wise man who built his house on rock. . . ."
James 4:12: There is one lawgiver and judge who is able to save and to destroy. So who, then, are you to judge your neighbor?	**Matt. 7:1:** "Do not judge, so that you may not be judged."

James 5:12: Above all, my beloved, *do not swear, either by heaven or by earth or by any other oath,* but *let your "Yes" be yes and your "No" be no,* so that you may not fall under condemnation.

Matt. 5:33–37: "Again, you have heard that it was said to those of ancient times, 'You shall not swear falsely, but carry out the vows you have made to the Lord.' But I say to you, *Do not swear at all, either by heaven,* for it is the throne of God, *or by the earth* for it is his footstool, *or by Jerusalem,* for it is the city of the Great King. And do not swear by your head, for you cannot make one hair white or black. *Let your word be 'Yes, Yes' or 'No, No';* anything more than this comes from the evil one."

There is also exhortation material similar to that in 1 Peter, as in this example:

James

James 4:1–2: Those conflicts and disputes among you, where do they come from? Do they not come from your *cravings that are at war within you?* You want something and do not have it; so you commit murder. And you covet something and cannot obtain it; so you engage in disputes and conflicts. You do not have, because you do not ask.

1 Peter

1 Pet. 2:11: Beloved, I urge you as aliens and exiles to abstain from the *desires of the flesh that wage war against the soul.*

Again, it is not that James necessarily knows the Gospels or 1 Peter, but rather that there is a tradition of exhortation into which sayings ascribed to Jesus in the Gospels have been taken up, although not in the form of sayings of Jesus.

Like the author of 1 Peter, the author of James uses Hellenistic Greek literary rhetorical devices. There are plays on Greek words, for example, 4:14, "That appears for a little time and then vanishes" (Greek: *phainomenē/aphanizomen*). This author uses the diatribe, which presents an argument in the form of a dialogue between the writer and an imaginary interlocutor (2:18–26; 5:13–15). The "letter" of James also contains a number of **aphorisms,** a form characteristic of Jesus' teaching.

This writing has a striking feature: It has very little that is distinctive of the Jesus Movement. Jesus Christ is mentioned only twice (1:1; 2:1), and both verses could be omitted without any harm to the flow of thought in the text. When the "coming of the Lord" is mentioned (5:7), there is nothing to denote there that it is Jesus; it could be a reference to the Lord *God.* "Faith" in this text is simply the acceptance of monotheism (2:19). These facts have led some scholars to suggest that the text is an Israelite homily touched up by a member of the Jesus Movement. Yet, contacts with the tradition of ethical exhortation in the movement and the discussion of the Pauline terms "faith" and "works" in 2:14–26, which seem to presuppose Gal. 3 and Rom. 4, suggest an origin within the movement. The discussion of faith and works in James 2:14–26 caused Martin Luther to contrast James unfavorably with the main texts in the New Testament as "a right strawy epistle in comparison with them, for it has no gospel character to it" (introduction to his German New Testament, 1522).

The author's use of Hellenistic Greek rhetorical devices, his lack of specific references to Jesus, and his tendency not to exhibit conservatism about Israelite Law, which was characteristic of Jesus' brother, pose problems for the identification of the author as that particular James. Moreover, if the issue of faith versus works (2:14–26) echoes Paul, which is very likely, a date a generation or so after Paul suggests itself, and this date does not easily comport with various traditions claiming that James was martyred in the 60s (Josephus *Antiquities* 20.9 197–203; Eusebius *Church History* 2.23.4–18).

A final problem for identifying this book as a "letter" of Jesus' brother is that the book was not widely known until it was popularized by the **Church Father** Origen in the third century C.E. By that time other pseudonymous books circulated under the name "James," for example, the *Protoevangelium of James* and the *Acts of James*. Perhaps the author of James developed some traditions that came from James, or he *thought* that his traditions came from Jesus' brother, but that does not add conviction to the view that James actually wrote the work. Thus most scholars are convinced that it is **pseudonymous.**

Key Ideas and Social-Historical Context of James

The author of the Book of James describes his addressees with language characteristic of Israelites living in Greco-Roman cities, that is, "the twelve tribes in the Dispersion [**Diaspora**]" (1:1) and the "synagogue" (2:2). Monotheism and the Law are important to him (2:19). The writing frequently combines Israelite and Hellenistic ethical exhortation. It is possible that the intended readers/hearers of this book were Israelite believers, although it is also possible that there were also some Gentile believers ("God-fearers") in the group.

The group is marked by internal social conflict. There are not only ethnic, but also economic and social differences. The author condemns the wealthy and defends the poor (e.g., 2:6–7; 5:1–6). He requires that his readers/hearers help the needy (2:14–17) and that they should love their neighbors as themselves (2:8–13). Finally, there appear to be power/status divisions between leaders—teachers (3:1–18) and elders (5:14)—and ordinary followers, although the function of "presbyter" or "elder" is important as part of a healing rite in which he anoints the sick with oil and prays over them (5:14–15). Nonetheless, "teachers" will be judged with greater strictness than others (3:1). This latter division suggests a certain degree of institutionalism.

The Pure and Holy Community

It is clear that cultural and social divisions in the community were leading to disruption, discrimination, and disunity. Members of the community sought to curry favor from outsiders, especially wealthy and influential patrons (2:1–4), and the writer of James considers them to be compromising their values. As the author admonishes the community, "Adulterers! Do you not know that friendship with the world is enmity with God?" (4:4a). The group also dishonored and exploited the poor (2:6–7), pursued selfish self-interest (4:1–10), and slandered brothers (4:11–12). There was gossip (3:1–12), hypocrisy (2:1–12), lack of serious commitment (1:6–8), and even apostasy and defection (5:19–20). In short, the community had become polluted or defiled.

In response, the author appeals to completeness and wholeness (NRSV 1:4: "mature and complete," cf. 1:17, 25; 2:22; 3:2), purity and holiness (e.g., 1:21, 26, 27; 3:6), which implies endurance (1:3–4), stability, and order. You will recall that holiness was one of the great themes of Israel (Chapter One). Here the appeal has personal, social, and cosmic dimensions (Elliott). Personal doubt must be offset by faith and trust (1:6). Personal division of mind must be counterbalanced by clean hands and a pure heart (1:7–8; 4:8). Instability (1:6–8) must bow to steadfastness (5:11). Quickness to anger (1:19–20) must be replaced by slowness to anger (1:21; 4:6–10). Individual gossip must be curbed by bridling the tongue (3:1–12). With respect to the socio-economic dimension, desiring wealth (4:13) must be countered by patience (5:7–12). Currying favor with the wealthy (5:1–5) must be replaced by showing no partiality (2:1). Dishonoring the poor (2:6a) must be corrected by loving one's neighbor as oneself (2:8–13). Further, teachers with unbridled tongues (3:1–12) should teach through wisdom by meekness (3:13). Securing the truth with oaths must be abandoned (5:12). Apostasy (5:19a) should be met with restoring repentant sinners (5:19b–20). Simple faith must be balanced with works (2:14–26). Similar contrasts can be drawn with regard to the cosmos or world as a whole. For example, alliance with the devil, impurity, sin, and double-mindedness (4:7b, 8b, c) must be met with resisting the devil, drawing near to God, and having purity of hands and heart (4:8a, b).

In short, the main thrust of James is to preserve and develop purity and unity in a polluted and divided community and in the process to distinguish it from values of society and the world at large. The author states his theme at the outset. One must face trials and tests with steadfastness, completeness, and wholeness (1:2–4). It is then developed in the body of the writing with hortatory expressions in response to negative, destructive behavior.

Structure

Some scholars have argued that James has little or no structure because it is simply a collection of ethical exhortations; thus it moves from theme to theme and makes connections by the association of ideas or catchwords. Here is one possibility:

1:1	Address
1:2–12	Holiness-wholeness theme and initial exhortations
1:13–5:12	Contrasts of behavior
5:13–20	"Conclusion"

Exegetical Survey

1:1:   *Address*   of James, God's servant, to the twelve tribes in the **Diaspora,** that is, those who believe that Jesus is the Messiah are addressed with a traditional metaphor for the true Israel.

1:2–12:   *Initial exhortations.*   The section contains *exhortations* to remain joyful and steadfast under persecution, which leads to perfection (1:2–4), to pray with wisdom and faith (1:5–7), and to boast of poverty, not riches. The stress on poverty may have spiritual overtones but is fundamentally economic. James stresses the downfall of the rich, thus reversing worldly human values (see 2:1–12, 4:13–16, 5:1–6). "Faith" means stability without doubt; passion leads to sin and death.

1:13–5:12:   *Contrasts of behavior.*

1:13–18:   *Temptation and divine gift giving.*

1:19–27:   *Both hear and do the word of God and bridle one's tongue.*   True religion is caring for orphans and widows and maintaining purity from worldly defilement.

2:1–12:   *Show no partiality, but fulfill the royal law of love.*   The literal poor are spiritually rich. Honor the poor, not the rich. The royal law is: "You shall love your neighbor as yourself" (2:8 [Lev. 19:18]; cf. Mark 12:31; Gal. 5:14). For Paul's view of the impossibility of keeping the whole law, see Gal. 5:3.

2:13:   *The necessity of mercy,*   a verse attached by a catchword to the preceding (Prov. 14:21; Tob. 4:10).

2:14–26:   *Faith without works is dead.*   This passage about works illustrates the central theme of actively overcoming impurity with purity and thus protection of the purity of the group. It is concerned to contest either the Pauline doctrine of "justification by faith" or, more probably, an extremist (mis)interpretation of that view, one that denied the necessity for "works" at all. To be sure, Paul and James see "faith" in very different terms. For Paul, faith is a dynamic relationship to the risen Lord allowing human beings to appropriate that which God has wrought through Jesus. For James, faith is subscription to a sound monotheism. Paul himself would never have denied the importance of works, as his sections on morality show, especially when freedom led to moral excesses; faith had to have consequences. Yet, in his struggles with the so-called Judaizers, Paul declared that works of the Law were insufficient for salvation and thus the emphasis on them, symbolized by circumcision, misplaced. In James, however, the tables are turned. Here the author argues *against* the libertarians of his own day. Thus the Book of James exposes early stages of institutionalism in the Jesus Movement. There can be no direct comparison between James and Paul because they come from different periods in New Testament history and correspondingly different social contexts.

3:1–12:   After a statement about the honorable role of teacher, the section exhorts: Guard your tongue, the potential damage of which is disproportionate to its size (cf. 1:19).

3:13–18:   Abandon earthly wisdom and seek heavenly wisdom (cf. 1:5; 1 Cor. 1–4).

4:1–10:   Avoid the conflicts brought on by the passion within and seek the peace that comes only from God.

4:11–12:   Do not speak evil against, or judge, one another.

4:13–16:   The business plans of rich, arrogant merchants who place commercial life first will be subject to God.

4:17:   Appended by catchword: the necessity of doing right.

5:1–6:   Woes upon the rich who defraud their laborers.

5:7–11:   Be patient until the coming of the Lord (the delay of the *parousia* theme). The judgment of God is imminent.

5:12:   Against swearing oaths (cf. Matt. 5:33–37).

5:13–20:   "Conclusion": The healing power of prayer. Be concerned for the erring brother. James has no formal epistolary conclusion.

THE PASTORAL LETTERS: 1 TIMOTHY, 2 TIMOTHY, TITUS

1 Timothy, 2 Timothy, and Titus are known as the Pastoral Letters because, like a shepherd who cares for his sheep, they claim to offer Paul's pastoral advice to Timothy and Titus, companions of Paul known from the Pauline Letters. They thus exhibit a serious, but sometimes affectionate, concern for churches, their leaders, and their ministry.

Timothy and Titus, Paul's Companions

Timothy is often mentioned as coauthor and close companion of Paul in the greetings of both Pauline and deutero-Pauline letters. For example, Paul sent his "brother" Timothy to Thessalonica from Athens, and he reported back, probably to Corinth (1 Thess. 3:1–5). He also sent Timothy from Ephesus to Corinth to remind the Corinthians of Paul's "ways" (1 Cor. 4:17; 16:10–11). Apparently he had preached to the Corinthians (2 Cor. 1:19). Paul also said that he would send Timothy to Philippi and told the Philippians of his trust and deep respect for Timothy (Phil. 2:19–24). This remark implied that Timothy was with Paul in prison (cf. Phil. 1:1). Acts adds some details about Timothy, although the historicity of all of them is uncertain. The Lukan writer says that Timothy met up with Paul in his hometown Lystra in southern Galatia. He had a Greek father and an Israelite mother (cf. 2 Tim. 1:5: his mother is named Eunice, his grandmother Lois). Also, Paul had Timothy circumcised because of Israelites in the area of Lystra and Derbe (Acts 16:1–3). Timothy then traveled with Paul (e.g., Acts 17:14–15; 20:4). Heb. 13:23 says, "our brother Timothy has been set free."

Titus was also Paul's trusted companion and emissary. He was a Gentile convert (Gal. 2:1, 3). Paul sent him to Corinth to help inaugurate the collection (2 Cor. 8:5–6, 16–24; 12:18). After Paul's "painful visit" to Corinth, Paul sent him back with a letter (2 Cor. 2:3–4; 7:6–8), and he reported to the anxious Paul that tensions between Paul and the Corinthians had eased (3:13; 7:6–16, especially 7:6, 13–14). Perhaps Titus himself helped to ease the tensions. Acts says nothing about Titus.

Church Traditions about the Pastoral Letters

The first reference to the composition of the Pastorals is in the **Muratorian Canon,** probably about 200 C.E. from Rome. It says that Paul wrote ". . . one [letter] to Titus, but two to Timothy for the sake of affection and love." Were the Pastorals quoted earlier in the century? There is a bit of parallel language between the Pastorals and Polycarp (martyred about 155/156 C.E.; cf. Martyrdom of Polycarp), but it is also possible that they simply shared oral or written traditions. Otherwise, we do not find certain quotations from the Pastorals before Irenaeus' *Against Heresies* about 185 C.E. Other Church Fathers accept them in the early third century. Eventually they were included in the Easter Letter of Athanasius in 367 C.E. They are also found in Codex Sinaiticus from the fourth century.

Missing references to the Pastorals in the early second century become historically significant because Marcion's "canon" of Paul's letters about 150 C.E. seems not to have included them. It is unlikely that he simply rejected them (as the Church Father Tertullian says in *Marcion* 5.21) if he knew them. Also, the early papyrus of the Pauline letter collection, **P**[46], about 200 C.E., omits the Pastorals, although it is not impossible that the manuscript was damaged because it breaks off at 1 Thess. 5:5 (before the Pastorals). Finally, the Muratorian Canon places them at the end of the Pauline Letters as a sort of appendix.

In short, reliable evidence for the Pastorals does not appear until the late second century C.E., about a generation before the time when they are included in the Muratorian Canon. Even then they are not yet firmly accepted everywhere.

Historical and Literary Criticism of the Pastorals

A few interpreters argue that Paul could have written these letters to Timothy and Titus late in his life when the church was changing. Another few try to solve some of the un-Pauline-sounding language and stylistic problems by attributing them to Paul's amanuensis, or secretary. However, no secretary is mentioned in the Pastorals, and, more importantly, where Paul does mention his secretary (1 Cor. 16:21; Gal. 6:11–18; Rom. 16:22), we do not encounter the problems listed next. Thus the majority of scholars reject Pauline authorship on the following grounds:

1. *Vocabulary.* Of 848 words (excluding proper names) found in the Pastorals, 306 are not in the rest of the Pauline letters, *including* the deutero-Paulines. Of these 306 words, 175 do not occur elsewhere in the New Testament. However, 211 are known to be part of the vocabulary of writers in the second-century Jesus Movement. Indeed, the vocabulary of the Pastorals is closer to that of Hellenistic philosophy than to that of Pauline or the deutero-Pauline letters. Furthermore, they have a special set of theological terms that does not sound like Paul (e.g., "piety"; "sound teaching"; "a good conscience"). Key Pauline terms are missing (e.g., "cross"; "covenant"; "freedom"). Finally, Pauline words are found but have a sense not otherwise found in Paul (*dikaios* does not mean "righteous" but "upright"; *pistis,* "faith," has become "the body of faith in the Movement").

2. *Literary style.* Paul writes dynamic Greek, with dramatic arguments, emotional outbursts, and the introduction of real or imaginary opponents and partners in dialogue (the diatribe). In contrast, the author of the Pastorals writes in a quiet, meditative style, far more characteristic of Hebrews, 1 Peter, and literary Hellenistic Greek.

3. *The historical context of the apostle implied in the letters.* In 1 Timothy, Paul is depicted as having written from Macedonia to the younger Timothy (4:11), whom he has left

behind in Ephesus to correctly instruct the people who have taken up false doctrines (1:3), probably Gnostic (6:20–21; cf. 1:4). In 2 Timothy, Paul is portrayed as imprisoned at Rome (e.g., 1:8, 16–17; 2:9), near death (4:6–8, 18); he has had a preliminary hearing, and most of his friends (except Luke) have abandoned him (4:16–17). He requests that Timothy, who is perhaps in Ephesus (2:17), come and bring Mark (4:11, 13). According to the letter to Titus, Paul is said to have left Titus behind on the Mediterranean island of Crete to organize the churches (1:5) and to have gone on to Ephesus (Titus 1:1; 3:12; cf. e.g., Col. 4:7; 2 Tim. 4:12).

However one imagines the sequence of these events and situations, there is no way they fit into any reconstruction of Paul's life and work as we know it from Paul's undisputed letters or the Acts of the Apostles. They can have happened only if they occurred *after* his Roman imprisonment (Acts 28). One might imagine that he carried out his intentions to go to Spain (Rom. 15:24, 28; cf. *1 Clement* 5:7) and somehow made it to Crete, Ephesus, Macedonia, and Rome for a *second* imprisonment (2 Timothy). However, the Pastorals do not mention two imprisonments. Most scholars conclude that a later writer deduced the events mentioned in the Pastorals from Paul's plans as detailed in Rom. 15:22–33.

4. *The author of the Pastorals seems to know the places that Paul went on his first missionary journey as described in Acts (2 Tim. 3:11; cf. Acts 13–14).* Acts is usually dated about 85–90 C.E., about twenty-five to thirty years after Paul's martyrdom.

5. *The letters reflect conditions typical of institutional development in the early church.* The preceding arguments are forceful, but a last consideration is overwhelming.

6. *Together with 2 Peter, the Pastorals are the most distinctive representatives of the emphases of emerging institutionalism in the very late first and early second centuries, that is, doctrine, officers, church decorum, and the like.*

The large majority of scholars conclude that the Apostle Paul did not write the Pastorals; they are pseudonymous.

Yet, vocabulary, style, viewpoint, and concerns in the three letters are homogeneous enough to make it almost certain that the same person wrote all three. The question is why the author chose to write in the name of Paul. The usual answer is that he believed himself to have been in the tradition of Paul. Thus he was a third-generation member of the Pauline School. Also, as opposed to false teachers he wished to present a true understanding of Paul.

A number of the preceding factors, especially the affinity between the Pastorals and 2 Peter and between the Pastorals and second-century writings of the early church, suggest a date somewhere in the first half of the second century. It is possible that Polycarp alludes to the Pastorals in his letter *To the Philippians,* usually dated about 125–135 C.E. Thus most scholars date them in the first quarter of the second century, that is, 100–125 C.E.

No precise place for the Pastorals can be documented. They seem to be related to the region connected to the Aegean Sea because the island of Crete (Titus 1:5) and the city of Ephesus (1 Tim. 1:3) are mentioned. In 2 Timothy, Paul is said to be in prison (1:8; 2:9), but that could imitate Paul's prison letters (Philemon, Philippians).

"Opponents"

It is difficult to be very precise about the "opponents" because they are portrayed in stereotypical terms. In Titus the author warns about those who are interested in Israelite myths, commandments (1:14), and "quarrels about the law" (3:9), and in 1 Timothy, they desire to be "teachers of the Law" (1:7). All of this sounds like Israelites, or like Israelite Christ believers: ". . . there are also many rebellious people, idle talkers and deceivers, especially those of the circumcision" (Titus 1:10). However, opponents also "forbid marriage and demand abstinence from foods" (1 Tim. 4:3), claim that the resurrection has already taken place (2 Tim. 2:18), and presumably are concerned about genealogies (Titus 3:9). This sounds like an ascetic form of early Gnosticism, and there is also the comment, "Avoid the profane chatter and contradictions of what is falsely called 'knowledge'" (*gnōsis;* 1 Tim. 6:20). Within the community, widows may have chosen celibacy, perhaps as a means to freedom from domineering males, a lifestyle perpetuated in some Gnostic groups. Thus either we have indications of a kind of syncretistic Israelite Gnosticism in the Jesus Movement, or there are several irreconcilable views that pious believers should avoid.

Social-Historical Context of the Pastorals

The Pastorals reveal several interrelated concerns. Various recommendations show that the author wants to put on a good face for the rest of society: The "overseer" or "bishop," for example, must "be well thought of by outsiders" (1 Tim. 3:7). The church is also threatened internally, as the section on opponents has just indicated. All of this leads to a focus on institutional development, or church order, which needs to be discussed.

You will recall that household management was very important in Greco-Roman society (indeed, the basis for political and economic thought), and specifically that the "household code" was the key pattern of social organization found in the large Greco-Roman household. The head of the family or head of the household (*paterfamilias*) ruled, and order was achieved primarily from three principles: wives subject to husbands, children subject to parents, slaves subject to masters. These traditional male-dominated, authoritarian family structures were believed to be necessary to preserve a stable social and political order. The Jesus Movement seems to have increasingly conformed to these cultural norms, values, and practices in the late first century and early second century, as the deutero-Pauline literature (see Chapter Seven) and 1 Peter show. A third area of importance is hospitality, or the gracious reception of visitors in the household (Chapter Eleven).

The family household and its organization and hospitality are also an important theme for understanding the social situation of the church community in the Pastorals: ". . . I am writing these instructions to you so that, . . . you may know how one ought to behave in the household of God, which is the church of the living God. . . . " (1 Tim. 3:14–15; cf. 2 Tim. 2:20). "Do not speak harshly to an older man, but speak to him as to a father, to younger men as brothers, to older women as mothers, to younger women as sisters—with absolute purity" (1 Tim. 5:1–2). Women should learn in silence in complete submission, never teach, and never have authority over men (1 Tim. 2:11–15). Older women should train younger women to love their husbands and children and to be good homemakers under control of their husbands (Titus 2:4–5). Church leaders should manage their households well and keep their children under control (1 Tim. 3:4, 12). Slaves should be under the control of their masters, not talk back (Titus 2:9–10), and regard their masters with honor, especially not taking advantage of masters who are "brothers" (1 Tim. 6:1–2). This latter norm implies on the one hand that some slaves in the Jesus Movement have "pagan" masters, and on the other that master-patrons deserve benefits from their slave-clients. As in 1 Peter, no recommendation is given to masters, perhaps suggesting further assimilation to normative cultural values, which is clearly not good news for slaves in the Jesus Movement.

The household model of organization in the Pastorals seems to reflect households of rather large size, influence, and wealth (2 Tim. 2:20). Yet, they have social diversity and thus mirror a cross-section of social strata found in any Hellenistic city. The house must be large enough and the householder wealthy enough to have slaves and take care of widows (1 Tim. 5:3–8). The wealthy are exhorted not to be haughty or put their trust in riches (6:17–19), and women are warned not to adorn themselves in worship with braided hairstyles, gold ornaments, pearls, and expensive clothes, implying that they were wealthy enough to do so (1 Tim. 2:9). There is also evidence that some positions of the church were paid (1 Tim. 5:17–18).

The author of the Pastorals emphasizes that the church must be decent and well ordered. In 1 Timothy, he describes qualifications of what is usually translated "bishop" (*episcopos;* 1 Tim. 3:1–7; Titus 1:7–9), "deacon" (*diakonos;* 1 Tim. 3:8–13), "elder" (*presbyteros;* 1 Tim. 5:17–25), and apparently also a special group called "widows" (*chēra;* 1 Tim. 5:9–11). An important and much-discussed question historically is the relationship of the "bishop"/"overseer" (Greek: *episcopos*) to the "elder"/"presbyter" (Greek: *presbyteros*). By way of cultural background, elders were local leaders in ancient Israel (Josh. 24:31; Judg. 2:7), Greco-Roman Israel, and the **Diaspora** (the *Mishnah;* Jerusalem synagogue inscriptions). The elder who claims to have written 2 and 3 John was clearly assuming authority in his region. In the Jesus Movement represented in the Acts of the Apostles, elders, along with the apostles, had decision-making roles at the Apostolic Assembly in Jerusalem (e.g., Acts 15:2–6, 22–23; 16:4). By the time the Pastorals were written, a *council* of elders had the right to "lay on the hands" (1 Tim. 4:14; 5:22; 2 Tim. 1:6)—and it was not to be done casually. As is known from other ancient texts, this was the power to transfer authority (e.g., Num. 27:18–23; cf. Acts 6:6; Acts 13:3). In 1 Timothy, they are called "elders who rule" and "those who labor in preaching and teaching"; they deserve to be paid (1 Tim. 5:17–22).

There are two problems. The first is whether the *episcopos* is being distinguished from the *presbyteros*. The second is that the relationship of the *episcopos* (/*presbyteros*) to the community is murky.

More precisely, the letter to Titus seems to equate the *episcopos* with the *presbyteros* (Titus 1:5–9), as does 1 Pet. 5:1. However, 1 Timothy discusses them separately, and *episcopos* is in the singular (1 Tim. 3:2; cf. Titus 1:7), suggesting to some interpreters that he had a higher status. Had the *episcopos* become more like a "bishop," or was he an "overseer" with virtually the same functions as the presbyter/ elder? If the former, the Pastorals might represent a group or groups in which "church offices" were beginning to emerge, although not yet clearly defined (cf. *1 Clement*). Another possibility that supports this theory is that there appears to be a modest development from Titus, where they are not distinguished, to 1 Timothy, where they are distinguished, thus suggesting that the "office" of *episcopos* was in the process of gaining some preeminence (contrast Phil. 1:1; cf. Acts 20:28). Was the *episcopos* the head of the council of elders? If so, there may have been an advance on the understanding of *episcopos* as "teacher"/"prophet" in the early second-century *Didachē* (chapters 13, 15) in the sense that there such a person is locally elected and has a right to financial support. Slightly earlier, *1 Clement* (ca. 96 or 97 C.E.) speaks about an ordained succession of the "bishops/presbyters"—again they are not clearly distinguished—in the sense of their authority as descended from the apostles (apostolic succession). Yet, he notes that there would be controversy over the title "bishop" (*1 Clement* 44). Finally, Ignatius of Antioch speaks of the emergence of the single *episcopos* as the leading authority in the local church, which historians call the "monarchial episcopate" or "monepiscopate" (*To the Smyrnians* 8:2; cf. *To the Trallians* 7:1). Here *episcopos* has clearly become a fixed *office* in a hierarchy. Was this beginning to happen in the Pastorals?

However one decides the question, the Pastorals offer an excellent example of growing institutionalization in the Jesus Movement of the early second century. They describe the *qualifications,* especially moral and organizational (again household management) and mention several roles, especially that of "overseer"/"bishop" with authority, a development that, precisely because of these listed qualifications, clearly goes beyond the Pauline churches (e.g., Phil. 1:1). Yet, the roles are not as clearly defined as they are in Ignatius.

Structure of the Pastorals

The structure of the Pastorals as letter genres was probably a stratagem by the author. They claim to be directed to the church or to churches in a particular area; the address to individuals known to be companions of Paul is a literary device to lend plausibility. Despite their literary structure, they are essentially manifestos like 2 Peter, written partly in response to the threat of a spreading Gnosticism within the churches, partly as an answer to the growing need for organizational structure in the church. Additionally, 2 Timothy approximates a genre known from Israelite literature as a "testament," that is, the last words of an eminent figure, often a father to his son, or a central person to his coworker, near the time of his death.

The structure of the Pastorals is related to their content. The author argues against false teachers and for organizational structure of the church. He exhorts "Timothy" and "Titus" to correct inappropriate behavior and practice as ministers of the church. He holds up the false teachers as bad examples to avoid and the Apostle Paul (= himself as writer!) as an exemplary model to follow.

The present order of the Pastorals in the New Testament is probably based on their length, from the longest to the shortest. The longest later received the name "1 Timothy," the next-longest "2 Timothy," and the shortest, "Titus." Again, the events portrayed in these letters cannot be coordinated with Paul's movements as known from his undisputed letters and Acts. Thus scholars have often rearranged them based on their content. Some have suggested a sequence of Titus, 1 Timothy, 2 Timothy because bishops/elders are not separated in Titus and then are separated in 1 Timothy, and because "Paul" expects his impending death in 2 Timothy. Other scholars place 2 Timothy first because it is more personal than 1 Timothy is and because Titus mentions no specific roles and functions. Thus the rationale is no specific roles/functions mentioned (2 Timothy) → bishops/elders not separated (Titus) → apparent separation of bishops and elders (1 Timothy). The important point in this rearrangement is the shift from Titus (no separation of roles/functions) to 1 Timothy (separated roles/functions), and separated roles/functions seem to lead toward offices.

There can be no certainty in deciding the sequence of composition, especially if these books represent a transitional stage in the evolution of church government. This textbook will follow the second suggestion and take them up in this order: 2 Timothy (most personal), Titus (no separation of bishops/elders), and 1 Timothy (apparent separation of bishops and elders). The basic reasons are that 2 Timothy may have been developed first on the basis of either a Pauline fragment about Paul's personal relations with Timothy, or the attempt to create this impression, as Luke does in Acts 20. In this chronological sequence, the letters are increasingly less personal and increasingly more concerned with separated church roles/functions: a move toward institutionalism and perhaps even offices.

Exegetical Survey of 2 Timothy

1:1–2:   *Address and greeting.*

1:3–5:   *Thanksgiving.*

1:6–2:13:   *Exhortation to witness on the basis of the example of Paul.*   In 1:6, the gift of God is said to be rekindled through "the laying on of hands," a transfer of power and authority. Verse 1:8 states that Paul is prisoner, and 1:9–10 contains elements of a liturgy. Verses 13 and 14 of chapter 1 exhibit the view of faith characteristic of the emerging institutional church. It is the "standard of sound teaching" (1:13), which was heard from the apostles and which is to be guarded and followed. Note also 2:2, which stresses preservation of the truth in later generations. 2 Tim. 2:8 sounds like an allusion to the Christological confession Rom. 1:3; the author seems to know a collection of the Pauline letters.

2:14–4:8:   *Exhortation to good behavior in all respects.*   The author now turns to the behavior expected of the true minister of God. Characteristically, the false teachers are examples to avoid; in contrast, the Apostle Paul is an example to follow. In this section we learn more about what the false teachers teach: It is "profane chatter" (2:16); it holds that "the resurrection has already taken place" (2:18); it features "myths" (4:4). Verses 3:2–4 contain a typical vice list. The emerging institutional church regards its time as the last time, separate from the time of the apostles (3:1; cf. Jude 18; 2 Pet. 3:3); it is coming to regard scripture in a very formal way as "inspired by God" and "useful" (3:16).

4:9–18: *"Paul's" personal situation.* This has been constructed to add a sense of realism to the pseudonymity.

4:19–22: *Closing greetings.*

Exegetical Survey of Titus

1:1–4: *Salutation.*

1:5–9: *The ordained ministry.* According to the author, Titus has been left in Crete to organize the church, and the letter functions of as a guide for him. This section is not a church order such as we find in 1 Timothy, but rather some directions with regard to bishops and elders. Titus seems to equate the bishop/overseer and the elder/presbyter, whereas 1 Timothy seems to separate them. Yet, there is some similarity to the description of the qualifications for becoming a bishop/overseer in 1 Tim. 3:1–7. If there is a development, the situation with regard to the relationship between the two offices was still fluid at the writing of Titus, and separation of the two was only beginning to take place at the time of the writing of 1 Timothy.

1:10–16: *An attack on the false teaching.* The false teaching apparently had some connection with Crete (1:12) and certainly with Israelites (1:10, 14; cf. 1:10). The comment about those from the island of Crete is an excellent example of an ancient ethnocentrism, here said to be uttered by a prophet of the false teachers. See the preceding discussion of the opponents.

2:1–3:7: *Exhortation to a proper behavior.* Verse 2:1 again mentions "sound doctrine." Here are the moral norms of the household and its organization similar to those in the "**household codes**" found in emerging institutionalism (cf. 1 Pet. 2:13–3:7). Earlier deutero-Pauline codes are in Col. 3:18–4:1 and Eph. 5:21–6:9 (Chapter Seven). Note also the renewed *parousia* hope and the description of Jesus as "our great God and Savior" (2:13; cf. 2 Pet. 1:1).

3:8–11: *Renewed attack on the false teaching.* The author appears to know Eph. 2:3–12.

3:12–14: *Personal notes.*

3:15: *Closing greetings.*

Exegetical Survey of 1 Timothy

1:1–2: *Salutation.*

1:3–20: *Attack on the doctrine of the false teachers.* The false teaching seems to be a form of early Gnosticism with a strong Israelite element (cf. 6:20; cf. 2 Tim. 2:17). The reference to "myths and endless genealogies" (verse 4) would fit Gen. 4–5, and the reference to the Law in verses 8–9 points to Israelite values. However, myths and genealogies could also reflect the Gnostic tendency to speculate about the hierarchy of heavenly beings. In verse 5, "sincere faith" can be read as "sincere profession of the religious belief" (see also 5:8; 6:10, 21). Moreover, faith has become a matter of accepting *doctrinal propositions* (verse 15). All of this is quite different from Paul's view of faith.

2:1–3:16: *A house-church order: Part 1.* 1 Timothy includes what is to all intents and purposes a church order, divided into two parts, 2:1–3:16 and 4:11–6:19. The first part covers worship in the house-church (2:1–15) and specific roles/functions or what may be emerging as fixed offices (3:1–16).

2:1–15: *Worship in the house-church and the role of women.* The regulation to pray "for kings and all who are in high positions" and the grounds given for it (2:1–2) reflect the movement's concern to conform to the larger society and its good reputation among outsiders. The ideal of "good citizenship" is a Hellenistic philosophical value. There follows a famous section on the role of women in worship (2:9–15). It charges that they must dress modestly in worship and forbids them to teach or have authority over men. The reason is that Eve, not Adam, was deceived in the garden (see Gen. 3:13; 2 Cor. 11:3). Women will be "saved" by bearing children. The passage, which does not sound at all like Paul (e.g., Gal. 3:28; Rom. 16), may have been an implicit attack on the opponents' ascetic denial of marriage and family (cf. 1 Tim. 4:3–5; 5:9). It is in any case an accommodation to traditional patriarchal values. Its author, or someone like him, may also have inserted a similar passage into 1 Corinthians (1 Cor. 14:33b–36). Both passages have become targets for modern feminist attacks on sexism in the Bible.

3:1–7: *Bishops/Overseers.* The church is the "household of God" and must be so ordered. In Titus, the "bishop/overseer" and "elder/presbyter" are not clearly distinguished, and his role is something like a pastor or minister (Titus 1:5–9). However, in the **Church Father** Ignatius of Antioch, roughly contemporary with the Pastorals, the bishop has emerged as the chief officer of the local church. Ignatius writes, "Nobody must do anything that has to do with the Church without the bishop's approval. You should regard that Eucharist as valid which is celebrated either by the bishop or by someone he authorizes. . . . Where the bishop is present, there let the congregation gather, just as where Jesus Christ is, there is the Catholic Church" (*To the Smyrnaeans* 8:1b–2a). In *Didachē* 15:1 (also roughly contemporary), both bishops and deacons are appointed, and their ministry is identical with that of prophets and teachers. The bishop/overseer's functions are not absolutely clear in this 1 Timothy passage, although he takes care of the household of God (3:5). Yet, the qualifications for "bishop/overseer" are described separately from the qualifications for "elder/presbyter" (5:17–25). Is this the beginning of separate roles/functions, as they are in Ignatius?

3:8–13: *Deacons.* The term "deacon" (Greek: *diakonos*) is found in Phil. 1:1, but there its exact meaning is unclear; it is often translated more generally as "minister," "servant," or "helper." In Rom. 16:1, Phoebe is called a "deacon," but her precise role, although clearly important, is not specified. In 1 Timothy, qualifications are spelled out in detail, but the precise function of the deacon is still not totally clear. In Acts 6, the deacons appear to be those in charge of the distribution of funds to members of the community; they also preach to others (Acts 7; 8:4–8, 26–40). In 1 Tim. 3:11, it is not clear whether "women" refers to women *deacons* (in which case there would be a deacon's office for women, as well) or to the *wives* of deacons.

3:14–16: *Ethics and Christology.* This section climaxes in one of the great New Testament Christological hymns (3:16), no doubt taken by the author from the liturgy of his church. Other hymns are Phil. 2:5–11, Col. 1:15–20, and John 1:1–16 (see Chapter Three).

4:1–10: *An attack on the ethics of the false teachers.* The writer contrasts the ethics of the false teachers with the behavior expected of the true teacher.

4:11–6:19: *A house-church order: Part 2.*

4:11–5:2: In the form of instructions to "Timothy," the author develops the ideal minister. "Timothy" should not neglect "the laying on of hands by the council of elders" (4:14; cf. 5:22; 2 Tim. 1:6).

5:3–16: *Widows.* The author details regulations concerning all widows (5:3–16; cf. Polycarp *To the Philippians* 4). The specific qualifications for widow in 5:9–10, which compares to bishop/overseer and deacon in the first part of the church order, suggest that there was at least a specific role, perhaps even an *office,* of "widow" (cf. "enrolled" or "put on the list"), as in the letters of Ignatius about this time. If this inner group chose celibacy as a means to freedom (already in 1 Cor. 7:8–9, 25–38?), there must have been a tension between their role/office and the other widows who were charged to conform to patriarchal standards.

5:17–25: *Elders.* In Acts and in Titus, the "elder/presbyter" appears to be indistinguishable from the "bishop/overseer" (Acts 20:17 plus 28; Titus 1:5–9; *1 Clement* 44, too?), but in this 1 Timothy passage, the qualifications for each are discussed *separately* (5:17–22; cf. 3:1–7). Elders rule and are especially responsible for preaching and teaching (5:17); they are worthy of pay (possibly implied by "double honor" and certainly implied by the scriptural reference; cf. 1 Cor. 9:9; Luke 10:7 [Deut. 25:4]). In 4:14, a council of elders is empowered to "lay on hands"; here, elders should not "lay on the hands" hastily (cf. 2 Tim. 1:6).

6:1–2: *Slaves.* As in the **household codes,** slaves are warned to honor their masters and not to take advantage of masters who are also brothers in the Jesus Movement. Compare Titus 2:9–10.

6:3–16: *Further instructions to the ideal minister.* Avoid false teachers and act in a pious way.

6:17–19: *Exhortations to the rich.*

6:20–21: *Conclusion.* Even in his concluding greeting the author continues his polemic against the false teachers. The reference to "what is falsely called knowledge (Greek: *gnōsis*)" strengthens the case that the false teaching was a form of Gnosticism.

THE LETTER OF JUDE

The author calls himself "Jude" (Greek: *Judas*), the "brother of James" (1:1). Unless "brother of James" was added, for which there is no manuscript evidence (**Textual Criticism**), this ascription would make him also the brother of Jesus, the Judas of Mark 6:3 = Matt. 13:55. Probably he was also a leader of the church and a missionary (1 Cor. 9:5: "brothers of the Lord"). Thus he would *not* be the Apostle Jude, son of James (Luke 6:16; Acts 1:13; cf. John 14:22: "Judas, not the Iscariot").

Church Tradition and Historical Criticism of Jude

With respect to the canon, leading scholars of the third (Clement and Origen, both of Alexandria) and fourth centuries (Eusebius of Caesarea) still listed Jude among the "disputed books" (Eusebius *Ecclesiastical History* 6.14.1; 6.13.6; 3.25). Yet, the book had appeared in the **Muratorian Canon** (ca. 200 C.E., Rome) and was included in Athanasius' **Easter Letter** of 367 C.E., which "closed" the canon.

However, ancient suspicions about the book were well founded. The Book of Jude *looks back* on the time of the apostles as in the *past* (verses 17–18); this, together with features of fine Greek, citation of several apocryphal sources, and especially institutional themes, makes authorship by Jesus' brother Jude impossible. The letter is therefore **pseudonymous.**

The identity of opponents suggests that Jude might have been written in Asia Minor, but the place of composition cannot be known with any certainty. The outer limit for Jude's date is indicated by its incorporation into 2 Peter, therefore about 125 C.E. (see following). Its thought represents institutionalism. In short, it was probably written sometime between 100 and 125 C.E.

"Opponents"

The letter of Jude is a tirade against a group of opponents whose members at one time seem to have been outsiders (verse 4) but who are now apparently insiders creating friction within the community (verses 4, 12, 18, 23). According to the author these persons claim to be charismatic prophets whose spiritual gifts and corresponding freedom make them and others like them superior to other Christ believers. In response, they are accused of vices (flattery, gluttony, greediness, godlessness, licentiousness, ignorance, sexual deviance, grumbling, etc.); as such, they fulfill prophecies about the ungodliness expected before the end (verses 14–15). Yet, they claim to be members of the movement and participate in the cultic meals of the community (verse 12). Who are they?

Identification of these opponents is very difficult, especially because the vices listed are very general, typical of such vice codes in antiquity, and not explained further. Moreover, the writer does not rationally argue against them, which might clarify them, but simply denounces them and threatens them with dire examples of punishment known from the scriptures. They were certainly libertarians; despising the world of the flesh, they saw no fault in abandoning themselves to fleshly practices (verses 7–8). Perhaps they were early Gnostics because they considered themselves to be superior to the angelic powers (verse 8: "the glorious ones"); this would be consistent with the word used of them in verse 19, *psychikoi* (NRSV: "worldly people"), a technical term used by Gnostics (cf. 1 Cor. 2:14).

Social Setting

Jude chronicles an example of early church conflict. The author holds to certain purity norms for insiders and calls his outsider-opponents names. In social-scientific terms he is drawing sharp social boundaries and is engaged in "negative labeling" of his opponents. However, probably the most interesting features of his attack are the implied characteristics of emerging institutionalism, that is, the instructions, implicit and explicit, for insiders. The letter speaks of "the faith that was once for all entrusted to the saints" (1:3); this description means that faith is the acceptance of authoritative tradition. In denouncing the heretics the author also admonishes the faithful based on the authority of that tradition. There is also evidence of a developing liturgy. In verses 20–21, ". . . pray in the *Holy Spirit;* keep yourselves in the love of *God;* look forward to the mercy of our *Lord Jesus Christ*" implies something like a Trinitarian formula in a liturgy. The closing doxology (verses 24–25) is a magnificent piece of liturgical language, so different in style and tone from the remainder of the letter that the writer has probably taken it from some existing liturgy in the Jesus Movement.

Jude's Use of Apocalyptic Documents

A remarkable aspect of Jude is its use of apocalyptic documents. You will recall that apocalyptic writing flourished throughout the New Testament period in both Greco-Roman Israel and the early churches. Jude is eloquent testimony to this relation because its author is aware of the myth of the fallen angels in Israelite apocalyptic, and he knows the myth of the burial of Moses from an Israelite apocalypse in the Jesus Movement, the *Assumption of Moses.* He also alludes to a major apocalyptic work, the Book of *I Enoch*, in the matter of the "wandering stars" (opponents who are without direction), and he explicitly quotes *I Enoch* 1:9. His own understanding of apostolic faith is notably apocalyptic. The letter shows that apocalyptic, revitalized in the late first century (as in Revelation), can still be a living force in the period of emerging institutionalism. Nevertheless, when Jude is reused in 2 Pet. 2, the author of 2 Peter is careful to remove all references and allusions to apocalyptic works that were excluded from the Israelite canon.

Structure

This polemical letter is an invective piece that defies structural analysis beyond the obvious fact that it opens with a greeting and closes with a doxology. The writer simply denounces the heretics and warns his readers against them.

Exegetical Survey of Jude

1–2:   *Address and salutation.*

3–4:   *The emergence of false teachers.*   This emergence makes it an urgent necessity to contend for the faith once and for all delivered to the saints.

5–7:   *Scriptural instances of sin and punishment.*   The writer warns his readers that God punishes sin. He uses as examples the traditions of God punishing the unfaithful Israelites in the wilderness (compare 1 Cor. 10:1–11; Heb. 3:7–4:11), the fate of the rebellious angels who wanted to mate with human women (Gen. 6:1–4), and Sodom and Gomorrah, sinful cities destroyed by God (Gen. 19:1–29). The reference to the fallen angels seems to exhibit an awareness of how this myth was developed in the apocalyptic works *Book of Enoch, Jubilees,* and *2 Baruch.*

8–16:   *Denunciation of the false teachers.*   The reference to the archangel Michael in verse 9 is a reference to a legend in an apocalyptic work, the *Assumption of Moses,* where

Michael digs a grave to bury Moses. Satan appears, accuses Moses of murder, debates with Michael about the law, and claims the body, although unsuccessfully. The envious Cain (Gen. 4) became famous in Israelite and early church tradition as the first heretic; similarly the greedy Balaam (Num. 22–24) was said to have led Israel into apostasy. Korah led a rebellion against Moses (Num. 16:1–11), and thus opposed legitimate authority. "Love feasts" are a form of the community's sacred meal in which the cultic aspect was blended into a regular communal meal. In Corinth, and no doubt elsewhere, this blending led to excesses and loss of the seriousness of religion (cf. 1 Cor. 11:20–22), and thus the cultic Eucharist was eventually separated from the communal meal. The reference to the wandering stars is from the apocalyptic *Book of Enoch*. The quote in verses 14–15 from the Pseudepigraphical work *1 Enoch* 1:9 is considered to be scripture.

17–23:   *Evils of heretics contrasted with attitudes required of the faithful.*   If verse 19 is a quotation, we do not know its source. It may represent the author's understanding of apostolic teaching and is notably apocalyptic in tone.

24–25:   *Closing doxology.*

THE SECOND LETTER OF PETER

Peter and Church Tradition

We have already given information about Peter, 1 Peter, and the Petrine circle. There is no church tradition about 2 Peter in the second century. Indeed, the first to mention 2 Peter explicitly is third-century Origen, who places it among the "disputed books" (*Commentary on John* 5:3 in Eusebius *Ecclesiastical History* 6.25). Fourth-century Eusebius also has this judgment (*Ecclesiastical History* 3.25.3). Also, in the fourth century Jerome, translator of the Latin Vulgate, notes the doubts of many, but he himself accepts it. It is included in Athanasius' Easter Letter of 367 C.E. Yet, some churches still rejected it in the fifth century.

Historical Criticism of 2 Peter

Ancient hesitations about 2 Peter were justified. Modern scholars doubt that Peter wrote 2 Peter, despite its emphatic claims to the contrary (1:1, 18; 3:15). There are a number of reasons. There is explicit mention in 2 Peter of 1 Peter (2 Pet. 3:1), and Jude 4–16 is copied into 2 Pet. 2 (see Chapter Three and following). The writer knows the synoptic gospels account of the transfiguration from the late first century (1:17–18). He also knows the letters of Paul as a collection and as scripture, also about the late first century (3:15–16). The first generation of believers has died (2:2). Although some scholars are willing to date 2 Peter to the last decade of the first century, most of them prefer a date in the early second century, many years after Peter's martyrdom. Moreover, as we shall see, 2 Peter shares with the Pastorals an emerging institutionalism. These facts make it impossible for the Apostle Peter to have written it; indeed, it is universally recognized among critical scholars as **pseudonymous.** Its author is probably the latest of all the New Testament writers. A date about 125 C.E. (some place it even later) is appropriate.

Literary Character

The form of 2 Peter is a manifesto with a letter-like greeting combined with elements of a "testament," or last words of instruction of a dying father to his sons and close acquaintances. The testament genre was well known in ancient Israelite literature (like English "last will and testament"; see e.g., 1:3–11, 12–15). 2 Peter is written in very good Greek but in a style quite different from that of 1 Peter.

Social Context of 2 Peter

The church to which this "letter" is written contains Christ believers of both Israelite and Greek backgrounds. It has a number of references to ideas that are in the Bible and in Greco-Roman literature and several Greek concepts. Such features of the work suggest that its social context is a Hellenistic, erudite urban setting, which corresponds to its stress on institutional features.

A key aspect of the content of the book is its attempt to reiterate the hope for the *parousia* against a growing skepticism (3:4). With respect to social context the author is attempting to combat false teachers who claim that the delay of the *parousia* has been too long and that nothing has changed since creation, thus God does not — and will not — intervene in history. These false teachers were probably Gnostic because they emphasized knowledge of salvation now and eventual translation to the heavenly sphere, and such views correspond to those of Gnostics who despised the world and the body and had no concern for a future *parousia*. The sheer passage of time and the continuing delay of the *parousia* had undoubtedly sharpened their polemic against the traditional apocalyptic hope in the Jesus Movement.

Structure

The structure of 2 Peter is simple.

1:1–2	Address and salutation
1:3–21	Exhortation to holiness
1:3–11	Exhortation
1:12–18	The certainty of the promise is grounded in the revelation the apostle encountered
1:19–21	An appeal to scriptural prophecy
2:1–22	Attack upon the false teachers
3:1–10	True teaching concerning the day of the Lord
3:11–18	*Parenesis* and concluding doxology

Exegetical Survey of 2 Peter

1:1–2: *Salutation.* The salutation is important for an understanding of the author's perspective and emerging institutionalism. It sees faith as available to those who stand in succession to the apostles represented by Peter.

1:3–21: *Exhortation to holiness.*

1:3–11: *Exhortation.* Note the characteristic Hellenistic emphasis on the corruption of the world and on escaping it to partake of the divine nature (verse 4). It is only a short step from this to the Gnosticism of the false teachers. The list of virtues in verses 5, 6, and 7 is an adaptation of the kind of virtue lists popular in the Hellenistic world. Verse 11 represents a Hellenizing of much earlier language about "entering the Kingdom of God."

1:12–18: *The certainty of the promise.* This is grounded in the revelation encountered by the apostle. This is a difficult passage, but its general meaning seems clear. The apostles were eyewitnesses to the Transfiguration of Jesus and so eyewitnesses of his majesty—that is, they saw him partake of the divine nature on one occasion in anticipation of the moment after his Resurrection when he would partake of it fully. Having been granted this vision, the apostles can testify to the reality of the promise that members of the Jesus Movement also will one day partake of that divine nature.

1:19–21: *An appeal to scriptural prophecy.* The promise is also guaranteed by the scriptures. All scripture is understood as prophecy, not only particular books or passages, and a very high, albeit somewhat mechanical, view of the inspiration of scripture is presented. In such a view the question of canonicity is crucial, and we shall see that 2 Peter is in fact our earliest witness to the development of a definite, distinct, and limited view of the canon of scripture in the Jesus Movement.

2:1–22: *Attack on the false teachers.* This section is based on Jude 4–16. It portrays what in Jude are the false teachers, and it uses many of his examples. However, 2 Peter purges Jude of references to books outside the canonical scriptures, that is, Old Testament. The myth of the burial of Moses from the *Assumption of Moses,* an allusion to the reference to the wandering stars in the *Book of Enoch,* and a quotation from *Enoch* 1:9 in Jude are all missing in 2 Peter. It is not that the author of 2 Peter does not like such apocalyptic myths; far from it! Rather, it appears that a canon was developing among the Israelites and that apparently he thinks that members of the Jesus Movement should accept it.

3:1–10: *True teaching concerning the day of the Lord.* This section begins with a renewal of the pseudonymous claim to Petrine authorship, which is at the same time a recognition that, for the writer, 1 Peter was already achieving the status of scripture (verse 1). It continues with a clear recognition of the sacredness of the apostolic age, which is now past (verse 2). The present of the writer is separated from that age, which he calls the time of "the last days" (verse 3; cf. Jude 17–18, where we have exactly the same distinction between the apostolic age and "the last time"). The scoffing of the false teachers is met by claiming that God's time is different from human time and that the *parousia* is imminent in God's time and certain in human time. It is an ingenious argument, but it loses the dynamic of the imminence of the *parousia* in Mark or of the attempt to make theological sense of the delay of the *parousia* in Matthew or Luke. Verse 10, the day of the Lord coming "like a thief (in the night)" represents a theme known from Paul (1 Thess. 5:2) and the synoptic gospels (Matt. 24:43 = Luke 12:39), except that it is considerably embellished.

3:11–18: *Ethical exhortation and concluding doxology.* The most interesting element in this concluding passage is the reference to Paul's letters. In verses 15–17, they are known as a collection and regarded as "scripture." We are approaching a canon that excludes

Israelite apocalyptic works that the Israelites themselves were excluding from their canon. The members of the Jesus Movement include the synoptic gospels (because 2 Peter refers to the gospel story of the transfiguration [2 Pet. 1:17] in a way in which it refers to scripture), 1 Peter (see 2 Pet. 3:1), and this collection of Paul's letters. Another important aspect of these references is the characterization of the letters of Paul as "hard to understand, which the ignorant and unstable twist to their own destruction . . ." (verse 16). This seems to imply that the false teachers against whom the author is directing his polemic are using the letters of Paul, or some aspects of them, as a basis for their position. The remainder of this passage is ethical exhortation based on reiterating the expectation of the "day of the Lord" in 3:1–10.

THE CHARACTERISTICS OF THE EMERGING INSTITUTIONAL CHURCH

The origins of the Jesus Movement can be located in an Israelite faction of the Greco-Roman period started by a Galilean peasant prophet named Jesus of Nazareth. The millennial prophet John the Baptizer baptized him. Jesus taught that the Kingdom of God was already beginning, recruited followers, spoke witty aphorisms and thought-provoking parables, exorcised demons, challenged the religious and political authorities in Galilee, and finally came into sharp conflict with the temple establishment and political powers of Jerusalem. His attempt to revitalize Israelite religion and life in the villages of Galilee led him to oppose, and be opposed by, these authorities. Ultimately, he met a cruel death by Roman crucifixion. Although there is much more that needs to be said about him (see Chapter Fourteen), for now it is important to note that his movement developed into a number of groups. Variety, not unity, characterized the Jesus Movement. Each wing of the movement developed its own responses to the meaning of Jesus. Some wings were more or less Israelites; some more or less Gentile; most some mixture of the two. Over time, especially as outside opposition and internal conflicts grew, there was an attempt to come to a greater consensus. This quest for unity implied a quest for self-definition in contrast to other, competing groups. Out of it came certain institutional developments—sacred texts, church roles and offices, and attempts to assimilate to the ways of the larger society. Let us characterize some of the main features of these emergent institutional churches.

Self-Definition

There is a great deal of negative labeling, or name-calling, in the literature of the growing institutional churches. Opponents in the Pastorals are accused of being greedy, deceptive, quibblers, sayers but not doers, full of vices, and appealing to women. In Jude we find denunciation of libertarian heretics described with traditional vices, condemned for despising the world of the flesh, and reviled for considering themselves to be superior to the angelic powers. In 2 Peter the opponents are said to emphasize knowledge of salvation now and eventual translation to the heavenly sphere and to despise the world and the body. Much of this sort of negative labeling can be found in contemporary philosophers' denunciations of the "sophists." This makes it difficult to identify with precision the opponent groups. Yet, these books are denouncing what will become in the second century "the Gnostic heresy," indications of which are already in Paul, the deutero-Paulines, and the Johannine letters. Clearly the institutional churches are in the process of self-definition over against those they believe to be "heretics." This eventually affected the very choice of books in the New Testament canon itself.

The Apostolic Tradition

Another obvious characteristic of the emerging institutional churches is the tendency to look back at the apostolic age and appeal to apostolic tradition as a way to combat opponents. The churches are now separated from the age of the apostles by a considerable period. The tendency is to remember that time as one of perfection, as the "golden age" of the church, as the time of revelation by God through Jesus to the church in the persons of the apostles. This process begins in the legends found in the Acts of the Apostles, but the author of Luke-Acts himself deliberately stresses the parallels between that heroic age and that of his readers, thus blurring the distance in time between them. The writers in this period, however, characteristically see themselves and their readers and hearers as separated from the age of the apostles. That time was the time of revelation and perfection; theirs is the time of the danger of apostasy, of falling away. For some, these are the "last days," and they are days of trial and corruption (Jude 17–18; 2 Pet. 3:3; 2 Tim. 3:1–5).

In many respects this understanding is strikingly parallel to the apocalyptic writers' understanding their days as the last days of a history hastening to its close. The representatives of the emerging institutional churches share the millennial hope of the *parousia.* Yet, there is an important difference. The apocalyptic writers look to the future *and live out of that future;* the representatives of the emerging institutional churches look to the future but *live out of the past,* the past of the apostolic age. An apocalyptic writer's expectation of the future dominates his whole understanding of things. A representative of institutionalism, such as the author of 2 Peter, has an expectation of the future but is dominated by the past of the apostolic age and the tradition that he believes comes out of the past.

Apostolic tradition must be guaranteed both in its origin and transmission. If it is to carry the authority of the apostles, then the apostles must themselves be the guarantors of the origin of the tradition. If it is to carry the authority of the apostles into the "last days," then there must be a separate agent guaranteeing its purity in transmission. That agent is the Holy Spirit. As the apostles are guarantors of the origin of the tradition, so the Spirit is the guarantor of its transmission (Jude 3; 2 Pet. 1:12–18; 2 Tim. 1:14).

These writers have a particular way of meeting what they believe to be false teaching. They do not argue the issues or debate with the false teachers. Instead they confront the teaching and the teachers and, standing squarely on the authority of the apostolic tradition, denounce both as not being in accord with the sacred, apostolic truth.

Faith as Revealed Truth

Emerging institutionalism conceives of revelation as given in the past, in the more or less pristine apostolic age, and handed on in the churches as a sacred object. Its concept of faith is very different from that of earlier periods of the church's history. It is no longer a belief in the imminent coming of Jesus as Son of Man, buttressed by experiences; it has become the acceptance of a revealed truth that can be expressed in little creeds. The Gospel of Matthew prepares for this with its concept of obedience to a verbal revelation authoritatively interpreted; and Hebrews, where faith is "the assurance of things hoped for, the conviction of things not seen" (Heb. 11:1), represents a transitional stage. But in the literature of emerging institutionalism, faith becomes the acceptance of authoritative tradition (Jude 20), something originally obtained by the apostles and available to those who stand in true succession to them (2 Pet. 1:1–2), and a synonym for more formalized religion (1 Tim. 1:5). 2 Tim. 1:13–14 stresses a "standard of sound teaching" to be guarded and passed on. 2 Tim. 2:2 emphasizes the same thing. Statements scattered through the Pastorals stress what is "sure," the adjective coming from the same root as the noun "faith" (1 Tim. 1:15; 3:1; 4:9; 2 Tim. 2:11; Titus 3:8).

The View of "Scripture"

The emphasis on authoritative apostolic tradition and on the Spirit as its guardian leads naturally to a high view of the written deposit of that tradition and of its Israelite counterpart, scripture. 2 Pet. 1:20–21 says that scripture does not come "by human will, but men and women moved by the Holy Spirit." 2 Tim. 3:16 says, "All scripture is inspired by God. . . ." These statements about Spirit-inspired texts naturally lead to defining what constitutes a sacred book.

The interest in sacred, authoritative texts was intensified by the beginnings of the Israelite definition of scripture in this period (about 90–100 C.E. at Yavneh or Jamnia) and also by the fact that the Gnostic false teachers depended on their own sacred books, which were often "secret." Believers in Christ as the Messiah were motivated by their own high view of "scripture" and no doubt challenged by the successful promulgation of the Israelite canon. Confronted by the Gnostic threat backed by secret books, the representatives of the emerging institutional church took the first step toward defining its own canon of scripture.

The most dramatic example is the contrast between Jude and 2 Pet. 2. Jude makes indiscriminate use of books being accepted into the Israelite canon—what would become the Old Testament—and the books that Israelites were rejecting, in this instance apocalyptic texts. Jude is here typical of earlier phases of the movement. But when Jude is used as the basis for 2 Pet. 2, all reference to anything outside the Israelite canon of scripture is carefully removed. The author of 2 Peter is apparently giving testimony to the importance of the Israelite example, and he is taking significant steps toward an equivalent for the Jesus Movement. By his treatment of Jude he reveals that he is the first to accept the Israelite canon or what was to become the "Old Testament" for Christ believers. Similarly, he is the first writer in the movement to refer to Paul's letters as "scripture" (2 Pet. 3:15–16). In his treatment of the transfiguration of Jesus (2 Pet. 1:16–19) and in his reference to "the second letter I am writing to you" (2 Pet. 3:1–2), he is also prepared to accept the gospels and 1 Peter as "scripture." Indeed, he is not too reluctant to put his own letter in that category!

Accommodation and Assimilation

When a group bears witness to its ideology to outsiders in the society, it must also define itself in relation to that society, as the author of Luke-Acts deals with the Roman Empire and its authorities. In the literature of growing institutionalism, there emerges a concern to represent itself to political authorities—governors, kings, and the like—as nonsubversive and to demonstrate to "those outsiders" that the church has a reputation to uphold (1 Pet. 2:11–17; Titus 2:7–8; 3:1–2).

The concern for what outsiders think and order within the group inevitably implies a certain level of accommodation and, at times, even assimilation to the established social order and its cultural beliefs, norms, and behaviors. The strong stress on the orderly pattern of the household and the ethics of the household codes in the Pastorals can be seen as accommodation and assimilation. Jesus' subversive attitude toward the family (see Chapter Fourteen) and Paul's famous "no longer Israelite (NRSV: Jew) or Greek, . . . no longer slave or free, . . . no longer male and female . . . in Christ Jesus" (Gal. 3:28), although not egalitarian in the modern sense, do not conform to this traditional pattern.

More Defined Roles and Functions; an Ordained Ministry

Development of church organizational structure implies more carefully defined roles and functions, if not yet offices, and thus an "ordained" ministry. There is in the Pastorals a lack of clarity about church roles, especially in Titus, but there is nonetheless an attempt to spell out the qualifications for "bishop/overseer" (3:1–7), "deacon" (3:8–13), and perhaps "widow" (5:9–6). "Elders/presbyters" who rule and preach are described (5:17–22), although their role as distinct from "bishops/overseers" is not yet clear. Yet, there is a council of elders/presbyters (1 Tim. 4:14; 5:22; 2 Tim. 1:6) engaged in ordination to the ministry by the "laying on of hands" (2 Tim. 1:6). In short, if it is difficult to demonstrate a full-blown institutionalization, it is quite clear that there is a move in that direction. One needs only to turn to *1 Clement* and especially the writings of Ignatius from generally the same period to see how in a somewhat different local context that development has already occurred.

The Letter Form

Striking in the literature of the emerging institutional church is the frequent use and transformation of the letter. Only one of the documents sounds something like an *actual* letter (1 Peter), and even the bulk of that letter may have been developed from a baptismal homily. Of the others, Jude, 2 Peter, and the Pastorals are less letters than manifestos. Why, then, are they all presented as letters? The answer is probably twofold. In the first place, at this time the letters of Paul are known and are now being circulated as "scripture." To imitate or develop the literary form is to use something familiar and hence more likely to be accepted. In the second place, and actually much more important, the letter genre provides an opportunity for pseudonymity—an opportunity to write in the name of someone from the apostolic age.

PSEUDONYMITY IN THE LITERATURE OF EMERGING INSTITUTIONALISM

The subject of **pseudonymity** has already been discussed at several points in this textbook, especially in connection with the deutero-Pauline literature (Chapter Seven). However, because it is a major characteristic of the literature of the period following the death of the original leaders/apostles, it is important to look briefly at the subject again.

Outside the literature of the emerging institutional church, actual pseudonymity is found in the New Testament only in the case of the deutero-Pauline letters: 2 Thessalonians, Colossians, and Ephesians. The synoptic gospels and the Acts of the Apostles were originally *anonymous,* not pseudonymous, that is, they were originally circulated without any author's name, and the names they now bear were ascribed to them later. Similarly, the literature of the Johannine School first circulated anonymously, although the writer of the second and third letters identifies himself as "the elder," and the author of the appendix to the gospel, chapter 21, identifies the evangelist as "the disciple whom Jesus loved." These writings are an instance of later scribal followers deliberately writing in the name of the venerated founder. This was a not unusual practice in the ancient world (again, see Chapter Seven). Analogous to the pseudonymity of the deutero-Pauline letters is the quite remarkable gospel practice of putting everything in the form of sayings of Jesus and stories about him. Finally, the apocalyptic author of Revelation identified himself as "John," and there is no reason to doubt that "John of Patmos" was its author, although there is every reason to doubt that he is any other "John" known from the early days of the church.

However, in the literature of the institutional development of the Jesus Movement pseudonymity becomes quite deliberate and predominant. Every single writing in this literature is pseudonymous in the narrow sense. There is no single writing in this literature that bears the name of its author; all without exception are written in the name of a figure from the apostolic age. Thus neither Jude, the brother of Jesus, nor Peter nor Paul authors any of these books.

In claiming authorship, the other literature of this period is also interesting. Clement of Rome does not write to the community at Corinth in his own name, but rather in the name of the community at Rome. The letter begins, "The church of God which sojourns in Rome to the church of God which sojourns in Corinth." The actual author is nowhere mentioned in the letter. Ignatius of Antioch writes in his own name, but he is writing personal letters to churches and to an individual

(Polycarp), like Paul. The *Didachē* (Greek: "teaching") is technically "The Teaching of the Lord to the Gentiles *by the Twelve Apostles.*" In other words, in this period there is a *reluctance to write in one's own name;* the important thing is not oneself, but rather the group whom one represents, or still more, the authoritative apostolic tradition in which one stands. This is not the authority of anonymity, but rather the authority of pseudonymity. Ignatius is the exception, but then his letters are distinctly personal letters; they are not simply ethical exhortation, manifesto, or incipient church order.

In short, the pseudonymity of the literature of emerging institutionalization is part of a pattern. One need only distinguish the highly personal from the remainder. Paul and Ignatius are writing very personal letters, and John of Patmos is giving an account of a personal revelation granted to him. The others are writing by the authority of the risen Lord, or of their community, or of an office within their community, or of their teacher, or of the apostolic age. So anonymity or pseudonymity is the rule; it is personal authorship that is the exception.

After we recognize this, the pseudonymity of the literature of emerging institutionalism becomes readily understandable. The writers view themselves as defenders of a faith once and for all delivered to the apostles and transmitted to their community by means of an apostolic tradition. So they write in the name of apostles and even go to considerable lengths to establish "authenticity," as when the author carefully constructs situations in the life of Paul out of which to write. The apostolic age and the apostolic tradition are the source of their inspiration and their authority. To write in the name of a person from the apostolic age is for them the next step.

THE INTERPRETATION OF THE LITERATURE OF THE EMERGING INSTITUTIONAL CHURCH

Many persons find that proper order and sound doctrine in their church or denomination are key elements in their faith. They may also find that the writers of these New Testament books speak directly to them. Others will be interested historically in the churches of this period hammering out a new vision of their faith and purpose in drastically changing historical circumstances. They may find that these texts speak to similar situations of drastically changing historical circumstances. Finally, still others may be interested in seeing how institutionalization affects a movement. They may be intrigued by how religious movements evolve. Whatever the point of view, the literature of the emerging institutional church has many lessons to teach.

STUDY QUESTIONS

1. What can you say about Peter and Babylon? What are some critical problems about the church's tradition regarding 1 Peter? What is the significance of the "house-church" for the interpretation of 1 Peter? How is 1 Peter related to the practice of baptism?

2. Who was James in early Christianity? How has historical criticism evaluated church tradition about James? What is the main content of James? How would you compare the Book of James to the writings of Paul? Does the book seem to be Jewish? How would you compare its teachings to those of the teachings of Jesus?

3. Who were Timothy and Titus? Who are opponents in these letters? Why do scholars place these letters in a third generation of Paulinists? What is a "**household code**"? What does 1 Timothy say about worship? bishops? deacons? widows? elders? slaves?

4. Why do interpreters think that the community represented by these letters demonstrates growing institutionalization in the Jesus Movement?

Courtesy of Joint Sepphoris Project

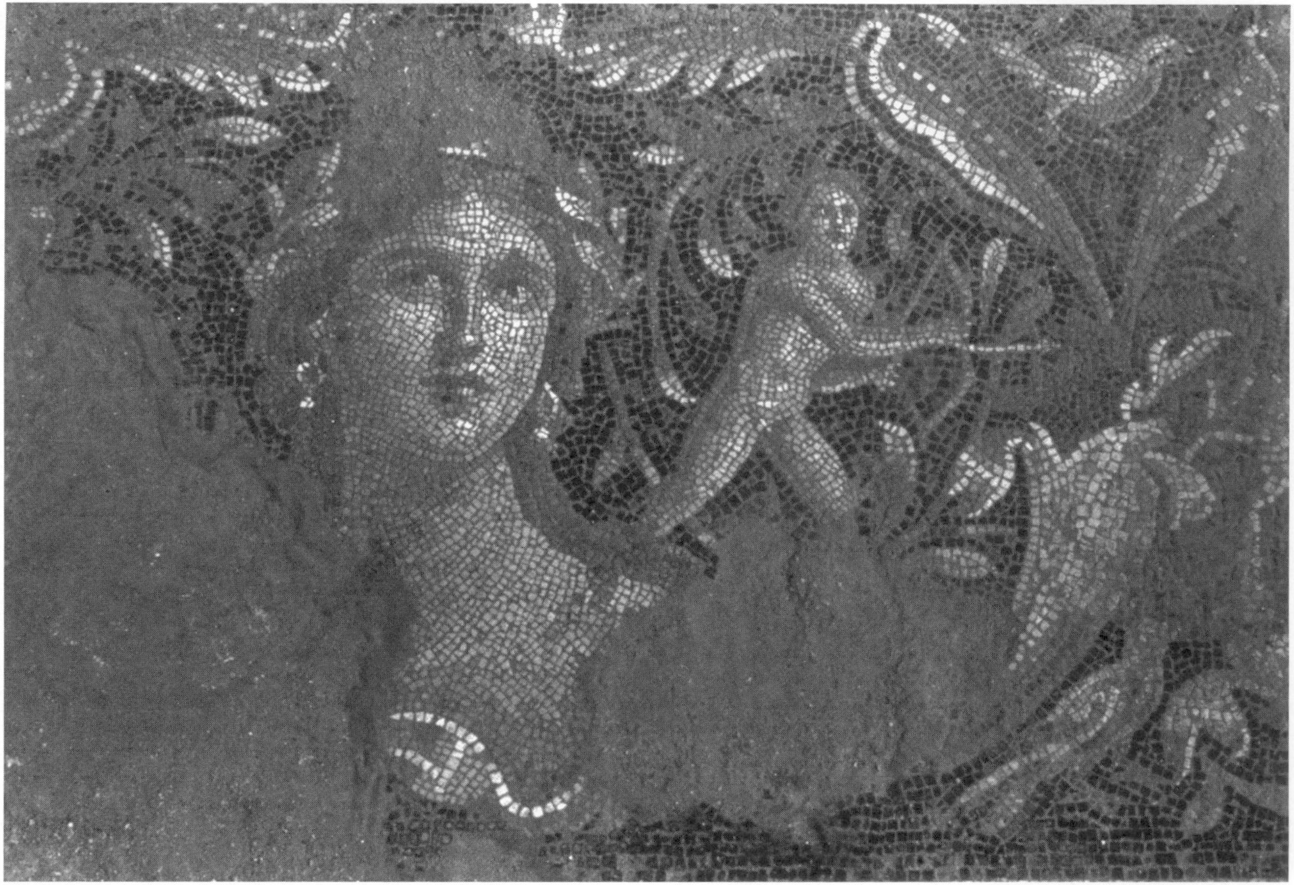

Photo 14.1 "The Mona Lisa of the Galilee." This beautiful woman was unearthed as part of a mosaic floor of a banquet hall (*triclinium*) featuring Dionysus, the god of wine, and the Dionysiac cult, in the villa of a very wealthy, influential person at Sepphoris (Hebrew Zippori), just three miles from Nazareth in Galilee. Her identity is not known. Herod Antipas (ruled 4 B.C.E. to 39 C.E.) rebuilt Sepphoris as his first capitol, renamed it "Autocratoris" ("imperial city"), and wanted to make it "the ornament of all Galilee" (Josephus *Antiquities* 18.2.1 [27]). This town was Israelite but excavations clearly show that it also had many Hellenistic influences, such as the mosaic that portrays this beautiful woman. There are competing theories about whether Sepphoris (never mentioned in the New Testament) had any cultural influence on Jesus of Nazareth.

CHAPTER FOURTEEN

THE PRESUPPOSITION OF THE NEW TESTAMENT: JESUS

Jesus of Nazareth is the presupposition for everything in the New Testament. Had the artisan not left his village and wandered about Galilee preaching, teaching, healing, and sharing meals with all sorts of people, had the Romans not executed him as a politically dangerous rebel, and had some of those devotees who heard him and followed him not come to believe that God had vindicated him, there would have been no Jesus Movement, no writings about his teachings, life, and significance.

Yet, followers of the groups who traced themselves back to him were less interested in the actual, historical Jesus who fascinates most modern historians than in his continuing presence among them. The sources that give us his "life" contain only a small selection of sayings, **anecdotes, parables,** and miracle stories, a selection that is overlaid with layers upon layers of interpretation. In the eighteenth century, however, Western intellectuals began to develop an intense pursuit of "what actually happened," and despite some contemporary intellectual trends to the contrary, that curiosity seems to persist, now fueled by new archeological discoveries and social-scientific insights. Scholars and nonscholars alike have become increasingly interested in "the historical Jesus," the Galilean who lived and taught, as distinct from the various beliefs about him, or "Christs of faith," found in the New Testament and developing creeds and confessions down through the centuries.

THE PROBLEM: THE VARIETY OF IMPRESSIONS ABOUT JESUS IN THE EARLY JESUS MOVEMENT

As our study of the New Testament has shown, there was a rich variety of individuals, groups, and practices and a corresponding variety of beliefs, oral traditions, sources, and writings in the Jesus Movement. There was correspondingly a great diversity of opinion and belief about the Galilean peasant's life and teachings. Paul of Tarsus recorded almost nothing of his teachings. Other believers, some of them probably Paul's opponents, stressed Jesus' life as a great and powerful miracle worker, and they collected miracle stories. Other believers handed down teachings attributed to Jesus, although some of them seem to have been spoken by the "living" Jesus through prophets in altered states of consciousness. These served as guides for life. Some reflected the image of Jesus as a millennial prophet; others recalled his witty aphorisms as a wise sage; still others made him sound like a learned rabbi. Collections such as **Q** and the *Gospel of Thomas* appeared.

Within a couple of generations, accounts of Jesus' life also appeared. The author of the Markan gospel, unlike Paul, recorded a few of Jesus' teachings and especially his miracles; yet, like Paul, he subordinated them to his emphasis on Jesus' Passion and death. Apparently writing for common folk, he saw Jesus as a miracle-working millennial Messiah–Son of God/suffering Son of Man who wished to keep his mysterious identity a secret. The author of Matthew elevated Jesus' status. He said that Jesus was descended from a long line of kings stretching back to King David and beyond to the beloved patriarch Abraham. His Jesus was also a new Moses who left for his followers the true interpretation of the Torah. Indeed, Jesus fulfilled the Torah and the teachings of the prophets about the Son of God and Son of Man. The writer of Luke-Acts, writing for elite Greeks and Romans, combined a number of images—a miracle worker like Elijah; the Spirit-filled prophet who, although innocent, must die in Jerusalem; and most important, the cosmic patron and liberator of all humanity. The author(s) of the Johannine gospel, writing antilanguage for an antisociety, combined images of the Israelite royal Messiah, the millennial Son of Man, and Wisdom to create an image of the heavenly Man who came to earth, taught, and returned to the heavens. He included other images—the Manna from heaven and the great "I AM." Others wrote other gospels not finally accepted in the canon, and still others stressed images such as the heavenly High Priest in Hebrews.

In short, the earliest storytellers and writers developed a great variety of perpetually reinterpreted Christ images. These make the task of recovering the historical Jesus who actually lived, taught, and was active in ancient Galilee very difficult. Indeed, some scholars think that this quest is doomed to failure. Yet, other scholars think some progress can be made. Because Jesus was a historical figure, they say, the attempt to find him is a legitimate and necessary historical task—whether the results directly affect how modern believers think or not. The first step in any discussion of the historical Jesus, then, is to learn a little about the course of that progress in the modern period.

MODERN QUESTS FOR THE HISTORICAL JESUS

Modern attempts to recover the historical Jesus had their origins in late eighteenth-century Europe and North America, the period of the intellectual Enlightenment and the Industrial Revolution. In the preceding century Europeans and Americans had learned something about native, tribal peoples. They usually judged them to be emotional, irrational, underdeveloped, and primitive. It is therefore no surprise that they concluded that Western civilization and Christianity were superior to tribal religions. However, they were also recoiling against the devastating seventeenth-century European religious wars among Christians themselves. By extension, many Western intellectuals judged that all traditional religions, including Christianity, were simply superstitious. One result was that ancient beliefs of the churches could no longer be accepted without criticism.

In this intellectual climate the scriptures and traditions of traditional Christianity were examined under the microscope of human reason. Was the supernatural Christ of traditional Christianity a fabrication of ancient peoples who were influenced by superstitions and pagan beliefs about the gods? Who was the historical Jesus—really? Such impulses awakened interest in historical study of the life and teachings of Jesus. What follows is a brief sketch of the main contours of this modern "quest of the historical Jesus."

The "Old" Quest ("The First Quest")

Sources for Doctrine or Human Historical Sources?

The first major question was this: Are the sources primarily sources for divine revelation and doctrine, or were they human sources? Were they "supernatural" or "natural"? If human, who wrote them, and when, where, and for what purpose? Could one trust what they said? Were they records of what "actually happened" or the products of pious imagination? Could one reconstruct real history from them? How?

The first intellectuals who tried to answer these questions were the Deists and Rationalists. In Germany the Rationalist Reimarus argued that Jesus believed himself to be a political messiah who would deliver the Israelites from the Romans and establish a temporal Kingdom in Jerusalem. When he was executed, his disappointed followers created the spiritual, supernatural savior who atoned for the sins of the world and was expected to return at the End to offer rewards and punishments. Reimarus' writings were so controversial that they were not published until after his death (1776).

The most troubling stories for the scientific-minded Rationalists were the miracle stories because they were thought to go against the natural, physical laws of the universe. Fifty-plus years after Reimarus, another German Rationalist named Paulus gave what he thought was the fundamental reason for these unbelievable accounts: The ancients did not yet scientifically understand the laws of nature. Paulus tried to find reasonable explanations for the miracle stories. Most troubling were the nature and feeding miracles. Jesus did not really walk on water; he was walking on a sandbar in a mist near the shore. Jesus did not really feed five thousand people; the rich shared their food with the poor. Jesus did not really rise from the dead; he was only in a deathlike trance, and, after the earthquake moved the stone, he revived, put on the gardener's clothes, and spent forty days with his disciples before mysteriously disappearing in a cloud. And so on.

The evaluation of the sources was resolved in favor of the "natural" explanation, not the "supernatural" one. The Rationalists' explanations of the miracle stories seem a little quaint today. Yet, their desire to know "what actually happened" was a historical motive, and today most critical scholars still try to explain the nature miracles in nonhistorical ("symbolic") ways.

John or the Synoptics?

The second major question followed on the first: Was the Gospel of John or the synoptic gospels the most historical? In 1835 David Friedrich Strauss published his famous *Life of Jesus*. It cost him his job and his career. Strauss sought to overcome the traditional supernatural and Rationalist natural alternatives by arguing that the gospels were "mythical," by which he meant they were products of religious experience developed by reflecting on the Hebrew Scriptures. The most mythical stories were the infancy narratives and the resurrection accounts; there was more history in the rest of the gospel narratives. Nonetheless, the net effect of Strauss' reading was to cast doubt on the historicity of the gospels. Because the Gospel of John was more "mythical" than the synoptics, it was correspondingly less valuable historically. From this point forward, the Gospel of John has been hardly used as a source for finding the historical Jesus. In the 1840s Bruno Bauer went further: All the gospels were pure literary fiction and thus virtually without value as historical sources; indeed, said Bauer, the historical Jesus never lived, but rather was the creation of the Jesus Movement!

Initially scholars did not take the path of the radical Strauss, let alone Bruno Bauer. In the same year that Strauss wrote his *Life* (1835), Karl Lachmann argued in contrast to the traditional view that the Gospel of Mark was the earliest gospel ("**the Priority of Mark**"). It, not Matthew, was closest to the time of Jesus. He also argued that the Matthean writer had used a now-lost collection of Jesus' sayings. Three years later Wilke (pronounced "Vil-kuh") and Weisse (pronounced "Vaissuh") defended this position, and in 1863 H. J. Holtzmann nailed it down. For New Testament historians the **Two-Source Theory** and **Priority of Mark** seemed to be the most satisfactory answer to **the Synoptic Problem,** and the historical skepticism of Strauss and Bauer for the Markan outline was considered to be basically historical. It was therefore the key to the historical Jesus' life and thought, which included his developing "**messianic consciousness.**" At Caesarea Philippi, they said, Jesus *redefined* his role as Messiah in terms of his own suffering as the Son of Man (Mark 8:27–9:1). This theory of the fundamental historicity of Mark and his developing messianic consciousness is called "**the Markan Hypothesis.**"

The stage was now set for the culminating act of the first quest for the historical Jesus. By the late nineteenth century, literally thousands of historical lives of Jesus were being written on the basis of the Markan Hypothesis. Adolf von Harnack's classic summary of Jesus in *The Essence of Christianity* (1901) is typical of what scholars said about Jesus' teaching:

1. The Fatherhood of God and the brotherhood of "man"
2. The ("spiritual") Kingdom within, as a matter of human experience
3. Ethical teachings, especially loving God, neighbor, and even enemy

This summary shows that the scholars were bypassing the doctrinal teachings of the churches about the supernatural Christ of faith and attempting to discover Jesus' true spiritual religion. For theologians—at least Protestant theologians—Jesus' own experience was the moral example for modern believers. The key was his deep personal religion and his love ethic. This historically based thinking about Jesus, whose ethics was easy for modern people to appropriate, was called "**Liberalism.**"

One might imagine that everyone accepted the newly discovered historical Jesus of the Liberals as the answer to historical skepticism. For Conservatives, however, the answer was insufficient. The French scholar Ernst Renan, a Roman Catholic whose historical *Life of Jesus* (1863) was so popular that it rapidly went through ten printings, was excommunicated. On the Protestant side, traditional Lutherans were suspicious of Harnack.

In summary, the second major choice, John or the synoptics, was answered in favor of the synoptics, and among them, the favorite for historical reconstruction was the Gospel of Mark on which the Markan Hypothesis was built, and thus many Liberal lives of Jesus were written.

Apocalyptic or Nonapocalyptic?

During the very same period when Harnack stressed Jesus' religious experience and ethical teaching, the **History-of-Religions School** (*Religionsgeschichtliche Schule*) developed in Germany. Its goal was to research and understand the various religions of the Greco-Roman world. Most important for understanding Jesus was the rediscovery of apocalyptic thinking among Israelites of the Greco-Roman period.

Johannes Weiss' little book, *Jesus' Proclamation of the Kingdom of God* (1892), argued in opposition to Liberals such as Harnack that Jesus was an apocalyptic prophet. Jesus' Kingdom teaching was not about the spiritual presence of God within and in human experience; rather, he taught that God would intervene in world affairs very soon to bring about his *supernatural Kingdom.* To be sure, Jesus seemed at times to have spoken about a present Kingdom, but these sayings, argued Weiss, were spoken in an ecstatic state. Jesus was really like many of his contemporaries, an apocalypticist. He was a strange, remote, unfathomable person, not one with whom modern people can easily identify. He was mildly "ascetic" (usually defined as denying bodily pleasures in pursuit of a higher spiritual goal). His mission was to prepare his people for the great "Day of the Lord," the day of judgment, when the forces of evil would be overcome and the good would receive their reward.

Weiss' view of Jesus' Kingdom teaching ran counter to the prevailing Liberal view of Jesus based on the Markan Hypothesis. It found support in the famous Albert Schweitzer (also organist and winner of the Nobel Peace Prize for medical work in Africa). Schweitzer even went further: The *whole course of Jesus' life* was determined by his apocalyptic ideas. Schweitzer focused on Matt. 10–11, a section that contained Jesus' speech to the disciples about the mission, and Matt. 10:23. The verse reads: "When they persecute you in one town, flee to the next; for truly I tell you, you will not have gone through all the towns of Israel before the Son of Man comes." Schweitzer reasoned that Jesus must have said this because otherwise his followers would not have preserved such an unfulfilled prophecy. When his prophecy did not happen, Jesus decided to go to Jerusalem to *force* God's hand to bring in the Kingdom. Of course, that did not happen, either! In Schweitzer's perspective, Jesus' ethical teachings were not meant for posterity but only for the short interim period before the End (called an "interim ethic"). Schweitzer named his view "**thoroughgoing eschatology.**" In short, apocalyptic eschatology was a blow to the Markan Hypothesis and the dominant Liberal view of Jesus as ethical teacher.

Mark Again: History or Not History?

Most scholars of this period—including Schweitzer—accept the Markan Hypothesis. Mark, they said, was generally historically reliable. However, in 1901 William Wrede published *The Messianic Secret* (1901), a book that convinced most scholars (in Germany at least) that the secret of Jesus' suffering, dying, and rising messiahship in Mark was not *Jesus'* secret, but a *Markan* secret. The Markan author expanded this traditional theme. He also put into Jesus' mouth the commands of secrecy to demons, recipients of cures, and disciples not to reveal his (Jesus') secret identity. Why? He was attempting to explain to his readers why some of the gospel stories about Jesus that he had received from oral tradition did not seem to be explicitly "messianic." Simply put, Jesus told them not to tell. In short: The Messianic Secret was a literary theme of the Markan evangelist, not a theme of the historical Jesus. The ghost of Strauss was still around!

In concluding this section, note that it was mainly Protestant scholars—Liberals and apocalyptic theorists—who carried on these early debates about the historical Jesus. Traditional Protestants and Roman Catholics rejected these "natural" attempts to go behind (thus bypass!) the "supernatural" divine Christ of the creeds. The French Catholic scholar Ernst Renan had been excommunicated. Another French Roman Catholic scholar, Alfred Loisy, in his *The Gospel and the Church* (1903), presented an apocalyptic view of Jesus. Despite his masterful rebuttal of the Protestant Harnack, he was excommunicated as a "Modernist."

Weiss', Schweitzer's, and Loisy's apocalyptic views of Jesus on the one hand and Wrede's questioning of the historicity of Mark on the other—each quite different—called into question the late nineteenth-century Liberal historical Jesus. Moreover, if Wrede was right, the ghost of skeptical Strauss was still haunting New Testament scholars. Would it ever be possible to write a historical "life" of Jesus?

The Quest for the Oral Tradition (1919–1953) ("No Quest")

The Written Framework for the Oral Tradition

In 1919 Karl Ludwig Schmidt's *The Framework of the Story of Jesus* argued that the technique of the Markan author was to link together the isolated oral traditions he had received with vague references to time and place ("and Jesus said . . . ," "then," "immediately," and the like). In other words, the Markan author *created* the gospel framework or outline of the Markan story, like stringing pearls. Mark was not a modern historical biography; the trail blazed by Strauss and widened by Wrede was becoming a major highway.

The History of the Oral Tradition

In that same year, 1919, Martin Dibelius published *From Tradition to Gospel,* a Form Critical analysis of the oral traditions behind the gospels. Two years later Rudolf Bultmann published *The History of the Synoptic Tradition*. His object was to write the complete oral history of every synoptic passage (see Chapter Two). Each scholar analyzed the small forms of the synoptic tradition (parables, miracle stories, and so forth) and showed that they developed and how they changed as they were transmitted in various socio-religious settings in the early churches. This approach to oral tradition put even more distance between the historical Jesus and the "final" interpretations of the evangelists.

For Bultmann, this distance was no problem for Christian faith. As an "existentialist" he argued that humans can never be absolutely certain, but rather must always remain open for life's challenges and possibilities. Indeed, this "openness to the future" is the best way to understand the historical Jesus' apocalyptic Kingdom teaching. "Authentic existence" is the best way to look at the biblical idea of salvation. As a Lutheran, Bultmann believed that faith does not demand absolute certainty, but rather simply requires risk and trust in God. This means that the scholar is free to pursue her/his critical studies with the confidence that (s)he need not be certain about the historical Jesus.

Another brief observation is in order. Some scholars have labeled the period between World War I and World War II as the "no quest" period. The label has some merit but can be misleading for several reasons. First, many scholars, especially in Britain and North America, continued to write "Liberal" lives of Jesus. Second, some Scandinavian scholars claimed that oral storytellers preserved rather accurate reminiscences. Third, "the Chicago School," independent of Form Criticism, pioneered work on concrete social contexts of Jesus, for example, family life, economics, and politics. Fourth, even in Germany some scholars continued the quest. Joachim Jeremias (pronounced "Yo-a-keem Yeyr-a-mee-ahs") argued that one could use Form Criticism to reconstruct the original forms of Jesus' parables and ask what they meant in Jesus' historical setting. For Jeremias, Jesus was a mild apocalyptic thinker, and the parables were his "weapons of warfare." Thus for Jeremias, Form Criticism could be used positively as a tool for rediscovering the historical Jesus. Fifth, and last, even Bultmann, the scholar whose work most suggested the "no quest" label, wrote *Jesus and the Word* (1926), a rather sizable book about the historical Jesus. He removed later layers of tradition and stressed Jesus' "distinctive eschatological temper." He concluded three very important things.

1. *Eschatology.* Jesus was an "*eschatological prophet.*" Bultmann followed Weiss' view that Jesus' teaching centered in the apocalyptic Kingdom of God, but he argued that Schweitzer's *thoroughgoing eschatological* view went too far. Jesus was not like his mentor John the Baptizer. The Kingdom was both other *and near,* both future *and present.* He called this "reduced apocalyptic." Jesus' distinctive message gave hope to the poor, hungry, and sorrowful.

2. *Ethics.* Jesus was also an *unconventional rabbi.* He did not attack temple sacrifices, prayer, almsgiving, and fasting, but rather distinguished what was essential in the Torah, stressing love of God and neighbor. His ethical teaching was therefore subversive. He also taught the Lord's Prayer and some parables. He accepted scripture. He promised rewards and punishments. Decision was required, which Bultmann called "radical obedience."

3. *Self-understanding and activity.* Bultmann rejected the possibility of knowing Jesus' "messianic consciousness." However, one *could* know something about how Jesus *understood* himself (existentialist philosophers stressed "existential self-understanding")

and what was *typical* of his "activity" or way of life. This included performing exorcisms, having laxity in the Sabbath commandment, rejecting ritual purification, challenging Israelite "legalism," holding fellowship with outcasts (tax collectors and prostitutes), and being open to women and children. Thus Bultmann also thought that Jesus was not an ascetic like John the Baptizer; rather, Jesus banqueted and drank a glass of wine with pleasure. He also gathered disciples, and his followers included both men and women. Finally, he encountered opposition by religious authorities at Jerusalem, suffered, and was crucified by the Romans.

But was this reconstruction inclusive enough?

The "New" Quest (The "Second Quest") (1953–1975)

New Discoveries

Before taking up the "New Quest" as such, it is important to recall two major discoveries that began to affect Jesus research in this period—and still do.

1. *The **Dead Sea Scrolls**.* In 1946 Bedouins discovered the **Dead Sea Scrolls,** which were heavily apocalyptic and messianic. For many scholars they confirmed the view that Palestine was filled with millennial, messianic fervor at the time of Jesus, and for some scholars this context made the possibility that Jesus was an apocalyptic prophet, whether "thoroughgoing" (Schweitzer) or "reduced" (Bultmann), very plausible.

2. *The **Gospel of Thomas**.* The *Gospel of Thomas* was discovered among the Nag Hammadi texts near Nag Hammadi, Egypt, in 1945. In contrast to the Dead Sea Scrolls, it was *not* strongly apocalyptic. Although there was some initial resistance to using *Thomas* as a source for Jesus' sayings, that judgment has changed for most scholars.

Käsemann's Essay

In 1953 Bultmann and the so-called post-Bultmannians—primarily his doctoral students teaching in universities—gathered for a conference in Marburg, Germany. There Ernst Käsemann (pronounced "Kay-za-mahn"), a former student of Bultmann, presented an essay agreeing with most of Bultmann's position but arguing that Bultmann had made the distance between "the historical Jesus" (Bultmann's "Proclaimer") and the Christ of faith in the gospels (Bultmann's "Proclaimed") too great. For Käsemann, Bultmann was in danger of isolating Jesus from both his ancient Israelite Palestinian context and what his followers later said about him. Käsemann stressed more continuity. He warned that Bultmann's views might lead to **docetism,** the ancient heresy that claimed that Jesus did not come "in the flesh" (see Chapter Eleven). Käsemann's essay is now regarded as the study that launched the "New Quest" for the historical Jesus.

Other post-Bultmannian students agreed with Käsemann, including Günther Bornkamm, who wrote the classic *Jesus of Nazareth* (1956). The discussion also migrated to North America. Helmut Koester, Bultmann's last student, took a position at Harvard and influenced scholarly understanding of oral tradition and the noncanonical gospels. James M. Robinson wrote a classic description of the New Quest and edited the Nag Hammadi Library. Norman Perrin promoted New Quest scholarship about Jesus. Scholars also took up **Redaction Criticism,** which extended the perception that the gospels were interpretations of Jesus, not literal history.

It should be observed that the "New Questers" had more similarities with Bultmann than differences. All used the **Two-Source Theory, Form Criticism,** and **Redaction Criticism.** All tended to focus on the teachings of Jesus because a biography and psychological knowledge (Jesus' "messianic consciousness") were impossible to know. Finally, all thought that the gospels contain layers of interpretation and that rediscovering Jesus requires applying carefully formulated criteria. This leads to the next point.

Criteria of Authenticity

Bultmann had formulated a criterion for isolating what was the earliest Palestinian form of Jesus' sayings, thus the earliest layers of tradition. Käsemann refined this criterion, now known as the "criterion of dissimilarity," as follows:

> . . . we have reasonably secure ground under our feet [for finding the historical Jesus] only in one particular instance, namely, when there is some way of showing that a piece of tradition has not been derived from Judaism and may not be ascribed to early Christianity, and this is particularly the case when Jewish Christianity has regarded this tradition as too bold and has toned it down or modified it in some way.
>
> (*Essays,* p. 37; trans. Perrin, *Rediscovering,* p. 42)

This statement implies that a scholar must know everything possible about first-century Israelites and the Jesus Movement, a daunting task. It also implies that Jesus was distinctive (the criterion in modified form is called the "criterion of distinctiveness"). Jesus was a radical whose teaching was tamed down by his followers. There were other criteria developed in the "New Quest," used not only by the post-Bultmannians, but also by others. They will be considered further later.

The post-Bultmannians or "New Questers" were in most respects like Bultmann. Jesus' "eschatological temper" was distinctive in relation to his environment. Yet, they thought Bultmann had gone too far in severing Jesus from his Palestinian Israelite context and what early believers remembered about him. The door was open for further reevaluations.

A Brief Pause (1975–1985)

Although there was nothing equivalent to the major pause when Form Criticism developed between 1919 and 1953, there was in the decade of 1975–1985 less interest in the historical Jesus among scholars. But the pause was not long.

The Post–"New Quest" Quest ("Third Quest") (1985–Present)

Assuming the standard discussions about the "First [Old] Quest" and the "Second [New] Quest," the British scholar N. T. Wright recently suggested that there has now been a "Third Quest." The "Third Quest" category, like "No Quest," can be misleading. Wright had in mind certain scholars who were returning to a historical approach inherited from Albert Schweitzer (thoroughgoing eschatology, based on

Mark) rather than William Wrede (Mark was a later interpretation). Wright put forward the "Third Quest" as a critical alternative to the "New Quest." This textbook, however, takes the position that the "Third Quest" label, if used at all, is more *chronological* than a description of a single orientation. There is, indeed, an vital new interest in the historical Jesus, but it is characterized by a *variety* of options. Therefore, the label "Post–'New Quest' Quest" is preferred.

At least two general and four specific factors can be cited for the new interest in the historical Jesus. The two general factors are:

1. The emergence of the Jesus Seminar

2. Social-historical and social-scientific methods

The four specific factors are:

3. A renewed study of the events of Jesus' *life*

4. Developments in **Q** research

5. Continuing research on the *Gospel of Thomas*

6. A renewed interest in Jesus' Galilean context as illuminated by archeology

Let us briefly consider each of these factors.

The Jesus Seminar in North America

In 1985 a prominent scholar, Robert Funk, invited a number of other scholars to the first meeting of the Jesus Seminar. They would henceforth meet twice a year, would prepare scholarly papers on Jesus in advance, circulate them (the emergence of e-mail fostered this), and debate them at the meeting. Most of the scholars operated with modified versions of the Second Quest criteria, although other criteria were developed. However, Funk asked the scholars to do something quite foreign to traditional individualistic, humanistic historical study, namely, to reach closure by *voting* on the authenticity/inauthenticity of Jesus' sayings. He developed a system of color-coding. Here is one version of it:

Red:	Jesus undoubtedly said this or something very like this
Pink:	Jesus probably said something like this
Gray:	Jesus did not say this, but the ideas contained in it are close to his
Black:	Jesus did not say this; it represents the perspective of later tradition

Scholars voted, the colors were mathematically weighted, and the votes were tallied. Over the course of several years' work, the seminar concluded that about 18 percent of all sayings—including those outside the canonical New Testament—were red or pink. Subsequently, the seminar used a similar process on the activities of Jesus.

The activity of the seminar was (and is) controversial. Some nonspecialists who did not know the complicated issues already developed in traditional Jesus research history were appalled. Conservative scholars who had never accepted the commonly used critical methods and criteria of the post-Bultmannians objected. Some scholars who used such tools found the voting and media attention given to the seminar distasteful. Occasionally criticism was vitriolic.

However one evaluates the Jesus Seminar—one should recall that Textual critics also decide on the Greek text of the New Testament by committee vote and that translators often work in teams—it provoked a wave of new interest in Jesus among scholars and public alike.

Social-History and Social-Scientific Interpretation

A second more general factor is the resurgence of the social sciences as a way of understanding and reconfiguring Greco-Roman, Israelite, and early church contexts. This method has already been explained and extensively used in this book; here is a brief word about its emergence and impact.

Study of the social "class" of Jesus was not new. A century before in Germany Adolf Deissmann had argued that followers of Jesus were generally from the lower social strata. Form Critics had been interested in the socio-religious settings (*Sitze im Leben*) of the developing oral traditions about Jesus. The Chicago School had attempted to understand politics, economics, family, and religious institutions in Jesus' world (S. Mathews, S. J. Case).

The new approach, however, was much more self-conscious about social theory and models (see Chapter Two). Social-historical and social-scientific exegetical groups emerged in the national and international guilds of biblical scholars. The Social Facets of the Ancient World Seminar, developed as a satellite of the Jesus Seminar, separated and began to meet yearly as the Social Context Group. Studies related to Jesus influenced by cross-cultural models used in the (Social) Context Group are Crossan's *Jesus of Nazareth: The Life of a Mediterranean Jewish Peasant* (1992), the Stegemanns' *The Jesus Movement* (German, 1995), and Hanson and Oakman's *Palestine in the Time of Jesus: Social Structures and Social Conflicts* (1998). Such work continues to affect the way that scholars perceive the ancient Galilean setting for Jesus, as well as Jesus himself.

Consider now the four more specific factors.

Galilee and the Archeology of Galilee

The social context for Jesus was Galilee. An earlier generation of scholars tended to think that Galilee was a cultural backwater inhabited by ignorant "people of the land" (Hebrew: *'am ha-aretz*) who did not observe the Torah and had little contact with Greeks and Romans. Relatively isolated Galilee spawned rebels, charismatic holy men, and miracle workers. The implications for "Jesus the Galilean" are obvious.

A new generation of archeologists has now painted a somewhat different picture of Galilee. Upper Galilee (north) was indeed somewhat isolated, although it had some commercial contact with the Mediterranean coast. Lower Galilee (south) was more in contact with urbane Hellenistic culture. Herod Antipas rebuilt Sepphoris as his first capital. It was only three miles from the village of Nazareth. Excavations indicate many Greco-Roman cultural influences there—Greek language; Hellenistic architecture, art, and theaters; posh villas, and the like. Then Herod built another capital, Tiberias, on the Sea of Galilee to replace Sepphoris. In short, although Galilee seems to have been *somewhat* more rural and provincial than the regions surrounding it, it was also influenced by a more urban "pagan" cultural presence. Yet, continuing archeology study shows that its villages and their economies seem to have been relatively self-sufficient.

This modified archeological picture of Galilee has produced several important questions. First, did the new cities influence the peasants in the countryside, and, if so, how? Second, did Greco-Roman culture have any influence on the Galileans? Third, did the presence of "pagan" religion influence the Galileans to be less oriented toward the Jerusalem temple and traditional Torah laws? Finally, and most important for the historical Jesus, did the artisan from Nazareth find work in such cities, and, if so, did Hellenistic culture, philosophy, and religion have any influence on him? Such questions are hotly debated and will be taken into account in our following sketch of Jesus.

Q

Q was known to contain two types of sayings: future apocalyptic judgments and hopes on the one hand and practical wisdom for everyday life on the other. Earlier studies had argued that the earliest layer in Q was Palestinian and apocalyptic, whereas the later redaction added Hellenistic wisdom material. This tended to support the apocalyptic prophet image of Jesus. In the 1980s John Kloppenborg urged the reverse hypothesis, namely, that the wisdom sayings were Israelite and earlier ("Q1"), whereas the apocalyptic sayings stressed judgment and were added when the community faced opposition ("Q2"; see Chapter Two). Although Kloppenborg himself was reluctant to draw direct historical conclusions about Jesus from this literary sequence, some other scholars have argued that the wisdom sayings, not the apocalyptic ones (e.g., B. Mack), best represent the historical Jesus. In other words, Jesus was a wise sage, not an apocalyptic prophet. That conclusion is often correlated with a high evaluation of sayings in the *Gospel of Thomas,* which contains very little apocalyptic.

The Gospel of Thomas

The discovery of the **Gospel of Thomas** in 1945 eventually had a profound effect in the evaluation of the historical Jesus, for several reasons. First, it offered empirical evidence that members of the Jesus Movement made collections of Jesus' sayings like **Q.** Indeed, about one-third of the *Thomas* sayings have parallels in Q. Second, many *Thomas* scholars argued that the *Thomas* sayings were independent of the canonical gospels. This led historical Jesus scholars like Norman Perrin to the view that *some Thomas* sayings were early and more likely to have represented what Jesus said than their synoptic variants. More recently, a few scholars have dated the original version of *Thomas* itself to the first century. This strengthens its importance as an analogy for Q and as potentially containing very early Jesus sayings. In short, those who view Jesus as a sage or wisdom teacher rather than an apocalyptic prophet lay much weight on early Q (Q1) and *Thomas* (a *Thomas*–early Q Axis).

Reawakened Interest in the Events of Jesus' Life

The New Questers focused on Jesus' *teachings* from the perspective of Bultmann's "reduced apocalyptic." To be sure, exceptions to the New Questers emerged — R. Hiers' defense of Schweitzer's radical apocalyptic Jesus, S. G. F. Brandon's radical political Jesus, G. Vermes' charismatic healer Jesus, and M. Smith's magician Jesus—but the dominant orientation remained the New Quest approach.

In 1985 E. P. Sanders made a direct assault on this position. Stressing God's covenant with the Israelites through the Torah (covenantal nomism) and the view that God would make Israel a great people once again (restoration theology), Sanders stressed several well-accepted historical facts about Jesus' *life:*

1. Birth about 4 B.C.E.
2. Childhood and early adult years in the Galilean village of Nazareth
3. Baptism by John the Baptizer
4. Recruitment of disciples
5. Teaching in Galilean villages and towns
6. Preaching the Kingdom of God
7. Journey to Jerusalem for the Passover about 30 C.E.
8. Creation of disturbance in the temple
9. Last meal with the disciples
10. Arrest and interrogation by Israelite authorities, specifically the high priest
11. Execution on orders by the prefect, Pontius Pilate
12. Fleeing of disciples
13. Disciples "saw" him after his death and believed he would return to found the Kingdom
14. Formation of a community to wait for his return and to recruit others to believe in him as the Messiah of God

Sanders focused on two of these facts. First, Jesus selected *twelve* disciples (number 4), a selection that symbolized the twelve tribes of Israel. They would rule over (or judge) Israel (Q 22:28–30), implying that Jesus shared in the hope that Israel would soon be restored (restoration theology). In the tradition of Schweitzer, Jesus was a *radical* ("thoroughgoing") apocalyptic prophet. Second, Jesus overturned the money changers' tables in the Jerusalem temple (number 8), which, Sanders argued, was not simply a symbolic cleansing, but rather an anticipation that God would *totally destroy and rebuild the temple* (destruction: Mark 13:2; *GTh* 71; rebuilding: Mark 14:58; Matt. 26:61; John 2:13–22). This was a return to *apocalyptic,* a view taken up by several other scholars. Since Sanders' study, several other scholars have attempted to revive Schweitzer's radical apocalyptic views.

Summary

The modern quest for the historical Jesus has traversed more than two and a quarter centuries. In that quest, scholars first learned to treat the gospels as "faith documents" that reflect the historical and social contexts of the transmitters of the Jesus tradition and the authors of the gospels, not just as factual historical events about the life and teaching of Jesus. They realized that there are many layers of interpretation that must be removed to get to Jesus. They came to focus primarily on Jesus' teachings. However, several scholars in recent years have been willing to see a little more history in the events. A variety of perspectives on his life and teaching has therefore arisen, not only because of newer methods, but also because of new archeological discoveries. This textbook takes the perspective that finding the historical Jesus requires multiple methods and criteria that reflect both archeology and the multiple layers of tradition and redaction found in the gospels. It accepts a mediating position: that Jesus was indeed influenced by apocalyptic, but in a less radical way that allows room for his distinctive wisdom.

HISTORICAL, SOCIAL, AND CULTURAL CONTEXTS

One legacy of the History-of-Religions School, **Form Criticism,** the Chicago School, and especially of recent social-history, social-scientific method, and archeology, is the necessity of understanding Jesus in his historical, social, and cultural contexts. We have covered this general background in Chapter One. For convenience, here is a very brief summary.

Ancient Mediterranean society was an advanced agrarian society in which the Roman emperor and ruling families controlled the land and its agricultural surplus. The emperor could honor a local "client king" as "friend" or "ally" of Caesar. These families were in turn supported by local aristocratic families. All these elites together probably made up only about 1–2 percent of the total population.

There was no "middle class," although there was a sort of middle stratum. About 5 percent of the people served the elite as "retainers" (priests, scribes, administrative officials, financial experts, tax collectors, household managers ["stewards"], judges, professional soldiers, and educators). They lived in urban areas and shared some in the economic surplus. The growth of commerce led to the emergence of traders and merchants, a few gaining a little status. About 90 percent of the people were in the lower strata, and about 75 percent of them were peasants, poverty-stricken urban poor, and tenant farmers. Another 5 percent or so were artisans. Their manual labor was considered by the elite to be distasteful. At the very bottom were the "unclean" and the expendables—beggars, prostitutes, and the destitute—perhaps another 10 percent, mostly all living at a bare subsistence level. One must also mention slaves, freedmen, and freedwomen. If one inserts into this picture the local client Herodian kings, this sort of social stratification also characterized Palestine. Palestine was in effect a Roman "client kingdom" of the great patron, Caesar. From time to time parts of it—Judea and Samaria—were ruled directly by Roman governors. Those parts became in effect small imperial provinces.

Roman estates and Greco-Roman towns were scattered here and there. Roman soldiers were everywhere present. Cities named after the emperor were often built. All this required vast sums of money. The temple in Jerusalem also required taxes. The burden fell chiefly on the peasants and urban poor. Note that this whole system went against the native ideal that the "land of Israel" belonged to God and was promised to the Israelites; it was sacred to them as God's chosen people. The sacred center was Jerusalem with its holy temple and Holy of Holies, the very special place of God's holy presence. Roman-period Israelites believed that Roman control was an abomination. Many thought that God himself would remedy the matter; the question was "how soon?"

In this context there emerged various geographical, ethnic, and religious factions and larger, more permanent groups, whose interests often centered on issues of Torah purity. The cooperative Sadducee party was the most established politically and economically. It formed a core of the aristocratic elites. The reformist Pharisees and the isolationist Essenes offered alternative beliefs and lifestyles for the disaffected. A number of resistance groups emerged. Some were interested in "social reform"; the most radical were eager to start a war against Rome, believing that God would terminate it in their favor. Sporadic, violent activity eventually led to the outbreak of war against Rome in 66 C.E., and tragically it included a civil war among the Palestinians themselves. Israelite murdered Israelite in the name of God and Torah, and there was a vicious internecine strife in Jerusalem that aided the Romans in their siege of the city. Ultimately, Rome won and crucified those responsible.

In this context, Jesus of Nazareth, a wandering artisan/peasant who carried out his reforming activity primarily among the lower social strata of Galilee in the early decades of this period, met opposition and was executed as a political dissident on a Roman cross. Before turning to his life and teaching, some references to him outside the New Testament need to be noted and problems of method need to be refined.

JESUS IN ANCIENT SOURCES
OTHER THAN THE NEW TESTAMENT

The major references to Jesus outside the New Testament are of three types: Roman, Israelite, and noncanonical sources of the Jesus Movement. There are also a few scattered, isolated sayings attributed to Jesus (**agrapha**).

Roman Sources

The Roman historian Tacitus wrote about 112–113 C.E. When he described the great fire in Rome that took place in 64 C.E. under the emperor Nero, he said that the emperor scapegoated the devotees of Christ. In the process he gave a brief account of this "sect" (see Chapter Twelve). As part of that description, he says,

> The founder of this sect, Christus, was given the death penalty in the reign of Tiberius [14–37 C.E.] by the procurator Pontius Pilate [ruled 26–36 C.E.]; suppressed for the moment, the detestable superstition broke out again, not only in Judea where the evil originated, but also in the city [of Rome] to which everything horrible and shameful flows and where it grows.
> (Tacitus *Annals* 15.44)

If Tacitus' information is based on members of the Jesus Movement, it is not independent information; if it is not so based, it is the most valuable piece of Roman evidence about Jesus.

The Roman historian Suetonius (75–160 C.E.), who published his *Lives of the Twelve Caesars* around 121 C.E., says that Claudius, who was emperor 41–54 C.E., "expelled from Rome the Judeans who were constantly rioting at the instigation of a certain Chrestus" (Suetonius *Life of Claudius* 25.4; cf. Acts 18:2). Suetonius understood "Chrestus" to be the individual responsible for the riots. If the expulsion is dated to 49 C.E., either "Chrestus" was some other person, or, more likely, Suetonius was misinformed or confused about conflicts between Israelites who believed that Jesus was the Messiah and those who did not.

These most important Roman sources do not offer us any significant information beyond that found in the New Testament. Only Tacitus says anything about Jesus, and his information may have come indirectly from members of the movement. Their testimony does, however, confirm that missionaries from the Jesus Movement reached Rome quite early (cf. Paul's Letter to the Romans), and they make the fictional view of Jesus held by Bruno Bauer (see preceding) very untenable.

Israelite Sources

There are references to Jesus in Josephus and the Babylonian Talmud. In reporting the execution of James, Josephus (37–100? C.E.) refers to him as "the brother of Jesus, who was called Christ" (*Antiquities of the Jews* 20.9.1 par. 200). Most scholars have seen this offhand reference as having been written by Josephus himself, not some later Christian copyist. Josephus' second passage, however, has raised problems for historians. It says:

> About this time there lived Jesus, a wise man, *if indeed one ought to call him a man.* For he was one who wrought surprising feats and was a teacher of such people as accept the truth gladly. He won over many Israelites and many of the Greeks. *He was the Messiah.* When Pilate, upon hearing him accused by men of the highest standing among us, had condemned him to be crucified, those who had in the first place come to love him did not give up their affection for him. *On the third day he appeared to them restored to life, for the prophets of God had prophesied these and countless other marvelous things about him.* And the time of the Christ-ies, so called after him, has still to this day not disappeared.
>
> (Antiquities of the Jews 18.3.3–4, par. 63–64)

Because Christian copyists copied Josephus' works down through the centuries, it is plausible that either they created this whole passage or added the italicized phrases because they could scarcely have come from an ancient monotheistic Israelite. If only the italicized phrases were added, which is the majority scholarly opinion, Josephus did indeed have a note about Jesus as a wise man who gathered followers, taught, worked miracles, and was crucified under Pontius Pilate.

In the Talmud, the second type of Israelite source, there are traditions from about the first or second century C.E. These remembered Jesus as having practiced "sorcery," that is, magic; that Jesus had a popular following among the people; that Jesus' death was linked with **Passover;** that there was some sort of pleading in his defense, probably implying a formal trial before authorities; and that he was "hanged," which presumably refers to crucifixion (cf. Gal. 3:13).

In summary, the ancient Israelite literary sources tell us seven things about Jesus. First, Jesus had a brother named James, who was executed. Second, Jesus was a wise man. Third, he practiced magic and was popular among the people. This must mean that Jesus had a reputation as a miracle worker. Fourth, Jesus made disciples (and was reasonably successful). Fifth, Israelite authorities tried Jesus. Sixth, he was crucified the evening before Passover. Finally, the execution took place when Pontius Pilate was governor. These references offer no new information about Jesus, but they confirm what is known from the canonical gospels. A very important implication is that the ancients never doubted that Jesus actually existed, as a few modern interpreters have suggested (Bruno Bauer; the "Christ Myth" school).

Apocryphal Gospels

There are many apocryphal gospels. One common classification is: (1) New Testament–type gospels; (2) Gnostic gospels; and (3) gospels that are legendary supplements to New Testament stories, for example, Jesus as the miracle-working child, or Mary as a virgin child-bride of old Joseph. Most of these gospels offer nothing of value about Jesus himself but offer fascinating information about what various groups believed in the early centuries of the Jesus Movement.

An exception to this statement is the *Gospel of Thomas*. It has versions of sayings and parables of Jesus considered by many to be independent of those in the New Testament; they are therefore important for reconstructing the original form of these sayings or parables. Some of these will be included later.

Some scholars attempt to include a few other noncanonical gospels or gospel fragments, specifically, the Egerton Papyrus 2, the *Gospel of Peter*, and the *Secret Gospel of Mark*. Positive judgments about these apocryphal gospel fragments do not necessarily mean that the sayings or episodes they record are all historical. They must be evaluated critically, just as are the canonical gospels.

Isolated Sayings Attributed to Jesus (Agrapha)

Agrapha are isolated sayings attributed to Jesus in sources inside and outside the New Testament. One that looks valuable is:

> When on the same day he saw a man doing work on the Sabbath, he said to him: Man, if you know what you are doing then you are blessed. But if you do not know what you are doing then you are cursed and a transgressor of the law.

This saying is found after Luke 6:4 only in Codex D of the New Testament. Otherwise unattested, it is nonetheless very much like the challenge of Jesus to make one's own decisions. Another possibility is Acts 20:35, also in Codex D: "To give is more blessed than to receive."

Oral tradition was valued at least down to the middle of the second century C.E. Therefore, in some cases it is very important to compare isolated gospel sayings with variant forms of the same sayings preserved in the canonical gospels or in the early **Church Fathers.**

CRITERIA OF PROBABLE AUTHENTICITY

Criterion of Distinctiveness (Dissimilarity)

Bultmann put forth a criterion for isolating Jesus' sayings in the earliest layers of the gospel traditions. Käsemann refined it, and it became known mainly as "the criterion of dissimilarity." This criterion was used to isolate authentic sayings that were *different or unlike* teachings known to have been current among Jesus' Israelite contemporaries and the early Jesus Movement.

Many recent scholars are reluctant to accept this criterion in the hard form in which the Second Questers articulated it. Some make the valid point that its use can lead to the rejection of sayings that might accurately portray Jesus as *like* his Israelite contemporaries or that were accurately preserved in the Jesus Movement. In other words, the criterion is circular: By concentrating on what is new, unusual, shocking, or radical, it discovers a Jesus who is new, unusual, shocking, or radical. This becomes especially pungent when several points are remembered. First, "laws" of developing tradition (from simple to complex) are sometimes inaccurate. Second, scholars simply do not possess everything that ancient Israelite and Jesus Movement teachers—or Jesus himself—said. Third, as is definitely affirmed by another criterion, "linguistic and environmental tests," Jesus could not have been so distinctive that he failed to communicate to his Israelite peers. Some critics are also concerned about modern Christian anti-Semitism in scholarship, that is, tendencies to describe "the Israelites" as "legalists" or "ritualists" and then to see dissimilar (unique!) Jesus as the "spiritual" purifier of "the Israelite religion," which was inherited by the Jews. Jesus was certainly an Israelite operating within the context of his ancestral religion, as the other criterion, "linguistic and environmental tests," says. Fourth, it cannot be denied that the Jesus Movement did retain features of Israelite religion. Fifth, it is now generally accepted on the basis of archeology that Palestine had many Hellenistic influences. Therefore, a criterion that tends to reject what Jesus said on the basis of Hellenistic influence is not as certain as it once was. Indeed, one school of scholars sees the closest analogy to Jesus' lifestyle as the "countercultural" lifestyle of the Cynic philosophers.

Yet, other scholars still use a "softer" version of the criterion and call it the "criterion of distinctiveness," a name already used by "Second Quester" Reginald Fuller. The argument that Jesus must have said *something* distinctive is powerful. If he simply said what his Israelite contemporaries said, why did he develop a following? Moreover, sayings that are distinctive in both content and form are more easily remembered in oral tradition. On the other side, if he said simply what the Jesus Movement said he said, did he teach so many contradictory things? If a scholar gives up attempting to find the most probable version of what he said and did, the quest for the historical Jesus is futile. Furthermore, distinctiveness should not be reduced to theological prejudice; it is a historical probability. Jesus was not the only distinctive teacher in antiquity, and indeed not the only distinctive *Israelite* teacher. Others were remembered. Social-scientific interpreters view such teachers as "deviant," that is, as distinctive persons who did not accept commonly held, everyday beliefs, values, and behaviors. Consider, for example, radical Israelite millennialists (the Teacher of Righteousness or John the Baptizer), Israelite "charismatic" miracle workers (Honi the Circle Drawer or Hanina ben Dosa), and Hellenistic philosophers (the Pythagorean Apollonius of Tyana or the Cynic Diogenes). Each of these figures is *very distinctive.*

In short, some criterion of distinctiveness is difficult to avoid. Distinctiveness in *content* has led to a quest for the distinctive *forms* of Jesus' sayings: short, pithy, pungent, and witty aphorisms and radically challenging parables. It is not surprising to find that this criterion tends to focus on sayings that challenge culturally accepted beliefs, values, and practices. Parables that disturb, provoke, or simply tease or shock the imagination, like a business manager who plays fast and loose with his master's debtors, are especially important possibilities for going back to Jesus. Similarly, pithy wisdom sayings and aphorisms that challenge accepted values, such as "Blessed are you poor" (Q 6:20) or "Leave the dead to bury their own dead" (Q 9:60b), are plausible distinctive teachings. Finally, the distinctiveness criterion can be extended to Jesus' nonnormative, deviant *lifestyle.* Jesus does not accept the norm of following in the footsteps of one's father, or the normative patterns of family, home, trade, and village life, or associating with people who most would think were ritually clean or socially acceptable. This criterion also observes the tendency to *tone down* Jesus' more radical message and lifestyle, to accommodate him to more conventional and acceptable beliefs, values, and practices. Did Jesus forbid divorce (Mark 10:11), or did he allow it in the case of "unchastity" (Matt. 19:9; 5:32)? Did Jesus really say that one should "hate" parents (Luke 14:26) or, somewhat milder, not to love family more than him (Matt. 10:37)? Did Jesus tell his disciples to travel about barefoot (Matt. 10:10) or to wear sandals (Mark 6:9)?

The criterion of distinctiveness has its weaknesses; however, it also has its strengths. Used cautiously and judiciously, it can be a valuable tool in the quest for Jesus. Moreover, it is only a starting point; it must always be supplemented by other criteria.

The Criterion of Multiple Independent Attestation

The criterion of multiple independent attestation was traditionally called simply "multiple attestation." It originally referred to material that is found in several synoptic sources—Mark, **Q**, **Special M,** and **Special L**—where these sources are independent of each other (hence the addition of the word "independent"). Today it is usually extended to noncanonical sources. The theory is that the more widespread a tradition is—attested in several sources that are not dependent on each other—the greater chance it has of going back to an earlier point of origin. The criterion has usually been thought to be most successful in determining the probable authenticity of *themes* that occur frequently in the message or lifestyle of Jesus rather than of particular sayings or events. As in the case of distinctiveness, it has been extended to multiple *forms* of the same or similar themes. So, for example, Jesus' association with structurally marginal, unclean people, often called "tax collectors and sinners," is most likely to be authentic because it occurs in all of the synoptic sources, and it is attested in multiple forms (sayings, parables, and controversy anecdotes). Similarly, a parable that used a hated Samaritan's helping an Israelite in distress

(Luke 10:29–37) has a parallel in loving one's enemies (Matt. 5:44). Thus parable and aphorism tend to reinforce each other.

With the reevaluation by some scholars of the antiquity and independence of some sayings in the apocryphal gospels, multiple independent attestation, an essentially *quantitative* approach, is being used in relation to other versions of sayings. Thus, for example, a saying found in multiple sources and in multiple forms, some of them *outside* the New Testament, leads to an attempt to critically reconstruct the original form as possibly going back to Jesus. This is especially the case if the extracanonical units are judged to be from a very early period, such as a parable in the *Gospel of Thomas.*

Again, a note of caution is in order with respect to this criterion. The quantity of sayings or forms does not *prove* that Jesus said them. Recall that modern Textual Critics have determined that the *quantity* of manuscripts or readings does not prove a particular version of the text in them to be correct. The majority of manuscripts were actually produced later—*after* many changes had already "corrupted" them. In other words, the majority does not rule. *Both age and quality* must be assessed. Similarly, multiple independent attestation of sayings or themes alone will not be decisive. Judgment calls about quality (distinctiveness) and age must also be made.

Nonetheless, multiple independent attestation has become very important, and for one major Jesus scholar, Dominic Crossan, multiple independent attestation combined with age is *the* criterion, not distinctiveness (qualitative).

The Criterion of Coherence

The criterion of coherence grew out of a desire to go beyond what can be established through distinctiveness and multiple attestation. Essentially it says that material that on other grounds is uncertain can probably be accepted as generally authentic if it is *consistent with* ("coheres with") the core material established as probable by the other two criteria. For example, sayings in the *Gospel of Thomas* not found elsewhere—they are *not* multiply independently attested—might plausibly go back to Jesus *if* they sound very much like what Jesus would have said, given the material already isolated in the canonical gospels by the other two criteria. A noncanonical example is the parable of the Assassin in the *Gospel of Thomas* 98.

The Criterion of Cultural Environment and Language

The criterion of cultural environment and language has tended to be negative rather than positive, and only supplementary. In other words, material is *rejected* if it is *not* compatible with the languages or immediate environment of ancient Palestine. For example, although Jesus' teaching on divorce in Mark 10 is distinctive, it is not likely that *all of it* goes back to Jesus *in its present form* because it concludes with ideas based on Roman and not Israelite divorce law, that is, that a woman can divorce her husband. To be sure, it is possible that Jesus knew Roman divorce law because there were towns in Palestine dominated by Roman military personnel; the greater probability, however, is that the teaching was supplemented in a social environment influenced by Roman law. As for language, the allegorical interpretation of the parable of the Sower in Mark 4:13–20 hardly goes back to Jesus because it uses so much language known to come from the later technical vocabulary of the Jesus Movement. *This criterion does not work in the opposite direction.* Material cannot be accepted as authentic *only* because it reflects the linguistic or environmental circumstances of the Palestinian ministry of Jesus. The obvious reason is that the earliest Palestinian followers of Jesus shared his language and culture.

Other Criteria

The criteria of distinctiveness and multiple independent attestation have been extended from substance to form. Other criteria have also been proposed. One is the so-called criterion of embarrassment or criterion of contradiction. It is argued that in some cases, sayings or episodes may have been preserved in a somewhat conservative manner even though they created some embarrassment for members of the Jesus Movement. A clear example is that John the Baptizer, considered in the Jesus Movement to be inferior to Jesus, was said to have baptized Jesus, which would suggest that he was superior to Jesus. Jesus Movement believers explained the event by saying that John was a mere "forerunner" of Jesus the Messiah, thus Jesus' inferior, and the Matthean author explains that the baptism was according to God's will ("fulfilling all righteousness"; cf. Matt. 3:14–16). The embarrassing event is kept but explained. Another clear example is the crucifixion of Jesus, a horrible punishment, usually for sedition. That embarrassing event, too, is said to be according to God's plan, and Paul adds that the prophesied "cursed is everyone who hangs on a tree" (Gal. 3:13 [Deut. 21:23]) means that Jesus took the curse upon himself for believers. The crucifixion of Jesus would seem to be the most solid historical event we have, yet we can see Christ believers struggling with it. The obvious problem with this criterion is that what would be "embarrassing" to an ancient Mediterranean person is a judgment call, and not all scholars agree.

There are other attempts to add new criteria and break up the preceding criteria into more refined, extensive lists, but for purposes of simplicity, we shall remain with these.

MAJOR FEATURES OF JESUS' LIFE

Date of Birth

Although there are a number of chronological problems with the Lukan infancy story—the census is most likely to be dated at least ten years *after* Jesus' birth—the birth narratives agree in putting Jesus' birth sometime prior to the death of Herod the Great (Matt. 2:1; Luke 1:5). According to modern chronologies, Herod died in 4 B.C.E. Thus one must say what initially sounds odd, that Jesus was probably born about four to six years "before Christ." However, this is only an apparent oddity. In the sixth century a Scythian abbot, Dionysius Exiguus, on whose calculations our calendar is based, miscalculated the birth of Jesus by at least four years.

Ancestry, Parents, and Siblings

Both the gospels of Matthew (1:1–17) and Luke (Luke 3:23–38) trace Jesus' lineage to David and Abraham (Luke on back to Adam). The Matthean genealogy, which after David takes the descent line through the kings of Israel, is constructed on the basis of three "historical" divisions of fourteen generations each (1:17). The 3 × 14 schema seems to be built on the number of David's name in Hebrew (*D-V-D: D* = 4; *V* = 6; *D* = 4, a total of 14), and three kings are omitted. Furthermore, by modern historical standards, these three divisions are very unequal (about seven hundred years in the first fourteen; about four hundred years in the second fourteen; about six hundred years in the third fourteen, which includes Jesus himself). Thus the divisions do not make mathematical sense. The Lukan genealogy does not trace Jesus' line through the kings of Israel, although David is in the line, and pushes the genealogy back to Adam, who is the Son of God. In contrast, opponents of Jesus in the Johannine Gospel claim that Jesus was *not* from David's line (cf. John 7:40–42). Thus modern scholars see the genealogies, which cannot be conformed to each other, as status claims that Jesus was descended from the Son of God (Luke), the honorable patriarch Abraham, and the first important king, David.

Jesus' father is named Joseph. In Matthew, he is considered to be a peasant artisan (13:35), but that is an inference from the description of Jesus himself in Mark 6:3 (see following). Also in Matthew, Jesus' father Joseph receives messages from God through dreams. He is thereby associated with the ancient Joseph of the sacred scriptures, also a dreamer and dream interpreter (e.g., Gen. 37:5–10). Jesus' mother is called Mary (Semitic: Miriam). The Gospel of Matthew stresses that she was a virgin by interpreting a messianic prophecy (Isa. 7:14; Matt. 1:18–25); the Gospel of Luke mentions the virgin birth (1:27, 34) but focuses more on the parallels between Jesus' birth and John the Baptizer's birth (Luke 1–2). These accounts cannot be made to agree and are generally held to be interpretations, not history. The historical core is probably Jesus' parents, Joseph and Mary.

In a Markan passage where Jesus' village and family members did not accept him, Jesus is said to have had four brothers, who are named by name (Mark 6:1–6 = Matt. 13:53–58). One of them, James, became a prominent leader in the Jerusalem wing of the Jesus Movement (e.g., Gal. 1:19; 2:9, 12). The New Testament pseudonymous book called "James" may have been meant to refer to him. Another was "Judas," and the pseudonymous New Testament book called "Jude" may have been meant to refer to him. Sisters are also mentioned in Mark but not by name (Mark 6:3). Do references to at least six siblings have any merit? The **Apostolic Fathers** held different views on the matter. One view was that Jesus had actual brothers and sisters. Another was that they were children of Joseph by a previous marriage. A third was that they were "brothers" and "sisters" in the symbolic, spiritual sense, thus fictive kin. The latter two explanations support the notion that Mary did not have sex. Therein lies the basis for the Catholic view of the "perpetual virginity" of Mary (Mary not only was a virgin at Jesus' conception, but also she remained a virgin).

Place of Birth: Nazareth

In the ancient world, place of birth could be an important indication of status. The Lukan writer, for example, says that Paul claimed that he was from Tarsus (southeastern Turkey), "no mean city" (Acts 21:39). The infancy stories of Matthew and Luke place Jesus' birth in Bethlehem of Judea (Matt. 2:1–12; Luke 2:1–7). By most ancient standards, a small village like Bethlehem would not have been an important place. However, Roman-era Israelites knew that it was King David's birthplace (1 Sam. 17:12), and an ancient prophecy said that the Messiah would be born there (Mic. 5:2 [1]). Thus the claim that Jesus was born in Bethlehem gave a person of relatively low social status (a peasant artisan) the prerequisites for a very high—in this case, royal   social status. As David, the first great King Messiah, was from Bethlehem, so Jesus, the new King Messiah, was from Bethlehem.

However, the New Testament is not unanimous on Jesus' Bethlehem birthplace. The Gospel of John says that opponents thought that Jesus was not the Messiah precisely because he did *not* come from Bethlehem and because he was *not* from David's line (cf. John 7:40–42). (For the writer, that makes no difference; Jesus was really "from above," a still higher status!) Most scholars conclude that the Bethlehem birth was an inference from the belief that Jesus was a messiah descended from David and *must* therefore have been born in David's city (cf. Mic. 5:2; cf. Rom. 1:3–4; Acts 2:36).

A more historically plausible place for Jesus' birth was Nazareth of Galilee because Jesus was known as "Jesus of Nazareth" or "a Nazorene" (cf. Mark 1:24; 10:47; John 18:5; Matt. 2:23). Nazareth was located about twenty miles inland from the Mediterranean Sea and fifteen miles west of the southern tip of the Sea of Galilee. Curiously, Nazareth is not mentioned in the Hebrew Scriptures or ancient writings contemporary with the New Testament. However, there is archeological evidence for the presence of Israelite burial sites there. The village was also situated in one of the most fertile sections of Galilee, and Jesus frequently used agricultural images in his teachings, especially in the parables. A reasonable conclusion is that Nazareth was a small, relatively insignificant Israelite peasant farming village. Yet, it was not far from major highways, and nearby was Sepphoris, which, as archeology has shown, was an Israelite city with much Hellenistic cultural influence (see Photo 14.1).

In short, it is likely that the Bethlehem birth was an inference from the belief that Jesus was the Messiah from the line of David. Jesus was most probably born and reared in Nazareth of Galilee.

Native Language: Aramaic

Jesus' native language was Aramaic. Aramaic gradually replaced Hebrew, from which it was descended, as the vernacular language of ancient Israelites in the Persian period (532–332 B.C.E.). Hebrew had become difficult to understand for Aramaic speakers, and eventually the Hebrew Scriptures read in worship had to be "translated" into Aramaic so that people could understand them. Interpretive Aramaic "translations" of the Hebrew Bible from the period during and just after the rise of the Jesus Movement, called **Targums,** still survive.

Aramaic would have been the language usually spoken by rural peasants, although the vast majority could neither read nor write, except perhaps for a few necessary business matters (craftsman's literacy). The gospel writers emphasize Jesus' Aramaic language background by retaining some Aramaic expressions in Greek transliteration (English transliteration: *'Abbā'* ["Father"]; *talitha cumi* ["my daughter rise"]; *eloi eloi lama sabacthani* ["my God, my God, why have you forsaken me?" [Ps. 22:1]). Whether he could speak Greek is not certain.

Luke claims that Jesus could read because he read from the book of Isaiah (4:16). Because artisan peasants would at best have possessed only craftsman's literacy, many scholars think that the Lukan story is a way of presenting Jesus for the writer's educated Gentile readers.

Trade: Artisan

In the ancient world, identity was often related to work or profession (e.g., "Simon the Tanner," perhaps a negative label, because the Mishnah says that [smelly] tanneries should be placed at least fifty cubits outside city walls). Mark calls Jesus a *tektōn,* "artisan" (Mark 6:3: "carpenter"), and Matthew deduces that he was the "son of a *tektōn*" (Matt. 13:55). If *tektōn* is not simply a metaphor for "teacher," as it can be in rabbinic literature (e.g., *J. Kiddushin* 66a), Jesus was probably a worker in wood and stone. His father Joseph, or perhaps a more distant ancestor, had likely been displaced from his ancestral plot of land. Like all artisans, Jesus was in the broad sense from the peasant strata; indeed, artisans who worked with their hands and had no farmland were generally considered lower in status than landed peasants and tenant farmers.

Galilee and Jesus' Peasant Roots

Jesus was a peasant from Nazareth in central Lower Galilee. Ancient rabbinic scholars made occasional pejorative comments about Galilean peasants who did not keep Torah regulations strictly. Offbeat "charismatic" miracle workers like Honi the Circle Drawer and Hanina ben Dosa came from Galilee. As noted previously, scholars of a previous generation concluded from such information that Galilee was a "cultural backwater" relatively free of Greco-Roman culture and Judean control. They assumed that most all Galileans were "people of the land" or uneducated peasants. Also, Galilee was associated with political unrest, as suggested by figures such as Judas the Galilean, who opposed enrollment for taxes instituted in Palestine in 6 C.E., and other rebels noted in Chapter One. Accounts of such political leaders have often led scholars to say that uneducated Galileans were also independent, less tolerant of outside influence, and prone to political rebellion. There is a substantial body of literature measuring the extent to which Jesus might have been a "political revolutionary," or at least sympathetic to rebels, a possibility that would certainly have contributed to his crucifixion for sedition by the Romans.

Today these generalizations must be qualified. As already observed, archeologists have shown that although "Upper Galilee" was more remote and a likely outpost for resistance to Rome, Lower Galilee was not totally isolated from Hellenistic and Roman presence. This suggests to some historians that Jesus of Nazareth might have come into contact with more cosmopolitan and urbane Hellenistic ideas than had previously been supposed. A few scholars are now willing to imagine that he was influenced by Hellenistic culture and perhaps by Greek philosophy. The lifestyle of the wandering, Cynic sages provides a close analogy to his unconventional lifestyle. Nonetheless, Jesus was from the peasant strata of Greco-Roman Palestine and, as study of his teaching indicates, seems to have held peasant values about politics, economics, religion, and family. Again, the Romans crucified him, and this was a punishment most often reserved for political rebels. In short, the reevaluation of Lower Galilee opens the possibility that Jesus came into contact with Hellenistic culture, but the questions about his response to it must be answered by a critical reconstruction and interpretation of his teachings and actions (see following).

John the Baptizer: Millennial Prophet

The gospels portray John the Baptizer as a fiery millennial prophet of judgment who was active in the remote and desolate wilderness of Judea along the Jordan River (Mark 1:4 = Matt. 3:4; Luke 3:3–4). This view is reinforced by the writings of the ancient Israelite historian Josephus (*Antiquities of the Jews* 18.5.2 par. 116–119). The core of John's apocalyptic message seems to have been the call to repent and be baptized in preparation for "one who is coming" (Mark 1:7; Matt. 3:11; Luke 3:16; Luke 7:19 = Matt. 11:3). The descriptions of John's garb and diet are instructive. He is said to have worn camel's hair clothing with a leather belt around his waist (Mark 1:6 = Matt. 3:4) and to have eaten locusts and wild honey (Mark 1:6; cf. Lev. 11:22). This description is clearly an attempt in the Jesus Movement to identify John with the ancient prophet Elijah. Recall that according to sacred texts, Elijah did not die a natural death; rather, he was taken off in a chariot in a whirlwind (2 Kings 2) and was expected to return at the great and terrible "day of the Lord (God)" (2 Kings 1:8; Zech. 13:4; Mal. 3:1, 4:5). The Lukan author adds that John came from a family of priests (Luke 1:5) and was born shortly before Jesus, his relative (Luke 1:26, 36). From a critical perspective, John's diet and priestly connections are not elsewhere attested and are at best uncertain, an uncertainty not relieved when it is remembered that in the Jesus Movement, John was demoted to role of the Elijanic forerunner.

One further point should be made. The Judean wilderness, priestly, baptizing, and millennial associations are intriguing when it is recalled that the Qumran community existed in the Judean wilderness, just south of one of the traditional sites associated with John's baptizing activity in the Jordan River. The majority of scholars think that this group consisted of Essenes, a priestly, millennial sect who baptized. The New Testament never mentions the Essenes, and the surviving Dead Sea Scrolls do not know the New Testament. Yet, the possible association of John with the Essenes is a plausible hypothesis.

Finally, John was imprisoned and executed at the hand of the Galilean client king, Herod Antipas. The gospels say that the reason was that he criticized Herod's marriage to his brother Philip's wife (Mark 6:17–29). Josephus says that John was imprisoned at a Herodian fortress, Macherus, east of the Dead Sea and was killed because Herod feared that John's popularity might lead to rebellion (*Antiquities of the Jews* 18.5.2 par. 118–119); thus the reason was primarily political, not religious-moral. Whatever the reason—historians tend to trust Josephus in this case—Herod feared the prophet John, and John's demise anticipated that of Jesus.

Besides baptism, certain aspects of the lifestyle of John's core followers—prayer, fasting, abstinence from strong drink, and strict morality—can also be inferred from the gospels (Mark 1:6; 2:18; Matt. 11:16–18; Luke 11:1; 3:7–14). John's apocalyptic message about "one who is coming" noted earlier could have referred to the Lord *God* coming for final judgment (Matt. 3:11–12 = Luke 3:16b–17; cf. Luke 1:76; Mal. 3:1, 4:5). However, followers of Jesus developed the view that John meant the Lord *Jesus* (e.g., Q 7:18–19, 22–23; Mark 1.7–8; John 1:26b–27, 29–31). In short, John was portrayed as the returning prophet Elijah (e.g., Matt. 11:15); as such he is said to be "the beginning of the gospel" (Mark 1:1) and is made subordinate to Jesus.

Yet, there is some hint that Jesus and perhaps some of his disciples had once been followers of John (e.g., John 1:35–37). This is consistent with the tradition from Q that Jesus praised John (Matt. 11:18–19 = Luke 7:33–35). However, the interpretation of Jesus' teaching that follows will suggest that Jesus' message was less dramatically apocalyptic than John's. Certainly the memory in **Q** is that Jesus' lifestyle was not as "ascetic" as John's:

> For John the Baptizer has come eating no bread and drinking no wine, and you say, "He has a demon" [a "witchcraft accusation"]; the Son of Man has come eating and drinking, and you say, "Look, a glutton and a drunkard [the rebellious son accusation (Deut. 21:20; Prov. 23.21; 11QT 64)], a friend of tax collectors and sinners!"
> (Matt. 11:18–19a = Luke 7:33–34)

Whether Jesus actually spoke of himself as the "Son of Man" ("one like a human being") is much debated. If he did, he probably did not refer to himself as the apocalyptic Son of Man who would come on the clouds (Luke 12:8; Mark 8:38) or the suffering Son of Man, mostly likely a creation of the Markan author (see Mark 8:31; 9:31; 10:33–34). Rather, he would have used the Semitic idiom for "human being" (Ps. 8:4), probably including himself, as English sometimes uses "people [including myself] say." By the time Q was written in Greek, however, the phrase had become a title, indeed, a messianic title specifically for Jesus, and it was used in several senses. In the preceding Q quotation there was an implied contrast between John and Jesus, although both had the same opponents. The dominant view in the Jesus Movement became the view that John was the *forerunner* of the Son of Man = Messiah = Jesus. This evaluation probably contributed to the split between John's and Jesus' followers (cf. Mark 2:18–20). Indeed, there are indications that competition developed between John's group and Jesus' group (especially Matt. 9:14; John 3:22–30; Acts 19.1–7).

We can conclude that Jesus and probably some of his disciples had close connections with John the Baptizer and his disciples. They had probably been in John's millennial movement at one time. Jesus had been baptized by John (Mark 1:9–11 = Matt. 3:13a, 16–17 = Luke 3:21–22). Further, Jesus apparently maintained a high opinion of John, although he did not fully share John's strong millennialism and certainly not his "ascetic" lifestyle. We can also see the increasing tendency of the Jesus Movement to subordinate John as merely the forerunner of "the Lord" who was interpreted to be the Messiah Jesus. Indeed, there developed some competition between the surviving followers of John and the surviving followers of Jesus.

The Itinerant Holy Man

That Jesus did not follow in the footsteps of his artisan father at Nazareth was distinctive and can be multiply attested. He migrated to Capernaum on the northwestern coast of the Sea of Galilee, and from there he moved around from farming village to farming village, fishing village to fishing village, preaching, teaching, exorcising demons, healing the sick, and offering hope to the poor, the unclean, and the outcast. The synoptic gospels thus present Jesus as a Spirit-filled (some scholars say "charismatic") Israelite prophet, preacher, teacher, exorcist, and healer. Perhaps behind the baptism and temptation stories were experiences of altered states of consciousness. In most respects, this gospel image of Jesus conforms to that of an ancient "holy man"; paradoxically, he was not concerned about certain forms of holiness.

Jesus chose from among his recruits an intimate group, probably twelve, although some scholars think that the number, a symbol of Israel, may be a later interpretation. Members of this group followed the patterns he set forth. Thus arose the Jesus Movement. In its early phase it was a network of Galilean families led by those who went to the houses, villages, and towns of Palestine, preaching and healing and in general attempting to revitalize Galilean village life. Although Jesus' mission charge to his twelve disciples in Q may actually have been a model for the Jesus Movement missionaries later, after Jesus' death, it probably contains features of the radical lifestyle of Jesus himself and his first followers:

> He said to them, "The harvest is plentiful, but the laborers are few; therefore ask the Lord of the harvest to send out laborers into his harvest. Go on your way. See, I am sending you out like lambs into the midst of wolves. Carry no purse, no bag, no sandals; and greet no one on the road. Whatever house you enter, first say, "Peace be to this house!" And if anyone is there who shares in peace, your peace shall rest upon that person; but if not, it will return to you. Remain in the same house, eating and drinking what they provide, for the laborer deserves to be paid. Do not move about from house to house [in the village]. Whenever you enter a town and its people welcome you, eat what is set before you; cure the sick who are there, and say to them, "The Kingdom of God has come near to you." But whenever you enter a town and they do not welcome you, go out into its streets and say, "Even the dust of your town that clings to our feet, we wipe off in protest against you. Yet know this: the Kingdom of God has come near."
>
> (Q: Luke 10:4–11, 16 = Matt. 10:12–14, 40; cf. *GTh* 14.2)

The ideal in this passage, and others like it (e.g., Mark 6.7–13; 9.36–37; *Didachē* 11:4–5; John 12:44–50), is similar to the radical itinerant Cynic philosophy, noted earlier (for more on the Cynics, see Chapter One). "No purse" suggests the ideal of poverty, but it may as well represent solidarity with peasants, unclean, and social dropouts who were forced into poverty (cf. Luke 6:20: "Blessed are you poor . . ."). "No bag" recalls the Cynic's begging bag, a symbol of Cynic self-sufficiency. Its absence no doubt signifies that the Jesus missionary is not to beg for food, but to share meals together. "No sandals," that is, barefoot, was a familiar symbol of poverty. One is not to greet people on the road (a sense of urgency? security?), but upon entering a house say: "Peace (*Shālōm*) *be* to this house!" If anyone who shares in peace ("son of peace") is present, the greeting will be received, and the disciple will receive hospitality, including a meal.

Two other very important elements in the charge are "cure the sick" and "The Kingdom of God has come near to you," which will be considered in more detail later. Jesus' charge continues: If there is no hospitality extended, one either wipes off (Luke 9:5) or shakes off (Matt. 10:14) the dust from one's feet. This is the reverse of an act of hospitality in wealthier homes, that is, washing the guest's feet by the host's slaves (John 13:1–20). Thus Jesus and his earliest disciples engaged in a rural, lakeside, village mission. Again, such a mission was directed toward people on the margins of a society oppressed by the burdens of Roman, Herodian, and temple taxes, and to that extent it had political implications. By the time of Paul, the mission had been extended to major cities in the Roman Empire. It is clear that some women accompanied the men on the missions (1 Cor. 9:5: "sister-wives"), which might have been already developed in Jesus' day (e.g., Luke 8:1–3); see the following sections on eating together and healing.

Three special characteristics of the preceding description need to be highlighted: eating together (symbolized also by not carrying a bag), exorcising and healing, and proclaiming the Kingdom of God. They are interrelated (Crossan). The third belongs to Jesus' message, the first to Jesus' meal practices, and the second to Jesus' healing.

Eating Together

Social scientists often stress that meal practices symbolize social relationships. They analyze meal times and places, hospitality, who is invited, invitation customs, permitted and unpermitted foods, methods of food preparation, order of menu, persons with whom one may or may not eat, use of eating implements, seating place at the "table," and appropriate table talk. Major examples of meal practices in Greco-Roman antiquity are banquets and symposia. In Greco-Roman Palestine, important meals included festival meals, especially the Passover meal and, at Qumran, the Messianic Banquet. Among strict Israelites there was stress on kosher foods and purity, that is, not eating with Gentiles. The letters of Paul show that factions developed around meal purity. At Antioch, conservatives refused to eat with Gentiles, leading Peter to separate himself (Gal. 2:11–14). The Corinthians raised questions about whether one should eat meat sacrificed to idols (1 Cor. 8; 10:14–22) and whether the rich should eat with the poor at the Lord's Supper (11:17–22).

As the preceding quotation from Q indicates, the itinerant Jesus and his followers were often guests in the houses of those who received them with hospitality. They also shared meals in the open. Such common meals celebrated unity in the new relationship with God, a response to Jesus' proclamation of the Kingdom, reinforced by his gift of healing. The gospels also show Jesus banqueting with all sorts of people. The Lukan writer especially develops and expands this theme, but it is multiply attested. Jesus' meals were inclusive, not exclusive. This breaking of purity boundaries was distinctive.

Pure and polite society also despised the "tax collectors and sinners," and that theme is also multiply attested. As background, subjects of Rome hated tax collectors not only because of the economic reasons, but also because the tax collectors engaged in extortion. Judeans did not honor them for political and religious reasons: They worked for the "godless" Roman occupying powers. "Sinners" in this expression are more difficult to delineate. Apparently they were people whose activities or occupations were, according to strict interpretations of the Torah, offensive to God. The earliest forms of several gospel stories suggest that women sinners were sometimes present at meals. Prostitutes were an obvious example, especially if their "clientele" included Roman soldiers; thus Matthew has the expression as "tax collectors and *harlots*" (Matt. 21:31, 32). Whether the woman who showed up while Jesus was banqueting at a Pharisee's house, "a woman of the city, who was a sinner," as Luke says (Luke 7:27), was a prostitute, may be debated (Luke 7:36–50; cf. Mark 14:3–9 = Matt. 26:6–13). However, that she showed up at a male banquet at all is striking. In any case, within the spectrum of those considered most holy in the house of Israel (priests, levites) to those who were virtually beyond the bounds of the holy (e.g., eunuchs, those with deformed sexual features, hermaphrodites), "tax collectors and sinners" were near the latter end of the spectrum. Thus the expression "tax collectors and sinners" appears to have been a stereotypical phrase for marginal, unclean people in Greco-Roman-period Israelite society. To strict religious Israelites their activities or occupations were considered an offense to God.

The following anecdote illustrates Jesus' general practice; note that dining is correlated with healing, the following topic, by way of a metaphor:

> And as he sat at dinner in Levi's house, many tax collectors and sinners were sitting with Jesus and his disciples—for there were many who followed him. When the scribes of the Pharisees saw that he was eating with *sinners and tax collectors,* they said to his disciples, "Why does he eat with *tax collectors and sinners?*" When Jesus heard this, he said to them, "Those who are well have no need of a physician, but those who are sick; I have come to call not the righteous, but sinners."
>
> (Mark 2:15–17)

It appears that Jesus attempted to bring together such marginal people into a unified group no matter what their previous background or history, and apparently even their gender. We may also suppose that Jesus frequently ate with ordinary peasants and fisherfolk who could not always follow the strictest Torah observance. Even women, who normally ate separately, were included. From this perspective, it is not surprising to read that Jesus was accused by outsiders—in contrast to John the Baptizer—of being "a glutton and a drunkard, a friend of tax collectors and sinners!" (Matt. 11:19 = Luke 7:34).

Healing and Exorcisms

A second major activity of Jesus may be considered under the general expression "folk healing," which here includes exorcisms (when demons are present). You will recall that medical anthropologists analyze the reality "sickness" with reference to two concepts: disease, the abnormal functioning of bodily organs and organ systems, and illness, a social reality. Diseases are "cured" or not "cured"; illnesses are "healed" or not "healed" with reference to the whole self. In Chapter One, a variety of healers and healing options was cited, that is, health spas, prophetic healings, "charismatic healings," healing heroes, healing heroines, and magicians. Jesus was a folk healer.

As a folk healer, Jesus looked most like an Israelite "charismatic" healer. Examples of this type were Honi the Circle Drawer, who prayed to God and received rain, and Hanina ben Dosa, who prayed to God for healing. The evangelists say that Jesus could heal by touch or word, but it should be noted that more exorcism stories are told about him than any other ancient healer. His opponents accused him of deriving his power to exorcise from Beelzebul, the Prince of Demons (cf. especially Mark 3:22; Matt. 12:27 = Luke 8:19). Later opponents, the rabbis, called him a "magician" who led the people astray. Thus "magician" had become a sort of name-calling, a pejorative label for healers who were not part of one's own group ("we" heal; "they" practice magic). However, a "magician" was simply one kind of folk healer, a nonprofessional who is expert in powerful herbs, roots, animal parts, and especially pre-scientific formulas to protect. The recollection that Jesus was a magician was probably not just an outsider's accusation. Traces of "magical technique" appear in the exorcism and healing stories. For example, Jesus may have used spit to cure the blind (Mark 8:22–26; John 9:1–7). However, the Matthean and Lukan writers omitted such stories. This suggests that in some circles there was resistance to this form of folk healing, perhaps because of its polytheistic overtones. The main point is that in a world that believed in warring powers of good and evil on all levels, Jesus was able in the name of his God and God's Kingdom to help those who believed themselves to be possessed by demons and to heal illness. Jesus and the disciples offered gifts of health and healing, accompanied by their proclamation of the Kingdom and a new, inclusive community; what they received in return was hospitality ("generalized reciprocity").

Healing illness coheres with other practices of Jesus, for example, his opposition to exclusivity based on holiness. Among the early miracle collections certain miracle stories centered around meals that seem to have included women (Mark 6:34–44, 53). In another account, Jesus healed a woman who had a flow of blood (Mark 5:25–34). Still another female appeared to be dead (5:21–23, 35–43). The Syrophoenician Woman story deals with a Gentile woman and her daughter (Mark 7:24b–30). In addition, Jesus was said to heal the blind (Mark 8:22–26; 10:46–52), deaf and dumb (7:32–37), and those possessed with demons (5:1–20). Those who labored under the oppression of illness also labored under social and economic oppression—the two are related. In this light, it is important to take up the central message of Jesus.

THE MESSAGE OF JESUS

The Proclamation of the Kingdom of God

The third major element mentioned in the mission discourse to the disciples and mentioned in several other preceding passages was the proclamation of the "Kingdom of God." Scholars do not doubt that this proclamation was the central theme of the message of Jesus. The "coming" of the Kingdom is distinctive, and the theme itself is multiply attested. However, never do the texts describe it. To clarify its meaning, it is necessary to remember that in ancient Israel, prior to the time of the Babylonian Exile, there had arisen a myth about God and his Kingdom. This is not surprising. The form of government in the ancient Near East was the monarchy, and the Israelites had developed their own version of it. God was imagined as the greatest of all kings, a "Great King" (cf. Matt. 5:35) who was so powerful that he created the world, brought his enslaved people out of Egypt, guided them through the wilderness, defeated their enemies like a conquering warrior, and gave them the promised land. He was a universal king, judging the nations, and his rule was thought to encompass his whole creation. This is the theocratic ideal—divine rule—extended to the whole cosmos. This universal reign is the "Kingdom of God" (*malkuth Yahweh*), although the expression itself is not often found in the Hebrew Scriptures (1 Chron. 28:5). The myth of the God who created the world and constantly acted to preserve, protect, and judge the people became the very foundation of the people of Israel, which was formed as a theocracy. The myth was told and indeed acted again and again.

When Israel was finally destroyed and taken into exile by Babylon, the theocratic ideal that had expressed national solidarity began to be more of a future hope than a present reality. It became an "*eschatological* myth," a myth to which people clung in hard times, times of oppression and persecution, whether real or imagined. When millennial seers took up the myth in the years before the birth of Jesus, the tendency was to think in terms of "this (evil) age" and "the (good) age to come." "This age" was marked by a succession of four evil Kingdoms, which God, in one great cataclysmic and cosmic event, would overthrow and judge. Thus he prepared the way for an everlasting and victorious paradisiacal Kingdom like his Kingdom of old. For the millennialist, the more difficult and tragic conditions in this world became, the closer was the end of time—and all of this was observable by signs, the political and cosmic "signs of the times." Many apocalyptic scribes must have taken these signs quite literally. Examples of this kind of thinking were frequent in ancient apocalyptic writing, as we have seen. Apocalyptic eschatology would have been the normative way of perceiving the Kingdom of God.

However, not all of Israelite thinking stressed literal apocalyptic "signs to be observed" in connection with the coming of God's Kingdom. For example, the daily synagogue prayer, called the Kaddish prayer, said, ". . . May he establish his Kingdom in your lifetime and in your days and in the lifetime of all the house of Israel even speedily and at a near time." Whether apocalyptic signs were stressed or not, it is clear that the use of the phrase "Kingdom of God" would have called up the totality of the experience of Israel. It was a *symbolic phrase recalling the Kingdom myth,* the myth in which God created the world and the people, protected and sustained all of the creation, judged and defeated enemies, even judged the people when they did not conform to the covenant. It clearly had political, economic, and social implications. Its language would also give an accent to the future: The hope in Jesus' time was for the reestablishment of God's Kingdom when the good would be rewarded and the evil punished.

There are a number of important Kingdom sayings that pass the criteria of probable authenticity and that can be easily correlated with the activity of Jesus. Consider the following distinctive sayings in relation to itinerancy and homelessness:

> To another he said, "Follow me." But he said, "Lord, let me first go and bury my father." But Jesus said to him, "Let the (spiritually?) dead bury their own (physical) dead; but as for you, go and proclaim the Kingdom of God."
>
> (Luke 9:57–58 = Matt. 8:19–20 [see *GTh* 86]; Luke 9: 59–60 = Matt. 8:21–22)

This saying is extremely radical (distinctive!), no matter whether the term "dead" is literal or metaphorical. Among ancient Israelites the code of honor required burial of one's parents as an absolute necessity (e.g., Tob. 4:3–4; 6:13–15; *Berakoth* 3:1). In this distinctive saying, however, following Jesus and proclaiming the Kingdom take precedence over biological family and obligations to it.

Other distinctive sayings affirm that Jesus' "fictive" or surrogate family comes first and is potentially homeless. Note in the following sayings the mention of meals, the Kingdom, and the opposition to Jesus' exorcisms.

> Then he went into a house (NRSV: went home); and the crowd came together again, so that they could not even eat. When his family heard it, they went out to restrain him, for people were saying, "He has gone out of his mind." And the scribes who came down from Jerusalem said, "He has Beelzebul, and by the ruler of demons he casts out the demons. . . ." [the witchcraft accusation].
>
> Then his mother and his brothers came; and standing outside [the house], they sent to him and called him. A crowd was sitting around him; and they said to him, "Your mother and your brothers and sisters are outside, asking for you." And he replied, "Who are my mother and my brothers?" And looking around on those who sat about him, he said, "Here are my mother and my brothers! Whoever does the will of God is my brother, and sister, and mother." [*GTh:* "It is they who enter the Kingdom of my father."]
>
> (Mark 3:19b–22, 31–35 = Matt. 12:46–50 = Luke 8:19– 20; plus *GTh* 99)

Following Jesus "into the Kingdom" may require rejection of the customary values about home and family.

For many contemporary scholars of Jesus' teaching, the following are among the authentic Kingdom sayings:

> The Kingdom of God is not coming with things ("signs") that can be observed; nor will they say, "Look, here it is!" or "There it is!" For, in fact, the Kingdom of God is among you.
>
> (Luke 17:20b–21)

With this version can be compared a version in the *Gospel of Thomas:*

> His disciples said to him, "When will the Kingdom come?" [Jesus said,] "It will not come by waiting for it. It will not be a matter of saying 'Here it is' or 'There it is.' Rather the Kingdom of the Father is spread out upon the earth, and people do not see it."
>
> (Gospel of Thomas 113)

Both versions use the symbol of the Kingdom, and both deny the common millennial interpretation of the eschatological myth: Here, the Kingdom is *not* coming "with (cosmic, apocalyptic) signs to be observed"; no one will be able to say "Look, here it is!" or "There it is!" In a number of passages Jesus refused to give a sign (Matt. 12:39; 16:4; Luke 11:29–32). It was noted that the earliest form of the Sign of Jonah sayings was the refusal to give any cosmic sign whatsoever: "Truly I tell you, no sign shall be given to this generation" (cf. Mark 8:11–12). (The exceptions—preaching and resurrection—were added in connection with the story of Jonah later.) These sign passages cohere. Thus it is likely that this earliest form went back to Jesus and was related to his view of the Kingdom.

One implication of these sayings is that Jesus is not a thoroughgoing apocalyptic prophet like John the Baptizer: The Kingdom is not coming with "signs to be observed"; it is already mysteriously present "among you." The phrase "Kingdom of God" is symbolic; it may have called up the myth of God's Kingdom to at least some of Jesus' hearers. It is in the nature of such language that it cannot be limited to literal, descriptive statements. Symbolic language calls forth a whole set of interrelated ideas and emotions. In other words, the proclamation of Kingdom confronts the hearers of Jesus already in the present; one is not simply to expect it, but rather to respond to it now.

Another aspect of the Kingdom can be seen in the following saying:

> From the days of John the Baptist until now the Kingdom of heaven has suffered violence, and the violent take it by force.
>
> (Matt. 11:12)

Part of the eschatological myth in Israel involved a cosmic battle between God and Satan, between the forces of good and the forces of evil, in which God and the forces of good would ultimately triumph. In this light, the saying expresses the view that the death of John the Baptizer and the possibility of suffering of Jesus and his followers are part of the eschatological war. The future battle is already taking place, now, in the present.

Still another very important Kingdom saying is the following:

> But if it is by the finger of God that I cast out demons, then the Kingdom of God has come to you.
>
> (Q/Luke 11:20)

This Q saying refers to the activity of Jesus as exorcist in the battle against the forces of evil, the demons. Here Jesus acts as God's representative and manifests his power to defeat evil. Again, the Kingdom "has come" in this activity; it is a present reality, certainly for those who are exorcised, and more, for those who can accept the saying itself. One aspect of "Kingdom reality" is exorcism, and exorcism challenges the hearers of Jesus' message to recall the Kingdom myth and to take it seriously as an aspect of their own present experience.

To summarize, then, "Kingdom of God" is a symbol that evokes the whole range of meanings associated with the myth of God's activity as King. That means God's visiting and redeeming his people, not in the sense that it is just a future reality proved by the demonstration of literal signs. To be sure, it is possible to find Kingdom sayings that sound apocalyptic (e.g., Mark 1:15; 9:1; 14:25); but it is more likely that the Jesus sayings are the present ones, that is, the Kingdom is available already through the preaching and activity of Jesus. This Kingdom reality is the central theme of the message of Jesus. It will now be helpful to clarify it through a discussion of other aspects of his message.

The Parables

Intensive study of the synoptic gospels shows that, as noted previously, there are especially three other areas of Jesus' message where we can come close to the words of the historical Jesus. These are the parables, the aphorisms, and the Lord's Prayer. The parables reinforce the previous section because they are not highly apocalyptic.

Modern research on the parables of Jesus has established a number of points about them that may be stated in summary fashion.

1. As discussed in Chapter Three, scholars contrast parable and allegory. The parable makes its point as a whole story, not in its parts. Moreover, the main point of the parable can never be exhausted by any one understanding; the parable is, within certain cultural limits, "open ended," so that its meaning can be newly perceived in different situations. For that reason the parable, like a poem, cannot be translated into an exact meaning, or restated as a proposition or descriptive statement of fact; rather, it must be retold. The allegory, on the other hand, makes its point in the parts; each individual part bears a one-to-one relationship to what it represents. After that secret relationship is discovered, the message of the allegory becomes clear, and the allegory itself can be abandoned because its cryptic message can now be—and should be—expressed in noncryptic language. It is generally argued that Jesus taught in parables, but the early church understood them as allegories and in many cases revised them so that they became more allegorical.

2. Adjacent allegorical interpretations, transformations of the parables into allegories, and the present contexts and applications of parables in the gospels are the work of early Jesus Movement communities and evangelists. To interpret a parable as a parable of Jesus, therefore, one must first reconstruct the original nonallegorical form of the parable and then interpret it as a parable in the context of the message of Jesus without reference to its context or function in the gospel narratives.

3. The fundamental element in a parable is metaphor. *A* is compared to *B* so that meaning may be carried over from *B* to *A*. Normally, *A* is the lesser known and *B* the better known. For example, when the Kingdom of God is the lesser known, aspects of its meaning are illuminated by something better known or more readily envisaged: the story of a man finding a treasure in a field or of a merchant finding a pearl (Matt. 13:44–46).

4. There is, therefore, in the parable a literal point, the meaning of the story or image itself, and also a metaphorical point, that to which it is intended to refer.

5. The purpose of a parable is normally pedagogical; rabbis used it extensively to illuminate, illustrate, and instruct. In the case of Jesus, however, this normal use of the parable seems to have been subordinated to proclamation.

The best example of parable *followed by* its allegorical explanation in the New Testament is the Sower (Mark 4:3–8, 13–20), already analyzed in Chapter Three. An excellent example of progressive allegorizing is found in the parable of the Dinner Party in Luke 14:16–24, *Gospel of Thomas* 64, and Matt. 22:1–10. If one removes the interpretations that represent the interests of the writers, Jesus spoke simply of an anonymous, wealthy man of the elite classes who held a sudden dinner, and without the usual advance notice, invited guests (probably three sets, common in oral tradition) who could not come. So a servant was sent to invite anyone who could come. The story beckons the hearer into a world where the unusual, the dishonorable, the distinctive occurs: The invited elite do not come, the uninvited marginal people do. This reversal of the customary is like many of Jesus' parables, and the original version probably was something like it.

A second example is the famous parable of the Good Samaritan.

> A man was going down from Jerusalem to Jericho, and he fell into the hands of robbers, who stripped him, beat him, and went away, leaving him half dead. Now by chance a priest was going down that road; and when he saw him, he passed by on the other side. So likewise a Levite, when he came to the place and saw him, passed by on the other side. But a Samaritan while traveling came near him; and when he saw him, he was moved with pity. He went to him and bandaged his wounds, having poured oil and wine on them. Then he put him on his own animal, brought him to an inn, and took care of him. The next day he took out two denarii, gave them to the innkeeper, and said, "Take care of him; and when I come back, I will repay you whatever more you spend." Which of these three, do you think, was a neighbor to the man who fell into the hands of the robbers?
>
> (Luke 10:30–36)

This *form* of the parable is surely close to what Jesus taught. However, the present context of the discussion with the lawyer (10:25–29, 37) has been supplied by the Lukan author, who took it from a different context in Mark (Mark 12:28–31) and relocated it here. In its present context the parable is an example of how to live, illustrating the principle of good neighborliness to a man in need. This is absolutely in keeping with the use of parables by later rabbis. However, the Lukan context must be ignored in an attempt to understand the parable as a parable *of Jesus*. Then it is not an example. You will recall that the Israelites of Jesus' day despised the Samaritans on ethnic and religious grounds (see Chapter One), and relations between the two groups were such that no one could expect hospitality in a Samaritan village if he were on his way to Jerusalem (Luke 9:52–56). The parable confronts—indeed, shocks—the hearer of Jesus at the literal level with the combination *good* and *Samaritan*. It does not value the usual code of holiness emanating from the priestly hierarchy. It is asking the hearer, at least if he or she is pious, to rethink an accepted norm of behavior related to purity, to see the outsider as insider and the insider as outsider.

What happens when one is confronted by the demand to conceive what is inconceivable, to say what cannot be said? Either the demand is rejected, or the person confronted begins to question all that he or she has taken for granted up to that moment. It becomes necessary to reexamine the very grounds of one's being by a challenge that is effective at the deepest level of one's being.

A third, almost exact, parallel is the parable of the Unjust Steward, or Household Manager.

> "There was a rich man who had a manager, and charges were brought to him that this man was squandering his property. So he summoned him and said to him, 'What is this that I hear about you? Give me an accounting of your management, because you cannot be my manager any longer.' Then the manager said to himself, 'What will I do, now that my master is taking the position away from me? I am not strong enough to dig, and I am ashamed to beg. I have decided what to do so that, when I am dismissed as manager, people may welcome me into their homes.' So, summoning his master's debtors one by one, he asked the first, 'How much do you owe my master?' He answered, 'A hundred jugs of olive oil.' And he said to him, 'Take your bill, sit down quickly, and make it fifty.' Then he asked another, 'And how much do you owe?' He replied, 'A hundred containers of wheat.' He said to him, 'Take your bill, and make it eighty.'"
>
> (Luke 16:1–7)

Verse 8 says, "And his master commended the dishonest manager because he had acted shrewdly; for the children of this age are more shrewd in dealing with their own generation than are the children of light." A series of moral applications follows verse 8 (verses 9–13). Because the applications do not all equally relate to the parable, they were undoubtedly added later to attempt to explain Jesus' story about a character who was dishonest and compounded his dishonesty in the solution to his problem.

Instead of asking how this character can be seen as admirable, as did the author of these verses, we rather recognize the dramatic affront to morality that the Unjust Manager represents. In the case of the Good Samaritan, one needs to be aware of the situation between Galileans/Judeans and Samaritans at the time of Jesus. Putting together *good* and *Samaritan* would have been inconceivable. However, with the Unjust Manager, the character's decision and actions challenge the morality of business relationships and delegation of financial responsibility. The story itself focuses attention on the manager's dialogue with himself and his decision, and it implies that he was successful in his endeavor to avoid the evil consequences of his first dishonesty by compounding it. In a sense, then, the interpretation that concentrates on his "shrewdness" or the element of decision is correct. This is the focal point of the story. As the Good Samaritan challenges one to hear what cannot be said, this story challenges one to do what cannot be done.

A major theme of the parables is "reversal." In Luke 16:19–31, the Rich Man and Lazarus, the rich man is rewarded in this world, and poor man suffers; in the other world their fates will be reversed. In the case of the Pharisee and the Publican (Luke 18:10–14), the supposedly righteous man turns out to be self-righteous, and the sinner is the righteous man. For Jesus the parable becomes a form of the proclamation of the Kingdom. As the hearers are challenged to say what cannot be said, to applaud what should not be applauded, to recognize in the reversal of human judgments and human situations the sign of the breaking in of God's Kingdom, so the Kingdom "comes." The power of Jesus to transform the parable into a form of proclamation was at the same time a power to mediate to his hearers the experience of the Kingdom.

Yet, Jesus did not always use the parable form as a challenge to acceptable ways of doing things. Many of his parables instruct or teach. This must have been so, because the message of Jesus could never have been as effective as its historical consequences demonstrate had it not included the function of instruction.

Those of Jesus' day who listened to the Hidden Treasure and the Pearl parables (Matt. 13:44–46) would certainly have understood that the Kingdom evokes a response of overwhelming joy. The Tower Builder and the King going to War (Luke 14:28–32), along with the Assassin in the *Gospel of Thomas* 98, show how three very different people prepare themselves for their future responsibilities. The Friend Imposed Upon (Luke 11:5–8) and the Importuned Judge (the Unjust Judge, Luke 18:1–8) are rabbinical arguments "from the lesser to the greater." The metaphorical position in both is the same. The friend is no real friend at all—otherwise he would be out of bed immediately—and the judge is certainly no true judge. Yet, both could be pressed into doing what they should. If they can be so pressed, how much more can we trust God who does not need to be pressed?

There are many more parables of Jesus, but enough has been said to make the point that some of the parables of Jesus functioned as challenges to cheaply accepted values, and others functioned as moral instruction. Some mediated the experience of the Kingdom of God to those who heard them, whereas others instructed the hearer to respond in various ways. An aspect of the use of the parables by Jesus not yet discussed is the future; thus "Jesus and 'the future'" will be taken up later.

The Aphorisms: Countercultural Proverbs

Proverbs are short, pithy sayings that represent the collective wisdom of a culture. Therefore, they express easy-to-remember wise sayings about what is commonly accepted in the culture as the everyday truth—usually the wise, practical, and pragmatic way to live and succeed. A famous American example is "Early to bed, early to rise makes a man healthy, wealthy, and wise."

Collections of proverbial wisdom sayings can be found in the Hebrew Bible and in the Old Testament Apocrypha, for example, in the Wisdom of Solomon and the Wisdom of Jesus ben ("Son of") Sira. Consider the following proverb from ben Sira, about 180 B.C.E.:

> For the Lord honored the father above the children, and he confirmed the right of the mother over her sons. Whoever honors his father atones for sins, and whoever glorifies his mother is like one who lays up treasure.
> (ben Sira 3:2–4)

This proverb is an expression of conventional, cultural wisdom about everyday family relationships (its lesson about parental authority is taken for granted as "true").

It is seen to conform to God's just and orderly rule of the world (it is "the way things are," sometimes called "universal law" or "cosmic law").

An "aphorism" is a short, pithy, witty, sometimes humorous saying that looks like a proverb but does not function like a proverb. It is like a proverb in *form* but not in *content*. It does not conform to collective, conventional, cultural wisdom; rather, it is *counter*cultural, a challenge to conventional norms, values, and beliefs. It is thus quite distinctive.

A radical example is the following:

"Whoever comes to me and does not hate father and mother, wife and children, and brothers and sisters . . . cannot be my disciple."
(Luke 14:26 = Matt. 10:37; see *GTh* 55:1–2a; 101–103)

In this multiply attested saying, the word "hate" is very offensive. Most likely, the aphorism goes back to Jesus, even if it is an expression of hyperbole, or gross exaggeration. The Matthean variant softens it to "loves *more than me*," that is, one must place loyalty to Jesus above loyalty to one's family. The aphorism generally agrees with the other sayings about Jesus' "fictive" or surrogate family: those who do the will of God.

Another example was combined in Q with the radical saying cited earlier in connection with the Kingdom, "let the dead bury their dead." It expresses the homelessness of Jesus as an itinerant and in context reads:

"Foxes have holes, and birds of the air have nests; but the Son of Man has nowhere to lay his head."
(Luke 9:58 = Matt. 8:20; *GTh* 86:1–2)

Most likely this aphorism originally meant that whereas members of the animal kingdom have their "homes," "this human being" is "homeless" and rejected. It again indicates the radically distinctive quality of Jesus' life. Was the "fox" King Herod Antipas, as Luke suggests (Luke 13:32)? Yet, the saying appears to have already received a later Christological interpretation because the "Son of Man" no longer refers to a human being, but rather to "*the* Son of Man," the messianic figure from Dan. 7:13–14. Also, the variant in the *Gospel of Thomas* says nothing about itinerant followers of Jesus.

This, then, is the general background against which we must set Jesus' use of the aphorism. There are some aphorisms among the sayings already discussed. The following are important ones that Bultmann held to be authentic on the basis of what later came to be called the "criterion of distinctiveness/dissimilarity." They will be at least typical of Jesus' sayings. We examine these in groups according to our own analysis.

The Most Radical Sayings: Luke 9:60a, Matthew 5:39b–41

"Let the (spiritually?) dead bury their own (spiritually? physically?) dead."
(Luke 9:60a, discussed earlier)

"If anyone strikes you on the right cheek, turn the other also; and if anyone wants to sue you and take your coat, give your cloak as well; and if anyone forces you to go one mile, go also the second mile."
(Matt. 5:39b–41; cf. Luke 6:29)

These are not multiply attested, but they are the most radical, thus distinctive, of the aphoristic sayings of Jesus. Indeed, they overturn normal social behavior. To "let the dead bury their own dead" by any usual norm of family behavior is to act irresponsibly. Giving the "cloak as well" and going the "second mile" are moral imperatives that are at best difficult, if not impossible. Because the Palestinian peasant at the time of Jesus wore only those two garments, the result would have been indecent exposure! Moreover, it refers to the privilege of Roman soldiers to impress local citizens into service; the result of obeying it would be a lifetime of forced servitude.

As the message of Jesus, these are part of the proclamation of the Kingdom of God. They challenge the hearer to radical questioning. They jolt hearers out of normal ways of thinking and acting by creating a judgment against them. They exactly match the function of the parable as proclamation in the message of Jesus.

The Eschatological Reversal Sayings: Mark 8:35; 10:23b, 25; Matthew 20:16

> "For those who want to save their life will lose it; and those who lose their life [for my sake, (and for the sake of the gospel)] will save it." (The original may have been something like ". . . for the sake of the Kingdom of God.")
> (Mark 8:35 = Matt. 16:25 = Luke 9:24; Matt. 10:39 = Luke 17:33 [Q]; John 12:25)

In its present context in Mark, the saying is preceded by "following" and "self-denial" as "cross-bearing"; thus it seems to have received a specific meaning in the Jesus Movement. Probably the saying itself did not have the words "for the sake of the gospel," and perhaps also "for my sake" has been added. Without those lines, the aphorism is quite crisp.

> "How hard it will be for those who have wealth to enter the Kingdom of God! . . .
> It is easier for a camel to go through the eye of a needle than for someone who is rich to enter the Kingdom of God."
> (Mark 10:23b, 25 = Matt. 19:23, 24 = Luke 18:24, 25)

Although the critique of material possessions is not in itself distinctive in antiquity, the Kingdom relation combined with the striking aphorism about the camel is quite distinctive.

> "So the last will be first, and the first will be last."
> (Matt. 20:16 = Luke 13:30 [Q]; cf. Matt. 19:30; *GTh* 4b)

The Matthean version of this multiply attested saying is a little more radical than the Markan ("*many* who are first . . ."), and the Lukan version is similar to the Markan. The Matthean version is the crisp aphorism.

Summarizing, in these aphorisms the theme of eschatological reversal is one of the best-attested themes of the message of Jesus. It proclaims the Kingdom as reversal of *the present* and so invites, indeed *demands,* judgment on the present. Again, this use of the aphorism exactly parallels a use of the parable in the message of Jesus.

The Conflict Sayings: Mark 3:24–26, 27

> "If a Kingdom is divided against itself, that Kingdom cannot stand. And if a house is divided against itself, that house will not be able to stand. And if Satan has risen up against himself and is divided, he cannot stand, but his end has come."
>
> (Mark 3:24–26 = Matt. 12:25–26 = Luke 11:17–18; Mark/Q overlap)

This saying is a response to the opponents who claim that Jesus was himself possessed by Satan and exorcised by Satan's power (cf. also John 8:48–53; 10:20). The response is that the charge interprets the charge against itself by pointing to its faulty logic.

> "No one can enter a strong man's house and plunder his property, unless he first binds the strong man; then indeed the house can be plundered."
>
> (Mark 3:27 = Matt. 12:29 = Luke 8:21; *GTh* 35:1–2)

This saying is multiply attested and coheres with Jesus' activity as a folk healer/exorcist. The "strong man" refers to Satan.

Summarizing, these sayings express the same kind of thinking (cohere with) those discussed earlier in which the Kingdom is present in exorcisms, the fate of the Baptizer, and the potential fate of Jesus and his disciples (Luke 11:20; Matt. 11:12). They understand present human experience as an arena of conflict in which the Kingdom of God is present.

Moral Norms and Demands: Luke 9:62; Luke 13:24; Mark 7:15; 10:15; Matthew 5:44–48

> "Strive to enter through the narrow door; for many, I tell you, will try to enter and will not be able."
>
> (Luke 13:24 = Matt. 7:13–14)

Following Jesus will not be easy, and many will not succeed.

> "There is nothing outside a person that by going in can defile, but the things that come out are what defile."
>
> (Mark 7:15 = Matt. 15:11; *GTh* 14:5)

This multiply-attested saying challenges the traditional, very crucial norms about purity and pollution: Pollution is not external, but rather internal.

> "Whoever does not receive the Kingdom of God as a little child will never enter it."
>
> (Mark 10:15 = Matt. 18:3; Luke 18:17; see *GTh* 22a, 46b)

Jesus probably spoke some form of this saying about the Kingdom and childlike simplicity (see also Mark 10:14 par.), although "entering" it might be a later interpretation based on an entry rite—baptism—into the Jesus Movement.

> "Love your enemies and pray for those who persecute you, so that you may be children of your Father . . . ; for he makes his sun rise on the evil and on the good, and sends rain on the righteous and on the unrighteous. For if you love those who love you, what reward have you? Do not even the tax collectors do the same? And if you greet only your brothers and sisters, what more are you doing than others? Do

not even the Gentiles do the same? Be perfect, therefore, as your heavenly Father is perfect."

(Matt. 5:44–48 = Luke 6:27–36)

In these sayings, traditional proverbs appear, and Jesus uses the form in the same way as do his contemporaries. One great difference, however, is that these sayings are set in the context of Jesus' message about the Kingdom of God. Like all the moral demands of Jesus, they are concerned with response to the Kingdom. Jesus did not have a system of ethics in the usual sense. However, these sayings contain the seeds for ethical reflection: the radical questioning of one's easy acceptance of his or her current state of existence, the reversal of conventional morality, the battle against the forces of evil, and the necessity of responding to the Kingdom proclamation with spontaneous, radical, self-giving love.

The Lord's Prayer

The Lord's Prayer has been analyzed in great detail in Chapter Two. The reconstructed form was as follows:

Father,
Hallowed be your name.
Your Kingdom come.
Give us this day our daily bread.
And forgive us our debts,
As we also have forgiven our debtors.
And do not lead us to the test.

Clearly this prayer echoes Jesus' Israelite heritage. Yet, the simplicity and brevity of the prayer—some scholars have broken down the prayer into sentence fragments that came from Jesus independently—express a formal and majestic, but intimate, understanding of the relationship between the petitioner and God.

We note again that the three most distinctive elements in the prayer are use of the familiar Aramaic term for "father" (*'Abbā'*); the petition that the Kingdom "come"; and the willingness of humans to forgive as a condition for God's forgiveness of them. Jesus would also have viewed God's name as holy. As a poor peasant he would have petitioned God for "daily bread" or "bread for tomorrow" and have stressed God's forgiveness of actual "debts," which in Aramaic can metaphorically mean "sins." The setting of the prayer would probably have been Jesus' inclusive meals with his disciples and marginal people discussed earlier. In the villages of Galilee, the Lord's Prayer was revolutionary "wisdom" and "prophecy." Finally, for those who prayed the prayer, the Kingdom had to some extent already come.

JESUS AND "THE FUTURE"

We come now to an extraordinarily difficult theme in relation to the message of Jesus: his expectation and teaching concerning "the future." "The future" is put in quotation marks because from the perspective of peasant culture, "future" more often than not has to do with the agricultural seasons than with the *lineal* future, a characteristic of modern Western notions of time. Yet, there is a "future dimension" to eschatology, and that needs to be addressed.

In this textbook the sayings or teachings ascribed to Jesus in the gospels that give a definite form to the future fail the test of probable criteria for authenticity. This is an extremely important conclusion for understanding the historical Jesus. As noted, several scholars believe that Jesus was a radical apocalypticist and that as such he fits the millennialist context of Greco-Roman Palestine, for example, that found in the **Dead Sea Scrolls** and in the teaching of John the Baptizer. They conclude that he also fits the early Jesus Movement as represented by Paul's earliest letters. For example, the gospels are full of sayings about the Son of Man that appear to focus on his coming in "the future" for judgment. There are also sayings about the Kingdom that have been categorized as "future" sayings. Arguments are made that even if Jesus did not speak about *himself* as the coming Son of Man, he could have spoken about the apocalyptic Son of Man as someone *other than himself* (e.g., Luke 12:8; Mark 8:38). There is a powerful logic to this approach, but the position chosen here is that the "future" sayings are from the increasingly apocalyptic church.

However, the question is not just whether Jesus expected a future coming of the Son of Man, but whether he looked toward the future for something different from what was already present in the experience of those confronted by the reality of his activity and his message. To bring this question into focus we must call attention to one result of the preceding discussion, namely, that Jesus claimed to mediate the reality of the Kingdom of God to his hearers in a distinctive way. His proclamation of the Kingdom of God implies that claim, and some of his hearers responded to that proclamation. Jesus transformed the literary form of the parable in such a way that his peasant hearers saw it as a hopeful challenge for their lives. Similarly, Jesus transformed the proverb into an aphorism, a medium that possessed power to jolt the hearer into making sense out of human existence and hearing judgment on that existence. In this "jolting" the Kingdom is also "breaking in." Finally, the Lord's Prayer envisages and gives expression to a relationship with God different enough from that in the traditional Israelite prayers that for many persons who can pray that prayer the Kingdom has, in a real sense, already "come."

Yet, there is another aspect. Within the Lord's Prayer itself there is the petition "Your Kingdom come." Because it parallels petitions of Israelite prayers of hope, it cannot be denied that this petition looks forward in some way to the future. Furthermore, there is a group of parables, the Sower (Mark 4:3–9), the Mustard Seed (Mark 4:30–32), the Leaven (Matt. 13:33), and the Seed Growing of Itself (Mark 4:26–29), that challenges the hearer to put hope in what is coming. At the literal level they move from the present of the sowing, or of the leavening of the dough, to the future of the result of the sowing or of the leavening. At the metaphorical level they challenge the hearer to move from his or her present to a future. Finally, the eschatological reversal sayings seem to have an accent on the future in so far as the present is unacceptable. At this point it becomes important to note several things. As noted, modern conceptions of time and history need not be ascribed to Jesus, a peasant artisan of the first century. This consideration is reinforced by recalling that at one time, when first-century apocalyptic came very close to a modern understanding of signs as expressing a one-to-one relationship to temporal, historical events and figures, Jesus dissociated himself from such thinking. It is therefore plausible to claim that Jesus looked toward a future, but not necessarily a future conceived in temporal, historical terms. His message promised his followers a future that would be a consummation of what they already knew in the present as they responded favorably to what he announced. As part of their response, they subsequently came to interpret this message in terms of a temporal and historical event drawn from traditional apocalyptic expectations, the coming of the Son of Man, whom they now identified with Jesus. They were not correct in so doing, if the progression of history is allowed its rightful place.

THE LAST DAYS OF JESUS

Jesus' final days in Jerusalem received, like other narrative materials, a great deal of interpretation in the early Jesus Movement. In Chapter Three, it was suggested that the Passion Story was largely a creation of the evangelists. It is filled with prophecies that gave rise to events to fulfill them—after the fact. At the same time it is difficult to deny that there is some historical core behind the accounts. For example, the crucifixion of Jesus by the Roman authorities is judged by some historical scholars to be the most certain event of Jesus' life. Yet, its details often appear to be developed from reflections about the psalms of suffering and the Suffering Servant of Isaiah in the ancient scriptures. What sort of judgments can be made about Jesus' final days in Jerusalem?

Note again a well-known discrepancy. The Gospel of John does not agree with the synoptic gospels that Jesus made only one trip (as an adult) to Jerusalem. Rather, he made several trips and attended several festivals, suggesting that the length of his public life was more than one year. A more important focus, however, is Jesus' *final* visit.

In an oriental temple state, the seat of holiness in Greco-Roman Israel was the holy city Jerusalem, its holy temple, and ultimately the "Holy of Holies," the sacred space where the most holy God was said to reside. Holy persons, the Jerusalem priests, controlled all in the name of God. The ideal was a theocracy with the priests as God's earthly representatives. Recall that Jesus' Kingdom message, his healings, and his meal practices opposed the tendency toward exclusivity based on holiness. Thus Jesus' message and practice implied an anti-temple stance. Moreover, Jesus' healings opposed oppressive evil powers, which in antiquity could also be the realms of evil economic, political, and social powers. These powers had a basic distrust of political and religious groups of those considered to be outside the mainstream. Indeed, at times there were Roman laws against newly formed "secret societies." As Jesus' following among the peasants and outcasts grew, he naturally aroused opposition among the political, economic, and religious elite of his day, as well as those who served them, the "retainers." Some of them were members of religious parties, such as the Pharisees. In short, it is not so surprising that Jesus' Kingdom message—drawn from a political metaphor—contributed to an opposition that culminated in his arrest, trial, and final execution by the Romans on a charge of treason against the state.

Still, what happened? The facts are difficult to recover. Probably Jesus rode into Jerusalem on a donkey. However, the gospel portraits of his tremendous reception and acclamation as the King Messiah have undoubtedly been expanded by reflection on the classic prophecy of the procession and entry of the humble messianic king into the holy city (Zech. 9:9 [Matt. 21:5; John 12:15]). The Hosannas from the familiar and often-used texts in festival liturgies (e.g., Ps. 118:25–26) were no doubt added and received messianic interpretation.

An important event in the synoptics, one much debated today, is Jesus' so-called cleansing of the temple (Mark 11:15–19; Matt. 21:12–13; Luke 19:45–48). In its present form, Jesus enters the temple, drives out the money changers, and overturns their tables, as well as those of pigeon sellers. He then quotes scripture: "My house shall be called a house of prayer for all the nations" (Isa. 56:7c) and "You have made it a den of robbers" (Jer. 7:11). However, there are some critical problems with the story. The outer precincts of the Jerusalem temple had become a place where sacrificial animals could be purchased and money exchanged in order that sacrificial animals might be bought without coins, on which there were forbidden images. This was accepted practice. Indeed, it was necessary practice to preserve purity.

What lay behind Jesus' violent act? Scholars often tie the event to a key prophecy supposedly spoken by Jesus. The gospel writers say that false witnesses accused Jesus of having spoken this prophecy: "I will destroy this temple [made with hands] and in three days I will build another [, not made with hands]" (*GTh* 71; Mark 14:58 = Matt. 26:61; cf. Mark 15:29–30 = Matt. 27:40–41; cf. John 2:19). The same prophecy is echoed in Stephen's temple polemic: "The Most High does not dwell in houses made with human hands . . ." (Acts 7:48). The *Gospel of Thomas* has what appears to be another variant: "I shall [destroy this] house, and no one will be able to build it [. . .]." The Markan version's "in three days" is no doubt an interpretation after the fact based on early belief in the Jesus Movement that Jesus rose from the dead on the third day (or after three days), also found in John 2:21–22. The *Thomas* version has no rebuilding at all. Either it is more original, or it is an interpretation based on the destruction of the temple in 70 C.E. Although there is no absolute certainty, perhaps Jesus symbolically enacted in deed what he prophesied, all of which would have been consistent with critique of purity norms associated with the temple. Indeed, some scholars conclude that this was more than a symbolic act designed to indicate its impurity. Rather, they say, Jesus opposed the temple and its sacrificial system altogether. If so, the gospels have toned down Jesus' views considerably. As they stand, the temple is only "cleansed," the words about its destruction are said by *false* witnesses, the event is further interpreted by the resurrection, and his opposition in the temple is from a variety of "religious"—not political—opponents (Mark 12). An even more extreme view is that Jesus launched a guerrilla-style attack against the temple. This view cannot easily be supported in the texts as they stand. In any case, it seems very likely that his act, however extreme it may have been, combined with the temple destruction prophecy, engendered opposition by the Jerusalem priestly establishment supported by the client kings and the Roman governor.

A second major event of Jesus' Jerusalem period was his last meal with his disciples. The synoptic gospels' overall view portrays Jesus as eating a **Passover** meal with his disciples on the first evening of the Passover feast (Mark 14:22–25). Later he was arrested and condemned for blasphemy at a late night "trial" before the Sanhedrin (Mark 14:53–72) and then crucified the next afternoon, still the first day of Passover (Nisan 15; Mark 15:22–41). Matthew and Luke follow this general Markan Passover emphasis.

Yet, some scholars think that the comment in Mark 14:2, which says that the chief priests wished to arrest Jesus *before* the Feast of Passover began, "lest there be a tumult among the people" (Mark 14:2), hides a strong historical probability: Jesus did not eat a Passover meal. This opinion receives support from a number of other factors. First, neither of the two eucharistic rituals in the *Didachē* (10, 9) links Jesus' final meal with the Passover, and neither does Paul (1 Cor. 11:23–26). Second, the Gospel of John explicitly contradicts the Passover meal view by placing Jesus' crucifixion on the Day of Preparation, when the Passover lambs were slain, *before* the Passover evening meal (13:1; 19:31). The objection that John's version has symbolic significance—Jesus is the slain Passover lamb—has validity but is not a sufficient explanation because the synoptic version also has symbolic significance: A new Passover instituted a new Israel. Thus it is also an interpretation. Third, crucial features of what later became the Passover meal, particularly the Passover lamb and the unleavened bread, are not mentioned in the synoptic account. Fourth, in Israelite law, at least in slightly later sources, night trials and single sessions of the Sanhedrin were strictly prohibited for capital cases; indeed, the courtroom was locked at night, and capital cases required a second verdict on a second day. Fifth, according to the same law, Jesus said nothing at the "trial" that was blasphemous (he said nothing against the Divine Name); moreover, the traditional Israelite punishment for blasphemy was execution by dropping a large stone on the convicted person standing in a pit ("stoning"). This problem, to be sure, is complicated by the question of whether the Judeans could themselves carry out capital punishment in this period (cf. John 18:31, which says that it was not lawful).

Some scholars still defend the Passover meal view of the synoptics, but the greater historical probability is that Jesus ate one of his customary meals, perhaps with only his disciples, sometime before the Passover began (the previous evening, as the Gospel of John suggests?). This would explain a well-known problem, namely, that the earlier *Didachē* version (*Didachē* 10) of the Last Meal appears to be a common meal of food and drink. It would also explain why neither version (*Didachē* 10, 9) refers to Jesus' body and blood, the symbol for his death. Finally, it would also explain the traditions in Paul. There the cup was drunk "after supper" (1 Cor. 11:25), Paul complained about the social distinctions at the meal, and such fellowship meals are mentioned elsewhere as having been practiced in the early church (e.g., Acts 2:46). Paul exhorts the Corinthians that if people (the elite?) could not wait (for the poor?) and get drunk, they should eat at home, a recommendation that contributed to the eventual separation of the ritual from the common meal (cf. 11:17–22, 33–34). Meanwhile, the proximity of Jesus' death to the time of the Passover contributed to the development of a "Jesus Movement Passover" and thus the synoptic tradition.

A third major historical question is this: Who was directly responsible for the execution of Jesus? The tradition that one of Jesus' disciples betrayed him may be accurate, although we can only guess at the motive. It is also possible that he was arrested in the Garden of Gethsemane by Israelite authorities as a threat to the temple establishment. If so, they handed him over to the Roman authorities as a potential political threat, as they had done with John the Baptizer before him. Although it is not unreasonable to think that the Jerusalem elite who controlled the temple were deeply involved, it must be seen that the Gospels attempt to exonerate the prefect Pontius Pilate. This distinctly pro-Roman, pro-Gentile position does not comport with what is otherwise known of Pilate's nasty character. Josephus relates several dramatic episodes where Pilate crushed Israelite and Samaritan demonstrations (see Chapter One), and Philo says that Pilate was responsible for ". . . acts of corruption, insults, rape, outrages on the people, arrogance, repeated murders of innocent victims, and constant and most galling savagery" (*Legation to Gaius*). It may be assumed that after the Roman-Israelite wars of 66–70 C.E., the Gospel writers took a distinctively pro-Roman stance. Thus they fixed the guilt for the death of Jesus much more directly on the Israelite participants, all colored by belief in the Jesus Movement that Jesus was the Messiah.

It should not be doubted that the Romans crucified Jesus, who was apparently deserted by his followers. Their motive was probably his supposed sedition. Probably a sign was carried about his neck, as was the custom, and affixed to the cross. It read, "King of the Israelites."

The Date of Jesus' Death

The stories of Jesus' crucifixion say that he died on a Friday (e.g., Mark 15:42 and par.; John 19:31, 42). As noted, in the synoptic gospels this Friday was the first day of the Passover Festival (Nisan 15), and Jesus ate the Passover meal the evening before. In the Gospel of John, however, this Friday was the Day of Preparation, the day before the Passover Festival, when the paschal lambs were sacrificed (Nisan 14), and Jesus did not eat the Passover meal. Most scholars prefer the Johannine chronology. However, the precise year of his crucifixion is probably not recoverable.

FROM JESUS TO THE NEW TESTAMENT

The Jesus who can be reconstructed historically from the New Testament proclaimed the Kingdom of God. More than that, he had the power to mediate to his hearers that which he proclaimed and how to respond to it. On this basis he taught those who responded to the proclamation to look to "the future" with confidence.

There are two striking things conspicuously absent from this picture, if it is compared to that found in the gospel accounts. The first is a specific claim by Jesus to be the Messiah. In modern historical research there is general agreement that the messianic claims put into the mouth of the Jesus of the gospels are exactly that: claims *put into* the mouth of Jesus. Jesus proclaimed the Kingdom of God, exorcised demons and healed the sick, gathered together and ate with disciples, outcasts, and his peasant brothers and sisters, but he made no explicit claims for himself. Of course, the very fact that he proclaimed the Kingdom of God and challenged his hearers as he did no doubt *implied* certain claims about himself, but historians think that Jesus did not make such claims explicit. The explicit claims in the gospels reflect the understanding of the early churches and the writers of the gospels, not historical data about Jesus of Nazareth.

The second element conspicuously absent from this picture is Jesus' interpretation of his own death. The fact is that we simply do not know how Jesus thought about his own death. In view of the fate of the Baptizer and the plausible comparison of John and Jesus (e.g., Matt. 11:12), it is inherently probable that Jesus did recognize the dangers to himself of his last visit to Jerusalem. However, the sayings in the gospels and in 1 Cor. 11 that reflect on his death are also products of the piety and understanding of the early Jesus Movement about martyrdom. They do not tell us anything about Jesus himself.

Within a short time after his death the followers of Jesus were claiming that God had raised him from the dead. Whereas he himself had proclaimed the Kingdom of God, they were proclaiming not only that, but Jesus himself. The Proclaimer had become the Proclaimed (Bultmann). He was, among other descriptions, the one who was about to return on the clouds of heaven as Son of Man and agent of God's final judgment and redemption of the world (so millennial forms of the Jesus Movement). He was also the one who "died for our sins and was raised for our justification" (so Paul). Finally, he was "the lamb of God, who takes away the sin of the world" (so the Johannine School). The historical details of the movement, from the wandering peasant who proclaimed the Kingdom of God to the various views that Jesus was "the Christ" in the New Testament and beyond, are probably forever lost to us.

STUDY QUESTIONS

1. How does the variety of images in the New Testament contribute to the problem of the historical Jesus? What are some of the main issues that have arisen in the quest of the historical Jesus during the last two centuries? What are some important critical problems about trying to find the historical Jesus, and how do criteria of probable authenticity help to solve them? What three kinds of external information exist about the historical Jesus?

2. What was the cultural and social-historical context of the life of Jesus? What are some of the major features of the life of Jesus, as historically reconstructed? How would you describe his early years? His relation to John the Baptizer? His meals with others? His healings?

3. How would you describe Jesus' teaching about the Kingdom? What is the main *form* of Jesus' teaching? What is the content of some of Jesus' major parables? What is an aphorism, and what do some of Jesus' aphorisms teach? How does the Lord's Prayer fit the overall impression of Jesus' message? What is Jesus' teaching about the future?

4. What are some of the difficulties in reconstructing what happened to Jesus in Jerusalem? Why do you think Jesus went to Jerusalem? Did he know he was a messiah? What can you say historically about Jesus' last meal in Jerusalem? Why was he arrested? Did he have a "fair trial"? Who was really responsible for Jesus' death?

Appendix One

Form and Contents of the Q Source

In this appendix is a list of the Q passages from J. Kloppenborg's chart of Q in his *Q Parallels*. Note several points. First, sayings of *uncertain but probable* origin in Q are marked with parentheses, transitions that *might* have been in Q but are unrecoverable are marked with angle brackets, and materials of *improbable* origins are put in Q with brackets. Second, H. C. Kee's simplified forms in Q in his second edition of *Jesus in History* have been listed as follows:

Narratives	Na
Parables	Pa
Oracles	Or
Beatitudes	Be
Prophetic Pronouncements	PP
Wisdom Words	WW
Exhortations	Ex

Third, asterisks after the formal abbreviations indicate that the section contains what J. D. Crossan has identified as "aphorisms," that is, short proverbial-type sayings that go against conventional proverbial wisdom. Fourth, because Q and the *Gospel of Thomas* are similar in genre, another column indicates passages they have in common. Fifth, certain blocks of material are in boldface type (nos. 7–14; nos. 21–28; nos. 35–42; nos. 50–57). The boldfaced and nonboldfaced sections indicate what some scholars (especially Kloppenborg) think are two different layers or sources that have been combined in Q. Sixth, we use the following symbols (*sigla*) to identify what some Q scholars think was or was not originally in Q:

( ) = probably originated in Q

[ ] = probably did *not* originate in Q

* = saying is, or unit contains, aphorism(s) [Crossan]

Section and Name	Form	Q Text	Matthew	Luke	*GTh*
Incipit and the Preaching of John					
1. Incipit		<Incipit>	[no text]	[no text]	
2. [The Coming of John the Baptist]		[3:2−4]	3:1−6	3:1−4	
3. John's Preaching of Repentance	PP	3:7−9, [10−14]	3:7−10	3:7−9, 10−14	
4. John's Preaching, the Coming One	PP	3:16b−17	3:11−12	3:15, 16−17	
5. [The Baptism of Jesus]		[3:21−22]	3:13−17	3:21−22	
The Temptations of Jesus					
6. *The Temptations of Jesus*	*Na*	*4:1−13*	*4:1−11*	*4:1−13*	
Jesus' Inaugural Sermon					
7. Introduction		<6:20a>	5:1−2	6:12, 17, 20a	
8. Blessing and Woes	Be*(****)	6:20b−23, (24−26)	5:3−12	6:20b−26	54, 69b, 68, 69a
9. On Retaliation	WW****(*)	6:27−33, (34−35b), 35c (Q/Matt. 5:4)	5:38−47; 7:12	6:27−35	95, 6b
10. On Judging	WW**	6:36−37b; (Q/Matt. 7:2a); (6:37c−38b), 38c	5:48; 7:1−2	6:36−38	
11. Blind Guides, Teachers and Pupils	WW**	6:39b−40	15:13−14; 10:24−25	6:39−40	
12. On Hypocrisy	WW*	6:41−42	7:3−5	6:41−42	26
13. Good and Evil Men	Pa*****	6:43−45	7:15−20; 12:33−35	6:43−45	43b, 45a, b, c, d
14. The Parable of the Builders	Pa*	6:46−49	7:21−27	6:46−49	
John, Jesus, and This Generation					
15. *The Centurion's Son*	*Na*	*7:1a, 1b−2, (3−5), 6−10*	*8:5−13*	*7:1−10*	
16. John's Inquiry	PP	7:18−19, (20), 22−23	11:2−6	7:18−23	
17. Jesus' Eulogy of John	PP*	7:24−28	11:7−11	7:24−28	78, 45
18. The Kingdom Suffers Violence	PP*	16:16	11:12−15	16:16	
19. John and the Tax Collectors	PP	[7:29−30]	21:28−32	7:29−30	
20. The Children in the Agora [Marketplace]	Pa	7:31−35	11:16−19	7:31−35	
Discipleship and Mission					
21. Three Followers of Jesus	PP*(*)	9:57−60 (61−62)	8:18−22	9:57−62	86
22. The Mission Speech	PP*****	10:2−12	9:36−38; 10:1−16	10:1−12	73, 14b
23. Woes on the Galilean Towns	Or*	10:13−15 (Q/Matt. 11:23b−24)	11:20−24	10:13−15	
24. The Authority of Missionaries	PP*	10:16, [18−20]	10:40	10:16−20	
25. Thanksgiving for Revelation	PP*	10:21−22	11:25−27	10:21−22	
26. Blessing on the Eyewitnesses	Be*	10:23b−24	13:16−17	10:23−24	

Section and Name	Form	Q Text	Matthew	Luke	*GTh*
On Prayer					
27. The Lord's Prayer	Ex* (4a)	11:2–4	6:7–13	11:1–4	2, 92, 94
28. Confidence in Prayer	WW**	11:[5–8], 9–13	7:7–11	11:5–11	
Controversies with This Generation					
29. The Beelzebul Accusation	PP**	11:14–18a, 19–20, (21–22), 23	12:22–30; 9:32–34	11:14–23	
30. The Return of the Evil Spirit	Or*	11:24–26	12:43–45	11:24–26	
31. True Blessedness	Be	(11:27–28)	[no parallel]	11:27–28	
32. The Sign of Jonah	PP*	11:16, 29–32	12:38–42	11:16, 29–32	
33. The Lamp and the Eye	Pa**	11:33–35, (36)	5:14–16; 6:22–23	11:33–36	33b
34. Woes against the Pharisees	Or********	11:39b–44, 46–52	23:1–39; 13:34–35	11:37–54; 13:34–35	39a, 102, 89
On Anxiety					
35. Hidden and Revealed	PP**	12:[1], 2–3	10:26–27	12:1–3	5b, 6b, 33a
36. Appropriate Fear	Or/Pa***	12:4–7	10:28–31	12:4–7	
37. On Confessing Jesus	PP*	12:8–9	10:32–33	12:8–9	
38. Blasphemy of the Spirit	PP*	12:10	12:31–32	12:10	44
39. The Spirit's Assistance	PP*	12:11–12 [Q/Matt. 10:23]	10:17–20, 23	12:11–12	
40. Foolish Possessions		(12:13–14, 16–21)	[no parallel]	12:13–21	
41. Earthly Cares	Pa***	12:22–31	6:25–34	12:22–32,	36, OxyP 655
42. Heavenly Treasure	Pa**	12:33–34	6:19–21	12:33–34	76b
Sayings on the Coming Judgment					
43. Watchful Servants		[12:35–38]	[no parallel]	12:35–38	
44. The Householder and the Thief	Pa**	12:39–40	24:42–44	12:39–40	21c, 103
45. Faithful and Unfaithful Servants	Pa*	12:42b–46	24:45–51	12:41–48	
46. Fire and Division on Earth	PP(*)*	12:(49), 51–53	10:34–36	12:49–53	10, 16
47. Signs of the Times	Pa*	12:54–56	16:2–3	12:54–56	91
48. Agreeing with One's Accuser	Pa*	12:57–59	5:25–26	12:57–59	
Two Parables of Growth					
49. The Mustard and the Leaven	Pa	13:18–21	13:31–33	13:18–21	20, 96
The Two Ways					
50. The Narrow Gate and the Closed Door	WW*(*)*	13:24, (25), 26–27	7:13–14, 22–23	13:22–27	
51. Gentiles in the Kingdom	Pa***	13:28–30	8:11–12; 20:16	13:28–30	4b
52. Lament over Jerusalem	PP*	13:34–35	23:37–39	13:31–35	
53. Livestock in a Pit		[14:5]	12:11–12	14:1–6	
54. Exalting the Humble		14:11/18: 14b	23:6–12	14:7–12; 18:14	
55. The Great Supper	Pa	14:16–24	22:1–10	14:15–24	
56. Being My Disciple	PP**	14:26–27; 17:33	10:37–39	14:25–27; 17:33	55a, 101a, 55b
57. Savorless Salt	PP*	14:34–35	5:13	14:34–35	

(continued on page 554)

Section and Name	Form	Q Text	Matthew	Luke	GTh
Miscellaneous Sayings					
58. The Lost Sheep	Pa	15:4−7	18:10, 12−14	15:1−2, 3−7	
59. The Lost Coin	Pa	(15:8−10)	[no parallel]	15:8−10	
60. God and Mammon	WW*	16:13	6:24	16:13	47a
61. The Kingdom, the Law and Divorce	PP/WW/**	16:16−18	11:12−13; 5:18, 32	16:16−18	
62. On Scandals	*	17:1b−2	18:6−7	17:1−2	
63. Forgiveness	Ex**	17:3b−4	18:15−17, 21−22	17:3−4	
64. On Faith	Ex*	17:6b	17:19−20	17:5−6	
The Eschatological Discourse					
65. The Presence of the Kingdom		[17:20b−21]	[no parallel]	17:20−21	
66. The Coming of the Son of Man	Or****	17:23−24, 26−27, (28−29)	24:23−28, 37−42	17:22−37	3a, (22b, 46b), 51, 113, 61a
	**	30, 34−35, 37b			
67. The Parable of the Talents	Pa*	19:12−13, 15b−26	25:14−30	19:11−27	41
68. Judging Israel	Or	22:28−30	19:27−29	22:24−30	

Appendix Two

The Canon of the New Testament

One use of the term *canon,* derived from a Greek word for "reed" (*kanōn*), refers to holy or sacred books. In antiquity, a reed was often used as a ruler, measuring rod, or "yardstick." Metaphorically it can mean a rule, a standard, a model, a paradigm, and so on.

The formation of a New Testament canon of twenty-seven books began in the later first century C.E. and reached its climax in the late third century C.E. Many books used by Christ believers from this period were rejected; some churches in the Middle East still resist accepting the Book of Revelation. It should be observed that the emergence of the canon paralleled the development of the Western orthodox church, as the conflict with Gnosticism shows. The canon became—and still is—the church's book. To study the Jesus Movement historically and literarily, however, one must include books from the same period outside its canon. The selection in this textbook has included the *Gospel of Thomas* and a few of the earliest Church Fathers.

THE FIRST COLLECTIONS OF PAULINE LETTERS

Some sort of collection of letters attributed to Paul, the earliest writer in the New Testament, probably existed by the end of the first century C.E. By then Ephesians, attributed by most scholars to an admirer of Paul *who knew the other Pauline letters,* was in existence, and the Acts of the Apostles featured Paul as its hero. Moreover, about 95 C.E. a formal letter sent from Rome to Corinth, *1 Clement,* contains references to Romans, 1 Corinthians (*1 Clement* 47.2–4), and perhaps also the Letter to the Hebrews (*1 Clement* 17.1–6; 36.1–6). Similar evidence about collections can be found about 115 C.E. (Ignatius *To the Ephesians* 12.2: "all his letters") and slightly later (*Letter of Polycarp* 3.2). 2 Peter, about 100–125 C.E., mentions "all his [Paul's] letters" as an addition to "scripture" (2 Peter 3:15–16).

It is possible to deduce that by the end of the first century C.E. a collection of ten Pauline letters existed, that is, 1, 2 Thessalonians; 1, 2 Corinthians; Romans; Galatians; Philippians; Colossians; and Philemon, plus Ephesians, perhaps as a cover letter. Marcion knew some such a collection by about 150 C.E. The four other letters attributed to Paul are not listed as such before about 200 C.E.

THE FIRST ACCEPTANCE OF GOSPELS

A collection of gospels is more difficult to track. The **Two-Source Theory** implies that at least the second gospel and other sources such as collections of Jesus' sayings (Q) were known and used by the authors of Matthew and Luke. Indeed, the latter explicitly notes that other gospels were in existence (Luke 1:1–4). Meanwhile, oral tradition continued. The four gospels were probably not known by the names that we know them before the middle of the second century (see Chapter Two).

The earliest testimony to gospels as "scripture" comes from the early second century (2 *Clement* 2:4 [Matt. 9:13 = Mark 2:17; cf. Luke 5:32]). Somewhat later, a Church Father named Justin Martyr, writing about what is read in worship, speaks of the gospels as "the memoirs of *the apostles*" along side the prophets (Justin, *Apology,* pp. 66, 67).

THE INFLUENCE OF MARCION
AND GNOSTICISM

Marcion flourished in the middle of the second century C.E. Influenced by Gnosticism, he held that the creator deity was the God of the Old Testament, the God of judgment, but that Jesus had revealed another, supreme God, the God of love, previously unknown. Thus Marcion flatly rejected the God of the Hebrew scriptures and thus the Old Testament (Septuagint) for Christ believers. He further believed that the revelation by Jesus had been hopelessly corrupted by the Twelve but correctly preserved by Paul. To support his views Marcion drew on the ten-letter collection of the Pauline corpus and an edited version of the Gospel of Luke that he believed represented Paul's gospel and was written by Paul's companion (see Chapter Ten). Marcion apparently edited down his text of Luke, and perhaps also that of the Pauline letters, to bring it into line with his own understanding of the revelation of God's love by Jesus. The point here is that something new occurred: a set of authoritative writings distinct from the Hebrew scriptures, consisting of two parts, "the gospel" and "the apostle." Although condemned as a heretic by the emerging orthodox churches, Marcion attracted a wide following.

By the late second century, Gnosticism had become more developed and very influential. Marcion limited his "canon," but most Gnostic believers used a greater number of books. The orthodox churches responded by expanding their canon in relation to Marcion but limiting it in relation to other Gnostic groups. They appealed (as did the Gnostics!) to "apostolic" writings, that is, those thought to have been written by apostles but also used in public worship in churches thought to have been founded by apostles and believed to support "apostolic" or orthodox ideas. In this same period (ca. 140–150 C.E.) Papias, bishop of Hierapolis, was the first to write about Matthew and Mark (see **Historical Criticism,** Chapter Two).

OTHER PAULINE LETTERS

The three Pastoral Letters (1 Timothy, 2 Timothy, Titus) and Hebrews were added to the ten-letter collection sometime in the second half of the second century C.E. The Pastorals were undoubtedly more easily accepted because of their opposition to (Gnostic?) Docetism. The **Muratorian Canon** (named for its discoverer) was an official list of the books of the New Testament, perhaps written at Rome toward the end of the second century. It is opposed to Gnosticism. It accepts the Pastorals, but not Hebrews, which was not easily accepted in the West. Yet, Origen, head of the Catechetical School in Alexandria in 203, reports that Hebrews was accepted everywhere. Although he had doubts about Pauline authorship, he justified its acceptance because he thought that its thought was Pauline.

Although other letters circulated in Paul's name (e.g., the Letter to the Laodiceans), the Pauline part of the canon (fourteen letters) was now complete. The Muratorian Canon refers to several "which cannot be received into the catholic church, for gold ought not to be mixed with honey."

THE FOUR GOSPELS AND THE *DIATESSARON*

Many gospels were produced and in use in the movement that went back to Jesus. About 170 C.E. a Syrian Christ believer by the name of Tatian wove four gospels—those that were eventually accepted into the canon—into a single narrative called the *Diatessaron* (Greek for "through the four"). This shows that these four gospels had been initially accepted in the East; yet, the popularity of the *Diatessaron* in Syria for more than three centuries was a clear challenge to the acceptance of four separate gospels, which eventually came with the Syriac *Peshitta*. In the West, about 185, Irenaeus, bishop of Lyons (in modern France), refers to the "fourfold gospel" (Greek: *tetraeuangelion*) and makes the following comment:

> And it is impossible that the gospels can be either more in number or, on the other hand, less than they are. For since there are four zones of the world in which we are, and also four principal winds, and [since] the church is scattered throughout the whole world, and since the pillar and support of the church is the gospel and the Spirit of life, it is natural that she should have four pillars breathing out immortality all over the rekindling of people.
> (Irenaeus, *Against Heresies* 3.11.8)

THE MURATORIAN CANON

The Muratorian Canon, an official list of books perhaps from Rome toward the end of the second century, is anti-Marcionite in tone. It speaks of a letter "to the Laodiceans, another to the Alexandrians, forged in Paul's name for the sect of

Marcion." This canon lists the four gospels, Matthew, Mark, Luke, John; the Acts of the Apostles; thirteen letters of Paul (omitting Hebrews); Jude; 1 and 2 John; the Wisdom of Solomon (in the Old Testament Apocrypha!); and two apocalypses (Revelation and the "apocalypse" of Peter).

From this point forward the church in the West maintained only the four gospels as canonical. Acts also had a firm place in the canon, as did thirteen letters attributed to Paul. Other books remained in dispute for some time. Some were dropped and others added. The tendency was to accept literature used in emergent Catholicism, an understandable tendency because of its orthodox characteristics.

THE CANON IN THE THIRD CENTURY

In the third century, Tertullian (about 160–220), writing in Latin (not Greek), is the first writer to speak of the "New Testament." Compared with the Muratorian Canon, he omits 2 John, the apocalypse of Peter, and the Wisdom of Solomon, but adds 1 Peter. Origen (185–254), who wrote in Greek in the East, mainly in Alexandria, distinguishes between twenty-two "acknowledged" books (four gospels, all fourteen letters attributed to Paul [adding Hebrews], Acts, 1 John, 1 Peter, and Revelation) and five often "disputed" books (James [mentioned for the first time], Jude, 2 Peter, 2 and 3 John). These are all the books that finally constituted the canon of the New Testament.

A feature of the later third century in the East was a dispute about the Book of Revelation. It was rejected in Alexandria and Antioch, and although it was eventually restored to the canon it never achieved the same status as the other books in Greek-speaking Christianity, and it has never achieved full canonical status in the Syrian churches.

THE CANON IN THE FOURTH CENTURY

About 325, Eusebius of Caesarea completed his famous *Ecclesiastical History.* In it he reports on the state of the New Testament canon in the Greek-speaking churches of the eastern Mediterranean. He is the first writer to speak of a distinct group of the "seven so-called Catholic epistles" (1, 2, 3 John; 1, 2 Peter; James; Jude), but he agrees with Origen that James, Jude, 2 Peter, and 2, 3 John are "disputed." He is ambiguous about Revelation, and he notes that because Hebrews is not accepted as Pauline at Rome, some also reject it.

The most important event in the fourth century in the East was, however, **the Festal Letter of Athanasius,** bishop of Alexandria, circulated among the churches under his charge in 367. In it, he listed as "scriptures of the New Testament" precisely the twenty-seven books now accepted in the West, with none "disputed." When Jerome made his Latin translation in the latter part of the fourth century, he followed the Athanasian canon of the New Testament, although in a letter to Paulinus written about 385, he acknowledged the difficulties some had with Hebrews and Revelation.

FURTHER HISTORY OF THE NEW TESTAMENT CANON

The *Festal Letter* of Athanasius in the East and the work of Jerome in the West settled the extent of the New Testament canon everywhere except Syria, where the *Diatessaron,* Acts, and fifteen letters of Paul (including a third letter to Corinth) prevailed. In the early fifth century, however, the four separate gospels replaced the *Diatessaron,* 3 Corinthians was omitted, and James, 1 Peter, and 1 John were added. Thus the Syrian church agreed with the rest of the orthodox churches except for Jude, 2 Peter, 2 John, 3 John (four of Origen's five "disputed" books), and Revelation. The accommodation would doubtless have gone further, but in the fifth century fierce controversies about the doctrine of Christ split the Syrian church and separated it from the rest of the churches. These five books, especially Revelation, were never fully accepted in Syrian Christianity.

The only other factor that needs to be mentioned here is that for some time other books were sometimes accepted in some places. For example, the fifth-century manuscript Codex Alexandrinus includes *1 Clement* and *2 Clement* in its New Testament.

In short, with the exception of Syria, the twenty-seven-book canon gained general acceptance. The acceptance was by common consent rather than by formal pronouncement of general church council.

EXTRACANONICAL EARLY CHURCH LITERATURE

In Chapter Two it was noted that "**Patristic citations**" are part of the evidence for reconstructing the original text of the New Testament. The **Patristic Literature** contains the writings of the **Church Fathers** (or **Apostolic Fathers**). Several of these writings hovered on the edge of acceptance into the canon of the New Testament, for example, *1* and *2 Clement,* the *Shepherd of Hermas,* the *Epistle of Barnabas,* and the *Didachē.* Although these were finally rejected, they continued to exercise considerable influence in the early churches.

A large quantity of other literature in the churches, some but not all of it Gnostic in character, was once in use among Christ believers of the early centuries, but it was eventually rejected by the orthodox churches. This literature included other gospels, letters attributed to Paul and others, acts of various apostles, and apocalypses. Those that survive are now collected in the **New Testament Apocrypha.** Furthermore, it is necessary to note the Nag Hammadi Library (see Chapter Two and Appendix Three). Logically it belongs with the New Testament Apocrypha. However, it is customarily discussed in isolation because it is a single discovery. It contains the *Gospel of Thomas.* Some scholars also value very highly the *Gospel of Peter* (mainly an account of Jesus' resurrection), the *Secret Gospel of Mark* (probably a longer version of Mark, passages of which are purported to have been discovered in 1957), and *Egerton Papyrus 2* (a few variant passages of the gospel stories).

Finally, there are various isolated sayings of Jesus found here and there, for example, in Acts 20:35 ("To give is more blessed than to receive"), in select manuscripts of New Testament books (Manuscript D of Luke 6:34), or in various other documents of the early churches. These isolated sayings are called **Agrapha.**

Appendix Three

Major Archeological and Textual
Discoveries and Publications

ARCHEOLOGY

In the narrow sense, *archeology* refers to the science of recovering (by planned field excavations) and evaluating the material remains of everyday life from past civilizations. In the broader sense, *archeology* includes manuscripts that have been discovered apart from field excavation, whether by searching or by accident. Because archeological and textual discoveries and publications relating to the period of the New Testament are much too numerous to describe in a short appendix, only some of the most important ones will be noted.

The Dead Sea Scrolls and Khirbet Qumran

In the spring of 1947 two Arab shepherd boys of the Bedouin Ta'amireh tribe were grazing their flocks of sheep and goats at the foot of the cliffs about a mile west of the Dead Sea, about twelve miles east of Jerusalem. The site, the lowest land point on the earth's surface, is adjacent to the ancient ruins of the Wadi Qumran (a *wadi* [Arabic] is a dry riverbed that fills up in the rainy season). As the story goes, according to the boys, one of the animals strayed, and in their search for it, Muhammed ed-Dib threw a stone into one of the cave openings high up the face of a cliff. He heard a shattering sound and, perhaps fearful of demons, fled. Later, Muhammed and Ahmed Muhammed returned to the cave and found elongated jars partly buried in the cave floor, one of them containing leather scrolls. Muhammed ed-Dib had discovered the first of the Dead Sea Scrolls, which W. F. Albright later called "the greatest manuscript discovery of modern times. . ." (letter to John Trevor).

Secret, illegal excavations by the Bedouins and illegal buying and selling characterized the following period. Professor E. L. Sukenik purchased some manuscripts in a Jerusalem antiquities shop for the Hebrew University in Jerusalem. The Syrian Orthodox metropolitan of Jerusalem acquired another lot from the Bethlehem shoemaker and middleman Kando. It was subsequently identified by scholars at the American Schools of Oriental Research, taken to the United States by the metropolitan, and finally sold to an agent of noted Israeli archeologist Yigael Yadin on behalf of the Hebrew University for $250,000 in 1954. Meanwhile, Arab-Israeli fighting frustrated attempts to carry out scientific excavations in the caves or near the place of discovery, Khirbet Qumran, until 1949. The fantastic episode seemed closed. However, further digging by Arab Ta'amireh tribesmen in 1951 uncovered more scrolls in caves at nearby Wadi Murabba'at. More bargaining with antiquities dealers took place, and a series of scientific excavations of the caves in the general area was begun.

In 1951 the first excavations at the nearby ruins known as Khirbet ("ruin") Qumran took place. Eventually excavations of other sites were undertaken. Two miles south at Khirbet Feskhah was an agricultural complex. Nine miles inland at Khirbet Mird was a Hasmonean fortress. Twelve miles south at Wadi Murabba'at were four caves containing Greek, Aramaic, and Hebrew materials related to the bar Cochba Revolt of the Israelites in 132–135 c.e. They included letters of the revolutionary Israelite leader, Simon bar Kosibah (see Chapter One). A few other valleys and caves to the south were explored.

More discoveries by the Ta'amireh tribesmen and further scientific explorations in eleven caves by the Wadi Qumran, as well as at several other nearby sites, led to the remains of about eight hundred books, mostly in small fragments, but including about ten complete scrolls. This was a library of significant proportions. Most of the manuscripts were written on parchment (leather), although a few were on papyrus, and two were on copper. The most valuable finds were discovered in Cave I (the first discovered), Cave IV, and Cave XI. After many years of delay marked by scholarly controversy, intrigue, and pressure from outside scholars who were not on the original team of paleographers (backed by the journal *Biblical Archaeology Review*), all the texts have now been published.

About one-fourth of the scrolls are books that found their way into the Hebrew Bible, all thirty-nine books of that Bible being represented except the Book of Esther. Four other categories of literature in the scrolls are Apocrypha and Pseudepigrapha (see following); biblical commentaries exemplifying the *pesher* method of interpretation; apocalyptic, sectarian writings such as the War of the Sons of Light against the Sons of Darkness; and Rules for the Community (the Manual of Discipline). All three languages—Hebrew, Aramaic, and Greek—are found in the scrolls, Hebrew by far predominating. The presence of books from the Apocrypha and Pseudepigrapha is further testimony that prior to 70 c.e. a much larger and more diversified body of sacred literature was in use and that there was as yet no fixed text.

Scroll discoveries led to further excavations of Khirbet Qumran. The site originally contained a water supply system with aqueduct, cisterns and baths, an assembly and banquet hall, kitchen and pantry, laundry, scriptorium (a room for copying texts), pottery workshops, storerooms, stables, watchtower, and a cemetery nearby. The first period of occupation, 135 to 31 b.c.e., ended with an earthquake. The second period of occupation, 4 b.c.e. to 68 c.e., ended with its destruction by the Romans.

The attempts to identify the authors of the Dead Sea Scrolls and the original inhabitants of Khirbet Qumran are related. Although there are arguments that the scrolls came from the Sadducees or represent a Jerusalem library relocated to the site at the time of the advance of the Romans in 68 c.e., most scholars still hold that the scrolls belonged to, and represent the ideas of, the Essenes, a sect described by the ancient writers Josephus, Philo, and Pliny the Elder. Similarly, although arguments have been put forward that Khirbet Qumran was originally a Roman villa or a Roman fortress, most scholars still hold that it was originally the ancient settlement of the Essenes.

The organization of the Qumran community is based on several texts, especially the Manual of Discipline. It included divisions into priests and laity; the domination of the priests, including a priest-president who presided at the sacred meal; an overseer who had power over admissions, instruction, and various practical matters; a guardian of all the "camps"; a council of the community; a future lay leader (perhaps a royal messiah); a Court of Inquiry to try offenders; an annual assembly at the Feast of the Renewal of the Covenant; nightly study and prayer; and a two-year initiation for new members. Several important beliefs and practices were that the community is the elect, purified remnant of Israel that will be vindicated in the final days (apocalyptic eschatology); that the Jerusalem temple and its priesthood are polluted and are replaced by the community and its worship life; close adherence to ritual laws and seasonal festivals according to a solar calendar; the maintenance of purity by ritual baths; a sacred meal in which bread and wine are served and which anticipates the Messianic banquet; a dualistic eschatology that opposes light, good, and angelic powers against darkness, evil, and the demonic powers; the hope for a prophet, as well as a Messiah of Aaron (priestly) and a Messiah of Israel (royal); and the anticipation of a post-Messianic age that includes a new Jerusalem.

The discovery of the Dead Sea Scrolls was an amazing event. Uncovered were Old Testament texts in Hebrew that predated previously known texts by a thousand years; the history of the Old Testament textual traditions was dramatically changed; knowledge of a little-known Israelite sect was impressively revealed; the understanding of pre-70 C.E. Israel was totally transformed; and a sectarian movement parallel to the Jesus Movement was uncovered, one that continues to provide invaluable information for the environment of the origins of the Jesus Movement.

Photos: http://www.kchanson.com/LINKS/ancweb.html#11

http://orion.mscc.huji.ac.il/

http://www.ibiblio.org/expo/deadsea.scrolls.exhibit/intro.html

Masada

About thirty miles south of Khirbet Qumran along the Dead Sea is a magnificent mesa, the flat top of which covers about twenty acres, with steep rock cliffs rising about 600 feet on the west side and about 820 feet on the east. This natural fortress was accessible only by two paths. One is the treacherous "snake path." The other narrows at one point, making it easy to defend. On the top of the mesa Herod the Great built a walled fortress that he named "Masada" ("mountain stronghold"). The Israelite writer Josephus has immortalized the location with his exciting, but tragic, tale of the last stand of the revolutionaries and their mass suicide in order not to be taken alive by the Romans (Josephus *Wars* 7.8–9). Although some scholars question Josephus' story, the site remains symbolic of Israeli patriotism to this day.

Initial surveys of the well-known site in 1953 and 1955–1956 led to a full-scale archeological expedition in 1963–1965 headed by Israeli archeologist Yigael Yadin. The discoveries revealed three main periods of occupation: (1) Herodian (37–4 B.C.E.); (2) the period of the Israelite Rebellion against Rome and its aftermath (66–73 C.E.); and (3) the Byzantine period (fifth–sixth centuries C.E.). Because there was no water supply, Herod built dams on two small *wadis* below, and in the rainy season the water flowed by channels to two huge reservoirs cut into the cliff on the northwest side. From there the water was carried by slaves to cisterns on the top, all together the cisterns holding about 1,400,000 cubic feet of water. Herod's casemate wall surrounding the top (except for the villa) had thirty towers and four gates. Also on the top Herod constructed a series of storerooms for provisions, an intimate and luxurious three-tiered palace-villa at the north end, a huge western palace for administration and ceremony, several small palaces for family members and high-ranking officials, a luxurious bathhouse, and a swimming pool.

Prior to the revolt in 66 C.E., a Roman garrison was bivouacked in Masada, but, at the outbreak of the revolt, the insurrectionists took it by trickery and adapted it for themselves and their families. They also constructed ritual baths, a synagogue, and what may be a "religious study house." Excavators have uncovered in the western palace many burnt arrows and coins and in the smaller palaces scrolls of the scriptures of the famous second-century B.C.E. sage, ben Sira, and of some Qumran literature, indicating that some point of contact existed between the Essenes and the Masada resistors. About seven hundred *ostraca* (pieces of pottery often used for ballots) show not only Hebrew and Aramaic writing, but also Greek and Latin. Built into Masada there is still visible a gigantic dirt ramp on which a huge battering ram was brought forward by the Romans in their siege of the fortress. A Roman garrison remained after the siege. Subsequently, Masada was deserted until some Christian monks settled there and built a church, as well as a few rooms and cells. See the photo at the beginning of Chapter One.

Photo: http://faculty.smu.edu/dbinder/masada.html

The Nag Hammadi Texts (the Nag Hammadi Library)

The Nag Hammadi Library is not a library in the usual sense, but rather ancient books found near the southern Egyptian village of Nag Hammadi. The precise details of their discovery are not clear. One account is that late in 1945, an Egyptian peasant boy, Abu al-Majd, discovered twelve papyrus codices plus part of a thirteenth (tucked into Codex VI) bound in portfolio-like leather covers and stored in a ceramic jar under an overhanging rock at the base of the Jabal el-Tarif. This cliff is located in southern ("Upper") Egypt near the Nile River villages of Chenoboskia (once a monastic center) and Nag Hammadi. The peasant boy was said to be accompanied by six others, one of whom was his oldest brother, Muhammad 'Ali, who took charge. Muhammad broke open the jar and, upon finding the codices, decided to divide them up among the seven camel drivers present. When the fearful and unknowing drivers refused their shares, Muhammad put them in a pile, wrapped them in his white headdress, and, slinging them over his shoulder, mounted his camel and headed for his home in Chenoboskia. The usual confusion and intrigue followed: The scrolls made their way to middlemen, then to antiquities dealers, and finally to the Coptic Museum in Old Cairo, Egypt. The "Jung Codex" was an exception; it was taken to the United States and then to Brussels, Belgium, where it was purchased for the C. G. Jung Institute in Zurich, Switzerland, and presented to the eminent psychiatrist Carl Jung as a birthday present. Subsequently (after its publication) the codex was returned to Cairo.

The official announcement of the discovery of the Nag Hammadi "library" was in 1956. It consists of copies of Coptic translations of fifty-one Greek texts (Coptic is an Egyptian language written with mostly Greek letters). In their present form as copies, they date from about the fourth/fifth century C.E., but some of the original autographs are much older and the Greek originals still older. The collection represents many literary genres, some like those found in the canonical New Testament. It contains gospels, apocalypses, acts, letters, dialogues, secret books, speculative treatises, wisdom literature, biblical interpretations, revelation discourses, and prayers. The texts also represent various types of Gnosticism known from the early Church Fathers, as well as the Egyptian Hermetic literature and non-Gnostic writings, such as Plato's *Republic*. Yet, they often show strong influence of biblical traditions and interpretations, for example, the Genesis myth of creation, the Wisdom myth, various techniques of scriptural interpretation, and the apocalyptic periodization of history.

Scholars fiercely debate the origins of Gnosticism. These texts simply add to the debate. Some of them seem to be "pagan," but this does not answer the question of whether their originals were earlier than the Jesus Movement. Nonetheless, it has been demonstrated that a pagan text in the collection (*Eugostos the Blessed*) was reworked for Christ believers (the *Sophia of Jesus Christ*). This is all the more interesting when it is observed that the Nag Hammadi text called the *Apocalypse of Adam* appears to be pagan, maybe dating as early as the second century C.E., yet it contains the full-blown "Gnostic Redeemer Myth." This would seem to support the *possibility* that those who interpreted Jesus as the divine Christ could have been influenced by such a myth.

The most important text for the interpretation of the Jesus Movement is the Coptic *Gospel of Thomas* from Nag Hammadi. It contains a collection of Jesus' sayings, including some thirteen parables that are variants of synoptic gospel parables. The discovery of a "sayings gospel" is important for the hypothesis that Q was such a collection (see Appendix One); moreover, a comparison of the forms of the *Thomas* parables with those of the synoptic tradition shows that *Thomas* has often preserved simpler, probably earlier, forms of some of Jesus' parables. Its value for interpreting the Jesus tradition is therefore immense (see Chapters Three and Fourteen).

Until the discovery of the Nag Hammadi texts, what was known about Gnosticism came primarily through the attacks of anti-Gnostic Church Fathers. Now what some Gnostics believed can be learned from a set of Gnostic texts. In short, these texts are immensely valuable for the light they shed not only on the Gnostic movement, but also on the history of the Israelites and Christ believers in the Greco-Roman period. (See the photo at the beginning of Chapter Seven.)

Gospel of Thomas: http://home.epix.net/~miser17/Thomas.html (S. Davies)

THE OLD TESTAMENT PSEUDEPIGRAPHA

The term *Pseudepigrapha* means literally "false writings" because they are non-canonical writings that for the most part are inspired by, written in honor of, and attributed to Old Testament heroes who did not write them. In other words, they are pseudonymous. The term *Pseudepigrapha* is not totally satisfactory because Old Testament writings, like those in the New Testament, are also pseudonymous, and not every book in the Pseudepigrapha collection is pseudonymous. Yet, no better term has been found for these books.

Briefly, they are books that come from either Israelites or Christ believers from the approximate period 250 B.C.E. to 250 C.E., books that are normally considered to be inspired or related to the Hebrew Bible (Old Testament) and are usually attributed to some Old Testament figure. Usually excluded are most (but not all) of the books from the same period, called the Old Testament Apocrypha (although most of the Old Testament Apocrypha is the Roman Catholic Old Testament; see Appendix Two). Also excluded are the Dead Sea Scrolls and the Coptic Gnostic Nag Hammadi Texts because they are special discoveries, although some would like to include the (apparently pagan) *Apocalypse of Adam,* and certainly *by definition* many of the Dead Sea Scrolls could be included. The rabbinic literature (especially the Mishnah and the Talmuds), preserved for centuries by Jewish scholars, is also excluded, although this body of literature has some traditions that go back to the period covered by the Pseudepigrapha.

The Pseudepigrapha or parts thereof can be found in a number of modern editions. The classic is volume 2 of the two-volume collection by R. H. Charles called *Apocrypha and Pseudepigrapha of the Old Testament.* It contains seventeen writings, introduced and extensively annotated. More recent and comprehensive is the two-volume edition edited by J. H. Charlesworth, *The Old Testament Pseudepigrapha.* Because of new discoveries, publications of little-known manuscripts, further evaluation of previously known documents, and the inclusion of a few documents that might fall outside the dating boundaries, this edition contains sixty-three documents with introductions and annotations.

The Pseudepigrapha contains a wide variety of forms and genres, including apocalypses, testaments, prayers, psalms, hymns, odes, oracles, and legends, and the material contains not only apocalyptic eschatology, but also much information about some of the more esoteric aspects of Greco-Roman Israel and the Jesus Movement, for example, astrology and magic. In short, although the Pseudepigrapha is not a completely new discovery in the sense of the Dead Sea Scrolls or the Nag Hammadi Texts, much of it is either new or scarcely known, and it is an important addition to the noncanonical materials of the period.

SINAITICUS

An especially interesting example of a "rediscovery" of a manuscript is Codex ("Book") Sinaiticus, a fourth-century manuscript. Originally it contained the whole **Septuagint,** as well as the New Testament, and two noncanonical works, the *Epistle of Barnabas* and the *Shepherd of Hermas.* Indeed, Codex Sinaiticus contains one of the two most important more or less *complete* manuscripts of the New Testament. The usual story of its discovery is that in 1844 a German textual critic, Constantin von Tischendorf, went to the Sinai Peninsula east of the Red Sea looking for manuscripts. There he saw in the Monastery of Saint Catherine at the foot of Jebel Musa ("Mount of Moses," the traditional site of Mount Sinai) a basket of manuscripts that had been used by the monks to start fires. Permitted by the monks to examine them, von Tischendorf discovered that they included the **Septuagint** of four books of the Old Testament, as well as Tobit and 2 Esdras, a total of forty-three pages. The monks claimed that some baskets had already perished. The excited von Tischendorf was granted permission to take these forty-three pages to the University of Leipzig, where they were presented to his patron, the king of Saxony, and where they remain in the university library. Keeping silent about their place of origin, he returned in 1853 but was unsuccessful in being able to see the rest of the codex. However, on the last day of a third visit in 1859, von Tischendorf showed the steward of the monastery his own 1846 printed edition of the other pages, whereupon the steward showed him a great portion of the rest of the codex, 347 leaves, wrapped in a red cloth. The secretly excited von Tischendorf stayed up all night looking at its contents and discovered that it also contained the New Testament. Refused permission to buy it, he went to Cairo, prevailed upon the abbot to have it sent there, and then copied it, eight pages at a time. Eventually, for certain monetary gifts and ecclesiastical favors to the Greek Orthodox monks by the czar of Russia, von Tischendorf's current patron, the codex was presented to the czar and a facsimile edition published at Leipzig. Almost half of the manuscript (Genesis to 1 Chronicles in the LXX) is missing. Finally, after the Russian Revolution, the Russian government, in need of cash, sold this part of Sinaiticus to the British Museum, whence it was finally delivered in 1933 and where it is now prominently displayed. Curiously, a dozen more leaves of the codex (from Genesis) turned up in 1975 in the wake of a fire at the monastery, but they have not been formally published.

Photo: http://www.earlham.edu/~seidti/iam/tc_codexs.html

MISCELLANEOUS PALESTINIAN ARCHEOLOGY

Herod the Great's Building Projects

The Jerusalem temple. Herod the Great began the rebuilding of the magnificent Jerusalem temple about 20 B.C.E. and, although the basic construction was completed in about eighteen months, work was still being done probably until the Romans destroyed it in 70 C.E. Because of the destruction, reconstruction is partly imaginary and must be done with the aid of 1 Kings and Josephus' works as literary sources. The bottom sections of the Western Wall are Herodian, and on it can be seen evidence of Robinson's Arch and Wilson's Arch. There is also an excavation from Roman times on the North Wall at the Damascus Gate.

http://www.erskine.edu/seminary/lowe/biblical_theology/sld009.htm (Erskine Seminary, Lowe's slide 9 [L. Ritmeyer's reconstruction])

http://www.bibleplaces.com/templemount.htm (Bibleplaces.com) http://www.bibleplaces.com/westernwall.htm (Bibleplaces.com)

http://www.kchanson.com/PTJ/temple.html (K. C. Hanson)

http://faculty.smu.edu/dbinder/jerusalem.html (D. D. Binder, "Jerusalem")

Masada. Herod's most famous palace-fortress complex (see preceding).

Herodium. Another of Herod's opulent palace-fortresses built atop a high hill not far from Bethlehem.

http://faculty.smu.edu/dbinder/herodium.html (D. D. Binder)

Jericho. Herod's luxurious winter palace in the warm Jordan valley.

Photo: http://faculty.smu.edu/dbinder/jerusalem.html (D. D. Binder)

Caesarea Maritima. A seaport-city on the Mediterranean Sea, the "Roman capital of Judea."

http://www.padfield.com/tours/cmphoto1.html (Church of Christ, Zion, IL)

http://www.greatcommission.com/israel/CaesareaMaritimaPilateInscription.jpg (Pontius Pilate Inscription)

http://www.greatcommission.com/israel/CaesareaMaritimaRomanAqueduct.jpg

Other Discoveries in and near Jerusalem

The Herodian Palace Area, City Buildings, Streets.

The James Ossuary. Bearing the inscription in Aramaic, "James, son of Joseph, brother of Jesus," this 20-inch-long "bone box" may be the earliest archeological evidence for Jesus.

http://www.kchanson.com/ANCDOCS/westsem/james.html

Theodotus Inscription. One important find is the Theodotus Inscription (pre-70 C.E. date now debated). It is a dedicatory inscription that shows that a Greek-speaking synagogue had existed in Jerusalem.

http://faculty.smu.edu/dbinder/jerusalem.html (D. D. Binder)

The crucifixion of Jehohanan. A small slab containing a spike and heel bones discovered in tombs northeast of Jerusalem represents the only surviving archeological remains of the crucifixion of a first-century Israelite.

http://www.pbs.org/wgbh/pages/frontline/shows/religion/jesus/crucifixion.html (J. H. Charlesworth)

http://www.uncc.edu/jdtabor/crucifixion.html (J. H. Tabor)

The tomb of the High Priest Caiaphas.

http://www.bibleplaces.com/westernwall.htm (Bibleplaces.com)

http://www.livius.org/caa-can/caiaphas/caiaphas.htm (J. Lendering)

The "Burnt House." Jerusalem house destroyed by the Romans in 70 C.E.

http://www.abu.nb.ca/courses/NTIntro/images/Burnthouse.htm (B. D. Smith)

Israelite Synagogues

Archeological evidence that synagogue buildings existed in Palestine before 70 C.E. is sparse. (There is, however, first-century evidence for synagogues outside Palestine.) Palestinian evidence is limited to a few rooms (Masada, Herodium, Magdala, Gamla), possibly a third-century structure underneath a fourth/fifth-century synagogue at Capernaum, and possibly a Greek-speaking synagogue in Jerusalem (note the uncertain date of the Theodotus Inscription). Because this small amount of evidence conflicts with Josephus' writings and the New Testament, the problem may be one of definition: There may have existed rooms in houses used as synagogues ("house-synagogues" similar to "house-churches").

http://faculty.smu.edu/dbinder/index.html (D. D. Binder)

Galilean Towns/Cities and Other Sites

Excavations in "Lower (southern) Galilee" and along the Sea of Galilee show that much of Galilee was not a "cultural backwater," as once thought.

Discoveries at **Sepphoris,** an administrative capital along a major trade route, reveal a Greco-Roman cultural and religious presence only four miles from the village of Nazareth, Jesus' hometown. Such excavations play a role in the discussions about possible Greco-Roman ("Hellenistic") influences on Jesus and the Jesus Movement. One example is the use of Greek as well as Hebrew and Aramaic. Another is unconventional "wisdom" in Q.

http://www.centuryone.org/sepphoris.html (Century One foundation)

Sea of Galilee harbors and anchorages.

http://www.urantiabook.org/graphics/sogports.htm (Bibleplaces.com [M. Nun])

Galilee boat.

http://www.leaderu.com/theology/craftmatches.html (S. Moore)

http://www.israel.org/mfa/go.asp?MFAH0gc00 (State of Israel)

Capernaum, a center of Jesus' activity, preserves the remains of a house under which may be more remains of a house belonging to Jesus' disciple Peter. It also has the ruins of a fourth- or fifth-century synagogue, although under it are Early Roman walls, probably from the third century.

Photos: http://www.bibleplaces.com/capernaum.htm (Bibleplaces.com)

http://faculty.smu.edu/dbinder/capernaum.html (D. D. Binder)

Bethsaida, fishing village, another center of Jesus' activity.

Photo: http://www.bibleplaces.com/bethsaida.htm (Bibleplaces.com)

http://www.greatcommission.com/israel/BethsaidaFishermanHouse.jpg

Nazareth, Jesus' hometown.

Photos: http://198.62.75.1/www1/ofm/san/TSnzarc2.html (franciscan cyberspot)

Cana, story of Jesus changing water to wine

http://www.nexfind.com/cana/index.html (Carrie Reed)

http://www.ups.edu/community/cana/sitepg.htm (D. R. Edwards)

Other Greco-Roman Cities and Religious Sites

Forums, main streets, town squares, marketplaces, theaters, baths, stadiums, hippodromes, aqueducts, coliseums, houses, banquet rooms, and the like give glimpses of "urban" social life throughout the Roman Empire. Temples, groves, caves, theaters, mosaics, vase and wall paintings, and the like reveal the awe and mystery of Greco-Roman religious life.

Glossary

Abomination That Makes Desolate A pagan altar erected by the Seleucid Greeks over the Jerusalem temple alter, on which the Seleucids offered sacrifices to Zeus, thus defiling the temple (Dan. 11:31; 1 Macc. 1:54; Mark 13:14). See **Hanukkah, Feast of; Maccabean Revolt.**

Actium, Battle of A battle on the Mediterranean Sea near Actium, 31 B.C.E., in which Octavian's forces defeated Antony's, setting the stage for establishing the Roman Empire.

Agrapha Isolated sayings of Jesus outside the New Testament canon.

Allegory A comparison story, the several parts of which symbolically point to persons, virtues, and other realities outside the story.

Amanuensis A secretary, especially one to whom a letter is dictated.

Anecdote A brief, reputedly biographical episode, often ending with a punch line.

Anonymity, Anonymous From Greek *a-*, "without" or "no," and *onoma*, "name," thus to have no known name, to be unknown. See **Pseudonymity.**

Antilanguage In sociolinguistics, the intentional use of language in new and distinct ways by marginal groups, for example, (1) new metaphorical uses, (2) different words for the same concept, (3) wordplay, (4) symbol, (5) irony, (6) repetition, (7) antitheses, (8) **intercalations,** and (9) **chiasms.** See **Chiasm, Intercalation, Antisociety.**

Antioch Incident Paul claimed that Peter was a hypocrite for refusing to eat with Gentiles when conservative Israelite believers from Jerusalem arrived (Gal. 2:11–14).

Antisociety A marginal social group that consciously sets itself apart from the larger society, distinguishing itself in part by antilanguage. See **Antilanguage.**

Aphorism A short, pithy, challenging wisdom saying.

Apocalypse From the Greek *apokalypsis,* "an uncovering" or "revelation" (Rev. 1:1), a book or part of a book that records visual and auditory revelations of a seer in an ecstatic state about the future or the heavenly world, believed to come from an otherworldly medium, sometimes in the form of dreams. See **ASC.**

Apocalyptic An adjective derived from *apocalypse,* but often used as an umbrella term to encompass (1) apocalypses; (2) apocalyptic eschatology; and (3) apocalypticism. See **Apocalypse, Apocalyptic Eschatology, Apocalypticism.**

Apocalyptic Eschatology A particular kind of thought that stresses revelations about the "end" (Greek: *eschaton*). See **Apocalyptic, Apocalypticism, Eschatology.**

Apocalypticism Describes a social movement, sometimes political, that is typified by apocalyptic eschatology. See **Millennialism, Apocalyptic Eschatology.**

Apocrypha From the Greek *apocryphos,* "hidden," used of books that were not accepted into the final canon of scripture. Such books were "hidden" from the faithful in the church. Used alone, it refers to the **Old Testament Apocrypha.**

Aporia Greek for "difficulty," interruptions in the flow of a narrative, such as sudden shifts in geographical location, time, theme, language, or style.

Apostle From the Greek *apostolos,* "envoy," "messenger," or in the religious sense, "missionary," used for Jesus' immediate disciples in Luke-Acts.

Apostolic Decree Cultic requirements for newly converted Gentiles in Acts 15:20.

Apostolic Fathers See **Church Fathers.**

Apostolic Succession The conviction that a leader's authority in the churches is passed on through "laying on of hands" going back to the original apostles.

Aramaic Descended from ancient Hebrew, an international language of the East that became the vernacular of most eastern Israelites, including Jesus and the first disciples, in the first century C.E. See **Targums.**

Archeology See Appendix Three.

ASC Abbreviation of *altered states of consciousness,* a social-scientific designation for many types of consciousness other than "normal" states.

Ascension In the Lukan writings, Jesus' going up to heaven to the right hand of God, which is distinguished from his prior, intermediate resurrection to earth.

Asceticism From Greek *askēsis,* "exercise," "training," the practice of disciplining one's self not to yield to bodily pleasures such as sex or uncontrolled eating.

Astrology From the Greek *astēr,* "star," the study of heavenly bodies, which are also deities, to ascertain the heavenly pattern for earthly or future events.

Augustus An honorific title bestowed on Octavian by the Roman Senate. See **Caesar.**

Azazel In the Hellenistic/Roman period, probably a demonic being, but traditionally associated with the Day of Atonement ritual. See **Day of Atonement.**

B.C.E. "*before the common era* [of Israelites and Christ believers]." Traditionally B.C. ("before Christ"). See C.E.

Babylonian Exile, 587–539 B.C.E. The deportation of Judean leaders to Babylon by the Babylonians after the latter destroyed Jerusalem and the temple.

Bar Cochba Revolt, 132–135 C.E. Second rebellion of Israelites against Rome, led by bar Cochba (Aramaic for "son of the star"). See **Israelite Rebellion.**

Beatitude A short literary expression that begins with a word usually translated "blessed" and honors a person who is promised a divine reward. See Matt. 5:3–12.

Bethlehem David's hometown; the village of Jesus' birth in Matthew and Luke.

Bible From Greek *biblion,* "book," the collection of books held sacred by Israelites or Christ believers. See **Canon, Jewish Bible.**

C.E. "*common era* [of Israelites and Christ believers]," the traditional Christian designation being A.D. (*Anno Domini,* Latin for "in the year of the Lord"). See **B.C.E.**

Caesar Latin for "emperor" (German *kaiser;* Russian *czar*).

Calendar Inscription of Priene Dated 9 B.C.E., it honors Octavian (Caesar Augustus) with language also used of Jesus in the New Testament. See **Gospel.**

Canon From the Greek *kanōn,* "reed," often used to measure like a yardstick; by extension a list of authoritative books to "measure" correct belief and practice.

Catholic From the Latin *catholicus,* "universal" or "general." See **Catholic Epistles.**

Catholic Epistles Letters addressed to the church in general rather than to individual house-churches or individuals. See **Catholic.**

Challenge and Riposte (Response) Public verbal sparring between social equals in which the winner gains honor. See **Honor, Shame.**

Chiasm, Chiastic Patterns From the Greek letter *chi* (*x*), formal "criss-crossing" or "ring" patterns, for example, A B C B′ A′, often used by ancients to structure their (biblical) narratives.

Christian Bible, The For Protestants, the thirty-nine books of the Hebrew Bible (Old Testament) plus the twenty-seven books in the Greek New Testament; for Catholics the Old Testament section includes most of what the Protestants call the Apocrypha. See **Bible, Canon, Septuagint, Vulgate.**

Christological Hymn A poetic New Testament passage that honors Jesus as a supernormal figure, often thought by scholars to have been sung or chanted. See **Christology.**

Christological Titles Titles of honor taken over from the culture and used to describe Jesus, for example, "Christ" (Hebrew Messiah), "Lord," "Son of God."

Christology From Greek *Christos* (= Hebrew *Messiah,* "Anointed") and *logos,* "word" or "teaching," teaching concerning Jesus as "the Christ."

Church From the Greek word *kyriakon,* "that which belongs to the Lord," an English term that translates Greek *ekklēsia* (Greek *ek,* "out," *kaleō,* "I call"), a community "called out" for a particular purpose. See **House-Church.**

Church Fathers Important writers in the early churches, a few of whose works almost became canonical. See **Canon, Patristic Literature.**

Church Order (A document containing) the organization and discipline of a church with regard to its officers and members. See **Church.**

Circumcision "Cutting around" or off (some of) the prepuce as a rite of passage, especially of Israelite baby boys (the sign of the covenant). See Gen. 15:18–21; 17:10–13; **Covenant.**

Collection, The Paul's gathering of money offerings from his wealthier Gentile congregations for poor Christ believers in Jerusalem. See Gal. 2:10; 1 Cor. 16:1–4; **Jerusalem Conference; Jerusalem Compromise.**

Composition Criticism Analysis of the literary composition of a whole book, rather than its parts, written sources, or oral traditions. See **Genre Criticism, Literary Criticism.**

Coptic An ancient Egyptian dialect written with Greek letters. See **Nag Hammadi Texts.**

Corpus Latin for "body," used of a comprehensive body of writings, for example, the "Pauline corpus" attributed to the apostle Paul.

Covenant An ancient agreement or contract between two people or peoples, or between an emperor (patron) and less-powerful kings (clients); in the Bible a sacred contract between God and his people. See **Patron/Client Relations.**

Cynics, Cynicism Counterculture, wandering street preacher-philosophers who tried to convert people from their quest for fame, fortune, and pleasure to a life of austere virtue as the path to true enlightenment, freedom, and happiness.

Day of Atonement In the Bible a sacred festival day on which the priest offers sacrifices to atone for the sins of the priests and the people. See Lev. 16:3–34; 23:27–32.

Dead Sea Scrolls Manuscripts discovered near the Dead Sea, 1947–1956. See Appendix Three.

Deutero-Pauline "Secondary" literature attributed to Paul but not written by him. See **Pseudonymity, Pauline School.**

Diaspora Greek *diaspora,* "a dispersion," meaning the community of Israelites living outside their ancestral homeland, the "Land of Israel."

Diatessaron Greek "through the four," referring to a version of all four gospels woven together by Tatian of Syria, 170 C.E.

Disciple Pupil; student. See **Apostle.**

Divination A communication with supernormal powers by using natural materials (stars, entrails, the liver, etc.) or human-made objects (arrows, lots, etc.) in order to learn from them God's answers to questions or the future.

Docetism From *dokeō,* "I seem," an ancient view claiming that the divine Jesus only "seemed" to be human. Orthodox believers considered it to be heresy. See **Heresy.**

Doxology From the Greek *doxologia,* "a praising," in the New Testament formal praises of God found in prayers, letters, and the liturgy of the churches.

Dualism A type of thinking that views reality as a conflict of opposites, that is, good versus evil, light versus darkness, life versus death, and the like.

Easter Letter See *Festal Letter.*

Edict of Claudius An edict of the emperor Claudius, ca. 49/50 C.E., commanding all Israelites (including Christ believers) to leave Rome. See Acts 18:2.

Eisegesis From Greek *eis,* "into," and *hēgeomai,* "I lead," "I bring," thus to "bring (read) into" a text one's own private, preformed meaning. See **Exegesis.**

Eschatology From the Greek *eschatos,* "furthest," and *logos,* "word" or "teaching," teaching about the last things, the end of the world and history.

Essenes Possibly from Aramaic *Hāsayyín* = Greek *Essaioi,* "Pious Ones," a strict ascetic sect living along the Dead Sea, described by Pliny the Elder, Philo, and Josephus. See **Dead Sea Scrolls.**

Ethnocentrism, Ethnocentric Generalized judgments about other groups based on the biased opinion that one's own ethnic group is the "center," or superior. See **Stereotype.**

Evangelist From the Greek *euangelion,* "good news," a preacher of the gospel; in the New Testament, the author of one of the four canonical gospels. See **Gospel.**

Evil Eye (A belief that evil persons can cast) a gaze upon innocent people that harms them.

Exegesis From the Greek *ex,* "out of," and *hēgeomai,* "I bring," to "bring out" an author's intended meaning of his or her writing. See **Eisegesis.**

External Evidence Historical evidence outside of document that helps to establish matters such as authorship and date. See **Internal Evidence.**

Festal Letter (**Easter Letter**) Composed by Athanasius, bishop of Alexandria, distributed at Easter in 367 C.E., listing the twenty-seven books now in the canon. See **Canon**.

Form Criticism (German: *Formgeschichte,* "form history"). The analysis of the form, historical development, and successive socio-religious contexts of oral traditions.

Formula Quotations In the Gospel of Matthew, strategically placed (inserted) scriptural quotations preceded by a formula stating that events in the story context of the quotation fulfill them.

Fundamentalism A modern mind-set or movement that stresses certain necessary religious beliefs and practices (fundamentals) necessary to be a true believer; among Protestant Christians these include the view that the Bible is literally true.

Gallio Inscription Discovered at Delphi, Greece, an inscription that helps to fix the arrival of Paul at Corinth (Acts 18:2, 11–17) and thus Pauline chronology.

Genre From the French for "form," the general classification of longer literary types or forms according to structure, content, length, and emotional tone (e.g., gospel, history, letter, apocalypse).

Genre Criticism Theory and comparative analysis of genres, for example, apocalypse.

Glossolalia From the Greek *glossa,* "tongue," and *laleō,* "I speak," literally "speaking in tongues," that is, noncommunicative, pulsating noises that issue from the mouth of persons in altered states of consciousness (1 Cor. 12–14). See **ASC.**

Gnosticism From the Greek *gnōsis,* "knowledge," a dualistic religious movement that cuts across and combines many streams of thought and stresses special mythical knowledge about the origins, situation, and destiny of the universe and humanity, especially salvation from this evil world and body. See **Dualism, Syncretism, Nag Hammadi Texts, Thomas, Gospel of.**

Gospel From the Middle English *godspell,* which translated Greek *euangelion,* "good news," the oral proclamation of what God did in Christ, then the literary genre created or developed to narrate that story. See **Genre.**

Great Commission In Matt. 28:16–20 the command of the resurrected Jesus to his disciples on a Galilean mountain to go forth, teach his teachings, and baptize.

Great Omission The Lukan writer's omission of Mark 6:30–44 and 8:1–10.

Greater Insertion The Lukan writer's insertion of 9:51–18:14, mostly from Q and Special L; it makes up almost all of his special journey-to-Jerusalem narrative. See **Lesser Insertion, Great Omission, Q, Special L.**

Hanukkah, Feast of Hebrew for "dedication," the rededication of the defiled temple in 164 B.C.E.; later called the "Festival of Lights." See **Abomination That Makes Desolate, Maccabean Revolt.**

Hebrew An ancient Semitic language spoken by pre-Exilic and some post-Exilic Israelites; the language of almost all the Jewish Bible or Old Testament. See **Hebrew Bible.**

Hebrew Bible, The A collection of thirty-nine books written almost exclusively in Hebrew; the Jewish Bible and the Protestant Old Testament. See **Bible, Jewish Bible, *Tanak,* Canon.**

Hellenization From the Greek *Hellas,* "Greece," the spread of Greek language and culture, sometimes under force, in the regions conquered by Alexander the Great.

Heresy, Heretic From the Greek *hairesis,* "sect," "party," "school," but over time came to mean persons who engage in wrong thinking. See **Orthodoxy.**

Hermeneutics From the Greek *hermēneutēs,* "an interpreter," the general theory of interpretation, especially of written texts.

Hero, Heroine Figures to whom are attributed supernormal powers, especially miracle working, found in many Greco-Roman religions.

Herodians Most likely the families and retainers of Herod and his sons.

History of Religion From German *Religionsgeschichte,* the history and comparative analysis of religions, especially during the Hellenistic-Roman period.

Honor The claim of worth and the social recognition of that worth, especially related to power, status, and religion. Family honor is critical. See **Honor, Acquired; Honor, Ascribed; Shame.**

Honor, Acquired Honor achieved, especially by besting opponents in debate. See **Challenge and Response.**

Honor, Ascribed Honor bestowed by birth or a grant from an honorable person.

Hospitality The social custom of warmly welcoming guests.

House-Church A community of believers that meets in a house. See **Church.**

Household Code The scholarly designation for rules of ancient household management, considered critical for political stability: husbands over wives, parents over children, and masters over slaves.

Intercalation Also called a "sandwich," one story inserted inside another.

Internal Evidence Historical evidence within a document that helps to identify its author, date, location, and recipients. See **External Evidence.**

Interpolation An insertion into a text by a later scribe or copyist.

Israelites From "Israel," inhabitants of Palestine, people who are associated with Palestine, those who have beliefs associated with Israel, and the like; some prefer "Judeans"; ancestors of modern Jews.

Israelite Rebellion (66–70 C.E.) Revolt of Israelites against Rome, resulting in the second destruction of Jerusalem and the Jerusalem temple. See **Babylonian Exile.**

Jamnia (Yavneh) Academy A school started during the Israelite Rebellion by the Pharisees led by Johanan ben Zakkai. See **Prayer against the Heretics.**

Jerusalem The sacred city of the Israelites since King David conquered it (2 Sam. 5:5–10).

Jerusalem Compromise The decision at the Jerusalem Conference: Peter would carry out his mission to the Israelites, Paul to the Gentiles. See **Jerusalem Conference, Collection, Circumcision.**

Jerusalem Conference A meeting of Paul and the pillars in Jerusalem to decide the strategy for the mission (Gal. 2:1–10; cf. Acts 15). See **Jerusalem Compromise, Collection, Circumcision.**

Jewish Bible, The Thirty-nine mainly Hebrew books that are authoritative for the life, faith, and practice of the Jewish people. See the **Hebrew Bible.**

Judean Translation of *Ioudaios,* which can mean: (1) an inhabitant of Judea; (2) an inhabitant of all Palestine; (3) any ancient person who has connections with Judea; (4) anyone who professes the official religion of Judea; (5) an elite person from Judea.

Kerygma Greek for "proclamation," theologically used to denote proclamation or central message of the Jesus Movement or of any part of it.

King James Version (KJV) Influential English Bible translation, 1611 C.E.

Kingdom of God, The Central theme of the teaching of Jesus in symbolic language not defined, but that evokes the whole range of meanings associated with God's activity as King.

Koinē Greek for "common," describes the commonly spoken form of Greek that became the international language of the Hellenistic world. See **Aramaic.**

Lesser Insertion A non-Markan section found in Luke 6:20–8:3. See **Greater Insertion, Great Omission.**

Letter Fragments Parts of letters that are embedded in, or that make up, another letter.

Levite Originally a person from the tribe of Levi, the hereditary tribe of the priests; in the New Testament period, temple functionaries and musicians.

Liberationist Hermeneutics Interpretations of the New Testament that challenge any form of oppression of women, minorities, and "colonial" peoples. See **Hermeneutics.**

Literary Criticism (Old Literary Criticism) Analysis of vocabulary, grammar, syntax, and style of whole documents and genres. See **New Literary Criticism.**

Lord's Prayer Prayer attributed to Jesus, Matt. 6:9–13 and Luke 11:2–4 (Q).

Maccabean Revolt (167–164 B.C.E.) Revolt of Maccabean (Hasmonean) Israelites against forced Hellenization and oppression by the Seleucid Greeks.

Magic Attempt to influence the powers for good or evil by religious rituals that include use of plants and animals and careful recitation of formulae.

Markan Hypothesis Based on the Markan Priority, the hypothesis that the Markan Gospel is basically trustworthy history and reveals Jesus' developing Messianic Consciousness. See **Markan Priority.**

Markan Priority The hypothesis that the Gospel of Mark is the earliest of the three synoptic gospels. See **Synoptic Problem, Markan Hypothesis.**

Messianic Consciousness of Jesus The view that Jesus was conscious of being a Messiah; it is usually thought that it evolved during the course of his life. See **Markan Hypothesis.**

Messianic Secret Especially in the Gospel of Mark, describes Jesus' command of demons, the cured, and disciples to keep quiet about his Messianic identity.

Metaphor A literary comparison of two kinds of reality that are quite different but that figuratively make a point. Example: John *is* an eager beaver. See **Simile.**

Millenialism Social-scientific term for apocalypticism, based on Latin *mille,* "1,000." See **Apocalypticism.**

Mishna(h) Israelite legal interpretations of the Torah codified about 200 C.E. which later became part of the Talmud. See **Rabbinic Literature.**

Monarchial Episcopate From Greek *monarchos,* "ruling alone," and *episkopos,* "bishop," the hierarchical ordering of authority with growth of the rule of bishops.

Monotheism From Greek *mono,* "one," and *theos,* "god," the belief that there is only one true God. See Deut. 6:4 (the *Shema‛*).

Muratorian Canon The first "official" canonical list of New Testament books, probably written about 200 C.E. at Rome. Named after its founder.

Mystery Religions Popular, dramatic, ritualistic religions located at local Mediterranean worship sites, featuring myths about heroes and heroines and the agricultural seasons, as well as both public and private (secret) rites of initiation.

Nag Hammadi Texts ("Library") Mainly Gnostic manuscripts written in the Coptic language representing the thought of Israelites, Christ believers, and pagans, discovered in 1945 near Nag Hammadi, Egypt. See **Coptic, Thomas, Gospel of.**

Nazareth The village in central Galilee where Jesus was reared.

New Testament Apocrypha See **Apocrypha.**

Old Testament Apocrypha See **Apocrypha.**

Old Testament Pseudepigrapha See **Pseudepigrapha.**

Orthodoxy From Greek *orthos,* "straight," and *doxa,* "opinion," a correct opinion; see **Heresy.**

P^{52} The earliest surviving papyrus fragment of the New Testament, John 18:31–33, 37–38, from Egypt, usually dated about 125 C.E.

Paleography From Greek *palaios,* "ancient," and *graphō,* "I write," the academic field that analyzes ancient writing and attempts to put scripts in chronological sequence.

Papias Tradition Written by Papias of Hieropolis (recorded by the ancient historian Eusebius), in this textbook, the earliest surviving comments about Matthew and Mark.

Parable From Greek *para,* "beside," and *ballō,* "I throw," literally "to throw beside," a short comparison story that compares an indescribable reality to nature or everyday life and that teases, provokes, disturbs, or shocks the hearer into response.

Parousia A Greek word for "presence" that became a technical term for the visit of a high official to a province and, by transference, for the expected return of Christ.

Passion Story "Passion" refers to the suffering and death of Jesus; "Passion Story" or "passion narrative" is the account of that suffering and death.

Passover An Israelite pilgrim festival commemorating the "passing over" the houses of Israelites by the angel of death, making possible their exodus from Egypt and slavery to freedom. See Exod. 12:1–41.

Pastorals (Pastoral Epistles or Letters) Pseudonymous letters attributed to Paul and addressed to Timothy or Titus about pastoral oversight of their churches. See **Pauline School, Pseudonymity**.

Patristic Literature See **Church Fathers, Apostolic Fathers.**

Patron/Client Relations Customary informal relations between social superiors (patrons) and social inferiors (clients) at all levels of the social hierarchy.

Pauline School Describes the hypothesis that in analogy with Israelite scribal schools and Hellenistic philosophical schools followers of Paul wrote letters in his name to honor his memory and interpret his views. See **Pseudonymity, Deutero-Pauline.**

Pentateuch The first five books of the Hebrew Bible. See **Torah.**

Pentecost (Weeks) A pilgrim festival at the end of the grain harvest approximately fifty days after the beginning of Passover, later associated with God's giving the Ten Commandments to Moses on Mount Sinai. In the New Testament, the day when the Spirit descended on the Jerusalem church; see Acts 2.

Pericope From the Greek *peri,* "about," and *koptein,* "to cut": an extract cut from a larger work, thus a unit of narrative or discourse, a passage.

Pharisees A religious party or sect that emphasized application of strict Torah-based behavior in everyday life. See **Sadducees, Essenes, Zealots, Sicarii.**

Physiognomics Physical attributes—posture, skin color, facial features or expressions, hair, voice, overall physique—that to certain ancient writers supposedly reveal an understanding of personality types. See **Stereotype.**

Polytheism From Greek *poly,* "many," and *theos,* "god," belief in many gods.

Prayer against the Heretics (*Birkat ha-Minîm*) A prayer against Israelite sectarians who did not hold normative Pharisaic views; inserted into the synagogue prayers called the Eighteen Benedictions (*'Amîdâh*) in the late first or early second century C.E.

Prefect Governor of a district appointed directly by the Roman emperor.

Procurator a later term for *prefect.* See **Prefect.**

Proto-Luke The scholarly source theory that the writer of Luke first combined Q and Special L before he inserted Mark into it. See **Synoptic Problem, Q, Special L.**

Pseudepigrapha Greek for "false writings," usually refers to a collection of Old Testament-type books not found in any canon, from about 200 B.C.E. to 300 C.E.

Pseudonymity From the Greek *pseudos,* "false," and *onoma,* "name," attributed authorship (literally, "false name"). Adjective: *pseudonymous.*

Q Perhaps from *Quelle* (German for "source"), a hypothetical source used by the authors of the gospels of Matthew and Luke. See **Two-Source Theory.**

Rabbinic Literature The umbrella term for literature composed by rabbis over several centuries; includes the Mishna (interpretation of the Torah, mainly legal [*halakah*]), the Gemara (commentary on the Mishna), which together with further commentary make up the Talmud, as well as the Midrashim, or more practical and homiletic commentaries on the books of the Hebrew Bible. See **Rabbis, Mishna(h).**

Rabbis From Hebrew for "my great one," refers to eminent Torah scholars.

Redaction Criticism From German *Redaktionsgeschichte,* "redaction history," the study of the purposeful redaction or editing of traditional oral or written sources.

Roman Empire 27 B.C.E.–410 C.E. See Chapter One and map, p. 9.

Sadducees From Zadok, a priest in the Hebrew Bible (1 Kings 1:32–34), the wealthy, powerful, priestly party that sacrificed in the temple. See **Sanhedrin.**

Samaria Palestinian region between Galilee in the North and Judea in the South. See **Samaritans.**

Samaritans Inhabitants of Samaria considered by purist Israelites to be ethnically mixed and therefore impure, to be avoided.

Samaritan Pentateuch The sacred Pentateuch of the Samaritans in which Mount Gerizîm, the Samaritan holy temple mount, stands in place of Mount Zion, the Israelite holy temple mount. See **Samaria, Samaritans.**

Sanhedrin An Israelite court, but mainly the high court in Jerusalem controlled by the Sadducees. See **Sadducees.**

Septuagint (LXX) From the Latin *septuaginta* ("seventy"), the Greek translation of the Hebrew scriptures, based on the legend that seventy (or seventy-two) Israelite priests independently translated them, but their translations agreed, word for word!

Sermon on the Mount The first of five major speeches attributed to Jesus in the Gospel of Matthew (Matt. 5–7); it includes the Beatitudes, the Lord's Prayer, and Jesus' ethical teachings, many related to the Torah. See **Torah.**

Shame Negative: the state of one who does not recognize commonly accepted social boundaries; positive: the state of one who has the appropriate sense of his or her place and has sensitivity to others.

Sicarii From Latin *sica,* "dagger," thus "dagger men," or terrorist rebels at the time of the Israelite Rebellion. See **Israelite Rebellion.**

Signs Source A miracle story source reconstructed by scholars and thought to have been used by the author of the Gospel of John.

Simile A figure of speech that contains the comparison word *like* or *as.* Example: John is *like* an eager beaver. See **Metaphor.**

Sitz im Leben German "setting in life," this expression is used in Form Criticism as a technical term for the socio-religious context in which a given oral tradition functions. See **Form Criticism.**

Social Bandits The social-scientific term for rural bandit-chiefs and their followers who rise from the ranks of the peasants, rob the rich, and sometimes give to the poor.

Social-Historical Criticism The analysis of the history of communities from the perspective of their social relations as understood in the social sciences.

Social-Scientific Criticism The analysis of individuals and groups, especially from the perspective of observers' models developed from cross-cultural comparisons in the social sciences.

Son of Man Literally, "one like a human being" (Ps. 8:4); a human-like being in the sky (Dan. 7:13–14); a title of honor derived from the latter, frequently used in the gospels, usually to describe Jesus.

Soteriology From the Greek *sōtēr,* "savior," and *logos,* "word" or "teaching," teaching about the death of Jesus as the means of a person's salvation.

Source Criticism The analysis of writings to isolate and reconstruct their written sources. See **Two-Source Theory.**

Special L A reconstructed source used by the author of the Gospel of Luke. See **Two-Source Theory.**

Special M A reconstructed source used by the author of the Gospel of Matthew. See **Two-Source Theory.**

Standard Text A text type that, scholars agree, is the best reconstructed Greek text of the New Testament (primarily an Alexandrian text type). See **Textual Criticism,** *Textus Receptus.*

Stereotype A generalized attitude or impression about another group or other groups of people based on limited information; typecasting.

Stoicism A highly ethical philosophy based on the view that the world and humans are rational; founded by Zeno, who taught under a colonnade (Greek *stoa*) in Athens.

Structuralist Analysis The analysis of texts from the perspective of constructed models based on the tendency of human minds to think in oppositions.

Synagogue, House-Synagogue From Greek *syn,* "together," and *agō,* "I lead," "I bring," that is, a place (sometimes a house) to bring people together for prayer and worship. See **Church, House-Church.**

Syncretism In the formal study of religion a scholar's term used to describe the combining and fusing of disparate beliefs—gods, goddesses, myths, ideas—and practices, often by "diffusion," usually from distinct religious movements.

Synoptic Gospels From Greek *synoptikos,* "seeing together," seeing the three gospels of Matthew, Mark, and Luke together because they tell the same general story in the same kind of way in contrast to the Gospel of John. A book called a "synopsis" puts them in parallel columns for comparison and contrast.

Synoptic Problem The problem of the literary relationship between the first three (or "synoptic") gospels because they are similar and different in both content and order. See **Synoptic Gospels, Two-Source Theory.**

Synoptic Tradition Traditional material, usually oral, that has been used by the synoptic gospel writers.

Tanak An acronym for the Hebrew Bible based on its three ancient divisions, *Tōrāh* ("instruction"), *Nabî'îm* ("prophets"), and **Kitubîm** ("writings").

Targums Ancient Aramaic paraphrases of the Hebrew Bible for use in worship when Aramaic had replaced Hebrew as the vernacular language of Israelites. See **Hebrew, Aramaic.**

Textual Criticism Analysis of ancient manuscript copies, arranging them in families, dating them, and reconstructing from them a hypothetical original. See **Standard Text, *Textus Receptus.***

Textus Receptus Latin for the "received (Greek) text" of the New Testament from the sixteenth to the nineteenth centuries, used for early English translations, but now known to be based on late, slightly less reliable, cursive-script Greek manuscripts. Text Critics prefer the Standard Text. See **Standard Text.**

Thomas, Gospel of Discovered in 1945 among the Nag Hammadi Texts, a Coptic translation of an extremely important Greek book that contains 114 sayings reputedly spoken by Jesus (originally in Aramaic). See **Gnosticism, Nag Hammadi Texts,** Appendix Three.

Torah Hebrew for "instruction," it usually refers to the first five books of the Hebrew Bible ("the books of Moses"; modern scholars: "Pentateuch"). Though the Torah contains many laws, the common translation, "Law," obscures the other kinds of literature in these five books.

Transfiguration The gospel story that Jesus' clothes glowed brightly as he was talking with Moses and Elijah, and God called him "Son" on a Galilean mountain. See Mark 9:2–10.

Two-Source Theory (Four-Source Theory) The most widely held "solution" to the **Synoptic Problem,** namely, that the authors of Matthew and Luke used the Gospels of Mark and **Q** (plus their own unique sources, **Special M** and **Special L**) as sources.

Vulgate Latin for "common vernacular," a Latin translation of the Bible by Jerome, completed about 405 C.E., which eventually became the official Bible of the Roman Catholic Church. It included the extra books and portions of a few books also found in the Septuagint. See **Canon, Septuagint (LXX).**

Yavneh Academy See **Jamnia Academy.**

We Passages First-person plural passages in the Acts of the Apostles, suggesting to ancient and a few modern scholars that a companion of Paul wrote Acts.

Wisdom Myth The myth that God's heavenly Wisdom came to earth but, not being at home, returned to God. See *1 Enoch* 42:1–2; *ben Sira* 24:8–10.

Witness One who bears testimony to his or her faith, or the act of bearing testimony. The Greek word is *martys,* and later it came to be used specifically of those who "witnessed" to their faith to the point of dying for it (*martyr*).

Zealots From Greek *zealos,* "zeal," zealous Israelite rebels, often leaders, in the Israelite Rebellion. See **Israelite Rebellion.**

Selected Bibliography

For a complete bibliography of this book and further reading visit the on-line student resources for this book at http://religion.wadsworth.com.

Chapter 1: This chapter is especially indebted to the studies of D. E. Aune, D. L. Balch, S. S. Bartchy, S. J. D. Cohen, J. D. Crossan, R. A. Culpepper, D. C. Duling, L. Feldman, D. A. Fiensy, B. Fiore, S. Freyne, J. H. Elliott, J. G. Gager, J. S. Hanson, K. C. Hanson, P. D. Hanson, R. A. Horsley, G. Lenski, S. Mason, B. J. Malina, F. Millar, J. H. Neyrey, D. Oakman, C. Osiek, J. Pilch, T. Rajak, R. D. Rhoads, R. Rohrbaugh, E. Schürer, E. M. Smallwood, J. E. Stambaugh, V. Tcherikover, G. Theissen, G. Vermes, and Y. Yadin.

Chapter 2: This chapter is especially indebted to the studies of J. Capel Anderson, D. Aune, F. F. Bruce, A. Culpepper, J. R. Donahue, D. C. Duling, R. Fowler, J. H. Elliott, J. A. Fitzmyer, J. G. Gager, H. Y. Gamble, J. Jeremias, D. A. Kille, J. D. Kingsbury, R. H. Klein, A. J. Levine, B. J. Malina, W. A. Meeks, B. M. Metzger, E. M. Meyers and J. F. Strange, J. H. Neyrey, J. Z. Smith, D. Oakman, C. Osiek; D. Patte, N. Perrin, D. Rhoads and D. Michie, V. K. Robbins, J. M. Robinson, E. P. Sanders and M. Davies, E. Schüssler Fiorenza, W. R. Tate, H. Taussig, G. Theissen, H. Thurston, and D. O. Via.

Chapter 3: This chapter is especially indebted to the research of P. J. Achetmeier, D. E. Aune, M. E. Boring, J. D. Crossan, C. H. Dodd, D. C. Duling, R. A. Edwards, R. T. Fortna, R. Fuller, L. Hartman, L. Hurtado, J. Jeremias, W. Kelber, J. Kloppenborg, H. Koester, B. M. Mack, N. Perrin, R. Piper, V. K. Robbins, J. M. Robinson, R. C. Tannehill, J. T. Sanders, B. B. Scott, D. E. Smith, and G. Theissen.

Chapter 4: This chapter is especially indebted to the studies of R. A. Atkins, R. Banks, S. S. Bartchy, J. Beker, H. D. Betz, G. Bornkamm, R. E. Brown, J. K. Chou, K. P. Donfried, D. C. Duling, J. H. Elliott, J. A. Fitzmyer, D. Georgi, F. A. Judge, R. Hock, B. Holmberg, G. Lüdemann, B. J. Malina, W. E. Meeks, J. P. Meier, M. Mitchell, A. D. Nock, J. Neyrey, J. Pilch, E. R. Richards, R. Scroggs, K. Stendahl, N. Perrin, E. P. Sanders, W. Schmithals, H. J. Schoeps, A. Segal, R. Stark, S. Stowers, G. Theissen, and B. Witherington III.

Chapter 5: This chapter is especially indebted to the research of D. L. Balch, S. S. Bartchy, H. D. Betz, G. Bornkamm, A. D. Callahan, W. Doty, D. Duling, P. Esler, B. Fiore, J. T. Fitzgerald, R. Jewett, J. H. Elliott, A. J. Harrill, L. Keck, P. Lampe, N. Lewis, A. Malherbe, R. Martin, W. A. Meeks, M. Mitchell, E. J. Murphy-O'Connor, J. Neyrey, C. Osiek, R. Richards, C. Roetzel, J. Sanders, K. Stendahl, S. Stowers, D. Watson, and J. L. White. M. E. Boring, K. Berger, and

C. Colpe, *Hellenistic Commentary to the New Testament,* has been especially helpful for comparative texts.

Chapter 6: This chapter is especially indebted to the research of R. Bultmann, S. S. Bartchy, H. D. Betz, G. Bornkamm, J. H. Elliott, V. P. Furnish, P. Esler, E. Käsemann, W. A. Meeks, H. Moxnes, N. Perrin, P. Richardson, C. Roetzel, R. Scroggs, K. Stendahl, and B. Witherington III. M. E. Boring, K. Berger, and C. Colpe, *Hellenistic Commentary to the New Testament,* has been especially helpful for comparative texts.

Chapter 7: This chapter is especially indebted to the research of H. Attridge, J. A. Fitzmyer, F. O. Francis, R. H. Fuller, G. Krodel, E. Lohse, W. Meeks, N. Perrin, J. T. Sanders, R. Smith, and D. C. Verner.

Chapter 8: This chapter is especially indebted to the research of P. J. Achtemeier, D. Aune, F. Belo, R. Burridge, D. R. Cartlidge, D. Chapman, J. Dewey, J. R. Donahue, D. Duling, D. Dungan, R. Fowler, M. Hadas, L. Hartman, J. Jeremias, H. C. Kee, F. Kermode, V. Kelber, H. Koester, B. Mack, E. S. Malbun, B. Malina, W. Marxsen, C. Myers, P. Shuler, D. Michie, J. Neyrey, N. Perrin, N. Petersen, J. Pilch, D. Rhoads, V. K. Robbins, R. Rohrbaugh, M. Smith, C. H. Talbert, R. C. Tannehill, V. Taylor, M. A. Tolbert, C. Tuckett, H. C. Waetjen, T. Weeden, W. Wrede, and A. Yarbro Collins.

Chapter 9: This chapter is especially indebted to the studies of D. C. Allison, B. W. Bacon, D. L. Balch, G. Barth, H. D. Betz, G. Bornkamm, R. E. Brown, W. Carter, S. J. D. Cohen, K. E. Corley, W. D. Davies, D. C. Duling, R. A. Edwards, D. E. Garland, R. H. Gundry, D. Hagner, D. R. Hare, D. J. Harrington, H. J. Held, R. A. Horsley, J. Capel Anderson, J. D. Kingsbury, A. J. Levine, J. L. Kugel, U. Luz, B. J. Malina, J. P. Meier, J. Neusner, J. H. Neyrey, D. E. Orton, J. A. Overman, A. J. Saldarini, P. L. Schuler, E. Schweizer, D. Senior, D. Slingerland, G. N. Stanton, K. Stendahl, G. Strecker, J. Suggs, B. V. Viviano, E. J. Vledder, and E. M. Wainwright.

Chapter 10: This chapter is especially indebted to the research of H. J. Cadbury, H. Conzelmann, R. Cassidy, F. Danker, M. Dibelius, D. C. Duling, P. E. Esler, J. A. Fitzmyer, F. J. Foakes-Jackson, E. Haenchen, M. Hengel, R. A. Horsley, J. Jervell, R. J. Karris, L. Keck, W. G. Kümmel, K. Lake, J. L. Martyn, P. Minear, H. Moxnes, J. H. Neyrey, D. Oakman, N. Perrin, J. Pilch, V. K. Robbins, C. Talbert, R. Tannehill, D. Tiede, and P. Vielhauer.

Chapter 11: This chapter is especially indebted to the research of C. K. Barrett, P. Borgen, R. E. Brown, C. H. Dodd, P. D. Duke, R. T. Fortna, R. Bultmann, A. Culpepper, D. J. Harrington, E. Käsemann, R. Kimelman, R. Kysar, B. Lindars, G. Macrae, A. Malherbe, B. J. Malina, W. A. Meeks, M. Meyer, J. H. Neyrey, P. Perkins, J. Pilch, R. L. Rohrbaugh, J. L. Martyn, R. Schnackenburg, D. M. Smith, C. Talbert, and S. G. Wilson. Very helpful for comparative texts is M. E. Boring, K. Berger, and C. Colpe, *Hellenistic Commentary on the New Testament.*

Chapter 12: This chapter is especially indebted to the research of D. E. Aune, M. E. Boring, D. Barr, J. J. Collins, J. M. Ford, J. G. Gager, B. J. Malina, J. Pilch, E. Schüssler, Fiorenza, L. Thompson, and A. Yarbro Collins. Very helpful for comparative texts is M. E. Boring, K. Berger, and C. Colpe, *Hellenistic Commentary on the New Testament.*

Chapter 13: This chapter is especially indebted to the research of P. J. Achtemeier, D. L. Balch, J. Bassler, R. J. Bauckham, J. Beker, R. E. Brown, H. Conzelmann, N. A. Dahl, F. W. Danker, M. Dibelius, J. H. Elliott, H. Greeven, J. L. Houlden, A. J. Hultgren, M. Jackson-McCabe, S. J. Joubert, R. J. Karris, G. Krodel, J. H. Neyrey, N. Perrin, D. Schroeder, G. S. Sloyan, S. K. Stowers, D. C. Verner, and R. A. Wild. Very helpful for comparative texts is M. E. Boring, K. Berger, and C. Colpe, *Hellenistic Commentary on the New Testament.*

Chapter 14: This chapter is especially indebted to the research of M. Borg, R. Bultmann, J. D. Crossan, M. Dibelius, D. C. Duling, R. Fuller, R. Funk, A. von Harnack, Käsemann, W. J. S. Kloppenborg, H. Koester, G. Kümmel, A. Loisy, B. L. Mack, S. Mathews, E. Meyers, J. M. Robinson, N. Perrin, D. E. Oakman, S. J. Patterson, H. S. Reimarus, J. L. Reed, A. Schweitzer, J. S. Strange, L. Vaage, G. Vermes, W. Wrede, and N. T. Wright. Very helpful for comparative texts is M. E. Boring, K. Berger, and C. Colpe, *Hellenistic Commentary on the New Testament.*

Credits and Acknowledgments

We wish to thank the following for the photographs included in this edition:

Page xviii	Wadsworth / Thomson Learning
Page 3	Courtesy of U.S. Geological Survey, EROS Data Center
Page 13	AKG London / Peter Connolly
Page 27	© Sonia Halliday Photography
Page 52	Courtesy of the Masters and Fellows of Trinity College, Cambridge
Page 94	Steimatzky Group Ltd., Israel
Page 138	Alinari / Art Resource, NY
Page 175	Courtesy of Carolyn Osiek
Page 178	Photo Garo Nalbandian
Page 218	Scala, Art Resource, NY
Page 256	Institute for Antiquity and Christianity, Claremont, California
Page 292	Wadsworth / Thomson Learning
Page 328	Copyright © by Archie Lieberman
Page 362	Alinari / Art Resource, NY
Page 402	Reproduced courtesy of the director and university librarian, John Rylands University Library of Manchester
Page 442	The Pierpont Morgan Library, New York. M644, F174v.
Page 466	Bettman / CORBIS
Page 502	Courtesy of Joint Sepphoris Project

Index